ARARAT
• Van
CASPIAN
SEA
• Nineveh
SYRIA KASSITES
• Nuzi
R. TIGRIS
(Akkad)
BABYLONIA
•bylon
(Sumer)
Larsa •
• Ur

MADAI

ELAM

PERSIAN

GULF

A
R
K
T
A
Z
A

B
I
A

HAVILAH
• Uzal
• Timna
HAZARMAVETH
SHEBA

palacios

ON GENESIS:
A NEW READING

ON GENESIS:
A NEW READING

By BRUCE VAWTER

1977
DOUBLEDAY & COMPANY, INC.
GARDEN CITY, NEW YORK

Library of Congress Cataloging in Publication Data

Vawter, Bruce.
On Genesis.

Includes index.
1. Bible.   O.T. Genesis—Commentaries.
I. Title
BS1235.3.V38   222'.11'077
ISBN: 0-385-06104-8
Library of Congress Catalog Card Number 76–26354

In affectionate memory of
Joseph L. Lilly, C.M.
and
Daniel W. Martin, C.M.

Laudemus viros gloriosos,
et parentes nostros in generatione sua.

Contents

Preface

In 1956 we published *A Path Through Genesis* (New York: Sheed & Ward), which in the following year appeared in a British edition (London: Sheed & Ward) and in 1971 in Spanish translation, having meanwhile undergone several reprintings in hardcover and paperback. Kindly reviewers and some private communications have indicated to us that the book responded to a felt need in its time. That time has now passed from us. There could be no question of merely revising that book and somehow putting it in tune with 1977. If there is to be another book on Genesis— and, of course, whether there should be another book can be a debatable question—it must be really new, done afresh and without advertence to what was written over twenty years ago. We have tried to honor this principle in composing the book that unfolds in the following pages: during this time we have carefully refrained from rereading a single word of *A Path Through Genesis*.

It was easier to write about Genesis in 1956 than it is today. What then could be accounted exciting and venturesome may now be thought commonplace or, worse, an attempt to prolong beyond its time a critical view of Genesis with which one has learnt to live comfortably against the encroachment of newer views that others have made the exciting and venturesome of this moment. Neither in 1956 nor in 1977, however, have we endeavored to cast ourself in the role of advocate, of either a new or an old orthodoxy, critical or confessional. What we have wanted to do in each instance is represent as honestly and as responsibly as we can the best current thinking on the significance of Genesis as we have been given to see it. This is the bond that unites our two efforts: the perennial fascination which this biblical work holds for every kind of reader, as has been continuously demonstrated over the years, and the consequent challenge which such an unflagging interest continually issues to anyone professionally concerned with Genesis, to respond to it with the resources that are at his disposal. And of course, while the attraction of Genesis has not changed, most everything else has. The most everything else, in which the mind of the present author is very definitely included, necessitates this new book.

We cannot pretend to be on top of all the scholarship and research that have conspired to make a rereading of this kind both desirable and necessary. We have managed a good deal, certainly enough to persuade us to undertake a new pathfinding *vingt ans après*. But there is no doubt that details, even important details, have escaped our attention here and there. Failure to acknowledge views dissentient from ours, of course, need not invariably mean that they have not been noted along the way: some have indeed been looked at and simply passed by. On the other hand we have referred from time to time to the persons and facts that have contributed to the making of this commentary; but only by exception have we offered any specific citations. For the most part we have been concerned here with professional literature, especially periodical literature, which can have only a limited interest for the general reader for whom this commentary is mainly intended.

However, we must certainly give credit to various basic works that have determined the course of this book and to which we have referred more than once in the writing of it. The as yet uncompleted commentary of Claus Westermann, *Genesis* (Biblischer Kommentar I; Neukirchen: Erziehungsverein, 1966–   ), must hold pride of place in this list. But we have also profited from Umberto Cassuto, *From Adam to Noah* and *From Noah to Abraham* (Jerusalem: Magnes Press and Oxford University Press, 1953–64), from E. A. Speiser, *Genesis* (Anchor Bible I; Garden City, New York: Doubleday, 1964), from Gerhard von Rad, *Genesis* (The Old Testament Library, 3rd Edition; Philadelphia: Westminster Press, 1972), and from Robert Davidson, *Genesis 1-11* (The Cambridge Bible Commentary; Cambridge University Press, 1973). Originally published in 1934 but unavailable for many years, the massive *Genesis* of Benno Jacob has recently been brought back into print (New York: Ktav Publishing House, 1974); this work has been helpful to us in numerous ways. (An English abridgment of the commentary made by Jacob's son and grandson was also published at the time of the reprinting.) Finally, every commentator on Genesis must acknowledge his indebtedness to Hermann Gunkel, whose *Genesis* (Göttingen: Vanderhoeck & Ruprecht, originally 1910, most recently reprinted in 1964) remains after all these years the final arbiter of more than one interpretative dispute and the opening assertion of most others. The commentary was never translated into English, but its lengthy introduction was, under the title *The Legends of Genesis* (New York: Schocken Books): it still provides a good initiation into the literary forms of Genesis and their spirit.

The parallel literatures of antiquity to which we refer so frequently in this commentary appear integrally and in reliable translation under the editorship of James B. Pritchard, *Ancient Near Eastern Texts Relating to the Old Testament* (3rd edition; Princeton University Press, 1969). Parallels in greater abundance, many of them less certain, but all of them suggestive, are to be found with Theodor H. Gaster, *Myth, Legend, and Custom in the Old Testament* (New York: Harper & Row, 1969), which has incorporated generous portions of Sir James G. Frazer's classic *Folklore in the Old Testament* of 1918. The geography of Genesis has been admirably presented by Yohanan Aharoni, *The Land of the Bible* (Philadelphia: Westminster, 1967); this or another good Bible atlas will prove serviceable to the reader in supplement to the minimal information provided by the endpaper maps. A final reference that should not go unmentioned is that of Ignatius Hunt, *The World of the Patriarchs* (New York: Prentice-Hall, 1967).

As the copyright page indicates, the biblical text cited throughout this book is that of The New American Bible (NAB) Copyright © 1970 and used with permission of the Confraternity of Christian Doctrine, Washington, D.C. An accurate and conscientious translation of the Bible has already halved the labor of a commentator by doing much of his work before him. For this self-serving reason in addition to some others, we have selected this version to focus our commentary.

When it has been necessary to transliterate Hebrew words or phrases in the course of the commentary we have observed no rules of consistency or scholarly convention. We have done what T. E. Lawrence did with Arabic and have made our transliterations correspond in each case with what we felt was most appropriate to the comprehension of the reader.

It would be ungrateful of this author not to acknowledge his indebtedness to DePaul University and his Vincentian Community which have afforded him the resources to make this work possible. He can only hope that they will deem their trusts to have been requited in its execution.

ON GENESIS:
A NEW READING

Introduction

1. The Sources of Genesis

A generation ago—and it is with a mild kind of shock that we realize it was, indeed, a short generation ago that we first produced a commentary on Genesis—the task of introducing Genesis to the general reader and the reader to Genesis was at once simple and complex. It was simple because the issue was a simple one: the uncritical view of Genesis as a literary unity called the First Book of Moses had to be replaced by the critical view, the view of scholarly consensus, which recognized the book to be a compilation from three major sources, none of which could have any literary connection with the Moses of thirteenth-century B.C. Israel. The complexity of the task lay, of course, in achieving the knack of communicating this simple fact.

Today the task is not simple at all. It is true, Mosaic authorship no longer forms a problem for practically anyone, and therefore that part of the issue has been resolved. In whatever diluted a sense we may continue to talk about a Mosaic influence on the Pentateuch, an influence which in the analysis may be no more profound than that of the barons of Runnymede on the American Revolution, we are not discussing authorship as our contemporaries understand authorship. Historical and literary criticism have ruled on this matter once and for all and finally. Genesis is a monument hewn of stone that Moses may have descried but which he certainly never quarried, and there is no point in trying to breathe new life into an ancient formula by inventing new meaning for either "Moses" or "authorship."

The complexity of the present task rises from the fact that there is no longer a comfortable scholarly consensus to communicate. There were always scholars who swam against the current, commentators like Umberto Cassuto and Benno Jacob, for example, whom the following pages will leave no doubt that we hold in the highest regard, who rejected the "documentary" approach to the composition of Genesis which they caricatured as a scissors-and-paste concept of authorship at home perhaps in the nineteenth-century Europe where the theory evolved but alien to the world of the Bible. Today their once thin ranks have been increasingly swelled by other distinguished scholars who have added their names to the lists, who for various and sometimes contradictory reasons—the supposed laws of literary structuralism or of oral epic, the analogy of other literatures that grew and developed by successive *haggadah* or interpretative supplementation, disenchantment with the postulate of an ancient preliterary tradition that underwent successive and traceable literary refinements in the process of scriptural fixation, and historical skepticism pure and simple—have cast serious doubt on the validity of the neat J, E, and P divisions of Genesis, distinct in point of time and ethos, which were finally assembled by a Redactor to make up the book as we now know it and have known it for over two thousand years. The judgments and reservations of these scholars must certainly be respected, and they do forbid us from pretending to a consensus that no longer exists.

We remain convinced of the documentary hypothesis, nevertheless, despite all its shortcomings and the obvious objections against it. Working through Genesis once again for the purpose of this commentary, we have become convinced of it more than before. Genesis *is* a scissors-and-paste composition, if that is the expression we must use. It was by such a process that the Semite Tatian found it natural to put together his *Diatessaron* in the second Christian century. And as Jeffrey H. Tigay has recently pointed out,* it was the process followed in editing the proto-Samaritan texts found at Qumran and in the composition of the Samaritan Pentateuch itself, close to the time when the Hebrew Bible was being written in its present form. We are convinced that independent sources, in principle, were combined to make up Genesis and that Genesis, in principle, did not come about through a succession of amplifications and commentary on some basic, primal text. The sources of Genesis do fall apart linguistically and by other measurable constants that even the most casual reader of this book should be able to verify for himself. We are well aware of the many avenues that may be traveled down in pursuit of alternative explanations of the literary phenomena in question: the avenues were always open, only more recently they have been widened and improved. Our objection is to being asked to take so many of them in order to arrive at the same destination. The documentary hypothesis offers a less scenic but also a less roundabout route.

One reason for the present-day questioning of the basic premises of the documentary hypothesis, or at least for a serious revision of its conventional terms, has been the growing challenge asserted against the antiquity

---

* "An Empirical Basis for the Documentary Hypothesis," *Journal of Biblical Literature* 94 (1975), 329–42.

and reliability of much of the traditional data preserved in Genesis. The hypothesis assumes the antiquity and long oral transmission of these traditions in order to account for the variations which they separately took on before they became the literary sources of Genesis. The assumption is still that of probably most Old Testament scholars today. Against it, however, are now some ably argued reassessments of the evidence which maintain that nothing in Genesis antedates the mid-first millennium B.C.,† or in other words, that there is no preliterary Genesis to speak of and therefore no parallel sources could have developed. We shall have to confront some of these weighty objections in our commentary. For the moment we shall merely recapitulate the literary situation of Genesis as we see it, in terms of the old consensus to which we still subscribe.

The J tradition. The genesis of Genesis the literary work has been generally credited to the creative activity of the unknown author whom we know as the Yahwist (*Jahwist* in the German spelling which originally gave rise to the critical symbol "J"). This author, so named for his lavish use of the divine name Yahweh—though this is now recognized to be neither his chief nor most distinguishing trait—has been at times regarded as the father of Israelite historiography, the earliest exponent of an historical sense that distinguished Israel from the rest of its Near Eastern neighbors and that had been acquired through its unique experience of a God of historical revelation. He has been judged to have flourished during the heady period of the united kingdom of David and Solomon (tenth and ninth centuries B.C.) when Israel, newly emerged into nationhood from a series of tribal coalitions, took its place amid the other states of its world and thus, so to speak, entered into history. Having entered into history, it began to write it as well: not history merely in the sense of kingly annals and lapidary boastings with which the Near East was already replete, but history in a proper sense which would define for a people who and where it was by describing whence and how it had come to be.

Practically all of these judgments about the Yahwist and his world must now be qualified. He was very likely preceded by other historians in Israel, particularly by the author of the tendentious succession narrative of 2 Samuel 9–20 and 1 Kings 1–2. The history which he produced owes quite as much to the non-Israelite world of his times as it does to the peculiar Israelite experience which sundered Israel from that world; the sense of history that separated Israel from its neighbors seems to have been more a thing of degree than of kind. This history, furthermore, with which Israel more than the other peoples of the Near East carried on a continuous dia-

† For example, Thomas L. Thompson, *The Historicity of the Patriarchal Narratives: The Quest for the Historical Abraham* (Berlin: de Gruyter, 1974), and John Van Seters, *Abraham in History and Tradition* (Yale University Press, 1975).

logue, was a rather different commodity from that which has been marketed under that name since Herodotus and Thucydides had another idea. As we have already observed, the Yahwist's date is also in dispute. Of one fact only can we be quite sure, that J is the first responsible author of the book we now know as Genesis, on which he has imprinted indelibly his personality and his genius, making the work his more than it could ever be that of any other.

J is a very Israelite history. Naïvely so, it has sometimes been held. See, for example, how (as in 4:26) it has the name of Yahweh put on the lips of pre- and non-Israelites as though there were no other word by which God might be called, in distinction to later traditions which would quite properly restrict that name to the Mosaic revelation which had formed the religion of Israel as one apart from those of the Gentiles (explicitly in Exodus 3:13–15, 6:2, both P). Naïveté is not really one of the Yahwist's qualities, however. Rather, writing for other Israelites, he simply assumed unself-consciously as they did, as the prophet Amos also did in his utterances (cf. Amos 1:3–2:16), that the God of Israel's faith was in fact the Lord and Judge of all mankind (cf. Genesis 18:25, J), whether or whatever the Gentiles knew or thought about that fact. J's Israelite history was intended not for the Gentiles but to explain Israel to Israel, to flesh out ancient historical creeds of the type still preserved in passages like Deuteronomy 26:5–9, the story of the liberating act of a saving God who had freed Israel from political and religious bondage and settled it in a land of its own in fulfillment of a primordial pledge to its remote ancestors. This he could not have done had he not been the master of a history that was larger than Israel's own, even though it was exclusively through its own history that Israel knew its God.

It was this vision of the universality of Israel's God, a vision which J shared with the great prophets, that made the Yahwist produce the work that in turn has made Genesis a book for everyman. For he was not content merely to flesh out the historical creeds which had joined patriarchal legends with the message of Israel's exodus from Egypt to form the kerygmatic history of a people's salvation: the history that begins with chapter 12 of Genesis. He reached even further back into the past in order to show Israel's ancestors' origin in mankind itself, and by so doing he crystallized and passed on to Genesis a theology of historical man in relation to his world which is entirely without parallel in the context of its times. Within this history and theology the "children of Eber" (10:21), the putative ancestors of the Hebrews, certainly play an important role, but only one role among the many which are played by the other races and families of men to whom they are related. The single thread that connects all the data which the Yahwist has drawn together into his history is that of election, which is as far removed as may be from the notion of a superior people or race. Not through any mystique of blood or soil was Israel worthy of consideration, but only as it exemplified what the power of God could effect in it. It is this fact of chosenness as a truth of life that the Yahwist finds demonstrated in Israel's history, and before Israel's history in the mankind that had gone before: Cain and Abel, Noah in his generation, the sons of Shem, Abraham of the seed of Terah, Isaac and Ishmael, and the rest.

The particularities and virtues of the Yahwist's work will best be seen as we proceed through the commentary step by step. It will suffice for the present for us to recognize in this work the originating genius of Genesis as a whole. Had nothing further been done to fill out the larger unity with which we are concerned in this study, even had not the rather new structure been imposed upon it through its subsequent redaction and supplementation, we should still have in the Yahwist's theology of history the essence of all that has made and continues to make the reading of Genesis an exciting experience to so many people. By explaining Israel to itself this author did far more than he could possibly have known. He has enabled the men and women of more than two millennia to a better understanding of themselves and of one another and of the world in which they maintain an existence that is at one and the same time so sure and so precarious.

The E tradition. From the standpoint of literary chronology, though not certainly from the standpoint of earlier modification of the Genesis structure, and certainly not from the standpoint of its ultimate determination, we may consider at this point the contribution made to Genesis by the Elohist (originally so named because of his preference for a generic divine title for Israel's God: Elohim="God"). At best the Elohist is a shadowy figure in relation to the final make-up of Genesis, even though there is no doubt whatsoever of his presence. Was there ever an independently existing E history of Israel's experience with its God, just as there was most certainly an independently existing J history? Or does E rather add up to editorial modifications that were later made on the J history—leaving aside the question as to when those modifications might have been made during the time of Genesis' composition? Probably both of these hypotheses could be separately sustained. To many critics it does appear that there was at one time an Elohist history roughly paralleling that of J, possibly from a northern Israelite point of view as distinct from the Judahite-dominated J story that had come earlier. If so, the same critics will acknowledge, however, that mostly only in fragmentary form has this tradition been introduced into the final text of Genesis, and that largely by melding it with J passages that were in parallel. In favor of the editorial hypothesis we might instance the comparable situation of the so-called Elohistic Psalter, Psalms 42–83, which at some point in time were systematically submitted to a redaction that consisted at least in altering the name of Yahweh to Elohim throughout (easily seen in Psalm 50:7, where the present "God your God" was obviously originally "Yahweh your God," or in Psalm 53, which is the Elohistic duplicate of Psalm 14). On the other hand, the E presence in Genesis (and the Pentateuch) quite frequently goes beyond mechanical name-changing and editorializing. Thus, while the fact of the E element in Genesis is without doubt, the nature and contours of this element are extremely hazy.

Often the presence of E can be detected simply through the evidence that more than one hand has been at work in a combined narrative, even though it may be impossible in a given verse or series of verses to decide whether J or E is the responsible author. But at the same time, most critics would be willing to concede chapter 20 to E beyond doubt, and in other parts of the narrative it is E rather than J who assumes the major responsibility for the common story. One thing is sure: E, whether a supplement or a distinct source, has entered Genesis *in medias res,* which tells us that if indeed there was originally an E history wholly parallel to J, it has not been equally utilized in the composition of Genesis. The same must be said with regard to the forehistory that has played such an important role in the accounts of J and P. If E had had the same insight that prompted J to integrate the history of Israel into the history of everyman, his work has been lost to us since it went unused by the Redactor of Genesis. More likely is it that E never contained such a section but rather followed the conservative lines of the ancient creeds which began with the legends of the fathers. In any event, we are brought to the recognition that by whatever route, E has been joined to Genesis largely as a supplementation and modification of J. By the same token, it is problematical, even unlikely, that there was ever a combined JE narrative prior to the composition of Genesis. Though E probably existed in some form before the writing of P or the redaction of the book of Genesis, and in fact may represent quite as venerable a tradition as that of J itself, it would appear to have been saved from oblivion, to the extent that it was saved, only through the efforts of that unsung workman of whom we know the least, who put the book of Genesis together and used E in the process for more than casual patchwork.

What we have said should not be allowed to prejudice the reader against the E element as though it were of small account. Even if it does not possess the habitual excitement of J's elaborate constructions or even the occasional grandeur of P's carefully chiseled periods, it is not without virtues of its own. Those virtues have often been exploited in the redaction of Genesis, as when an E narrative has been used to round off some of the rough edges of a J parallel. Possibly reflecting the influence of the northern prophetic movement, E displays a sensitivity to certain theological nuances that are often lacking in J and sometimes even in P. It must be admitted, nevertheless, that E's general appearance in the combined narrative is by way of filler, to make an interesting story more interesting through the addition of other details or by heightening its suspense by prolonging its conclusion. Even such a contribution has been considerable, since the other sources of Genesis sometimes anticipated the ultimate Redactor by handling their own materials in the same fashion. The commentary will have to supply the particulars.

The P tradition. If J is the true author of Genesis from the standpoint of the bulk of its content, it is P who has imposed upon the book the order and system by which we identify it as a work in its own right in its present form. P receives its name from the sacral or priestly interests which it largely reflects, especially in the lengthy legal sections which are ascribed to it in the subsequent books of the Pentateuch, but also and already in the tenor of some of the narrative sections of Genesis. Actually, the P narrative in Genesis is relatively sparse, with the notable exceptions of the creation and flood stories, but the stamp of these interests is unmistakably present there all the same. The priestly concerns that are in question are those of the exilic and postexilic circles and communities which codified and updated Israel's ancient cultic and moral traditions and attached them firmly to the restored Jerusalem temple liturgy which was then ideally construed as having been the only one divinely intended for Israel from the beginning. These concerns make the literary date of P, sometime approximately in the fifth century B.C., of somewhat more importance than the separate literary fixations of J or E. Venerable though much of its material may be, as old or older than some of the material of the other two sources, in this tradition we are never allowed to lose sight of those later preoccupations which had been forced in upon Israel through the trauma of exile, the loss, however temporary, of the promised homeland, and the contempt and ridicule of oppressors and persecutors. P cannot treat in the casual way of J with the myth and ritual elements that connect Israel with its ancient contemporaries, or with the conceptions of deity which they shared in common. Its monotheism is hard-line because it had been hard-won, hammered out fine on the anvil of bitter experience in which no quarter could be given at the cost of national and religious dissolution. It is, for this reason, exclusivist, intent on telling Israel what it is by defining what it is not. For the same reason, though it has dredged its materials from the same Near Eastern sources as did J and E, it has transformed them in ways that these other traditions have not.

Like J—and in imitation of J?—P begins with the beginning, not with Abraham but with man himself, and even with the world before man. As it happens, because it does begin with the world before man, it is the younger P rather than the elder J which the Redactor of Genesis has chosen to set at the head of this book. From a literary standpoint the choice was most apt. We are often told, as a consequence, that Genesis begins with two separate stories of creation. In a sense this is true, but we shall also have to see the sense in which it is not true, when we examine the two stories and determine the various ends toward which each was directed. The same choice that made Genesis begin with P also imposed upon it from the outset P's "outline" of its history: the tenfold *toledoth* (literally, "generations," a word peculiar to P and the postexilic literature) first found in 2:4 (of the heavens and the earth) then repeated in 5:1 (of Adam), 6:9 (of Noah), 10:1 (of Noah's sons), 11:10 (of Shem), 11:27 (of Terah), 25:12 (of Ishmael), 25:19 (of Isaac), 36:1.9 (of Esau), and 37:2 (of Jacob), variously translated "story," "descendants," or "family history."

Besides the distinctive preoccupations of P which make it so easily isolable among the traditions of Genesis, we must take note of its entirely particular style. P has not only thoroughly transformed the materials that were at his disposal to a greater extent than J or E, he has also imposed upon them the stamp of a peculiar vocabulary and literary technique. It is not a style that a modern reader finds especially exciting, though it has its moments; but it is unmistakable and therefore highly useful in sorting out the message of Genesis. From these points of view, even though P's contribution to Genesis has been quantitatively less than that of J, he eminently deserves to be considered a major author, even more so than the ultimate Redactor of the book.

The redaction of Genesis. P has, as a matter of fact, sometimes been identified with this ultimate Redactor, the R of the critics. Certainly the two could not have been far separated in time, and it is to be presumed that many if not most of their presuppositions were the same. It does appear, however, that P and R are more than two separate ciphers: they were also separate persons. P assuredly was acquainted with the work of J and at times he presupposes it, accepting its premises without need of repetition, while at other times he "corrects" it or at least improves upon it from what was obviously his point of view. It is quite understandable, given this premise, that he himself should have laid his work side by side with J's or mingled the two together, exactly as we now find the situation in Genesis. What is less understandable, and perhaps not understandable at all, is that in the process he would have left lying about in his book so many unresolved conflicts between his construction of the materials and the one J had made. He could so easily have removed the conflicts as he went along, and from what we can otherwise judge of his proclivities it would have been his disposition to remove them. The more probable conclusion from the state of Genesis as it actually is is that, rather, someone else put the book together from the separate P and J (and E) traditions, treating them with fair impartiality, refusing to allow either one to dominate the other entirely but instead utilizing what he obviously thought were the better insights of both. To explain Genesis, then, it seems that we need an R as well as a P.

He is, however, an R: the hand that readied Genesis in its final form is rightly regarded as that of a redactor and not of an author. If it is true that the juxtaposition of several sources has sometimes given a new nuance to the combined text—the shading of intention that results from the confluence of viewpoints without any single one given the priority—still, we would be hard pressed to assign to R very many fresh ideas that have been introduced into Genesis. He has shown us what was important to him and, at times, what was not important; but whatever he accepted or rejected, whatever he deemed important or dispensable, he found in his sources. The ideas proposed by Genesis are those of J and P, and, occasionally, of E. (As we shall see, the work of R was not the simple one of assembling these three naked sources, but the simplification will serve for the present.) It is this fact that justifies the procedure we follow in this commentary, taking Genesis piece by piece as it may be redivided into its sources. That is where the message of Genesis is.

The message of Genesis, we repeat. We are frequently reminded of the fact we ourselves have noted, that Genesis is only the first part of the larger work we call the Pentateuch or Hexateuch, that is, the five- or six-part national and religious epic of Israel now divided into as many "books," the first books of the Hebrew Bible in its traditional form. J, E, and P, joined later on by D (for the Deuteronomic historian), continue their way through these subsequent books to bring the story to a (provisional) conclusion: the conclusion of a people's pilgrimage of which Genesis is the promise and foreshadowing. The R of Genesis, therefore, is the creator of a far greater unity, and in bringing Genesis into being he had far larger designs in mind. Nevertheless, though Genesis is an introduction, it is also an integral composition in its own right, and this both by reason of its content and in virtue of the materials of which it was composed.

Though the threads of source continuity are sufficiently clear to compel us to an acceptance of the J-E-D-P hypothesis of Pentateuchal composition operative throughout, nevertheless the same criteria that commend the hypothesis also indicate that beginning with the first chapter of the book of Exodus a rather different provenance of the sources must be presupposed than of the ones of Genesis. For that matter, as we shall see later on, a rather different provenance of the J and E traditions must be presupposed once we reach chapter 37 of Genesis. The same sources are there, yet in ways less than subtle they are different. In other words, Genesis itself forms a natural unit in view of its own internal structure and make-up, and in view of the same internal structure and make-up we may find other equally natural divisions within the book of Genesis.

In the following commentary we shall divide Genesis into four more or less equal parts: chapters 1–11, then 12–25, then 25–36, and finally 37–50. The divisions are both convenient and have been dictated by the composition of the book. First of all, from the very earliest editing of Genesis it has been apparent that chapters 1–11 form a prehistory that is separated from the following patriarchal history alike by subject matter and by the way the compositional materials of the several sources have been handled. Chapters 37–50, the Joseph story, as just mentioned separate themselves from the rest of the patriarchal history through an orientation and inspiration that are peculiarly theirs, which betray an influence at work that has not touched the sources elsewhere. Finally, while chapters 12–36 are in many respects a unity, in others they are not. It is not simply that 12:1–25:18 contain the saga of Abraham while 25:19–36:43 contain that of Jacob (with Isaac and Ishmael playing shadow roles in the first section and Isaac and Esau in the second): what seems to be involved is the rather more important evidence that these separate segments give of origins in the cult centers of Israel's forehistory, of Hebron and the south on the one hand and of Bethel and the north on the other. These natural divisions reflecting the varied use made of the Genesis source materials might cause us to qualify the judgment ventured above concerning R's qualities as author. Even though he has left his sources more or less as he found them, he has also selected them with imagination and by no means mechanically. He sought them out where they were best to be employed— we recall, he may have made the first joining of J and E—and he created from them that excellent combination that became the book of Genesis.

2. The Materials of Genesis

We come now to a consideration of the materials of which Genesis has been compounded. Materials, now, rather than the sources into which the materials had been poured. The materials of Genesis are the raw bits and pieces of myth, legend, saga, and whatnot out of which the J and E and P authors shaped their several sources: they are the stuff from which the true authorship of Genesis emerged. As raw components they are almost entirely and without exception identifiable in terms of the literary and thought-forms common to the ancient Near Eastern culture of which Genesis and Israel were a tiny part. In virtue of their transformation into the continuity of the biblical sources they have usually assumed a rather new and different character, precisely the kind of character that has given to their appearance in Genesis the universal and perennial human appeal that they possess not at all outside it. The same forms outside the Bible are of intense interest today, it is true, to the student of comparative religions and cultures, and we shall have occasion to recognize that interest from time to time in this book. For the most part, however, they had ceased for centuries to be included in any living literature until they came to be recovered by the quite modern techniques men have devised to reconstitute the—relevant and irrelevant—memorabilia of antiquity. In Genesis they were there all along. The forms did not survive simply as forms, obviously, but because of what they had been made to say that somehow struck an answering chord in the minds and emotions of those who heard them say it in Genesis.

For the moment a couple of examples of what we are talking about will suffice. In Genesis 6:1–4 the J author has picked up a story that is fairly routine in the mythologies of ancient peoples throughout the world, a somewhat disedifying tale of divine and human miscegenation that led to the birth of a monstrous growth of supermen. Had he done this only, only repeated the story, it would be nothing especially memorable that he accomplished. Why the story in J has remained memorable is that the Yahwist chose to fit it into a picture of cosmic disorder, of a world strangely out of joint, that did then and has afterward continued to correspond with what man's historical experience of the world has caused him to sense that the story has something true about it. Another example is the P story of origins in Genesis 1:1–2:4a. Every ancient literature has its share of such creation myths, in which man was put in his place amid the awesome spectacle of the generation of the gods and cosmic forces which were thought to rule over him. As we shall see, P has also put man in his place within the story as he told it, but in a vastly different kind of place indeed, a place which had been revealed to him through the perspectives on God and man which were communicated through Israel's religion. In such ways did the compilers of the Genesis sources assume the functions of genuine authors in creating a unique literature out of the common Near Eastern materials.

It is in order now to consider what were the kinds of materials that were assembled by the sources.

Genealogies constitute one of the forms whose importance it is easy to underesteem, even though they are so prevalent that they cannot be ignored. They are, first of all, an almost exclusive Genesis characteristic, one of those traits which distinguish Genesis from the rest of the books of the Bible. Not that there are no genealogies elsewhere in the Bible, since as a matter of fact they play more than an occasional role in both the Old and the New Testaments. It is that in Genesis they play a special role which is neither perfunctory nor merely statistical but one that gives direction and

provides the structure of the entire work. We associate the genealogy in
Genesis with the P source first of all (recall the *toledoth* divisions noted
already), but in point of fact it is J who has used the form most imaginatively, especially in the prehistory section of chapters 1–11. Properly
speaking, as would seem obvious, the genealogy pertains to the patriarchal
history rather than to these chapters which introduce it: it is precisely the
kind of form that would reflect the concerns of the tribal society out of
which that collection of sagas derived. Its extended and highly sophisticated transferral into prehistory serves as a continual reminder of the intent of Genesis to set its sights firmly on a human *history* and, contrary to
the disposition of ancient myth to drift toward never-never lands peopled
with unearthly beings, to play upon a stage both earth- and time-bound
with a cast of real characters.

In Genesis the genealogy assumes various specific formulations, which
need not concern us at this time, and it also is applied to varied functions.
Sometimes, indeed, it is merely a list of names and generations, as it almost universally is outside Genesis. But it may also take on such tasks as
exploring the sweep and progress of history, the origin and names of peoples and their relationship one to another, the development of the arts and
crafts and other institutions of man, and the like. In many of these adaptations it perforce becomes mingled with one or another of the narrative
forms which generally carry out the development of the book.

Narrative as a matter of course accounts for the lion's share of the materials that have been taken up by the authors of Genesis' sources. The book
is, after all, fundamentally a story and a series of connected stories. Many
of the narratives, especially those of the Yahwist or of the JE compilation
but sometimes others as well, along with their surrounding or intermingled
genealogies, still bear the marks of a prior, independent existence, and
even of a prior, independent meaning, which they enjoyed before being
woven into the sources. As we have already admitted, we shall have to
revert to this issue frequently in the commentary. If the sources of Genesis
deserve separate treatment because of the separate authorships involved,
similarly a division of the text almost story by story for the purpose of
commentary can be justified not only for the sake of convenience but also
on the more pressing grounds of these components' pre-existence as independent narratives that were either adapted or reworked. It is evidently
the duty of a commentator to observe where his material has been as well
as where it now is.

We shall deal with the complex variety of Genesis narrative forms as we
come to them. However, we may now make some preliminary remarks on
the more prominent of the forms and the categories into which they fall.

There is, first of all, especially in the early chapters, a considerable
amount of *myth*. This term ought not to be a frightening one for the per-

son who wishes to take Genesis seriously; quite to the contrary, the more seriously he wishes to take Genesis the more inevitable this literary category will appear and appeal to him in his reading of the book. The intention of Genesis, as we have said more than once, was to produce a work directed to historical man to help him to a better self-understanding by responding to the resonances of his own genuine historical experience. But it could not do this by amassing historical documentation, for there was none. Even the patriarchal legends which begin with chapter 12 of Genesis are not historical documentation, even though they doubtless have preserved their share of history in the banal sense of Things That Really Happened. Far less was it possible to document the creation of man and his world, the origin of his unique dignity and his dependence on God, his many successes and failures in a primordial and misty past that antedated even the vaguest kind of historical memory. For all of this there was only myth. The genius of Genesis is not simply to have made use of myth to write its history of man, since it could do no else; the genius of Genesis was to have chosen the right myths and to have discarded the others. Myth, in its most acceptable definition, is simply a society's attempt to dramatize its faith in its own identity and its institutions, and as such it can be positively good, indifferent and trivial, or unspeakably vicious. The comparative study of ancient mythologies which modern research has made possible has confirmed what more than two millennia of the readers of Genesis long knew without knowing, that this book chose its myths wisely and well.

The myths of Genesis are not of one piece. Myth in one of its purest forms is encountered in the P creation story of Genesis 1:1–2:4a. As we shall see, there are several creation stories in Genesis (not just two), and all of them are necessarily mythological, though not in the same way or to the same degree. This story of the Priestly author, even though it has as one of its purposes to polemicize against the spirit and details of the Babylonian myths of creation, nevertheless has retained much of the ritual aspect of re-enactment and reiteration which was the essence of such myths. As will be evident from the reading of this passage, it is less a story than it is a prose poem celebrating certain dominant Israelite convictions about the nature and consequences of creation: it is a recitation of dogma, in other words. Whether it ever actually accompanied a ritual or simply owes its form to having been modeled on myths that did accompany rituals cannot be determined.

Other creation motifs in Genesis are properly identifiable as stories of origins. Here, whether they deal with out-and-out mythical characters such as those of 6:1–4, or the putatively historical race of man in 11:1–9, or typical or eponymous characters such as those of chapter 4, myth readily melds into *the etiological story,* one of the most common of the art forms to be found in ancient literatures. The function of the etiological story is to tell how things began: languages, tribes, the arts, human crafts, and other accomplishments, as well as the deeper mysteries of the human short-comings and the disordered world in which man finds himself. In the lack —and a lack that continues to this day, of course—of authentic information about such beginnings, the stories were told, and because they lack authentic information they are in that sense mythical. One primary assertion of the stories in Genesis, however, must be accounted anti-mythical, and that is their insistence that all such matters do, indeed, pertain to human history that was acted out on the solid earth of man's experience. Human beings, not gods, people the stories of Genesis.

Epic is undoubtedly the best category under which to classify the flood story of Genesis 6:5–9:17 (J and P combined into one). It is true, in this story we have one of our most sustained parallels with a portion of the great Babylonian myth cycle of Gilgamesh, a parallel which descends to rather minute details at times and could hardly be the result of chance. It is quite clear, in other words, that the myth and the stories assimilated by the sources of Genesis have a common ancestor that could not have been too remote. As we shall see when we compare the stories, however, they have an entirely different motivation and direction in their separate usages. The flood story of Genesis is no longer, if ever once it was, part of a myth of divine and human commerce dealing with the theme of man's quest after immortality and godship, the character that the episode has in the Gilgamesh story (and which has a partial parallel in the Yahwist's portrayal of man in the garden of God in chapters 2–3 of Genesis). It has become instead a piece of primitive human history acted out on the grand epic pattern but in what was considered to be the workaday world of strictly natural if not ordinary events and occurrences.

Most of the patriarchal history is best described as *saga*. Saga, as the word might indicate, is the tales, legendary and historical, which were first said, told orally, about great or notorious personages of the past (another clear, if quite brief, instance of saga occurs in the Lamech poem of Genesis 4:23–24). It is the nature of saga that it focuses attention on the single hero, to whom other characters in the stories play subordinate roles, and that it gathers about this hero stories that may once have belonged to someone else or which may be "typical" stories assimilated to him from disparate origins. As we have already indicated, the cycles of sagas which have been assembled to make up the patriarchal history are roughly three, those of Abraham, Jacob (already combined with the figure of a patriarch Israel), and Joseph. The three cycles, however, as we have also indicated, are of no single school or source of storytelling, even independently of the fact that they cut across the sources of traditions of Genesis as a whole. Even though they now have been bent into other directions, and already were when they were gathered into cycles, much of the sagas of Abraham (and Isaac) and Jacob (and Israel) still gives evidence, when it is looked for, of origins in cult legends associated with one or another of the southern or central Palestine sanctuaries which obviously retained great significance for the sources of Genesis, especially the Yahwist. (An interest, incidentally, which is in significant contrast with the polemics of prophetical preaching and even more so with the thrust of the Deuteronomic reform and of postexilic exclusivism.) The "novel" of Joseph, on the other hand, is by comparison "secular" in its inspiration: Joseph is noteworthy not for having erected altars or anointed sacred stones but for having proved to be an astute statesman and courtier, the ideal of the "wise man" of Israel's wisdom tradition, which was neither prophetic nor priestly in its interests.

The above will give some idea of the kinds of materials we expect to meet as we read Genesis. There are others, of course, bits of poetry scattered here and there or gathered into sequences, some stories that seem to have been told for the sheer joy of the telling, with no other excuse, and other tales and pieces of prose that defy any more precise categorization. We shall make the attempt to define them as accurately as possible when we take them up one by one in the commentary.

The sources of the sources of Genesis is another way of saying what these materials are. They have usually been quite satisfactorily assimilated into the sources to which they belong, but sometimes they have not. Because of the sheer wealth of the materials and their variety as taken up by the Yahwist it is often that in his work we discover internal tensions and inconsistencies from one story to another, or at least difficulties that we create for ourselves when we attempt to impose a unity upon the materials that he did not see fit to impose. A celebrated instance is the sudden appearance of Cain's wife (Genesis 4:17) into a context to which she originally belonged not at all, to the consequent chorus of claims and counterclaims of biblical contradiction. Of course there will be contradiction, if we persist in reading the Yahwist's story without advertence to the sources which he has gathered into his source. Already in the same context (4:14) a whole host of other interlopers are presumed who, we might think, have no business in a story that has been adapted to tell of the first generation of the human race (4:1–2). These are the most trivial examples of the blithe disregard for internal cohesion which is typical of the Yahwist's handling of his materials. The other sources display a regard for consistency that is to our tastes more sophisticated, which is to say that they have more thoroughly reworked or recast their materials in favor of larger unities. Even in these, however, we sometimes encounter, albeit more rarely, variations on the same theme: witness, for example, the chronological note of Genesis 11:10 which strangely jars with the numerical sequences which the Priestly author has otherwise worked out in such loving detail—and, it must be confessed, in a fairly tedious detail when measured by contemporary interests and priorities. P too, as it eventuates, has not bothered to smooth away all the conflicting unevennesses of its source materials.

The combination of the materials into the sources of Genesis, not unlike the juxtaposition of the sources themselves one to another, is part of the key to the interpretation of this book. Neither the book nor its sources nor the sources of the sources have been harmonized into a whole according to the canons of classical or modern historiography. By their own lights all these units were intended to be read as unities, and unities they are, but only by those lights. The refusal to resolve the incidental conflict indicates to us, whether the refusal was that of J or P or R, what in his mind was the veritable unity and what was, on the contrary, the dispensable detail. Dispensable, that is, from the standpoint of conveying information; from the standpoint of good storytelling it may have been, indeed, indispensable. Therefore, as we have already observed, it is necessary to read the story as it was put together, vignette by vignette, narrative following narrative, not merely as a convenience of procedure, but as entering into the spirit of the composition itself.

3. The Interpretation of Genesis

We have now broached the delicate question of interpretation. We do not intend to say very much about this question here and now, since we feel that the principles on which we venture interpretations of Genesis will be made plain as we proceed through the commentary. A preliminary remark or two are in order, however, especially as regards our reading of the book for a mainly Christian audience.

We do not enter into the spirit of Genesis unless we recognize from the outset that its intention was to write a history. We have said this before, but it bears repeating, since the temptation is ever present to have it otherwise, particularly in view of the fact that there is so much in Genesis which a modern mind can hardly accept as history. Nevertheless, a modern mind that would attempt to resolve the historical situation for itself by treating Genesis as a series of more or less elaborate allegories and by transferring this treatment to the authors of Genesis themselves would end by compounding a series of mistakes. Genesis took itself seriously as serious history, the beginning of a history that its authors had seen triumphantly fulfilled in their own lifetimes.

The myth, legend, and folklore of which the early chapters of Genesis have been composed, not to mention the sagas which account for most of the patriarchal stories, form no obstacle, as we have argued, against taking this history at its own face value. When all is said and done, such is the usual stuff of history, and not only the history of the Old Testament. More important, however, is it that Genesis has been written out of an historical experience that was independent of the materials of which it fashioned its history, or better, which found in these materials resonances and insights that corresponded with the experience. Genesis did not present creation as an historical fact because it had any human witness or record of creation, quite obviously, even though human witness and record are conventionally the sources on which history draws. It presented it as an historical fact because it depended on the historical experience of a God who had revealed himself in such ways that were readily recognizable in the creation myth. It was this historical experience that dictated the choice of materials of which we have spoken above, the choice which was made so wisely and so well that Genesis stands apart from the rest of Near Eastern myth and folklore to which it is otherwise so evidently related. The historical experience has imposed its character upon materials that were not of themselves or in content originally historical.

One reason for our stressing this historical intention is to justify the first of the major segments into which we divide Genesis for the purposes of this commentary. That major segment is the first eleven chapters of the book, not the first three only. In a non-historical interpretation of Genesis the Christian might be tempted—and Christian readers have indeed succumbed to this temptation on many occasions—to isolate the first three chapters at the expense of the rest because these chapters deal with myths which the church has appropriated and developed independently of biblical history: in this instance, the myths of creation and the fall of man. The historical interpretation, on the other hand, will insist that these myths cannot be isolated from what follows them. Creation and fall are not in Genesis simply theologoumena; they are events like other events that succeed them, the events of Cain and Abel, of the descendants of Cain and Seth, of the children born to the daughters of men by the sons of heaven, and of the flood and its aftermath in the scattering of the nations throughout the world. In turn, this complex history is presented as a preface to the patriarchal story that both anticipates and desiderates the later history of Israel that lies outside the scope of Genesis. The historical approach to Genesis forbids us from mining its texts for adventitious purposes that are unrelated to its authors' grand designs.

Genesis is, then, a history—a preface to the history of Israel. But is it thereby our history: the history of a people or of a church that lays no claim to lineal descent from Abraham yet feels itself countable among the true sons of Abraham (cf. John 8:31–59)? We believe that it is, and that for several reasons, the first of which is already apparent in the posing of the question itself. Christianity no less than Judaism has appropriated the Old Testament as its prior history, a fact that is patent in the foundation literature and the record of the mission of the earliest church. It may be argued that the fact is due in no small measure to some incidental circumstances of New Testament origins, and the argument does have a certain validity. From parts of the New Testament itself it is plain that history could have taken another turn, that the Christian kerygma could have been phrased in terms of a religious experience other than that of Israel, just as it is entirely conceivable that it can be phrased or rephrased today in such other terms for those peoples or cultures for whom the history and the God of the Hebrew Bible are alien and unknown. Nevertheless, for all that its circumstances may have been incidental, the fact remains a fact. From the beginning, the New Testament as a whole has been wedded to the Old Testament as a whole, and the one has been seen as the continuation of the other. Israel's history and Israel's God were the history and God of Jesus and the first disciples, and from them of the primitive church, whether Gentile or Jewish. The history of Genesis, therefore, has an ancient title to consideration as Christian history, and even if we must concede that it is not the only possible Christian history, it is a Christian history nevertheless.

The best reason, however, is that which we have already brought out in the discussion of the composition and make-up of Genesis. The book forms a history unto itself, and a history that may be rightly appropriated by everyman, since it is truly everyman's history. The principle of this assertion is most readily apparent in the first eleven chapters, where its authors have professedly related the history of their people to the history of mankind as a whole. It is no less present, however, in the patriarchal history, which though the story of Israel's ancestors is not the story of Israel alone. The patriarchal history is the story of the Semites, an ethnic group which we may find it intriguing to recall in these times embraces the numerous Aramean and Edomite tribes who later came to be known as Arabs alongside other Hebraic tribes who later came to be known as Jews. From its very inception, therefore, it is no exaggeration to call the patriarchal history anything other than an ecumenical venture. It is no exaggeration at all, particularly if we have enough historical sense to know that the opposition between Jew and Arab was no less fierce in the age that witnessed the final redaction of Genesis than it has become in our later times. As a consequence, it should not be difficult to enter into the spirit of this ecumenicity by recognizing the intent of Genesis to deal with the broadest possible scope of human history. In its own fashion and within its own historical limitations, Genesis tried to treat of a universal human history.

The interpretation of Genesis for the Christian reader should be no different from its interpretation for anyone else. If Genesis is to appear as a relevant literature it can only do so when its original purposes are taken seriously and it is interpreted historically. This does not mean that we call history in the case of Genesis what our better information has convinced us cannot be literally considered history. To the contrary, one of the implications of taking the book seriously on historical principles is that we must distinguish in it the various non-historical forms out of which it shaped its history. What is meant is that we not allow our later insights whether derived from a more sophisticated knowledge or from confessional commitment to impede the message of Genesis by imposing upon it categories that were not of its ken. It must take its place within a process of development in which it was neither the first nor the final stage. When it is thus firmly placed, and only then, we hear the sounds that have always been the voice of its universal appeal.

I. The Book of Origins

1. The Story of Creation

We begin at the beginning, with the P story of the creation of man's world.

> **1** In the beginning, when God created the heavens and
> **2** the earth, the earth was a formless wasteland, and
> darkness covered the abyss, while a mighty wind
> **3** swept over the waters. Then God said, "Let there be
> **4** light," and there was light. God saw how good the
> light was. God then separated the light from the
> **5** darkness. God called the light "day," and the dark-
> ness he called "night." Thus evening came and morn-
> ing followed—the first day.

The reader is, of course, immediately aware of some differences between this version and the "traditional" translation of these first few verses of Genesis. "In the beginning God created the heavens and the earth" is the initial line of familiar resonance. It is the programmatic assertion of a creation that then immediately unfolds in the vision of a cosmic chaos upon which order is speedily imposed: God is the author of an as yet formless earth which he proceeds to organize. It is possible that the same sense may still be extracted from the text as we have it above. The "when" of God's creation, it would seem, could at choice either presuppose the condition described in vs. 2 or define it as a consequence: "when God created the heavens and the earth, the earth was (already? then and there became?) a formless wasteland." In its most normal acceptation, however, and the one that we believe to be correct just as we believe the translation itself to be correct, what vs. 2 is concerned with is the raw material of divine creation and not its effect. A better understanding of the biblical notion of creation and a better awareness of the place of the Priestly narrative within a recognizable pattern of Near Eastern literature lead us to this conclusion.

Though the parallel is not exact in every detail, these verses may be aptly compared with the opening lines of *Enuma elish,* the Sumero-

Babylonian creation hymn that was ritually recited during the annual new year's festival in Mesopotamia:

> When on high the heaven had not yet been named,
> firm ground below had not yet been called by name,
> naught but primordial Apsu,* their begetter,
> and Mummu-Tiamat,† she who bore them all,
> their waters commingling as a single body;
> no reed hut had been matted, no marsh land had appeared,
> when no gods whatever had been brought into being,
> uncalled by name, their destinies undetermined:
> then it was that the gods were formed within them . . .

The Babylonian hymn is a theogony, a recital of the birth of the gods, which has no counterpart in the Genesis story. First the gods, then the heavens and earth and underworld, and only at the end man, who is to serve the gods—such is the structure of the Babylonian myth. The similarity to Genesis is nevertheless apparent, just as is its similarity to other ancient creation stories, Greek and Roman as well as Semitic. At the beginning of all there is a vision simply of unformed chaos, with no attempt made to account for its presence. The myth of creation, in other words, does not speculate about the origin of matter; it rather attempts to account for the emergence of an ordered, livable universe.

In this sense *God created the heavens and the earth,* these terms being merely the cumbersome way the Hebrew has of designating the visible world about us, sky and land. It has often been observed that the Hebrew word translated "created" (*bara*) does not necessarily mean making something out of nothing, that it can be used (cf. Isaiah 41:20, for example) to refer to a re-creation, the remaking of something that already exists. The observation is correct, but also fairly otiose, since it is doubtful that any language of man has a verb "create" which all by itself expresses the recondite notion of the eduction of matter *ex nihilo sui et subiecti.* Nevertheless, the parenthetical reference to Isaiah 41:20 is quite in order. There it becomes evident that the sense of *bara* is pre-eminently a soteriological one, that the essence of creation is that it be a saving action. The Second Isaiah, on whose theology the Priestly author is dependent or with which at least his own stands in strong parallel, is a firm believer in a Creator God whose initial act of creation is the model of his act of election in saving and re-creating Israel in the Babylonian captivity:

> For thus says the LORD,
> The creator of the heavens,
>   who is God,

---

* A personification of the primordial sea of sweet water.
† Personification of the primordial salt-water ocean.

The designer and maker of the earth
  who established it,
Not creating it to be a waste,
  but designing it to be lived in:
I am the LORD, and there is no other.
  I have not spoken from hiding
  nor from some dark place of the earth,
And I have not said to the descendants of Jacob,
  "Look for me in an empty waste."
I, the LORD, promise justice,
  I foretell what is right (Isaiah 45:18–19).

In these lines that contain several verbal and conceptual links with the first verse of Genesis we undoubtedly have one of our best commentaries on what creation meant to the Priestly author. It has to do with a wonderful act of divine mercy: *bara* is never used in the Hebrew Old Testament with other than God as its subject. It is conceived as the first in a long history of saving acts of which, as we have asserted, Israel had had experience and which served as the model of the conception. We should not lose sight, in the parallel of *Enuma elish* which we have made above, of all that separates the story of Genesis from the Babylonian myth. Creation is not just a happening, not the random formation of divine beings out of primordial chaos. It is an act *of God*, of the same God who, as the story develops, will be seen to have been the God of Israel's forefathers and the same who appeared to Moses to call Israel out of Egypt, to form to himself a people just as he had first formed the land (cf. Exodus 3:4–17). Although he is forbidden by his self-imposed schema from invoking the sacred name of Yahweh at this early stage (Yahweh, in his purview, is the name of God reserved for the Mosaic revelation), what the Priestly author is insisting on most strongly is that the God of Israel is the one who has given mankind the goodly earth in which it was to lead a productive and meaningful life—not the mindless deities of Babylon with whom Israel had lately become acquainted to its sorrow, and not the chthonic gods of Canaan which had always exercised a powerful attraction on Israel in its land of promise (cf. Hosea 2:7–11).

When we understand creation in this way, as primarily an act of redemption (see also Isaiah 43:1, 45:11–13), a conquest of primordial chaos which other Old Testament poetical texts have not hesitated to express in far more mythological terms (cf. Psalms 74:12–17, 89:10–12; Isaiah 51:9), we are prepared to see what is the image entailed in the parenthetical vs. 2 above. When God began the work of creation, says the author, *the earth was a formless wasteland.* "Formless wasteland" translates the famous *tohu wa-bohu* whose very sound even outside translation suggests disorder and aimlessness. And that, very probably, explains the origin of the expression. *Tohu* is a fairly common word in the Hebrew Old Testament, where it usually refers to the empty and the unproductive (in Job 26:7 to the "empty space" which parallels "nothing at all"). In Isaiah 34:11 and Jeremiah 4:23 besides this second verse of Genesis *bohu* has been added, doubtless as a simple alliterative strengthener of the primary idea, without any separate meaning of its own. There is no reason to look for a hidden mythological allusion, such as to the Phoenician goddess Baau on the one hand or the Babylonian Tiamat on the other. The Priestly author has modeled himself so far on the prevailing mythological pattern and is in the process waging a subtle polemics against the mythological presuppositions, but his performance throughout is low-key and never obtrusive. He is simply picturing the mess he conceived to be the lot of the world apart from the creative, saving, and sustaining intervention of God. Similarly, when he says that *darkness covered the abyss,* he doubtless intends no personifications but simply another effort at describing primordial chaos. Contrary to the surface sense of Isaiah 45:6, the Priestly author does not consider the darkness to be part of the creative work of God but rather the exemplification of disorder that is to be banished by his first creative word. The "abyss" (Hebrew *tehom*), though at one time it may have had some relation to the Babylonian figure of Tiamat (in Genesis 49:25 and other poetic passages *tehom* is accorded some personal characteristics), has no such relation here. It is merely the lowest level of a primitive cosmology, the "waters beneath the earth" (Exodus 20:4) which were thought to be the source not only of the salt seas (Genesis 1:10) but also of the fresh waters as well (Deuteronomy 4:18). Before creation the abyss covered all, which was also clothed in darkness. After creation (vss. 6–9 below), it was divided in two by the dome of the sky, giving rise to those waters beneath the earth just mentioned as well as to the waters above the earth (i.e., above the solid bowl of heaven), the "flood" (*mabbul*) where God was thought to have his dwelling (Psalm 29:10) and whence the rains came (cf. Psalm 104:5–13). Most of the details of this cosmology and its related mythology (e.g., the waters below as the guardian of the realm of the dead, Job 26:5) are not pursued by the Priestly author in his evocation of the precreational abyss.

The *mighty wind* that *swept over the waters* (that the prosaic "waters" parallels "abyss" indicates how impersonally P thought of the latter) forms some special problems of its own. "Mighty wind" comes out literally something like "a divine wind," and it is taken to signify a wind that was superhuman, almighty, inconceivable in ordinary terms—like the "divine panic" of 1 Samuel 14:15 that is translated "beyond human endurance," or Nineveh the "divinely large city" that turns out to be "enormously large" in Jonah 3:3, or even perhaps the "cedars of God" of Psalm 80:11

that were so large they were thought to have been planted by God himself (Numbers 24:6: the popular "as old as God" is not far from this kind of superlative). In this probably correct assessment of the expression, we have a final stroke added to the picture of initial disorder, with the world-to-be as yet inundated by the dark primordial waters and whipped into a vortex by a driving wind. It must be confessed, however, that here again another "traditional" translation is conceivable that would alter this interpretation considerably. For the wind of divine proportions might also be "the spirit [i.e., the life-giving breath] of God" moving upon the waters preparatory to the beginning of creation. "For the spirit of God has made me, the breath of the Almighty keeps me alive" (Job 33:4): in Hebrew the words for spirit, breath, wind, all symbols of power, are one and the same. Against this alternative translation, however, besides the already remarked parallelism between the darkness of the abyss and the wind-swept waters, are at least two other considerations of some weight. First of all, "swept" seems to be the correct word to translate the Hebrew participle rather than the hovering or brooding concept we would expect were the spirit of God in question. Even more decisively, what next takes place is not an infusion of the spirit of God but rather the pronouncement of a divine word: "Let there be light." It seems preferable, therefore, to let the translation given above stand, and to find the first act of creation in the making of light.

Then God said is the constant refrain of this creation story, the usual corollary of which is *and so it happened* or its equivalent. "By the word of the LORD the heavens were made . . . he spoke, and it [the earth] was made" (Psalm 33:6.9). The "let there be" of the creative command equates with the "made" and "created" scattered elsewhere through the story and is no warrant in itself of a superior or more sophisticated conception of the relation of the Creator God to the object of his creation (the Babylonian creation myth and other ancient myths as well could imagine things coming to be through the word of a god): they are simply different ways of making explicit what was entailed in the "created" of vs. 1. What doubtless does lie behind this particular formulation is the common Semitic conception of the built-in efficacy of the uttered word. In the Old Testament "word" and "deed" are, or frequently are, one and the same: blessings, curses, prophetic pronouncements all obtain their efficacy from their very assertion and from then on lead a life of their own. There is, no doubt, to the modern taste at least some vestige of magic underlying a conception of this kind, though the biblical authors may have been unaware of it. They were, rather, in a society where written documents and instruments were few, testifying to the dynamic effect which perforce had to be attributed to the spoken word. Word is power: the same idea has penetrated the New Testament and is at the base of the Christian conviction of the efficacy of the word in preaching and sacrament. In the instance at hand, the sheer repetition of the formula along with the occasional "made" or "created" is doubtless intended to emphasize the transcendence of this Creator God of the work of his creation. Though creation by word is not unknown in the ancient myths, it is rare there. Ordinarily the myths depict divine creation as a slow, laborious process in which things are made from other things, indeed, from divine things more often than not.

The first of God's creations is *light*. It has often been remarked that the Priestly author is not disturbed by the incongruity of the existence of light prior to the creation of the sources of light which takes place only on "the fourth day" (vss. 14–19). Partly, of course, this is accounted for by a lack of scientific knowledge concerning the nature of the light of day; but there is more to the question than that. Dominating the ancient world and corresponding to some still recognizable instinct buried deep in the human psyche was the dualism of darkness and light, in which the former stood for everything fearful and hidden, unknown and therefore frightening, or morally bad and unstable, while the latter stood for all the opposites. Light, it was agreed, was the proper sphere of divinity. In the myths light was, in fact, a god. The Bible is also capable of identifying God with light (see 1 John 1:5), but it is not in the Priestly author's interest to do so. Rather he must insist that light, like everything else that is good in man's world, is a creature of God. It is the first of his creatures, however, since it is the condition of the rest of his creation, all of which must be deeds of light. Also, as we see in a moment, the creation of light makes possible the beginning of time, and with it that history of which creation is the first act. *God saw how good the light was* images the divine satisfaction over a work well done. The line occurs sevenfold in the creation story and serves two purposes. First of all, it underscores a belief in creation as a deliberate overflowing of God's goodness, not the adventitious or even capricious happening that it could appear to be in the myths. Secondly, it insists that man's ordered world is indeed good, not in ontological or moral opposition to the designs of God as pagan pessimism early and late might have it. It is not said, of course, that the darkness is equally good; as we have seen already, darkness is probably not in the vision of P part of God's creation, though he dominates and controls it as we are immediately reminded.

The creation of light is accompanied by a work of division: *God then separated the light from the darkness*. Partly this is another evocation of mythological motifs, according to which the beginning of the cosmos was the result of the (sometimes violent) separation of heaven and earth, or sea and sea, or sea and land. In *Enuma elish* Marduk the creator god "split [Tiamat] like a shellfish into two parts," of which the upper was made into the heavens, the lower into the earth and underworld. Separation thus takes its place alongside creation by word, fashioning, and other traditional creational themes which the Priestly author has combined with fair impartiality. The theme of separation permits him, however, to show the creative power of God at work even over those parts of the universe which he did not (explicitly) make: here the darkness as well as the light, and in the following section the primordial waters. The same function is performed by the bestowal of names that immediately ensues: *God called . . . "day," and . . . "night."* It was the common persuasion that name-giving signified control, dominance, taking possession. "I have called you by name: you are mine," said Yahweh to Israel (Isaiah 43:1). So in the Yahwist's story man asserts his domination over the rest of animal creation by giving to each creature its proper name (Genesis 2:19–20). It is significant that in vs. 10 below after the recession of the waters God calls by name the earth and the sea, both of which in their unformed state preceded the utterance of God's first creative word.

Now that day and night have been defined, the cycle of time begins and we have *the first day.* ("Day" does double duty in biblical Hebrew, just as it does in most other languages, both to distinguish the daylight hours from the night and to refer to the period of time that includes the night as well.) It is likely enough, given the background of P, that *evening came and morning followed* implies a day that stretches from sunset to sunset, in keeping with the ritual pattern (Leviticus 23:32, for example). In any case, the rationale of the division of the creation story over a series of days we shall examine below.

> 6 Then God said, "Let there be a dome in the middle of
> the waters, to separate one body of water from the
> 7 other." And so it happened: God made the dome,
> and it separated the water above the dome from the
> 8 water below it. God called the dome "the sky." Eve-
> ning came, and morning followed—the second day.

This translation follows the ancient Septuagint Greek version of the Hebrew Bible in transferring *and so it happened* from the end of vs. 7 to the end of vs. 6 where it more logically and consistently belongs, whatever may have been the logic and consistency of the original author. It does not follow the Septuagint when it adds "and God saw how good it was" as the divine verdict on the creation of the dome. We might expect such a verdict to have been rendered, as the Septuagint obviously expected it. Why was it not? Perhaps because the creational purpose of the dome was not thought to have been entirely fulfilled until the separation of the waters led finally to the emergence of a habitable earth (cf. vs. 10). Or perhaps because the author had allotted to his story only a sevenfold "good" which he felt should be otherwise distributed. We should not easily accede to the temptation to improve on the story as it has come down to us.

Similarly with the other particulars of these verses. As though to recompense for any shortcomings in properly dignifying the dome as God's good creation, the author has combined no less than four of his customary motifs to herald its appearance. We hear the creative command as before: *let there be . . . and so it happened;* but now it is added that *God made the dome* (from the parallel in vss. 21 and 25 below it is evident that the author draws no distinction between "made" and "created"). Furthermore, this turns out to be a work of separation of *one body of water from the other.* And finally, there is the giving of a name. We need not draw the conclusion from this proliferation of formulas that the text of Genesis has conflated various versions of the same creative event. What we should conclude, however, is that the author attached great importance to this particular event.

The rearing of the dome, as a matter of fact, after the creation of light that is its condition, marks the first stage in the ordering of the universe as the Priestly author conceived of it. He obviously thought of the sky as some kind of burnished, metallic bowl suspended above his earth (cf. Job 37:18). This dome ("firmament" in the older translations) had to have solidity in order to sustain in normal times *the water above the dome* which in abnormal times surged through floodgates to produce torrential rains (Genesis 7:11). *The water below* the dome, as we have already pointed out, following the additional creational word of vs. 9 becomes the seas and (though not taxatively accounted for in these few verses) the fresh-water springs of the earth. The rearing of the dome makes possible the final appearance of a livable world by a taming of the waters even as darkness had been tamed.

That *God called the dome "the sky"* (in the Hebrew "sky" is the same word as "the heavens" of vs. 1), that he felt the need to claim it as his own even though he has already been shown to have created it thrice over, is partly explained by the fact that the totality of the sky now embraces some of the primordial waters that anteceded creation. What seems to be at issue here is an insistence on the creaturely status of the heavens, a protestation against any dualistic conception of man's world that would oppose to the solid earth beneath his feet extraterrestrial powers from on high that could dominate and influence him. The Old Testament is capable of localizing God in the heavens (Psalm 11:4) and even of surrounding him there with a ceremonial court of supernatural beings (1 Kings 22:19); and such ideas have penetrated the New Testament as well. Later language could in consequence make of "heaven" a metonym for "God" (cf. Matthew's "kingdom of heaven," our "heaven knows"). These are neither the language nor the thoughts of the Priestly author. In vss. 14–18 below he carefully demythologizes the astral deities who infected so much of the religious thinking of his contemporary world and who in other guises have infected men's thinking since. For the present he is content to define the heavens simply as the sky, simply as a compartment of the familiar universe round about, neither a source of fear or dread nor an object of reverence or worship. He was many worlds removed from the apocalyptic mentality which viewed life as a battle "not against human forces [literally, "blood and flesh"] but against the principalities and powers, the rulers of this world of darkness, the evil spirits in regions above" (Ephesians 6:12). The heavens and the earth of the Priestly author are rather different from this kind of perspective, and rather more recognizable to present-day eyes which view them across the centuries.

> 9 Then God said, "Let the water under the sky be gathered into a single basin, so that the dry land may appear." And so it happened: the water under the sky was gathered into its basin, and the dry land
> 10 appeared. God called the dry land "the earth," and the basin of the water he called "the sea." God saw
> 11 how good it was. Then God said, "Let the earth bring forth vegetation: every kind of plant that bears seed and every kind of fruit tree on earth that bears
> 12 fruit with its seed in it." And so it happened: the earth brought forth every kind of plant that bears seed and every kind of fruit tree on earth that bears fruit with its seed in it. God saw how good it was.
> 13 Evening came, and morning followed—the third day.

This translation has slightly departed from the reading of the existing Hebrew text, mainly following the Septuagint; but the changes are not so important as to warrant comment. Here again we have a creative command and a work of separation. At last *the dry land* appears through the recession of the waters from the earth with which they were formerly mingled, and God claims as his own the now separated *earth* and *sea* by imposing upon them their names. Now that the primal elements have redistributed themselves by divine fiat into the structure of an ordered world, there will be no further need of name-giving: everything that follows will be new, called into being, made, created.

The creation of the habitable earth, for all its importance, is recorded fairly laconically. It is typical of the Priestly author that neither here nor elsewhere does he dwell on cosmological details or seek to "rationalize" the cosmos as is done in other Old Testament texts. Cosmology is of interest to him only as it illustrates creation as the beneficent act of a God who has presented man with a world in which he can and should live. The *God saw how good it was* of vs. 10 must be considered the benison accompanying the appearance of such a world.

But another "work" occurs on this third day: the earth is commanded to *bring forth vegetation.* At first glance this may appear to be a quite natural development, a necessary complement to the production of a land on which man can live and thrive. And so indeed it has become, an integral element in the creation story as the Priestly author finally told it. Nevertheless, we receive the impression that it is something of an afterthought, the redressing of an imbalance that was effected by the modification of an earlier outline that had assigned one work only to each day. The unique formulation that accompanies this particular work reinforces this impression. We may be able to justify this impression better when we encounter the same situation in the narrative of the sixth day, when the interruption of the pattern caused by the creation of man evidences a far more innovative revision of the tradition.

This time there is no simple "let there be," but rather a command to the fecundity of the earth: *the earth brought forth* the vegetation whose existence God had decreed. Obviously there is some echo here of the "mother earth" figure common to most ancient peoples and a frequent enough motif of biblical poetry (cf. Sirach 40:1, Job 1:21), though it must be observed that in the vision of P the earth fructifies only when God demands that it do so. What must also be remembered is that in the Hebrew scheme of things the bloodless, unbreathing, and unmoving vegetation of the earth did not fall under the rubric of life or of the living. It was considered to be simply a part of the earth itself, given the normal conditions of rain and cultivation (cf. Genesis 2:5). Its special "creation" in this story is in view of its relation to the truly living beings which God is about to bring into being (see vss. 29–30 below).

Vegetation is divided between *every kind of plant that bears seed and every kind of fruit tree on earth that bears fruit with its seed in it,* that is, between those growths like wheat and barley which bear their seeds exposed and those like the fig and olive trees which enclose them within fruits. It is an elementary kind of categorization in which the Priestly author frequently indulges. He has a particular liking for pairs, as we have already seen and will see again: the heavens and the earth of vs. 1, the earth and the abyss of vs. 2, the light and darkness of vs. 4, the waters above and below the dome in vs. 7, the earth and the sea of vs. 10, the two kinds of vegetation in this passage, the two great lights of vs. 16, the water creatures and the birds of vs. 20, and so forth. Every author must be permitted his own idiosyncrasies which do not necessarily have a lasting theological import. Some other of P's idiosyncrasies with numbers we shall explore below.

14 Then God said: "Let there be lights in the dome of
   the sky, to separate day from night. Let them mark
15 the fixed times, the days and the years, and serve as
   luminaries in the dome of the sky, to shed light
16 upon the earth." And so it happened: God made the
   two great lights, the greater one to govern the day,
   and the lesser one to govern the night; and he made
17 the stars. God set them in the dome of the sky, to
18 shed light upon the earth, to govern the day and the
   night, and to separate the light from the darkness.
19 God saw how good it was. Evening came, and morning followed—the fourth day.

In the following three days of creation, now that the various compartments of the newly formed universe are to be "peopled" with their respective denizens, the Priestly formula is universally one of a creative word followed by the description of a creation in act. God first decrees that a thing
should be, and as though the decree were not enough he is immediately
said to have made (or created) the object of the decree. The reason for
this dual formulation is amply justified in each case, and, as before, there
is no reason to suspect that originally alternate versions of a common creation story have been combined to make up a composite narrative. The
Priestly author thought it important, first of all, to continue to portray his
Creator God as ontologically aloof from the mundane realm in which
man must live and move, which he is challenged to dominate but to which
he must also be subject in divers fixed and defined ways. The succession of
day and night, the determination of *the fixed times* (the ability to set
dates, sacred and profane), *the days and the years,* and the shedding of
light upon the earth, man knew were determined by the sun, the moon,
and the stars above him. God's part in this orderly process, the part of the
one who has already created light and separated it from the darkness, who
has made possible the beginning of time, is to declare the process a further unfolding of his grand design. Marduk did no less in *Enuma elish*
after arching the upper part of the dead Tiamat into the dome of the
heavens:

> He constructed stations for the great gods,
> fixing their astral likenesses as constellations.
> He determined the year by designating the zones . . .
> In her belly he established the zenith.
> The moon he caused to shine . . .

and so on in great detail.

But the Israelite author could not let the story rest at this point. It was vital to him that *God made the two great lights, the greater one to govern the day, and the lesser one to govern the night; and he made the stars.* We are so far removed from the world of Genesis that we can scarcely comprehend how revolutionary was such a statement uttered to those who were habituated to a universe whose heavens were peopled with gods and demons, benign and malign tutelary spirits. The sun, the moon, the other stars and planets (no distinction, of course, was recognized between the two) were accorded primordial divine status, and they were thought to govern man's destiny as well as to determine his times and seasons. The prevailing superstition was always a temptation to Israel (see Deuteronomy 4:19, 17:3; Job 31:26–28). An ancient bit of poetry like Judges 5:20 could conceive of the stars as friendly supernatural forces aiding Israel in its wars, and a late bit like Isaiah 47 had to ridicule (as a cautionary example to Israel) the astrology in which the supposedly superior people of Babylonia took refuge. Thus it is essential that the Priestly author should demote the celestial bodies to pieces of created matter adhering to the dome of the sky, governing nothing except the sequence of light and darkness, times, and seasons which God has already set in motion. It is obvious, too, that neither the sun (Shemesh) nor the moon (Yarah, Sin, Nannar) nor any of the stars (cf. Amos 5:26) can be given any of the common names under which they were then the object of worship.

> 20 Then God said, "Let the water teem with an abundance of living creatures, and on the earth let birds fly beneath the dome of the sky." And so it hap-
> 21 pened: God created the great sea monsters and all kinds of swimming creatures with which the water teems, and all kinds of winged birds. God saw how
> 22 good it was, and God blessed them, saying "Be fertile, multiply, and fill the water of the seas; and let
> 23 the birds multiply on the earth." Evening came, and morning followed—the fifth day.

Following the Septuagint, this translation has added to the end of vs. 20 *and so it happened,* even though the words do not occur in the Hebrew text. Whether or not the phrase was originally included by the author seems to be of little consequence: again there is a creative word accompanied by the description of a creative act. There is also something of a difference, however. *Let the water teem* is not precisely the same kind of injunction that is addressed to the earth in vs. 24 (and already in the supplementary vs. 11 above): there was for the ancient Hebrew no conception of a "mother sea" corresponding to "mother earth," let alone a "mother sky" which was only a space and not a place. The *living creatures* of the water and the *birds,* another of P's pairings, the beginning of true life on earth, must be made by God, and for this act he reserves his strongest expression: *God created.*

What God created was first of all two types of swimming life, *the great sea monsters and all kinds of swimming creatures with which the water teems,* along with *all kinds of winged birds. On the earth let birds fly beneath the dome of the sky* is the fairly cumbersome expression necessary in a language that lacked the ability to say simply "in the air." We can leave aside as of secondary interest the reasons for the Priestly author's groupings and concentrate on the act of creation that he doubtless deemed as of the greatest importance, that of the *tanninim* or sea monsters.

A creation myth that does not much impinge upon the Priestly author's story of origins—in his version God deals with the waters by a quiet word of command—but which was nevertheless widespread in the literatures of both Mesopotamia and Canaan involved a cataclysmic struggle between the creator god and the sea personified as a monster, to which names like Rahab or Leviathan (Lothan in the Ugaritic literature of Canaan) were sometimes given. The struggle ended in victory for the god and therefore in creation, as a version of the myth like Psalm 74:12–17 proclaims:

> Yet, O God, my king from of old,
>   you doer of saving deeds on earth,
> You stirred up the sea by your might;
>   you smashed the heads of the dragons in the waters.
> You crushed the heads of Leviathan,
>   and made food of him for the dolphins.
> You released the springs and torrents;
>   you brought dry land out of the primeval waters.
> Yours is the day, and yours the night;
>   you fashioned the moon and the sun.
> You fixed all the limits of the land;
>   summer and winter you made.

Other passages of the same kind are in Isaiah 27:1, 51:9; Job 26:13, 38:8–11.

It is not at all to be unexpected that the mythical sea monsters over which the God of Israel was known to exercise full control (cf. Amos 9:3) should be represented as having formed no problem for him from the first, as much the creatures of his hand as the placid fish of the seas and lakes and the twittering birds of the skies.

A new note is struck on this fifth day, however, for with the first appearance of living things God not only remarks on the goodness of his creation but also he *blessed them* with the injunction to *be fertile, multiply, and fill the water of the seas; and let the birds multiply on the earth.* In the creation of life something more has been done than to call a thing into being.

A dynamism has also been evoked which thrives on this word of benediction. It is a divinely ordained perpetuation of life that will challenge man in his commission to continue the ordering of the universe.

24 Then God said, "Let the earth bring forth all kinds of living creatures: cattle, creeping things, and wild
25 animals of all kinds." And so it happened: God made all kinds of wild animals, all kinds of cattle, and all kinds of creeping things of the earth. God
26 saw how good it was. Then God said: "Let us make man in our image, after our likeness. Let them have dominion over the fish of the sea, the birds of the air, and the cattle, and over all the wild animals and all the creatures that crawl on the ground."
27 God created man in his image;
    in the divine image he created him;
    male and female he created them.
28 God blessed them, saying: "Be fertile and multiply; fill the earth and subdue it. Have dominion over the fish of the sea, the birds of the air, and all the living
29 things that move on the earth." God also said: "See, I give you every seed-bearing plant all over the earth and every tree that has seed-bearing fruit on
30 it to be your food; and to all the animals of the land, all the birds of the air, and all the living creatures that crawl on the ground, I give all the green plants
31 for food." And so it happened. God looked at everything he had made, and he found it very good. Evening came, and morning followed—the sixth day.

As we come to this lengthiest of the day divisions of creation we are quickly made aware of certain anomalies. Again we begin with a creative word—this time clearly complemented by the confirmatory *and so it happened*—followed by the description of a creative act. But there is no blessing of the land animals which we might expect to correspond with the blessing of the sea creatures in vs. 22. It is possible that the author practiced deliberate frugality by dispensing the divine blessing three times only (in 1:22, 1:28 of man only, and 2:3 of the sabbath), but if so the distribution remains curious. It appears more likely that the story of the creation of the animals has been truncated in favor of that of man which now accounts for the major emphasis of the sixth day. As for the creation of man, it assumes an entirely different form from any of the creational motifs that have preceded it. The difference is no doubt calculated in view of the special role assigned to man in the cosmos; nevertheless, the entire structure is remarkable. Finally, while the reference to the plant life in vss. 29–30 is quite natural in respect to the food of man, in keeping with a mythical history of his diet which the Priestly author adopted and adapted (see below on 9:3–7), its extension to the animals of land and air as well looks like a rationalizing afterthought already prepared for in the final version of the work of the third day. All in all, when we examine the outline of the six-day creation story as it now appears in Genesis:

I	II	III	IV	V	VI
separation of light and darkness= creation of light	separation of *waters* by the dome of the *sky*	eduction of the *dry land*	creation of the heavenly *lights*	creation of *fish* and *birds*	creation of *earth life*
		appearance of the plants			creation of man

we have more than a suspicion that behind it we can discern an older outline which was concerned only with the production of an orderly cosmos whose various "compartments" or areas created on the first three days were systematically occupied by their appropriate denizens on the second three days. This earlier arrangement was first disturbed by the introduction of the lengthy account of the special creation of man along with the dietary note of vs. 29. Then, partially to redress the balance of the original outline, the dietary rule was extended to the animals as well and the whole was anticipated by the rather anomalous appearance of the plants in vss. 11–12 of the third day.

The suspicion that some alteration of this kind took place is confirmed by a comparison of the Genesis story with the models which the Priestly author had at hand in his contemporary world—including, it may be noted, the Yahwist's story of the creation of man that follows in chapter 2—and which were certainly well known to his readers. In these models cosmogony, the story of the origin of the world, is not coupled with the myth of human creation, but the two are kept separate. *Enuma elish,* as we saw, begins like Genesis with a primeval chaos, but the final issue is a theogony, not the emergence of human life. Only much later, after a cosmic struggle between the gods, does Marduk even old scores by literally rending hostile deities to produce both the earth on which man will live and man himself, not as a chef-d'oeuvre of creation but as a "savage" who "shall be charged with the service of the gods that they might be at ease." Creation is really incidental to the myth, which is a piece of propaganda to explain how the formerly minor deity of Babylon assumed hegemony among the gods.

The epic of Gilgamesh, which we shall consider below in connection with the flood story, presupposes both the generation and the creation of men, or part men, by the goddess Aruru, but the scene is always the familiar firm earth, with no hint of a cosmogony to explain its presence. The same is true of the legend of Atra-hasis, an older Babylonian version of the flood epic, in which the mother goddess Mami creates *lullu* ("savage"=man) "that he may bear the yoke" and "carry the toil of the gods." Again the creation of the world plays no part in the story. Both in these examples which could have easily influenced the Priestly author and in countless others of a cognate nature where influence is not to be expected, the pattern seems to have been the same. Creation of the world was one thing, and creation of man was another. Rarely if ever were the two brought into the same myth.

And therefore we see the new thing that P tried to do in combining the two themes into the one story of creation. Not only did he set man firmly in the midst of a purposefully created universe which he has repeatedly declared good and blessed by God, he set him there not as a plaything of demonic forces or as a slave to the capricious deities of a god-ridden heaven and earth but as the crowning effort of a creative power that spends itself finally in what can only be termed the very image and likeness of God himself. In a world he never made man is not doomed to walk bewildered and afraid but is summoned into being at the very end of a creative process that declares him, after God himself, lord of all he beholds. The many parallels that connect the Priestly account of creation with the myths on which he drew as models should not be allowed to obscure the very real differences that make this story unique amid the literature of its time, all of which differences are due to the superior vision of man and his place in the universe as the religion of Israel rather than the myths had revealed them. We shall see the unicity of this revelation borne out in the following verses.

The creation of the life of earth is quickly described, the result of a creative word and a creative act. *Let the earth bring forth* repeats the injunction of vs. 11, but this time it is not said that "the earth brought forth" but rather that *God made* the animals: we are now concerned with life in the true sense, which must be created. (Similarly, in vs. 28 man's dominion over the entire universe need be expressed simply in terms of the living things of the earth, the rest being taken for granted.) P's penchant for categorization shows up in his division of *living things* into *cattle, creeping things, and wild animals*—the variation in order from verse to verse is of no consequence. While we naturally think of cattle as simply the domesticated form of wild animals, in the static world of the biblical author they were no less naturally thought of as separate creations which along with the crawling things of the earth made up *all kinds* of living creatures in what was presumably the original conclusion of the story of earth's beginning.

But now comes the creation of man, and with it entirely new creational formulas. *Then God said* appears just as it introduces every work of creation, but it is not followed by a creative word. Rather, God engages in counsel: *"Let us make man . . ."* But with whom does he take counsel, and with whom does he share the "our" of the divine image and likeness in which he contemplates the creation of man? These are celebrated questions to which no fully satisfactory answers have yet been given. We can probably dismiss a couple of the proposed answers out of hand. There is not, quite obviously, contrary to what some of the early fathers of the church thought, any allusion in these pronouns to the later Christian doctrine of a Trinity of persons in the one godhead. Only a thoroughgoing unhistorical reading of the Bible could allow such an interpretation. Neither, however, does it seem possible to reduce the matter to a simple matter of grammar, as the late E. A. Speiser tried to do. It is true, the word *elohim* which we translate here "God" and which does multiple duty in Hebrew to designate one or many gods (in 1 Kings 11:5 also a goddess, biblical Hebrew lacking any more precise term for such a being), or supernatural beings of various types (the "preternatural being" of 1 Samuel 28:13, for example), as well as Yahweh, the single God of Israel, is a plural in form and is sometimes, though rarely, construed with a plural adjective or verb even when it has but one individual in view. The use of a plural pronoun, however, does not occur in such connections; and besides, we have here the further anomaly that God is not being spoken of in the plural but that he is addressing himself in the plural.

Grammarians usually call the formation we have been speaking of something like a "plural of majesty." (It is by no means restricted to *elohim:* in Hosea 12:1 "the Holy One, who is faithful" actually involves a plural: *qedoshim,* "holies." "Faithful," it may be remarked, is here a singular.) Père Marie-Joseph Lagrange, who did so much to enlighten the world about Genesis, doubtless was reflecting on the implications of such a usage when he opined: "If [God] employs the plural, this supposes that there is in him such a fulness of being that he can deliberate with himself just as several persons deliberate among themselves." An attractive thought, perhaps, but probably not that of the Priestly author. The use of the magisterial first person plural which we take so much for granted was slow in arriving in Hebrew speech: the first instance of it in the Bible occurs in Ezra 4:18, in a quotation from an Aramaic letter of a Persian king.

It is natural to suspect, as some have, that the plural form in which God speaks is due to a reminiscence of an originally polytheistic source which the Priestly author used or at least on which he modeled his story. In the creation myths with which both P and his readers were undoubtedly famil-

iar counsel among the gods before their important undertakings was a
fairly routine procedure. But it is precisely this kind of reminiscence, if we
may judge from the rest of his work, that P would have been sensitive to
and would have tried to avoid. For much the same reason we may dis-
count the associated possibility that what the author had in mind as God's
counselors was the divine "council" or "court" that is sometimes pictured
as surrounding him and his heavenly throne (the "host of heaven" and
"spirits" of 1 Kings 22:19-22; the "sons of God" of Job 1:6; the "assembly" and "council of the holy ones" in Psalm 89:6-8, etc.): these, in the
popular mythology, were the lesser *elohim* that a later theology would conceive of as "angels." There is simply no evidence that the Priestly author
shared this popular mythology and, on the contrary, every reason to suppose that he would have excluded it from his picture of the sternly serene
monotheistic Creator of his story—more reason than ever in view of what
he is about to say concerning man's unique situation in being created in
God's image and likeness.

After discounting these various possibilities, it may come as an anticlimax when we conclude that in our opinion the "us" and the "our" of
vs. 26 are nothing more or less than rhetorical devices which the author
surely never thought would provoke the controversy that has surrounded
them. They are rhetorical devices which are not foreign to our own modes
of speech. A man today who deliberates over some course of action and
eventually arrives at a decision on a course of action is as likely to say
"Let's do it!" as he is to say "I'll do it!" "What shall we do?" comes as
naturally to the lips of the perplexed soul as "What shall I do?" The psy-
chological explanation of such language is probably the tendency of the individual to visualize his personal quandaries as general ones. At all events,
it is the deliberative sort of language that turns up elsewhere in the Bible.
In Genesis 11:7 (J) the divine counsel finds expression in a "let us" when
it is nevertheless evident that Yahweh alone is speaking to himself. Isaiah
6:8 manages to combine singular and plural in the same self-query:
"Whom shall *I* send? Who will go for *us?*" Presumably nothing more is at
stake here than the same kind of rhetoric.

Much more important questions are enmeshed with these verses under
our present consideration. That God proposes to make man *in our image,
after our likeness* involves, as we shall soon see, extremely bold language,
but we can appreciate its boldness the better when we recognize the background against which it was uttered and the crudities which it has avoided.

That man has something godlike about him, that he is a compound of
the divine and the earthy, is one of those transcultural myths that seem to
have occurred spontaneously in the minds of primitive men of all races
and boundaries, among peoples as spiritually akin to the Hebrews as the
Egyptians and Mesopotamians, and among peoples as hopelessly alien to

them as the Australian aborigines and the American Indians. Very often the myth took the form of a tale in which clay was used as the base material (a motif preserved by the Yahwist in Genesis 2:7) which was then animated by the breath of a god (also a theme of the Yahwist) or mingled with the blood of a god (a myth known to P, as we shall see in 9:6 below). In *Enuma elish* Marduk tells the other gods,

> "Blood I will mass and cause bones to be.
> I will establish a savage, 'man' shall be his name.
> Verily, savage-man I will create . . ."

The blood, as it develops, comes from the severed blood vessels of the rebel god Kingu who is slaughtered in reprisal for the occasion. In the legend of Atra-hasis the mother goddess Nintu or Mami collaborates with the earth-god Enki to bring man into existence out of a mixture of clay and the flesh and blood of another slain god. The hapless deity in this instance was the otherwise unknown We-ila who paid the forfeit because of the dubious distinction that he "had personality" (*temu*="mind"). Stories of this kind were certainly familiar to those for whom the Priestly author wrote his account of creation, and it was against them that they judged his account.

It is not inconceivable that the motif of god's blood (*dam*) has influenced the biblical author in his insistence that man was created after God's "likeness" (*demuth*). The word *demuth* can frequently point to nothing more significant than a vague similitude, a simile, something that resembles something else in some way, as in Psalm 58:5 ("like") or in Ezekiel 1:5.26 ("resembling," "something like," respectively). But it can also signify a "model," a blueprint, an exact copy, as in 2 Kings 16:10. In this sense it is used by the Second Isaiah, in a passage that was doubtless in the mind of P: "To whom can you liken God? With what equal (*demuth*) can you confront him?" (Isaiah 40:18). There is no contradiction between the protestation of the Second Isaiah that no would-be idolater can ever equal the only true God and the assertion of the Priestly author that God himself could make such an equation at will; but it is instructive to see that they were at basic agreement on the principle involved.

Thus we have already spoken of vs. 26 as containing a bold expression, and it becomes bolder the more we consider the context in which it has been put. For the "image" of God in which man is to be created, and which qualifies the "likeness" after which he is made, is a word (*selem*) found more often than not in the Old Testament (Numbers 33:52, Amos 5:26, for example) to mean a forbidden image, an idol. The etymology suggests a sculptured statue; in the Septuagint it generally lies behind the word *eikon* (as it does here), which is not a mere semblance but an exact visual reproduction, a surrogate of the otherwise unseen (cf. Christ the *eikon* of the invisible God in Colossians 1:15). And so we see that the hendiadys of P's "image and likeness" is not all that "spiritual" a portrayal that it has often been made out to be, not all that much of a departure from the mythic conceptions of his contemporaries. It has avoided details which his readers and we would find grotesque and strange in this account of a God who is elsewhere wholly transcendent of the work of his creation, even such details as the Yahwist found acceptable in his story of the creation of man; but it has not budged from the core of the myth, which was to define man as carrying about with him something of the divine. The idea, therefore, is not new to Genesis. What may be new is what Genesis did with the idea.

It ought not to be necessary to insist, though even some scholarly opinion still makes it necessary to insist, that the Priestly author did not think of God as human in form, so that by simply being man man is the image and likeness of God. It is a bit of impertinence to assume that the human form or man's erect posture or whatever else there is about him automatically qualifies him as godlike even in the mind of primitive peoples; and the theriomorphic deities of Egypt, for example, prove that no such idea occurred spontaneously to one ancient people of higher cultural attainments than the Israelites. The law of the Decalogue prohibiting the representation of the Deity under any form (Exodus 20:4–6, Deuteronomy 5:8–10), a law which as far as we know had no extra-Israelite parallel, seems like Isaiah 40:18 to rest on the premise that nothing in nature is capable of being an image of God in this sense. (One version of the Decalogue, we might recall, appears in a Priestly redaction: cf. Exodus 20:11.) Besides, unlike the Yahwist the Priestly author is not describing the shaping of the human form but the creation of the human species. There is no indication that he thought of one man only as the object of this creation or even of a single human pair. The contrary is suggested by the context into which he has inserted this story of creation—"all kinds" of wild animals, cattle, etc.—and also by the language of the story itself: *Let us make man . . . Let them have dominion . . . God created man . . . male and female he created them.*

Commentators old and new have sought the source of man's imaging of God in his "spiritual" nature that separates him from the beasts and approximates him to the divine in the possession of mind and will. We might add emotions, too, which the Bible does not hesitate to ascribe to God. This interpretation would be just as wrong as the preceding if it were to ascribe to the biblical author a later analysis of the human person in which he did not share or if it were to dwell in its own way on one part only of the human composite at the expense of another. We say again, what the text is concerned with is the creation of mankind, not of a spiritual soul. It is on the right track, however, the more it tries to isolate what is distinct about man with respect to the rest of creation by causing him alone to ask what is his relation to it and to his Creator. The very asking of the question, the ability to ask it and to venture some kind of response do, one might think, image the God whose relation to Israel was that of self-revelation and disclosure. Man is not only a creature but a conscious creature, and in the consciousness of his creaturehood he mirrors in some fashion that supreme consciousness with whom he can dialogue. The author of Psalm 8 (the relationship of this psalm to the Priestly creation story, whether one of dependence or of influence, is not certain) shares this awe of self-realization when he reflects first of all on his puniness in the face of the vastness of the universe that teems about him:

> When I behold your heavens, the work of your fingers,
> the moon and the stars which you set in place—
> What is man that you should be mindful of him,
> or the son of man that you should care for him?

Yet he recognizes as well a triumphant countertruth:

> You have made him little less than the angels [*elohim*],
> and crowned him with glory and honor.
> You have given him rule over the works of your hands,
> putting all things under his feet:
> All sheep and oxen,
> yes, and the beasts of the field,
> The birds of the air, the fishes of the sea,
> and whatever swims the paths of the seas (vss. 4–5.6–9).

Perhaps neither Genesis nor the psalmist were able to phrase completely to our satisfaction in what consisted this likeness to God which they attributed to man. It is instructive, however, to observe that both have uttered in one breath their affirmation of man's divine likeness together with his dominance over the rest of nature: *let them have dominion* . . . Whether this dominion was thought of as in synonymous parallel with creation in the image and likeness of God or whether the one was rather judged to be the consequence of the other, it is certainly significant that the two appear in concert. At least part of man's similarity to God resides in his share over his own sphere in a totality of power which in God's case extends to every sphere, including man of course.

"Have dominion" is a Hebrew verb (*radah*) of some vehemence: it does not imply some kind of benign presidency over a docile and pacific nature. It occurs in sufficient rarity in the Hebrew Bible that its frequent usages in connection with kingship (1 Kings 5:4; Psalms 72:8, 110:2; Isaiah 14:6; Ezekiel 34:4, for example) convince us that it was part of the technical language of royal rule—and royal rule, it hardly need be pointed out, was an absolute in the world of Genesis. ("Putting all things under his feet," quoted in Psalm 8 above, expresses the general idea.) Paradoxically, therefore, the man who according to the myths was created to be the slave and yoke-bearer of the gods according to Genesis is created to be the lord of all he surveys.

The extension of royal language to all mankind is often instanced as an example of the Priestly author's "democratization" of ancient motifs. It is this, indeed, but it is even more. As we shall see later on, the language chosen to describe God's covenant with Israel's ancestors, the patriarchs, was also appropriated from the royal mandate of court prophecy—an earlier form of "democratization." Only the Priestly author has anticipated the patriarchal covenant with the Semites by applying it to the aftermath of the flood and centering it upon the figure of Noah, who in his purview was the ancestor of the entire existing human race (cf. Genesis 9:1–17). His earlier portrayal of an incomparable dignity bestowed upon the whole of mankind is only one facet of the truly ecumenical spirit in which he has approached the story of origins and which has helped immeasurably to give Genesis its universal appeal.

The ancient Near Eastern king always had about him some aura of the divine. Here man as such is declared created in the image and likeness of God. It was conventional to ascribe to the king universal and absolute rule. Here man is assured complete dominance over all his world. But what kind of dominance? As we have already explained, it made sense to the author to speak only of the living things of the earth that fell under man's dominion: in these are included all else. But it is not to be domination of exploitation, not an arbitrary rule however absolutely it might be phrased. (In fact, from the Priestly author's present perspective man was not yet permitted even to slay the animals for food, as we see below.) It was to be, rather, a domination modeled on God's own, of which it was a part. Here again the royal motif serves us in stead, when it describes the total power of the king as it was ideally to be exercised:

> Not by appearance shall he judge,
>   nor by hearsay shall he decide,
> But he shall judge the poor with justice,
>   and decide aright for the land's afflicted.
> He shall strike the ruthless with the rod of his mouth,
>   and with the breath of his lips he shall slay the wicked.
> Justice shall be the band around his waist,
>   and faithfulness a belt upon his hips (Isaiah 11:3–5).

If power tends to corrupt and absolute power corrupts absolutely, this has been the melancholy conclusion of historians who have unfortunately had to observe man as he has made himself. Genesis has tried to imagine man as he was made by God, when the ideal could be entertained as a possibility. The possibility—let us never despair that it has disappeared—is that power should be exercised in the cause of right and justice and equity, the way that God exercised it in Israel's history and the way that he intended that man should exercise it as his surrogate. This means, in modern terms, a rational, sensible, humane, intelligent, and thoughtful ordering of God's ordered world, dispensing correctives where they are necessary and furthering propriety where it is clearly proper. Dominion is not a license to caprice and tyranny but, in its best sense, a challenge to responsibility and the duty to make right prevail. If Genesis is attended to carefully, we see that it gives every encouragement to the present-day ecologist who believes that the earth has been delivered into man's hands as a sacred trust that he can perpetuate in a nature- or God-given order which he has been given the capacity to learn and improve upon. It gives no encouragement at all to a concept of man that puts him at the disposal of nature, that effectively reduces him to his former status of yoke-man to the natural forces from which Genesis declared him free. Genesis, had it known about them, would have shed no tears over the disappearance of the dinosaur and the saber-toothed tiger. Such "endangered species," it would have concluded, were encompassed within the *radah* of man, to deal with as he saw fit, or to deal with as he should see fit. Man, of course, had nothing to do with the evolutionary process that decreed the demise of these and countless other species of living beings that perished along the route leading to the existing world of man and beast. That is hardly the point. The point is that in the faith of Genesis man is the norm of what an ordered world ought to be, not some cluster of supposedly higher abstractions that are presumed to govern him. If man is created in the image and likeness of God he shares in the unpredictability of God that often clashes with the inexorable predictability of nature. Man is not permitted to succumb to the cyclic routine of nature but is destined to make decisions which may be for good or ill but which in any case are his decisions that cannot be dictated by any science exact or inexact. (God, too, makes mistakes according to Genesis. Not only did he "regret" having made man according to the J story of 6:6, in the following vss. 11–12 [P] he suddenly discovers that the world which he has repeatedly pronounced good and ideal is now filled with lawlessness and corruption.) Genesis put its faith in man as it put its faith in God, not that it believed every decision would be equally profitable, but because it preferred free decision to any mystique of nature. The mystique of nature was the myth from which Genesis felt that it was declaring man and his world free.

Only of man is it specified that God created them "male and female." The same is obviously presupposed in the description of the rest of the animal creation that has gone before, but no point was made of it. The difference is partly explained, no doubt, by the separate sources that the Priestly author has combined in bringing together this story of the creation of the world and of man. It may also be true that he considered his formulation an improvement over the more primitive portrayal of the Yahwist as he knew it, which pictured a single creation of one man and one woman at the beginning.

The blessing imposed on human fertility is after the model of the one pronounced over the animals before, but there is also a more than subtle difference that disappears in the translation given above. Following the Hebrew text literally, *God blessed them and said to them:* what he had merely commanded of the beasts becomes a form of conversation when addressed to man. This is appropriate, of course, for the creature which has been made in God's image and likeness and with whom he can speak face to face. To the injunction to man to *fill the earth* is added the significant command *and subdue it.* "Subdue" (*kabas*) is part of the same uncompromising rhetoric within which "have dominion" falls: literally it implies trampling under one's feet, and it connotes absolute subjugation (cf. Jeremiah 34:11.16; Zechariah 9:15; Nehemiah 5:5; 2 Chronicles 28:10). Probably no distinction is intended between the two terms even though one is applied to the earth itself and the other to the animals. Man's dominance is declared absolute, subject always to the example of the supreme dominance of God after which it has been imaged.

An apparent reservation governing man's dominance over nature is found in the following verses, where his food, like that of the other animals, is restricted to the plant life of the earth. However, another theme entirely is introduced here, and a certain ideal as well. It was a common persuasion of the ancient myths that vegetation had followed the creation of man (as in the Yahwist's story) and that in his long-lost "golden age" man had been a vegetarian. The ideal behind such a conception was not as quaint as it might seem. Seen from the opposite direction it is expressed in the continuation of the picture of the royal ideal which we saw above:

> Then the wolf shall be a guest of the lamb,
>   and the leopard shall lie down with the kid;
> The calf and the young lion shall browse together,
>   with a little child to guide them.
> The cow and the bear shall be neighbors,
>   together their young shall rest;
>   the lion shall eat hay like the ox.
> The baby shall play by the cobra's den,
>   and the child lay his hand on the adder's lair.

> There shall be no harm or ruin on all my holy mountain;
> for the earth shall be filled with knowledge of the LORD,
> as water covers the sea (Isaiah 11:6–9).

This is the myth of *Urzeit-Endzeit,* the idea that at some future age there will be a return to a bygone era of utter peace and tranquillity. Unrealistic? Most certainly: completely mythical from both ends. The ideal that it enshrines, however, is worthy of consideration. In the only world historical man has known the law of survival, the price of life, has been the expenditure of other life: life has existed only through death, that is the paradox. In Genesis 9:1–3 the Priestly author recognizes this fact of the real world. In the present passage he makes his sole concession to the paradisaical vision of man's beginnings of which the Yahwist has made so much in chapters 2–3 of Genesis. There could be, there could have been, another way, is what he is saying. We say that the other way never was, and therefore that the ideal of restoring it is illusory. Yet mankind lives by unrealizable ideals, even mythical ideals, as much as he does by realities. There is nothing wrong, surely, in dreaming impossible dreams, if the alternative is not to dream at all but simply to acquiesce in what is.

See, I give you continues the direct discourse of God to the man he has created in his image and likeness and concludes the major insertion which the Priestly author has made into the original six-days story of cosmic creation. The reference to the animals in vs. 30, on the other hand, is part of his own redaction to tie together, or to retie together, the works of the third and sixth days, as we have argued above. *God looked at everything he had made, and he found it very good,* with or without the addition, comes fittingly as a final benediction on the whole work of creation.

> **2** Thus the heavens and the earth and all their array
> 2 were completed. Since on the seventh day God was
> finished with the work he had been doing, he rested
> on the seventh day from all the work he had under-
> 3 taken. So God blessed the seventh day and made it
> holy, because on it he rested from all the work he
> had done in creation.
> 4a Such is the story of the heavens and the earth at
> their creation.

Finally, on this seventh day when no work is done, do we obtain the explanation why the whole of creation has been divided over a six-day span. The biblical author has pictured God as going about his work like a faithful Jew—specifically, like a faithful Jew of his own time to whom the externals of his religion were all-important—laboring six days a week continuously at his allotted tasks but reserving the seventh day as a holy

Sabbath of rest. The word "Sabbath" itself is not named, in keeping with the Priestly author's studious avoidance of strictly Israelite terms until their appropriate appearance in history, but it is suggested at least by popular etymology when it is observed that on this day God *rested* (*shabath*) from the work of creation. The institution of the Sabbath, which as far as we know has no extra-Israelite origins, is shrouded in the mists of antiquity. It already existed when Israel's earliest literary documents were composed (cf. Amos 8:5) and is included in its oldest law codes (Exodus 23:12, 34:21). Its original meaning has doubtless even been forgotten. But at the time of the Priestly author when so many other identifying characteristics of his people had either been shattered utterly into tiny pieces or were in immediate jeopardy of dissolution—possession of the land, the holy temple, the Davidic succession, the Mosaic traditions, and so much else—refuge was taken in such externals of religion as the Sabbath observance to form a hedge about religious and national identification that, it was thought, would preserve it against the onslaughts of assimilation and syncretism. Nervous Christians in our own times have displayed the same syndrome, often enough having selected some accidental of religious practice of far less consequence than the Sabbath rest, and of far more recent provenance.

It is to be observed, however, that as the Priestly author is telling the story of all mankind, by implication he is declaring the Sabbath rest proper for men in general and not simply an important observance of Judaism. Because of their early appearance in these pre-Israelite pages of their national history, the prohibition of blood (Genesis 9:4) as well as the institution of the Sabbath were regarded by later Jews, and, indeed, by some early Christians as well (cf. Acts 15:20) as laws binding all persons of whatever religion, whether or not they were recognized as such: non-Israelites resident in Israel were held to the Sabbath like everyone else (so Deuteronomy 5:14). However, it is not simply a matter of legalities with which we are confronted here. The author quite obviously thought it as something naturally appropriate that man should periodically rest from his daily toil, and therefore permitted himself one of his rare anthropomorphisms by having God "rest" to serve as his example. Some humanitarian consideration like that of Deuteronomy 5:12–15 may very well have motivated this thought. Interestingly, the later rabbis proposed the Sabbath as a mark of man's basic equality, since on that day all became one, rich and poor, those to whom leisure was a way of life and those for whom it was a surcease from backbreaking labor.

Probably nothing too much should be made of the twofold assertion that God "rested" having "finished" with the work he had undertaken on the seventh day. The anthropomorphism is clear and is not to be got rid of by alternative translations. We may be quite certain that a writer of the sophistication of P was well aware that he has otherwise portrayed a God who is always "at work." Of somewhat more importance to us is the statement that *the heavens and the earth and all their array were completed.* By the "array" that fills the universe the author doubtless meant its entire composition, all that is, both the few details that he had brought into his six-day scheme and all else as well. It implies, of course, a static conception of nature and existence that is in conflict with the dynamic, evolutionary world of constant change with which the sciences positive and social have acquainted us. It is not merely a question of opposing Darwin to the Bible: the question of the biological evolution of the human species is but a tiny fraction of the totality of the disparity between these two world views. Attempts to remove the disparity by making Genesis say what it evidently does not have been just as misguided as those which have sought a solution by ignoring whatever is in conflict with Genesis. Genesis has many exciting insights to contribute to our view on God and man, but it also has its serious limitations, and no service to human understanding is performed by overlooking the one or the other.

Such is the story (literally, "generations") is the first of P's series of ten *toledoth,* as we have noted earlier. (There are other numerical devices included by the author in this story, such as the sevenfold declaration of the goodness of creation, the sevenfold use of the word "create" in various forms, and so forth, which we have not bothered to dwell on.) In keeping with the pattern elsewhere, it is conceivable that this final half verse once stood at the beginning of the creation story and that it was moved to this place by the Redactor to serve as a transition to the following story.

2. Man and the Garden

As we have seen, despite a fairly obvious revision of an earlier outline, the Priestly author has exercised rather rigid control over his material. It is unmistakably his just as everything else that he has done is unmistakably his, his vocabulary, his style, even his idiosyncrasies. Such is not entirely the case with the writing of the Yahwist to which we now turn. The Yahwist, too, has made his story thoroughly his own; but he has dealt with much more disparate material than P had at his disposal. J has not composed a free and new myth in the manner of P but has knit together a number of mythological motifs without P's concern for internal consistency and without bothering to conceal the sutures and connectives that betray the original contours of separate stories and fragments of stories. For better understanding of what follows it is necessary to do some preliminary sorting out of this material used by J—a procedure which was not required in view of the tighter weave of the P story.

First of all, it seems hardly necessary to insist that in chapters 2–3 of Genesis we are indeed reading a new author with new techniques and preoccupations. Nowadays hardly anyone would attempt to defend the original unity of the first three chapters of Genesis. Secondly, it does seem necessary to insist that these verses which we assign to the Yahwist are indeed his, that is, that there is not in them a composite of J with some other independent source. The J story that follows was meant to be taken as a whole in its present form and was so known to the Redactor of Genesis and doubtless to P as well. In separating the components of the story we are not attempting to change its over-all message but simply trying to ascertain how the message came to be put together from its earlier elements. Both the message itself and the preliminary elements are of relevance in telling us what the Yahwist and Genesis are about in this enterprise.

While practically everyone is in agreement about the composite nature of the story we are about to read, there is a variety of suggested redivisions into its original parts. Here as so often is the case it is necessary to choose an hypothesis that seems to square best with the facts, and that is what we have done. Having considered various alternatives, the hypothesis we have selected is basically that of Herbert Haag.

According to this hypothesis there is a basic story which we will designate A. It is the story of creation and fall that dominates the entire two chapters, and it is only mildly mythical. It proceeds in these stages: (1) First, the world is described in its wild, uncultivated state prior to the creation of man (Genesis 2:4b–5). (2) Man is created as the living being who will till the soil (vs. 7). (3) Vegetation appears, including "the tree of the knowledge of good and bad" which will figure in the story of temptation and fall (vs. 9). (4) Man is given free rein over the vegetation of the earth except for the tree of knowledge which he is forbidden to eat under penalty of death (vss. 16–17). (5) The animals are created to be subject to man (vs. 19). (6) One of the animals, the serpent, precipitates the temptation which leads to man's contravention of God's prohibition in respect to the tree of knowledge. As a punishment, the earth is "cursed" because of man and the intended idyllic harmony of nature is broken (chapter 3 *passim*).

Woven into this story is a secondary one, probably not complete in itself, and much more akin to the mythologies surrounding the origins of man. We may call this story of the garden story B. (1) God plants a garden in which he places man, and in the midst of which is "the tree of life" (vss. 8–9). (2) After man's settlement in the garden (vs. 15) something now undisclosed in the total story occurs that leads eventually (3) to God's banishment of man from the garden and from the tree of life from which he is perpetually blocked (Genesis 3:22–24). Behind the remnants of this story, as we shall note later on, it is easy to discern the theme of man's missed opportunity at immortality, a motif that pervades ancient Near Eastern myth.

Both story A and story B have been expanded on by the Yahwist in the process of his drawing the entire biblical narrative together. The most important addition is in A, where he has taken occasion of the creation of the animals to introduce a special creation of woman, with some interesting theological implications. In B the somewhat puzzling geography of 2:10–14 has been added to the description of the garden, a description that we might think dispensable but which the Yahwist doubtless valued for its "demythologizing" effect. And there are obviously smaller additions and changes here and there to weld the narrative into a more or less consistent whole.

It is difficult in these few lines and without recourse to the original text to show the reader in every case why the analysis just offered should be accepted. We hope to offer additional clarifications as we go along in the verses that follow. And we would insist again that the purpose of the analysis is not needlessly to disintegrate the biblical text but rather to show the rather marvelous creation that the Yahwist brought into being out of materials that in isolation were never so well suited to his purpose.

> 4b At the time when the LORD God made the earth and
> 5 the heavens—while as yet there was no field shrub
> on earth and no grass of the field had sprouted, for
> the LORD God had sent no rain upon the earth and
> 6 there was no man to till the soil, but a stream was
> welling up out of the earth and was watering all the
> 7 surface of the ground—the LORD God formed man
> out of the clay of the ground and blew into his nos-
> trils the breath of life, and so man became a living
> being.

At the time when (literally, "on the day that") clearly begins with a temporal clause like *Enuma elish* and asks no questions about the antecedent of the "when" God *made the earth and the heavens* (there is probably no significance to be attached to the reversal of P's "the heavens and the earth"). We do not begin with a watery chaos but, perhaps more in keeping with a Palestinian origin, a bare land badly in need of rain. There is as yet no vegetation, since in the view of the author both rain and cultivation are required both for *field shrub* and *grass of the field*. It ought to be noted, however, contrary to what some commentators have concluded, that the text does not really represent here or in the following verses the earth as a dry and parched landmass. It is simply a desolate, uninhabited, uncultivated land.

With the beginning of the Yahwist's story we expect to read regularly about the LORD (such being the conventional translation regularly given in English Bibles to the divine name "Yahweh"); but only in this story and in Exodus 9:30 (where the reading is uncertain) is *God* regularly added to the divine name. It is most likely that we owe this combination to the Redactor, who has used it to tie the Priestly and Yahwistic creation stories together, despite the essential differences between the two.

Though it has appeared so to some commentators, there is no real contradiction between vs. 6 and what has gone before. What has gone before, as we have seen, has not presupposed a moistureless earth but an earth without the rain which alone can guarantee the vegetation which digs its roots deep into the land. Here we are told only that there was *a stream* which *was welling up out of the earth and was watering all the surface of the ground*. The surface of the ground is not whence the plants draw their existence, but it is the source of the clay from which man is next to be formed. "Stream" is undoubtedly a correct word to correspond with the *ed* of the original (found elsewhere only in Job 36:27 where it is translated "mists"): it corresponds with the *'edu* or *id* of Mesopotamian texts which designate the underground source of the springs of the earth, not unlike the eventual picture understood by P after the separation of the waters. This underground source of water makes possible a cohesion of soil on the surface of the land to allow for the clay out of which man is first shaped. This is what J is really interested in, not the greening of the earth but the production of man.

According to the Yahwist, God *formed man* ("formed" is almost, though not quite, as much a word reserved to God in the Hebrew Old Testament as "created") *out of the clay of the ground*. As we have seen already, this is a fairly common mythical motif for which the author can claim no originality. There are, however, some variations. There is a play on words: man (*adam*) derives from the ground (*adamah*). And an unusual word (*'afar*) is used for "clay," even though the image is evidently of a potter shaping into form a figure which (since he is divine) he will later make live. Why the unusual word? The noun *'afar* ordinarily means "dust," the discrete bits of soil that collect on our unused books and bookshelves or in the nooks and crannies of our rooms, hardly the material to be shaped into any plastic form. It is true, it can sometimes indicate something more cohesive, as in Leviticus 14:42 ("mortar") or Genesis 26:15 ("dirt") or Isaiah 34:7.9 ("earth"). But what was probably uppermost in the author's mind was another play on words, according to which the destiny of man was to become dust (cf. Job 17:16; Psalm 22:16.30; Ecclesiastes 12:7, etc.)—a conclusion that could be verified from the accidental exhumation of any Palestinian tomb. The exact passage we want is that which occurs in Job 10:9: "Oh, remember that you fashioned me from clay!* Will you then bring me down to dust† again?" There is certainly here an insistence on the earthiness of man which has nothing in common with P's preoccupation with him as containing a spark of the divine. What J has to say about man as something special in creation will have to be seen in the latter part of our story.

Something special is, it is true, insinuated in the final words of vs. 7 according to which God *blew into* [*man's*] *nostrils the breath of life, and so man became a living being.* What is special is not the action itself but the solemnity of the formula, contrasting with the simple "formed out of the ground" that is predicated of the other animals in vs. 19. The "breath of life" itself which God blows into the nostrils of man is no different from the "breath" or "spirit" which he bestows on the rest of animal creation (see Ecclesiastes 3:18–20). Breath, like blood, in the elementary physiology of ancient man was the sign of life and therefore equated with life itself: to have breath was to be "a living being." Thus far, therefore, the Yahwist has said nothing to distinguish man from the other animals who will also share a bodily form shaped from the earth and breathe the breath bestowed on them by the Creator.

> 8 Then the LORD God planted a garden in Eden, in
>   the east, and he placed there the man whom he had
> 9 formed. Out of the ground the LORD God made var-
>   ious trees grow that were delightful to look at and
>   good for food, with the tree of life in the middle of
>   the garden and the tree of the knowledge of good
> 10 and bad. A river rises in Eden to water the garden;
>   beyond there it divides and becomes four branches.
> 11 The name of the first is the Pishon; it is the one that
>   winds through the whole land of Havilah, where
> 12 there is gold. The gold of that land is excellent;
> 13 bdellium and lapis lazuli are also there. The name
>   of the second river is the Gihon; it is the one that
> 14 winds all through the land of Cush. The name of
>   the third river is the Tigris; it is the one that flows
>   east of Asshur. The fourth river is the Euphrates.

* *homer,* the classic word for plastic, malleable clay.
† *'afar,* the word which we have been discussing.

We now hear of the *garden* which in the present form of his story the Yahwist has made the scene of all that follows. That God *planted* this garden is, of course, part and parcel of the author's unself-conscious anthropomorphism of a Deity who shapes clay like a potter, breathes, and walks about taking the air in the cool of the day. The garden is said to have been planted *in Eden, in the east.* "In the east" doubtless is in reference to Palestine, therefore the region generally known as Mesopotamia, where the rest of the Yahwist's history is played out till the time of Abraham. The geographical notation is not without purpose: it is part of the author's "historicizing" of the myths with which he works.

"Eden," which may at one time have referred to some real land, appears in the Bible as a place of proverbial lushness (Ezekiel 36:35; Joel 2:3) and sometimes as the garden where God himself dwells (Isaiah 51:3; Ezekiel 28:13, 31:9). The reader should consult especially Ezekiel 28:11–19 if he would find what is undoubtedly the closest parallel in the Hebrew Bible to chapters 2–3 of Genesis. It is not that either passage depends on the other, but that both have drawn on a common mythology from which the one has appropriated some of the details, the other some of the rest, and in a few instances the details are the same. On the whole, the Yahwist has been more sparing in his appeal to the myth than has Ezekiel. Both stories deal, as we shall see in the development of the Yahwist's tale, with the theme of the "missed opportunity" at immortality, a motif that haunts the mythologies of antiquity. We must call to the reader's attention that it is never said in Genesis, despite what an uncritical construction of vs. 16 might lead him to believe, that prior to his "fall" man had been created immortal by God.

Having *placed there the man whom he had formed,* that is, in the garden, God causes various fruit trees to spring up from the ground. *The tree of life in the middle of the garden* is most assuredly the most significant of all these trees, but we never hear of it again until Genesis 3:22. In the present structure of the story it is *the tree of knowledge of good and bad,* which originally had nothing to do with the garden, which bears the burden of the narrative, and we shall hear much about it in the following verses.

The "tree of life," that is, a tree whose fruit confers idyllic life or immortality, is a mythical conception found both in the Old and New Testaments and, as might be expected, in the contemporary literatures of the Gentiles. It is often simply a figure of speech: "[Wisdom] is a tree of life to those who grasp her" (Proverbs 3:18, cf. 11:30, 13:12; Revelation 2:7, etc.), or in an Assyrian inscription: "Ashur rendered Adad-Nirari [III]'s government as good as the plant of life." But it also appears as a serious mythic motif more than once. In the Gilgamesh epic the now-divinized hero of the flood Utanapishtim directs Gilgamesh seeking immortality to discover a "plant of life" that lies at the bottom of the ocean. Gilgamesh does in fact obtain this plant, but it is stolen away from him by a serpent. Thus he loses his chance at immortality. In the Babylonian myth of Ea and Adapa we have instead a "water of life" and a "bread of life." Because of false counsel Adapa refuses these foods proffered by the gods and thus is told in derision that he has forfeited an opportunity to become immortal. In the original story of the garden used by the Yahwist there was undoubtedly the detail of some mishap or misunderstanding that led to man's neglect to profit from the tree of life in whose proximity he had been placed.

Of vss. 10–14 which the Yahwist seemingly has added to his first description of Eden and whose precise relevance in their context has baffled more than one commentator, Claus Westermann has made the interesting proposal that they serve an analogous function to genealogies in providing periodic information to structure the narrative, only this time the information is geographical. The picture is, by the author's lights, a fairly prosaic one, designed not to enhance the mystical aura surrounding Eden or God's garden but rather to bring them quite literally "down to earth." Therefore we should resist the temptation to find here an echo of the Canaanite myth which placed the residence of God at the source of all the waters of the earth. (In any case, when Israelite poetry localized "the mountain of God" where was Eden, his garden, according to Ezekiel 28:13.16, it put it in the far north rather than in the east; cf. Isaiah 14:13; Psalm 48:2.) The text does not say that the garden produced a river that watered the whole earth, as some commentators have seemed to think. It says, rather, that *a river rises* in Eden (which as yet has not been identified with the garden but it is simply where the garden is) which first waters the garden then divides to become four tributaries—or, if we look at the map in reverse, is fed by four tributaries that cause the river to "rise" in Eden. What is now called the Shatt el-'Arab, the confluence of the *Tigris* and *Euphrates* before they empty into the Persian Gulf, seems to have been the region the author had in mind. The traveler to that region—which the Yahwist undoubtedly had not been—might be inclined to dispute its paradisaic candidacy, at least from the standpoint of climate, but there is no doubt that it is munificent in trees, since a major part of the world's dates come from the area. North, west, and east of the Shatt el-'Arab there are all manners of rivulets and streams that flow into the Tigris and Euphrates, and it would be impossible as well as pointless to try to identify which of these the author had in mind as *the Pishon* and *the Gihon,* neither of which is elsewhere mentioned in the Hebrew Bible. By a benign interpretation, however, they can all be related to the same general region. The Pishon *winds through the whole land of Havilah:* Havilah, whether north (Genesis 25:18) or south (Genesis 10:7.29) is in the vast Saudi-Arabian peninsula contiguous to Mesopotamia. Cush normally means Nubia, the ancient Ethiopia, the southern part of Egypt, but in this case it might refer to the land of the Cassites who inhabited northern or central Babylonia. We must remember that, with all the best intentions in the world, this is a primitive geography done by someone who was not personally familiar with any of it. We may be one hundred and eighty degrees wrong in our replotting of it just as he may have been one hundred and eighty degrees wrong in plotting it in the first place.

The translation offered for the precious metals/stones/spices associated with these regions is partly based on the Septuagint readings and partly guesswork.

> 15 The LORD God then took the man and settled him
>   in the garden of Eden, to cultivate and care for it.
> 16 The LORD God gave man this order: "You are free
> 17 to eat from any of the trees of the garden except the
>   tree of knowledge of good and bad. From that tree
>   you shall not eat; the moment you eat from it you
>   are surely doomed to die."

That the garden, which has now become the garden *of* Eden, here and elsewhere through the rest of the story is a secondary addition is easily seen from an examination of the Hebrew text, quite over and above the fact that as the text now stands vs. 15 is a doublet of vs. 8. The *it* (which twice occurs in the Hebrew) which man was set *to cultivate and care for* is an objective feminine pronoun which goes very well with an original "earth" or "land," both of which are feminine nouns in Hebrew, but not at all with "garden," which is a masculine. In joining the various themes together the Yahwist has not bothered to remove these inconsistencies. By the same token, *any of the trees* from which man is *free to eat* according to vs. 16 does not include "the tree of life" of vs. 9 and 3:22 (where, for that matter, it is made clear that man has not yet eaten from this tree), which originally had nothing to do with these verses. Rather, man is set over the earth—and in a garden, since the Yahwist will have it so—to tend it and to eat of its fruits. This is in part at least the equivalent of the Priestly author's proclamation of man's dominance over the rest of creation. But just as before man's rule was subject to responsibility even though absolute, here a condition is laid upon him: *the tree of the knowledge of good and bad* is excepted from the fruits of which he may eat. We should not think of this as an arbitrary whim on the part of the Almighty, but rather try to understand what is meant by "the tree of the knowledge of good and bad."

Obviously the "tree" of knowledge is to be taken with the same force as the "tree" of life, that is, one whose "fruit" conveys the knowledge of good and bad. Undoubtedly we are also meant to assume that "knowledge" in this context has its Semitic rather than its "Greek" or otherwise "Western" connotation, namely of experience rather than of merely intellectual awareness. And finally, "good and bad" is not a disjunctive but a collective, as in Numbers 24:13 or Deuteronomy 1:39: it means the whole area of what is encompassed by "good and bad," the good as well as the bad.

These preliminaries understood, it is evident that the knowledge of good and bad does not necessarily entail some kind of immorality in the conventional sense as so many readers at first assume. "Good and bad" can run the gamut of literally everything. The prophet who can do neither good nor evil of his own accord but only what God commands is simply incapable of any independent action whatsoever. Little children who as yet do not know good from bad are, in other words, innocent, without the experience of the discretion which comes with maturity. The thoughtless inhabitants of Jerusalem who say in their hearts, "Neither good nor evil can the LORD do" (Zephaniah 1:12), affirm in their foolishness that God will do nothing at all. In short, though it may seem to be an unnecessarily cumbersome way of saying something quite simple—a trait that the casual reader sometimes suspects to be verified more than once in the Bible— "the knowledge of good and bad" may signify nothing more or less than "knowledge" full stop.

Nevertheless, there has been a venerable persuasion not only on the part of readers but on the part of commentators as well that some moral question is connected with this tree of knowledge, and specifically one with a sexual overtone. It is not that the use of sex itself has been considered to be the moral issue—at least not by anyone who is capable of sharing the healthy outlook of the biblical author. It is inconceivable that an Israelite author would portray sexual experience as something morally reprehensible. Besides, at least as the story has been laid out in its present form, woman as distinct from man has not yet made her appearance on the scene. Rather, it has been thought that the Yahwist could have used his story to wage a polemics against the fertility cult of Canaan which always held such a fatal attraction for Israel. According to this construction the serpent, the tempter who later makes his appearance to cajole man into transgressing the divine prohibition, would stand for the fertility god Baal (who often enough was in fact associated with the serpent as fertility symbol), who was ever present to lead the Israelite astray into some forbidden byway of sexual deviance connected with the popular agricultural cult. We are reminded that in one instance at least the penalty for having eaten the forbidden fruit has sexual overtones (3:16); thus according to the Hebraic principle *midda keneged midda* (loosely translated, "let the punishment fit the crime"), the offense might have been sexual as well. Some less compelling arguments are that the fruit of the tree could have been figured as one of those that bestow sexual potency (as in Genesis 30:14), and that after consuming the fruit the man and woman experience shame at their mutual nudity (Genesis 3:10–11). Robert Davidson also points out a "Tempting parallel" (by which, however, he is not tempted to the point of acceptance) in the Gilgamesh epic. Gilgamesh's rival and later friend Enkidu, who is first created as a wild man more akin to the beasts than to other men, through union with a (cult?) prostitute first becomes separated from the beasts (cf. the theme of the next passage in Genesis) and then is proclaimed to have acquired wisdom like the gods (that is, by exercising generative power): cf. the verbal parallel with the words of the tempter in Genesis 3:5.

There is much to be said for this line of interpretation (and much more, indeed, than has been said for it in these few lines), but it is also subject to some major difficulties. Just to mention a few of these difficulties, we must observe, first of all, that the "man" of this story, whether or not with the separate presence of the woman who later appears, is everyman, mankind in general, and not merely Israelite man. The Yahwist has not written an elaborate allegory to bring a narrowly Israelite problem into focus, but, as the further development of his history shows, he has tried to tell a story in which Israel's problems and hopes are set in the perspective of a totality of human destiny that begins with man at his most basic, as a creature of God. Furthermore, as Genesis 3:1 makes very clear, the serpent/tempter of the story is merely another of God's creatures, a wild animal albeit an astute one, and is not, therefore, an immediately obvious candidate to represent a rival deity or, indeed, a force of evil of any kind. Even more fundamentally, as Umberto Cassuto has pointed out, the knowledge of good and bad which is prohibited to man is also—and not by the tempter's "exegesis" alone (3:5) but by God's as well (3:22)—a prerogative of the Deity. It can therefore hardly stand for a moral failing. Cassuto likewise protests that while God quite properly can forbid man to do what is bad, he could not—not in the biblical perspective of the freedom and relative autonomy which are bestowed on man—forbid him the option of choosing between good and bad, if that were what this knowledge was all about.

All in all, we are brought back to the opinion that by "the knowledge of good and bad" vs. 17 did not envisage something immoral but rather something highly moral indeed, what other biblical traditions would characterize as "wisdom." What man is being forbidden is simply what is not in his power to obtain and therefore what is not proper for him to aspire to. It is not that wisdom of a kind does not lie within the grasp of man; man is exhorted over and over to acquire wisdom, and much of the Old Testament has been written to extol its incalculable worth (cf. the first verses of Proverbs and *passim* the entire book). What is the fact, however, as the book of Job, for one, was composed to proclaim in majestic poetry (see, for example, the opening lines of Job 40) and as the work of Ecclesiastes concluded more cynically, is that however useful and desirable wisdom may be, this taking of prudent thought and sage reflection on the lessons of experience, these alone of themselves do not and cannot ultimately locate man in his universe, explain himself finally to himself or himself in his relation to God. To have it otherwise is to turn wisdom into folly, to exchange it for an arrogant claim to equality with God, whose prerogative it is alone to know the ultimate rationale of things (cf. Job 15:7–9; Proverbs 30:1–4). It is in this same sense that Paul (repeatedly) condemns "the wisdom of the world" (see 1 Corinthians 1:20–21, for example), which gets in the way of the gospel. For Paul as for the Yahwist the only proper posture of man if he would be truly wise and lead a full life is faith in God and not a professed self-sufficiency of knowledge. It is in this latter acceptation, then, that man is forbidden "the tree of the knowledge of good and bad." We believe that this construction of what the Yahwist meant will be verified as the story subsequently develops in chapter 3.

A too literal translation of the final part of vs. 17 could cause an unintended difficulty. The Hebrew has it that "on the day that you eat of [the tree] you shall surely die." In the event, as we see later, man (and woman) does not die, let alone on that day of eating, but rather other consequences follow. The translation above has correctly rendered the sense: *the moment you eat from it you are surely doomed to die.* This is the declaration, as we would say, of a capital offense; but capital punishment is not actually inflicted.

18 The Lord God said: "It is not good for the man to
19 be alone. I will make a suitable partner for him." So
   the Lord God formed out of the ground various
   wild animals and various birds of the air, and he
   brought them to the man to see what he would call
   them; whatever the man called each of them would
20 be its name. The man gave names to all the cattle,
   all the birds of the air, and all the wild animals; but
   none proved to be the suitable partner for the man.
21 So the Lord God cast a deep sleep on the man, and
   while he was asleep, he took out one of his ribs and
22 closed up its place with flesh. The Lord God then
   built up into a woman the rib that he had taken
23 from the man. When he brought her to the man, the
   man said:

   "This one, at last, is bone of my bones
      and flesh of my flesh;

This one shall be called 'woman,'
  for out of 'her man' this one has been taken."
24 That is why a man leaves his father and mother and
  clings to his wife, and the two of them become one
  body.
25 The man and his wife were both naked, yet they
  felt no shame.

We now resume the story that was interrupted at vs. 9, the burgeoning of the earth; what follows is the creation of the animals. In the present
form of the story as the Yahwist has decided to tell it, however, the animals have become almost of secondary interest to the new and primary
thrust of his narrative, which is to dwell on a separate creation of woman.
It is not good for the man to be alone does not immediately tell us that
woman is to be created; rather, man's social nature is in view (cf. Ecclesiastes 4:9–12): he needs *a suitable partner* (a masculine in the Hebrew).
Thus we have a charmingly suspenseful little narrative leading up to man's
triumphant exclamation in vs. 23 after a series of "false starts" in which
God has *formed out of the ground* (as he formed man) the various animals which he has then *brought to the man to see what he would call them*
—will this, or will that be the "suitable partner"? As we saw previously,
this action also is the equivalent of the Priestly author's proclamation of
man's dominance over the rest of creation. Not only does man possess
such a dominance, he proclaims it by assigning the names of all other
creatures in which are contained their identities; he orders the (living)
world in which he has been placed. None of the names he calls, however,
acknowledges kinship with himself.

Thus the stage is set for the creation of one who will be truly like man,
and appropriately the creation assumes an entirely new form. Imper-
ceptibly we have begun to move, though the Hebrew word (*adam*) has not
changed, from the conception of man the species to man the male who will
be complemented by woman.

The *deep sleep* (*tardemah*) into which God casts the man might
superficially be regarded as an anesthesia if we were expected to take at
face value the details of these wonder stories of creation. Actually, the
word is almost invariably used in the Hebrew Bible to describe a sleep in-
duced by God for his own purposes (1 Samuel 26:12; Isaiah 29:10) during which he often does marvelous things (Genesis 15:12; Job 4:13,
33:15). The marvelous thing that he does in this instance is to create
woman. The Yahwist has probably borrowed his image of the Deity
"building" (the *built up into* of our translation seems to reflect another
idea) a woman out of *the rib that he had taken from the man* from creational motifs common in the mythologies with which he was familiar. That

it should have been a "rib" that was chosen for the raw material of woman is perhaps due to a wordplay that has been lost in Hebrew (and of course in the English) but which existed in an assumed Sumerian prototype of this story. (In Sumerian the same cuneiform symbol represents both "life" and "rib.") That the creator deity is the "builder" of his living creatures is a conception familiar from both Mesopotamian and Canaanite religious language.

As we have warned before, we should not permit the naïve description of the creational act to beguile us away from the profoundly religious meaning of what is being described and which is brought to the fore in the semi-poetic exclamation with which the man greets this masterpiece of God's creation. *At last!* he cries, at last *this one* (feminine, and three times repeated) *is bone of my bones and flesh of my flesh.* The literalness of the reference in this case conceals a frequent figure of speech (see Genesis 29:14, for example) which signifies kinship and—it should also be stressed in these days of a more enlightened attitude toward woman— equality as well. Woman and woman alone is declared the "suitable part- ner" of man, his complement. In the same spirit, while the name-giving to which man proceeds serves as before to assert dominance, such being the realistic appraisal which the Yahwist gives to the social order within which he moved, it should not be separated from the primary assertion that woman is indeed man's only compeer amid the rest of creation. Indeed, the point is driven home by the play on words by which *woman* (in Old English, *wife* [=female]-*man* [the human species]) is derived from *man* (that is, here the male of the species). The etymology is actually more factual in English than it is in the Hebrew. The translation above, how- ever, has probably correctly read the text with the Septuagint and other ancient sources to make the apparent etymology more precise: she is called woman (*ishshah*) because from *her* man (*ishah*), i.e., from her husband, she *has been taken.*

These assertions made more or less by indirection are confirmed by the Yahwist's own comment in vs. 24. *That is why,* namely, because of the natural affinity and complementarity of man and woman, *a man* (*ish* again this time, rather than *adam,* to leave no doubt that it is about man the male he is speaking) *leaves* his own family to form a new one with *his wife.* That *the two of them become one body* should not be too narrowly interpreted as referring exclusively to the physical side of marriage. Biblical Hebrew actually has no separate word for "body": "flesh" is used instead. But the flesh of man is his very being itself, his identity, his heart and soul. "My soul yearns and pines for the courts of the LORD. My heart and my flesh cry out for the living God" (Psalm 84:3). The union of man and woman in marriage, therefore, is set on the highest and most integral plane: it is a union of persons who together make up a new person. It is not possible, again given the social background against which the Yahwist wrote, to insist positively that he was thinking of monogamous marriage as the ideal. The kind of interpersonal relationship of which he was speaking was also conceivable within the institution of polygamy (cf. 1 Samuel 1:1–8). We must be chary of reading back into any ancient author ideas whose time had not yet come. Nevertheless, there was a respectable strand of tradition even in polygamous Israel which always prized monogamy (Proverbs and the "wisdom" literature in general seem to regard it as having been the rule rather than the exception in the society for which they were written), and it is likely enough that the Yahwist was of a similar mind despite his matter-of-fact acceptance in the patriarchal history of the facts as they had been.

The final vs. 25 of this section forms a bridge to the story of the "fall" of chapter 3 when it asserts that *the man* (once again *adam*) *and his wife were both naked* (*'arummim*), instigating a play on words that is picked up by the *cunning* (*'arum*) serpent who is already waiting in the wings. What is meant by connecting this state with the disclaimer that *yet they felt no shame?* As we see below, it is after the eating of the tree of "knowledge" that they do recognize their nakedness and are ashamed of it. As yet, however, they are without "knowledge," whether licitly or illicitly gained: they react to their situation like children who find nudity, man's original state, to be quite natural and therefore sense no shame about it. Shame, it should be observed, while its lack is a mark of innocence, is not in itself necessarily a mark or consequence of personal sin; it is likewise an indication of a sense of responsibility and of adulthood. A shameless man is either a conscienceless monster or an idiot child. Nudity, we must bear in mind, was particularly abhorrent to adult Israelite mores in distinction to the ways of other peoples. It was sometimes inflicted as a form of shameful punishment (cf. Hosea 2:5) or an insulting humiliation (cf. 2 Samuel 10:1–5). That the man and his wife were perfectly at ease in their naked state underscores the idyllic character which the Yahwist ascribes to man and his world at their primordial state of existence.

3 Now the serpent was the most cunning of all the animals that the LORD God had made. The serpent asked the woman, "Did God really tell you not to eat 2 from any of the trees in the garden?" The woman answered the serpent: "We may eat of the fruit of the 3 trees in the garden; it is only about the fruit of the tree in the middle of the garden that God said, 'You 4 shall not eat it or even touch it, lest you die.'" But the serpent said to the woman: "You certainly will 5 not die! No, God knows well that the moment you eat

of it your eyes will be opened and you will be like
gods who know what is good and what is bad."
6 The woman saw that the tree was good for food,
pleasing to the eyes, and desirable for gaining wisdom.
So she took some of its fruit and ate it; and she also
gave some to her husband, who was with her, and he
7 ate it. Then the eyes of both of them were opened,
and they realized that they were naked; so they sewed
fig leaves together and made loincloths for themselves.

That the separate creation of woman narrated in the preceding section
was a later elaboration of the Yahwist is indicated by the fact that here she
is aware of the particulars of the prohibition of 2:16–17: the man (*adam*)
to whom it was originally addressed incorporated both male and female, in
the same fashion that the Priestly author thought of man at the moment of
his creation. To describe a "fall" of man J has found it convenient to tell
the story of a primordial human pair, a theme which apparently had no
appeal for P. There are other signs of a progressive development through
which the eventual story which we read was created out of originally
discrete elements. The "tree of the knowledge of good and bad," for example, which is never again explicitly called that in chapter 3, has now
been moved to the middle of the garden, displacing the "tree of life" temporarily (3:3, cf. 2:9). It is likely that the story of the serpent once dealt
with a tree of death that was deceitfully passed off as a tree of life, in a
variation on the Ea and Adapa story. We are also reminded of the Gilgamesh epic in which a serpent stole away the plant of life which Gilgamesh had obtained at such pains. As the story now stands, in any case,
the tree in question is one of "knowledge," and the rest of the narrative
has been shaped to accommodate the theme.

The serpent was the most cunning of all the animals: we have already
indicated why we believe this characterization disqualifies the serpent from
consideration as a representative of the Canaanite fertility god Baal. Later
Jewish (cf. Wisdom 2:23–24) and early Christian thought would identify
him with the devil, whose machinations brought death into the world and
an end to the incorruptibility of man. Such a dualism of supernatural
agents is foreign to the Yahwist's thinking, however, and as we have already seen, the story of Genesis 2–3, at least in its present form, is not really concerned with the origins of death. Furthermore, the figure of the
serpent here is not so much one of a force of evil as of mischief, trouble-
making: he is a trickster, or, in the biblical phrase, "cunning." We need
look no further than to this putative trait to explain why the Yahwist
chose to cast him in the tempter's role vis-à-vis a human couple as yet innocent of knowledge for their good or their bad. The serpent was regarded

with some amazement as a creature of craft and cunning who could apparently move effortlessly with no means of locomotion (cf. Proverbs 30:19) and whose habit of changing his skin credited him with the secret of immortality (and thus made him a fertility symbol). That he is depicted here with the powers of speech and conversation as well is, of course, part of the unearthly attributes that are ascribed to the earthly paradise that was thought once to have been man's.

It has often been remarked how this story as it unfolds acts out the "psychology" of temptation. The serpent begins his assault on the woman's defenses with a deliberate caricature of the divine prohibition: *Did God* really *tell you not to eat from* any *of the trees in the garden?* This is almost a total reversal of what God actually had said in 2:16: "You are *free* to eat from *any* of the trees of the garden." (Of course, in the conversation between the serpent and the woman the name of Yahweh, LORD, does not occur.) The woman is a match for this misrepresentation, or at least nearly so. Is there, however, a touch of resentment lurking in the refinement that she adds to the original stipulation, namely, that they may not *even touch* the forbidden fruit? In any case, she is unable to counter the temptation as it reaches its culmination.

That temptation is twofold, consisting in what the tempter suggests along with what the woman's own eyes confirm, or, in her state of unknowing, seem to confirm. *You certainly will not die!* is typical of a trickster's language: the words can also be read in Hebrew: "You will not die certainly," i.e., "It is not certain that you will die." So also is the ambiguity of the serpent's claim that eating of this tree will make the man and woman *be like gods* (or, *be like God:* in either case *elohim*), knowing *what is good and what is bad.* On the one hand, there is an insinuation of the vulgar theme familiar from the mythologies, that the gods guarded jealously their special prerogatives, usually knowledge and immortality, that alone separated them from mortal men. On the other hand, there is that element of truth that makes the temptation effective. God has indeed reserved to himself this particular knowledge to which man can aspire only by attempting to transcend his creaturehood and verily declaring himself "like God." The essence of the tempter's trick is that he should persuade man to look for what he can never possess, for what he can only experience an unrequited lust.

That is the second part of the temptation, that *the woman saw that the tree was good for food, pleasing to the eyes, and desirable for gaining wisdom.* It is not true, as we see, that man and woman in their primordial state were conceived as in such a condition of innocence that they were incapable of contemplating transgressions even on their own. The tempter has made the suggestion, but the woman has made the decision, based on her own judgment—"this thing is good to have." In other words, while this story depicts a "fall" of man in the sense that he commits a sin, misses the mark, transgresses a commandment imposed upon him—and, since the perspective is of the first man and woman, it can be viewed as the first sin and first transgression—still, it is not a fall in the sense that man after has become anything else than man was before. The potential for transgression is always present, for it is man's nature to be prone to wrongdoing (cf. Genesis 8:21, J). In the ultimate analysis no explanation is given for this undoubted fact of life, either by the Yahwist or by the Priestly author. The biblical sources merely confirm what several millennia of human history have not been slow to spell out in meticulous detail, that man was created defectible.

She . . . ate . . . gave some to her husband . . . and he ate: It is perhaps in order to point out that the woman, contrary to the misogynistic interpretation of Ben Sira (cf. Sirach 25:23), is not really portrayed by the Yahwist as a temptress who beguiles man into misdeeds. Genesis does not share in the motif common in ancient mythologies according to which a woman was the cause of the miseries of a disordered world ("Pandora's box" is one familiar example). The "fall" as J depicts it is collective, a social act. If the conversation of the serpent has been with the woman rather than with the man it has been so largely in view of the sentence that is to be pronounced in vss. 14–15 which sets up enmity between their separate offsprings. Ancient literary conventions dictated that there be dialogue between two persons only "on stage" at one time.

The eyes of both of them were opened fulfills the promise of the serpent, but at the price of what anticlimax! They had been told that they would share the knowledge of gods, and what in fact they now see is the fact of their mutual nakedness. They have indeed gained knowledge, but what a paltry knowledge at the expense of what they have lost, as is soon to be shown. They have matured: even illicit experience can bring this gift. But it is a gift that has been purchased through the loss of innocence. And not only innocence, for they have lost much else. The first making of clothing, therefore, which the Yahwist doubtless saw as the beginning of one of the marks of civilized man as he knew him, is accompanied by a sadness that anticipates the soon to be lost Eden of man's origins.

> 8 When they heard the sound of the LORD God moving about in the garden at the breezy time of the day, the man and his wife hid themselves from the
> 9 LORD God among the trees of the garden. The LORD God then called to the man and asked him, "Where
> 10 are you?" He answered, "I heard you in the garden; but I was afraid, because I was naked, so I hid my-

11 self." Then he asked, "Who told you that you were
naked? You have eaten, then, from the tree of which
12 I had forbidden you to eat!" The man replied, "The
woman whom you put here with me—she gave me
13 fruit from the tree, and so I ate it." The LORD God
then asked the woman, "Why did you do such a
thing?" The woman answered, "The serpent tricked
me into it, so I ate it."
14 Then the LORD God said to the serpent:

"Because you have done this, you shall be banned
　　from all the animals
　　and from all the wild creatures;
On your belly shall you crawl,
　　and dirt shall you eat
　　all the days of your life.
15 I will put enmity between you and the woman,
　　and between your offspring and hers;
He will strike at your head,
　　while you strike at his heel."

16 To the woman he said:

"I will intensify the pangs of your childbearing;
　　in pain shall you bring forth children.
Yet your urge shall be for your husband,
　　and he shall be your master."

17 To the man he said, "Because you listened to your
wife and ate from the tree of which I had forbidden
you to eat,

"Cursed be the ground because of you!
　　In toil shall you eat its yield
　　all the days of your life!
18 Thorns and thistles shall it bring forth to you,
　　as you eat of the plants of the field.
19 By the sweat of your face
　　shall you get bread to eat,
Until you return to the ground,
　　from which you were taken;
For you are dirt,
　　and to dirt you shall return."

Now comes retribution, which proceeds in an orderly fashion, with the
contestation of guilt, its confession and verification, and the meting out of
punishment.

The man and the woman confess their transgression and acknowledge their feeling of guilt by what they do rather than by what they say, since what they say is actually an attempt to exculpate themselves. When they hear the sound of God making his way through the lush undergrowth of the garden on what is presumably his daily stroll in the coolness of the evening breeze, they show at one and the same time their old familiarity with his habits and their new feeling of embarrassment at his presence. We should not permit the extreme naïveté of this picture story to distract our attention from the rather keen insight it manifests into the ways of human conduct. The semi-comical aspect of the first human pair skulking about in *the trees of the garden* reveals the novelty of the relation to God in which they now find themselves, in which shame and fear predominate. Even this much of self-awareness, however, must be elicited and made explicit by the divine summons: *Where are you?* Man's answer is a grudging confession of guilt, since his conduct can sustain only one explanation: *you have eaten, then,* of the forbidden fruit!

If there was a psychology of temptation implicit in the conversation between the woman and the serpent, there is also a psychology of self-justification manifest in the interchanges between God and man and God and woman. Yes, the man finally brings himself to admit, he did eat, but only because of *the woman whom you put here with me.* The man manages to insinuate that the goodness of God in making for him a partner has been at least partially responsible for the present contretemps. The woman's response, though somewhat more straightforward, is nevertheless in like vein, for is not the serpent one of God's creatures as well? *The serpent tricked me into it, so I ate it.*

Curiously, as it might first seem, the serpent is not interrogated at all; it is merely condemned. Therefore no explanation is given why the serpent chose to interfere in the affairs of men or to assist in the disruption of good relations between God and man. The Yahwist is not interested in the subject, not even to the extent of inventing a halting plea of half-guilt of the type he has ascribed to the man and the woman. The serpent remains as a consequence the symbol of an unexplained source of mischief and wrong for which no accounting is given. As we saw in the commentary on vs. 6 above, this story does not seek to expose the origins and causes of wrongdoing in general, but only to record how quickly mankind was and has been disposed to wrongdoing when given the chance. The fact that no inquest is held over the serpent's duplicity demonstrates for one thing that the Yahwist is interested in a history of man and woman and not of serpents. It also demonstrates that, despite his keen appreciation for etiologies, the etiology of evil, as Claus Westermann has rightly held, is not one of his concerns.

As the transgression occurred, in like order the punishment is decreed: first the serpent, then the woman, then the man successively receive their sentences. In these sentences the etiological interest of the Yahwist does reassert itself, for they are explanations—as, of course, they made sense to the mind of an ancient author—of how a presently existing series of situations had come about.

First the serpent, which is cursed. The translation above correctly renders the sense of the doom pronounced over this creature when it asserts that it *shall be banned* from the society of all the other animals of the earth. Thus was interpreted the proverbial isolation of the serpent in its haunts, the result of a banishment on the part of the rest of the animal species. In the same way was construed the serpent's way of slithering about in the dusty soil of Palestine, a manner of life that the biblical author regarded with mingled fascination and repugnance. This, too, must be the effect of a curse: *on your belly shall you crawl, and dirt shall you eat.* It would be to miss the point of the story to ask whether the author thought the serpent had once walked on legs or flew with wings. He only wants to account for a present state of things, as he does with man and woman.

In vs. 15 we have a further etiology. Aside from assorted herpetologists and other special people who form the inevitable exceptions to every human rule, there has traditionally been and still is for most men and women some kind of instinctive revulsion at the presence of a snake. Benighted and irrational the attitude may be, in view of the harmlessness of the vast majority of the serpentine clan, and in view, in fact, of the sturdy service which this vast majority performs in maintaining the ecological balance of nature; but reason, ancient or recent, has never dictated prejudices. Thus the Yahwist in his age understood the *enmity between* the serpent *and the woman* and between their separate *offspring,* that is, between the serpent species on the one hand and the human on the other, as having been *put* there by an angered Deity to make total the ban that would separate the tempter and his kind from all the rest of creation. He adds a graphic description to underscore the intensity of the enmity. Yahweh is made to say to the serpent: *He,* the human race, *will strike at your,* you serpents', *head, while you strike at his heel.* The image is of a man seeking to tread on the head of a snake and crush it out of existence while the snake in turn tries to bury its fangs in the man's foot. Thus we have portrayed not merely a passive hostility between man and serpent but also a continuous and violent confrontation.

Is it also a confrontation that leads to or implies the victory of one party over the other? From early Jewish times, as we have already seen, the serpent of this piece was already viewed as a surrogate of the principle of evil. It was only a small step, one might think, for interpretation to proceed to the conclusion that this principle in its satanic personification would ultimately be crushed through some representative of the human race acting with the power of God. However logical this step might seem, however, it was apparently never taken in Jewish times either before or after the coming of Christianity. Jewish tradition knows of no "messianic" exegesis of Genesis 3:15. That interpretation, which became extremely popular during the Middle Ages and has penetrated many ecclesiastical documents, not excluding those of the Second Vatican Council, we owe to the allegorizing of early Christian writers—not, it must be pointed out, those of the New Testament nor their immediate successors.

Irenaeus of Lyons (about A.D. 130–200), it seems, was the first to see in this passage a prophecy of the victory of Christ, the Messiah, over Satan, a construction that led to the coining of the term *Protoevangelium* ("beginning of the gospel") used by later Catholics and Protestants alike to refer to it. In making his interpretation Irenaeus was doubtless influenced by the personal "he" (*autos*) by which the Septuagint had rendered the pronoun applied to the woman's offspring (we would normally expect to read "it," *auto*). This rendering had been faithfully carried over (as *ipse*) in the Old Latin version (a translation of the Septuagint) in which the Old Testament was read in the early Western church. As we have already seen above, it has also been carried over in the translation we follow in this book. (The Hebrew is ambiguous, since "offspring" is a masculine in this language rather than a neuter as it is in Greek and Latin.) This translation is justifiable, however, for it seeks merely to enter into the spirit of the figure involved by personifying the offspring of the woman as the human race, mankind; and that is all that the Septuagint had intended by its rendering. A further complication was contributed by the later Latin Vulgate reading of "she" (*ipsa*) rather than the "he" of the earlier text. This change led to a mariological as well as a messianic interpretation: it was Mary, the mother of the Christ, who would be the one to crush the head of Satan, so thought many who read Genesis 3:15 in their Latin Bibles, assisted, no doubt, by the mysterious portrayal of the woman (the church) and the dragon in Revelation 12:1–6. But the "she" translation originally had nothing to do with the Virgin, as we might expect. It came into the Vulgate through Ambrose of Milan (about A.D. 339–97), who was following the thought of his Jewish mentor Philo of Alexandria (about 20 B.C.–A.D. 50). Philo argued that the rules of parallelism made it more appropriate that the pronoun refer back to the woman of the woman-serpent opposition rather than to her offspring; on his side he had mathematical precision if nothing else (you: the woman; your offspring: her offspring; she and your head: you and her heel). Neither Ambrose nor, obviously, Philo attached any messianic or mariological significance to the passage.

Despite the vogue which Genesis 3:15 enjoyed as a *Protoevangelium* for the medieval church and the church of the Reformation, it cannot be said that it had been firmly fixed in this light by the earliest Christian tradition. Less than half of those who are accounted "fathers" of the church imitated Irenaeus' exegesis, and the majority of those who did not includes the chief doctors of both the Eastern (Basil, Gregory of Nazianzus, John Chrysostom . . .) and the Western church (Ambrose, Augustine, Jerome, Gregory the Great . . .). And rightly so, it would appear. Whatever may have been the values for christological and mariological piety which the allegorical reading of this verse has provided in the unofficial and official pronouncements of the church—and in its official pronouncements the church has never claimed that its reading was more than allegorical—it seems best to agree with Oswald Loretz that it is advisable no longer to use *Protoevangelium* in connection with Genesis 3:15. The passage is part of a curse and a condemnation, not a prognosis of future blessings. It predicts a protracted hostility, even a protracted battle, but not a victory of one side or the other. Neither does it seem profitable to attempt to salvage the allegory by critical appeal to the Yahwist's theology as has been recently done by Béda Rigaux and Walter Wifall. The offspring of the woman, despite the "he" of its personification, is a collective body, not an individual, not David any more than it is Christ. And the serpent and its offspring are precisely those, neither the personification of Baal nor of Apophis, the Egyptian serpent of darkness. Thus far and no further runs the literal sense of vs. 15, the only sense with which we have to do in this book.

In vs. 16, the author's attention turns properly to the woman, not precisely with a curse but with what he considered to be the dire consequences of her transgression that now would affect her in her natural role of mother and wife. *I will intensify the pangs of your childbearing,* says Yahweh. Childbirth itself was accounted a blessing, a sharing in the mystery of creation and fruitfulness with which God had endowed his creatures: the Yahwist would have had no problem at all with the fertility blessing pronounced over mankind by God according to the Priestly author in Genesis 1:28. But the paradox was that such a blessing should be accompanied by excruciating *pain*. Even in the male-dominated society of the Old Testament the suffering of childbirth was proverbial to evoke the idea of supreme anguish (cf. Isaiah 13:8, 26:17; Jeremiah 6:24, 13:21, etc.). This state of affairs, in the Yahwist's mind, must be due to no initial intention of a beneficent God but was rather one consequence of the disordered world of man in the making of which man and woman had had their part.

The rest of the fate meted out to woman involves another paradox. Regardless of the pain of childbirth, the *urge* for man which results in childbirth will constantly remain with her. Now this "urge" (*teshuqah*) is the desire to possess: compare its other uses in Genesis 4:7 and Song of Songs

7:11 (where "his urge" is translated "he yearns" in the NAB). In the woman's case, however, she is destined not to possess but to be possessed by man: *he shall be your master.* The Yahwist recognized, and doubtless cheerfully acquiesced in, the social order of his people which accorded to woman an inferior status and declared her, in theory at least, the chattel of her husband. But he was sensitive enough to regard this order, too, as a dis-order that derived from human mismanagement rather than from a divinely decreed ideal. As we saw above, the Yahwist represented as the creative intent of God that woman be man's "suitable partner," his complement and peer. That she in fact was not, he had to ascribe to human interference with a higher design.

The condemnation of the man in vss. 17–19 is the lengthiest of all, but it is the simplest in import: it is the Yahwist's etiology of the paradox that the kindly earth from which man was taken and which he was set to till is so niggardly in return for all his labor. Neither is man any more than woman declared accursed, but *cursed be the ground because of you!* That is to say, man is set at variance with his natural environment. The *toil* by which he shall *eat its yield* corresponds with the "pain" of woman's childbearing (the two words are closely related in Hebrew, and in the Samaritan Pentateuch they are the same). It is not, obviously, that work and labor are being presented as punishments, for according to the Yahwist man was created with work in mind—not that he was to substitute for the work of the gods, to be sure, but that he should care and tend for the earthly home in which he had been placed by his Creator. What now occurs is that enmity is put between man and the soil, just as enmity was put between the offspring of the woman and the serpent. The author may have been thinking, in his existential situation, of the rocky, inhospitable soil of the Palestinian countryside, but the geography is totally irrelevant. What is the essential is that man's life in whatever capacity is to be hard and difficult, the very opposite of the idyllic existence that was projected in the story of his creation. The Yahwist, whatever his own social standing may have been, sympathized with the generally unenviable lot of the contemporary peasant; but he believed that it was a lot due to man's own false devisings.

This condition was to be, as it had proved to be, permanent. *Until you return to the ground, from which you were taken* corresponds with the *all the days of your life* of vs. 14. Death (which is in fact not specifically mentioned) is not itself viewed as part of man's punishment: we have already seen that a natural immortality for man did not belong to the Yahwist's myth. Death is simply the termination of man's life of toil. *You are dirt, and to dirt you shall return* refers to historical, sinful man, the only man that the biblical author knew. It would not have been stated otherwise, however, had the condition of man not changed one whit from the condition in which he was created according to Genesis 2:7. It is the supreme paradox, nonetheless, that the knowledge which was supposed to make man like the immortal gods ends in revealing to himself his hapless mortality.

> 20 The man called his wife Eve, because she became the mother of all the living.
> 21 For the man and his wife the LORD God made
> 22 leather garments, with which he clothed them. Then the LORD God said: "See! The man has become like one of us, knowing what is good and what is bad! Therefore, he must not be allowed to put out his hand to take fruit from the tree of life also, and thus
> 23 eat of it and live forever." The LORD God therefore banished him from the garden of Eden, to till the
> 24 ground from which he had been taken. When he expelled the man, he settled him east of the garden of Eden; and he stationed the cherubim and the fiery revolving sword, to guard the way to the tree of life.

The conclusion of our story reverts once more to the tree of life for which the garden is the proper locale. In the present form of the story, of course the garden has been the scene all along, though it was not so from the beginning as we have explained above. We must content ourselves as before with studying the text as it lies before us, since we cannot perfectly separate the elements out of which the Yahwist fashioned his story.

It is generally agreed that vs. 20 forms special problems. The woman is given a proper name, which the man has not yet (the NAB translation has rightly refrained from naming the man "Adam" in vss. 17 and 21 even though the extant Hebrew reads there simply "man" without the article which has therefore been supplied). Her name is said to designate her *mother of all the living: Eve* (our traditional English approximation of the Hebrew *hawwah*) resembles the Hebrew word for "life" and was so translated (*zoe*) by the Septuagint; yet no birth has occurred or will occur until 4:1. By many commentators the verse is deemed to be out of place, and they transfer it elsewhere.

However, we may suggest a couple of reasons for the verse to be right in its present place according to the intentions of the author, no matter what may have been its original signification before he took it over. First of all, it has been placed as immediately as possible after the lines that proclaimed woman's condition as one of subjection to her husband, and name-giving is, as we know, the prerogative of one in dominance. Secondly, there may be here another of those wordplays in which the Yahwist took pleasure. Just as in Genesis 2:25 there was a linguistic bridge built between the nakedness of the human pair and the craftiness of the serpent, something similar may have been attempted here as the story takes leave of the serpent and dwells on the consequences of its perfidy. Not in the Hebrew preserved by the Bible, but in the cognate Arabic and Aramaic languages a word related to *hawwah* means "serpent" (in Aramaic, *hiwya*). This consonance has been pointed out from the times of the earliest Jewish commentators on the text. Whatever may have once been the sense of the *hawwah* (serpent-mother=mother goddess?) which the Yahwist decided to read as "mother of all the living," and whatever the route by which the term came to him in the first place, he may very well have recognized its etymological appropriateness for the present context. What the woman is in her historical state, after all, for good as well as for ill, she owes to the intervention of the serpent.

Also vs. 21 presents its problems. At first glance it seems to duplicate unnecessarily vs. 7. If they were already clothed, why is it that *for the man and his wife the* LORD *God made leather garments?* And why should the solemn word "made" which the Yahwist otherwise reserves for the great creations of God be reduced to the paltry fashioning of breechcloths out of the skins of animals? (Obviously, the Yahwist had no knowledge of the Priestly author's prohibition at this time of the exploitation of the animal kingdom.) And finally, it is to be remarked that this "creational" act violates the otherwise inflexible rule of J to attribute to men—not to the gods or to a God—the successive developments in human progress marked by the invention of clothing, of the forge, of pastoral and urban life, and so forth. What seems to account for all these anomalies and to recompense for them is the author's intent to demonstrate God's continued solicitude for his creatures despite all. Even when on the point of banishing the man and woman from his presence in the garden, God manifests his care for their progress and well-being.

In vs. 22 a bridge has been built to connect the tree of knowledge again with *the tree of life*. We note *the man* has once more become a collective, referring to the human species of both men and women, as it originally did in 2:7–9.15–17 before the motif of the separate creation of woman was brought in through the insertion of 2:18–25. The present verse is perhaps the most "primitive" of all those in the Yahwist's account. The man who *has become like one of us* obviously presupposes a plurality of *elohim* that cannot be explained away as we did the plural employed by P in 1:26. Neither do we have any reason to take as ironic or sarcastic Yahweh's agreement with the serpent's contention in 3:5 that mankind's experience of good and bad has made him "like gods." We must candidly confess that in this instance the Yahwist has incorporated into his story a myth which he has barely or hardly assimilated with his monotheism. In the Gilgamesh epic, the legend of Ea and Adapa, and other mythological sources, knowledge and immortality were the prerogatives which the gods jealously guarded to themselves away from men, and so it is in this story. Knowledge man has acquired, illicitly and through his own devices. He must not now be permitted to seize the gift of immortality as well. So reasons Yahweh in the council of the *elohim,* and for this reason he *banished him from the garden of Eden, to till the ground from which he had been taken* and for which he had been created in the first place.

In vs. 24, which is partly a doublet of vs. 23, the NAB follows the Septuagint when it has God settle man *east of the garden of Eden* and station *the cherubim and the fiery revolving sword* at the entrance to the garden *to guard the way to the tree of life;* but the difference between this reading and that of the extant Hebrew is of little importance. The verse is highly mythological. Cherubs are not in this context the little winged angels with which Renaissance painters decked their canvases: these latter were borrowings from a very different mythology. As Theodor Gaster correctly says of the cherub: "The word is identical with the Mesopotamian *karibu,* which denotes a winged monster—somewhat like a griffin—such as stood before the portals of Babylonian and Assyrian palaces, just as similar creatures stand before temples and palaces throughout Southeast Asia." These mythical creatures were thought of as the servitors of Deity (cf. Psalm 18:11) and especially as the guardians of sacred things such as the ark of the covenant (see Exodus 37:7–9) and of sacred and therefore forbidden places, as here (so also Ezekiel 28:14.16). A personified twisting and flaming sword completes the picture in this composite account of a garden of life forever after barred to man. The sword of God's wrath is likewise a mythical motif found elsewhere in the poetry of the Bible (cf. Isaiah 27:1, 34:5, etc.). Thus on this inexorable note ends the narrative of man's first testing and of his failure and its consequences.

Now that we have concluded the Yahwist's story about man and the garden, it remains for us to say a few words concerning the relation of the story to the later Jewish and Christian notion of an "original sin" that constituted a "fall" of man. It is not our purpose to trace the development of this doctrine in the church or to justify it: to do so would be to invade the precincts of systematic and historical theology. We must, however, restate the message of Genesis to which, in the past, this doctrine has appealed for its formulations and see to what extent the appeal has been warranted.

With the basic affirmation of the doctrine itself, with the assumption that lies behind it, there can hardly be any problem. It is, basically, a repudiation of the Pelagian heresy which claimed that man was sufficient unto himself for his salvation, that he could achieve his destined end apart from the quickening grace of God. The doctrine affirms that man is born into a sinful world and into a sinful race, and that from both of these he stands in need of redemption. This is quite plainly the sense of biblical religion, the teaching of both the Old and the New Testament, and with it there can be no quarrel.

It is rather another matter, however, to imagine that we can reconstruct a history of how this state of affairs came to be or to suppose that Genesis does, indeed, record that history. Genesis did not, in fact, attempt such a history. As we have seen above, the Yahwist presupposed that mankind was capable of transgression from the beginning, even without outside help. There was, therefore, no "fall" in the sense that men and women became something other than what they had been created. The story does try to account for man's alienation from God, why his life is bounded with frustrations, and why he is under sentence of death. According to the story, however, immortality was not a gift that he forfeited but rather one that he failed to obtain. There is nothing in Genesis concerning those "preternatural gifts" of "our first parents" about which later theologians would speculate. There could be some foundation for that kind of speculation in the portrayal of primal man applied to the king of Tyre in Ezekiel 28:11–23, if that passage were to be viewed as sober history rather than the poetic myth that it is; but we have seen that the Yahwist made a sparing and varied use of the mythological motifs that are also found there. The man and the woman of Genesis 2–3 are intended to represent everyman, but an everyman no different from that of the Yahwist's time and our own.

A further consequence of reading the traditional doctrine of original sin back into the Yahwist's narrative has been to attribute to Genesis a biological theory of which it was neither guilty nor capable: monogenism, the postulate that views all mankind as the descent from a single pair of original ancestors. As late as 1950 in his encyclical letter *Humani generis* Pope Pius XII, after conceding within limits that the hypothesis of the biological evolution of man was an open question, denied the same freedom of discussion to the theory of polygenism—the scientific hypothesis which holds that the human race is the result of multiple origins—"since it is in no way evident how such an opinion can be squared with what the sources of revealed truth and the pronouncements of the church's teaching state in regard to original sin." The pope's argument, as he went on to explain, was based on the assumption made in the traditional doctrine (traditional, that is, since Augustine of Hippo in the fifth century) that original sin is transmitted by human generation from parent to child in an unbroken succession going back to "Adam," the first man. This is what Paul was thought to have said in Romans 5:12, where we read that "through one man sin entered the world and with sin death, death thus coming to all men inasmuch as all sinned." Nor is Paul alone with such thoughts among his contemporaries. A Jewish author writing toward the end of the first century also cried out: "O Adam, what have you done? Although you [alone] sinned, the fall was not yours alone, but ours, too, who descended from you" (2 Esdras [4 Ezra] 7:118, translation by Jacob M. Myers in the Anchor Bible).

We do not propose to deal at this time with the exegesis of Paul and the ecclesiastical pronouncements to which Pope Pius referred. Suffice it to say that in the quarter century and more since *Humani generis* numerous exegetes and theologians have examined both and have come to other conclusions than the one at which the pope arrived. The reader who is interested in exploring the whole question would do well to consult the book *Is Original Sin in Scripture?*‡ by Herbert Haag, who states toward the end of his study: "Whether mankind originated in monogenism or polygenism is a question which only science can answer; it is not a theological question."

Our interest in the matter here is exclusively as it concerns Genesis. We have seen how for dramatic effect and to enunciate certain convictions about women as well as men the Yahwist introduced "the woman" into a story which originally spoke only of "man" or "the man" in a collective sense, to mean all of humanity, like the Priestly author's "man" of Genesis 1:26. The man formed from the ground and destined to return to it is all mankind, men and women together, as is the man who is driven from the garden of Eden. Among the reasons that prompted the Yahwist to introduce a woman into his story, to inculcate monogenism was not one. He may very well have thought that the human race originated in such a fashion, but if so he simply took it for granted and did not make it part of his message. The story of the "fall" is a paradigm of human conduct in the face of temptation, not a lesson in biology. We conclude, therefore, that just as it has long been recognized that the imagery of Genesis says nothing either *pro* or *contra* the scientific hypothesis of the evolution of man from lower species, it should be recognized as well that neither does it pronounce anything for or against the hypotheses of single or multiple origins of man's own species.

In sum, the traditional doctrine of original sin is not to be found in Genesis, though as we have said the assumption that lies behind the doctrine definitely is: we shall see this contention borne out in what follows. It remains for the theologians to redefine the doctrine in such a way as not to historicize unduly the myth of Genesis or to create out of Romans 5:12 a new myth of Adamic origins for all of mankind. (As Stanislas Lyonnet has shown, the "inasmuch as all sinned" of Romans 5:12 was interpreted by all of the early church fathers aside from John Chrysostom [about A.D. 347–407] to refer to the personal sins of universal humanity, not to a single sin that had been committed by their "father" "Adam.") As we

‡ New York: Sheed & Ward, 1969.

have already suggested, this kind of redefinition is going on apace. Its fruition cannot but help to restore Genesis to its position as illustrating the frailty of the man we know and the mercy of the God with whom he places himself in contest.

3. Cain and Abel

4 The man had relations with his wife Eve, and she conceived and bore Cain, saying, "I have produced
2a a man with the help of the LORD." Next she bore his brother Abel.

This verse and a half are the beginning of a genealogy which is continued in vs. 17 below. Through the addition of vs. 2a the Yahwist has created a bridge to connect with the preceding story of the "fall" that which follows, which he has derived from another of his sources and inserted within the genealogy. As becomes immediately evident on reading, Cain is the focus of interest throughout, while Abel is a passive figure who appears only to disappear in almost the same breath. This fact may explain the latter's name (in Hebrew *hebel*), even though no etymology is suggested for it anywhere in the text: *hebel* means "breeziness," "emptiness," and may therefore allude to Abel's brief and transitory appearance on the stage set up by the narrative. Others, however, point to the Syriac *habla*, "shepherd," as indicative of the underlying meaning of the name, describing the calling of Abel as represented in the following story.

The man had relations with his wife is literally "the man *knew* his wife." The expression, common enough in the Old Testament, underscores the total involvement which the Hebrew associates with "knowledge" and to which we have already referred above. Knowledge is the prerogative of man vis-à-vis the beasts, the rest of the animals, and means a personal encounter and experience. Accordingly, in this sense of sexual relations the expression is never used of the mating of animals, only of the shared experience of man and woman.

I have produced, in Hebrew *qanithi,* offers a popular etymology for the name of Cain. The true meaning of the name is disputed; but see below. *With the help of the* LORD presupposes an uncertain translation of the Hebrew preposition *eth* which normally means simply "with." This entire saying of Eve is somewhat curious, including the designation of her offspring as *a man* rather than a boy. We are hearing the jubilant cry of the mother of all the living who now finds herself fulfilled by sharing in the creational work of God. But we hear also, perhaps, a bit of the old arrogance that led to the eating of the forbidden fruit, the lusting after autonomy and equality with the gods. Along with Yahweh who created the first man, she boasts, now she too has produced a man. *Next she bore* has seemed to some to indicate that Cain and Abel were thought of as twin brothers, a conclusion which in turn has caused them to institute parallels between this story and others such as the legend of Romulus and Remus. Actually, however, vs. 2a has been introduced into the genealogy of Cain only to tie it to the story of vss. 2b–16 which was originally independent of it, and therefore the relationship of Cain to Abel should be determined only from the story itself, which states merely that they were brothers.

2b Abel became a keeper of flocks, and Cain a tiller of
3 the soil. In the course of time Cain brought an of-
4 fering to the LORD from the fruit of the soil, while
Abel, for his part, brought one of the best firstlings
5 of his flock. The LORD looked with favor on Abel
and his offering, but on Cain and his offering he did
not. Cain greatly resented this and was crestfallen.
6 So the LORD said to Cain: "Why are you so resent-
7 ful and crestfallen? If you do well, you can hold up
your head; but if not, sin is a demon lurking at the
door: his urge is toward you, yet you can be his
master."
8 Cain said to his brother Abel, "Let us go out in the
field." When they were in the field, Cain attacked
9 his brother Abel and killed him. Then the LORD
asked Cain, "Where is your brother Abel?" He answered, "I do not know. Am I my brother's keeper?"
10 The LORD then said: "What have you done! Listen: Your brother's blood cries out to me from the
11 soil! Therefore you shall be banned from the soil
that opened its mouth to receive your brother's
12 blood from your hand. If you till the soil, it shall
no longer give you its produce. You shall become
13 a restless wanderer on the earth." Cain said to the
14 LORD: "My punishment is too great to bear. Since
you have now banished me from the soil, and I
must avoid your presence and become a restless
wanderer on the earth, anyone may kill me at

15 sight." "Not so!" the LORD said to him. "If anyone
    kills Cain, Cain shall be avenged sevenfold." So
    the LORD put a mark on Cain, lest anyone should
16 kill him at sight. Cain then left the LORD's presence
    and settled in the land of Nod, east of Eden.

It is evident on first reading that this story did not originally describe the immediate descendants of the first man and woman. The existence of other people, indeed of organized society and civilization, is presupposed: the separate callings of shepherding and agriculture, the institution of sacrificial worship, and the rest. The purpose of Cain's enticing Abel into a field is obviously that he might perform a covert act in seclusion from others. As we shall see, Cain is a variant of the Kenan of the Priestly author's genealogy in 5:9, and the latter appears considerably down the line from "Adam." (The two names Cain and Kenan are in Hebrew more clearly the same than would appear from our English approximations.) The story introduces a long interruption into the Yahwist's genealogy, which is continued in vs. 17 below. Even so, however, it is a story that shows signs of having been abbreviated in the telling.

It is intriguing to speculate about the original meaning of the story. It, too, tells of a temptation and "fall," though the crime in this case is murder and fratricide rather than the unlawful acquisition of esoteric knowledge. It, too, speaks of a banishment from God's presence: the parallels between chapters 3 and 4 of Genesis are, in fact, more than several. Of the many suggested origins for this history of the fate of Cain, one especially deserves consideration for having a great deal of probability on its side. That is, that the story was once the etiological accounting for the nomadic existence of the people known as the Kenites (Hebrew *qeyni*), descendants of an eponymous ancestor Cain (Hebrew *qayin*). The Kenites were a non-Israelite people who were nevertheless closely associated with Israel on numerous occasions and in divers ways which the Bible does not always make clear. According to Judges 4:11 they were the descendants of Hobab, Moses' father-in-law. In Exodus 18, however, Moses' father-in-law is called Jethro and he is designated a Midianite. (In Exodus 2:15b–22, for good measure, the same Midianite is named Reuel: we are dealing with separate and parallel traditions.) It is probable that the Kenites are to be identified in some fashion with the Midianites, another non-Israelite people to whom the Israelites were akin and with whom they were alternatively on friendly or hostile terms. Because of the considerable influence that Moses' priest-father-in-law is represented as having had on the decisions of Israel's traditional lawgiver and founder of its religion, the so-called Kenite hypothesis has sometimes prevailed among critical students of biblical history, namely, that it was from the Kenites that the

Israelites derived their worship of the God Yahweh. We need not enter into the hypothesis here. Suffice it to say that the Israelites always showed a special regard for the Kenites (cf. 1 Samuel 15:6, 30:29) and were involved with them in some special way. The Kenites were indeed a nomadic tribe living on the fringes of civilization, and it has been conjectured with some probability that they were itinerant smiths and tinkers (*qayin* can mean "smith," cf. vs. 22 below concerning Tubalcain). There is a whole literature not only of antiquity but also extending down to recent times regarding the superstitious awe or dread in which workers in metals have often been held by "primitive" settled peoples, frequently constituting the smiths a pariah class within society. The reasons for this attitude are buried somewhere in the past, but they probably had to do with the powers for good or evil that were popularly associated with metals—witness the lucky coins and horseshoes still carried or nailed over doors in these days of enlightenment.

Others have seen in the story an exemplification of the traditional animosity that the farmer (Cain starts as a farmer) extends to the shepherd or herdsman, an attitude that is reciprocated by the latter. In this acceptation, the story tilts the scales in favor of the pastoral life, a calling in which many Israelites were engaged and for which many professed a nostalgia, even though it probably had a broader basis in romantic legend than it did in any fact. Whatever may have been the first meaning of this passage, however, is now of secondary interest when compared with the meaning which the Yahwist attached to it; and this meaning is not hard to find. The Yahwist has used the story to illustrate the further alienation of man from God that inevitably follows after the first rebellion against the divine decrees. Man who will not respect the limits set on his existence by his Creator God will also not respect the limits set on his activity by the rights of his brother and fellow. It is also brought out that the assault of one human person upon another is an assault upon the divine law which makes men answerable to God.

That *Abel became a keeper of flocks, and Cain a tiller of the soil* seems to indicate merely the separate pursuits followed by men in their common calling to labor upon the earth; the Yahwist has not made any value judgment ranking either vocation over the other. Neither is it explained why God *looked with favor on Abel and his offering, but on Cain and his offering he did not* when the two brothers brought these offerings to him *in the course of time* (an expression which in the Hebrew seems to suppose some prior events which the Yahwist has left out of the story). The reason for the divine choice preoccupied the attention of later Judaism and the Christian church (cf. Hebrews 11:4; 1 John 3:12; Jude 11), but Genesis says nothing about Cain's lack of faith or unrighteous deeds prior to the rejection of his offering as these sources would have it. For the Yahwist the story of Cain and Abel is part of a pattern in which one brother is favored over another or the others, Abel over Cain, Abraham over his brethren, Isaac over Ishmael, Jacob over Esau, and so on. Reasons for the divine selection are not given; they are known only to God and hidden from men. Again, there are limits placed on man's knowledge and wisdom which he must not overstep. In trying to overstep them in his own case Cain is led to resentment, envy, and eventually to murderous rage and murder itself. (We are not told in this abbreviated story how the Deity manifested his pleasure and displeasure respectively to the two brothers.) The warning which God issues in vs. 7 is to a man whose *hybris* in the face of the divine judgment has now made him prone to the onslaught of overt evil.

That Cain *was crestfallen* is expressed in the literal Hebrew with the words "his face fell." Thus the congruence of the divine caution that by doing well and rejecting the temptation to which he is already receptive *you can hold up your head* (a single word in the Hebrew), that is, he can be serene in the knowledge that he is righteous in God's eyes. On the contrary, if he does not do well, *sin is a demon lurking at the door.* This translation supposes that sin (a feminine word in Hebrew) is here personified as a lurking or crouching being (*robets,* a masculine) which in turn is to be identified with a demon *rabitsu* known from Assyrian sources. There are objections to this rendering of the text, not the least of which is the isolated character of such a concept in the Yahwist's work—and, indeed, in most of the Bible as a whole—but at this writing it seems to represent the best interpretation that can be given this difficult verse. To lie in wait "at the door" means to plot someone's harm (cf. Job 31:9). Cain is warned of the demon's *urge* toward him (the same word also appears in 3:16, though in a different sense) to become his master, but he is also assured of the power to counter these designs and so turn the tables on their designer.

However, he does not do so. Abruptly the story turns to Cain's next action, which speaks more eloquently than any verbal reply he could make to the divine warning. *Cain said to his brother Abel* is all that appears in the Hebrew text, which, as we have already seen, gives evidence of having been abbreviated and compressed. *"Let us go out in the field"* has been supplied from the Septuagint and other ancient parallels to fill out what was presumably the intended sense of the verse. Cain strives to ensure that there will be no witness to the bloody deed he contemplates. That deed itself is passed over with the utmost brevity. It is as though the author is saying that what he tells is too frightful for words, that brother should slay brother, and that so soon after both had made their offerings to the same God. Cain's sin, nevertheless, is intended to represent a paradigm of the human condition as it was in the Yahwist's time and unfortunately as it has remained thereafter. Mankind is the only species within the order of creation that systematically destroys and preys upon itself out of envy, greed, selfish unconcern, or denial of its own commonalty, and does this so often to the accompaniment of lip service paid to supposedly common principles of justice and mercy. The Yahwist was probably testifying to an early breakdown of old convenantal laws premised on tribal brotherhood which had never been able to accommodate to Israel's original sin in becoming a nation.

As in 3:9, after the commission of an act an interrogation follows. This time, however, the guilty party does not merely dissemble or reply evasively but rather counters the question with a direct lie. To this he adds the insolent and sarcastic retort that has become proverbial to express the ultimate in callous disavowal of human responsibility: *"Am I my brother's keeper?"* To this bit of impudence the divine interrogator does not deign to make reply, for his and the Yahwist's views on the matter are implicit both in his initial question and in the sentence that he proceeds to mete out. It has been frequently observed that Cain's whole posture in this interchange betrays the disposition of one who had already sundered himself from his fellows before he was led to murder and to the consequent ostracism with which his deed is punished.

Your brother's blood . . . from the soil and *the soil that opened its mouth . . .* in vss. 10–11 involve some ancient notions that have in part survived the passage of time. One is this idea that the blood of someone foully murdered will find some means of testifying against the murderer: it may "cry out," for example, by flowing afresh when he is brought into the corpse's presence. Murder will out, we say. In the story as the Yahwist tells it, the meaning is that however covert a crime may be, it cannot be hidden from the God who sees and hears all and judges all. Abel, who said nothing at all before, has now become eloquent in death. Another notion is that blood, the sacred substance of life, renders taboo the land on which it falls until expiation is made for it. "Bloodshed desecrates the land, [and] the land can have no atonement for the blood shed on it except through the blood of him who shed it" (Numbers 35:33). Yahweh is more merciful than the law. Instead of condemning Cain to death he decrees that the profaned soil shall no longer sustain him with its produce in the quiet agricultural life which he had begun to lead. Cain is *banned from the soil* to *become a restless wanderer on the earth*. As we suggested earlier, the original meaning of this story may have been to account for the nomadic existence of the Kenites. Whether or not this be the case, for the Yahwist it marks an increasingly severe judgment passed on the increasingly ugly conduct of sinful man.

Yahweh's mercy, however, is not exhausted simply by his sparing Cain's life. Although Cain acknowledges that he must *avoid* God's *presence*, nevertheless the divine protection will accompany him. Cain's protestation at the severity of the punishment he has received which will have as a consequence that *anyone may kill me at sight* pictures a society in which the isolated wanderer is fair prey for the settled population which fears and hates him, a society in which "stranger" and "enemy" are synonymous terms. To save him from his fate Yahweh *put a mark on Cain* that indicated, presumably, that as a deterrent to any would-be slayer *Cain shall be avenged sevenfold*. It is hard not to see in these details an original meaning which referred to a tribal sign or taboo that proclaimed its bearer one for whose death blood vengeance would be exacted. As Theodor Gaster has observed in this connection, the nomadic smiths of the Sudan are distinguished to this day by a cross-shaped mark on their brows. What the Yahwist may have made of the mark in his transmogrified version of the story is not at all clear, but in any case it was some kind of protecting sign, not a badge of shame as has been so often thought. In primitive societies which lack the safeguards of laws and courts the threat of sure retribution in kind is the keeper of the peace.

And so Cain *left the* LORD's *presence and settled in the land of Nod* (which means "wandering"), still farther, presumably, *east of* that *Eden* where God had first placed man and encountered him. The story of the first murderer and slayer of his brother which has roughly paralleled the story of the "fall" in the preceding chapter has served the valuable purpose of showing how the way of the transgressor eventually has social implications and cannot be restricted to a private and personal offense against God alone. In the intention of the Yahwist Cain is every bit as possible an everyman as were the man and the woman in the garden.

4. The Genealogy of Cain

17 Cain had relations with his wife and she conceived and bore Enoch. Cain also become the founder of
18 a city, which he named after his son Enoch. To Enoch was born Irad, and Irad became the father of Mehujael; Mehujael became the father of Methusael, and Methusael became the father of La-
19 mech. Lamech took two wives; the name of the first was Adah, and the name of the second Zillah.
20 Adah gave birth to Jabal, the ancestor of all who
21 dwell in tents and keep cattle. His brother's name was Jubal; he was the ancestor of all who play the

22 lyre and the pipe. Zillah, on her part, gave birth to
Tubalcain, the ancestor of all who forge instruments of bronze and iron. The sister of Tubalcain
was Naamah.

23 Lamech said to his wives:

"Adah and Zillah, hear my voice;
wives of Lamech, listen to my utterance:
I have killed a man for wounding me,
a boy for bruising me.

24   If Cain is avenged sevenfold,
then Lamech seventy-sevenfold."

The genealogy begun in 4:1 and interrupted by the Cain and Abel story
now continues. It is evident that the genealogy originally had nothing to
do with the story: here rather than a "restless wanderer" on the earth Cain
is the *founder of a city*. On the other hand, it is just as evident that "the
song of Lamech" which has been appended to the genealogy does presuppose at least vs. 15 of the story of Cain the murderer protected by God.
As usual, the Yahwist has woven his narrative out of varied and diverse
skeins of tradition.

Besides bridging the gap between the creation story with its sequelae
and the story of the flood which the Yahwist begins in chapter 6, this
genealogy has as one of its functions to account for the beginning of various institutions and human accomplishments. Despite the preceding story
which had Abel a keeper of flocks, the genealogy designates a man six
generations later as *the ancestor of all who dwell in tents and keep cattle,*
thus describing the nomadic or semi-nomadic life of the shepherd and
drover. Husbandry, Cain's original calling according to the story, will not
be mentioned again by the Yahwist until 9:20, in connection with Noah
after the flood. Probably of chief importance to the biblical author, as we
have suggested earlier, is that these are indeed *human* accomplishments,
not prizes wrested or stolen from the gods or gifts bestowed by them on
men. Thus, however naïve it may seem to us to find these separate works
assigned each to some single "ancestor," the force of the biblical narration
was to demythologize man's primitive history. We note that there are eight
generations from the first man to the sons of Lamech in this genealogy,
which might make it correspond with one of the Babylonian lists of eight
kings separating the flood from creation. However, as we shall see later,
this number in the Yahwist's genealogy may have been accidentally
brought about in the process of redaction and therefore represent nothing
more than a coincidence.

Embedded in the genealogy there may be wordplays of a subtler kind
than the folk etymologies that are so often explicitly drawn for the reader.

Thus when Cain is said to have *named* the city he built *after his son Enoch* (in Hebrew *hanok*) we may be supposed to think of the verb *hanak,* which means "to found," "to dedicate" (in 1 Kings 8:63 used of a building), even though it does not occur in the text. Similarly the Jabal (*yabal*) of vs. 20 could evoke the Hebrew root *yabal,* "to lead" (in Jeremiah 11:19 the participle is used of a sheep led to slaughter), and the Jubal (*yubal*) of vs. 21, *ancestor of all who play the lyre and the pipe,* might call to mind the word *yobel,* which first meant a cattle horn and then by association the musical instrument fashioned from one (cf. Exodus 19:13). As has already been observed, the latter part of the name of *Tubalcain, the ancestor of all who forge instruments of bronze and iron* (bronze is correctly placed before iron in keeping with the history of metallurgy) can mean "smith." It is also intriguing to note that Tubalcain figures in the genealogy as the half brother of Jabal, which for some has provoked speculation about a doublet of the Cain and Abel story.

The true etymologies of the names in this genealogy are unknown or sharply disputed. We shall re-examine the names, however, in our treatment of the Priestly author's parallel genealogy in chapter 5.

Probably nothing should be made of the first mention of polygamy in vs. 19. Even if the biblical author favored monogamy as an ideal (which cannot be proved) he undoubtedly accepted polygamy as a fact of life and did not for this reason intend to set Lamech in an unfavorable light or to insinuate anything pejorative about either of the two wives or their separate children. Quite another judgment has to be rendered, however, about the Lamech of vss. 23–24. With the progress of mankind in the arts and crafts, alongside there has been a progress in antisocial conduct and violence. Lamech boasts to his wives that the blood vengeance that had protected Cain he has now extended to counter even the slightest affront to his person or his "honor." Behind these verses we doubtless hear the vaunt-song of some tribal chieftain bragging to his womenfolk of his prowess and invincibility in battle and of the dread that his name conveys to all his enemies. What the Yahwist means by incorporating these lines into his history, however, is something else, to bring the Cain saga to its logical if somewhat gloomy conclusion. The institution of tribal blood vengeance which was designed to keep the peace now instead promotes and instigates bloodshed in an ever increasing scale. Rather than serving as a deterrent to murder it now encourages the arrogant and powerful to slaughter at whim or caprice. Without saying so at this juncture, the author undoubtedly looked on the Law of Moses as having brought about redemption from his chaotic regimen by establishing the rule of talion (Exodus 21:24). We often fail to recognize that "eye for eye, tooth for tooth, hand for hand," etc. is nothing else than the law of strict indemnification by which courts and judges still dispense justice: the meaning is that for an eye or whatever *only* an eye or whatever is placed in jeopardy, that a life is not forfeit for a mere wounding. It would remain for a greater than Moses to direct the spirit of this toward an ideal higher than that of strict justice (cf. Matthew 5:38–42, 18:21–22). The biblical author now turns away from the Cainites and their history of good and evil and shifts his gaze in another direction.

5. The Sethites

25 Adam again had relations with his wife, and she gave birth to a son whom she called Seth. "God has granted me more offspring in place of Abel," she
26 said, "because Cain slew him." To Seth, in turn, a son was born, and he named him Enosh.
At that time men began to invoke the LORD by name.

For the first time the Yahwist or, more probably, the Redactor of Genesis uses *Adam* as a proper name for him who thus far has been regularly referred to as "the man." The word, of course, means "man," as does the *Enosh* of vs. 26 also used as a proper name. For *Seth* (Hebrew *sheth*) a popular etymology is found in the mother's jubilant cry that *God has granted* (*shath*) another son to replace the murdered Abel. As Robert Davidson has nicely put it: "In English we might say he is called Grant, because God granted him." We are somewhat surprised to find "God" rather than "Yahweh" (in vs. 25) in these lines that unmistakably come from the Yahwist. This, too, may be due to the Redactor, assimilating this brief genealogy to the lengthy one of the Priestly author which he has placed after it. In fact, the entire presence here of these verses from the Yahwist's work may be ascribable to a redactional use of the work rather than to the Yahwist himself. Certainly this is only a fragment of what must have been a longer genealogy which may have been related to the preceding one in a fashion other than it now is. Just as certainly, as we shall see in our examination of the Priestly genealogy that follows, the name of Noah once appeared somewhere in the Yahwistic genealogy and was removed by the Redactor lest he spoil the effect of his composite story by introducing prematurely the hero of the flood. The Yahwistic Noah passage is now found at 5:29, where it rests uncomfortably and quite obtrusively in its Priestly surroundings. We can only guess where Noah originally figured in the generations calculated by the Yahwist.

The chief difficulty of these verses, however, is framed in vs. 26b: *At that time men began to invoke the* LORD *by name.* This statement, which ascribes the cult of Yahweh to primeval times, apparently conflicts with the E and P traditions of Exodus 3 and 6:2–9, according to which the worship of God under the name of Yahweh was a revelation reserved to Mosaic times. The contradiction may be allowed to stand. Or we may agree with Claus Westermann that the essential point intended by the Yahwist is that the cult of the true God was also present at man's origins, along with the other cultural accomplishments to which he had attained. For the Yahwist, the name of the true God could only be Yahweh—the LORD. And this regardless of whatever other names men may have used at the time.

6. The Genealogy of Adam

5 This is the record of the descendants of Adam. When God created man, he made him in the like-**2** ness of God; he created them male and female. When they were created, he blessed them and **3** named them "man." Adam was one hundred and thirty years old when he begot a son in his likeness, **4** after his image; and he named him Seth. Adam lived eight hundred years after the birth of Seth, and he **5** had other sons and daughters. The whole lifetime of Adam was nine hundred and thirty years; then he died.

6 When Seth was one hundred and five years old, he **7** became the father of Enosh. Seth lived eight hundred and seven years after the birth of Enosh, and **8** he had other sons and daughters. The whole lifetime of Seth was nine hundred and twelve years; then he died.

9 When Enosh was ninety years old, he became the **10** father of Kenan. Enosh lived eight hundred and fifteen years after the birth of Kenan, and he had other **11** sons and daughters. The whole lifetime of Enosh was nine hundred and five years; then he died.

12 When Kenan was seventy years old, he became the
13 father of Mahalalel. Kenan lived eight hundred and
forty years after the birth of Mahalalel, and he had
14 other sons and daughters. The whole lifetime of
Kenan was nine hundred and ten years; then he
died.
15 When Mahalalel was sixty-five years old, he became
16 the father of Jared. Mahalalel lived eight hundred
and thirty years after the birth of Jared, and he had
17 other sons and daughters. The whole lifetime of
Mahalalel was eight hundred and ninety-five years;
then he died.
18 When Jared was one hundred and sixty-two years
19 old, he became the father of Enoch. Jared lived
eight hundred years after the birth of Enoch, and he
20 had other sons and daughters. The whole lifetime of
Jared was nine hundred and sixty-two years; then he
died.
21 When Enoch was sixty-five years old, he became the
22 father of Methuselah. Enoch lived three hundred
years after the birth of Methuselah, and he had
23 other sons and daughters. The whole lifetime of
24 Enoch was three hundred and sixty-five years. Then
Enoch walked with God, and he was no longer here,
for God took him.
25 When Methuselah was one hundred and eighty-
seven years old, he became the father of Lamech.
26 Methuselah lived seven hundred and eighty-two
years after the birth of Lamech, and he had other
27 sons and daughters. The whole lifetime of Methuselah was nine hundred and sixty-nine years; then
he died.
28 When Lamech was one hundred and eighty-two
29 years old, he begot a son and named him Noah, saying, "Out of the very ground that the LORD has put
under a curse this one shall bring us relief from our
30 work and the toil of our hands." Lamech lived five
hundred and ninety-five years after the birth of
31 Noah, and he had other sons and daughters. The
whole lifetime of Lamech was seven hundred and
seventy-seven years; then he died.
32 When Noah was five hundred years old, he became
the father of Shem, Ham and Japheth.

We now rejoin the Priestly author, who has likewise used a genealogy to separate the creation story from the story of the flood. *The record of the descendants* is, literally, "the book of the *toledoth*": cf. 2:4a where *toledoth* was translated "story." Here we do not have a story but rather a list of generations. At the same time, however, summary reference is made in vss. 1–2 to the earlier account of the Priestly author, so constituting these verses a creation story in miniature, concerned now only with man and not with the surrounding cosmos, and introduced by the conventional *when.* We see immediately the ambiguity of the word *adam.* For the purposes of the genealogy it is made, as before, into a proper name, but the artificiality of this device becomes apparent when the author reiterates in the same breath that God created *them male and female* and that it is a they to whom he has given the name "man."

Probably nothing is to be made of the fact that man is said to have been made in *the likeness of God* and not, as before, "in the image of God, after his likeness." The two terms have now been equated and for all practical purposes have the same meaning. This equation is confirmed by vs. 3, where the former order is reversed and it is said that Adam *begot a son in his likeness, after his image.* Man in all his dignity and in all his shortcomings descends generation by generation as he was constituted in the beginning.

Before proceeding further, let us look at the relevant names in the two genealogies of chapters 4 and 5 and see what we believe has taken place in their transmission by the two authors.

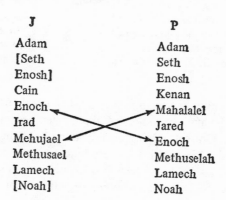

J	P
Adam	Adam
[Seth	Seth
Enosh]	Enosh
Cain	Kenan
Enoch	Mahalalel
Irad	Jared
Mehujael	Enoch
Methusael	Methuselah
Lamech	Lamech
[Noah]	Noah

It is not really difficult to see what has happened here. Both J and P possessed what was essentially the same list of ten "antediluvian patriarchs." J passed over the second and third of the names in order to begin with Cain in the amplified version of the Cain and Abel story. Thus the names of Seth and Enosh which were left over had to be made into a separate genealogy after the Lamech generation (also in an amplified form) had been reached. As we shall see below, the J genealogy also originally possessed the name of Noah, but its reference to this final generation has been mixed in with its counterpart in the P version. P, for its part, switched the order of Enoch and Mahalalel in the list in order to accord Enoch a symbolic seventh place for reasons we shall see. Otherwise the two lists contain the same names, or obvious variants on the same names, and in the same order.

It is noted that there are ten generations in the genealogy, explicitly so in the Priestly writing, and in the Yahwist's chronicle by reconstruction. Berossos, a Babylonian priest of the third century B.C. whose work in Greek has come down to us by devious routes and fragmentarily, has long encouraged the belief that the Babylonians also counted ten generations from creation to flood, not of mere human beings, to be sure, but of dynasties of kings "who came down out of heaven." We give here Berossos' list of the kings together with the fantastic number of years assigned each (one of Berossos' intentions was to show the Greeks the great antiquity of Babylonian culture), since the numbers assigned to the biblical generations will soon occupy our attention.

Aloros of Babylon	36,000
Alaparos, son of Aloros	10,800
Amelon of Pautibibla	46,800
Ammenon of Pautibibla	43,200
Megalaros of Pautibibla	64,800
Daonos, shepherd of Pautibibla	36,000
Evedoranchos of Pautibibla	64,800
Amempsinos of Laracha	36,000
Otiartes of Laracha	28,800
Xisouthros, son of Otiartes	64,800
	432,000

At first glance it may not seem that this list of exotic names has anything to contribute to the understanding of the biblical genealogies. However, long ago Hermann Gunkel, relying on the state of the then available erudition, suggested several interesting correspondences, some of which seem to have been proved wrong, but others just as surely vindicated. Gunkel attempted to restore the Babylonian words or names that were the putative originals hiding behind the Hellenized form that they took on in Berossos' work. For example, he thought that the Amelon in Berossos' third place might represent an original *amelu,* a Babylonian word for "man" which could equate with the Enoch of the Hebrew tables. For the original of the Ammenon in the fourth place he proposed *aminanu/ummanu,* the Babylonian for "craftsman," which could correspond with the Hebrew Cain/ Kenan, "smith." By a possibly inspired guess he saw in the name Evedoranchos the Mesopotamian Enmeduranki, an ancient hero who according to Babylonian legend had been initiated into all the divine mysteries and become the founder of the *baru*-priests (diviners who played an important role in that society): he could be, thought Gunkel, the counterpart of the Hebrew Enoch who "walked with God." With less good fortune he conjectured as lying behind Amempsinos the Babylonian Amel-Sin, "man of Sin" (Sin being the name of the moon-god), which could find its opposite number both in the Methuselah of P (*mutu-shelah,* "man of Shelach," a Canaanite god of the underworld) and the Methusael of J (*mutu-sha-el,* "man of [the] god"). Finally, in Otiartes, revised to Opartes, he correctly saw the Ubartutu of the Gilgamesh epic, the father of the hero of the flood who is called in Babylonian sources Atra-hasis or Utanapishtim, and in Sumerian Ziusudra (cf. the Xisouthros of Berossos), and in the Bible Noah.

Since Gunkel's day the horizons of our vision on the antediluvian kings have been immeasurably broadened by the decipherment of cuneiform tablets that place us in direct contact with the sources of the tradition handed on by Berossos. It turns out that the names were all Sumerian, not the Semitic that Gunkel imagined for many of them. Their origins, therefore, are to be found in the very oldest, pre-Semitic culture that once flourished in Mesopotamia. The tablets both confirm Berossos in some areas and part company with him in others:

W.B. 444*		W.B. 62*	
Alulim of Eridu	28,800	Alulim of Subaru	67,200
Alalgar of Eridu	36,000	Alalgar of Subaru	72,000
Enmenluanna of Badtibira	43,200	. . . -kidunnu of Larsa	72,000
Enmengalanna of Badtibira	28,800	. . . -alimma of Larsa	21,600
Dumuzi, shepherd of Badtibira	36,000	Dumuzi, shepherd of Badtibira	28,800
Ensibzianna of Larak	28,800	Enmenluanna of Badtibira	21,600
Enmenduranna of Sippar	21,000	Ensibzianna of Larak	36,000
Ubartutu of Shuruppak	18,600	Enmenduranna of Sippar	72,000
		Ubartutu of Shuruppak	28,800
		Ziusudra of Shuruppak	36,000
	241,200		456,000

What these lists seem to make plain, first of all, is that there is no direct connection between the Old Babylonian chronologies and the genealogy of P. Doubt is also raised as to whether there was any firm Mesopotamian tradition that set the number of generations between creation and

---

* W.B. with an appropriate number recognizes that the document in question belongs to the Weld-Blundell collection of cuneiform tablets housed in the Ashmolean Museum at Oxford.

the flood at ten. Claus Westermann has argued that the two Larsa names of W.B. 62 were interpolated into an original eight-generation list like that of W.B. 444 in order to enhance the prestige of that Mesopotamian city. Certainly political and other considerations have governed the transmission of the materials. It is no accident that in the list of Berossos, a Babylonian priest, the city of Babylon is mentioned in the first place rather than Eridu or Subaru. We cannot decide on the basis of the evidence available to us whether the Old Babylonian king list comprised exclusively eight generations which were later expanded to ten, or whether eight and ten coexisted together in variant lists. If the latter is true, the Priestly author may have taken from Babylonia the precedent for his numbering of ten generations before (and after, in his calculations) the great flood story that is shared by Babylonia and the Bible alike. He may also have taken from this source the idea of the inflated figures which characterize each of these generations, a matter to which we are about to turn our attention. And he may have taken an additional idea or two, which we will discuss later. But we must emphasize that the association, if any, is slight. (In addition it is interesting to observe that the oldest Assyrian version of the legend of Atra-hasis seems to have prefaced to the story of the flood no king list at all, whether of eight or ten.)

The reader will have noticed, perhaps, that all the numbers in the Babylonian lists, Berossos' included, are divisible by six. This is in accord with the six-base mathematical system that was used in Mesopotamia along with the decimal system: things tended there to be counted in sixties. (Without always realizing it, we adhere to the six-base principle ourselves as heirs to antiquity, when, for example, we continue to count 360 degrees in a circle.) This is not true of the biblical numbers, which march to some other, more elusive drummer. The sole resemblance, or practically the sole resemblance, which the biblical numbers have to the Babylonian is that they all represent impossible ages. Even this resemblance is lessened by the fact that while the Babylonian numbers deal in tens of thousands, the figures of P never attain to one thousand. Nevertheless, the discrepancy may have been deliberate on the part of the Priestly author with an eye to the Mesopotamian tradition. The worthies of the king lists were, after all, gods or demigods, whose ages could consequently be recorded astronomically. P deals only with men, and therefore the ages he assigns them are comparatively modest. A thousand years is a perspective proper to Deity (cf. Psalm 90:4) and consequently is denied to any mere man.

The Priestly genealogy follows a relentlessly monotonous schema. First is given the age at which each patriarch sired the first of a new generation, then the number of years he lived thereafter, and finally the sum total of his years. The sum of the first set of numbers amounts to the number of years from creation to flood. If the reader's patience has not been too much taxed by the arithmetic which we have inflicted on it thus far, we shall test it a final time with the following tables which list the first and the third series of numbers in the genealogy as they are attested to by our three ancient witnesses to the biblical tradition: the "standard" or Masoretic Text of the Hebrew Bible (MT), the Samaritan Pentateuch† (SP), and the Septuagint (LXX).

	MT		SP		LXX	
Adam	130	930	130	930	230	930
Seth	105	912	105	912	205	912
Enosh	90	905	90	905	190	905
Kenan	70	910	70	910	170	910
Mahalalel	65	895	65	895	165	895
Jared	162	962	62	847	162	962
Enoch	65	365	65	365	165	365
Methuselah	187	969	67	720	167	969
Lamech	182	777	53	653	188	753
Noah	500		500		500	
	100	950	100	950	100	950
	1656		1307		2242	

What do these series of tables tell us? First, as seems apparent, the LXX or the Hebrew original on which it depended has tried to round the numbers off into a more or less consistent pattern. The SP, for its part, appears to have diminished some of the numbers in the first column in order, perhaps, to render them more "believable." Secondly, however, the comparison of the three separate listings indicates that even if the numbers as preserved in the MT be original and correctly handed down, the key to their esoteric meaning, if any, has largely been lost and had already been lost shortly after their devising.

Certain things do stand out in the MT chronology. For one, Noah is the first man to be born (in the "year of the world" 1056) after the death of Adam (in the year of the world 930). This marks the beginning of the new generation of man that follows the flood. The construction is only strengthened by the consideration that Methuselah, the longest-lived of the antediluvians, dies precisely (in the year 1656) at the time that the flood begins. A clean sweep, therefore, is made of all the patriarchs that preceded Noah and the flood, and there is no reason to conclude that any of them were included in the combined judgment of both J and P that the

---

† At some undetermined time in the postexilic age Samaritan and Jew were definitively separated. A small community of Samaritans still survives at Nablus (the Shechem of today) in northern Palestine. The text of the Pentateuch which they have preserved escaped the MT redaction and differs from it in many details.

whole earth had become a *massa corruptionis* that had to be destroyed. It may also be interesting to note, for what it is worth, that all the numbers in the P list according to the MT aside from the total age of Methuselah are in multiples of five or in multiples of five after the removal of seven.

Beyond these easily recognizable intimations, we hesitate to venture further. Every commentator on Genesis, including the present writer, has spent hours over pencil and paper, and recently with a pocket calculator, trying to wrest some sense or pattern out of the figures with which the MT supplies us. The best conclusion drawn from this effort is that there are other pursuits more rewarding. There undoubtedly is, or was, a key to these numbers which the Priestly author intended his readers or hearers to grasp, but whether it has disappeared in transmission or simply now eludes us is impossible to determine.

Two of the names in this Priestly genealogy demand our attention. First, in vss. 23–24 the *Enoch* who *walked with God, and was no longer here, for God took him*. The Priestly author has put Enoch in a potentially significant seventh place and has assigned him a potentially significant age of 365 years; unlike the rest of the series he is not said to have died. It may be indeed that the Enmeduranki or Enmenduranna of Babylonian myth has influenced the Hebrew legend of Enoch, a figure which captivated the imagination of early Judaism (cf. Sirach 44:16, 49:14; see also Hebrews 11:15). The apocryphal book of Enoch which was composed sometime in the intertestamental period exercised enormous influence and is quoted (Jude 14–15) in the New Testament. The passage in the Priestly genealogy may reflect a fairly early form of the speculation which continued to surround this shadowy figure. Enoch "walked with God": the same expression is used of Noah in 6:10 (P) and presumably means the same thing, namely that his life was one of complete righteousness. It may be that for this reason while he did not die at all, his son Methuselah is accorded the longest life of all in the list of the antediluvian patriarchs. His own life-span of 365 years could have some connection with the fact that Enmenduranna of the Babylonian lists is associated with Sippar, the city of the sun-god, and therefore with the solar calendar of 365 days, a "perfect" number. That Enoch "was no longer here, for God took him" has suggested to most commentators that, in consequence of his perfect life, he was spared the common lot of mortals and taken by God from this earth to be with him, as Elijah had been (2 Kings 2:1.9–11). Therefore, whether or not the biblical portrayal of Enoch is remotely tributary to a motif of Babylonian mythology, it has at any rate been thoroughly divested of alien attire and clad in the familiar garb of biblical religion. As R bert Davidson has said, "the priestly writer has firmly closed the door on much speculation. For him, the supreme honour is not esoteric knowledge or the gift of divination, but the life of faith, a life lived in intimate communion with God."

The other name at which we must look in this list is that of Noah in vs. 29. As has already been intimated, while it is undoubtedly true that Noah was part of this P list from the beginning, as it stands this verse has been extracted from somewhere in the work of J. It employs the name Yahweh, it refers to the J passage of 3:17–18 and looks forward to the J passage of 9:20, and unlike P but in the wont of J it attaches a popular etymology to the name. The true meaning of "Noah" is unknown. The popular etymology lies in Lamech's words that he *shall bring us relief* (*yenahamenu*): the similarity is not very close, but neither is it in many other such etymologies, so that it is not necessary to conjecture another reading as some commentators do. The "relief" refers to the gift of the vine, which will be attributed to Noah in 9:20. Though this gift has some unhappy results for him personally in that instance, it was biblical man's conviction that the purpose of wine was to gladden men's hearts (cf. Psalm 104:15). Hence Noah was remembered for something else than his character as hero of the flood.

As in the Babylonian king lists, so in Genesis the ages of men after the flood will be sharply reduced. The flood thus marks a decisive watershed —no levity is intended—in the prehistory of man which the Bible has prefaced to the history of Israel's more immediate ancestors, this congeries of myth and legend out of which it spun from conviction the story of how God and man must have been in the ages—far vaster than the Bible could ever know—before history in any true sense could be written. The tremendous ages ascribed to the folkloric heroes of old gradually become less and less incredible the closer the story arrives at the threshold of familiar fact and reality. The story of the flood, taken from the same common Near Eastern folklore that has supplied the other materials with which we have been concerned, has an importance that is revealed by the relative space that has been accorded it in both the J and the P traditions, now combined by the Redactor of Genesis into a single narrative. It is to this narrative that we now must turn.

7. The Story of the Flood

6 When men began to multiply on earth and daughters
2 were born to them, the sons of heaven saw how beautiful the daughters of man were, and so they took for

3 their wives as many of them as they chose. Then the
LORD said: "My spirit shall not remain in man forever, since he is but flesh. His days shall comprise
one hundred and twenty years."

4 At that time the Nephilim appeared on earth (as
well as later), after the sons of heaven had intercourse with the daughters of man, who bore them
sons. They were the heroes of old, the men of renown.

5 When the LORD saw how great was man's wickedness
on earth, and how no desire that his heart conceived
6 was ever anything but evil, he regretted that he had
made man on the earth, and his heart was grieved.
7 So the LORD said: "I will wipe out from the earth the
men whom I have created, and not only the men, but
also the beasts and the creeping things and the birds
8 of the air, for I am sorry that I made them." But
Noah found favor with the LORD.

Though it first does not appear so, this passage is the Yahwist's beginning of the story of the flood. It becomes clearer when we recognize that
vs. 5 is the interpretation he wishes to give to the preceding four verses,
and therefore the reason for his including this rather curious myth in his
chronicle. The myth itself, though it is relatively brief, appears to have
been both truncated and conflated, not to say interpolated: the biblical author has combined some snatches of parallel myths which he has bent to
convey his own message, which appears mainly in vs. 3.

The original sense of the myth is not difficult to determine, as it has
many parallels in the mythologies of antiquity, including the Canaanite
mythology from which the Yahwist doubtless took it. It tells of the miscegenation of divine and human beings which led to the rise of a mongrel
race of superhuman attainments, frequently depicted as giants. It was a
common belief of ancient man that among the aboriginal inhabitants of the
earth or of his land there had been giants (cf. Numbers 13:34). The origin
of this belief may have been the larger-than-life effigies that these bygone
peoples had left behind, such as the great stone images of Easter Island
which remain something of a puzzle to this day. The giants of this Genesis
story were portrayed in later Jewish tradition as proud rebels against God
who had been swept away from the earth by the flood (Wisdom 14:6;
Sirach 16:7; Baruch 3:26–28). This later tradition goes beyond the
apparent intention of the Yahwist in making use of the myth.

When men began to multiply on earth is the Yahwist's equivalent of the
reiterated "other sons and daughters" of the Priestly author's genealogy of

the preceding chapter. It is interesting to observe that in the Atra-hasis legend the flood also is the eventual sequel to a time "when the land extended and the peoples multiplied." In the Mesopotamian story the problem is that the noise and uproar of mankind disturbs the serenity of the gods. In Genesis the problem is quite different, as we see. *The sons of heaven* are, literally, "the sons of God" or "sons of the gods," inferior deities which the earlier Israelitic monotheism had no hesitation about picturing as making up the heavenly court of Yahweh (cf. Job 1:6, 2:1, 38:7; Psalm 89:7, etc.). The expression is, however, obviously polytheistic in origin, and later it caused embarrassment in times of greater theological sensitivity. Hence the Septuagint translated "angels of God," and most Jewish and early Christian interpretation followed suit in regarding the "sons of heaven" of Genesis 6:2 as angels. In times of even greater theological sensitivity, of course, when angels came to be defined as "pure spirits" and thus incapable of what is ascribed to the sons of heaven of this passage, a further reinterpretation had to be made by those who wanted to take these verses as representing sober history. It was then that "the sons of God" were thought of as good men *v.* bad women who were "the daughters of man," or as the Sethites *v.* the Cainites, or simply men in general (created in the likeness of God) *v.* women in general (made from man). There can be no doubt, however, that in the myth used by the Yahwist the sons of heaven were as we first defined them, gods, who cohabited with *the daughters of man,* human women. The biblical author undoubtedly had no difficulty about accepting the story as he found it; however, his first purpose in repeating the myth, or repeating it partially, was not to provide an etiology for a race of giants but rather to continue his representation of man as a creature constantly trying to overstep the boundaries that separate him from God and to usurp the divine prerogatives.

That this construction is the right one we see immediately from what follows in the Yahwist's narrative. Instead of vs. 4 which is presumably the original point of the myth, describing the consequence of the traffic between the sons of heaven and the daughters of man, the author has inserted vs. 3, which renders a judgment on man. It is a judgment that is somewhat puzzling, to be sure. It is not puzzling in its substance. *My spirit shall not remain in man forever* without doubt refers to the life breath of God by which man has become and remains a living being (Genesis 2:7). Man shall not live forever, says Yahweh, reiterating the judgment previously expressed on the occasion of man's expulsion from the garden, away from the tree of life (3:22–24). *He is but flesh:* "flesh" is the badge of creaturehood, comprising all that limits man and separates him from the divine realm. *His days . . . one hundred and twenty years:* most likely this sentence refers to the life-span of man rather than to a waiting period prior to the flood. The Yahwist, of course, was not privy to the great ages ascribed to men both before and after the flood by P, all of which, even in patriarchal times, exceed his 120. Neither did he have the interlocking series of individual ages related to events that characterizes the work of P all the way through Genesis. He is simply laying down, in opposition to an unlimited immortality, a fixed and "round" number of years. As Theodor Gaster has observed: "One hundred and twenty occurs elsewhere in the Old Testament as a conventional round number. Thus, the total weight of gold dishes in the Tabernacle is 120 shekels. Both Hiram of Tyre and the Queen of Sheba send Solomon 120 talents of gold. There are 120 priestly trumpeters at the dedication of the temple . . . This round number is probably to be explained as thrice forty, i.e., as an hyperbolic exaggeration of what is elsewhere in the Bible the typical round number."

What is puzzling about the judgment passed on man is that it is indeed passed on man. Coming as it does as an evident commentary on what has been described in vss. 1–2, we would naturally expect vs. 3 to condemn, if anyone, "the sons of heaven" who *took for their wives as many of [the daughters of man] as they chose.* It is only these to whom any positive action has thus far been attributed. And the judgment, be it noted, is passed on man as a whole, on mankind, not simply on the supermen who were the product of the mating of divine with human beings. It is difficult to agree here with Westermann's usually admirable commentary, which succeeds in identifying after all "the sons of heaven" with a would-be superior class of men in despite of all that it has tried to do to prove that they are not men but gods. Rather, it would seem that we are in better company with Oswald Loretz when he places the emphasis on the Israelite and Canaanite background against which this myth has been evaluated by the Yahwist. The biblical author is, throughout these early chapters of Genesis, describing the coming to be of everyman, not just Israelite man. But neither can he divorce himself from the Israelite experience that made the description possible in the first place. Man aspires to the divine: and this aspiration is not necessarily *hybris,* but can be a legitimate desire for communion with God. One route to such communion, however, which any true Israelite would recognize as leading to a cul-de-sac was that of ritual marriage or sacred prostitution in which the aspirant after godliness would unite himself or herself with an hierodule or her male counterpart who served as surrogates for the divinity. The practice was widespread in Canaan and in Babylonia, where it was elaborately regulated by law. Occasionally it penetrated popular Israelite religion (cf. Hosea 4:14). It was this present peril, therefore, that the Yahwist was quite conceivably concerned with first and foremost rather than with an ancient tale of philandering among the gods.

If this interpretation is correct, then it is not required that we decide who were the "guilty" parties, the sons of heaven who were captivated by the beauty of the daughters of man and took them for wives, or the latter who became willing brides. What was wrong was the persuasion that man could become more than man by means of a sacralized mystique of sex. (A persuasion that has not entirely disappeared in the history of man subsequent to the Bible.) It was for this reason that man had to be reminded that he was and is but man, and once again to be told that the path of his glory leads inevitably to the grave.

In vs. 4 we are not told explicitly that giants were the product of the union of divine and human beings, though that was the obvious intimation of the myth. The biblical author is not all that much interested in pursuing the story, which he has now used for his own purposes. *Nephilim* occurs here and in Numbers 13:33 in the sense of giants (in the latter passage paralleled with Anakim who are explicitly called giants). The words *as well as later* are doubtless a gloss to account for the later appearance of the Nephilim in the time accounted for by Numbers 13:33. The Nephilim are identified here with *the heroes of old* (the *gibborim*) and *the men of renown,* probably through a combination of sources, all of whom, like the Nephilim ("those who have descended"?), were thought now to reside in Sheol, in the underworld of the dead (cf. Ezekiel 32:21.27).

In vs. 5, as we have already suggested, we come to the ultimate judgment that the Yahwist rendered on the preceding story as a preface to his account of the flood. It is not, however, that only because of what is described in vss. 1–4 did Yahweh see *how great was man's wickedness on earth, and how no desire that his heart conceived was ever anything but evil;* rather, we are expected to see in this incident simply the most recent in the series of failures by which man has shown himself inept to the promise that was held out for him in the act of creation. As we have remarked before and shall have occasion to remark again, no real explanation is ever given of this fact. Evil exists without any accounting for it, and man is ever susceptible to it and conquered by it. Therefore the Yahwist does not shrink from the anthropomorphism that says of God that *he regretted that he had made man on the earth, and his heart was grieved.* God confesses, in effect, to his own failure with man, is willing to cut his losses, and like the potter of Jeremiah's vision (Jeremiah 18:1–11) he is prepared to start all over again. His first step necessarily will have to be to *wipe out from the earth the men whom* [he has] *created* (this verse, particularly when it goes on to include not only men but the other creatures of the earth as well, reflects the language of P, which is doubtless attributable to R).

But Noah found favor with the LORD. Noah, originally present in the Yahwist's genealogy and now in any case part of the combined story of Genesis prepared by R, needs no introduction beyond this one. It is important to note, however, that in this first mention of Noah that the Redactor has permitted the Yahwist to make in his own right, in the midst of a totally corrupt generation of man he is identified merely as one who "found favor" with God. Noah is not characterized by J as a completely righteous man as P characterized him. It is part of the message of J, as we have seen before, that the choices and favors of God, the dispensation of his grace, are not based on discernible qualities possessed by the recipients, but are hidden in God's own salvific designs.

And so, we now begin the story of the flood. The tradition of a great, world-destroying flood has been handed down not only from the Sumero-Semitic Near East, but also from the mythologies of Greece, Egypt, India, Polynesia, and even the American Indians, not to mention other peoples who have produced analogous tales. It is not profitable to try to discover a single beginning for all these stories, as though they might go back to some aboriginal happening that had somehow involved the prehistory of such widely distributed and unrelated human cultures. Most of the similarities in the stories are casual, as they turn out to be when one is compared with the other. That prehistoric mankind had, once or twice or multiple times, been wiped from the face of the earth by fire or by flood or by drought seems to have been a general persuasion of ancient peoples who expressed their belief in mythopoeic accounts which are inevitably similar. The proliferation of flood stories should no more surprise us than does the proliferation of stories describing the creation of man from a base material of clay or wood or whatever, breathed into or otherwise vivified by the power of God. The ideas are similar, and they invite similar expressions.

It is not so—as far as the biblical evidence is concerned—with the Mesopotamian accounts of the flood. Here we have a tradition that has been handed down in at least ten different Babylonian versions that constitute a very close parallel with the biblical story. The most complete and the best-known of the Babylonian sources is the Gilgamesh epic. In this epic we have the following correspondences with the biblical story:

the *occasion* is the same: divine causality has decided on the flood;

the *principals* are the same: one man and his family are to be saved;

the *revelation* of the flood is made by divinity;

the *construction* of the ark is dictated by deity;

animals are taken aboard according to dictate;

the *end of the flood* is determined by birds;

the ark rests on a mountain;

a *pleasing sacrifice* concludes the story.

There is no question at all that anyone who is familiar in any way with the Genesis story will recognize immediately that we have before us what is essentially a common tradition. The Babylonian texts come from the library of King Ashurbanipal (seventh century B.C.) at Nineveh and probably go back to a millennium or so before, therefore to a long time prior to the separate J and P narrations with which we now have to do. This is not to say that the biblical narration has simply been borrowed from Mesopotamian legend—there are too many incidental and irrelevant differences in detail to make such an hypothesis likely—but rather the biblical and the Babylonian stories have somewhere a common ancestor. The no less essential differences that separate the biblical from the non-biblical stories will best be brought out in the following commentary. We say "stories" both as regards the Mesopotamian and the biblical writings, for it is plain that in both cases we are confronted by multiple traditions. The Genesis account of the flood is a rather admirable combination of the J and P histories which R has sutured together in a quite credible fashion. Nevertheless, he has left behind the traces of his disparate sources:

God twice observes the malice of man (6:5, J; 6:12, P);
he announces the flood twice (6:13.17, P; 7:4, J);
he orders Noah twice to enter the ark (6:18–20, P; 7:1–3, J);
Noah obeys twice (6:22, P; 7:5, J);
Noah enters the ark twice (7:7, J; 7:13, P);
God twice resolves to destroy mankind (7:11, P; 7:12, J);
twice the waters increase and raise the ark (7:17, J; 7:18ff., P);
all living beings die twice (7:21, P; 7:22, J);
the waters abate twice (8:1, J; 8:3a, P);
God promises no more floods (8:20–22, J; 9:8–17, P).

Besides these replications there are the obvious discrepancies between the biblical traditions which reveal them as two. In 6:19–20 and 7:15–16 (P) the animals taken aboard the ark are one pair of each species; in 7:2 (J) a distinction is made between the clean (seven pairs) and the unclean (one pair) animals. In 7:4.12, 8:2b (J) the flood is caused by rain: by *geshem,* the winter rain, as it happens. In 7:11, 8:2 (P) it is the "fountains of the abyss and the floodgates of the sky" that reverse the order effected by creation and again bring chaos into the cosmos. And, according to P, this takes place (7:11) "in the second month," i.e., May–June (the same time that the flood occurred according to Berossos). In 8:5 (P) the mountains appear, and yet in 8:9 (J) the waters are still over the whole earth. Noah learns of the end of the flood in two ways: in 8:6.12.13b (J) he finds this out by the use of birds, while in 8:14–16 (P) he is instructed by God. According to J the rain which caused the flood lasted forty days and forty nights (7:4.12) and the flood itself endured for sixty-one days (cf. 7:10, 8:8–12). In P the flood crests after 150 days (7:24, 8:2a3b). Then the waters begin to descend. In the 601st year of Noah, in the first month, the first day of the month, the waters have disappeared (8:13, P). Since the flood began according to P in the 600th year of Noah, the second month, the seventeenth day (7:11), the whole "cleansing" process would have taken ten and a half months. The earth, again according to P, eventually became dry on the twenty-seventh day of the second month (8:14). Thus the total duration of the cataclysm would have been a year and eleven days.

We point out these discrepancies not because they are important but rather in order to suggest that they are not—not, at any rate, to the biblical author or redactor who has given us this composite story. The biblical author, who was well aware of the differences in the traditions he used long before modern critics rediscovered them, was obviously disinterested in such details. He handed on the stories as they had come to him not because he was concerned over water sources or dimensions of time and space, but because he found in this legend from the distant past a suitable means of illustrating a deeply held religious conviction: the conviction that evil is requited by a just God who is at the same time a God of mercy. In the Mesopotamian stories of the flood no real motivation is ever offered to explain why the gods brought about this particular disaster, not even in the legend of Atra-hasis where the flood is the last of a series of calamities visited on man by one set of gods and mitigated by another set. In the biblical story the divine motivation for the flood is of its essence. What the Bible has done is to turn an amoral myth into a highly moral parable of God's retribution and grace responding to the challenge of his creatures' willfulness and evil-doing. There and there alone lies the biblical message intended by the flood story.

We have seen the Yahwist's introduction to the story. Now we read the Priestly author's version to the same effect:

> 9 These are the descendants of Noah. Noah, a good
> 10 man and blameless in that age, for he walked with
> 11 God, begot three sons: Shem, Ham and Japheth. In
> the eyes of God the earth was corrupt and full of
> 12 lawlessness. When God saw how corrupt the earth
> had become, since all mortals led depraved lives on
> 13 earth, he said to Noah: "I have decided to put an
> end to all mortals on earth; the earth is full of law-
> lessness because of them. So I will destroy them
> and all life on earth."

These are the descendants of Noah: P has placed the flood story within his series of *toledoth.* Perhaps he makes a special point of it in this present instance. The Babylonian Noah, Utanapishtim, was received after the flood into the fellowship of the gods. The biblical Noah, it is emphasized, remained throughout a man with human progeny who eventually died (9:29, P). Noah, along with Daniel and Job, figured in Hebrew folklore as an example of extraordinary virtue (cf. Ezekiel 14:14.20), therefore it is not surprising that P so characterizes him here. Like the mysterious Enoch of 5:24 (P), *he walked with God* (see the commentary above). Though God has resolved to destroy all that he has created, nevertheless he will not allow the innocent to perish with the guilty. For the sake of the innocent, indeed, he will preserve a whole family in order to give mankind a fresh start.

With the family of Noah we shall be concerned later on. For the moment, we must pause to remark on the really shocking character of what we read in vss. 11–13 above. Nothing in the Priestly narration thus far has prepared us for anything like this. With almost tiresome repetition we are told that *the earth was corrupt and full of lawlessness* and that *all mortals* (literally, "all flesh") *led depraved lives:* the Priestly author depicts God's creation as having become a mass of corruption in a more thoroughgoing fashion than does the Yahwist. And this with no warning at all. This is the same creation which the same author in the first chapter of Genesis had God bless over and over again and find that it was all very good (1:31). This is the same creation which the same author in the fifth chapter of Genesis showed burgeoning in fulfillment of the divine injunction to increase and multiply, when men led fabulously long lives in apparent fruitfulness and tranquillity. This author has offered no hint of the transgression of divine prohibitions, no hint of murder or violence, no instance of *hybris* or disorder. And now all is changed in the twinkling of an eye, and what was once all good is now suddenly all bad.

It is conceivable, of course, that the Priestly writing at one time contained some intervening material that has been omitted by the Redactor; but this hypothesis is gratuitous and lacks probability. Rather, it would appear that P has deliberately left the mystery of iniquity appropriately shrouded in an embracing sequence of events that rejects logical analysis and explanation. At the same time, this author has emerged with a rather different concept of sinfulness than that of J. Sin, in this construction, is not the transgression of one or many divine prescriptions, cumulatively or climactically describable. It is, rather, a turn of existence that is a standing offense to the blessing and order willed by the Creator, a reversal of that order that has already anticipated the return of primeval chaos which God will soon offer as his response. And it is, be it noted, a willful and culpable turn of existence, since Noah, *a good man and blameless in that age,* is proof positive that it need not have been so. In much the same fashion, the prophet Amos cried woe against a complacent Israel whose life-style had already brought about the decay and ruination which Yahweh could only ratify by his sure retribution (Amos 6:6–7).

According to P, God announces to Noah from the beginning his intention to bring an end to life on earth. As we shall see, the situation is somewhat different in J, or in what we can surmise was the version of J. We shall have to make a similar surmise about the construction of the ark according to J. What we have in the narrative that R has effected is a continuation of the P story:

> 14 "Make yourself an ark of gopherwood, put various
> compartments in it, and cover it inside and out with
> 15 pitch. This is how you shall build it: the length of
> the ark shall be three hundred cubits, its width fifty
> 16 cubits, and its height thirty cubits. Make an opening
> for daylight in the ark, and finish the ark a cubit
> above it. Put an entrance in the side of the ark,
> which you shall make with bottom, second and third
> 17 decks. I, on my part, am about to bring the flood
> [waters] on the earth, to destroy everywhere all
> creatures in which there is the breath of life; every-
> 18 thing on earth shall perish. But with you I will es-
> tablish my covenant; you and your sons, your wife
> 19 and your sons' wives, shall go into the ark. Of all
> other living creatures you shall bring two into the ark,
> one male and one female, that you may keep them
> 20 alive with you. Of all kinds of birds, of all kinds of
> beasts, and of all kinds of creeping things, two of each
> shall come into the ark with you, to stay alive.
> 21 Moreover, you are to provide yourself with all the
> food that is to be eaten, and store it away, that it
> may serve as provisions for you and for them."
> 22 This Noah did; he carried out all the commands that
> God gave him.

The Priestly author, as we know, loves to fiddle with numbers. Therefore he has devoted considerable attention to the divine specification according to which the ark was to be constructed. He was following precedent, however. First of all, what was this *ark* that Noah was instructed to create? The Hebrew is *tebah,* a word which by general scholarly consent seems to have been borrowed from an Egyptian term meaning "box" or "cask": it is the faithful and literal Latin translation *arca* which has given us our "ark." (It is probably not by accident that outside Genesis the only occurrence of *tebah* in the Hebrew Bible is in Exodus 2:3 where it designates the reed basket daubed with pitch in which the baby Moses was saved from destruction.) It is interesting that in Genesis the vessel of preservation is never termed a ship but rather a box, even though its dimensions correspond to those of a ship, whereas in the Gilgamesh epic it is indeed called a ship but could hardly be one, since it seems to have been a perfect cube:

> Tear down (this) house, build a ship! . . .
> Aboard the ship take the seed of all living things.
> The ship that you shall build,
> Her dimensions shall be to measure.
> Equal shall be her width and her length . . .
> On the fifth day I laid her framework.
> One (whole) acre was her floor space,
> Ten dozen cubits the height of each of her walls,
> Ten dozen cubits each edge of the square deck . . .
> I provided her with six decks,
> Dividing her (thus) into seven parts.
> Her floor plan I divided into seven parts . . .

So spoke Utanapishtim to Gilgamesh, adding too the biblical note that he *cover[ed] it inside and out with pitch*. The Gilgamesh version of the flood story is a leisurely and fanciful elaboration of the Atra-hasis legend, according to which a reed house was literally fashioned into a reed boat—the same kind of boat still used in the Middle East and which has been recently floated across the seas by Thor Heyerdahl to prove the seaworthiness of such a craft. Somewhere in between Gilgamesh and Atrahasis, and with its own variations, the P story describes its ark. It is made of *gopherwood* (cypress? teak?) rather than reeds, but it has *compartments* as in the Gilgamesh story, and it is calked with pitch, Mesopotamian style. Its length is *three hundred cubits, its width fifty cubits, and its height thirty cubits*. The cubit, or ell (cf. the English elbow or the Latin *ulna*) is the length of the forearm, roughly a foot and a half, or something less than a half meter. As we see, Noah's ark is much smaller than Utanapishtim's.

Make an opening for daylight in the ark, and finish the ark a cubit above it presupposes a translation with which not everyone will agree but which is just as probable as any alternative that has been suggested. As we shall see, it is rather important that in the P story Noah has a means of looking outside, whereas in the J version he does not. The three *decks* of Noah's ark, we notice, describe a rather modest boat in comparison with the liner floated by Utanapishtim.

In vs. 17 God specifies the means by which he will bring the end to the residents of earth that he has already announced in vs. 13, though this means should have become obvious by now. He is about to bring upon the earth once more the *mabbul* (the "waters above the dome" of 1:7, here translated *flood* and therefore not needing the gloss "waters" which has been placed in brackets in the NAB). It will be a return of the primitive chaos that had been banished by creation, *to destroy everywhere all creatures* (the same *kol basar*, "all flesh," that was translated "all mortals" in vss. 12–13 above). The Priestly author's view of the depravity of the world, we point out once more, embraces a concept of the world that is not limited to man alone.

In vs. 18 we have our first biblical reference to *covenant*. No doubt the author's primary intention in making this reference is to point us forward to the covenant that will be established in 9:9–11 (P). It can also be argued, however, that a covenant is being proclaimed here and now. In English, covenant (from the Old French *covenir*=agree) usually means a mutually agreeable arrangement, a bi- or multilateral understanding that has been reached after negotiation. However, it translates a Hebrew word (*berith:* etymology uncertain) which in the Bible can mean not only this but various other things besides. Specifically, when it is a question of covenant between God and man, or God and people, the initiative is always ascribed to God alone, who has extended covenant as a sign of his grace and mercy. In other words, God voluntarily binds himself to be held accountable to the terms of a promise which he has made out of his goodness. Thus the point does not rise whether Noah's wife or his sons or his sons' wives were "deserving" of the divine consideration shown them: even though Noah himself has been designated "a good man and blameless in that age" and therefore singled out for salvation, it does not follow that the same qualities have to be credited to his family. God's election, in P as in J, is an act of his sovereign will which cannot be merited by man. Also, for the sake of a good man the guilty can be allowed to go free. Such was the teaching of the Second Isaiah on whom the Priestly author was dependent, but as we shall see below (in the course of the Yahwist's narrative in chapter 18), it was an older teaching as well.

We may be tempted to smile at the naïveté of our story which decrees a place in the ark for specimens of all the species of the denizens of the earth, *one male and one female, that you may keep them alive with you.* In vs. 20 the living creatures in question are tallied as *all kinds of birds, all kinds of beasts,* and *all kinds of creeping things;* with simple logic only the fish go unmentioned, since they can presumably fend for themselves without outside help. It is likely enough that the biblical author also found his story naïve in this respect, though of course he could not have known as we do how completely impossible would be such an undertaking at any time and under any circumstances. It is futile to attempt to rationalize the story here or elsewhere, for example to try to estimate how much would be *all the food that is to be eaten* by Noah's family and their floating zoo— vegetarian food, we remember, in the perspective of P, if such details were supposed to be recalled from one story to the next. Neither must we marvel at how expeditiously Noah seems to have *carried out all the commands that God gave him.* The ultimate origin of the flood story taken over by P is myth, and no matter what the biblical author has done with the story, he has not changed its nature. It is the nature of a story-myth to mingle the real with the unreal, the possible with the impossible, verisimilitude with phantasmagory, and it is silly and unnatural to think we can segregate and retrieve for "fact" by some species of concordism a selected few of these elements while we let the others go. The biblical story of the flood has indeed a message for man on this earth, but the *locus* of the story is the never-never land of fancy and not one that was ever mapped or plotted by everyday and real experience.

In the Priestly narrative, as we see, we are not told how long it took for Noah to make his ark and prepare for the flood. Both in the Atra-hasis legend and especially in the Gilgamesh epic we are assured that the entire process required only an incredible seven days. The seven days also turn up in the Yahwist's account, though apparently only as a recollection without significance, since when we are introduced to his story *in medias res* the ark seemingly has already been constructed.

> 7 Then the LORD said to Noah: "Go into the ark, you
>   and all your household, for you alone in this age
> 2 have I found to be truly just. Of every clean animal,
>   take with you seven pairs, a male and its mate; and
>   of the unclean animals, one pair, a male and its mate;
> 3 likewise, of every clean bird of the air, seven pairs, a
>   male and a female, and of all the unclean birds, one
>   pair, a male and a female. Thus you will keep their
> 4 issue alive over all the earth. Seven days from now
>   I will bring rain down on the earth for forty days
>   and forty nights, and so I will wipe out from the
>   surface of the earth every moving creature that I
> 5 have made." Noah did just as the LORD had com-
>   manded him.

The J narrative has not been preserved in the section which must have corresponded with P in describing the building of the ark in keeping with the divine blueprint. Instead, we immediately hear Noah commanded to *go into the ark* along with his *household*. Yahweh adds that Noah *alone in this age have I found to be truly just*. Though we have no way of being sure and can only speculate about it, it would fit entirely with the Yahwist's theology if this missing portion of his narrative contained the injunction to build an ark—a big box, we recall—without a revelation of its purpose until now, in vs. 4, so that Noah's faithful execution of Yahweh's command in blind obedience would be (like Abraham's obedience in 12:1 and 14:6, both J) the source of his being declared "just." Thus the interpretation of Hebrews 11:7: "By faith Noah, warned about things not yet seen, revered God and built an ark that his household might be saved. He thereby condemned the world and inherited the justice which comes through faith." In any case, there is here no major divergence of the Yahwist from the Priestly construction of things: in both sources it is God who takes the initiative in choosing his own.

The difference that does stand out between the two stories is the distinction which J makes of "clean" from "unclean" animals (the comparable distinction of the two classes of birds is not in the extant Hebrew text but has been supplied in the translation above, probably correctly, with the assistance of the Septuagint) and which P does not, with a consequent discrepancy in the numbers of the creatures that are to be saved. Just as J has already repeatedly invoked the name of Yahweh by which Israel knew its God, and rather explicitly in 4:26, and has presupposed the institution of sacrificial worship (4:3–4) as he will do again in the flood story (8:20–22) and thereafter in the patriarchal legends, with equal study P avoids doing any of these things, all of which he has reserved for the Mosaic era. It is not a question of deciding who is right here and who is wrong, but simply of recognizing different religious values. J says that what was distinctive about Israel was rooted in man's origins. P says that these same distinctive qualities were first manifested at a definite point in time of man's history.

As we have already noted, the coming flood in J is to be the result solely of a lengthy rain. The P version which we shall see below presents a rather different picture.

In this picture which follows, the J and P versions of prehistory have no longer been laid side by side in parallel sections but have become somewhat mixed. P sustains the major part of the story while J has been used to supplement it. Accordingly we will set the P part of the narrative in roman type and indicate the J insertions with italics.

> 6 Noah was six hundred years old when the flood
> 7 waters came upon the earth. *Together with his sons,*
> *his wife, and his sons' wives, Noah went into the ark*
> 8 *because of the waters of the flood. Of the clean ani-*
> *mals and the unclean, of the birds, and of everything*
> 9 *that creeps on the ground, [two by two] male and*
> *female entered the ark with Noah, just as the* LORD
> 10 *had commanded him. As soon as the seven days*
> *were over, the waters of the flood came upon the*
> *earth.*
> 11 In the six hundredth year of Noah's life, in the second month, on the seventeenth day of the month: it was on that day that
> > All the fountains of the great abyss burst forth,
> > and the floodgates of the sky were opened.

12 *For forty days and forty nights heavy rain poured
down on the earth.*

13 On the precise day named, Noah and his sons Shem,
Ham and Japheth, and Noah's wife, and the three

14 wives of Noah's sons had entered the ark, together
with every kind of wild beast, every kind of domes-
tic animal, every kind of creeping thing of the earth,

15 and every kind of bird. Pairs of all creatures in
which there was the breath of life entered the ark

16 with Noah. Those that entered were male and female, and of all species they came, as God had commanded Noah. *Then the* LORD *shut him in.*

17 The flood continued upon the earth *for forty days.
As the waters increased, they lifted the ark, so that*

18 *it rose above the earth.* The swelling waters increased greatly, but the ark floated on the surface

19 of the waters. Higher and higher above the earth
rose the waters, until all the highest mountains ev-

20 erywhere were submerged, the crest rising fifteen cu-

21 bits higher than the submerged mountains. All creatures that stirred on earth perished: birds, cattle, wild
animals, and all that swarmed on the earth, as well as

22 all mankind. *Everything on dry land with the faint-*

23 *est breath of life in its nostrils died out. The* LORD
*wiped out every living thing on earth: man and cat-
tle, the creeping things and the birds of the air; all
were wiped out from the earth. Only Noah and
those with him in the ark were left.*

The *six hundred years* of Noah (recall the six-base of the Mesopotamian chronologies) when the flood begins are part of the Priestly author's
complicated numerical computations which, as we already saw in commenting on chapter 5, permit the return of chaos to the cosmos only after
the last of the antediluvian patriarchs save Noah and his family have
disappeared from the earth. In vs. 11, in pursuit of a further specification
and calendar whose purpose now escapes us, both the month and the day
of the month are also spelt out. The flood takes place one hundred years
after the birth of Noah's sons (cf. 5:32), therefore allowing ample time
for the latter to have begun families of their own, even when taking into
account the extraordinary life-spans of the men (and women?) who lived
before the flood. At the same time, if P intended his version of the flood
story to be consistent with the rest of his narrative (cf. 10:1), the sons of
Noah are presumed to have been childless when they entered the ark.

We have italicized the intervening vss. 7–10 because they pertain more to the Yahwist than to the Priestly author, but it might be more accurate to concede them to R, who has combined some scraps of J with some of the language of P to fill in this gap. Actually, in vs. 9 "God" rather than "Yahweh" is the reading of the conventional Hebrew text, but the NAB has followed here, probably correctly, the reading of the Samaritan Pentateuch. The distinction of *the clean animals and the unclean* is clearly J's, and so probably is the unnecessarily bracketed *two by two* which is followed by the *male and female* we find in both J and P. As we know by now, the biblical flood story as it stands is the work of the Redactor of Genesis, who has brought together the parallel narratives of J and P. What we must also recognize is that he has brought them together in varying ways, usually quite integrally, but occasionally by virtually rewriting them, selecting his vocabulary from both sources. We shall see other instances below of this process of Redactor-becoming-author. The same process accounts for the fact that along with the obvious discrepancies that have always made the separation of the Genesis sources inevitable, there is concomitantly an illusory agreement between them throughout the story even on certain rare key words like *tebah* (ark), *mabbul* (flood). Redactor is a modern word, of course, just as the concept of redaction is a modern one. From his own standpoint the R of Genesis was its responsible author, and sometimes he becomes precisely that, by anybody's accounting, within the limits stipulated in our Introduction.

In vss. 11 and 12 we see together the two concepts of what constituted the flood. For P it was a return to the chaos out of which the world had first been ordered in creation. *The fountains of the great abyss* and *the floodgates of the sky*—the dome which had been erected to separate the two bodies of water (1:6–8, P)—are released from their restraints, and once again the earth is covered by a watery mass. J, on the other hand, thinks simply of a *heavy rain* of *forty days and forty nights* which *poured down on the earth,* a fairly simple-minded accounting for a cosmic cataclysm that altered human history for all time.

In this respect it is evident that P's story has taken on a theological coloration linking it to the story of creation whereas J's has not. Correspondingly, J's version of the flood is closer to the putative original from which all these stories derive: both in Atra-hasis and in Gilgamesh the flood is the result of a prolonged rain, in these cases a rain of seven days and nights. It is entirely appropriate that these developments should have occurred as they did. Only P, as we observed when studying the creation story, has combined and integrated into one vision the beginnings of man as they relate to the origins of the cosmos in which he lives, moves, and ideally dominates as the surrogate of God. The Mesopotamian myths had made no such integration, nor had J. In keeping with this vision is the cosmic sweep of P's concept of the depravity that provoked the flood: man gone wrong means a world out of joint, and vice versa. The one is the sign and the inevitable complement of the other. We should by no means minimize the implications which such a view of the conjoined destinies of man and matter has held out for the contemplation of Judaism and, later, Christianity. In their authentic traditions derived from the Bible there has been no room for a Gnostic or Manichean dualism that would segregate man from his world of life, growth, and death, from his world in which all his potentialities for good and ill are tested, tried, and evaluated.

In vss. 13–16 the entry into the ark is described in the language of P, a parallel to the mainly J description of vss. 7–10. In this description the *on the precise day named* of vs. 13 is probably deserving of note, since the same expression occurs in Genesis 17:23.26 (both P, translated by NAB "on that same day") and Exodus 12:17.41.51 (all P, NAB "this very day," "this very date," "that same day") to signify the fulfillment of a divine command, and especially the celebration of a religious act of worship. In keeping with the Septuagint witness, NAB has somewhat shortened the ending of vs. 14, but the sense of the verse is in no wise altered. What is more important is the insertion of vs. 16b from J, to the effect that Yahweh *shut* [Noah] *in* the ark. In the J description of the ark which we no longer have, it seems most likely that a craft was envisaged in which Noah would be completely boxed in, with no more vision of what was taking place outside than he had had of the purpose of the ark in the first place (see above, on 7:1–5). The Yahwist wants to make the point that God is in total control, not only of the flood itself but also, every step of the way, of the salvation and new hope for man that was afforded him in the preservation of Noah and his family. In this detail the biblical story stands in marked contrast with the Babylonian myths. The Gilgamesh epic has Utanapishtim say (after laying in provisions of meat, wine, oil, and precious metals), "I boarded the ship and battened up the gate." Similarly Atra-hasis, after taking a test of the weather, "severed the hawser and set the boat adrift." But it is not only such apparently trivial differences of scenario that the Bible draws the line of separation between the God of Genesis and the gods of the Gentiles. In the Mesopotamian myths the gods are mercurial, sometimes favorable and sometimes inimical to man, and the preservation of the human species from the flood is due more to their intramural rivalry and jealousy than it is to any genuine interest in mankind. The biblical story, on the contrary, is shot through with divine purpose which is ultimately determined by what is for man's best interests and which reconciles God's destroying action with his saving will. What the Yahwist wants to add, here and there, is that man's proper posture in the face of this purpose is one of faith, trust, and utmost reliance on the good designs of God.

The description of the flood in the remaining verses of the section above is fairly consistent as regards the totality of the destruction of life on earth. It can be argued that P stresses more the flood's universality, as by having its *crest rising fifteen cubits higher than the submerged mountains.* (As Hermann Gunkel recognized long ago, the meaning is probably that the ark, which was thirty cubits high [6:15, P], drew fifteen cubits of water, or half its height.) However, there is really very little reason to choose between J and P, since the cosmologies of both were much the same, limited to what we now know as a tiny segment of a world that they thought was flat and we know is round. (Neither Pikes Peak nor Mount Everest, quite obviously, was included in P's mental catalogue of "submerged mountains.") The laws of physics were also not in question: there was no need to explain whence, from the closed atmospheric system of earth, all these new waters came together, or whither they disappeared once their end had been accomplished. It is rather more important to concentrate on what the sources believed to be the meaning of the flood, for God and for man. In the Babylonian myths the flood hardly has a meaning for either. According to the Gilgamesh epic, "the gods were frightened by the deluge" they had let loose, "the gods cowered like dogs." Similarly in the Atra-hasis story, the gods repent their decision and try to cast blame on one another. Once again, in the biblical account the divine purpose is clear, and at the end come the words of J, indicating the sure hope that is soon to be fulfilled because *Noah and those with him in the ark were left.*

> 24 The waters maintained their crest over the earth
> 8 for one hundred and fifty days, and then God re-
> membered Noah and all the animals, wild and tame,
> that were with him in the ark. So God made a wind
> sweep over the earth, and the waters began to sub-
> 2 side. The fountains of the abyss and the floodgates
> of the sky were closed, *and the downpour from the*
> 3 *sky was held back. Gradually the waters receded*
> *from the earth.* At the end of one hundred and fifty
> 4 days the waters had so diminished that, in the
> seventh month, on the seventeenth day of the month,
> the ark came to rest on the mountains of Ararat.
> 5 The waters continued to diminish until the tenth
> month, and on the first day of the tenth month the
> tops of the mountains appeared.

Above we have the account of the ending of the flood according to P (and, as before, we have indicated the small J contribution by the use of italics).

That *God remembered Noah* (*and all the animals* adds an engaging touch) is an anthropomorphic way of saying that he has responded to a prayer addressed to him (cf. 30:22, P) or otherwise acknowledged an obligation of favor he has voluntarily assumed (19:29, P, "he was mindful"). God now turns his attention to the salvific end which he had in mind when sending the flood. That he *made a wind sweep over the earth* may tempt us to recall the "mighty wind" of Genesis 1:2 (P) that swept over the waters prior to the first act of creation; but the sense is really different, and here the wind(s) appears to be tributary to the common Near Eastern flood story on which the biblical and the Mesopotamian versions have depended. Both in P and in J, the ending of the flood is ascribed to the drying up of its respective primal source.

The ark came to rest on the mountains of Ararat. Ararat, the ancient Urartu, is the mountainous region of what is now Armenia. No particular mountain in the Ararat chain is singled out, but there are two peaks in it which are of singular height and were probably thought by the Hebrews to be the highest mountains in the world. The Gilgamesh epic placed the landing of the ark on Mount Nisir, south and east of Ararat.

In the following section, we reverse our previous procedure. The passage is J most of the way. The single P verse we indicate in italics.

> 6 At the end of forty days Noah opened the hatch he
> 7 had made in the ark, *and he sent out a raven, to see*
>   *if the waters had lessened on the earth. It flew back*
>   *and forth until the waters dried off from the earth.*
> 8 Then he sent out a dove, to see if the waters had
> 9 lessened on the earth. But the dove could find no
>   place to alight and perch, and it returned to him in
>   the ark, for there was water all over the earth. Putting
>   out his hand, he caught the dove and drew it back
> 10 to him inside the ark. He waited seven days more
> 11 and again sent the dove out from the ark. In the
>   evening the dove came back to him, and there in
>   its bill was a plucked-off olive leaf! So Noah knew
> 12 that the waters had lessened on the earth. He waited
>   still another seven days and then released the dove
>   once more; and this time it did not come back.

It seems to have been a common practice in ancient times, before the invention of the compass and other means of navigation, for mariners to release birds in order to determine the nearness and direction of dry land. Certainly this practice is a feature of both the biblical story of the flood and the epic of Gilgamesh. The latter reads:

When the seventh day arrived,
I sent forth and set free a dove.
The dove went forth, but came back;
There was no resting-place for it and she turned round.
Then I sent forth and set free a swallow.
The swallow went forth, but came back;
There was no resting place for it and she turned round.
Then I sent forth and set free a raven . . .

and by the fact that the raven did not return, Utanapishtim knew that the dry land had appeared.

At the end of forty days marks the duration of the flood according to J. Then *Noah opened the hatch he had made in the ark:* probably this "hatch" means an opening in the roof of the ark. As we have remarked more than once before, we do not know what was the Yahwist's conception of the ark. It is likely, however, as we have also remarked, that it was a conception that allowed of no outlook on the horizon, hence the need of birds to ascertain whether or not the dry land had reappeared. The sequel, therefore, to vs. 6 is vss. 8–12 in which the exploration by the dove is detailed in its various stages.

In vs. 7, which is from P, the NAB above has added to the translation *to see if the waters had lessened on the earth,* a clause that is not in the Hebrew but which appears in the Septuagint Greek. Here we believe that the NAB and the Septuagint are wrong, that they have simply harmonized vs. 7 with vs. 8. In the P construction of the ark, there was a window a cubit below its roof from which the outside could be viewed just as easily as it admitted light to the inside (cf. 6:16). Hence in the P story there was no real need for sending out a bird to learn the lay of the land. Nevertheless, the release of a bird or birds was an integral part of the flood tradition, as we have seen in the Gilgamesh citation above. As we see it, P has retained the detail in fidelity to the tradition, but without any purpose to serve, the raven simply *flew back and forth until the waters dried off from the earth.* Quite obviously, in the biblical story the raven had no information to convey to Noah.

On the contrary, *the dove* of the J version fulfills a very important role. We may admire the cleverness of the storytelling in which the dove first returns to the ark and is retrieved by Noah's hand, then returns again with an olive leaf in its beak (the dove of peace!) to indicate that *the waters had lessened,* and finally returned no more as evidence that the earth was habitable once again. It would be a mistake, however, to rhapsodize on this "co-operation between man and animal" as though some profound theological message were meant to be conveyed thereby. In these details the Yahwist is merely handing on a traditional and stylized story.

In the following section we again have an account that is essentially P with only a half verse that is J, which we indicate by italics:

13 In the six hundred and first year of Noah's life, in the first month, on the first day of the month, the water began to dry up on the earth. *Noah then removed the covering of the ark and saw that the surface of the ground was drying up.*

14 In the second month, on the twenty-seventh day of the month, the earth was dry.

15/16 Then God said to Noah: "Go out of the ark, together with your wife and your sons and your 17 sons' wives. Bring out with you every living thing that is with you—all bodily creatures, be they birds or animals or creeping things of the earth—and let them abound on the earth, breed-18 ing and multiplying on it." So Noah came out, together with his wife and his sons and his sons' 19 wives; and all the animals, wild and tame, all the birds, and all the creeping creatures of the earth left the ark, one kind after another.

First of all, it is evident that vs. 13b (J) easily follows on the preceding J narration: having determined by the flight of the dove that the flood was ended, *Noah then removed the covering of the ark and saw that the surface of the ground was drying up.*

It is a little more difficult to reconcile the twin chronological data of P in vss. 13a and 14. The NAB translation above has tried to do so by its rendering that *the water began to dry up on the earth* in vs. 13a as opposed to its reading of vs. 14 that *the earth was dry.* But the most natural reading of the Hebrew of vs. 13a is that "the water had dried up on the earth." Thus we are confronted by two separate chronologies of the flood within the same source, a fact that should not too much disturb us in view of the complicated history of the legend. *The first month, on the first day of the month* (vs. 13a) would be New Year's Day, a fitting time for the beginning of a new race of man after the flood. It is less easy to determine what was meant by *the second month, on the twenty-seventh day of the month* (vs. 14), but this is hardly the only number in P that challenges our imagination.

In vss. 15–17 we see the inauguration of a new creation in the terms of P (cf. 1:22.28). Noah is obedient to the injunction and follows it to the letter (in vs. 19 above the translation has had recourse to the Septuagint, probably correctly).

The following passage is purely J, and it can be indicated as such without recourse to different typefaces:

20 Then Noah built an altar to the LORD, and choosing from every clean animal and every clean bird, he
21 offered holocausts on the altar. When the LORD smelled the sweet odor, he said to himself: "Never again will I doom the earth because of man, since the desires of man's heart are evil from the start; nor will I ever again strike down all living beings, as I have done.
22   As long as the earth lasts,
          seedtime and harvest,
          cold and heat,
       Summer and winter,
          and day and night
          shall not cease."

In the Babylonian myths a pleasing sacrifice ended the flood story. It was, however, an offering of food to the bewildered deities who had set in motion a devastation that they could not control. Atra-hasis: "The gods sniffed the smell, they gathered like flies over the offering." Gilgamesh: "The gods smelled the savor, the gods smelled the sweet savor, the gods crowded like flies about the sacrificer." The Yahwist has included this traditional ending because he could work it into his theology of a Yahweh who from the beginning had been worshiped by name, whether acknowledged or not (4:26b, J). And thus we have the first mention in Genesis of an *altar,* even though one was doubtless presupposed in the story of the offerings presented by Cain and Abel (4:3–5, J). The Priestly writer had no room in his chronicle of the flood for these particulars since in this theology there was no legitimate cult of Yahweh prior to the Mosaic age.

We now see both why J distinguished between the clean and the unclean animals and why he admitted more of the former to the ark than he did the latter. From the ritually acceptable animals Noah *offered holocausts* to God. The holocaust was a complete immolation, a total sacrifice in which no part at all of the offering was reserved for any other purpose. In the context, it seems obvious that the sense of this particular holocaust was to express thanksgiving to God for what he had wrought. Animal sacrifice is not easily explained to a modern Western audience. The whole idea has remote roots in magical and animistic concepts, of the release of *mana,* a life-giving force produced in death, or of food or placation proffered to hostile deities. What the Bible understands by a holocaust, however, is sacrifice in a truly spiritual sense, the wasting of something that man holds valuable, which he does not preserve for his own needs however pressing, but simply abandons to God (see Leviticus 1, P). It was a sacrifice which made allowances for the relative means of the worshiper (cf. Luke 2:22–24, Leviticus 12:6–8, P). The notion of sacrifice involves a paradox, whether the sacrificer puts his purse or his life on the line of decision. "The man who loves his life loses it, while the man who hates his life in this world preserves it to life eternal" (John 12:25). Faith is the essential concomitant to sacrifice, without which it has no meaning.

In vs. 21 Yahweh *smelled the sweet odor* of the holocaust. Only here in the Hebrew Bible does this expression occur, and it is plain that it derives from the same tradition on which the Babylonian stories depended: almost the same words are found there. We can wonder how literally the Yahwist expected the statement to be taken. He can surprise us, we know, by the way he can mingle apparently childish anthropomorphisms with highly elevated assertions of the transcendence of God. However, even in the admittedly more sophisticated theology of much later times (Exodus 29:18, for example, or Leviticus 1:9, to mention only two instances out of some forty in the Priestly narrative, or Ezekiel 20:41 of roughly the same period, or the even later Sirach 45:16), the "sweet odor" of sacrifice remains a formulaic expression to signify merely something that is acceptable to God. There is no reason to suppose that the Yahwist meant anything other than this in vs. 21a.

Also in the Babylonian stories the gods repent themselves for having unleashed the flood upon the world. Their repentance, however, takes the form of mutual recriminations on the one hand at having been beguiled into precipitate action, and on the other hand of profound regret at having been ineffective in bringing on a flood that had not properly done its work but instead had left survivors. Here in the Yahwist's vs. 21b Yahweh meditates over what has transpired and concludes to his own satisfaction —*he said to himself:* it is not a pledge to man as in 9:15 (P)—that the flood had really changed nothing. The mankind which had overcome the flood offered him worship as was originally intended (4:26b, J), and therefore justified his salvation of Noah and his family; but he also knows that *the desires of man's heart are evil from the start.* What has happened before will surely happen again. A flood of devastation, therefore, is not a remedy for the future, and by implication it must be equally admitted that it was not a remedy in the past. (There is something engaging about this portraiture of a God who can learn by his own "mistakes.") Whatever may be the proclivity of man to deviate from the way, God must learn to live with the deviation and recognize the fallibility of the creature into whose lungs he first breathed the breath of life. Whatever may be the destiny of man (our history, these thousands and millions of years), it does not consist in an extinction of our species by the Almighty by flood or by any other means of destruction.

Yahweh has already said that he will *never again doom the earth* (*adamah*) *because of man* (*adam*), recognizing that the earth was a kind of innocent bystander in the deluge directed against man, though man and earth had been inextricably bound together from the beginning (so 2:7, J). In vs. 22 in reciprocity, a benison is pronounced over the earth which will also affect man. It is not, as some commentators have suggested, a departure from the usual biblical concept of time as linear and terminal as opposed to the cyclic idea of eternal return presupposed by the nature religions: *as long as the earth lasts* understands a coming-to-be when there will be no earth, thus an end to all. Nevertheless, this little poetic measure invokes the recurrence of the seasons and other earth-tied intervals to underscore the perpetuity of the divine resolution never again to destroy. More than one commentator has recognized that by invoking the regularity of nature in this utterance, Yahweh is expressing his intention to deal henceforth with all men evenly, whether they are bad or good. Or, in the words of Matthew 5:45: "his sun rises on the bad and the good, he rains on the just and the unjust." The time of God's "forbearance" with man and his transgressions, as conceived by Paul (Romans 3:26), has now begun.

The Priestly version of the ending of the flood takes a quite different form:

9 God blessed Noah and his sons and said to them:
2 "Be fertile and multiply and fill the earth. Dread fear
   of you shall come upon all the animals of the earth
   and all the birds of the air, upon all the creatures that
   move about on the ground and all the fishes of the
3 sea; into your power they are delivered. Every
   creature that is alive shall be yours to eat; I give them
4 all to you as I did the green plants. Only flesh with
5 its lifeblood still in it you shall not eat. For your
   own lifeblood, too, I will demand an accounting:
   from every animal I will demand it, and from man
   in regard to his fellow man I will demand an accounting for human life.
6   If anyone sheds the blood of man,
       by man shall his blood be shed;
     For in the image of God
       has man been made.
7 Be fertile, then, and multiply; abound on earth and
   subdue it."

This little section forms a unit, noted by the "inclusion" that occurs between the first and last verses, enclosing those which intervene: *be fertile and multiply and fill the earth . . . into your power* [*all the creatures* of the earth] *are delivered* in vss. 1–2, and *be fertile, then, and multiply; abound on earth and subdue it* in vs. 7. First of all, therefore, the initial blessing of creation and the role destined to be played by man in the created world (cf. 1:28, P) are reaffirmed in this new and second act of creation. (In vs. 7 the NAB has correctly read "subdue" [*redu*] instead of a redundant "multiply" [*rebu*] of the extant Hebrew text.) To this extent the Priestly author agrees with the Yahwist that God is ready to begin once more with the fallible man with whom he started the ordering of the universe and to whom he is now willing to recommit it, with full recognition that the same kind of "corruption" and "lawlessness" (6:11, P) will reoccur all over again (vss. 5–6).

What is new in this reconstructed earth is the proclamation of the rule of life with which we are familiar, that animal shall feed upon animal: *every creature that is alive shall be yours to eat.* The myth of a primal golden age of the peaceable kingdom of man and beast is now firmly quashed. But at the same time P inserts some theological prejudices into the account. *Flesh with its lifeblood still in it you shall not eat* (Leviticus 17:10–14, P). *For your own lifeblood, too* (a small correction of the Hebrew text is supposed), *I will demand an accounting: from every animal I will demand it* (cf. Exodus 21:28, E), *and from man in regard to his fellow man I will demand an accounting for human life* (Genesis 4:2–16, J). Because ancient legalisms like these turn up in the Noah story, long before the Bible imagines the emergence of the people Israel, early Jewish teachers concluded they were divine prescriptions imposed on all peoples, Jew and Gentile, and were included, therefore, in a set of seven commandments thought to apply to the whole human race: no eating of blood, no murder, no idolatry, no blasphemy, no incest, no thievery, no repudiation of authority. (Acts 15:29, we have seen, indicates that some of these rules were honored in the early Christian community. The same rules, we know from patristic sources, prevailed even in completely Gentile churches well into a later Christian era.)

Both in vss. 4–5 and in vs. 6 a sacred quality is ascribed to blood. Along with breath (2:7, J), blood was considered in a primitive anthropology to be the sign and source of life, therefore taboo to man and reserved to God. In the later legislation (Leviticus 17:10–14, P) the law was spelt out in considerable detail. Here in Genesis a somewhat surprising explanation is given why *if anyone sheds the blood of man, by man shall his blood be shed.* The explanation is not simply, as we might expect, that a *quid pro quo* is demanded, according to the law of strict justice and reciprocity. Instead, we are informed that it is because *in the image of God has man been made.* At first glance, this offers us no explanation at all: the "image of God" picks up part of the figure contained in 1:26–27 (P).

What we are reminded of, however, is that the "image" and "likeness" of which the Priestly author speaks in his creation story is undoubtedly a refinement of what was originally a description of man created from the *blood* of deity: so it was in *Enuma elish*. The P tradition, it seems, has preserved only a faint and chastely strained recollection of this older idea (see above on 1:26–27).

> 8/9 God said to Noah and to his sons with him: "See, I
> am now establishing my covenant with you and
> 10 your descendants after you and with every living
> creature that was with you: all the birds, and the
> various tame and wild animals that were with you
> 11 and came out of the ark. I will establish my cove-
> nant with you, that never again shall all bodily
> creatures be destroyed by the waters of a flood;
> there shall not be another flood to devastate the
> 12 earth." God added: "This is the sign that I am
> giving for all ages to come, of the covenant be-
> tween me and you and every living creature with
> 13 you: I set my bow in the clouds to serve as a sign
> 14 of the covenant between me and the earth. When
> I bring clouds over the earth, and the bow appears
> 15 in the clouds, I will recall the covenant I have
> made between me and you and all living beings, so
> that the waters shall never again become a flood to
> 16 destroy all mortal beings. As the bow appears in
> the clouds, I will see it and recall the everlasting
> covenant that I have established between God and
> all living beings—all mortal creatures that are on
> 17 earth." God told Noah: "This is the sign of the
> covenant I have established between me and all
> mortal creatures that are on earth."

In vs. 11 we have a close parallel with the narrative of 8:21 (J)—*never again. There shall not be another flood to devastate the earth* is the reiteration of the J conclusion to the flood story, here a promise offered as a *covenant . . . with every living creature* (vss. 8–11). Covenant (as observed above on 6:18) in the sacred sense is an act of divine grace. According to the Priestly author, God extends this grace freely, commits himself as by oath (cf. Isaiah 54:9), and promises irrevocably that his future dealings with man and his world will be to their eventual good and not to their ill, regardless of the deserts of those involved. The model of covenant for any Israelite author was, presumably, in the first place the word of God at Sinai which had said: "If you hearken to my voice and keep my covenant, you shall be my special possession, dearer to me than all other people, though all the earth is mine. You shall be to me a kingdom of priests, a holy nation" (Exodus 19:5–6, E). But another model, especially for the Yahwist, was the promise made by God to David: "I will raise up your heir after you, sprung from your loins, and I will make his kingdom firm . . . I will be a father to him, and he shall be a son to me . . . Your house and your kingdom shall endure forever before me" (2 Samuel 7:12–16, cf. Psalm 89:20–38). The Yahwist, as we shall see, thought of this promise to David ("covenant" in Psalm 89:29) as the realization in remembered time of a covenant first made in the dim past with Abraham and the other Israelite patriarchs. Abraham, of course, he regarded as the Father not only of the Israelites but of all Semites—Arabs, Nabateans, Midianites, Asshurim . . . (cf. Genesis 25:1–4, J). The Yahwist extended the sacred concept of covenant to include other peoples than Israel, as did the prophet Amos (9:7):

> Are you not like the Ethiopians to me,
> O men of Israel, says the LORD?
> Did I not bring the Israelites from the land of Egypt
> As I brought the Philistines from Caphtor
> and the Arameans from Kir?

Amos—with the Yahwist—was saying that the election of a people owes nothing to nature or peculiar merit but only to grace. The Priestly author, on his part, picks up this ecumenical gesture and carries it a great distance beyond. According to him, the whole human race and everything that is associated with it, which is to say the whole of the cosmos, have been embraced by God's covenant so that they should survive and prosper under his providence.

The sign of the covenant—every covenant had to have a sign of the compact reached (like the heap of rocks in Genesis 31:45–49)—here is said to be the rainbow, or, as the Priestly author puts it, speaking in the name of God, *my bow in the clouds.* The repetitiveness (minimized by NAB in its translation of the Hebrew) with which the covenant and its sign, its universality and irrevocability, are stressed in these verses is doubtless intended to enhance the solemnity of God's promise, but it also seems to be true that the passage abounds in "doublets," i.e., that the Priestly author has combined at least two parallel versions of this conclusion to the flood story to produce his narrative. Neither of these versions has any counterpart in the Babylonian myths, however. The details of the covenant and its sign are uniquely those of P and, evidently, of the sources on which P immediately depended. Theodor Gaster has suggested a possible parallel in *Enuma elish,* the Babylonian story of creation rather than of the flood, therefore, in which the god Marduk is said to have hung up his bow in the heavens as a sign of his having vanquished Tiamat (the personified great deep or abyss) and the monsters which she had created to do battle with the gods. However, though elsewhere in the Old Testament the God of Israel may be represented as a warrior with bow and arrow (see Lamentations 2:4, 3:12) and the victor in a struggle with the primordial watery chaos (see above on 1:1–5, P), neither of these poetic images appears to correspond precisely with what the Priestly author has in mind here and now. The "bow in the clouds" is exactly that, a rainbow, not a discarded weapon of war. Quite to the contrary, it is a sign of peace, a warrant of God's pledge to perpetuate his covenant with the world. In the flood story he has not battled with and overcome the waters but rather has sent them to cleanse the earth and make a new start possible. It seems that we need no more *recherché* explanation of the rainbow as sign of God's covenant than the one that is most obvious and is experienced by us today when we see it in our own clouds: it indicates that the rain is over, the waters are gone, we can walk once more on our familiar ground without fear of what can happen to us and to ours from alien elements.

Nevertheless, we may be somewhat set back by the fact that the Priestly author, of all people, has selected this means of publicly validating the covenant between God and all mankind, especially when we read that it is not so much intended to be a sign of reassurance to man as it is a reminder to God himself: *I will recall the covenant I have made between me and you and all living beings, so that the waters shall never again become a flood to destroy all mortal beings . . . I will see it and recall the everlasting covenant . . .* Even though by exception, the Priestly author can be quite as anthropomorphic as the Yahwist in his depiction of God. We really should not complain about this. It was part of the Bible's *via affirmationis* about the divine attributes that stands in conflict with the *via negationis* of later theology, which tried to define God by removing from him every ascription we make to a human and finite being. Both "ways" (*viae*) have their values and defects, and both are necessarily mythological, since they both begin with the human experience that we are alone aware of, and transfer it, by saying aye or nay, to the divine sphere into which we have not entered. We can do no more, if we are to talk about God at all.

So ends the story of the flood (except, perhaps, for vss. 28–29 [P] below which are actually the end of Noah's genealogy with which P began the story). The influence of the story on subsequent Jewish and Christian thought has been enormous. The idea of eventual salvation through water (we have already remarked on the correspondence of *tebah*, the ark, with the basket in which Moses the founder of Israel was preserved from drowning) continues in significant ways. The crossing of the Reed Sea

(Exodus 14:10–22, JEP), by which Israel passed from the slavery of Egypt into freedom, was also a salvation through water, and it would be difficult to say whether this tradition has more influenced the story of the flood or has been more influenced by it reciprocally. In the New Testament, the theme is picked up and applied to baptism, another salvation through water: ". . . Noah's day, while God patiently waited until the ark was built. At that time, a few persons, eight in all, escaped through the water. You are now saved by a baptismal bath which corresponds to this exactly" (1 Peter 3:20–21). This typical application is over and above the meaning which the Noahitic covenant and "commandments" had for both Jewish and early Christian thought.

8. The Postdiluvians

First, a Yahwistic section complemented by the conclusion to the Noah idyll which we indicate in italics:

18 The sons of Noah who came out of the ark were
   Shem, Ham and Japheth. (Ham was the father of
19 Canaan.) These three were the sons of Noah, and
20 from them the whole earth was peopled. *Now Noah,*
   a man of the soil, was the first to plant a vineyard.
21 *When he drank some of the wine, he became drunk*
22 *and lay naked inside his tent. Ham, the father of*
   Canaan, saw his father's nakedness, and he told his
23 *two brothers outside about it. Shem and Japheth,*
   however, took a robe, and holding it on their backs,
   they walked backward and covered their father's
   nakedness; since their faces were turned the other
24 *way, they did not see their father's nakedness. When*
   Noah woke up from his drunkenness and learned
25 *what his youngest son had done to him, he said:*
   "Cursed be Canaan!
      The lowest of slaves
      shall he be to his brothers."
26 *He also said:*
   "Blessed be the LORD, the God of Shem!
      Let Canaan be his slave.

27   May God expand Japheth,
        so that he dwells among the tents of Shem;
        and let Canaan be his slave."
28 *Noah lived three hundred and fifty years after the*
29 *flood. The whole lifetime of Noah was nine hundred*
    and fifty years; then he died.

The passage is somewhat complicated. The Yahwist's contribution to it
is not of one piece, and this fact has led to the perplexity of many readers.
In vss. 18–19 we have the immediate J sequel to the flood story and an introduction to the J portions of chapters 10 and 11. While P (in 5:32,
6:10, and 7:13) has already listed the sons of Noah as *Shem, Ham and
Japheth,* in vs. 18 we find them for the first time in the Yahwist's narrative, in the same order, which would be, according to Hebrew usage, the
order of their relative ages (see below). The parenthetical *Ham was the
father of Canaan* is an addition to the text which serves as a suture to connect vss. 18–19 with vss. 20–27. What we are told in these two verses is
that Noah's sons were the ancestors of all men who now live and breathe; it
was *from them* that *the whole earth was peopled.* This is the story that will
be taken up below.

On the contrary, vss. 20–27 seem to present an independent story which
originally had nothing to do with the preceding flood epic nor with what
follows in chapters 10–11. It is a story that involves a rather different
Noah and partly different sons (who rather than married men on their
own seem to be youths still resident *inside his tent,* in the Bedawin fashion). The sons here are Shem, Japheth, and Canaan (the last mentioned,
in vs. 24, is *his youngest son*): in vs. 22, *Ham, the father of* is another suture to impose a literary unity on the complex of vss. 18–27. We must
admit that this story was once an etiological tale sufficient to itself. But we
also have to recognize that its incorporation into J has been the work of
the Yahwist himself, not of a later redactor or interpolator. In vs. 20 without question there is an advertence to 5:29 (J): the vine, and its natural
product of wine, were then and now, by most men, regarded as one of
God's blessings designed to offer man a relief and surcease from his work
and toil. And the curse under which Canaan has been placed (vss. 25–27)
will pervade the rest of the Yahwistic narrative: in J pre-eminently, it is
under the designation of "Canaanites" that the indigenous population of
Palestine was named which had to be removed before the Promised Land
could become that of Israel.

There is a temptation to transfer to an ancient author prejudices that
have been inherited only from a later experience than his. The temptation
must always be resisted. The Bible did not include among its demons to be
exorcised the destroying effects of alcoholism on the individual human

body and soul and on family and general society as well. That Noah *became drunk* (vs. 21) is a simple statement of fact, not a moral judgment. As in many other societies, drunkenness was regarded in Israel as a social *gaffe*, not a crime, a thing that could expose an otherwise sensible person to the ignominious condition in which Noah was found by his youngest son (cf. Habakkuk 2:15; Lamentations 4:21). Thus it is not necessary to excuse Noah of his "sin" on the score that he was *the first to plant a vineyard* and therefore was unaware of the potency of the drink he consumed. (It should be noted, perhaps, that the discovery of wine and the vine is, like the discoveries of Genesis 4:17–22 [J], the work of man and not of the gods—Dionysos in Greek mythology was the inventor of wine—and all these works were directed ultimately to the good of man.) On the other hand, *nakedness*, as we have seen before, was an abdication of the right to human respect, a shameful thing in itself. To this stage Noah's drunkenness led him.

It is difficult to tell whether in vs. 22 Canaan (the original of the Ham of the addition to the text) simply *saw his father's nakedness* or proceeded to do something about it, something that the biblical author refused to narrate. In any case, when *he told his two brothers outside about it*, they were revolted at what he had done or at what he had failed to do. With truly filial reverence, his elder brothers *took a robe, and holding it on their backs, they walked backward and covered their father's nakedness*. They tried to repair whatever harm had been done to their father's reputation and dignity.

The real point of this story is reached only in vs. 24 and following. *When Noah woke up from his drunkenness and learned* (how?) *what his youngest son* (Canaan) *had done to him*, he pronounced blessings and cursings which were, in the Yahwist's perspective, prophetic of the divers peoples that then existed in his world.

Cursed be Canaan!—and, we say again, Canaan is conceived of as the eponymous ancestor of the Canaanites, the aboriginal or indigenous population of Palestine displaced by the Israelites—is probably intended to be less an evocation of ancient relationships than it is a continuous warning to Israel to hold to its religious traditions and despise as vile and contaminating the contrary influences which were proffered to it daily by the heathen "people of the land" which continued to live in its midst. From the earliest of the Israelite prophets whose names have been preserved in the literature of the Bible (Hosea 4:14, for example) down to legislation that took its final form in Israel's last days as an independent people with its own cult and religion and land (Deuteronomy 23:18–19, for example), the Israelites had to be bullied, cajoled, and force-fed to protect them against the abominations of the Gentiles which tempted them on every side. After all, Canaan represented the "old religion" which had stood the test of unknown centuries long before Israel was heard of and had preserved the bountiful land which it had inherited. The religion of Canaan, flesh of its flesh and bone of its bone, tugged at Israel just as surely as the religion of the Roman *pagani* tugged at the nascent and interloping Christian faith of the third and fourth centuries, or as witchcraft and covens and curious rites tugged at the Christendom of the Middle Ages. Often the old religion never really surrendered but, as in the case of many a "Christian tradition," became assimilated and absorbed by the new faith with only a halfhearted gesture at reinterpretation. Israel had an assimilative power, as any student of comparative religions knows very well. But there were elements, obviously, both for Israel and for Christianity, which were unassimilable. It is about these that the Yahwist is thinking in this passage. When we recognize, as critical studies now make us do, that probably most of the Israelites were the same people as the Canaanites, the former having rallied to the newly imported God Yahweh while the latter had not, we have a new light in which to view Canaan's status as *the lowest of slaves . . . to his brothers.* Yahweh had won; the Israelite coalition had succeeded, and the dissidents had been reduced. Those who did not subscribe to the new religion were made secondary citizens of the land (cf. Joshua 9:3–27). Such, says the Yahwist, was Yahweh's will.

In vs. 26 we expect *Shem* (the ancestor of the "Semites," which in Genesis is a much more restricted concept than it is in modern linguistic or ethnic categories) to be blessed, just as surely as Canaan was cursed. Instead, with biblical delicacy, it is rather Yahweh, *the God of Shem,* who is blessed. The sense is the same in either case. It is the Semites in the biblical acceptation, that is, those peoples with whom the Israelites acknowledged kinship, who are welcomed into the company of the elect. For that matter, in view of the fragmentary preservation of the J narrative in these verses, it turns out that for all practical purposes Shem is simply equated with Israel (see below), in which event the second part of the verse has its sense: *Let Canaan be his slave.*

But who is the *Japheth* of vs. 27? Or who are his descendants? There is no clue in the J story. He is, evidently, someone who corresponds neither with the cursed Canaan nor with the blessed Shem. He is in between. *He dwells among the tents of Shem* and, like Shem, he has Canaan as his servitor. Historically, the people which would seem best to correspond with these attributes are the Philistines, that advanced, non-Semitic race which was establishing a colony on the coast of southern Palestine ("the land of the Philistines") at about the same time the federation of Israelite tribes was being formed inland. At one or another stage of its expansion, this maritime and mercantile people, in virtue of its superior weaponry (iron: 1 Samuel 13:19–22) and, perhaps, its superior culture as well, bade fair to wrest control of the heartland of Canaan from the less organized and less sophisticated Israelite tribes. Certainly the Philistines dwelt "among the tents of Shem." Even when they were eventually contained by David they remained an enclave in the Land of Promise which was never dislodged throughout the entire history of Israel and Judah, and, after all the Palestinian lands had been invaded and laid waste by foreign powers, when once again a vestige of Israel and Judah reappeared about Jerusalem, alongside it was a vestige of Philistia (cf. Nehemiah 13:23–24, the "Ashdodites," and Sirach 50:26) which remained to achieve some final triumph in giving its name to the whole land. Thus the Philistines satisfy eminently the criteria of a people dwelling among the tents of Shem to which it could be said "let Canaan be his slave"—had this verse been written by a disinterested observer. Since it was written by no disinterested observer, however, but rather by a devout son of Israel, in the light of the books of Judges and of 1 Samuel, not to mention the judgment of Ben Sira cited above, all of which profess an impartially even loathing for these heathen, the "uncircumcised" *par excellence,* it is impossible to imagine that *may God expand* (Hebrew *yapht,* a popular etymology) *Japheth* could ever have been uttered in favor of the Philistines.

Another possible identification is with the people that the Bible calls "Hittites." These are not the Hittites known to the scholars of archeology or paleography, the inhabitants of Asia Minor (modern Turkey) who developed a flourishing Indo-European culture there around the beginning of the second millennium B.C., long before Israel became a nation. There is no evidence that this people, in any of its successive developments, ever penetrated as far south as the land of Palestine. Besides, these true Hittites began to disappear about the same time the Philistines and Israelites began to appear. The "Hittites" with which Genesis deals—we will see them in chapter 23, but better and more historical examples are to be found in David's servants Ahimelech (1 Samuel 26:6) and Uriah (2 Samuel 11:3)—were non-Israelite foreigners who were nevertheless allowed to live in Israel on a basis of equality and who even intermarried with Israelites without prejudice (cf. Ezekiel 16:3: "By origin and birth you [Jerusalem] are of the land of Canaan; your father was an Amorite and your mother a Hittite"). They were called Hittites for approximately the same reasons that we nowadays call Egyptians the Arabs who inhabit the upper reaches of the Nile, who have little connection with the Hamitic cultures responsible for Karnak and Abu Simbel, Memphis, the Valley of the Kings, the Great Pyramids, the Sphinx, or Thebes. In other words, just as Egypt became a geographical rather than an ethnic denominator, so did Hatti ("the land of the Hittites") centuries before. Who the "Hittites" of the Old Testament were, over and above the fact that they had come from a region that could be vaguely designated as "theirs" by origin, is the subject of debate. At any rate, these "Hittites" may be the friendly aliens that

J had in mind in this passage. Other conjectures are possible, of course, especially if we are willing to assign the Yahwist to a period of activity later than that of the Davidic-Solomonic era.

As noted above, vss. 28–29 follow on 9:17 and conclude the P story of the flood with appropriate numbers that fit the Priestly author's earlier figures. We now proceed to his table of the nations—the result of God's covenant with all mankind in the persons of the sons of Noah—and to their distribution in a new world that has so recently been re-created.

Again we indicate the dominant text (P) with roman typeface and show the usually obvious J insertions by using italics:

10 These are the descendants of Noah's sons, Shem, Ham and Japheth, *to whom sons were born after the flood.*

2 The descendants of Japheth: Gomer, Magog, Madai, Javan, Tubal, Meshech and Tiras.

3 The descendants of Gomer: Ashkenaz, Riphath and Togarmah.

4 The descendants of Javan: Elishah, Tarshish, the Kittim and the Rodanim.

5 These are the descendants of Japheth, and from them sprang the maritime nations, in their respective lands—each with its own language—by their clans within their nations.

6 The descendants of Ham: Cush, Mizraim, Put and Canaan.

7 The descendants of Cush: Seba, Havilah, Sabtah, Raamah and Sabteca.

The descendants of Raamah: Sheba and Dedan.

8 *Cush became the father of Nimrod, who was the*
9 *first potentate on earth. He was a mighty hunter by the grace of the* Lord; *hence the saying, "Like Nimrod, a mighty hunter by the grace of*
10 *the* Lord." *The chief cities of his kingdom were Babylon, Erech and Accad, all of them in the*
11 *land of Shinar. From that land he went forth to Asshur, where he built Nineveh, Rehoboth-Ir*
12 *and Calah, as well as Resen, between Nineveh and Calah, the latter being the principal city.*
13 *Mizraim became the father of the Ludim, the*
14 *Anamim, the Lehabim, the Naphtuhim, the Pathrusim, the Casluhim, and the Caphtorim from whom the Philistines sprang.*

15 *Canaan became the father of Sidon, his first-*
16 *born, and of Heth; also of the Jebusites, the*
17 *Amorites, the Girgashites, the Hivites, the Ar-*
18 *kites, the Sinites, the Arvadites, the Zemarites*
   and the Hamathites. Afterward, the clans of the
19 *Canaanites spread out, so that the Canaanite*
   borders extended from Sidon all the way to
   Gerar, near Gaza, and all the way to Sodom,
   Gomorrah, Admah and Zeboiim, near Lasha.
20 These are the descendants of Ham, according to
   their clans and languages, by their lands and nations.
21 *To Shem also, Japheth's oldest brother and the*
   ancestor of all the children of Eber, sons were
   born.
22 The descendants of Shem: Elam, Asshur,
   Arpachshad, Lud and Aram.
23 The descendants of Aram: Uz, Hul, Gether
   and Mash.
24 *Arpachshad became the father of Shelah, and*
25 *Shelah became the father of Eber. To Eber two*
   sons were born: the name of the first was Peleg,
   for in his time the world was divided; and the
   name of his brother was Joktan.
26 *Joktan became the father of Almodad, Sheleph,*
27 *Hazarmaveth, Jerah, Hadoram, Uzal, Diklah,*
28/29 *Obal, Abimael, Sheba, Ophir, Havilah and*
   Jobab. All these were descendants of Joktan.
30 *Their settlements extended from Mesha all the*
   way to Sephar, the eastern hill country.
31 These are the descendants of Shem, according to
   their clans and languages, by their lands and nations.
32 These are the groupings of Noah's sons, according to their origins and by their nations. From
   these the other nations of the earth branched out
   after the flood.

As we speedily see, the Priestly author, whose work seems to have been preserved fairly integrally, has incorporated this "table of the nations" into his narrative as another of his *toledoth* (vs. 1): *These are the descendants of Noah's sons, Shem, Ham and Japheth.* He then proceeds, in reverse order, to explicate this genealogy by the use of essentially the same repeated formulas: *the descendants of Japheth* (vss. 2–5), *the descend-*

ants of Ham (vss. 6–7.20), and *the descendants of Shem* (vss. 22–23.31), concluded by a summary statement referring to all three sons' descendants and reiterating like the second half of a parenthesis or set of quotation marks the language of vs. 1 (vs. 32). The Yahwist's parallel narrative/genealogy, which was much richer in names of peoples and places and which had its own characteristic language and formulas, has been employed by the Redactor, it appears, in a kind of random fashion to augment and supplement the text of P. It has been used spottily and not in its entirety: there is, for example, no supplement to P's genealogy of Japheth, but a quite extensive one to the genealogy of Ham, and a briefer one to that of Shem. J's contribution, it is evident, contains more narrative material, more geography, and more etiologies than P, which assumes externally a fairly rigid genealogical form. The intentions of the Redactor who combined these two sources were approximately those of the Priestly author who provided the basic structure of the chapter: first of all (as summed up in vs. 32) to show the fulfillment of the divine blessing on the new creation of man which emerged *after the flood,* that it should "be fertile and multiply and fill the earth" (9:1, P); and secondly, to indicate by the climactic order in which the descendants of Shem appear in the final place (confirmed by the genealogy of the "postdiluvian patriarchs" in 11:10–26, P) that it is in this line pre-eminently that the designs of God toward man are to be made manifest in a history of divine grace, promise, and election. The intentions of J were probably not far removed from these, even though in this source there was no such explicit doctrine of a new creation of mankind.

The descendants of Japheth are, in the primary line, seven, to which three and four, again equaling seven, are added in two instances in the secondary line. Aside from the name of Japheth itself, whose real meaning is unknown (as we have seen, a popular etymology is offered in 9:27, J), the names of vss. 2–4 are exclusively those of peoples, not of individuals. They are, in addition, the names of peoples who were fairly remote from the life, the geography, and the history of the people of Israel. We must recognize that it was factors like these, and no real genetic or ethnic distinctions that were then unknown, that dictated the attribution of these peoples to this or that "son of Noah." *Gomer* represents the Assyrian Gimirrai or the Greek Kimmerians, a people of the Black Sea region (modern Russia), who have given their name to the Crimean peninsula. *Magog* (also in Ezekiel 38:2, 39:1.6 associated as here with Meshech and Tubal) is either a people of the same general area or a corruption of the name Gog (cf. the Ezekiel texts), which certainly applied to such a people known from Assyrian tablets ("the land of Gaga" or "of Gugu"). The *Madai* are the Medes, an Indo-European people who lived side by side with their relatives the Persians and eventually formed with them a common kingdom and empire (the modern Iran). *Javan* (cf. "Ionian") is the Hebrew word for Greece. *Tubal* and *Meshech* (found together in Ezekiel 27:13, 32:26, 38:2–3, 39:1) are probably to be identified with the *moschoi* and *tibarenoi* whom Herodotus, a Greek historian of the fifth century B.C., located somewhere southeast of the Black Sea. *Tiras* is mentioned nowhere else in the Old Testament and cannot be identified in the Mesopotamian sources. It is likely, however, that they were a people named in Egyptian texts (the *turusha*, or in Herodotus the *tyrsenoi*), one of the "peoples of the sea" who, like the Philistines, appeared out of the Mediterranean to colonize the littoral *orbis terrarum* which constituted most of the world known to ancient man.

The descendants of Gomer are probably quite correctly identified geographically. *Ashkenaz* (the Scythians?) by Jeremiah 51:27 is to be connected with the Black Sea region, somewhere in the vicinity of Armenia. *Riphath* is unknown, but *Togarmah* (*takarama* in Hittite, *tilgarimmu* in Assyrian) was without doubt a people and a district in the neighborhood of Tubal (Ezekiel 27:13–14).

The descendants of Javan are certainly identified with geographical exactness. *Elishah* is the island we know as Cyprus. *Tarshish,* a name that occurs with some frequency in the Old Testament, was doubtless applied to various ancient cities on the Mediterranean coast and exported from one place to another. In Isaiah 23:1.6 there is a Tarshish which is associated with Tyre and Kittim. Of *the Kittim* and *the Rodanim* (Hebrew has "Dodanim," but the Septuagint and the Samaritan Pentateuch make it clear that the letter ר [*r*] has been confused with ד [*d*] somewhere in the transmission) we have little doubt: they are the people of Cyprus (Kition was the name of a Phoenician colony in Cyprus) and of Rhodes, both Greek islands. We have somewhat more difficulty in deciding why only Gomer and Javan in the primary line should have been singled out for progeny in the secondary line when the other five have not.

These are the descendants of Japheth summarizes the foregoing. *From them sprang the maritime nations:* this notice can hardly apply strictly except to "the descendants of Javan," the primary name that has been most recently mentioned. In any case, however, in speaking of this class of peoples distributed *in their respective lands—each with its own language—by their clans within their nations* Genesis obviously intends to designate those who were both historically and geographically remote from Israel, as we have seen above.

The descendants of Ham, on the contrary, are listed by P as four, of which the last named is *Canaan* (cf. 9:18–25, J). The others are *Cush* (southern Egypt or Nubia, the classic—not the modern—Ethiopia), *Mizraim,* which is Egypt itself, and *Put,* which is either Libya or the Somali coast, in either case a land and a people closely associated with

Egypt. It becomes quite evident that the common denominator of these peoples, Africans on the one hand and Asiatics on the other, is not their ethnic relationship but rather their historical encounter with Israel: all of them were remembered as enemies and oppressors.

One primary name in this case is given progeny by P, that of Cush. But the secondary names do not follow a geographic plan but rather hew to the ideological line. *Seba* is a part of Egypt, but *Havilah* was a part of Arabia (cf. 10:29, J; 25:18, "J"). *Sabtah, Raamah and Sabteca* are again probably Arabian place-names. All of them are non- and anti-Israelite. Similarly the tertiary names in this instance: *Sheba* and *Dedan* are Arabian peoples who, though related to Israel by ties of blood (chapter 16), had been separated from it by more than one trauma of history.

In vss. 8–19 there is an insertion from the J source which differs both in form and content from the surrounding P context. It takes up various "descendants" of Cush, Mizraim, and Canaan, omitting the Put who is also mentioned in vs. 6. In the inserted material we see perhaps better than before the kind of historical and national presuppositions that lie behind these "genealogies" both in P and J. It is as though we were to record our history in this fashion: "The descendants of Europe: Britain, France, Spain . . . Britain became the father of America, Canada . . . To Spain also children were born: California, Mexico . . . The descendants of America: Virginia, Georgia, Carolina . . . Georgia became the father of Atlanta, Augusta, and Savannah . . . ," and so forth.

However, the first part of the J insertion seems to deal with an individual human person rather than with a people. Furthermore, the passage (vss. 8–12) takes the form of a narration rather than a genealogy. *Nimrod . . . was the first potentate on earth.* The NAB has used the word "potentate" (literally, "mighty man" or "warrior") probably because the translator has assumed that the biblical Nimrod corresponds with the historical character Tukulti-Ninurta I, the first (in the thirteenth century B.C.) Assyrian conqueror of Babylonia, noted, as all the Assyrian kings were as *a mighty hunter* (*by the grace of the* LORD would seem to be, like the "wind of God" of Genesis 1:2, a means of expressing the superlative): Ninurta was also the name of the Babylonian god of war and the hunt. The identification is as probable as any other that has been suggested. According to Micah 5:5 Assyria is "the land of Nimrod," and certainly all of the cities and places listed in vss. 10–12 are Assyrian and Babylonian (reading *kulannah*, "all of them," in vs. 10 instead of an otherwise unknown place-name *kalneh* in the extant Hebrew text). Of course, an Egyptian or Arabic origin (vss. 6–7 above) does not fit well with an Assyrian king, but it is likely that for the Yahwist *Cush* meant the land of the Kassites, conquerors of Babylonia several centuries before the Assyrians. All in all, it seems very probable that in these verses the J tradition had remembered an ancient and proverbial tyrant from the distant past.

The J supplement to the genealogy of *Mizraim*—Egypt—in vss. 13–14 resumes the format of a descent of peoples, not all of whom, however, can be identified. The *Ludim*, who in vs. 22 below (P) are "Semites," are in this context unknown. By Jeremiah 46:9 and Ezekiel 30:5 Lud is, indeed, associated with other "Hamitic" peoples, as here; but for good measure, in Isaiah 66:19 it seems to be included among the "Japhethite" peoples (cf. vss. 2–4 above) of the north and west. In this latter acceptation, at least, it is likely that the Ludim may represent those who in classical times were known as the Lydians, Indo-European inhabitants of Asia Minor.

Neither are the *Anamim* known. (The word occurs only in this verse and in 1 Chronicles 1:11 which has copied it.) The *Lehabim*, however, may with fair certainty be identified with the Libyans (the same as the Lubim of Daniel 11:43 and Nahum 3:9), the neighbors and allies of the Egyptians then as they are today. The *Naphtuhim* are probably the people of Lower Egypt (i.e., the north and the Nile delta) and the *Pathrusim* are certainly the inhabitants of Upper Egypt (i.e., the south, cf. Isaiah 11:11): the Hebrew Mizraim is a dual, recognizing a twofold Egypt which the Egyptians themselves insisted upon in their art and architecture, their history, and their laws. The *Casluhim* are likewise unknown. The people that stand out in this paragraph are the *Caphtorim* (the translation above has rightly reread the Hebrew text to make them rather than the Casluhim the ancestors of *the Philistines*). Caphtor was an Aegean region, probably the island of Crete, which in the Old Testament is more than once (Amos 9:7, Jeremiah 47:4) named as the original homeland of the Philistines. The Philistines, as we have observed above (see on 9:27), were a highly civilized people who undeniably were related to the other Indo-European and Mediterranean "peoples of the sea" who spread throughout what we now know as the Greek isles and the adjacent coastlands in the thirteenth and twelfth centuries B.C. Genetically they had nothing to do with the Egyptians, but they harassed and partly settled the Egyptian coast just as they did more permanently the coast of Canaan. They are included as "Hamites" and associated with the hated Canaanites because of historical reasons, since they were among the inveterate enemies of Israel during its formative years.

In vss. 15–19 *Canaan* is featured (see above on 9:25). Again, the Canaanites in the modern ethnic and linguistic sense of the word were Semites just like the Israelites. In the history of human encounter, however, they were for Israel "Hamites" *par excellence*. In these verses we have a mixture of genealogy and geography. *Canaan became the father of Sidon, his first-born:* Sidon, a city which still survives under the name of Saida, was indeed from olden times the metropolis of northern Canaan, the classical Phoenicia, the modern Lebanon, a city which often gave its name to the whole region over which it presided (cf. Judges 18:7). *Heth* is the eponymous ancestor of "the Hittites" in the acceptation of 9:27 above: that they are here "Hamites" (probably also in Genesis 23, 25:34, 27:46, certainly in 36:2 and Ezekiel 16:3.45), whereas in 9:27 they may have been regarded as "Japhethites," should not by now disturb us at all. These "genealogical" relationships which derived from history also changed with history and were undoubtedly revised by it from time to time and from source to source.

Aside from the *Arkites*, the *Sinites*, and the *Zemarites*, who are mentioned only here in the Old Testament (except for the copywork in 1 Chronicles 1:15–16), the rest of the names in vss. 16–18 are fairly commonplace in the Hebrew Bible to designate various populations of greater Canaan. It might be added that the three not otherwise listed in the Old Testament, along with the *Girgashites*, the *Arvadites*, and the *Hamathites*, who are, are amply attested in ancient non-biblical documents as genuine locales in Phoenicia, Syria, and Palestine. What remain are the *Jebusites*, whom the Bible regularly identifies with the pre-Israelite inhabitants of Jerusalem and its environs, and the *Amorites* (Babylonian Amurru, "westerners"), which once referred simply to Western Semitic people in general, but which the Bible (mainly E) has made a term either for the indigenous Canaanite population of Palestine as a whole, or sometimes for a distinctive part of it, such as the inhabitants of the hill country (Numbers 13:29, JE).

The final Yahwistic supplement is a fairly prosaic description of the borders of Canaan. *From Sidon*—a later source would probably have set the border farther north—*to Gerar, near Gaza:* Gerar is south of Gaza, but less well known, as it is to this day, hence the parenthetical note. On the other hand, the eastern extent of the land is determined as *Sodom, Gomorrah, Admah and Zeboiim,* all of which cities we shall see later in the Yahwist's narrative and which we know at least were in the Dead Sea region, while they are presumably for easy reference's sake located *near Lasha*—a place that we do not know at all.

The Yahwist in vs. 21 begins the genealogy of *Shem, Japheth's oldest brother and the ancestor of all the children of Eber.* The name of Eber is picked up again in vss. 24–25, where it occurs in the fourth generation (now that vss. 22–23 from P intervene), as it does in the P genealogy of 11:10–26. What may have been the original connection between Shem and Arpachshad in the J name list we cannot know. At any rate, it is worthy of some note that in this final portion of the "genealogy" of the sons of Noah, many (not all) of the Yahwist's names are intended to indicate individual persons, real or not, whereas most (not all) of the Priestly author's names indicate peoples or places. In particular, the name Eber

(Hebrew *heber,* adjective *hibri*) is undoubtedly intended to designate the eponymous ancestor of the Hebrews. "Hebrew," as we shall see later, was possibly a social before it was an ethnic term. In the Bible, there is no doubt, it has sometimes been made an ethnic term. Here (cf. vss. 25–30) it is an ethnic designation that obviously includes many other peoples besides the Israelites, though eventually it comes to be applied to the Israelites alone (cf. Exodus 3:18, 5:3, 7:16, 9:1.13; Jonah 1:9). But in any case, it is to be observed that even if considered here as a gentilic of Israel, the name of Eber is rather thoroughly buried in the list, and it is given no special prominence.

In vss. 22–23 *the descendants of Shem* according to P are mainly the names of peoples, or more properly, of the lands where these peoples lived. *Elam* was an ancient country lying east of Babylonia and north of the Persian Gulf, inhabited by a people which was frequently at war with its Mesopotamian neighbors. The Elamites were not Semites in the modern sense of the term. *Asshur* is, of course, the name of Assyria and of its capital city, north of Babylonia and transected by the Tigris River. The Assyrians were, indeed, Semites; but we recall that in vss. 8–12 above the Yahwist listed them among the "Hamites." *Arpachshad* is persistently identified with Babylonia by many commentators, but without convincing proof. In 11:10–13 (P) below, Arpachshad is definitely intended to be a personal name. *Lud* we have already considered: see above on vs. 13 (J). *Aram* represents the Arameans, at first a federation of nomadic tribes, later a sedentary league of city-states, which occupied northern Mesopotamia and the land west of the Euphrates which was later known as Syria. The Arameans were ethnically related to the Israelites and were closely involved both in Israel's origins (Ezekiel 16:3) and in its subsequent history. We shall see more of them in the patriarchal history. Of the "descendants" of Aram in vs. 23, *Uz, Hul, Gether and Mash,* only the first can be identified with any degree of probability. Uz was an Edomite and therefore Semitic district (Jeremiah 25:20; Lamentations 4:21) south of Palestine, the homeland of the biblical Job (Job 1:1). In Genesis 22:21 (J) Uz is put into closer relationship with Israel, being named the "nephew" of Abraham. In Genesis 36:28, on the contrary, in the midst of Edomite genealogies and tables of disparate origin, Uz is called a Horite, considered to be one of the aboriginal inhabitants of the land who were displaced by the Edomites.

As already mentioned above, many of the names in the J supplement of vss. 24–30 are intended to be those of individual persons remembered from the distant past, and for most of these no commentary is possible. *Arpachshad* we have seen before, and also *Eber. Peleg* deserves some attention, since *in his time the world was divided* (the passive of a verb *palag*), though to be sure we do not know what meaning this statement has beyond providing for the Yahwist an obvious play on words. Is it a reference to the J story in 11:1–9? Or is it, as some think, a dimly remembered recollection of the time when the desert land between the Tigris and the Euphrates was cut by an enormous series of irrigation canals, constituting one of the wonders of the ancient world? (In Isaiah 32:2 *peleg* in the plural means "streams" or "runnels" of water. The canal system of ancient Mesopotamia, charted out by the pre-Semitic civilization of the Sumerians in the third millennium B.C., long ago reverted to the desert through the successive rule and misrule of invading and departing peoples of all kinds. Vestiges of it, however, can still be perceived by means of aerial photography, and in part it is being restored by the people of modern Iraq.)

The "sons" of *Joktan* (vss. 26–30) seem to be place-names, some of which can be identified. Joktan itself may be the same as the Jokshan of 25:2–3 (J), associated there as here with Sheba. *Hazarmaveth* is undoubtedly Hadramaut, a district on the southwest coast of the present-day Saudi Arabia, east of Yemen. *Sheleph* and *Uzal* (for the latter, cf. Ezekiel 27:19) are also known as Arabian sites. So is *Sheba,* which in vs. 7 above (P) is listed as Hamite. So is *Ophir,* probably a trading seaport on the Arabian coast, frequently mentioned in the Old Testament (1 Kings 9:28, etc.) as the source of gold and many other imports into the land of Palestine. And so is *Havilah* (cf. on vs. 7 above), which again according to P is Hamite. With all these identifiable names serving as precedent, it is not rash to conclude that the others remaining are also Arabic, as some of them would lead us to suspect in any case. *Mesha* (the Massa of Genesis 25:14?=one of Ishmael's "sons," i.e., Arabian) and *Sephar,* an Isfar south of Hadramaut, can also safely be located within the geography of Arabia.

Given the mixed character of the sources that have gone into the production of this listing of "Noah's sons," it is impossible to recapture the rationale by which some in the first, second, or third generation have been credited with progeny whereas others have not. We can, however, perhaps see the purpose, or part of the purpose, of the Redactor who drew the sources together. It happens, when we eliminate the repetitions, that the "decendants" of Japheth are fourteen: two times seven. The "descendants" of Ham are thirty-one: four times seven plus three. And the "decendants" of Shem are twenty-five: three times seven plus four. All together, then, there are seventy "descendants": seven times ten. More important, however, than this mathematical gamesmanship is the theological lesson that peers through the bewildering and at times tedious catalogues of persons, peoples, and places dredged up from the memories and imaginations of half-forgotten generations that made up the long ago for Yahwist, Priestly author, and Redactor alike.

That lesson is, that Israel was not the first, not the greatest, and not the most accomplished of the nations which in God's providence had been granted their moments on life's stage. Quite to the contrary, even their remote origins, which for that matter they shared with others who in time proved to be their superiors in divers ways or who took a retrograde path and ended in obloquy, were never so sharply defined as to give any hint of what they might become as vessels of divine election. Practically no other people of antiquity was able to avoid the temptation to look upon itself as the darling of the gods, equipped with some innate genius to possess at last hegemony over its own world, to assert to itself its "manifest destiny." The Semitic and European empires of the ancient West and East have all shared in common with their modern counterparts the conviction that some unique combination of blood or genes along with nerve, toughness, and self-reliance decreed them fit to govern where others could not, and they imposed their reign because it was inevitably the best of reigns. Israel never had such a temptation, and not only because it was a tiny nation enmeshed between others far more powerful (so was England before the Tudors, or Prussia before Wilhelm II). Israel avoided the temptation because it had inherited a healthy sense of its shortcomings, of its frequently disreputable ethnic connections, and of its many vulnerabilities on every side. Israel was never permitted by its geography or its history to assume a natural superiority of any kind. "It was not because you are the largest of all nations that the LORD set his heart on you and chose you, for you are really the smallest of all nations. It was because the LORD loved you and because of his fidelity to the oath he had sworn to your fathers, that he brought you out with his strong hand from the place of slavery, and ransomed you from the hand of Pharaoh, king of Egypt" (Deuteronomy 7:7–8). Seen in this light, the notion of divine election has nothing of smugness about it but rather is an encouragement to national humility.

11 The whole world spoke the same language, using
2 the same words. While men were migrating in the east, they came upon a valley in the land of Shinar
3 and settled there. They said to one another, "Come, let us mold bricks and harden them with fire." They
4 used bricks for stone, and bitumen for mortar. Then they said, "Come, let us build ourselves a city and a tower with its top in the sky, and so make a name for ourselves; otherwise we shall be scattered all over the earth."
5 The LORD came down to see the city and the
6 tower that the men had built. Then the LORD said: "If now, while they are one people, all speaking the same language, they have started to do this, nothing will later stop them from doing whatever they pre-

7 sume to do. Let us then go down and there confuse
their language, so that one will not understand what
8 another says." Thus the LORD scattered them from
there all over the earth, and they stopped building
9 the city. That is why it was called Babel, because
there the LORD confused the speech of all the world.
It was from that place that he scattered them all
over the earth.

In the preceding chapter the Priestly author has repeatedly
(10:5.20.31–32) spoken of the distribution of the nations of mankind
"according to their clans and languages, by their lands." Now the Yahwist
—and there can be no doubt that the story above is the work of the
Yahwist—accounts for the same distribution and differentiation, and it is
not surprising that his account takes the form of an etiology or series of
etiologies. As we shall see, however, the etiologies do not constitute the
primary reason for which the story was told.

The tale of the Tower of Babel, a page from the book of Genesis with
which almost everyone is familiar to some degree, turns up in a myriad of
forms in the folklore of many unrelated peoples, somewhat comparably
with the story of the flood. That is to say, the separate motifs of the story
turn up here and there: there is no single account anywhere that even approximately replicates all that we read in Genesis 11:1–9. The same thing
is true, and even in a greater measure, of the folklore of those peoples that
we might expect to have exercised a more than indirect influence on the
biblical narrative. As a matter of fact, however, until less than a decade
ago no Sumerian, Akkadian, Assyrian, or Babylonian story was known that
could serve as a non-biblical parallel to the Tower of Babel episode. In
1968, to mark a new development in comparative religion and to fill an
otherwise perplexing lacuna, Samuel Noah Kramer published "a Sumerian
version" of the Babel story, gathered from Ashmolean fragments some of
which go back to the period of the Third Dynasty of Ur (2065–1960
B.C.), which professed that in one point of time the language of man
which before had been one was by divine agency confused and distinguished. The Sumerian story has the linguistic discrepancy depend on a rivalry between the gods Enki and Enlil, just as the Mesopotamian stories of
creation and the flood were essentially the outgrowth of internecine
conflict within the Sumero-Babylonian pantheon. The Genesis story, of
course, has no such polytheistic background but deals with a relationship
between God and man. Furthermore, what Kramer called "a Sumerian
version" of the "Babel of tongues" is precisely that: this one motif of the
Genesis story is featured and no others. It is still true to say, therefore,

that as far as we know there is no genuine parallel outside the Bible to the story of Genesis 11:1–9.

In former times of biblical criticism, extending down to the great commentary of Hermann Gunkel in the first decade of this century, it was assumed with what appeared to be good reason that the Genesis story was the product of at least two separate narratives, one of which had been concerned with the building of a city, the other, or others, with the building of a tower. Nowadays it is more readily recognized that while the story may indeed have been assembled from originally separate themes, the net result is a rigid unity which the Yahwist has made thoroughly his own and stamped with the indelible marks of true authorship. These marks consist in the structure(s) given to the story and in the wordplays, assonances, and other rhetorical devices which have been scattered through it.

First of all, the structures. Umberto Cassuto has correctly pointed out that with vss. 2–4, man's resolution and action, correspond vss. 5–8, God's resolution and action, completed by the author's commentary in vs. 9. But the structure can be further refined, by recognizing in vss. 1–4 on the one hand, and in vss. 6–9 on the other, two complementary sections that refer back and forth to each other by the use of the same catchwords or expressions. In this construction, vs. 5 is the line of division and connection, the watershed on either side of which the two primary sections rise and fall. The whole process may be better clarified if we offer another, more literal translation of the passage, identifying the correspondences back and forth with the use of italics, and putting it in the colloquial form that accords with the spirit of the Hebrew text. Lest this procedure become too complicated, we will deal afterward with the other verbal and literal crisscrosses.

> 1 Once upon a time, *the whole earth,*
> *the language was one,* and the words were *one.*
> 2 And it happened, as they marched from the east,
> that they found a plain in the land of *Shinar,*
> and they settled down there.
> 3 *And they said, each one to his friend:*
> *"Come on!* let us brick bricks,
> and let us bake them with baking."
> So they had brickwork for stone,
> and pitch they had for mortar.
> 4 *And they said:*
> *"Come on! let us build us a city* and a tower,
> *whose head is in the heavens,*
> and let us make us *a name,*

> *lest we be scattered*
> *on the face of the whole earth."*
> 5 Then Yahweh came down to see
> both the city and the tower
> which the sons of man had built.
> 6 *And Yahweh said:*
> "See! the people is *one,*
> and *the language is one* for them all.
> And this is the beginning of their doing,
> so that now will not be withheld from them
> all that they scheme of doing.
> 7 *Come on! let us go down,*
> and confuse there *their language,*
> so that they will not understand
> *each one the language of his friend."*
> 8 And Yahweh *scattered them from there*
> *on the face of the whole earth,*
> and they left off *building the city.*
> 9 Wherefore he called *its name Babel,*
> because there Yahweh made a babble
> of *the language of the whole earth,*
> and from there Yahweh *scattered them*
> *on the face of the whole earth.*

The argument for structural unity seems to be quite incontrovertible. The other literary devices which interlock with such frequency as to constitute a strong argument for an original single authorship of the entire passage are in large part incapable of intelligent discussion without bringing in the Hebrew text, which it is not practical for us to do in any detail in a commentary of this kind. We have been able to point up some of the wordplays involved, at the expense of idiomatic English, in the translation immediately above: "brick bricks," "bake them with baking," "Babel . . . made a babble." But it has not been equally possible to indicate that in Hebrew "brickwork" and "for stone" have a similar sound, and that the words for "pitch" and "mortar" contain precisely the same consonants, or that "there" and "name," which together occur seven times in the story and which are ideologically related in its development, have the same spelling in the Hebrew Bible. It has not been possible to suggest that in Hebrew "the sons (of man)" in vs. 5 joined with "had built" form in sequence a poetic line. Nor can we show in any translation the chains of assonances constructed about the letters *b-l-n* in various combinations (evoking the name of Babylon), or the sibilants *s* and *sh* (a single letter in the Hebrew Bible), involving such interrelated elements as "name," "there," "language," "Shinar," "whose head is in the heavens," etc., or, finally, the assonances surrounding the letter *l* in itself, which are quite numerous and which in at least one instance (in vs. 4) come in a sequence that suggests the original connection of "a city and a tower" (the latter *migdoL* in Hebrew). The reader will have to take most of this on faith. He can also, of course, consult a more detailed commentary, such as Cassuto's, on whose philological observations we have mainly depended for the construction of this paragraph.

The whole world spoke the same language: in the necessarily highly imaginary evocation of the prehistory of man in precritical ages—"once upon a time"—it was taken for granted that the many languages of mankind were so many variations on what must have once been a common tongue—literally, in Hebrew, "the same lip." This was taken for granted just, of course, as it was taken for granted that the races, the peoples, and the many nations that made up the human species had descended in a direct line from one common stock. P as well as J, we know, thought of the whole commonalty of man as descendants of the three sons of Noah. The Yahwist, therefore, reproduces his version of the etiology of tongues which, we have already seen, was a fairly universal possession of ancient man, including ancient Near Eastern man.

While men were migrating in the east reaches back to the geography of 2:8, 4:16 (J), according to which the origins of man were remotely "in the east": the episode of the flood has not altered this geography, and, to be more precise, the flood story probably never even thought about it. In the present story we find men still wandering in the east, like Cain, till they come *upon a valley in the land of Shinar.* This gives us the locale of our narrative. Shinar, which may or may not have some linguistic connection with the name Sumer, referring to the pre-Semitic civilization of lower Mesopotamia, in the Hebrew Bible designates that same region which in classical times came to be known as Babylonia, a regional term derived from the then capital city of Babylon (Babel in Hebrew, vs. 9, or in Akkadian Babilu). Babylonia, or Sumer, in the times of the Yahwist was the southern part of Mesopotamia only; the northern part was known as Akkad, after a city and a people (Semites) who succeeded the Sumerians and contributed the generic name (Akkadian) to the Eastern Semitic language in which most of the cuneiform documents of ancient Mesopotamia have been written, whether from Akkadian, Assyrian, or Chaldean times. In later periods the whole of Mesopotamia was known as Babylonia (more properly, Chaldea), but only after it had first been Assyria (after the Asshur which we have seen repeatedly above). Assyrians, Akkadians, Chaldeans, Babylonians were all Semitic peoples related to the Israelites and represented successive waves of conquest and immigration within the land between the two rivers of the Tigris and the Euphrates from which the Israelites themselves, or many of them, also ultimately derived.

They used bricks for stone, and bitumen for mortar. This is quite evidently a Palestinian story told by someone who had heard about the strange ways of Mesopotamia. The building of Palestine was and is precisely one of stone and mortar: stone is hardly a blessing but rather the curse of much of the Palestinian soil. On the contrary, sun-dried or baked mud brick was almost the cultural emblem of Mesopotamia, used alike for its writings and records and for its buildings. Mud bricks joined together with asphalt produced structures which have remained amazingly intact through millennia and owe less of their ruin to the elements and the vicissitudes of time than to the depredations of ignorant marauders and learned treasure hunters and antiquarians. The point is, in this story, that the author has to explain an exotic building technique for his readers. It is a story, in other words, that must have risen in the land of Israel with a recollection only of Mesopotamian origins that will be noted in vs. 9. The Mesopotamian origins can by no means be ignored, but it should also be quite obvious that they do not carry the major burden of the story. That is to say, an etiology of the city of Babylon is most definitely not the paramount concern of the biblical storyteller, if indeed it is a concern at all.

Let us build ourselves a city and a tower may, as we have suggested above, combine two themes which the Yahwist found originally separate in his sources. It is doubtful, however, that in any case he considered them to be all that disparate and disconnected, even if they were separate. Rather, it would seem that he thought of them as twin symptoms of an ancient desire and effort of primeval man, namely, that by his own devices he might build this city and tower *with its top in the sky, and so make a name for* himself on his own initiative, independent of the intentions of God, even as he had aspired to do in the garden of Eden. *Otherwise we shall be scattered all over the earth:* it was undoubtedly the Yahwist's conviction that it was precisely the divine will that mankind be "scattered" over the face of the earth, just as it finally comes about in vs. 8. By trying to prevent the fulfillment of God's will for man in favor of a destiny which he prefers to carve out for himself, the creature man not only repeats his antediluvian history, he also ratifies the gloomy prediction held out for him by his Creator and Savior in the aftermath of the flood: "the desires of man's heart are evil from the start" (Genesis 8:21, J). It is the exemplification of this continuously sad state of affairs that appears to be the meaning intended by the biblical author in retelling this ancient story inherited from a scantly remembered past.

By recognizing what, indeed, is the biblical message, we are dispensed from dwelling overmuch on many of the other details of Genesis 11:1–9, except to the extent that they possess an antiquarian interest for shedding light on the background of the story. The "tower" of which the story tells was without a doubt a Mesopotamian ziggurat (more properly, *ziqqurat,* "pinnacle"), a stepped pyramidal structure built of baked bricks rising to a topmost shrine or temple, which was the characteristic of the Sumero-Babylonian city-states (much like the abbey-towns of feudal Europe): the religious center from which the city derived its identity and vitality. The ziggurat was in material fabric the counterpart and symbol of the mythical "mountain of God" (Ezekiel 28:16—recall Mount Sinai in the Israelite history, Mount Olympus in the Greek mythology, the Mount of the Beatitudes and the Sermon on the Mount in the New Testament revelation, etc.) where the divine was thought to reside and the human able to make contact with it (as in Jacob's dream at Bethel in Genesis 28:10–19 and its New Testament application in John 1:51). As far as we can see, the Yahwist has retained no recollection of the original religious sense of the ziggurat to characterize his "tower." For him it was merely a symbol of *hybris,* which might just as well have been a gigantic smokestack or a water tower—any landmark, in fact, would do.

For the same reason we have no cause, except again for antiquarian purposes, to attempt to determine what particular ziggurat and its fate may have originally given rise to the story which the Yahwist has so faintly remembered. Was it Esagila ("the house which raises its head," cf. vs. 4), the temple of Marduk at Babylon? In *Enuma elish* it is said that the head of Esagila was raised up "towards heaven." Known in Sumerian as Etemenanki ("house of the foundations of heaven and earth"), this ziggurat was restored by a later Babylonian king who willed thereby once more to "make its summit like the heavens." Or, since the excavator's spade has revealed for the temple and ziggurat of ancient Babylon rather more modest dimensions than those which both Semitic and Hellenistic (Herodotus) sources would have led us to expect, could the legend have confused it with one more truly spectacular, like the Ezida of the nearby temple-city of Borsippa (the modern Birs Nimrud)? It is really not that important to decide. What alone is important, perhaps, is to recognize that by the time of the Yahwist's writing the ancient Babylonian civilization had been so thoroughly wiped from the screen of Near Eastern vision (by the Hittite invasions of the sixteenth century B.C., for one thing) that memories of it were no longer reliable. In short, the "tower" of the Genesis story no longer has much to do with the ziggurat of the Mesopotamian originals. "Babylon," we see in vs. 9, obviously signified for the biblical writer something like the oldest city in the world, just as Greece and Rome to similarly ill-informed nineteenth-century scholars epitomized "the ancient world" until the chronicles of several prior millennia began to be discovered.

In vss. 5–7 Yahweh reacts to the building of the city and the tower in

the same manner that he reacted to man's gaining of "knowledge" in
3:22–24. He reacts, moreover, in a way that marks him quite the same
Yahweh of the earlier story. Again, almost with a start of surprise, he observes what man has done in his absence. Again he muses on the consequences that may befall man's deed. And again, finally, he resolves in con-
ference—*let us then go down*—on a course of action that will frustrate
man's plan and restore the proper order of things intended from the beginning. *Thus he scattered them from there all over the earth* it is said in vs.
8, and we are left in no doubt that such was the divine purpose built into
the instinct of mankind as already implied in the P sections of the preceding chapter 10. *That is why* [the city] *was called Babel,* the story concludes. Quite obviously, Genesis took it for granted that Babylon was
where it had all begun, just as later centuries and cultures would take it for
granted that it had all begun at Rome, or Athens, or Troy. Babel-babble is
the almost inevitable English approximation of the Hebrew *babel-balal*
("confused") wordplay which the NAB has unaccountably avoided. The
Hebrew "etymology" of the city's name is, of course, unscientific and contrived. But so, for that matter, was the "Babylonian" name itself: Babilu,
"gate of the gods," doubtless meant something rather different in the
Sumerian which preceded it.

> 10 This is the record of the descendants of Shem.
> When Shem was one hundred years old, he became
> the father of Arpachshad, two years after the flood.
> 11 Shem lived five hundred years after the birth of
> Arpachshad, and he had other sons and daughters.
> 12 When Arpachshad was thirty-five years old, he
> 13 became the father of Shelah. Arpachshad lived four
> hundred and three years after the birth of Shelah,
> and he had other sons and daughters.
> 14 When Shelah was thirty years old, he became the
> 15 father of Eber. Shelah lived four hundred and three
> years after the birth of Eber, and he had other sons
> and daughters.
> 16 When Eber was thirty-four years old, he became the
> 17 father of Peleg. Eber lived four hundred and thirty
> years after the birth of Peleg, and he had other sons
> and daughters.
> 18 When Peleg was thirty years old, he became the
> 19 father of Reu. Peleg lived two hundred and nine
> years after the birth of Reu, and he had other sons
> and daughters.
> 20 When Reu was thirty-two years old, he became the

21 father of Serug. Reu lived two hundred and seven
   years after the birth of Serug, and he had other sons
   and daughters.
22 When Serug was thirty years old, he became the
23 father of Nahor. Serug lived two hundred years after
   the birth of Nahor, and he had other sons and
   daughters.
24 When Nahor was twenty-nine years old, he became
25 the father of Terah. Nahor lived one hundred and
   nineteen years after the birth of Terah, and he had
   other sons and daughters.
26 When Terah was seventy years old, he became the
   father of Abram, Nahor and Haran.

This *toledoth* of the "Semites" bears the unmistakable marks of the
Priestly author's schematics. It has been modeled on the P genealogy of
chapter 5, though the structure has been greatly simplified and the astro-
nomical ages assigned to the antediluvian generations have here been
slimmed down in deference to the approach of historical times. "Modeled
on" is doubtless the correct characterization to be applied to this genealogy in relation to that of chapter 5, for more than one reason. If we include Abraham—the Abram of vs. 26 who is so designated in all the
sources of Genesis until 17:5 thanks to the harmonization of the Redactor
—as representing the tenth generation in the list of the postdiluvians, we
have an obvious correspondence with the antediluvian genealogy of chapter 5 with its ten generations that preceded the flood. As we saw when we
were considering the genealogy of chapter 5, the ten-generation formula
adopted there was in all likelihood the invention of P or of his immediate
Israelite source: it is not probable, as it once seemed, that the Priestly author was for this conception dependent on an older Babylonian tradition.
Certainly, there is no Babylonian precedent for counting ten generations
between the flood and the commencement of historical times. The Babylonian lists of the kings who reigned after the flood show an indiscriminate
and unschematic use of names and ages, both of which appear in generous
profusion. Indeed, in his 1939 publication of the Sumerian king list
Thorkild Jacobsen had already concluded that the antediluvian parts of
the Babylonian list which do, in various forms, display a schematic structure were originally independent of it and responded to separate ideas of
their own.
A rather more obvious reason for thinking this genealogy to have been
modeled on that of chapter 5 and to reflect no extrabiblical tradition preceding it is its function within the strictly Israelite history of the Priestly
author's narrative. Unlike the genealogy of chapter 5 which purported to
list the generations of all mankind from creation to the flood, this one

claims to be merely the record of the race of Shem, of only one of the sons of Noah, listing the immediate ancestors of Abraham. It does count ten generations after the flood, therefore, but only obliquely.

It seems to be a fair assumption that the Priestly author has built this genealogy up from the Yahwist's data in 10:21.24–25, perhaps with the help of additional and parallel traditions. From the Yahwist we had already the first five names of the P list, ending with Peleg. At 10:26–30 Peleg's "brother" Joktan and his descent captured the interest of the J tradition, which therefore did not continue to develop the line of Shem through and after Peleg. P has done what J did not. No doubt the biblical author thought of all these names as those of individual persons, and in some part they may have been such, though it matters very little whether they were or not.

These are the names with their "ages" listed according to the three ancient witnesses to the biblical tradition which we utilized in chapter 5:

	MT		SP		LXX	
Shem	100	500	100	500	100	500
Arpachshad	35	403	135	303	135	430
[Kenan]					130	330
Shelah	30	403	130	303	130	330
Eber	34	430	134	270	134	370
Peleg	30	209	130	109	130	209
Reu	32	207	132	107	132	207
Serug	30	200	130	100	130	200
Nahor	29	119	79	69	79	129
Terah	70	135	70	75	70	135
	390		1040		1170	

If it was obvious before in how highly cavalier a fashion these biblical figures were handled in the process of their transmission, it should be even more obvious now. First of all, it would appear that LXX, through a dogged determination to have ten generations *between* the flood and Abraham just as there had been between creation and the flood, invented another Kenan (borrowed, of course, from 5:9–14) to fill in the supposed gap in the line which links Shem to Terah (cf. Luke 3:36, which follows the LXX). For good measure, LXX has added "then he died" to the end of vss. 11.13ab.15.17.19.21.23.25 to heighten further the resemblance of this passage to the genealogy of chapter 5. For even better measure, SP has in vss. 11.13.15.17.19.21.23.25 inserted the phrase "the whole lifetime of . . . was . . . years; then he died," to underline the relationship still more. There can be no question that the calculus of probabilities favors the existing MT in these instances as the more respectable depository of an unadulterated tradition. There can also hardly be question that the SP and LXX together, partly tributary to an originally common effort and partly in independence each of the other, partly by obvious design and partly by nothing more abstruse than honest error and the metathesis of ciphers, have initiated changes in the numerical patterns that vitiate the first intentions of the biblical author. This is not to say that the MT has necessarily preserved the original numbers with an accuracy and credibility quotient of 100 per cent. It is to say, however, that the MT (which has been followed almost invariably by our NAB) holds the best chance to have done this work of preservation over all its rivals.

As before, when we grappled with the similar formulations of chapter 5, it is possible to perceive some of what is being aimed at in the interlocking numbers of 11:10–26, but we must confess that most of it defies analysis. For one thing, it is doubtless not without intention that these computations leave all the postdiluvian patriarchs, Noah included, alive and well at the time of the birth of Abraham. There is no question here of the passing away of an earlier race of man prior to the cataclysmic new beginning brought in by the flood; rather, it would seem that we are being told that the new race of man begun by Noah and blessed in him is permitted to see within its own "lifetime" the fulfillment of its blessing in the appearance of him who will be the father of many nations and the embodiment of God's special relationship with man through grace and faith. On the other hand, with the appearance of Jacob (to arrive at the correct computation of dates, add the hundred years of 21:5 and the sixty of 25:26, both P), who is born a hundred years after the death of Noah, only Shem, Shelah, and Eber remain of the line from Shem to Terah. It is easy to understand why Shem (=the Semites) and Eber (=the Hebrews) should coexist with and extend partway into the lifetime of Jacob (=the Israelites); it is not equally clear why Shelah (not the same in spelling as the Judahite Shelah of chapter 38, 46:12, etc.) should be the other survivor. The LXX and SP, and whatever prior tradition they may have had in common, have resolved all such difficulties by stretching the relevant numbers out to such lengths as to put all of Abraham's immediate ancestors on more or less the same plane and also, without doubt, to make more "realistic" the span of years that separated him from the flood.

A few other significant numbers peep through the tables, or are presupposed by them. Three hundred and sixty-five years after Arpachshad, the first generation to follow the flood, Abraham enters the Promised Land, or, more accurately, the land that was soon to be promised (note 12:4b, P). The time from Shem to Terah is 320 years, just twice that of the time from Abraham to Jacob which we have already noted above. Both of these numbers are multiples of forty, the "ideal" count of a generation of years. In the first column of generational dates above (MT) we have the sequence 35-30, 34-30, and 32-30 (no 33-30 or 31-30, however), making room for the twenty-nine years assigned Nahor at the birth of Terah. There are, of course, many other combinations and correspondences which ingenuity might suggest and which, indeed, could have some foundation in the biblical author's real intents; but it seems hardly worthwhile to try to pursue them further.

One very clear-cut and precise date that seems to have no explanation is the *two years after the flood* of vs. 10. This chronology is in clear conflict with the other P data of 5:32 and 7:11, and there is no better explanation for it than the supposition that the Priestly author has here incorporated into his narrative another and variant tradition about Arpachshad which he did not bother to harmonize with the rest of his writing. It may seem strange that an author who is otherwise so captivated by numbers should have permitted this oversight, and it is strange; but there is no other persuasive accounting for the fact. If, as some have thought, the "two years" of vs. 10 are due to a later "corrective" glossing of the text, the insertion was singularly inept, since it created rather than resolved a chronological problem.

It remains to take note of the names that appear for the first time in the Priestly genealogy. *Reu* is otherwise unknown, but it is possible that it is a shortening of Reuel, a theophoric name common to Edomites (36:4, etc.) and Midianites (Exodus 2:18, etc.). *Serug* (Sarug), *Nahor* (Nahur), and *Terah* (Turahi) are all northern Mesopotamian names well attested in cuneiform documents, where they refer to sites in the vicinity of Haran (vs. 31 below), an important city of which we shall soon be speaking in connection with the origins of Abraham and his people. (The *Haran* of vs. 26 who appears as Abraham's brother differs in Hebrew spelling from the city designated Haran in vs. 31 just as the Shelah of chapter 11 is not the Shelah of chapter 38; but the separation of the two Harans may be due to a deliberate change in the Hebrew text in order to distinguish between person and place.) That these names refer in our sources to locales rather than to peoples or persons has relatively minor significance, given the facility with which personal names came to be attached to the regions where these persons resided and vice versa. What is more important is that as we reach the end of prehistory and enter upon the terrain of "real" history, even though admittedly a still highly legendary history, which introduces into our consideration real and personally identifiable protagonists—for there can be no doubt that Abraham and those who follow him are meant to be historical personages and not the personifications of peoples or places—we are brought face to face with a series of names that rings exactly true, that fit precisely where they ought to fit. "My father was a wandering Aramean," sang the ancient historical creed of Israel (Deuteronomy 26:5). It was from these peoples and from these regions of

Aram Naharaim, from the Serug and the Nahor and the Terah and the Haran of northern Mesopotamia, that the patriarchal legends took much of their beginnings. It is to the patriarchal history, therefore, that we now turn. The Book of Beginnings has concluded.

II. The Saga of Abraham

1. The Terahites

The *toledoth* of Terah, the father of Abraham, is, of course, taken from the Priestly source. There is also in our redactional text, however, a fairly extensive insertion borrowed from the Yahwist, which we indicate below in italics:

27 This is the record of the descendants of Terah. Terah became the father of Abram, Nahor and Haran, and Haran became the father of Lot.
28 *Haran died before his father Terah, in his native*
29 *land, in Ur of the Chaldeans. Abram and Nahor took wives; the name of Abram's wife was Sarai, and the name of Nahor's wife was Milcah, daughter of*
30 *Haran, the father of Milcah and Iscah. Sarai was barren; she had no child.*
31 Terah took his son Abram, his grandson Lot, son of Haran, and his daughter-in-law Sarai, the wife of his son Abram, and brought them out of* Ur of the Chaldeans, to go to the land of Canaan. But when
32 they reached Haran, they settled there. The lifetime of Terah was two hundred and five years; then Terah died in Haran.

As has already been observed, a great number of these names betray their origin in the ambient of northern Mesopotamia, in Aram Naharaim, "the land between the two rivers" of the Tigris and Euphrates, circling the famous city of Haran that first appears in vs. 31. Before we consider any of these names in detail, however, it might be profitable for us to contemplate the family tree of the Terahites as it is presupposed here and in the following chapters of Genesis:

* *Or,* and they went out with him from: so the MT, contrary to the LXX and the SP.

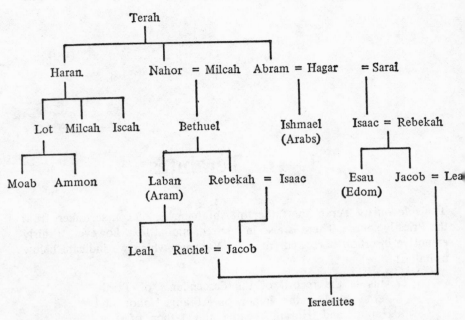

The interrelationships within this family become more apparent when they are viewed in this table, especially perhaps as they indicate a tendency toward endogamy, a practice which is explicit in some of the patriarchal stories and is implied in others. But in addition we have an overview of names which have some significant historical import.

"In times past your fathers, down to Terah, father of Abraham and Nahor, dwelt beyond the River and served other gods," ran another of the old historical creeds of Israel (Joshua 24:2). The family tree of the Terahites leaves us in little doubt that one of the other gods, if not the chief of the other gods, whom Abraham's fathers and brethren served was the moon-god Sin, the tutelary deity of the cities of Ur and Haran in southern and northern Mesopotamia. Sin (the Sumerian for it had been *zu-en,* "knowing lord"), also called Nannar ("the man in heaven": quite literally "the man in the moon"), had as his consort Ningal ("the great lady"), and both of these appear to have been honored many times over in the names which the Terahites chose for themselves. *Sarai,* for example, which in the Eastern Semitic of Mesopotamia meant "queen," translated the Sumerian Ningal. *Milcah* ("princess") was an alternative title with similar significance as was also—probably—*Iscah. Abram,* which doubtless has its Hebrew or Western Semitic counterpart in the Abiram of Numbers 16 and 1 Kings 16:34, *may* have a connection with Sin: the name means "the father [i.e., the father god] is exalted." The name *Laban* ("white") almost certainly has this connection (in Isaiah 24:23,

30:26, and the Song of Songs 6:10, and only there in the Hebrew Bible, the word *lebanah* occurs with the meaning "moon").

The association of the Terahites with the cult of the moon-god is not without some import as regards other historical details which Genesis presumes to lie at the background of these beginnings of the patriarchal story. In the received text of Genesis both J and P name *Ur of the Chaldeans* the Terahites' original homeland (though in the opinion of some scholars the reference in vs. 28 is redactional rather than original with the Yahwist). That by any account the designation is an anachronism there can be no doubt: not until centuries after the presumed time of Abraham did the people known in Akkadian as the Chaldeans (in Hebrew, *kasdim*) invade and impose their name on the southern Mesopotamia of Ur. (Genesis 22:21–22, J, quite properly identifies as relatives of Abraham both Aram—the Arameans—and Chesed, the eponymous ancestor of the *kasdim:* all of these were Western Semites. With that relationship we are not at present concerned.) Ur, in any case, though without the later qualification "of the Chaldeans," was an ancient and still flourishing city when the Terahites first made their appearance in the Near Eastern scene that has been portrayed by Genesis 11–12. But was this Ur indeed the Terahites' first homeland, even as the existing text of the Bible claims? Many are disposed to doubt this, principally, perhaps, because the patriarchal legends otherwise display little or no acquaintance with the traditions and geography of southern Mesopotamia, whereas on the contrary they are quite conversant with those of northern Mesopotamia, those of Aram Naharaim, whose chief city was Haran. Hence "Ur of the Chaldeans" is by some regarded as an unhistorical intrusion into the tradition or—a more recent hypothesis—as the deformation of another Ur which had lain to the north of Canaan and which was later confused in the tradition with the better-known Ur in Chaldea.

In favor of the accuracy of the biblical tradition as it stands, however, is the strong indication that the Haran of the patriarchs was a daughter city of the famous Ur which came to be known as "of the Chaldeans." Though the origins of Haran remain obscure (until the inscriptions of Ebla mentioned below, the first references to it occurred in commercial documents of the nineteenth century B.C., in the records of a trading company situated in Asia Minor that had earlier been founded from Ur), there is good reason to believe that it owed its existence to a migration from Ur. As already mentioned, the gods of Ur were also those of Haran, a phenomenon which finds its readiest explanation in the assumption of a sizable movement of people and culture from one center to the other. Haran was located at the intersection of trade routes in a region that had long been dominated by Ur, and therefore it is quite understandable how and why there could have been a migration up the Euphrates valley to more hospitable climes once the parent city had lost its attraction for some of its population. There is nothing inherently improbable, therefore, in the thought that Genesis may have preserved an authentic recollection of the past in making Ur of the Chaldeans the "native land" of the Terahites before they ever settled in Haran.

The reason for indulging this possible historical reconstruction is not the dubious advantage of favoring one ancient Ur over another but rather the conditioned capacity of placing some of the ancestors of the Israelite people within a defined era of the known history of mankind. Precisely what that "defined era" may be, it is true, can be the subject of legitimate debate. John Van Seters, for example, who also accepts the Ur-Haran connection, argues that only in the time of Nabonidus (555–539 B.C.) of the Neo-Babylonian empire were there such conditions as are presupposed in the narrative of the patriarchal migration. On this basis he must, of course, prenounce the patriarchal stories devoid of any genuine historical reminiscences, since they can only be archaizing fiction spun out of events of a fairly recent past. Such a position can be quite plausible, simply because we know more about the Neo-Babylonian empire than we do about the Old Babylonian and consequently have less need for educated guessing. Educated guessing is still necessary, however, to sustain either hypothesis. In our judgment, the guessing that is necessary to sustain the hypothesis that the patriarchal narratives testify to an historical tradition older than the monarchical Israel is not stretched so thin as to strain credibility, and we believe also that the positive evidence here and there of venerable antiquity in these legends cannot be written off as invention or coincidence.

At the time these words are being written both the scholarly and the general press have begun to take note of the discoveries by Italian archeologists at ancient Ebla (the modern Tell Mardikh) in northern Syria, some thirty miles south of Aleppo. The excavations, carried out during the past several years and still continuing, have revealed the existence in the *third* millennium B.C. of a *Western* Semitic empire of extensive commercial and cultural influence which had left hardly a trace in human history till this decade of our present century, more than four thousand years later. Unfortunately, it is impossible at this time to assess what, if anything, the records of this northern Canaanite state will have to contribute positively to the study of the patriarchal history: no less than twenty thousand clay tablets have thus far been found, but as yet nothing has been officially published. We do know that some of the patriarchal nomenclature turns up at Ebla in routine fashion—names like Eber, Abraham, Ishmael, Israel, and Esau, along with other geographical and personal names found in Genesis and other parts of the Hebrew Bible. We also know, very interestingly, that at Ebla a deity was invoked under the name Yah or Ya'u.

And we know that Ur and Haran were related sites which had dealings with Ebla. But above all we know—the best that we can say under the present circumstances—that Ebla and, perhaps, the other Eblas that still await their finding, caution us against too hastily misbelieving the indications of great antiquity that are scattered through the patriarchal stories.

If we accept, at least for argument, that the patriarchal history is in its origins premonarchical with roots in the second rather than the first millennium B.C., the Ur with which the Terahites are putatively to be associated was the so-called Third Dynasty of Ur, or Ur III, a Sumerian culture with strong Semitic overtones. The Sumerians, neither Semites nor Aryans, were invaders who had entered Mesopotamia sometime toward the end of the fourth millennium B.C. Bearers and developers of a superior culture with a fair claim to have been the inventors of writing, law, and mathematics, the Sumerians ruled southern Mesopotamia through the polity of a series of dominant city-states, the last of which, beginning about 2500 B.C., was Ur. The Semitic color that was to characterize the later Ur III was owed to the Akkadians, also invaders into Mesopotamia, who from about 2360–2180 B.C. supplanted the Sumerians in Near Eastern politics by establishing the first world empire and a centralized government that embraced not only southern and northern Mesopotamia but also parts of Asia Minor as well. (They were contemporaries and rivals of the Eblaite kingdom which we mentioned above.) After the collapse of the Akkadian empire caused by the inevitable barbarian incursion from the north, Ur eventually emerged as the chief city of a reborn Sumer, the heir and cheerful carrier of venerable and sophisticated cultures political, literary, and artistic. It is just as well that we reflect on this fact, which has definite implications for the background of the patriarchal narrative that we try to reassemble from the sometimes conflicting strands of biblical testimony. If the tradition which links the Terahites with Ur of the Chaldeans is reliable, it may have more to suggest to us than simply a chronological tie with the Near Eastern past. It also associates the patriarchal ancestors with a city which possessed awesome credentials to the title of having been one of the foundresses of civilization as we know it. This thought must be weighed in the balance of probabilities when we assess the cultural and sociological slots into which the patriarchal history may with the most likelihood be fitted.

The renaissance of Ur III was short-lived. By 1960 B.C., the city was already in decline, and it was not to regain its prestige until a couple of centuries later when Elamite kings declared it a sacred place. The period of Ur's wane in the face of Elamite invasion also coincides with the incursions of the Amorites in the Near East, and it is likely that this development, too, has something to say with regard to the dating of the patriarchal history. The Elamites and Amorites ended by dividing the "empire" of Ur III between them. To this same period belongs the founding of the city of Babylon which was finally to lead to the rise of the Old (Amorite) Babylonian empire under the celebrated King Hammurabi (1728–1686 B.C.).

The Amorites (Sumerian *Martu,* Akkadian *Amurru*="westerners," i.e., people who lived west of Babylonia) were Semites who over a period of several centuries systematically invaded the so-called Fertile Crescent of lands surrounding the great Syrian desert from which they doubtless originally came. They formed only a part of one of those general reshufflings that occurred periodically in the ancient Near Eastern world, but there can be no doubt that theirs was one of the most lasting and influential of the political and cultural changes that emerged from the resultant ethnic turmoils. There was never, however, anything like an Amorite league or federation: the pattern of Amorite expansion became one of independent city-states often at rivalry with one another, a pattern which prevailed to the end in the west of the Fertile Crescent (Phoenicia and Canaan) and was ended in the east (Mesopotamia) only with the establishment of Hammurabi's empire. One of the chief Amorite city-states which we shall have occasion to mention later on was Mari on the Euphrates, the apogee of whose culture was reached about 1700 B.C. But—as might be expected from the consideration of their desert origins—the Amorites counted among their ranks not only builders of cities and adapters and improvers of the great civilizations that had preceded them in Sumer and Akkad, but also semi-nomads, people who lived on the fringes of settled society and served it in various capacities without, however, being a real part of it. We have to insist on all these complexities involved in the history of the times in order to suggest both the likelihoods and the obscurities which it presents for an interpretation of the biblical story of the patriarchs.

On the one hand, it might seem that in the history of Ur and Haran and of the Amorite incursions east and west throughout the Fertile Crescent we have a convincing framework in which to situate the story of Terahite origins as Genesis tells it. Like the Hebrews and later Israelites, the Amorites were Western Semites. It does not strain the probabilities to imagine Abraham's ancestors forming part of an Amorite population settled about Ur during the latter period of that city's Sumero-Akkadian existence, a population which moved with other elements of the declining Ur III up the Euphrates to Haran where again it settled, en route *to the land of Canaan* in one of the successive waves of Amorite migration. Ezekiel 16:3.45 counts the Amorites among the forebears of Israel and Judah, though to be sure it has in mind Amorites of the later Canaanite ethnic mixture rather than those of the earlier incursions. It is in keeping with the usual pattern that the satellite population we imagine should have shared the culture and religion of the Ur and Haran to which it was attached before it moved on farther west and south. In terms of the general plausibility of this historical background and in view of other chronological considerations which will appear later, we tend to concur with those who assign to Abraham a beginning date somewhere in the mid-nineteenth century B.C. This we could do with greater confidence were the evidence confined simply to those data we have sketched out above.

On the other hand, the patriarchal tradition is not of one piece but rather is a composite of disparate origins. It has remembered real people, perhaps, and has not simply personified symbols. But it has remembered these people faintly, and the sequence and structure within which it has placed these people and related them are at times conflicting and often quite artificial. As we shall soon see, the traditions are not at all agreed on the vital issue of the social class to which patriarchal society belonged, even though they usually portray it as pastoral and mobile, lending credibility to the hypothesis that it best corresponds with the less sedentary elements among the Amorite populations. Therefore we must conclude this initial attempt to situate the Terahites in world history with cautionary notes. At the same time, the surprising thing is not that we have to settle for conjecture and conditioned probabilities, but rather that in these matters we can realistically conjecture at all.

Sarai was barren; she had no child anticipates a theme to be developed in the Abraham story, concerning Isaac as a child of promise. However, in this J genealogy the obvious purpose of the note is primarily to explain why, as yet, no issue is to be ascribed to Abraham.

The lifetime of Terah was two hundred and five years: this is, of course, part of the P schematic chronology, according to which Abraham's lifespan was thirty years less than that of his father (cf. 25:7), in keeping with the usual policy of P to reduce the patriarchal ages progressively as they enter into historical times. If Abraham was born in Terah's seventieth year (11:26), and if he himself was seventy-five years old when he left Haran for Canaan (12:4), then it appears to be the meaning of the biblical author that Terah lived on in Haran for another sixty years after Abraham had departed his father's house. This conclusion conflicts with later Jewish tradition (reflected in Acts 7:4), which assumed that what is described in Genesis 12 all took place after *Terah died in Haran.* Sensitive to such an assumption, the Samaritan Pentateuch, no doubt through a deliberate alteration of the text, sets the lifetime of Terah in this verse at one hundred and forty-five years. However, there is no reason to wonder that the Priestly author should have found it appropriate for Terah to have continued the old life of the clan in Aram Naharaim whilst Abraham was beginning an entirely new era in Canaan: the separation between the two ways is thus made all the more real as both remained living options. Of the one hundred years which the biblical chronology allots to Abraham in

Canaan, the last forty only, a generation, would have been spent there after Terah's death. This calculation, too, may have had some significance for the mind of P.

2. The Call of Abraham

The narrative of the next two chapters is Yahwistic throughout with only occasional supplementary verses added from P. The latter have been indicated by italics.

12 The LORD said to Abram: "Go forth from the land of your kinsfolk and from your father's house to a land that I will show you.

2   "I will make of you a great nation,
        and I will bless you;
    I will make your name great,
        so that you will be a blessing.

3   I will bless those who bless you
        and curse those who curse you.
    All the communities of the earth
        shall find blessing in you."

4 Abram went as the LORD directed him, and Lot went with him. *Abram was seventy-five years old*
5 *when he left Haran. Abram took his wife Sarai, his brother's son Lot, all the possessions that they had accumulated, and the persons they had acquired in Haran, and they set out for the land of Canaan.*
6 *When they came to the land of Canaan,* Abram passed through the land as far as the sacred place at Shechem, by the terebinth of Moreh. (The Canaanites were then in the land.)
7 The LORD appeared to Abram and said, "To your descendants I will give this land." So Abram built an altar there to the LORD who had appeared to him.
8 From there he moved on to the hill country east of Bethel, pitching his tent with Bethel to the west and Ai to the east. He built an altar there to the
9 LORD and invoked the LORD by name. Then Abram journeyed on by stages to the Negeb.

There are some interesting contrasts between the vivid Yahwistic story of Abraham's call and the flat, matter-of-fact prose that is typical of the Priestly author's parallel contributions here and at other points in the patriarchal narrative. P's is simply the account of a man, his wife, and a nephew who continued a journey to Canaan that had been interrupted by a prolonged stay at Haran; the account continues in 13:6.11b–12 with an equally laconic narration of the need of Abraham and Lot to separate once they had reached Canaan, since the land was hardly able to sustain them both in one place in view of the greatness of their possessions. The J story is something quite different from this, telling of a divine summoning to grace and faith, the call of a man to desert his homeland and journey into the unknown and unfamiliar, into a land which at the last he is assured will be the possession of his descendants. In keeping with the theme of a man wholly dependent on providential designs, the Abraham of J cuts a modest figure, one that might be easily imagined of a shepherd leading his flocks to the best pasturelands and *pitching his tent* there: *Shechem, Bethel,* and *Ai* were all in the hill country of Palestine, where the land is plentifully watered. On the contrary, P almost goes out of its way to depict Abraham and Lot as oriental potentates, rich in slaves and other possessions, rulers over considerable material and personal domains. There are also other differences both in tone and content.

Perhaps of even greater importance is it to discern in the Yahwist's account of Abraham's entry into Canaan here and in the following chapter a pattern that reoccurs later on in a cross-section of all the sources when they tell the story of the patriarch Jacob. These are the significant parallels:

Abraham		*Jacob*	
12:6	the sacred place at Shechem	33:18	Shechem
	the terebinth of Moreh		
	the Canaanites in the land		in the land of Canaan
12:7	theophany: promise of the land	33:20	El, the God of Israel
	an altar built		a memorial stone
12:8	Bethel	28:11	Bethel
	an altar built	28:18	a memorial stone
		28:13	theophany: promise of the land
13:4	Bethel again and its altar	35:7	Bethel again and its altar
13:15	promise of the land	35:12	promise of the land
13:18	the terebinth of Mamre	35:8	the oak below Bethel
	an altar built	35:27	Mamre

The remarkable agreement that we find in both geographical sequence and related details has suggested to more than one scholar that a certain standardization had been imposed on the narrative, even in a preliterary stage, which purported to describe the route of an earliest father of Israel proceeding from the homeland "beyond the River" into and through the Land of Promise. This standardization doubtless featured locales that had already become religiously significant to the Israelites even as the Yahwist celebrates their religious significance in the above story: Shechem, Bethel, and Mamre had been first Canaanite and then Israelite sanctuaries and places of pilgrimage. Furthermore, the standardized route also probably brought with it a standardization of patriarchal roles. While both Abraham and Jacob have been associated in the tradition alike with a coming into Canaan from Aram Naharaim and with a descent from Canaan into Egypt (the latter, as regards Abraham, represented by the little story in vss. 10–20 below), the best guess is that we have to do here with an historical amalgam. As seems to be borne out in the further development of the patriarchal narratives, the tradition of Abraham, tied in with the hill country and the Shephelah of Judah and with the Negeb of Palestine, originally derived from tribal elements which only at some time later came to know of the tradition of Jacob, a figure who had been remembered in the sanctuaries of Ephraim to the north. (Jacob is sometimes given the proper name Israel, and this fact, too, doubtless points to an even earlier amalgam of separate patriarchal progenitors.) When the traditions were brought together, the tendency to mix them up proved irresistible. Form-critical considerations of this kind are needed to temper the urge that so often presents itself to ascribe to the biblical narrative a kind of objectivized history to which it never really aspired. But they can also raise serious objections to a view of the patriarchal stories that would like to see them as projections from the thought-frame of a late monarchic or exilic age—which could hardly have evinced the slightest interest in the ancient shrines of Palestine and its places of pilgrimage, all of which had been excoriated by the great prophets for various reasons and abolished in favor of the Jerusalem temple by the Deuteronomic reform.

It is altogether in keeping with the Yahwist's theology that God should simply "say" to Abraham that he should depart his homeland and embark upon the unknown, going *to a land that I will show you*. Abraham is being portrayed as a man totally obedient to the promptings of the divine will, in whatever ways this may have been indicated to him. *The land of your kinsfolk* should perhaps be rendered more literally "your land and your kinsfolk": as already observed in the section above, it is possible that J did not originally reflect the tradition that placed the beginnings of the Terahites in Ur of the Chaldeans rather than Aram Naharaim.

In vss. 2–3 complemented by the theophanic promise in vs. 7a we have the first instance of the theme of the divine blessing extended to the patriarchs according to whose terms the land of Canaan in which they lived as sojourners was to become the eventual possession of their descendants the Israelites. The Yahwist author brought to term a tradition which had gone before him, which had already united into the single kerygmatic history of a people the originally distinct strands of historical remembrance which form the stages of the exodus, the desert wandering, Sinai, the conquest, etc. In this united history the patriarchs are featured as ancestors of Israel and related peoples in whose providentially guided lives Yahweh's later special relationship with Israel was foreshadowed in various ways. Often the foreshadowing takes the form of a patriarchal covenant anticipating the great covenant of Sinai which Yahweh would later extend to Israel (see the comments on covenant with respect to Genesis 8:8–17 above). Here there is no explicit mention of covenant, unlike the parallel traditions about God and Abraham preserved in chapters 15 (J) and 17 (P). The idea of covenant is, nevertheless, present, both because one of the root meanings of "covenant" was "oath" or "promise," and, secondly, because the language of these verses has ultimately been borrowed from the liturgy of kingship in which the king was pictured as the recipient of a covenant promising numerous progeny, an enduring name, and universal domination (see especially Psalms, 2, 45, 72, and 89). The association is not linguistic alone: the royal covenant, of relatively recent absorption in Israel's historical experience, became the model according to which the ancient patriarchal traditions were interpreted. This development was singularly appropriate for inclusion in the Yahwistic history, where so often Abraham appears as the foreshadower as well as the forefather of the great King David.

The *great nation* which Yahweh promises to make of Abraham is, in this context, Israel itself, though it is also added that *all the communities of the earth shall find blessing in you.* The latter probably means here simply that Abraham will be for all mankind the exemplar of divine blessing: "may God bless us as he blessed Abraham!" (cf. Genesis 48:20). In later tradition, however, the blessing of Abraham was understood to have descended from him to "all the communities of the earth" (cf. Sirach 44:21; Acts 3:25; Galatians 3:8), and that sense is not really foreign to the redactional message of Genesis even though it is not yet explicit there. The Abraham for whose sake Yahweh blesses all who are well-disposed to him (*I will bless those who bless you*) is but a step removed from the Abraham whose very blessing they will share. We have already seen how the Priestly author has extended the covenantal principle to embrace the entire human race in the person of Noah.

The Yahwist has incorporated into his story the mention of various sites which were sacred in the Israel of his time and which he is anxious to show connected with the patriarchal ancestors of Israel of so long ago. *The sacred place at Shechem,* which we shall later see more intimately connected with Jacob, was one of these sites; its history is inextricably interwoven with the origins of Israel in Palestine, but with complexities which modern scholarship has to date not successfully unraveled (some of the complexities can be readily appreciated by a reading of Judges 9 and Joshua 24). Whatever the history of Shechem, it was of course a place sacred to the Canaanites before it became Israelite, hence the note that *the Canaanites were then in the land* is not so parenthetical as it appears in the text above. *The terebinth of Moreh* may also be rendered "the oracle-terebinth." Sacred trees were then as they are now common in the Near East, reputed to be the places of divine communication with man (see, for example, Judges 4:5 and 6:11, and, as regards this special tree at Shechem, Judges 9:6 and Joshua 24:26, and possibly Deuteronomy 11:30). Not only must Abraham be associated with these sacred places, however, he must also be shown to have, as it were, claimed them for Israel, having both at Shechem and Bethel *built an altar there to the* LORD *and invoked the* LORD *by name* (on the anachronistic naming of Yahweh, the God of Israel, see our remarks above on 4:26). That Abraham's second altar was built not at Bethel itself but in *the hill country east of Bethel* and *with Bethel to the west and Ai to the east* possibly indicates the biblical author's recognition of the precise location of the sanctuary of Bethel. Bethel, a shrine even more important than Shechem both in Canaanite and Israelite religious history, we shall consider later in the story of Jacob where it more properly belongs. Ai, which means "the Ruin," was, on the best judgment of Palestinian archeology, exactly that during the time of the patriarchs and of early Israel (the story of Joshua 8 notwithstanding): a celebrated heap of ruins of a long-abandoned city near Bethel. There would seem to be no doubt that Ai is to be identified with the modern et-Tell ("the Mound"), a couple of miles east of Beitin (Bethel), which has disgorged the remains of a city that died forever about 2400 B.C.

The reference to Ai, therefore, is a misguided attempt at historical reconstruction—a thing not peculiar to the Yahwist in the biblical chronicle. The rest of Abraham's itinerary, however, rings true, including his journey *by stages to the Negeb,* to what is now the southern desert, following a route that J evidently intends to suggest as that of a shepherd moving seasonally from place to place with his flocks. The archeological excavations of Tell Balatah (Shechem) and of Beitin, as well as explorations in the Negeb, have shown that these sites were both habitable and inhabited during the period which we have proposed as plausible for the migration of the Terahites into Canaan.

> 10 There was famine in the land; so Abram went down
>   to Egypt to sojourn there, since the famine in the
> 11 land was severe. When he was about to enter Egypt,
>   he said to his wife Sarai: "I know well how beauti-
> 12 ful a woman you are. When the Egyptians see you,
>   they will say, 'She is his wife'; then they will kill

13 me, but let you live. Please say, therefore, that you
are my sister, so that it may go well with me on
your account and my life may be spared for your
14 sake." When Abram came to Egypt, the Egyptians
15 saw how beautiful the woman was; and when Pharaoh's courtiers saw her, they praised her to Pha-
16 raoh. So she was taken into Pharaoh's palace. On
her account it went very well with Abram, and he
received flocks and herds, male and female slaves,
male and female asses, and camels.
17 But the LORD struck Pharaoh and his household
with severe plagues because of Abram's wife Sarai.
18 Then Pharaoh summoned Abram and said to him:
"How could you do this to me! Why didn't you
19 tell me she was your wife? Why did you say, 'She
is my sister,' so that I took her for my wife? Here,
then, is your wife. Take her and be gone!"
20 Then Pharaoh gave men orders concerning him,
and they sent him on his way, with his wife and all
that belonged to him.

Following the pattern that has paralleled the migrations of Abraham
and Jacob (outlined in the section above), a *famine in the land* explains
why Abraham *went down to Egypt to sojourn there* (note the beginning of
the story of 42:1). If we are permitted in addition to suggest a genuine
historical *situs* for the story in the spirit of the biblical author, we can
hardly venture outside the age of the so-called Middle Kingdom of Egypt
(2052–1778 B.C.), or, more precisely, outside the second half of that age
known as the Twelfth Dynasty, a period during which Egyptian civilization reached one of its highest peaks. During the Twelfth Dynasty there
was considerable traffic between Egypt and Canaan. For its part, Egypt asserted at least nominal hegemony over various of the city-states of Palestine, and there is evidence that it sometimes vindicated its claim by force
of arms, penetrating at least as far north as Shechem. At the same time,
Egypt felt that it had to maintain constant vigilance against incursions
from these same Semitic peoples of Canaan, whom it termed "the Asiatics," and in whose face it built at the isthmus of Suez a fortification
named the Prince's Wall ("wall"=*shur;* see below on 16:7). The situation
was ambiguous in the extreme. Much of the success of the Twelfth Dynasty was due to its use of mercenary troops which it had drawn from this
same inimical Semitic east which had helped it in the overthrow of the
southern Theban dynasty which had preceded it: many Amorite names
turn up in the Egyptian records of this period. At any rate, the Twelfth

Dynasty presided over an extremely prosperous Egyptian society that had been enriched by conquests north and south and by exploitation of an extensive mining industry in the Sinai, a fact that makes the description of the wealth showered on Abraham according to vs. 16 not at all hard to believe. Nor is there anything inherently improbable about the visit to a royal court of Egypt on the part of a prominent Asiatic chieftain in the context of the Fertile Crescent of the early second millennium B.C.

Reproduced in practically every atlas of the Bible is the wall painting from the tomb of an Egyptian noble of the Twelfth Dynasty which was discovered in the heyday of Egyptian archeology at Beni Hasan (a place midway between Thebes and the Mediterranean) and which depicts a Semitic, Asiatic, Amorite family of thirty-seven persons who entered Egypt from Canaan about 1900 B.C. The picture of Beni Hasan is undoubtedly very like what the Yahwist had in mind as he brought Abraham down from Canaan through the Negeb into Egypt. The leader of the Semitic group at Beni Hasan is named in the Egyptian commentary Absha or Ibshai (cf. the Abishai who was the kinsman of David in 1 Samuel 26:6 and afterward), therefore a right Western Semite. W. F. Albright has thus described the scene*:

> Both men and women wear woollen tunics made by sewing together strips of cloth woven in brightly coloured patterns; these tunics are draped over one shoulder, leaving the other bare. The only difference between men's and women's tunics indicated by the artist is that the women's reach half-way between ankle and knee, while the men's stop at the knee. However, some of the men wear long white (linen?) tunics, and some of them wear short tunics reaching only from the waist to the knee. The men generally wear sandals, but the women are shown wearing low leather boots. For weapons they carry a composite bow, throw-sticks, and darts. The least expected items of luggage are a lyre carried by one of the men and two bellows carried (with other things) by the asses. Obviously we are dealing here with travelling metal-workers, something like the tinkers of later times, who were still a sufficient oddity in Egypt to be represented for posterity by the local prince.

It would be unwarranted, of course, on the analogy of the Absha painting to make out Abraham as the leader of a caravan of itinerant smiths. Other details in the picture, however, can be carried over with consider-

* *The Archaeology of Palestine* (Penguin, 1954), pp. 207–8.

able confidence, including the significant item that Abraham's would undoubtedly have been a donkey caravan. The *camels* mentioned in vs. 16 above and subsequently in the patriarchal history are an anachronism, since it appears to be quite certain that the camel was not domesticated in the Near East until about the thirteenth century B.C. It was only with the introduction of the camel, as a matter of fact, that true nomadic existence in the desert was made possible. The donkey nomads of this earlier time were of necessity more restricted in their wanderings and thus tied more closely to the centers of settled life than the true nomads who succeeded them, who could travel swiftly and far on beasts whose needs did not include a steady water supply. We should keep these facts in mind when we attempt to visualize patriarchal society. However tempting it is to think of Abraham, Isaac, and Jacob in terms of the Bedawin whose way of life had invaded many of the paths once trod by the patriarchs (and however much the Bible itself can encourage the temptation to think in these terms), it is a fact that in the days of the Terahites there were no Bedawin and they could not yet be.

In the minds of many readers Abraham cuts a rather sorry figure in the story that lies before us, safeguarding his own skin and increasing his material possessions at the expense of his wife's truthfulness and her honor. It is not only later Jewish and Christian sensibilities that have been offended by the story. In the Elohistic doublet that appears in chapter 20 the point is made that Sarah was indeed Abraham's sister as well as his wife (a situation imaginable even in the J account, given the endogamous pattern of Terahite relationships noted above) and that her identification of herself as his sister was habitual and by prior agreement, virtually a part of her marriage contract. Also in this doublet and in the further J doublet of chapter 26 (this time featuring Isaac and Rebekah rather than Abraham and Sarah) it is made clear that while the patriarchal wife's virtue had been put in jeopardy it had in fact, providentially, been preserved from compromise. These two doublets likewise summon up compassion for the foreign prince (Abimelech, in these cases, rather than Pharaoh) on whom the trick has been played and do not leave him, therefore, quite the cipher and foil that he certainly is in this story. Hence it would appear that biblical tradition itself was not entirely at ease with the moral tone achieved in this present episode.

It would, nevertheless, be a mistake to apply to it judgments based on a value system which it simply did not possess, however much we may deplore the fact. The Yahwist is capable elsewhere of sensitivity to all the moral pieties which we might like to find honored in this story, but he did not find them in the story and it was not for their sake therefore that he and the Redactor after him preserved the story for Genesis. It was preserved for other reasons, because it portrayed Abraham as a man of shrewdness and sagacity in his time, even by an outmoded scale of priorities, and because it showed him to be under God's specific and continuous protection. We must respect the narrative for what it does and excuse it for what it does not. It is not, of course, the whole portrait of Abraham, as painted either by the Yahwist or by the rest of Genesis.

The story is a mélange of the credible and the unexplained. It does not, obviously, presuppose the Priestly author's chronology, according to which Sarah would have been over sixty-five years of age at this time (cf. Genesis 12:4b and 17:17). No attempt whatever is made to account for Pharaoh's perception of a divine visitation in the plagues that had afflicted him and his household or for the connection that he established between this phenomenon and the presence of Sarah in his harem. And what revealed to him that she was a wife and not a sister? The storyteller, single-mindedly devoted to the chronicle of the fathers and not to other issues of logic or even fair play, would doubtless have looked on such questions as frivolous and quite beside the point.

> **13** From Egypt Abram went up to the Negeb with his
> wife and all that belonged to him, and Lot ac-
> 2 companied him. Now Abram was very rich in live-
> 3 stock, silver and gold. From the Negeb he trav-
> eled by stages toward Bethel, to the place between
> Bethel and Ai where his tent had formerly stood,
> 4 the site where he had first built the altar; and there
> he invoked the LORD by name.
> 5 Lot, who went with Abram, also had flocks and
> 6 herds and tents, *so that the land could not sup-*
> *port them if they stayed together; their posses-*
> *sions were so great that they could not dwell to-*
> 7 *gether.* There were quarrels between the herdsmen
> of Abram's livestock and those of Lot's. (At this
> time the Canaanites and the Perizzites were occu-
> pying the land.)
> 8 So Abram said to Lot: "Let there be no strife be-
> tween you and me, or between your herdsmen and
> 9 mine, for we are kinsmen. Is not the whole land
> at your disposal? Please separate from me. If you
> prefer the left, I will go to the right; if you prefer
> 10 the right, I will go to the left." Lot looked about
> and saw how well watered the whole Jordan Plain
> was as far as Zoar, like the LORD's own garden,
> or like Egypt. (This was before the LORD had de-
> 11 stroyed Sodom and Gomorrah.) Lot, therefore

chose for himself the whole Jordan Plain and set out eastward. *Thus they separated from each other;*
12 *Abram stayed in the land of Canaan, while Lot settled among the cities of the Plain,* pitching his
13 tents near Sodom. Now the inhabitants of Sodom were very wicked in the sins committed against the LORD.
14 After Lot had left, the LORD said to Abram: "Look about you, and from where you are, gaze to
15 the north and south, east and west; all the land that you see I will give to you and your descendants
16 forever. I will make your descendants like the dust of the earth; if anyone could count the dust of the
17 earth, your descendants too might be counted. Set forth and walk about in the land, through its length
18 and breadth, for to you I will give it." Abram moved his tents and went on to settle near the terebinth of Mamre, which is at Hebron. There he built an altar to the LORD.

The action of Abraham and Lot reaching an agreement over their separate spheres of interest is typical of the *ad hoc* covenants by which civilized life was made possible in a simple, pastoral society (cf. the more formalized covenant between Abraham and Abimelech as described below in 21:22–32). In the Yahwist's purview, the separation was necessitated only now, after both Abraham and Lot—though the latter was not mentioned in the story of Abraham in Egypt—had been enriched at the expense of the Egyptians (like the later Israelites departing Egypt according to Exodus 12:35–36). In the Priestly author's summary version of the narrative, as we have already seen, the patriarchal family was wealthy even before it entered Canaan for the first time.

The biblical author does not represent this new affluence as the occasion of a falling out between the kinsmen but rather as a source of *quarrels between the herdsmen of Abram's livestock and those of Lot's* which could be the harbinger of future, more serious family strife. Abraham, foreseeing this possibility, appears once more in the guise of a wise and prudent man in making his proposal to Lot. He appears also as a man of generosity and magnanimity, leaving the first choice to his nephew and family inferior. Lot is not cast in a correspondingly selfish or mean-spirited role: it is only the part of good sense to seize the opportunity that offers most for oneself and one's family. Nevertheless, there is irony in the scene, for Genesis knows Lot to be a man for whom luck sours, whose choices inevitably end up badly. Now, as from the height of Bethel he *looked about* to the east (and south?) *and saw how well watered the whole Jordan Plain was as far as Zoar, like the* LORD's *own garden*—J's lost Eden of chapter 3—*or like Egypt*—the proverbially lush delta of the Nile which was the scene of the preceding episode—the way of wisdom must have seemed pathetically simple: of course, choose the Jordan Plain! The Yahwist, however, both in vs. 13 and in the parenthetical note in vs. 10 that *this was before the* LORD *had destroyed Sodom and Gomorrah,* anticipates the later destiny of the region which Lot chose, the subject of the account in chapters 18–19. The precise geography of this region we can better discuss below. For the moment, it can be observed that J and P may have had different views about its location. Though they both use the term *kikkar,* the Plain, for P this seems to be outside Canaan (vs. 12), while for J it is simply the Jordan valley. Both for J and P, it must be added, it is likely that the region's fabled greenery owes more to legend and wistful speculation than it does to any historical recollection.

Again, it is not altogether parenthetically that vs. 7 takes note of the occupation of the land by *the Canaanites and the Perizzites:* we are being reminded that Abraham and Lot were "dividing" a land that was not yet theirs, which had not yet been bestowed as God's gift. The Perizzites usually appear in the Bible (including Genesis 15:20, J) simply as one of many names to designate the indigenous inhabitants of Canaan before and after the Israelite "conquest." Here, however, and in 34:30 (J), as well as Judges 1:5 (J in spirit if not J in fact), Canaanites and Perizzites are listed together as though they constituted an exhaustive table of the aborigines. Some scholars have concluded from this that a primitive attempt was being made to differentiate between the Semitic inhabitants of Canaan (i.e., the Canaanites) and those who were not Semites, in which case Perizzites (a name possibly of Hittite origin) would have been made into a generic designation for the latter. Whatever is to be said for the theory, it is certainly true that the mainly Semitic population of Canaan in the time of the patriarchs also admitted of a considerable admixture of non-Semitic peoples who occupied their own centers and formed their own city-states. The Amorite invasions, as already pointed out, had been only a part of a much greater migration of peoples which had come before and after. Later passages in Genesis will point up the ethnic mixture that characterized the land of the patriarchal sojourn, which historical sources verify and Hebrew tradition had remembered more or less accurately.

The promise of the land in vss. 14–17 is quite plainly in parallel with the blessing of Abraham in 12:2–3.7 above. What these verses add, perhaps, is a certain solemnity to the divine assurance—again communicated by the casual speech of God to man—of countless progeny and future inheritance. The passage seems to have been tacked on by the Yahwist from one of the many sources of tradition that were open to him: for one thing, in the present context it appears to adopt the P perspective that Lot had definitively departed and left Canaan to Abraham as his exclusive preserve. More important than the parallel, for all its poetic qualities, is doubtless vs. 18 with its association of Abraham with *the terebinth* (the standard Hebrew text has "terebinths," in the plural) *of Mamre, which is at Hebron.* Here probably for the first time do we have a Palestinian locale that was from the beginning connected with the Abraham tradition and not simply made part of it by later assimilation. (Reciprocally, the connection of Jacob with Mamre in 35:27 is probably an instance of the same kind of assimilation in the other direction.) As further reading will bear out, the figure of Abraham in the Bible is with the greatest likelihood the product of historical recollections that had been gathered from Israelite ancestors who had inhabited the highlands of Judah and the Negeb. The recollections, long before they reached the stage at which we encounter them in Genesis, had been thoroughly refracted through storytelling into the directions and emphases that we now find so familiar and "scriptural." The concerns still latent in many of the stories, however, and in some of them far more clearly than in this present one, were the shrines and other sacred places of the land which had once given the people their identity and in whose association they recalled the deeds of their fathers. As a consequence, it is to the seemingly incidental "terebinth of Mamre" and like geographical marginalia that we may be ultimately indebted for much of this literature that has given spiritual solace and direction to other ages, other peoples, and other religions.

Mamre is no exception to the rule that has doomed most of the cult places of the patriarchal stories to later oblivion. It had evidently been forgotten even before biblical times, since the author has found it necessary to identify it as "at Hebron." Hebron itself, a city famous in Israel's history, did not yet exist in the time when Genesis has Abraham walk the length and breadth of the Judean hills. Because of its biblical associations, however, it is known to this day as El-Khalil, that is, "[the city of] the Friend [of God]"—after the name by which the Muslim Arabs call the patriarch Abraham.

3. Abraham and the Kings

Without any question whatever, chapter 14 of Genesis is one of the most controversial of this entire work. One does not need to read very far into it to learn why this should be so. It interrupts the natural sequence of chapters 13 and 15 by intruding in their midst an Abraham quite different from theirs, an Abraham of such a different life-style that he might almost be thought to inhabit a different world. Despite the slight redactional touches that have tenuously connected the chapter with the surrounding Abraham-Lot story, it is quite plain that it originally had nothing in common with the concept of a providentially guided history that permeates the rest of the patriarchal narrative. On the contrary, for the most part it reads like a secular chronicle, full of places and events that have neither a direct nor an indirect religious import. It is not surprising, therefore, that most critics and commentators deem this section to be an isolated fragment of saga altogether independent of the nominal sources of Genesis, neither J nor E nor P. This conclusion can be easily drawn; it is the easiest of all to draw. The Redactor of Genesis has admittedly on occasion gone outside his usual sources to introduce fresh material—chapter 49 is one example of this—and he has also, here and there, made up free compositions from his sources. We intend to argue, however, that chapter 14 could just as easily have been inserted into the J narrative by the Yahwist as into the final Genesis by R. In any event, it will remain for us to show in the commentary why someone thought it important enough to disturb an earlier and more conventional story of Abraham by intruding upon it this highly unconventional piece of prose that had also chronicled (another?) Abraham.

Along with most present-day commentators we are persuaded of the antiquity of the data of this chapter. There is a growing number of critics, however, who are disposed to regard the production as a whole as an antiquarian reconstruction from fairly late times, and their arguments must be taken seriously and considerately. In the past, before the controls of archeology and paleography were applied to Old Testament studies, Genesis 14 could be cheerfully ascribed, fairly much at the whim of the literary critic, indifferently to eyewitness annals of a putative second-millennium age of Abraham or to midrashic imagination of the time of Judas Maccabeus (175–164 B.C.) or to practically anything in between. The past is now on the return, this time with the resources of archeology and paleography, which seem to lead to some rather contrary conclusions. Genesis 14 does breathe, geographically and historically, an ancient air; on this point there is no dispute. Whether it is the still-living atmosphere of historical memory or the musty exhalation of reconstituted matter has to be decided.

> 14 In the days of . . . , Amraphel king of Shinar,
>   Arioch king of Ellasar, Chedorlaomer king of Elam,
>   2 and Tidal king of Goiim made war on Bera king of
>   Sodom, Birsha king of Gomorrah, Shinab king of
>   Admah, Shemeber king of Zeboiim, and the king of

3 Bela (that is, Zoar). All the latter kings joined
forces in the Valley of Siddim (that is, the Salt
4 Sea). For twelve years they had been subject to
Chedorlaomer, but in the thirteenth year they re-
5 belled. In the fourteenth year Chedorlaomer and the
kings allied with him came and defeated the Rephaim in Ashteroth-karnaim, the Zuzim in Ham, the
6 Emim in Shaveh-kiriathaim, and the Horites in the
hill country of Seir,* as far as El-paran, close by the
7 wilderness. They then turned back and came to Enmishpat (that is, Kadesh), and they subdued the
whole country both of the Amalekites and of the
8 Amorites who dwelt in Hazazon-tamar. Thereupon
the king of Sodom, the king of Gomorrah, the king
of Admah, the king of Zeboiim, and the king of
Bela (that is, Zoar) marched out, and in the Valley
9 of Siddim they went into battle against them: against
Chedorlaomer king of Elam, Tidal king of Goiim,
Amraphel king of Shinar, and Arioch king of El-
10 lasar—four kings against five. Now the Valley of
Siddim was full of bitumen pits; and as the kings†
of Sodom and Gomorrah fled, they fell into these,
11 while the rest fled to the mountains. The victors
seized all the possessions and food supplies of
Sodom and Gomorrah and then went their way,
12 taking with them Abram's nephew Lot, who had
been living in Sodom, as well as his possessions.

Yohanan Aharoni represents one contemporary scholarly view of the
itinerary followed by the kings in this story: that it "describes faithfully the
main centres of occupation along the King's Highway in Transjordan and
also those in the Negeb. Therefore, the text probably has preserved a
memory of the event that put an end to the settlement there during the
twentieth century B.C., although the broad historical background is still
unknown." It is true that this broad historical background is unknown and
possibly it is forever destined to remain so; it was obviously not known to
the biblical author, whose anacoluthic text (*In the days of . . .*) is mute
testimony to the haze and mists through which this vision of the past, if indeed it is such a vision, had so barely worried its way. Nevertheless, the
historian must be grateful for his sources wherever he finds them, and even
if he has to wipe away the patina of countless unhistorical concerns before

* So the ancient versions. Hebrew: "in their mountains, Seir."
† So the ancient versions. Hebrew: "the king of Sodom and Gomorrah."

ever he can recognize them as sources. There is no reason that this chapter of Genesis should not have provided us with authentic information about an ancient event simply because it happens to be the only witness we have to the event—always provided that it carries with it credentials that can survive critical scrutiny.

The first part of the story is not, in the main, implausible. The invading "kings," to be sure, in a chronicle of less heroic and perhaps more factual proportions might have been identified as lieutenants acting in the interests of their overlords. But certain details that otherwise surround these individuals do ring true. After the collapse of Ur III and until the rise of Babylonian dominance under Hammurabi, the Elamites were more or less the masters of the old Sumero-Akkadian empire and the determiners of Mesopotamian politics. In this story it is the *king of Elam* who heads the punitive expedition of Mesopotamian kings, and it was to him that the Canaanite kings *had been subject for twelve years*. The name *Chedorlaomer* is genuinely Elamite: a modern transliteration would be *kudur lagamar*, "slave of Lagamar," an Elamite deity. It should be added at once that the name does not appear in the known king list of the Elamites, and that for that matter most scholars find the presence and hegemony of the Elamites in southern Canaan at this time unlikely in the extreme. *Amraphel king of Shinar* bears a Western Semitic name (*amar pi el*, "the mouth of the god has spoken") appropriate to the Amorite dynasty that was then abuilding in Babylon. (Both linguistic and chronological considerations forbid the once popular identification of Amraphel with Hammurabi, since Mari documents have made it certain that the latter did not reign for yet another couple of centuries.) *Arioch king of Ellasar* involves a known Mesopotamian proper name (Ariwuk, Eri-aku) and what just possibly could be Larsa, the city in southern Mesopotamia north of Ur. *Tidal*, it is generally agreed, corresponds with the name Tudhaliya found in many cuneiform texts. It was the name of several Hittite kings, but it also pre-existed Hittite times. This Tidal was *king of Goiim:* though capitalized by NAB, insinuating a geographical designation, *goiim* is simply the Hebrew for "nations." It may be the translation of an Akkadian term originally used to characterize various peoples (Elamites, among others) who came, usually as invaders, from beyond the pale of conventional and familiar society—almost the precise equivalent of what the Greeks and Romans of a later day would call the "barbarians."

The cumulus of this admittedly shaky alliance of biblical nomenclature with the data extracted from Mesopotamian cuneiform weighs in, first of all, in support of an opinion that we judge preferable to another, namely that Genesis 14 has genuinely preserved historical tradition rather than given us the historical fiction of a post-Deuteronomic theological writer (the ultimate verdict of the late Roland de Vaux, who earlier had brilliantly defended the antiquity of the passage). (We would argue: if one would like to test the accuracy with which a post-Deuteronomic author was able to reconstruct even the fairly recent past in the lack of authentic sources, let him reread the fantastic history and geography proposed by the books of Esther, Daniel, Judith, Tobit, and then compare these with Genesis 14. Yet at least one present-day scholar has put the Arioch of Daniel 2 and Judith 1:6—a name which, like those of Nebuchadnezzar, Arpachshad, Cyrus, Darius, et al., we would assume these anthological works derived from earlier biblical sources like Genesis 14—on a par with the Arioch of vss. 1.9 above as though they are of one piece in Israel's literary history.) What we know of ancient Near Eastern civilization outside the Bible we generally owe to discoveries that began only in the past two centuries of the era we call Christian. Until that time all this knowledge, incised on clay tablets or scratched on stone or mutely locked in a maze of walls and gates of forgotten cities which only a trained specialist can penetrate, had lain dormant under sand and soil almost from the moment that it ceased to have immediate relevance for its contemporaries. History—instant history—was possible in the ancient Near East to those who were in immediate proximity to it just as it is possible to us nowadays, but history—the documented reconstitution of the past for a later age—was neither possible nor even desirable in the intervening centuries and millennia. Aharoni may have his dates wrong in connection with this present episode, but he is probably not wrong in principle. Not, especially, if we try to relate this chapter, as the author of Genesis evidently thought it should be related, to the other historical suggestions gleaned from the traditions of Ur and Haran and Aram Naharaim which circumscribe it. So far we have talked only about the Mesopotamian kings. Now we might take a look at the geography of the passage, which is possibly of even greater significance in respect to its historical reliability, as was claimed by Aharoni above.

The *Valley of Siddim* is identified with *the Salt Sea*. For one thing, this identification may preserve an ancient name for the lower Jordan valley that was no longer in use at the time these verses were committed to writing. But it may also indicate a belief held by the biblical author, and possibly shared by J in 13:10 above, that in the patriarchal age, or at least until the destruction of Sodom and Gomorrah, there was as yet no Dead Sea. If that was, indeed, the belief, it was of course misguided, for the topography of Palestine has not undergone any appreciable change within the historical age of man. (It should also be observed that while the source used by J in chapter 13 thought of the Jordan valley and, perhaps, of the continuation of the valley in the Dead Sea declivity as universally lush pastureland, the present source more realistically has it that *the Valley of Siddim was full of bitumen pits.*) The other two sites whose names are given "modern" equivalents in vss. 1–12 are Bela=Zoar, of which in a moment, and *Enmishpat,* which is said to be the same as the famous *Kadesh* in the Negeb, a cult center (the Hebrew underlying Kadesh contains the idea of a "holy" place) which figured prominently in the formation of at least some of the tribal components of the later Israelite people (cf. Deuteronomy 1:2.46: Kadesh became the focus of the "forty-years wandering" as the tradition was assimilated into the kerygmatic history of Israel). The identification is probable enough. Enmisphat means in Hebrew "spring where judgment is given," a designation not at all inappropriate for an oasis popularly associated with the giving of divine oracles. The place that nowadays has the best archeological claim to have been the biblical Kadesh is, certainly, a spring: in Arabic, Ain el-Qudeirat.

Another device that has been used in this chapter to update the geography while at the same time preserving its ancient flavor is the laying of older and newer names side by side so as to form an historically unreal composite. *Ashteroth-karnaim* is undoubtedly Ashtaroth (named for the fertility goddess Astarte), the capital of Bashan (Deuteronomy 1:4, etc.), which has been identified with the nearby Karnaim ("horns," a frequent surrogate to express "power," especially divine power), which is probably mentioned for the first time in Amos 6:13. Ironically, Ashtaroth is perfectly recognizable today on a map of Palestine as a mound which goes by the name of Tell Ashtar, while Karnaim's name as well as its identity have been buried at a place called Sheikh Saad. *Shaveh-kiriathaim* is in all likelihood a composite of the same order. Shaveh, which almost certainly means "plain" (see on vs. 17 below), is not here otherwise particularized, but the place to which it once referred has been equated with Kiriathaim, a city which at one time pertained to the tribe of Reuben (Numbers 32:37) though it later entered the Moabite sphere of influence (Jeremiah 48:1). And as for *Hazazon-tamar,* in the first element we doubtless have to do with a name and a place of which only this text has preserved a memory, which was therefore identified for the reader with a Tamar which he did know, deep in the south of Judah (Ezekiel 47:19). The only other two ancient names in the itinerary which go unexplained for this later reader appear to be *Ham* and *El-paran, close by the wilderness,* and probably for the simple reason that no explanation was thought necessary. Ham, though it is a geographical term found only here in the Bible, is a place-name preserved to this day in the northern Transjordan, at just about the precise spot it ought to be according to the route of the kings described in this passage. El-paran, at the edge of the wilderness of Paran that lies between the Dead Sea and the Gulf of Aqabah in the eastern part of the Sinai, could hardly have suggested to the earliest biblical reader of this text any other location than the one that occurs to practically every sophisticated reader today, namely, the port which in Israelite times was known as Elath or Ezion-geber. It remains today, or nearby, as the resort town of Eilat, roughly two hundred kilometers down the Ghor fault to the sea.

We have deliberately introduced the consideration of distance because it has a direct bearing on the imputation of historical credibility that we may or may not be permitted to apply to this chapter of Genesis. We said above that the verses we have thus far seen do not tell a story that in the balance is implausible. We can repeat the assertion, which has been corroborated by particulars that we have already detailed and will be strengthened by others that we shall mention in a moment. But it must be admitted that the story contains enough internal caveats to justify the verdict passed on it nearly seventy years ago by Hermann Gunkel (even though on evidence that argued neither as positively nor as negatively as he believed) that it "contains in shrieking contrast that which may very well be believed and that which is totally impossible." Must we include the magnificent scope and sweep of the march from Ashteroth-karnaim to the Valley of Siddim as among those elements "totally impossible" of belief? It would doubtless have to be so were we to confine this historical remembrance to those narrow dimensions which were alone of interest to the biblical writer, simply of a punitive expedition against some relatively insignificant towns of southern Canaan. If, however, the event recalled was actually a much more comprehensive campaign in which the involvement of the five Canaanite kings had been merely one episode out of many, then both the distances traversed by the invaders and their apparently roundabout route can make their own sense. What we seem to have before us is the description of an elaborate *razzia,* a raiding expedition of hit and run, highly mobile and erratic by design, whose primary object was plunder and booty. The periodic appearance of the *razzia,* small and large, was a familiar experience in these times of transition and change, when newly sedentary populations so easily became the ready prey to predators among the many other peoples about them who were still in feverish movement.

The invasion about which Genesis 14 tells follows the classic pattern of entry from the north, through the upper reaches of the Fertile Crescent: it would be many centuries yet before invading forces would be capable of crossing the great desert to the east of Palestine. From Ashtaroth the raiders proceed south through Transjordan, following the so-called King's Highway (cf. Numbers 20:17), a natural route more or less dictated by the topography of the land, to Ham, then Shaveh, through Edom (Seir), all the way to the terminus at the Gulf of Aqabah. As they go, they plunder, defeating various peoples in each place they encounter. The best indications which the limited archeology of this considerable region has been able to provide do confirm, indeed, that from Ashtaroth to Edom the King's Highway passed through a region that was throughout densely settled during this period with which we are presumably concerned, Middle

Bronze Age I, or perhaps the earlier part of Middle Bronze II. Even more importantly, the same indications are that after this time there was no sedentary population in that area, not again till toward the end of Late Bronze II, when the Israelite people began to appear in Palestine. The further path of the invasion, from Enmishpat to Hazazon and the region of the Dead Sea, has revealed to the archeologist the same pattern of settlement interrupted by the same lengthy period in which the land lay mainly abandoned to none but nomadic life. In the circumstances of the time to which we wish to assign it, therefore, the itinerary of the invaders is not at all illogical; their route was a perfectly natural one. The names given the peoples whom they encountered, however, seem to have been borrowed by the biblical author from the catalogue of nations which later tradition listed as the pre-Israelite inhabitants of Canaan. All of them except *the Zuzim* (who may be the Zamzummim of Deuteronomy 2:20) appear elsewhere in the Pentateuchal traditions in a variety of relationships and localizations. *The Rephaim* (except for 15:20) and *the Emim* (exclusively in Deuteronomy 2:10–11) are heard of afterward only in the story of the Israelite conquest. *The Amorites* we have seen above, and *the Horites* and *the Amalekites* we shall meet again in Genesis.

Sodom, Gomorrah, Admah, Zeboiim, and *Zoar,* by which "modern" name an earlier *Bela* is identified, form the pentapolis which is the geographical focus of interest of this passage. Though the engagement in the Valley of Siddim where the leaders of the five cities *joined forces* seems by the logic of the story to have been simply the final of a successful series of skirmishes won by the invading "kings," the viewpoint of the tradition as it had been preserved for the biblical author was that the repression of the pentapolis had been the primary purpose of the invasion. Undoubtedly this viewpoint is a reflection of the local interests which ensured the preservation of the tradition in the first place, including the remembrance of four of the five names of the kings. (The names are not important as were those of their foreign counterparts, but that they are four and not five strongly argues that the four are genuine pieces of the past and not convenient figments.) All five cities of the pentapolis figure frequently in Scripture, usually as cautionary examples of the effects of divine wrath and retribution stemming from the famous story of Genesis 18–19. Genesis 18–19 (J) actually proposes Sodom alone for this exemplary character, with Gomorrah added as a kind of afterthought; the evocation in a parallel sense of Admah and Zeboiim in Hosea 11:8 may indicate an alternative, "Elohistic" tendency to make these other two cities the villains of the piece. In keeping with the Yahwistic emphasis, from vs. 10 on in this story concern with the five cities narrows down to Sodom and Gomorrah alone, and from vs. 17 on to Sodom alone. The story presupposes that the cities were in the Dead Sea area (or in what, from its standpoint, was the area later covered by the Dead Sea). We shall have to particularize on this presupposition below.

In vs. 12, as we ventured the opinion above, we probably have the redactional suture by which the biblical author integrated the Abraham of this story into the Abraham-Lot saga of the preceding chapter and of chapters 18–19.

> 13 A fugitive came and brought the news to Abram the
> Hebrew, who was camping at the terebinth of
> Mamre the Amorite, a kinsman of Eshcol and Aner;
> 14 these were in league with Abram. When Abram
> heard that his nephew had been captured, he mus-
> tered‡ three hundred and eighteen of his retainers,
> born in his house, and went in pursuit as far as
> 15 Dan. He and his party deployed against them at
> night, defeated them, and pursued them as far as
> 16 Hobah, which is north of Damascus. He recovered
> all the possessions, besides bringing back his kins-
> man Lot and his possessions, along with the women
> and the other captives.
> 17 When Abram returned from his victory over Ched-
> orlaomer and the kings who were allied with him,
> the king of Sodom went out to greet him in the Val-
> ley of Shaveh (that is, the King's Valley).

A fugitive is actually in the text *"the* fugitive": the reference is not to someone already mentioned but simply to the inevitable fugitive by whom the news of defeat is brought to the loser. In the story as it lies before us, Abraham is informed of the disaster because of Lot's involvement with it; however, it is likely that Lot has been introduced secondarily into vss. 14 and 16 as already in vs. 12, and we must probably look for another expla-nation of the original link between Abraham and the fortunes of Sodom and Gomorrah. Whether *the terebinth* of Mamre* is here a further redac-tional element of the biblical author or was integral to the story from the beginning and thus an aid in the association of its hero with the Abraham of the surrounding chapters, we cannot determine. What is interesting, in any case, is that the Mamre which in 13:18 is clearly a place here is no less clearly a person, *Mamre the Amorite, a kinsman of Eshcol and Aner.* Eshcol was likewise the name of a place (Numbers 13:22–24), a valley

---

‡ A conjectural translation based on the Septuagint. The Hebrew is obscure.
* As in 13:18 and again in 18:1 below, the NAB reads with the ancient versions a singular in each case. The plural of the existing Hebrew text is suspect of pious alter-ation designed to convert the memory of a now proscribed sacred tree into a harm-less secular grove.

near Hebron. (According to the Hebrew text of 1 Chronicles 6:55 there was even a city named Aner. However, NAB has rightly read there Taanach instead of Aner, adopting the parallel of Joshua 21:25. There are good text-critical grounds to cause us to suspect that some other name than Aner once stood at Genesis 14:13.) It would be difficult to scout the hypothesis that chapter 14 has invented some eponymous heroes to account for well-known places of the past whom it thereupon, in keeping with the military posture which Abraham assumes in the story, identified as native chieftains who *were in league with Abram* (or literally, his "covenant partners").

In truth, the Abraham of Genesis 14, introduced to us as though for the first time in vs. 13, is something else than the pastoral Abraham of the chapters before and after it, something else than even the pastoral Abraham enriched by the wealth of Egypt. He is called *Abram the Hebrew,* a designation that immediately calls for comment in view of the conflicting interpretations that have been given it.

In the Old Testament "Hebrew" does not seem to have been a term that the Israelites used of themselves but rather one that had been bestowed on them. As we saw at 10:24 above, nothing much was made about Eber as father of the Hebrews, even though the biblical author doubtless intended the eponymy to be noted. In 39:14.17 and 41:12 it is Egyptians who speak about "Hebrews," and in 40:15 Joseph identifies himself as a Hebrew only when accommodating himself to Egyptian language. The same phenomenon reoccurs outside Genesis in the Old Testament: always "Hebrew" is a foreign word, not one convertible with "Semite" or "Arab" or "Israelite." It is not, in other words, an ethnic determinant.

Neither is it, we believe, in the law of Exodus 21:2 developed and modified by Deuteronomy 15:12 (cf. Jeremiah 34:9.14), the legislation regulating the treatment of the "Hebrew slave." Contrary to the opinion of some commentators, "Hebrew" here does not distinguish from the ordinary chattel slave of foreign extraction one who had been taken from the ranks of Israel itself or from some people related to it by blood and history, whose servitude was of a different kind and subject to special protections and solicitudes. We side with scholars like Cassuto and Alt, who maintain that "Hebrew" was in the first place a social designation not *per se* connected with anything ethnic or national. It is in the light of their studies about "Hebrews" in general that we feel we have an insight as well into the sense of the "Hebrew" of Genesis 14:13.

Their hypothesis involves a consideration of the relationship of the "Hebrew" of Genesis 14:13 and Exodus 21:2—we leave out of consideration for the present other uses of the word in the Old Testament—with those who in the cuneiform literatures of the ancient Near East are called Habiru or 'Apiru. The discussion of this relationship is both an old one and a new one, and it has led to some very diverse scholarly conclusions. There is hardly any question in anyone's mind, however, that there is some kind of connection between the two terms, even though the simple equations that once seemed so obvious have had to be abandoned.

Let us summarize as briefly as we can some of the more pertinent data which the cuneiform sources have provided about the Habiru. They first appear in a text from Ur III where they are simply listed as foreign elements. In a text from Asia Minor of the nineteenth century B.C. they figure as prisoners of war destined for ransom. In eighteenth-century texts from the Amorite cities of southern Mesopotamia they are described as mercenary soldiers; the Mari texts frequently portray them as enemy marauders, but in Hammurabi's Babylon they are in the service of the king, under the charge of a royal official. In the fifteenth-century texts from Hurrian Nuzi beyond the Tigris they are foreigners who render certain services and who voluntarily sell themselves into slavery, presumably as a means of improving their social and economic security. In the fifteenth- and fourteenth-century Amarna letters (sent to the Egyptian Pharaoh by vassal kings in Canaan and Syria) the Habiru again emerge as bands of marauders, sometimes harassing the city-states of the land and sometimes in their hire as mercenary support. Also in Hittite texts of the fourteenth and thirteenth centuries they turn up as foreign mercenaries. There is much more, of course, but what we have now seen should be enough for our purposes. While the Habiru evidently are not always the same from century to century and place to place, there are nevertheless certain common denominators. They are foreigners in the regions which they inhabit, which they alternatively serve in various capacities or prey upon. They are not a single ethnic group: the names of the Habiru that have been preserved confirm what the geographical distribution would indicate, that while they were most frequently Semites they also numbered among themselves peoples of other extractions. Habiru, which appears to have been a Western Semitic or Amorite word originally, and whose exact meaning is still disputed, designated not an ethnic but a social class.

In Genesis 14 Abraham is portrayed as the commander of a sizable band of *retainers, born in his house,* allied with (other) Amorite chieftains of the region, who either on the spur of the moment or by prior agreement (in the original perspective of the story, probably the latter) commits his troops to the service of the king of Sodom and makes its cause his own. Just as the "Hebrew" slave of Exodus 21:2 corresponds with some of the phenomenology attaching to the survey of Habiru which we have reviewed above, so does the "Hebrew" Abraham correspond with some other of it. The Septuagint in this passage translated "Hebrew" by *perates,* which might be rendered "outlander." It is very likely that such was the import that "Habiru" had for the settled peoples of the ancient Near East when they used the term. Its use here in that sense, if we are correct in our understanding of it, enhances the flavor of antiquity of which this chapter is so often redolent. At the same time it does not argue against the contention of those who hold to another interpretation of "Hebrew" in their analysis of Genesis 14, namely that it is a token of a tale of non-Israelite provenance.

The number of Abraham's troops, according to vs. 14, was *three hundred and eighteen*. Is this meant to seem a small number, as the Old Testament so casually deals in random numbers, thus pointing up the magnitude of Abraham's victory over superior odds? Or is it a large number, relative to what were probably the actual dimensions of the raiding party of the "kings," thus testifying to Abraham's prowess as a musterer of fighting men? Exact numbers in ancient documents always rouse the suspicions of the commentator and tax his ingenuity in determining where they came from, since it seems to him so improbable that they really go back to sober historical fact. In 15:2 the household of Abraham—the much more modest Abraham of chapters 12–13 is there resumed—is epitomized in the person of his chief servant who is named Eliezer. It happens that the numerical value of this name (in Hebrew consonants, *'ly'zr*) is precisely three hundred and eighteen. But the coincidence is undoubtedly only that, a coincidence. Even though we tend to believe that both chapters 14 and 15 have felt the redactional hand of J and that the one is therefore aware of the other, still, it is not the wont of the Yahwistic author to anticipate P in playing the numbers game. Furthermore, it is altogether unlikely that the numerical shorthand employing the letters of the Hebrew alphabet already existed in biblical times. There is no compelling reason to reject the number three hundred and eighteen here as a traditional datum any more than there is to reject the traditional datum of "Hebrew." In like manner, there is nothing entirely unbelievable about Abraham's pursuit of the "kings" as described in vss. 15–16, extending from Hebron (i.e., Mamre) up the Jordan valley all the way to *Dan* (anachronistically named, cf. Joshua 19:47, Judges 18:29) and *Hobah* (unknown), *which is north of Damascus* (very well known indeed, one of the world's truly ancient cities). We are being told of a guerrilla operation, of repeated strikes particularly *at night,* by which eventually the enemy was worn down and persuaded to abandon its booty, or enough of it at least to satisfy the pursuers and so permit an unharried withdrawal to the north.

In vs. 17 Abraham is pictured returning fresh from victory over the invading kings and being met in *the Valley of Shaveh* by *the king of Sodom,* on whose behalf he had acted. The Valley of Shaveh ("the plain") may very well have been for the original source a locale in the vicinity of the Shaveh of vs. 5, there identified with Kiriathaim. If so, Abraham and the king of Sodom would have been brought together not far from the Valley of Siddim where the Canaanite kings had been defeated. The biblical author, however, less interested in history than he was in theology, has decided that the Valley of Shaveh should be *the King's Valley,* having in mind no doubt the place of that name near Jerusalem that had been so known from Davidic times (cf. 2 Samuel 18:18). That site cannot be precisely pinpointed by us on a modern map, but in any case it has been introduced only in view of the following Melchizedek episode which was not in original sequence with vs. 17. The narrative begun in vs. 17 is continued and completed in vss. 21–24 below.

> 18 Melchizedek, king of Salem, brought out bread and
>   wine, and being a priest of God Most High, he
>   blessed Abram with these words:
> 19   "Blessed be Abram by God Most High,
>   the creator of heaven and earth;
> 20   And blessed be God Most High,
>   who delivered your foes into your hand."
>   Then Abram gave him a tenth of everything.

These three verses tell a little story of their own and respond to interests which are not those of the remainder of the chapter. They likewise interrupt the account of Abraham's meeting with the king of Sodom and quite evidently have been inserted into a context with which they originally had nothing to do. Nobody to date has come up with a better explanation of the provenance of these verses than Hermann Gunkel, who expressed the opinion that they form a variant doublet on what are now vss. 17.21–24, making an alliance between Abraham and Melchizedek rather than between Abraham and the king of Sodom the historical situation lurking at the background of this chapter.

Various scholars, accordingly, have been disposed to agree with W. F. Albright in his conjecture that instead of *Melchizedek, king of Salem* which we have in the present Hebrew text and which was also read by the Septuagint, there was at one time a "Melchizedek, a king allied with him" (we would have to suppose that an earlier Hebrew *melek shelemo* had become deformed into *melek shalem*). Albright's hypothesis is not at all unlikely and might explain why the Melchizedek fragment was preserved in the first place. However, we may be sure that when this chapter was put together it was clearly understood that the story had to do with a king of Jerusalem, whether or not "Salem" had originally been in the text and, if so, whether or not it had originally referred to Jerusalem in any case. (An Egyptian record indicates that there was a Salem in northern Israel, which some scholars have located near Shechem [cf. John 3:23], thus conjecturing that the Melchizedek episode once had to do with a Shechemite priesthood and shrine.)

Melchizedek's name means "Zedek [a god, equivalent to the Greek *Dike*=Justice] is my king." Another king of Jerusalem whose name we know testifies to the cult of the same deity: Adonizedek (Joshua 10:1–3), "Zedek is my lord." (The Adonibezek of Judges 1:5–7 has been proposed as a corruption of the same name, though others have argued conversely that Adonizedek is the corrupted form of Adonibezek.) The prophet Isaiah, whose practice it was to invoke the ancient virtues and traditions of Jerusalem, spoke of it as the city where Zedek once lodged and which had now been pre-empted by murderers (Isaiah 1:21); this personification of justice possibly recalls a former title of Jerusalem that the prophet would like to have restored: City of Zedek, city of righteousness (vs. 26). On such grounds it has been thought appropriate that a king of Jerusalem in the time of Abraham should have been called Melchizedek.

"Salem," on the other hand and despite its reappearance in Psalm 76:3, probably was never a usual name for Jerusalem. In the Amarna letters the city is listed as Urusalim, an Eastern Semitic spelling which aids in the definition of its meaning: roughly, "Salim [the name of a god] has laid the foundation." The same spelling is said to turn up in the documents of third-millennium B.C. Ebla in northern Canaan. We cannot say for sure that the Salem of Genesis 14 was indeed Jerusalem in the original construction of these verses, but we can be quite certain that it was so for the ultimate author who found therein a means to bring Abraham and Jerusalem into association, an association he had to make even at the expense of interrupting the flow of his narrative. By this story Abraham, and in Abraham the seed of Israel, is brought into intimate contact with that which was destined to be the holy city of David, and accordingly Abraham receives the blessing of the Jerusalemite priesthood.

From Psalm 110:4 we know the important role that was played by the Melchizedek tradition in the Jerusalem temple liturgy of the Israelite monarchy. Obviously a remembered figure from the pre-Israelite past much as Genesis 14 portrays him, Melchizedek was held up as a prototype of the priest-king ideal that was thought to be realized in the divinely established Davidic dynasty. That the Canaanite king Melchizedek should also have been the chief priest of his realm was merely in keeping with the ancient Near Eastern conception of what a king must be. When the Israelites who at first had no king eventually adopted kingship they naturally took as their model the kingly estate that they saw all about them and in their midst, and this included the king's priestly character. Both David and Solomon officiated as priests (2 Samuel 6:13–14.18, 1 Kings 8:14–15.55), and David's sons were explicitly called priests (2 Samuel 8:18). Only by degrees did a separate, hereditary, professional priesthood—another institution which the Israelites shared in common with their neighbors—minimize and at last eliminate the priestly prerogatives that had once been conceded to the king, so that finally even their memory could be a source of embarrassment to a later theology (cf. the rewriting of 2 Samuel 8:18 in 1 Chronicles 18:17). Both Genesis 14 and Psalm 110 seem to antedate this later theology both in years and in spirit.

The author of Genesis 14 was doubtless as intrigued as the author of Psalm 110 by the possession of a bit of tradition that featured a priest-king in Jerusalem, a foreshadowing of the priest-king who now reigned there. However, the focus of interest for the author of Genesis is not Melchizedek but Abraham. Not Melchizedek but Abraham is for him the Davidic character. His chief purpose in retelling the story can probably be seen in at least three separate values that it held for him. First of all, it showed Abraham in pact with Jerusalem and blessed by its kingly and priestly authority. Secondly, it identified with the God of Israel (see vs. 22 below) the Name by which Abraham had been blessed in Jerusalem. And thirdly, it showed Abraham to be the recipient of Jerusalem's fealty and tribute.

In the final part of vs. 20 NAB has supplied a subject in translating *Abram gave him a tenth of everything.* Certainly this was the understanding of the passage in the use made of it by later Jews and Christians (cf. Hebrews 7:2): Abraham would have been offering to Melchizedek the tithe of his goods that was due the altar and the priesthood. The biblical text, however, is simply that "he gave him a tenth of everything," which by the logic of the context could suggest an additional action of Melchizedek in favor of Abraham and not the other way round. Melchizedek is first said to have *brought out bread and wine,* possibly as a ritual meal between two covenanted leaders, but in any case to convey the greetings and esteem of the Jerusalem in whose service, according to this version of the story, Abraham had pursued and defeated the invading kings. Then, *being a priest of God Most High,* Melchizedek *blessed Abram* in the name of his god, to whom he ascribed the victory that had been achieved. Finally, he gave him a tenth of the goods which had been retrieved for Jerusalem, even though, in the parallel version of vs. 21, the king of Sodom more generously offers Abraham the whole of his goods, desiring only the repatriation of his kidnaped people. This sequence, which makes the best sense of the fragment utilized by chapter 14, was probably as well the sequence intended by the biblical redactor. It is less likely, as some have imagined, that he had an interest in depicting Abraham as a donor of tithes and thus in some way confirming the legitimacy of the Jerusalem temple and priesthood.

The elaboration of the Melchizedek legend in the epistle to the Hebrews alluded to above is well known to every Christian reader. This is a Christian midrash corresponding to much Jewish midrash and allegory with which the figure of Melchizedek has been surrounded, which has through the ages resulted in the attribution to him of every conceivable quality, including the angelic and the divine. Because of his brief and unheralded mention in the Bible under somewhat mysterious and mystifying circumstances, Melchizedek like the Enoch of 5:21–24 became fair game for the speculation and unchecked imagination that have always followed in the wake of the scriptural word, mining both its utterances and its silences to build on it new and esoteric structures. The midrash of Hebrews, which makes of Melchizedek a prefiguration of Christ by ascribing to him a priesthood superior to that of Aaron and Levi, is quite restrained when compared with some of the allegory retrieved from Jewish sources; it restricts itself to the texts of Genesis 14 and Psalm 110, read for their typological possibilities. Later Christian speculation roamed far beyond Hebrews, however, first finding in Melchizedek's bread and wine a fore-shadowing of the Eucharist, then going as far as to conceive of the priest-king of Salem as an Old Testament appearance of Christ himself. However interesting some of the imaginative applications of the Melchizedek image may have been for the development of later theologies and pieties, they of course have no bearing on the historical interpretation of Genesis 14.

Melchizedek is said to be a priest of God Most High, and it is in the name of *God Most High, the creator of heaven and earth* that he blesses Abraham. This divine title and appellative is undoubtedly authentically Canaanite, the product of the same kind of assimilation that led to Israelite adaptation of identical religious language. There are three elements here: god (El), the most high (Elyon), and creator (perhaps, better, pro-creator, or possessor) of heaven and earth, and the three were probably once intended to specify separate deities. All three of the elements turn up in the mythological literatures of Canaan and Phoenicia which we now possess in generous measure, some of it known indirectly through ancient secondary sources, most of it the gift of fairly recent discoveries which have provided access to writings done when the myths were yet alive. The data are often fragmentary, sometimes inconsistent, always controvertible, and it would be rash in the extreme to attempt a neat summation of the state of the Canaanite pantheon when Abraham strode the land. Undoubtedly there was no single pantheon, even as there was no precisely single people or culture from city-state to city-state. We can surmise with some confidence, nevertheless, that in the Semitic Canaan of patriarchal times the worship of the high god El was the general rule, and that he in turn was usually identified with the local deities of the many shrines and sanctuaries, and finally that the common name El encouraged the assimilation of one local name to another. (Whether the net result, in the popular mind, was a multiplicity of Els or an El of multiple titles and attributes is another question.) Such is also the impression given by the traditions preserved in

Genesis, of which we shall see other examples later on. That Melchizedek's god should have been known as El Elyon, creator of heaven and earth, is, therefore, entirely believable.

The later Israelites appropriated the names and titles of Canaan's gods to their own Yahweh: as the sanctuaries became Yahwistic, so the religious language of Yahwism became Canaanized. Such a phenomenon has occurred time and time again in the history of religion, the history of Christianity forming no exception. Yahweh is called El Elyon in Psalm 78:35, Yahweh Elyon in Psalm 7:18, and simply Elyon in Numbers 24:16 (it is not clear whether the Elyon of Deuteronomy 32:8 was originally intended to be the same as the Yahweh of the following verse). It was in virtue of this thing that had happened that the biblical author of Genesis 14 could recount with equanimity the blessing of Abraham by a Canaanite priest. About Abraham's own religion, of which we shall have more to say, he had no trouble at all. He took for granted that the God of the patriarchs, by whatever name he was called (and the Yahwist, we know, did not hesitate to call him Yahweh), was the self-same God of Israel that he worshiped. That Melchizedek was a heathen king and priest was incidental to his being a king and priest in pre-Israelite Jerusalem. Melchizedek's blessing had invoked the name of God Most High. For the author and for his audience there was and could be only one God Most High, and Jerusalem was indeed his holy place.

> 21 The king of Sodom said to Abram, "Give me the
> 22 people; the goods you may keep." But Abram re-
> plied to the king of Sodom: "I have sworn to the
> LORD, God Most High, the creator of heaven and
> 23 earth, that I would not take so much as a thread or
> a sandal strap from anything that is yours, lest you
> 24 should say, 'I made Abram rich.' Nothing for me
> except what my servants have used up and the share
> that is due to the men who joined me—Aner, Eshcol
> and Mamre; let them take their share."

Taking up and concluding the story which was interrupted at vs. 17, these final verses make up an interesting little vignette in which in the best oriental tradition two men of means are shown trying to outdo each other in generosity and magnanimity. Unlike Melchizedek who in the parallel version distributed to Abraham the share of recovered property that was due him as his commission, *the king of Sodom* is willing to forgo his rights to the whole lot, asking only that the human booty that had been stolen away now be returned. It is *the people* who are important; *the goods* he dismisses with a wave of the hand. The king of Sodom thus appears here in an extraordinarily favorable light, given the usual tendency of the Bible to make of Sodom a byword for everything mean and wicked. This sympathetic portrayal would seem to stand in opposition to Benno Jacob's interpretation of Abraham's reply in vss. 22–24 as forming part of the anti-Sodom polemic which is so eloquently pursued in chapters 18–19 below. Jacob, who sees this entire chapter dominated by a desire to denigrate Sodom, a theme which he extracts from it by the discovery of rather subtly hidden clues, would stress that it is precisely Sodom that Abraham will not have as the source of his reward: *anything that is* yours, *lest* you *should say* . . . Such a nuance, however, must be intuited, if it is there at all. Abraham remains in this interchange the same person that he was in 13:8–12, one who has another beholden to him yet to whom he graciously condescends in a perfect gesture of *noblesse oblige*. Also, his is an act of personal abnegation: he does not make the mistake of other virtuous people who sometimes commit others unconsulted to the consequences of their deeds of generosity. He is careful to provide that both his servants and his allies who were partners in the joint enterprise shall be guaranteed their just due.

In vs. 22 Abraham states that he has confirmed his resolve by an oath to *the* Lord, *God Most High, the creator of heaven and earth,* thus joining the names of Yahweh and El Elyon and making the titles of Melchizedek's god those of his own Deity. The Septuagint witnesses to a text in which the name Yahweh did not appear, and therefore its presence in the extant Hebrew may be suspect. With or without the use of that name, however, it should be evident enough that the redactor of this chapter did not intend to insinuate that Abraham had invoked a new and hitherto alien deity but rather the God who had called him into the land of Canaan and who had directed his way since. For this God Abraham had a new title, provided by the redactor's inclusion of the Melchizedek episode into what is now the whole story of chapter 14, just as this God will be shown to acquire other titles subsequently; but for the biblical author and his readers, of course, the title was already old indeed, and it could only mean Yahweh.

We have devoted a good deal of attention to Genesis 14, though we have been careful to point out that some present-day critics consider it to be a romance that is historically worthless. Many of their arguments were anticipated in the commentary of Benno Jacob which we have already mentioned, who viewed the chapter as a parable whose catchword is Sodom. For Jacob it was significant that only the kings of Sodom and Gomorrah—those proverbial cities of doom—are featured, and that though the names of four kings of the cities of the plain are given, that of the king of Zoar, the city of Lot, is not. Further, he interpreted as caricatures the four names that are given, found it decisive that Abraham refuses any recompense from the king of Sodom, and observed numerous signs of artificiality: the first two names of the invading kings begin with *a* and the last with *t* (the first and last letters of the Hebrew alphabet), while the names of the four Canaanite kings begin with two *b*'s and two *s*'s, and each of the royal names contains the same number of Hebrew letters as the name of the respective city, etc. Ingenuities of this kind are intriguing, but they may be no more than measures of the arm of coincidence; and they get in the way of other factors that we have thought more relevant to the understanding of this passage.

4. The Covenant with Abraham

The three following chapters are fairly evenly divided between J and P. The covenant with Abraham according to J is the burden of chapter 15. In chapter 16 occurs the story of Hagar and Ishmael, a vivid and sprightly narrative of J supplemented by a bare-bones parallel from P which we have differentiated from the main text by the use of italics. On the contrary, chapter 17, though a continuation of the Hagar and Ishmael parallel of chapter 16, has been allowed to stand in regular type: it is entirely the work of P and is the P version of the covenant with Abraham.

In the judgment of many, perhaps most, of the commentators on Genesis, the first appearance of the Elohistic source or redaction takes place in chapter 15. If so, it is a gingerly, apologetic appearance, hardly more than a walk-on part, consisting of a few supplemental phrases which can add up to no recoverable narrative of its own. Such a situation constitutes no peremptory argument against the presence of E, it must be admitted, since very frequently this source has made its way into Genesis in relatively brief form, sometimes in a form that looks to be little more than a gloss or commentary on the larger narrative in which it is now embedded. However, as regards chapter 15 we have elected to follow the analysis of Norbert Lohfink and to agree with him that an appeal to E for the provenance of any part of these verses is superfluous and unnecessary. Lohfink has concluded that chapter 15 is entirely the work of J, not, however, as usually, a compilation by the Yahwist of previously existing sources, but a free composition made by him through the reworking of traditional materials. As we have seen by now, the distinction between these two kinds of literary activity must be one more of degree than of kind. The Yahwist is capable of handling his source material very freely, redacting it lavishly in the process to the extent of transmuting it into something else; and he is also capable of adhering to the original forms quite rigorously and even wood-enly. Most of what we know as J, particularly in the patriarchal narrative, lies somewhere in the center and at neither of the two extremes. In the present instance it may be true that the author which J undoubtedly was predominates over the compiler J which is the other undeniable element in his literary character. In any case, we have found no compelling reason to ascribe anything in this chapter to any other influence than that of J.

> **15** Some time after these events, this word of the LORD
> came to Abram in a vision:
> "Fear not, Abram!
> I am your shield;
> I will make your reward very great."
> **2** But Abram said, O Lord GOD what good will your
> gifts be, if I keep on being childless and have as my
> **3** heir the steward of my house, Eliezer?" Abram con-
> tinued, "See, you have given me no offspring, and so
> **4** one of my servants will be my heir." Then the word
> of the LORD came to him: "No, that one shall not
> **5** be your heir; your own issue shall be your heir." He
> took him outside and said, "Look up at the sky and
> count the stars, if you can. Just so," he added, "shall
> **6** your descendants be." Abram put his faith in the
> LORD, who credited it to him as an act of righteous-
> ness.

What are *these events some time after* which the vision of chapter 15 took place, in the mind of the Yahwistic author? In the opinion of many commentators the reference is simply to the call of Abraham and its con-sequences as recorded in chapter 12: in reward of his unquestioning obe-dience in departing his native land and going where his God would lead him, Abraham is now promised numerous progeny and the possession of the land of Canaan by his descendants. In this construction, chapter 15 might be considered a more elaborate and ritualized duplicate of the promise made to Abraham at Shechem according to 12:7. More probable is the opinion of those who insist that this chapter presupposes the narra-tive of chapter 13, particularly Abraham's taking up residence at the cult-place of Mamre-Hebron (13:18). As they point out, chapter 15 does definitely give all the signs of having a cultic background, and it would be strange that the holy place where such an important event occurred is not specified by the Yahwistic author unless, indeed, he did specify it at the conclusion of chapter 13. Hebron, for that matter, as has already been ob-served, is more properly associated with the Abraham tradition than is Shechem (see above on 12:1–9). If chapter 15 has been composed with chapter 13 already in mind, perhaps Lohfink's theory is better confirmed, that it was a freer production of the Yahwist drawing together miscellaneous traditions to suit the sequence of a narrative that he had thus far assembled. Recently, Martin Kessler has revived an older opinion that also includes chapter 14 among the material presupposed by the author of chapter 15 at the time it was written in its biblical form—a view, of course, that would argue for the Yahwistic redaction of chapter 14. Kessler's position is based on the recurrence of certain key words in chapters 14 and 15, something into which we can hardly enter in the compass of these pages, and also on some other possible connections which we shall mention below. (It can be remarked at this juncture that Genesis 14, too, doubtless understood Hebron to be the camping place of Abraham, even though in vs. 13 it had turned Mamre and Eshcol into ancestral figures of these nearby places.)

It has long been recognized that this present chapter 15 is a composite made up of disparate parts. In vss. 12 and 17 Yahweh reveals himself to Abraham at sunset, whereas in vs. 5 he had already directed him outside (the sanctuary? his tent?) to view the night sky. In vs. 8 Abraham expresses a doubt which is strangely disconsonant with the implicit faith that has just been credited to him in vs. 6. Yahweh makes known his name in vs. 7, but it is the name by which Abraham called him at the outset in vs. 2. There are other inconsistencies. The differences in narrative detail, however, do not correspond with the distinction of theological themes (the promise of the land in vss. 1.7–21, the assurance of a natural heir and of great progeny in vss. 2–6, a combination of the two in vss. 12–21), nor with the "mechanics" of the divine-human commerce that is involved (in vss. 1.12–16 a vision, in vss. 2–9.18–21 a dialogue, in vss. 10–11.17–18 a covenant ceremony, etc.). A distinction of consistent and independent sources is thus rendered impossible, and we must rather reckon with an author who has drawn his material from where he would without regard to whatever inner conflicts would inevitably ensue when he put it all together.

The *word of the* LORD *came to Abram in a vision:* this is the habitual expression used in the later language of Israel (and also in some of its earlier language) for prophetic inspiration (cf. Isaiah 1:1, Ezekiel 1:1, Amos 1:1, Obadiah 1:1, Habakkuk 1:1, etc.). For the first time the Yahwist seems to have become sensitive to the anthropomorphism of the man-to-man talk which thus far he has represented as the vehicle of divine revelation. Now—briefly, as it happens—he clothes the divine communication in the mysterious aura of the prophetic experience, the nature of which was never adequately explained even by the great prophets of Israel themselves. It is of statistical interest that in 20:7 Abraham is called a prophet by the Elohist ("spokesman" in the NAB), but only of statistical interest. The theme of the vision is resumed in vs. 12 below. Other devices that occurred to the biblical writers to substitute for the bald "God said" we shall see later on.

"Fear not, Abram!" Of what should Abraham be afraid (or Hagar in 21:17, Isaac in 26:23–24, Jacob in 28:13 [in the Septuagint] and again in 46:3, in all of which passages the same expression occurs)? Of his being alone in a new homeland and on a pilgrimage whose course he had not plotted, so thought the older commentators. Alternatively, of the awesome experience of hearing the word of the Almighty—an experience, however, which up to this point Abraham has accepted with remarkable *sang-froid*. The form-critical study of the Bible in relation to cognate religious cultures has given us a better answer. This is a formula, originally the address to the king by a prophet (cf. Isaiah 7:4, 37:6–7; Jeremiah 42:11–12) assuring him of victory over his enemies guaranteed by the national god. Extra-Israelite parallels exist in abundance. What is suggested is that the formula by degrees came to be usual in the sanctuaries to preface a favorable response delivered through a prophet, no matter what was the estate of the recipient or the matter of his petition. Such a development would agree perfectly with the other "democratization" of royal language which we have already observed beginning with 1:26–27. The biblical author in this case has applied to what he recognized as an ancient cultic encounter language which had become current in his time to describe such an encounter, even though it was not the language of a bygone patriarchal age.

"I am your shield" might appear at first glance to be an asseveration that would fit neatly and ineluctably into the format we have just found at the background of our text: the king who has first been told to fear no foe is now assured that Yahweh is his impregnable shield of defense. Certainly Yahweh is frequently named the shield of Israel in ritual texts which may have had their first application in the protection which the king could confidently expect as the elect of Yahweh (Psalms 3:4, 18:3.31, 28:7, etc.). However, it must be remembered first of all that in the perspective of Genesis Abraham is not a king, even though he might emblemize one; secondly, that in the context of this story he was not about to embark on a campaign of warfare against his enemies (quite to the contrary, if chapter 14 had already preceded, he had just soundly defeated them); and finally, that in Israelite language the royal formulas had already undergone the democratization of which we spoke above. "Holy war" is definitely not a theme of the patriarchal legends, neither of Abraham nor of Hagar nor of Isaac nor of Jacob. Hence it is that Martin Kessler may be quite in line when he proposes for the *magen* of vs. 1 (literally, "I am a shield to you") an original *mogen* (literally, "I am a deliverer unto you") corresponding with the *miggen* ("who delivered") of 14:20. Such a reconstruction would nicely identify the God Most High of chapter 14 with the Yahweh of 15:1.

"I will make your reward very great" might also receive a highly understandable interpretation in this acceptation. According to 14:23–24 Abraham returned to Hebron unrewarded and unenriched; now, however, Yahweh his deliverer promises to make his reward great indeed.

It is interesting that in vss. 2–3 no mention is made of Lot as a natural heir to Abraham. Probably in this passage the Yahwist drew on traditions which were independent of the Lot story, which in any case is only tenuously connected with the Abraham tradition. In protesting that he has no heir, an objection that would make better immediate sense if it occurred after the promises of 12:2.7, Abraham reminds the Deity that he is *childless* (cf. 11:30, J), and therefore that his presumptive *heir* would be one of his servants, the *steward of* his *house, Eliezer.* (In this translation the NAB makes conjectural sense of a corrupt Hebrew text, the general meaning of which, however, seems to be clear enough.) The arrangement to which Abraham alludes, in which a trusted servant was constituted the heir of a man who had no natural issue, is unknown elsewhere in the Bible and was not provided for in the Mosaic Law of Israel. Documents from Nuzi of the fifteenth century B.C., however, indicate that there was such a custom in Mesopotamia, which was often regularized by legal contract. Since our text is, after all, obscure, it would be rash to attach vast significance to this possible correspondence or draw large conclusions from it. Still, there is some reason to suspect that here the biblical tradition has preserved the memory of a way of life that once really was and that would hardly be the product of an inventive mind out of touch with the tradition.

The divine reply to Abraham's forceful remonstration is contained in the vivid lines of vss. 4–5. It is a promise not merely of great progeny as before in 12:2 but also a response to the pressing and urgent problem broached by Abraham: *your own issue shall be your heir.* That Abraham *put his faith* in Yahweh might better be rendered "he continued to believe," since in the biblical context Abraham has already been presented as one totally abandoned to the designs of God, who therefore epitomizes what the Bible understands by "faith." (The Hebrew verb in vs. 6 also suggests that a continuous rather than an incipient act is meant.) Faith, etymologically and really in the Hebrew of the Old Testament, denotes a state of complete reliance upon another person: one "takes a stand" upon the other and thus secures a new identity from this relationship. By saying that Yahweh *credited* Abraham's acquiescence in faith to his promise *as an act of righteousness,* the biblical author tells us that only an attitude of this kind can make a person "right" in the sight of God. Independent of this attitude neither he nor any of his deeds can be accounted "right," "since the desires of man's heart are evil from the start" (Genesis 8:21). On the basis of this text principally, Abraham has become the quintessential example and model of the man of faith, whose acceptance of God's word (Romans 4:3, Galatians 3:6) and fidelity to the commitment he had thereby incurred (Hebrews 11:8–10, James 2:23) constituted him the ideal for one who would be pleasing to God.

> 7 He then said to him, "I am the LORD who brought
>   you from Ur of the Chaldeans to give you this land
> 8 as a possession." "O Lord GOD," he asked, "how
> 9 am I to know that I shall possess it?" He answered
>   him, "Bring me a three-year-old heifer, a three-
>   year-old she-goat, a three-year-old ram, a turtle-
> 10 dove, and a young pigeon." He brought him all
>   these, split them in two, and placed each half op-
>   posite the other; but the birds he did not cut up.
> 11 Birds of prey swooped down on the carcasses, but
> 12 Abram stayed with them. As the sun was about to
>   set, a trance fell upon Abram, and a deep, terrifying
>   darkness enveloped him.

In vs. 8 as in vs. 2 Abraham addresses his God as Adonai Yahweh, Lord Yahweh, which in our English translations is given as Lord GOD, since "Lord" is the word already pre-empted to render "Yahweh," following the convention established in the Greek Old Testament long ago. Adonai Yahweh is a frequent combination in the Hebrew Bible, and the two names also often appear in parallel there. There is good reason to think that Adonai was once a divine name in its own right: the Great Lord. In the times when the sacred name Yahweh ceased to be pronounced, Adonai was uttered in its stead, which accounts for the LORD equivalent that was indicated in the Masoretic Hebrew and thus has made its way into all our Bibles. The combination Adonai Yahweh occurs in Genesis only in these two verses. It is a sign of the single authorship of this chapter, no doubt, but it does not conceal the separate origins of the components which the author has drawn together in writing the chapter.

Whereas vss. 2–6 above seem to be very well continued in vss. 13–16 below, probably with vs. 12 in the present pericope forming an interstitial transition, it is evident that vss. 7–11 (originally introduced by vs. 1?) begin a story that is only completed in vss. 17–21. The emphases of the two segments are distinct, even though there is some overlapping of ideas. The first is taken up with concern over Abraham's descent while the second, which begins here, tells of a solemn covenant ritual and oath by which Yahweh confirmed his promise of the land to an eventual Israel.

As befits the originally independent existence of this passage in the traditions which told of the promises made to Abraham, Yahweh appears as though for the first time in vs. 7 and introduces himself as the Providence which had directed the patriarch's steps to the land of Canaan. (The words *from Ur of the Chaldeans* may or may not be an addition of the Redactor of Genesis, depending on whether or not the Ur tradition was known to J as well as P: see above on 11:27–32.) Like the appearance to Isaac at Beer-sheba in 26:23–25, to Jacob at Bethel in 28:13–15, or to Moses at Horeb in Exodus 3:6–14, this is a theophany of recognition, whose language and form commend it to modern scholars as being drawn from cultic experience. In the God of this sacred place (Hebron, as we have assumed) Abraham would have recognized the guardian of his ways to whom he had committed his destiny. By whatever name Abraham might have known this God (Adonai? unlikely, but not impossible), the Yahwist of course wished to have it clear that, like the El Elyon of chapter 14, he was the Yahweh of Israel's faith, the only God who mattered. From his standpoint, the equation was inevitable.

As we pointed out above, Abraham's less than implicit acceptance of the divine assurance in vs. 8 is somewhat discordant with the portrait of the ideal man of faith and trust revealed in vs. 6. Nevertheless, it was considered to be perfectly proper that a "sign" be given to confirm a promise even of God (cf. 2 Kings 20:8–11, Isaiah 7:11). This is what Abraham asks for, and this is what he receives. Having first been told that he will have *this land as a possession,* a concession which in vs. 18 (and in the intervening vss. 13–16) is specified as pertaining to his *descendants* rather than to him personally, Abraham is instructed to some rather curious preparations. Not only does he fulfill the preparations to the letter, he also proceeds to ready them without further instruction in a fashion that indicates he knows very well what he is about. What is taking place is the elaboration of a covenant ritual by which an oath was ratified in the ancient Near East.

The ritual being described is alluded to in a charge by the prophet Jeremiah against the perfidy of Jerusalem: "The men who violated my covenant [i.e. Yahweh's] and did not observe the terms of the agreement which they made before me, I will make like the calf which they cut in two, between whose two parts they passed" (Jeremiah 34:18). It required the studies in comparative religions and cultures of the past century, however, both to elucidate this Jeremian passage fully and to reveal how general was the practice which explains why in biblical Hebrew "*cut* a covenant" means "make a covenant." The practice has been verified at Mari, at Alalakh on the Orontes (in northern Syria, roughly in the time of Mari), in Hittite texts from Asia Minor (from the fifteenth to the thirteenth centuries B.C.), in the Aramaic inscriptions of Sefire (from the Syria of about the middle eighth century B.C.), in Greek and Latin sources of the classical period, not to mention less relevant documentation pertaining to assorted Scandinavians, Africans, Indians, and other Asiatics. The significance of the rite is made very plain in the text of an eighth-century treaty between Ashur-nirari VI of Assyria and Matti-ilu the king of Bit-Agusi: "This head is not the head of a goat, but the head of Matti-ilu, the head of his sons, his nobles, and the peoples of his land. If any of these named sin against these vows, just as the head of this goat has been cut . . . may the head of these named be cut, his sons . . ." And in a Sefire inscription embodying a treaty between a certain Bir-Gayah and a vassal king of Arpad named Matiel: "If Matiel should prove unfaithful . . . just as this calf is cut in two, so may Matiel be cut in two and may his nobles be cut in two . . ." The kind of animal differs from place to place (at Mari it was an ass, a circumstance that has suggested to some a bearing on the interpretation of Genesis 33:19–34:29, see below), but in each instance the symbolism seems to have been the same and quite patent. The separated halves of the slain beasts in the midst of which oaths were taken were intended to provide a graphic illustration of the consequences the testators willed upon themselves should they fail to fulfill their commitments.

Abraham is told to bring *a three-year-old heifer, she-goat,* and *ram,* each of which he *split in two, and placed each half opposite the other* in keeping with the ritual prescriptions. The three-year-old rubric probably indicates that in the particular ritual tradition underlying this biblical story the use of adult animals was required for the ratification of the oath (it is so in one of the Hittite parallels). According to 1 Samuel 1:24 a three-year-old bull was the acceptable sacrifice at the primordial Israelite shrine of Shiloh (so, on ancient textual authority, in most modern versions of the Bible, contrary to the "three bulls" mentioned by the MT of this verse). It may well be that this association with sacrifice—though there is no indication that the slaying of the animals for the oath ceremony was sacrificial in the strict sense—accounts for the presence in this story of the *turtledove* and *young pigeon* with which Abraham seems not to know what to do. Under the Law of Moses only these two birds were admissible to the altars of sacrifice (Leviticus 1:14, 5:7, 12:8) along with such larger beasts as are listed in this same verse. At a later stage in the transmission of this passage when the ritual slaughter of animals had come to be confined almost exclusively to a sacrificial context, the birds could have been introduced into the story as what was thought to be a suitable complement. Obviously, they were ill-suited to provide additional material for the covenant spectacle which Abraham had constructed; hence, *the birds he did not cut up.*

The other birds, the *birds of prey* of vs. 11, doubtless appear as signs of ill omen. *Abram stayed with them* (i.e., with the animal carcasses threatened by the birds of prey) is translated by most other versions "he drove them away" (i.e., the birds). The difference is not important enough to require an explanation here. Neither is it entirely clear what precise significance this verse is intended to have in the Yahwist's narration. Does he merely want to say that Abraham was undeterred by or actively repulsed these intimations of misfortune? Or does he want to suggest that they presage a negative element in the divine promise and commitment: the oppression of Israel in Egypt before they may inherit the land (vs. 13)?

As we noted above, vs. 12 probably had nothing to do originally with the theme of the covenant ritual but rather introduces an account of revelation of an altogether different sort. The *trance* which *fell upon Abram* is the "deep sleep" (*tardemah*) of Genesis 2:21. We are about to hear in another version the divine assurance of a promised land for Abraham's descendants.

13 Then the LORD said to Abram: "Know for certain
   that your descendants shall be aliens in a land not
   their own, where they shall be enslaved and op-
14 pressed for four hundred years. But I will bring
   judgment on the nation they must serve, and in the
15 end they will depart with great wealth. You, however, shall join your forefathers in peace; you shall
16 be buried at a contented old age. In the fourth time-
   span the others shall come back here; the wickedness
   of the Amorites will not have reached its full measure until then."

Again Abraham undergoes prophetic experience, this time conveying to him knowledge of the Egyptian captivity of Israel, the only time that it is mentioned in Genesis. It is unusual for the Yahwist to offer a chronology: his *four hundred years* corresponds with the four hundred and thirty years that Israel stayed in Egypt according to Exodus 12:40 (P). However, like the highly abbreviated reference to the "plagues" of Egypt and the "spoiling of the Egyptians" in vs. 14, the notion of a return of Israel to Canaan *in the fourth time-span* was doubtless part of the exodus tradition long before it reached any of the biblical authors. An etiological explanation is also given why Abraham's descendants and not Abraham himself will inherit the land, and why it will be so long before they do: *the wickedness of the Amorites will not have reached its full measure until then.* Israel customarily regarded its possession of the land simply as the gift of its God, in whose power and right it was to bestow it upon whom he would. Constant vigilance against the corrupting influence of Canaanite ritual and moral practices, however, had also long persuaded the Israelites that they had displaced an aboriginal population whose vices had made them unworthy of all they had lost. A self-serving judgment, one might think, yet a reading of the great prophets, who were not disposed to let Israel itself off lightly, convinces us that its basis was a sound one.

For Abraham personally is promised the greatest consolation that the Old Testament can offer. He will *join* his *forefathers in peace*. Here the operative word is "peace": to join one's forefathers ordinarily means to be buried in the family tomb, which is not to be Abraham's destiny. In his case the conventional phrase merely signifies that he will enjoy a full life and then *be buried at a contented old age*. If he will never own the land, neither will he see the flowering of the evil of those who now possess it. He will live in tranquillity and he will die, as a man must, full of years, as is not granted to every man.

> 17 When the sun had set and it was dark, there appeared a smoking brazier and a flaming torch,
> 18 which passed between those pieces. It was on that occasion that the LORD made a covenant with Abram, saying: "To your descendants I give this land, from the Wadi of Egypt to the Great River
> 19 [the Euphrates], the land of the Kenites, the Keniz-
> 20 zites, the Kadmonites, the Hittites, the Perizzites,
> 21 the Rephaim, the Amorites, the Canaanites, the Girgashites, and the Jebusites."

The covenant ritual is quickly concluded. The *smoking brazier* and *flaming torch* revealed after *the sun had set and it was dark* (we are probably not to ask whether these for the Yahwist were real objects or parts of Abraham's vision) represent the divine presence: fire, in all mythologies a prerogative of the gods if not a god itself, is the almost invariable concomitant of Old Testament theophanies (cf. Exodus 3:2, Judges 6:21, Ezekiel 1:4, etc.). This fire *passed between those pieces* of the severed animals, solemnizing the promise of the land which is detailed in the following verses. Abraham himself does not walk between the pieces, for he is not in this passage assuming obligations but rather is the recipient of God's favor granted without restrictions. With high anthropomorphism the biblical author shows this God swearing an oath in a conventionally acceptable form, providing that "sign" which Abraham had requested in vs. 8. This episode strongly confirms Lohfink's contention that "oath" (that is, the strengthening by legal forms of a one-sided affirmation) is what was first meant by *covenant* (vs. 18), the same meaning that it evidently has in Jeremiah 34:18.

This land which is promised to Abraham's descendants appears here according to the "ideal limits" of the kingdom of David and Solomon, which claimed dominion *from the Wadi of Egypt to the Great River* (cf. 1 Kings 5:1). The Wadi of Egypt (it is necessary to read *nahal* in the Hebrew text, as in Numbers 34:5, Joshua 15:4, instead of *nahar*, "river": the River of Egypt is the Nile) is the Wadi el-Arish, which to this day is the dividing line between the traditional Palestine and the traditional Egypt. The Great River is correctly glossed in the text as *the Euphrates*. Listing the peoples whose land this is, however, the text goes on to shrink this territory to some historical limits instead of the ideal, possibly even to *the* historical limits which originally surrounded the figure of a patriarch of Hebron who had been promised the land as a divine gift. *The Kenites, the Kenizzites,* and, perhaps, *the Kadmonites* (who appear only here in the Bible) refer to peoples and areas which were certainly in the ambit of the Hebron and Judah which were formative of both Abraham and David and therefore doubly dear to the Yahwist. The Kenites we have discussed above under 4:2b–16. They dwelt in Judah and were later David's friends (1 Samuel 30:29). The Kenizzites, which Genesis 36:11.15 later lists as Edomites, are by other traditions (Joshua 14:14, for example) told among the Hebronite and Judahite clans which went to make up the later Israelite federation of tribes. *The Hittites* of this text are those of 9:27, 10:15 above: it will be remembered that there were "Hittites" in David's Jerusalem (2 Samuel 11:3–27) and that they had been his allies before he came to power (1 Samuel 26:6). *The Jebusites* (cf. 10:16 above) are particularly identified as the pre-Israelite inhabitants of Jerusalem (Joshua 15:63, Judges 1:21) and, indeed, as those who continued in its possession till the time of David (2 Samuel 5:6–9). *The Perizzites* we saw in 13:7 above and will see again in 34:30 below. Here they are probably nothing more than another name to assign to the pre-Israelite inhabitants of the Land of Promise. Along with *the Rephaim* (14:5), *the Amorites,* and *the Canaanites,* they have been brought in to "complete" what had now become a fairly stereotyped table of nations antedating the "conquest." The same is doubtless true of *the Girgashites*. Though we stated above (on 10:16) that this name has plausibly been verified in extra-biblical sources, to whom and to what it precisely referred were undoubtedly as unknown to the biblical author as they are to us today.

> **16** *Abram's wife Sarai had borne him no children.* She had, however, an Egyptian maidservant named Ha-
> **2** gar. Sarai said to Abram: "The LORD has kept me from bearing children. Have intercourse, then, with my maid; perhaps I shall have sons through her."
> **3** Abram heeded Sarai's request. *Thus, after Abram had lived ten years in the land of Canaan, his wife Sarai took her maid, Hagar the Egyptian, and gave*
> **4** *her to her husband Abram to be his concubine.* He had intercourse with her, and she became pregnant. When she became aware of her pregnancy, she

5 looked on her mistress with disdain. So Sarai said to
Abram: "You are responsible for this outrage
against me. I myself gave my maid to your embrace;
but ever since she became aware of her pregnancy,
she has been looking on me with disdain. May the
6 LORD decide between you and me!" Abram told Sarai: "Your maid is in your power. Do to her whatever you please." Sarai then abused her so much
that Hagar ran away from her.

This little interlude about Hagar and Ishmael serves the additional purpose of separating the J and the P versions of the covenant with Abraham,
thus putting them in sequence. The essential circumstances surrounding
Ishmael's origin and birth were preserved by P, as is evident from our distribution of the text above and below, but only in what appears to be a
radical and drastic summation of the J narrative in which all its life and
drama have disappeared.

The social and legal background presupposed by this story is once more
one that is not elucidated by the later Mosaic Law of Israel. When, however, the law code of Hammurabi was rediscovered in 1901, it became immediately evident that ancient Mesopotamian legislation had long provided for practically every detail in the life-situation described in Genesis.
Subsequent discoveries, particularly those of Nuzi, have confirmed the evidence and also filled it out in some part. Several concerns seem to be at
issue, all of which are dealt with explicitly in the Mesopotamian documents and are implied in our story.

First, Sarah's proffering of her maidservant to Abraham: in the P version, she *gave her to her husband*. It was the law that if a wife provided
her husband with a slave girl for the purpose of childbearing, the husband
was thereby precluded from taking a concubine on his own—which otherwise he almost surely would do, especially if he were afflicted with a childless wife. The purpose of this law was twofold, first to protect the wife's
status of undisputed mistress in the household, and again to prevent the
possibility of a divided inheritance, since the children got by the slave girl
would be legally accounted the wife's own. *Perhaps I shall have sons
through her,* Sarah says to Abraham. Hence what to some later readers
may have appeared to be something rather risqué and shocking in
Abraham's and Sarah's conduct was really nothing other than a normal
family matter involving a recurring problem that was met with the application of a quite routine solution. The Mesopotamian law likewise sheds
light on the denouement of the story as told in Genesis. It had anticipated
the situation, also probably quite routine, that a slave girl elevated to the
bedchamber of the master of the house and bearing him children tended to
aspire above her station and *looked on her mistress with disdain*. In such a

case, it was the prerogative of the wife to return the concubine to the company and the tasks of the ordinary household slaves. (If she had remained childless and nevertheless made herself the rival of her mistress she could simply be sold away.) Here Sarah vindicates to herself what she knows is her right—*May the* LORD *decide between you and me!*—demanding that Abraham return Hagar to her own control, which he speedily does. Abraham cannot be charged with an unfeeling and callous dismissal of the unfortunate woman who was to be the mother of his child, nor with a too easy bending to Sarah's willfulness; he was simply doing what custom said that he had to do. Legalities aside, however, it must be admitted that at least Sarah does not cut too happy a figure in this episode, neither in her recriminations over a development for which she herself was partly responsible and which was the miscarriage of a plan designed more for her benefit than anyone else's, nor in her vengeful treatment of Hagar after the fact. The lot of a slave is never a happy one, and quite obviously Sarah had no wish to change that rule.

> 7 The LORD's messenger found her by a spring in the
> 8 wilderness, the spring on the road to Shur, and he
> asked, "Hagar, maid of Sarai, where have you come
> from and where are you going?" She answered, "I
> 9 am running away from my mistress, Sarai." But the
> LORD's messenger told her: "Go back to your mis-
> 10 tress and submit to her abusive treatment. I will
> make your descendants so numerous," added the
> LORD's messenger, "that they will be too many to
> 11 count. Besides," the LORD's messenger said to her:
> "You are now pregnant and shall bear a son;
> you shall name him Ishmael,
> For the LORD has heard you,
> God has answered you.
> 12 He shall be a wild ass of a man,
> his hand against everyone,
> and everyone's hand against him;
> In opposition to all his kin
> shall he encamp."
> 13 To the LORD who spoke to her she gave a name,
> saying, "You are the God of Vision"; she meant,
> "Have I really seen God and remained alive after
> 14 my vision?" That is why the well is called Beer-
> lahai-roi. It is between Kadesh and Bered.
> 15 *Hagar bore Abram a son, and Abram named the*
> 16 *son whom Hagar bore him Ishmael. Abram was*
> *eighty-six years old when Hagar bore him Ishmael.*

The extraordinary attention given to Hagar and her son Ishmael points to another function of this story in its present place in Genesis, which is to heighten the suspense with which we wait on the Lord to make good his promises. When and how will this be done? Abraham has been assured many descendants in whose future glory he may rejoice. And despite the continuing barrenness of his wife, he has accepted God's word in all docility and trust. At last he has achieved a possible heir from his own loins, even as the Lord said he would, or so for the moment it seemed. Not an entirely satisfactory heir, to be sure, to be born of a surrogate wife and an Egyptian of all things. (The Yahwist undoubtedly thought of Hagar as one of those slaves which Abraham acquired in Egypt according to 12:16.) Now it appears that even this less than adequate response to his faith and prayers is to be snatched away from his eager grasp. Forced to accede to the abasement of his concubine, he now has to witness the inevitable sequel in her flight from his house and with her the only tangible hope he has been given to justify his confidence in the divine word. What now will ensue? Tantalizingly, the story refuses to tell us. It gently disengages our attention from Abraham and his worries (which, of course, are supposed to be our worries as well) and focuses it instead on the despised slave girl and her offspring. For the moment, at least, the exclusivism that tends to characterize biblical history is put in abeyance, and we are invited to empathize with the feelings and humanity of those who in its purview were destined not to stride its stage but only to view it from the wings or the pit. It is a rare performance for the Yahwist, and therefore all the more engaging.

The fleeing Hagar is met at a desert oasis *on the road to Shur*. Shur is the Hebrew word for "wall," and it is very likely that the reference is to the Prince's Wall that protected Egypt's eastern frontier against incursions by the "Asiatics" (see above, on 12:10–20). In Genesis 20:1 (J) Abraham—by which we may understand Abrahamic elements of the later Israel—is said to have dwelt for a time in the Negeb between Kadesh and Shur. We are doubtless to understand the present passage as showing Hagar midway on her flight from Hebron back to her native Egypt. She is met by *the LORD's messenger*. This expression translates the Hebrew *malak Yahweh*, which the Septuagint also rendered in literal Greek *angelos kyriou*, with the unfortunate result, however, that "angel" has tended to become associated with later theological speculations about God-man intermediaries that have absolutely nothing to do with Genesis. The "angel" of Yahweh of J ("angel of God" in E) does indeed stand between the divine and the human, but in a purely literary and anecdotal sense, as nothing much more than a figure of speech, with no ontological implications at all. The messenger of Yahweh who intervenes in vss. 7–12 is simply identified with Yahweh in vs. 13. We have already seen that the biblical author can sometimes evince nervousness over having God "speak" directly to man with quite the easy freeness that was more at home in the mythical world of Eden and Nod, now that man has been brought into the recognizable and familiar world of history where such a thing does not ordinarily occur. God can and does speak to a man in a dream or a vision, as he was, indeed, in biblical times speaking through his prophets (15:1.12). He can also speak through a "messenger," as here. He can speak in even more curious ways (18:1–5). Even with the admixture of the mythical with the real of which he had to put together his propedeuticon to history, the Yahwist was striving to attach some subtlety to the notion of what it means for God to make his will and disposition known to his human creatures.

There seems to be no question that vss. 9–10 above, though they are in the language of the Yahwist, are the work of the Redactor of Genesis and not of the Yahwist himself. The original J story, which has its E parallel in 21:9–21, undoubtedly took Hagar and her son out of Abraham's bosom and his household once and for all (contrary to the P version of the Ishmael chronicle in 16:15–16, 17:18.23–27, 25:9) and did not return them. They are returned here (along with a promise of progeny that recalls the one made to Abraham in 15:5) in order to provide a more or less reasonable sequence for the redacted narrative that follows.

In vs. 11 we have the introduction to an old poetic fragment (in vs. 12) which concerns the Ishmaelites. (The poetic structure of vs. 11 as it appears in NAB depends on a conjectural emendation of the text; other modern versions have it otherwise. What is evident beyond contest in the verse is relatively trivial: the popular etymology of Ishmael is "God has heard.") It is said of *Ishmael* that *he shall be a wild ass of a man:* the expression recalls the epithet "savage man" (*lullu*) predicated of primordial man in the ancient myths (see on 1:24–31 above). Ishmael, who represents the Arabian tribes who surrounded the southland of Judah (cf. 25:12–18), is here depicted as one whose lot it is to be in continual warfare and restless strife not only with strangers and foreigners who were normally accounted enemies, but also with his own kindred, with the peoples related to his own tribes and clans. In just such a light did the Israelites of their settled kingdoms view the Bedawin nomads and marauders—their own distant cousins—who inhabited the wild beyond their borders, who harassed them from time to time and who also embarrassed them by perpetuating a way of life which many Israelites themselves had once led before yielding to the blandishments of civilization and which they now regarded as a disreputable past better forgotten.

In vs. 13 Hagar—not, be it noted, Abraham—is allowed to identify Yahweh with yet another of the divinities of Canaan, this time *the God of Vision:* El Roi. In the rest of this verse the NAB tries to make sense of a Hebrew text that is patently obscure and probably corrupt. The source utilized by the biblical author tried to connect Hagar's experience with what must have been at one time a renowned site: *Beer-lahai-roi*. We can easily translate the components of this name ("Well," "life," "vision"), but we do not know how to reassemble them in the combination that once surely gave them some meaningful association. The location of the place had already ceased to have any pressing importance for the Yahwist, as is evidenced by his vague indication that it lay *between Kadesh and Bered*. (In modern times, the surface exploration of southern Palestine has suggested a plausible situation for Beer-lahai-roi at a well now known as Bir Mayin that lies between Ain Qedeis and Jebel Umm el-Bared in the Negeb.) As we shall see below, wells had equal importance along with sanctuaries in accounting for the geographical ties of the patriarchal legends: the recurring element which the German critics called *Ortsgebundenheit,* that is, the obvious interplay of site with event in the formation of these stories. In the parched land of southern Palestine wells and oases were doubtless very often one and the same as sacred places where there was a terebinth, a cult center, and a means of oracular recourse. But, like most of the other narratives in the patriarchal sequence, this one has lost whatever earlier cultic meaning it may once have had as a sacrifice to the storyteller's preference for persons over places.

> **17** When Abram was ninety-nine years old the LORD
> appeared to him and said: "I am God the Almighty.
> 2 Walk in my presence and be blameless. Between
> you and me I will establish my covenant, and I will
> multiply you exceedingly."

We have already concluded that chapter 17 can only be the work of the Priestly author, building off 16:15–16 (cf. 17:18 with 16:16). This is true despite the Yahweh (LORD) of 17:1, which must be attributed to the Redactor of Genesis, who has brought this story into concert with the surrounding J material. Possibly the Redactor put "Yahweh" in this place because of its earlier identification with the El Elyon of 14:22 and the El Roi of 16:13. Now there is a further identification: *I am God the Almighty:* El Shaddai.

Shaddai, however, is not for the Priestly author simply one of the random divine names extracted from Canaanite cult which were subsequently applied to the Yahweh of Israel's worship. Rather, as we see from 28:3, 35:11, and 48:3 below, as well as from Exodus 6:3, he has tried to assign this particular divine name an historical significance that elevates it into a category apart. Shaddai he considered to be the peculiarly patriarchal equivalent of the same God whom in his prepatriarchal forehistory he called Elohim and whom the later Israel knew as Yahweh. The schematism is, of course, artificial, and it is really not much pursued by P. In reality, the name Shaddai can hardly be distinguished from those other Canaanite and Near Eastern divine titles which the Old Testament has elsewhere appropriated to the God of Israel. The etymology of the word is debated ("mountain god" is one of the currently fashionable interpretations), and there is no hard evidence that it had any more direct connection with Yahwism than did the Elyon of chapter 14. Shaddai was translated by the Septuagint *pantokrator* (the "all-powerful" god of various myths), whence the Almighty of our English versions.

"I am God the Almighty," nevertheless, has its definite place in this Priestly account of the covenant with Abraham. In the suzerainty treaties of the ancient Near East which served as one matrix for the covenantal formulas of the Old Testament (the treaties by which a high king bestowed his favor upon a vassal), it was customary for the pact to show at its beginning the name and title of the lord who conceded the covenant. It was also customary to relate the past benefits which the overlord had showered on his underling and which, therefore, should guarantee a reciprocal loyalty (a thing which is not done here), and to demand a certain appropriate conduct in return (a thing which is done here): *Walk in my presence and be blameless.* The basic and very considerable difference that distinguishes the patriarchal covenant of P from that of J is that in this chapter 17 it is no longer the simple oath of a benign deity who promises, as before, to *multiply you exceedingly,* but is now a contract *between you and me,* an agreement which demands of its recipient a way of life and the fulfillment of divers stipulations that are part of its very nature and constitution. The difference reflects the tendency of the Priestly author to synthesize the various covenant traditions of Israel. He now structures the patriarchal covenant in such a way as to make it resemble the great covenant of Sinai which Yahweh was to confer on Israel, even as in 9:1–17 above he extended the covenantal privilege to all mankind in the blessing bestowed on Noah and his descendants.

3 When Abram prostrated himself, God continued to
4 speak to him: "My covenant with you is this: you
5 are to become the father of a host of nations. No longer shall you be called Abram; your name shall be Abraham, for I am making you the father of a host
6 of nations. I will render you exceedingly fertile; I will
7 make nations of you; kings shall stem from you. I will maintain my covenant with you and your descendants after you throughout the ages as an everlasting pact, to be your God and the God of your de-
8 scendants after you. I will give to you and to your descendants after you the land in which you are now

staying, the whole land of Canaan, as a permanent
possession; and I will be their God."

As the Priestly author proceeds in his rather plodding way to set the
stipulations of the Abrahamic covenant, it is interesting to note the revisions that have occurred in the tradition since it left the care of the
Yahwist. First of all, there is no covenant ritual, as there was in chapter
15. There may even be a significance in the fact that vs. 2 above has God
establish (literally, "give") a covenant rather than "cut" it as in 15:18
above. The ancient oath rite and its accompanying language may well have
seemed a touch too anthropomorphic for the theology of P. An alternative
"sign," however, is provided in the change of Abraham's name, which up
to this point has been spelled *Abram* (both in the J and the P elements of
Genesis, thanks to the standardization of the Redactor) but now picks up
an extra syllable and becomes *Abraham,* the additional "ha" being explained through popular etymology from the decree that he will be *the father of a host (ab hamon) of nations.* By the standards of genuine linguistics the two spellings undoubtedly simply reflected dialectical variations on
one and the same name. It is not impossible, however, that the tradition
had remembered an actual change of pronunciation that had taken place
as a consequence of migration into Canaan from beyond the Great River.
If so, a connection made between the new name and the new life of promise in Canaan was by no means a farfetched conceit. Such a change could,
indeed, quite legitimately be interpreted as a providential sign.

Another characteristic of the P version of the covenant is that it is declared perpetual (the *everlasting pact* of vs. 7). Again, the tendency of P
to assimilate the various covenant traditions one to another becomes evident: recall the "everlasting covenant" of 9:16 (Noah) and the "perpetual
covenant" of Exodus 31:16 (Sinai). But why the stress on perpetuity, in
any or all of these cases? The language comes from the same Davidic covenant tradition that inspired the Yahwist (cf. 2 Samuel 7:16.24–29;
Psalms 89:29–30.37, 132:12), even though he did not make use of it
when making that covenant the model of his portrayal of Yahweh's
dealing with Abraham. It has been very reasonably proposed by numerous
scholars that P's evocation of the Davidic covenant formula makes the
best sense when seen in concert with the stress laid on the same formula in
the consolation literature of exilic prophetic texts (cf. Isaiah 55:3, 61:8;
Jeremiah 32:40, 50:5; Ezekiel 16:60, 37:26). That is, in the traumatic
days of national and religious disaster when the Davidic dynasty was no
more and Israel had lost its land and identity (the *permanent possession*
of vs. 8), hoping against hope men of God reminded themselves that God
had once covenanted himself forever and unconditionally, and they therefore believed in a future that he would bring them to, even if by means

and in manners that they could not then discern. "Everlasting" and "perpetual," therefore, could easily have become for the Priestly author the epitome of what divine covenant was all about. It crystallized the same kind of faith that later apocalyptic writers professed when they reinterpreted the words of salvation prophecy that had to all appearances gone awry, knowing that the word of God must eventually come out right.

> 9 God also said to Abraham: "On your part, you and
> your descendants after you must keep my covenant
> 10 throughout the ages. This is my covenant with you
> and your descendants after you that you must keep:
> 11 every male among you shall be circumcised. Cir-
> cumcise the flesh of your foreskin, and that shall be
> the mark of the covenant between you and me.
> 12 Throughout the ages, every male among you, when
> he is eight days old, shall be circumcised, including
> houseborn slaves and those acquired with money
> 13 from any foreigner who is not of your blood. Yes,
> both the houseborn slaves and those acquired with
> money must be circumcised. Thus my covenant shall
> 14 be in your flesh as an everlasting pact. If a male is
> uncircumcised, that is, if the flesh of his foreskin has
> not been cut away, such a one shall be cut off from
> his people; he has broken my covenant."

The general and visible sign given to the Abrahamic covenant by the Priestly author is the circumcision of males. The practice is said to have existed in Egypt from the time of the ancient empire (about 4000 B.C.), and in biblical times it is characteristic of the Semitic peoples of Canaan and adjacent territories—not, notably, of the non-Semitic Philistines, who are proverbially "the uncircumcised." It was not a custom honored in Mesopotamia. Perhaps like the language change undergone in the voicing of Abraham's name, the adoption of circumcision was recalled as an effect of the passage of patriarchal society from its earlier homeland into the Land of Promise. If so, it could very fittingly and historically be invoked as a true covenantal sign. Its importance for the Priestly author, however, derives from much more proximate religious concerns.

Circumcision, often with a corresponding mutilation inflicted on the female, is a fairly universal human phenomenon, known to peoples ancient and modern, primitive and developed, black, white, brown, and yellow. Among these peoples it has taken on many guises and assumed contrary meanings: it can be a dictate of simple hygiene, an initiatory rite into the mysteries of puberty, and, in some instances, an ignorant and unhealthy tradition perpetrated with no rationality at all. Only among the Hebrews—

Jews and Arabs—does it seem to have become a religious rite practiced upon male infants. We do not know when and why this religious development took place, only that it did. The Priestly law of Leviticus 12:3 (and it is from this Priestly law that the Priestly author has drawn much of his name and reputation) furnished the precedent for vs. 12 above: *every male among you, when he is eight days old, shall be circumcised.* When P was being put together, the religious rite of circumcision, like the Sabbath observance (Genesis 2:2–3, Exodus 31:14–17), had become one of those externals by which, particularly in trying times, identity is established and preserved even at the expense of far more fundamental values. (Fish on Friday, the square tonsure, the sign of the cross from right to left, leavened bread, a choir without orchestral sounds, Yiddish and not Hebrew . . .) The *everlasting pact* which again turns up in vs. 13 therefore takes on added significance for the Priestly author. It is a reminder not only of a long-ago event but also of an enduring pledge and hope: the covenant once made with Abraham was now living in his own flesh and testified to his right to share in God's promise.

15 God further said to Abraham: "As for your wife Sarai, do not call her Sarai; her name shall be Sarah.
16 I will bless her, and I will give you a son by her. Him* also will I bless; he shall give rise to nations,
17 and rulers of peoples shall issue from him." Abraham prostrated himself and laughed as he said to himself, "Can a child be born to a man who is a hundred years old? Or can Sarah give birth at
18 ninety?" Then Abraham said to God, "Let but Ish-
19 mael live on by your favor!" God replied: "Nevertheless, your wife Sarah is to bear you a son, and you shall call him Isaac. I will maintain my covenant with him as an everlasting pact, to be his God
20 and the God of his descendants† after him. As for Ishmael, I am heeding you: I hereby bless him. I will make him fertile and will multiply him exceedingly. He shall become the father of twelve chief-
21 tains, and I will make of him a great nation. But my covenant I will maintain with Isaac, whom Sarah
22 shall bear to you by this time next year." When he had finished speaking with him, God departed from Abraham.

* So the LXX. The Hebrew refers to Sarah rather than to Isaac.
† The Hebrew text is truncated. The NAB translation follows the ancient versions.

The logical sequel to the covenant of circumcision detailed in vss. 9–14 is its immediate implementation as described in vss. 23–27. These intervening verses which appear above are equally part of the Priestly author's narrative and integral to the story as he wanted to tell it; but they also show that he has combined traditions of differing viewpoints that result in am ambivalence attaching to the covenant with Abraham as he has presented it finally.

As Abraham's new life under the covenant was marked by a change of name, so does it happen with his wife: *Sarai* becomes *Sarah*. This time no etymological reason is given for the change, which, as before, has its historical explanation in a dialectical shift. The main purpose of the author in introducing Sarah at this point is, in any case, to broach a new subject and not to protract an old one. For the first time in Genesis the birth of a son is foretold who will also be the offspring of Sarah. The Yahwistic parallel of this prediction will appear in the following chapter 18 where the Redactor has placed it. Here and now, however, in the redactional structure of Genesis, an answer is given to the question that was rather mysteriously raised by the assurance of 15:4 (J) regarding the natural heir that would be given to Abraham. Despite the assumption of Abraham reflected in vs. 18 above that that heir would be Ishmael, following 16:1b–2.4–8 (J) and the P narration of 16:15–16 which has Hagar's son duly born in Abraham's household (and such, we shall see, was also the Elohist version of the events), it now becomes plain, however, that this was not the Lord's design. The reward of Abraham's faith is to be more wonderful than he had imagined, for she who as early as 11:30 (J) was called barren is now to bear him a son. Ishmael is the answer that the reader has been tempted to apply to the implied question of 15:4, but it was the wrong answer.

In all three of the major sources of Genesis *Isaac* appears as a child of promise, of an unexpected and providential birth. In both J and P he is also represented as a child of his parents' old age, though J probably did not have in mind ages quite as advanced as those given by P. It is the factor of age, obviously, that in this story accounts for Abraham's having *prostrated himself and laughed* at the annunciation. His is a curious mixture of acceptance and doubt, the attitude of a man who wants to believe and whose instincts rebel against belief, forcing incoherences to unwilling lips. *Let but Ishmael live on by your favor!* might be accounted such an incoherence: touchingly, Abraham offers God the option of taking back the promise just made and of doing the less impossible thing by prospering the future of the heir who is already in hand. The exclamation permits a distinction to be drawn between the separate lots that are in store for Ishmael and Isaac. Ishmael's future will, indeed, be prospered, but he will not be Abraham's heir.

Parenthetically, we should note that the "laughed" (*yitshaq*) of vs. 17

contains a wordplay with the name Isaac that is a feature of all the Isaac stories, J, P, and E. It is a sign of the roots these stories have in a very primitive common tradition, however much they have later gone their separate ways.

The distinction of the respective providential futures of Ishmael and Isaac points up the ambivalence mentioned above which these verses introduce into the concept of the covenant which God has enacted with Abraham. Both sons, like Abraham himself, are assured a multitude of descendants. Isaac *shall give rise to nations, and rulers of peoples shall issue from him,* while Ishmael *shall become the father of twelve chieftains* (cf. 25:12–16, P) and be made into *a great nation.* But only with Isaac will God covenant; to him alone will be extended the *everlasting pact.* It is very evident that in 17:15–21 "covenant" and even "everlasting pact" is something different from what it is in vss. 1–14 above and in vss. 23–27 below. In this intervening section "my covenant" has ceased to be the covenant of circumcision which God entered into with the Hebrews (including Ishmael and his descendants) and has become instead the distinct inheritance through strict blood lines of a privilege that father could not transmit to son but could only deliver to legally acceptable candidates. Thus a Moabite and an Ammonite (cf. Genesis 19:30–38 below) could never become part of Israel (cf. Deuteronomy 23:4) according to Israel's later law. The same is doubtless true of Ishmael. A people that once shared in its patriarchal covenant, in view of a theology that tended to exclude it from this covenant when the covenant became more and more identified with Israel, simply came to be reckoned as outside the covenant. In these verses, the "covenant" means little more or less than the "inheritance" of 15:2–4: namely, those who are accepted in the direct line of Abraham-Isaac-Jacob and who will dominate the chapters that follow.

God departed from Abraham, says the text. Literally, "he reascended." The Priestly author allows himself an occasional anthropomorphism.

> 23 Abraham took his son Ishmael and all his slaves, whether born in his house or acquired with his money—every male among the members of Abraham's household—and he circumcised the flesh of their foreskins on that same day, as God had told 24 him to do. Abraham was ninety-nine years old when 25 the flesh of his foreskin was circumcised, and his son Ishmael was thirteen years old when the flesh of his 26 foreskin was circumcised. Thus, on that same day Abraham and his son Ishmael were circumcised; 27 and all the male members of his household, including the slaves born in his house or acquired with his money from foreigners, were circumcised with him.

The text reverts to a concept of the covenant which is dominant throughout the chapter, characterizing the Israel of an exilic and postexilic age which generously included among its members both natives and foreigners who were willing to live in peace within its realm and according to its laws. The covenant embraces not only Abraham and his natural heir Isaac, but also *Ishmael and all his slaves,* in which category was doubtless included the *ger* and *toshab,* the "sojourner" ("alien" in 15:13 as applied to Abraham) or the "transient" (Numbers 35:15), residents in Israel who were protected by its laws to which they conformed even as later Jews would conform to laws and customs of the Gentiles among whom they dwelt. Ishmael and his descendants, to be sure, the Arab peoples, Israel did not count as Gentiles but rather as Hebraic cousins.

We have already observed several times the artificiality of the Priestly author's chronology. It is worth noticing again in this place, however, since the *thirteen years* ascribed to Ishmael in this episode make absolutely no sense at all when transferred to the stories preceding or following, whatever may have been the Redactor's thought about the matter.

5. Sodom and Gomorrah

The story resumes the chronicle of Abraham and Lot and it is entirely J, except for a single summary verse indicated in italics as P.

18 The LORD appeared to Abraham by the terebinth of Mamre, as he sat in the entrance of his tent, while 2 the day was growing hot. Looking up, he saw three men standing nearby. When he saw them, he ran from the entrance of the tent to greet them; and 3 bowing to the ground, he said: "Sir, if I may ask you this favor, please do not go on past your ser- 4 vant. Let some water be brought, that you may bathe your feet, and then rest yourselves under the 5 tree. Now that you have come this close to your servant,* let me bring you a little food, that you may refresh yourselves; and afterward you may go on your way." "Very well," they replied, "do as you 6 have said." Abraham hastened into the tent and told Sarah, "Quick, three seahs of fine flour! Knead it

* The translation presupposes a slightly revised Hebrew text.

7 and make rolls." He ran to the herd, picked out a
tender, choice steer, and gave it to a servant, who
8 quickly prepared it. Then he got some curds and
milk, as well as the steer that had been prepared,
and set these before them; and he waited on them
under the tree while they ate.

These verses introduce what is at one and the same time one of the most
sophisticated and the most naïve of the portrayals of Divinity which it has
been given to the Yahwist to create. It begins with an appearance at *the
terebinth of Mamre* (cf. 13:18 above) of *three men standing nearby the
entrance of* Abraham's *tent, while the day was growing hot.* We are once
more confronted with Abraham the tent-dweller, the man of a childless
wife who inhabits a last homely house by the edge of the wild which is
open to every demand that may be made on it in the name of Bedawin
hospitality.

Here is an Abraham who runs eagerly to the flap of his tent, who bows
to the ground before the guests whom Allah has sent him, and who proceeds to overwhelm them with what he can offer: *a little food* deprecat-
ingly proffered, which amounts to *three seahs of fine flour* (roughly eight
gallons or a bushel, or again roughly, some forty liters) and *a tender,
choice steer,* along with *curds and milk,* rest under his tree from the blaz-
ing sun, water to wash their feet, and so on. We are completely overwhelmed by the munificence of this desert prince, as indeed we are intended to be. As we have long suspected must be the case, Abraham is
proved to be possessed of all the major virtues of nomadic society. We are
now to be told what happened to him in consequence of these virtues, as
had happened to many another hospitable person who entertained gods
unheralded.

For this, indeed, seems to have been the sense of the story that the
Yahwist has handed on with hardly an alteration. In vs. 3 Abraham
addresses his visitants as "sirs," which is the perfectly proper title of respect that a genial host will be expected to confer on his guest. The Hebrew for it, however, is Adonai, which can mean milord, or lords, or even
the Lord of 15:2. And such seems to have been the ironical twist which
the biblical author intended his reader or reciter to give this word when he
encountered it on Abraham's lips; for the "three men" of our passage, who
seem at times to become two men or even one man and eventually are
denominated angels, certainly signify in this story Yahweh, the only Lord
of Israel. It appears to be beyond doubt that the story derives from a
polytheistic source and that it has undergone a minimum of revision in its
adjustment to the Yahwism of the Bible. The theme of a god or gods traveling in disguise and rewarding the human hospitality they receive is very

common in mythology and folklore. "The classic parallel," as Theodor Gaster has pointed out, "is the tale, told by Ovid and Hyginus, of how Jupiter, Neptune, and Mercury (i.e., *three* visitors, as in the Biblical narrative!), while traveling through Boeotia, came in disguise to Hyrieus (or Hyreus), a childless peasant (or, as others say, a prince) of Tanagra, and, in return for his hospitality, granted him the boon of a son, who was in fact Orion."

9 "Where is your wife Sarah?" they asked him.
10 "There in the tent," he replied. One of them said, "I will surely return to you about this time next year, and Sarah will then have a son." Sarah was listening
11 at the entrance of the tent just behind him. Now Abraham and Sarah were old, advanced in years, and Sarah had stopped having her womanly periods.
12 So Sarah laughed to herself and said, "Now that I am so withered and my husband is so old, am I still
13 to have sexual pleasure?" But the LORD said to Abraham: "Why did Sarah laugh and say, 'Shall I
14 really bear a child, old as I am?' Is anything too marvelous for the LORD to do? At the appointed time, about this time next year, I will return to you,
15 and Sarah will have a son." Because she was afraid, Sarah dissembled, saying, "I didn't laugh." But he said, "Yes you did."

The story unfolds in the classic pattern. True to the ways of desert life, Sarah, though she had prepared the meal for her husband and his guests, would not have been present at the eating of it: men and women, in that society, did not and do not break bread in common. She remains *in the tent* while her lords and masters dine in the open. This, of course, does not prevent her overhearing their conversation, for which she evinces a normal curiosity. And so, she laughs (again, the play on words with the name of Isaac, even though, as in chapter 15, the actual name does not appear here) when she hears the prediction that she will bear a son, which she interprets as the type of pleasantry that one man will pass to another in ignorance of factual considerations such as the drying up of an aged wife.

The *one of them* of vs. 10 is doubtless a gesture of the author toward the Yahwism of the passage which becomes overt in vss. 13–14. Abraham, perhaps, should have been adverted to the supernatural character of his guests by their calling of his wife by name. Certainly Sarah begins to suspect when she discovers to her surprise and fear that her secret thoughts and emotions have been exposed. We can imagine, if we will, that she bursts forth from the tent, damaging protocol, to deny the undeniable in her confusion and anxiety.

16 The men set out from there and looked down toward Sodom; Abraham was walking with them to
17 see them on their way. The LORD reflected: "Shall
18 I hide from Abraham what I am about to do, now
that he is to become a great and populous nation,
and all the nations of the earth are to find blessing
19 in him? Indeed, I have singled him out that he may
direct his sons and his posterity to keep the way of
the LORD by doing what is right and just, so that the
LORD may carry into effect for Abraham the prom-
20 ises he made about him." Then the LORD said: "The
outcry against Sodom and Gomorrah is so great, and
21 their sin so grave, that I must go down and see
whether or not their actions fully correspond to the
cry against them that comes to me. I mean to find
out."

Abraham, the perfect host to the end, and still unaware of the character
of his guests, accompanies *the men* part of their way from his dwelling as
a courteous Bedawin will. Their way is set *toward Sodom*. Suddenly the
narrative gives way to a silloquy of Yahweh (who, however, speaks of
himself in the third person). The sililoquy celebrates the initial Yahwistic
blessing of Abraham that constituted him the friend of God (cf. 12:2–3)
and also (in vs. 19) brings out the moral and ethical demands imposed by
this friendship which were previously stressed by P (cf. 17:1). The major
point made by the soliloquy, however, is that God cannot keep hidden
from one such as Abraham his hidden designs. Again Abraham appears in
the guise of a prophet (cf. 15:12): "Indeed, the Lord GOD does nothing
without revealing his plan to his servants, the prophets" (Amos 3:7).

In vs. 20 the coming destruction of *Sodom and Gomorrah* is revealed as
the present plan of the Lord which will not be kept from Abraham. In the
section that follows below, a knowledge of this plan is presumed to have
been communicated to the patriarch. The language of vs. 21 is highly
reminiscent of Genesis 11:7 (J): as before, Yahweh must *go down* to ascertain the enormity of the crimes that have been committed and that cry
out for vengeance.

22 While the two men walked on farther toward
Sodom, the LORD remained standing before Abra-
23 ham.† Then Abraham drew nearer to him and said:
"Will you sweep away the innocent with the guilty?

† The Hebrew has "Abraham remained standing before Yahweh," which is a "pious"
scribal revision of the text.

24 Suppose there were fifty innocent people in the city; would you wipe out the place, rather than spare it for the sake of the fifty innocent people within it?
25 Far be it from you to do such a thing, to make the innocent die with the guilty, so that the innocent and the guilty would be treated alike! Should not the
26 judge of all the world act with justice?" The LORD replied, "If I find fifty innocent people in the city of Sodom, I will spare the whole place for their
27 sake." Abraham spoke up again: "See how I am presuming to speak to my Lord, though I am but
28 dust and ashes! What if there are five less than fifty innocent people? Will you destroy the whole city because of those five?" "I will not destroy it," he an-
29 swered, "if I find forty-five there." But Abraham persisted, saying, "What if only forty are found there?" He replied, "I will forbear doing it for the sake of
30 the forty." Then he said, "Let not my Lord grow impatient if I go on. What if only thirty are found there?" He replied, "I will forbear doing it if I can
31 find but thirty there." Still he went on. "Since I have thus dared to speak to my Lord, what if there are no more than twenty?" "I will not destroy it," he
32 answered, "for the sake of the twenty." But he still persisted, "Please, let not my Lord grow angry if I speak up this last time. What if there are at least ten there?" "For the sake of those ten," he replied, "I will not destroy it."
33 The LORD departed as soon as he had finished speaking with Abraham, and Abraham returned home.

This section of the story of Sodom and Gomorrah's destruction has all the appearances of being the Yahwist's personal contribution to the ancient saga (or series of sagas), his own insertion into it of a dialogue between Yahweh and Abraham in which he sought to safeguard certain theological values. The dialogue has been loosely harmonized with the surrounding narrative. We are doubtless supposed to think of *the two men who walked on farther toward Sodom* as the "two angels" of chapter 19 (however, the "two" of vs. 22 does not appear in the Hebrew but has been supplied by the NAB). They are now firmly distinct from Yahweh, who not since vs. 10 above has been identified with one or all of the three men who set the scene for the divine visitation by Abraham's tent but is always simply "present" under his divine title. Abraham, nevertheless, continues to use the ambiguous form of address Adonai with which he began in vs. 3: there "Sir," here "my Lord," even though he knows full well with whom he is conversing—the whole point of the dialogue, in fact. No explanation is attempted of how he has suddenly come to such knowledge or when he became privy to Yahweh's plan to destroy Sodom and Gomorrah. The Yahwist has been less interested in producing a coherent narrative than in honoring some religious values that were dear to him and with which he wished to embellish this story.

Chief among them, undoubtedly, is the quality of unstrained mercy that he ascribes to the God of Israel who is also, in Abraham's words, *judge of all the world*. It is proper that such a judge (*shophet*) should *act with justice* (*mishpat*): Yahweh is being "reminded" in this interchange of the Near Eastern ideal by which the judge or ruler was regarded in the first place as the one who made right prevail in his domain. He who has in his charge the whole of mankind cannot permit himself to fall short of an ideal that is expected of mortal kings and princes. Thus it must be evident that he does not act arbitrarily in imposing his rule, and specifically that in punishing the guilty he does not allow the innocent to perish, for otherwise *the innocent and the guilty would be treated alike,* a thing that can be tolerated in no judge.

As we have already seen, the destruction of the legendary cities of the plain was proverbial in Israelite tradition as exemplifying the dire consequences of divine wrath. What the Yahwist is anxious to bring out is how justified was this divine wrath, which had been withheld till it no longer legitimately could be (vss. 20–21), and which even now would be withheld again if the slightest counterindication for it could be found. No, Yahweh will not *sweep away the innocent with the guilty,* but he will spare the guilty for the sake of the innocent, however relatively few they may be. In vss. 26–32 Yahweh and Abraham are shown pitted against each other in a scene taken from oriental life, the bargaining ritual that produces the terms by which a deal is finally consummated. Abraham is highly skilled in the rules and the running of this serious game, but at the end, by implication, he loses; he cannot come up with the final, minimal coin that must be delivered to seal the bargain. By this device the Yahwist brings out, of course, how truly beyond the pale was the object of Yahweh's wrath, possessed of no redeeming quality whatever. He has also explored the mystery of the interrelation of divine judgment and mercy in relation to a people among which both guilty and innocent might be found, and in doing so he has at least hinted at the idea of a redemptive power which the just have for the unjust—an idea which meant much in an age when collective responsibility was a concept taken for granted, and which can mean something today now that the concept is being taken seriously again.

Besides, the Yahwist has presented Abraham in the guise of the prophetic pleader and mediator who stands between a vengeful God and a people deserving of doom (cf. Amos 7:1–6). In fact, Abraham appears as more disinterested than even the prophets, for while these pleaded for a people of which they themselves were part, he intercedes for aliens, simply out of a human sense of values that seem to him to be right (the *dust and ashes* presuming to speak to God in vs. 27). In conformity with this design, probably, is it that a consideration of Lot, Abraham's kinsman now resident in Sodom, is nowhere introduced into the conversation between the patriarch and the Lord of the earth. Abraham ceases his bargaining short of invoking any claim of special privilege with God for himself and his own, and only when he has pressed to that irreducible minimum beyond which justice would be bereft of all meaning along with mercy, since anything further would reduce them to empty words of no distinction.

> **19** The two angels reached Sodom in the evening, as Lot was sitting at the gate of Sodom. When Lot saw them, he got up to greet them; and bowing down
> 2 with his face to the ground, he said, "Please, gentlemen, come aside into your servant's house for the night, and bathe your feet; you can get up early to continue your journey." But they replied, "No, we
> 3 shall pass the night in the town square." He urged them so strongly, however, that they turned aside to his place and entered his house. He prepared a meal for them, baking cakes without leaven, and they dined.

The story is in sequence with the main tradition responsible for chapter 18, though there are some inconsistencies. The men of 18:2 continue their journey interrupted at Abraham's tent and now arrive at Sodom. They now appear as *the two angels*—"two" doubtless in deference to the distinction made at 18:22 (or 18:16) between Yahweh and the rest of the original trio, "angels" undoubtedly out of the same concern that dictated the "messenger" of 16:7 (the same Hebrew word is involved in both cases)—and they are angels also in vs. 15 below, but in vs. 12 (where, however, the NAB has translated "the angels," following the Samaritan Pentateuch) and in vss. 5, 8, 10 ("his guests" in the NAB), and 16 once more we hear of "the men." Yahweh makes the inspection announced in 18:21 still within the description of a human visitation. As before, from vs. 17 below and on, the symbolic presence of the men or angels is forgotten, and the words and action of Yahweh alone are featured. Also as before, Lot uses the ambiguous Adonai to address his visitants: "gentlemen" in vs. 2, "my lord" in vs. 18, though it is apparent that in the meanwhile he has acquired a better understanding of their more than human identity, even as Abraham did.

Lot himself, *sitting at the gate of Sodom,* fits into the narrative more loosely than any of the other elements that divide or separate chapters 18 and 19. When last seen (13:5–13) he had, indeed, been heading toward Sodom and had pitched his tent near there, but he was then a prosperous herdsman and semi-nomad. Now he is a townsman, pure and simple, presiding *in the evening* cool at the city gate, the equivalent of today's civic center or city hall, where the acknowledged leaders of the community gathered to discuss matters that affected them all, resolve difficulties, and exchange information that contributed to the common weal. His reaction to the unannounced presence of these strangers in his city is, quite evidently, modeled on the reaction ascribed to Abraham in 18:2–5. It already carries with it an implied rebuke of the boorish ways of the rest of the men of Sodom, an implication that will become quite explicit as the story continues. The personages to whom he extends his invitation have, of course, other purposes in mind than simply spending the night in Sodom and passing on, and therefore they indicate their intention to *pass the night in the town square,* to sleep in the streets rather than to seek the shelter of a house. Nevertheless, Lot's hospitality prevails. *They turned aside to his place and entered his house.* Lot further extends himself to make his guests comfortable: *cakes without leaven* are prepared for their food because, at such a late hour, there would be no time for the leavening of regular bread dough. There is no denigration here of Lot's offering against that of 18:6: Abraham's "rolls" were also unleavened.

> 4 Before they went to bed, all the townsmen of
> Sodom, both young and old—all the people to the
> 5 last man—closed in on the house. They called to
> Lot and said to him, "Where are the men who came
> to your house tonight? Bring them out to us that we
> 6 may have intimacies with them." Lot went out to
> 7 meet them at the entrance. When he had shut the
> door behind him, he said, "I beg you, my brothers,
> 8 not to do this wicked thing. I have two daughters
> who have never had intercourse with men. Let me
> bring them out to you, and you may do to them as
> you please. But don't do anything to these men, for
> you know they have come under the shelter of my
> 9 roof." They replied, "Stand back! This fellow,"
> they sneered, "came here as an immigrant, and now
> he dares to give orders! We'll treat you worse than
> them!" With that, they pressed hard against Lot,

10 moving in closer to break down the door. But his
guests put out their hands, pulled Lot inside with
11 them, and closed the door; at the same time they
struck the men at the entrance of the house, one
and all, with such a blinding light that they were utterly unable to reach the doorway.

We now learn what, in the view of the Yahwist, was the crime of the
cities of the plain that had called down on them divine vengeance and destruction—or at least what in his mind was one of the crimes of one of the
cities: we have already noted that Sodom alone tends to pre-empt the center of the stage in the portrayal of the ancient catastrophe that was held up
to Israel as an object of horror and shuddering and of an always imminent
retribution. The tradition about the cities was doubtless vague and indeterminate, inviting each storyteller to devise his own cautionary tale. Deuteronomy 29:22 and 32:22 speak of these places only in general terms, as
having richly deserved annihilation because of unspecified but notorious
offenses, and such is also the intelligence of Amos 4:11, Zephaniah 2:9,
Lamentations 4:6, and Hosea 11:8 (which speaks of Admah and Zeboiim
without reference to Sodom and Gomorrah). In Isaiah (1:9–10 and 3:9)
Sodom and Gomorrah are listed as earlier instructors of Judah in all the
vices, which in Judah's case were social and judicial vices, though they
were not necessarily so specified in the original magisterium (so also in the
later Isaiah 13:19, Sodom and Gomorrah are merely proverbial names to
designate cesspools of evil). Jeremiah 23:14 lists among Jerusalem's
Sodom-and-Gomorrah-like iniquities the shocking deeds of its prophets:
adultery, living in lies, siding with the wicked; but again it is not clear
whether the prophet intended to assert that Sodom and Jerusalem were
sinners of the same sin or were simply sinners together (as before, the
later Jeremiah 49:18 and 50:40 mention Sodom and Gomorrah only as a
byword). As for Ezekiel (16:46–56), with biting sarcasm Sodom is con-
trasted with its "sister" Judah as having, on the record, scored higher
marks for virtuous living even though it had also distinguished itself by
pride, conspicuous and wastrel spending in the face of crying human need,
and criminal callousness and complacency. It is possible that out of all
these biblical authors' grapplings with the legend of Sodom and Gomorrah, Ezekiel and the Yahwist emerge as the most successful in attempting
to assign to the old saga the parabolic role of defining a clear and present
evil that had once brought about a proud people's downfall and could
easily do so again.

Certainly there is no doubt about what the Yahwist believed that evil to
have been. It is what accounts for the presence in all our modern languages of "sodomy," which the best of our dictionaries defines as "an un-

natural form of sexual intercourse, esp. that of one male with another."
Before we comment on this, we might anticipate a modern reaction which
could easily judge that Ezekiel, and possibly the prophets before him, were
more sensitive than the Yahwist to the real evils that offend the sight of
God and may most fittingly, therefore, be proclaimed the seeds of a people's decadence and decay. Those whose ignorance of history tends to
match the frequency of their appeals to it are fond of the conceit that decline and fall have ever dogged the steps of what they call effeteness.
Effeteness for them is lack of nerve, loss of the homely, manly, family virtues, which they equate with permissiveness in the sexual and social arenas
of life. So went Rome, according to their paradigm, and so fell Rome as a
consequence. Edward Gibbon, whom they think they are quoting, surveyed the scene with somewhat different criteria. In his judgment decline
and fall coincided not with the rotting away of bourgeois virtues but with
the national cult of "immoderate greatness," a congeries of symptoms and
pathologies that is not far from what Ezekiel had in mind.

However, we are now concerned with Genesis and not Ezekiel. We must
try to understand the enormity of the sin of Sodom as it appeared to the
Yahwist and as he has featured it in his story.

In both the Old and the New Testament homosexuality is treated simply
as a perversion, an abomination punishable by death (cf. Leviticus
20:13). As Hans Walter Wolff tries to define the mentality behind such an
attitude: "Homosexuality is a failure to recognize the difference of the
sexes, and with it the basic way of arriving at a fruitful life through the
overcoming of self-love." For the same basic reason, transvestism was
condemned as a kindred aberration (Deuteronomy 22:5). In Romans
1:26–27 Paul, echoing the thought of other Jewish writers before and
after him, ascribes to the idolatry of the Gentiles and their perversion of
the true knowledge of God their consequent perversion in the practice of
lesbianism and male homosexuality. Throughout the whole Old Testament
period homosexuality was peculiarly identified with those other heathen
ways and practices which must not be allowed to contaminate Israel. Non-
Israelite indeed it was, from first to last. Babylonian inscriptions celebrate
it, the law code of Hammurabi protected it, and Plato praised it as a virtue. The Jews of Paul's time called it the Greek vice, though of course it
was far older than Greece.

The Bible did not know any of the facts that have been developed in our
modern studies of sexual behavior, which have revealed to us that the ho-
mosexual is most often what he or she is through no deliberate choice at
all but instead by a decree of birth. We do not expect to find in it, therefore, the compassion which it otherwise brings to the examination of the
manifold quality of the human condition in all its fundamental divergences, its pluses and minuses. Biblical religion would, of course, have us

exercise an understanding in this or in any other area that the Bible itself did not exercise, since we have knowledge that it did not, and knowledge carries with it the duty to understand. The Bible knew homosexuality only as the selfish perversion of one of man's highest goods, the product of an unholy lust, whether it was intended to slake a jaded appetite, or was the too easy resort of men and women confined overmuch to the company of their own sex, or—worst yet—was one of the dark rites of the religions of Canaan (cf. Deuteronomy 23:19).

We have probably already spent more time on the discussion of this question than the Yahwist would have intended that we do. There is no doubt that for him homosexuality was the characteristic "sin of Sodom" that provoked the cry reaching to heaven of which Yahweh spoke to himself in 18:20–21. There is likewise no doubt that, in keeping with the conversation of 18:23–32, he has designed to portray it as a universal, chronic, endemic vice, one of *both young and old—all the people to the last man.* Still, when he becomes explicit about it in this story he does so with the use of a single verb, and that a half euphemism. He is much more concerned with the heinous conduct of the Sodomites in violating the code of all civilized men, which ascribed an almost sacred character to "the stranger within the gates," the person who had taken refuge within the protection of their walls. Of this, under the circumstances far graver crime, their unnatural proclivities and desires had served only as the incitement and occasion. The priority accorded hospitality among the virtues and the consequent inviolability of the guest may strike a modern Western sensibility as exaggeration and oriental exuberance. But they were vital to the functioning of a society in which the reliability of various small sureties spelled the difference between death and survival. Outside in the desert everyone was everyone else's enemy until proved otherwise (cf. Genesis 4:14). With an enemy one knows how to deal: as an enemy. Once this same person had been received as a guest, however, he knew that he could relax his vigilance, secure in the company of his temporary friends. As for the host, tomorrow he might stand in need of the same succor which it was now his lot to dispense. The Sodomites, who had previously shown themselves to be clods, now reveal themselves as barbarians. Not only do they seek to brutalize the wayfarers who have put themselves under the protection of their city, they threaten even worse treatment to the one who had long dwelt in their midst as a fellow resident.

If the men of Sodom do not know what it is to be a host, the reader may be tempted to think that Lot knows a deal too much. Certainly to our tastes he proves himself to be more sensitive to the duties of hospitality than those of fatherhood. As we have suggested above in similar contexts, the spectacle of a father offering his virgin daughters to the will and pleasure of a mob that was seeking to despoil his household would not have seemed as shocking to the ancient sense of proprieties as it may seem to our own. (One commentator has also observed, tongue in cheek no doubt, that Lot, knowing well the sexual preferences of those with whom he dealt, confidently expected his invitation to be declined.) Really, there is no need to make excuses for him, as far as the biblical perspective is concerned. In all the stories about him, the soundness of Lot's judgment is never the point at issue; the opposite, in fact, is more than once indicated. He is a good and not a bad man, but neither is he heroic in any way. It is undoubtedly by no accident that in the rather distasteful story of vss. 30–38 below Lot's daughters treat in a singularly unfilial manner a father who had not exactly manifested to them the paternal ideal.

In the event, it is the guests who save Lot, not the other way round. To do so they must disclose their more than human identities, of which Lot is obviously aware in the verses that follow and conclude this story. The *blinding light* of vs. 11 (*sanwerim,* originally an Akkadian word) which they call down upon the Sodomites reappears in the Hebrew Bible only in 2 Kings 6:18, and in precisely the same sense: it is a divine emanation which protects the Lord's servants by frustrating his enemies. The punishment of impiety by temporary or permanent blindness occupies a well-thumbed page in the history of myth and folklore.

12 Then the angels said to Lot: "Who else belongs to you here? Your sons [sons-in-law] and your daughters and all who belong to you in the city—take
13 them away from it! We are about to destroy this place, for the outcry reaching the LORD against those in the city is so great that he has sent us to de-
14 stroy it." So Lot went out and spoke to his sons-in-law, who had contracted marriage with his daughters. "Get up and leave this place," he told them; "the LORD is about to destroy the city." But his sons-in-law thought he was joking.
15 As dawn was breaking, the angels urged Lot on, saying, "On your way! Take with you your wife and your two daughters who are here, or you will be
16 swept away in the punishment of the city." When he hesitated, the men, by the LORD's mercy, seized his hand and the hands of his wife and his two daugh-
17 ters and led them to safety outside the city. As soon as they had been brought outside, he was told: "Flee for your life! Don't look back or stop anywhere on the Plain. Get off to the hills at once, or
18 you will be swept away." "Oh, no, my lord!" replied
19 Lot. "You have already thought enough of your ser-

vant to do me the great kindness of intervening to save my life. But I cannot flee to the hills to keep the disaster from overtaking me, and so I shall die.
20 Look, this town ahead is near enough to escape to. It's only a small place. Let me flee there—it's a small place, isn't it?—that my life may be saved."
21 "Well, then," he replied, "I will also grant you the favor you now ask. I will not overthrow the town
22 you speak of. Hurry, escape there! I cannot do anything until you arrive there." That is why the town is called Zoar.

These verses are curiously connected and disconnected both within themselves and with the verses that have preceded them. Does what now happens presuppose the episode of vss. 4–11 (whence have the Sodomites so recently blinded disappeared?), or was it originally the immediate sequel to vss. 1–3 and parts of chapter 18 (cf. the "outcry" of 18:20 and 19:13, the "sweep away" of 18:23 and 19:15.17)? Who are the *sons* of Lot who surface for this moment only and then are again no more? The NAB has bracketed alongside them *sons-in-law*, doubtless correctly construing the Hebrew text which has introduced this gloss so as to harmonize vs. 12 with vs. 14. But even if Lot's sons dissolve into sons-in-law, what is he doing with sons-in-law anyway, who is the father of two virgin daughters? Are they only prospective sons-in-law? So the Vulgate interpreted the text, and after it many other versions and commentators. This is hardly the evident meaning of *who had contracted marriage with his daughters* (literally, "the takers of his daughters"), as the Septuagint had already recognized. Are they, then, men who had married other daughters of Lot, who are otherwise never mentioned? And if so, where do they all stand, shadowy sons, ambiguous sons-in-law, and putative daughters, in relation to "all the people" of Sodom who had lately tried to beat down Lot's door and were the fetid heap in which not even ten innocent could be found? The inquiring and attentive reader can easily suggest other questions that could be raised, all of which spring from conceptions of storytelling rules and proprieties that were obviously not shared by the Yahwist. The biblical author has taken very few pains to smooth away the evidence of the varied and contradictory narrative strands which he has combined and supplemented; he has simply allowed each segment of the story to make its contribution without much reference to the contribution of the others. He could do this, we suspect, in virtue of the wealth of traditional material that was at his disposal.

His sons-in-law thought he was joking: the same verbal root that in 18:12–15 was used to describe Sarah's laughter turns up here with a new twist. Sarah, too, had thought that a heavenly message was spoken in jest. Lot, of course, has a less immediate emissary of supernatural intelligence than Sarah had had. In both cases, nevertheless, a word from on high is unwittingly regarded as a source of amusement. Sarah, for her part, could afford to laugh: hers had been a word of good tidings portending a good that would inevitably be. Lot's sons-in-law are not so lucky. Their word will also come to be, but it is of such a nature that does not permit them the luxury of laughter.

Lot, in distinction to Abraham, is a man of hesitation and uncertain purpose. Even though he has accepted the angels' word as to what will occur and has even urged others to act on it, he cannot bring himself easily to do the same. Thus the graphic picture of the angels' seizing *his hand and the hands of his wife and his two daughters* and literally shoving them outside both their familiar house and the city walls. Then, while the angels shower words of urgency and immediacy about his ears, Lot still hesitates and wants to debate. *Get off to the hills*, he is told, for the Plain is utterly unsafe. But he will not have the hills (where eventually, according to vs. 30 below, he ends up anyway). Why is it that Lot *cannot flee to the hills?* Is it that they are too far away for his less than certain purpose? Has he become so used to the life of the city that he cannot abide any other existence? He does not help us discover what is in his mind, if indeed he knows, for his speech becomes babbling and incoherent. A small town is in view and catches his eye—*Look, this town ahead is near enough to escape to!* He is quite taken with the fact that it is small, too small perhaps to be worth the effort of divine destruction, or small enough to make an appeal to the Lord's magnanimity (cf. Amos 7:2.5). We can almost hear the sigh of exasperation with which Lot is humored by the divine power, which asks only that he get on with it and clear the way for the important and necessary business at hand. Yahweh, who will not destroy the innocent with the guilty, and who in fact preserves the guilty for the sake of the innocent, will go to any length to be consistent with his justice and mercy, even when a vessel of his election is as tiresome and dull-witted as Lot has proved to be. *I will also grant you the favor you now ask:* Lot, who has not recognized that he was asking for a favor, now receives this final one. He may go to this town, and because of him it will escape the general doom.

That is why the town is called Zoar: there is a play on words with the Hebrew for "small," which Lot has used twice in referring to this town. Zoar, according to the biblical traditions, was the only one of the five cities of the Plain that had been spared in the ancient conflagration. Another wordplay in this section involves the fivefold repetition of "flee" (or an English equivalent) in connection with Lot: *himmalet* and *lot*.

23 The sun was just rising over the earth as Lot ar-
24 rived in Zoar; at the same time the LORD rained
down sulphurous fire upon Sodom and Gomorrah
25 [from the LORD out of heaven]. He overthrew those
cities and the whole Plain, together with the inhab-
26 itants of the cities and the produce of the soil. But
Lot's wife looked back, and she was turned into a
pillar of salt.
27 Early the next morning Abraham went to the place
28 where he had stood in the LORD's presence. As he
looked down toward Sodom and Gomorrah and the
whole region of the Plain, he saw dense smoke over
the land rising like fumes from a furnace.
29 *Thus it came to pass: when God destroyed the Cities of the Plain, he was mindful of Abraham by
sending Lot away from the upheaval by which God
overthrew the cities where Lot had been living.*

Only in vss. 27–28 does Abraham rejoin the Yahwist's narrative, standing on the height of Hebron and staring with wild surmise down toward
the Jordan valley and the Ghor rift as the fumes from an earlier Hiroshima
rise slowly to the heavens. We have seen by now that there was little if
anything that originally connected the Lot of the Sodom traditions with
the nephew of Abraham of chapter 13. The connection has been made by
the Yahwist, sometimes skillfully and smoothly, sometimes less so. The
Priestly author's summary notice that compresses the whole story of Lot
and the cities of the plain into the single vs. 29 of this chapter reflects a
development of the tradition in which the connection had long been made
and which interpreted God's merciful dealing with Lot as entirely due to
his fidelity to Abraham.

There can hardly be any doubt that the biblical traditions about Sodom
and Gomorrah and about Lot and Sodom are only part of a complex of
ancient and hazy recollection that goes back to some actual event or
events, to some actual place or places that were involved in the events, and
to some actual person or persons whose lives had been enmeshed in both.
The names of Sodom, Gomorrah, and Zoar, it seems, turn up in the extensive records of ancient Ebla recently discovered. Zoar is also associated
there with Bela as in Genesis 14. A ridge near the southwest shore of the
Dead Sea in Palestine has been known from time immemorial as Jebel Us-
dum or Sdum (nearby is the Israeli town of Sedom), which has reasonably
been thought to have preserved the name of Sodom. The Dead Sea itself
is called by the Arabs the Bahr Lut, the Sea of Lot, and one or another of
the many salt formations resembling stalagmites that ring its shore will

be confidently pointed out to this day as Bint Lut, "the daughter of Lot," recalling a variation on the biblical story of *Lot's wife* who in violation of the taboo of vs. 17 *looked back* on the desolation of the cities of the Plain and as a result *was turned into a pillar of salt.*

But if there is something factual behind these stories, deciding what it is is another matter entirely. First of all, we must undoubtedly reject the assumption apparently made by some of the biblical traditions, that within the historical memory of man an area that had once been a garden spot (cf. 13:10) was transformed into the below-sea-level and landlocked salt and potash reservoir that we know now as the Dead Sea, surrounded as it is by salt slabs and desolate wasteland. Nothing like this took place in historical times, for there has been no essential change in the topography of Palestine since the earth ended the moanings and groanings of its birth pangs and settled down to being what it now is millions of years before man came to claim it. At whatever age we want to place them, when Abraham and Lot throve, there was already a Dead Sea.

It is possible, nevertheless, and in fact it is to be presumed, that within historical times the Dead Sea has changed its dimensions, just as within living memory rivers have changed their course and lakes have enlarged and diminished. The hypothesis hardly applies to the northern reach of the sea where the mouth of the Jordan empties: the attempt to locate the cities of the plain in this region has over the years proved to be singularly unpersuasive. The southern shore has proved to be more hospitable to the hypothesis for several reasons. First of all, while at its northern limit the Dead Sea may attain a depth of four hundred meters or so, its southern part is quite shallow, here and there only a few feet deep. Credibility is thus lent to the view expressed by W. F. Albright and other scholars that this is a "newer" part of the sea caused by land sinkage in historical times, quite likely as a result of one of the not infrequent earthquakes that occur along the fault line. The sinkage may even be measurable within the recent past: present-day Arabs are said to recall that their immediate ancestors could wade from el-Lisan (the "tongue" of land that juts out from the southeastern bank of the sea) to the opposite western bank, a thing which is no longer possible. Albright's thought was that the expanse of water that now forms the bay south of el-Lisan could very well cover the remains of cities that were part of a population system in what was then the southern extremity of the plain in the Early Bronze period (that is, the early second millennium B.C.).

What encouraged Albright in his view was the undeniable evidence of Early Bronze habitation of the Ghor and his suspicion that additional evidence would be found to show that the habitation had been extensive. Since the first quarter of this century an important site known as Bab edh-Dhra, located just about where el-Lisan begins on its east, has been the object of repeated archeological expeditions. These have shown conclusively that, whatever was its ancient name, Bab edh-Dhra had indeed been an impressive city of the Early Bronze age, but until the past several years there was no hard evidence to back up Albright's surmise that it had been only one of many such in its neighborhood. Now, since 1973, surface exploration has produced the evidence, at least for four sites fairly evenly distributed along the edge of the Ghor between Bab edh-Dhra and the beginning of the Arabah. One of these sites in Safi, some ten kilometers south of the Dead Sea, which on the Madaba map was identified with the biblical Zoar. (The Madaba map of Palestine is a floor mosaic in a Byzantine church of that Transjordanian town, dating from the end of the sixth or the beginning of the seventh Christian century.) All of these places add up to a likelihood of there having been other contemporary populations in this region whose vestiges remain undiscovered or indeed may be undiscoverable, which could lie at the background of the biblical legends of the cities of the Plain.

There is nothing, of course, to prove that Sodom and its sister cities now rest on the bottom of the Dead Sea, nor does the Bible say that they do. The *overthrew* of vs. 25 (cf. vs. 21 and the same terminology employed by P in vs. 29), however, can easily suggest the action of an earthquake; and the *sulphurous fire* which *the* LORD *rained down* on these wicked places at least suggests the presence of those pits of bitumen (cf. 14:10) which to this day permeates the Dead Sea and is often cast up to its surface in large masses. (In classical times, it may be remembered, the Dead Sea was known as Lake Asphaltitis.) All that we can conclude is that the local traditions which have pointed to the southern Dead Sea region as the historical theater of events recounted in Genesis 19 now have enough extrinsic corroboration to constitute their hypothesis respectable.

30 Since Lot was afraid to stay in Zoar, he and his two daughters went up from Zoar and settled in the hill country, where he lived with his two daughters in a
31 cave. The older one said to the younger: "Our father is getting old, and there is not a man on earth to unite with us as was the custom everywhere.
32 Come, let us ply our father with wine and then lie with him, that we may have offspring by our father."
33 So that night they plied their father with wine, and the older one went in and lay with her father; but he was not aware of her lying down or her getting up.
34 Next day the older one said to the younger: "Last night it was I who lay with my father. Let us ply him with wine again tonight, and then you go in and lie with him, that we may both have offspring by our

35 father." So that night, too, they plied their father
with wine, and then the younger one went in and lay
with him; but again he was not aware of her lying
down or her getting up.

36 Thus both of Lot's daughters became pregnant by

37 their father. The older one gave birth to a son whom
she named Moab, saying, "From my father."‡ He is

38 the ancestor of the Moabites of today. The younger
one, too, gave birth to a son, and she named him
Ammon,‡ "The son of my kin." He is the ancestor
of the Ammonites of today.

This story, tenuously connected with the preceding narrative, obviously
had little to do with the Sodom and Gomorrah saga and owes its preservation to other concerns. Those concerns, further, were somewhat different on the part of the original tellers of the story and those who are responsible for its inclusion in the present Abraham and Lot tradition of Genesis.

The Yahwist finds a bit of dark humor in the discovery of the citified
Lot now at home *in a cave;* he who would not live *in the hill country* (vs.
19) now must live there willy-nilly, suddenly *afraid to stay in Zoar,* the
city whose deliverance he had wheedled from the Lord and which had
been declared safe for him (vs. 21). A man of timid faith, destined to be
mastered by events rather than to master them, Lot now supinely sacrifices
the dignity of his person to unholy and forbidden relationships (cf. Leviticus 18:6–18) accomplished on him by voracious daughters whose dignity he had earlier disregarded (vs. 8 above). They reward his many
shortcomings as a man and as a father with the incestuous conception—a
conception in which he plays a grotesque, ludicrous, and unbelievably oblivious part—of those two peoples who, despite their ethnic connections
with Israel, were absolutely prohibited from ever being admitted into its
covenant community (cf. Deuteronomy 23:4). On this sad and somber
note Lot disappears from the biblical chronicle and is heard of no more.

We may safely assume that the story did not have these pejorative
Israelite connotations for those among and for whom it was first told. It is
a story of the origins of Moab and Ammon, proud peoples of the Transjordanian steppes, who traced their ancestry back to the famous Lot whose
name was primordially associated with the Dead Sea region and its adjacent territories. The catastrophe that had occurred as the story opens may
have been bigger in its original purview than now appears in the Genesis
context: *our father is getting old, and there is not a man on earth to unite
with us as was the custom everywhere.* Faced with the extinction of their
race, the daughters take extraordinary measures for survival, for which

‡ The Hebrew text has been revised here following the suggestion of the LXX.

they were doubtless applauded. They give birth to *the Moabites* and *the Ammonites,* both of whom are assigned eponymous ancestors out of popular etymologies developed in the text. Thus Moab=*from my father* (Hebrew *me abi,* or perhaps more hidden, *mu abi=*"the seed of my father"), and Ammon=*the son of my kin* (Hebrew *ben 'ammi*).

6. Isaac

In these remaining chapters of the Abraham saga the Elohistic source at last makes an uncontested appearance in the narrative and, at least at the beginning, assumes the major burden of the story. In the following chapter there is no need to look for any other source.

> **20** Abraham journeyed on to the region of the Negeb, where he settled between Kadesh and Shur. While
> **2** he stayed in Gerar, he said of his wife Sarah, "She is my sister." So Abimelech, king of Gerar, sent and
> **3** took Sarah. But God came to Abimelech in a dream one night and said to him, "You are about to die because of the woman you have taken, for she has
> **4** a husband." Abimelech, who had not approached her, said: "O Lord, would you slay a man* even
> **5** though he is innocent? He himself told me, 'She is my sister,' and she herself also stated, 'He is my brother.' I did it in good faith and with clean
> **6** hands." God answered him in the dream: "Yes, I know you did it in good faith. In fact, it was I who kept you from sinning against me; that is why I did
> **7** not let you touch her. Therefore, return the man's wife—as a spokesman he will intercede for you— that your life may be saved. If you do not return her, you can be sure that you and all who are yours
> **8** will certainly die." Early the next morning Abimelech called all his court officials and informed them of everything that had happened, and the men were
> **9** horrified. Then Abimelech summoned Abraham and

* The NAB corrects the text with the help of the LXX. The MT has "would you slay a people?"

said to him: "How could you do this to us! What wrong did I do to you that you should have brought such monstrous guilt on me and my kingdom? You
10 have treated me in an intolerable way. What were you afraid† of," he asked him, "that you should
11 have done such a thing?" "I was afraid," answered Abraham, "because I thought there would surely be no fear of God in this place, and so they would kill
12 me on account of my wife. Besides, she is in truth my sister, but only my father's daughter, not my
13 mother's; and so she became my wife. When God sent me wandering from my father's house, I asked her: 'Would you do me this favor? In whatever place we come to, say that I am your brother.'"
14 Then Abimelech took flocks and herds and male and female slaves and gave them to Abraham; and
15 after he restored his wife Sarah to him, he said, "Here, my land lies at your disposal; settle wherever
16 you please." To Sarah he said: "See, I have given your brother a thousand shekels of silver. Let that serve you as a vindication before all who are with you; your honor has been preserved with everyone."
17 Abraham then interceded with God, and God restored health to Abimelech, that is, to his wife and his maidservants, so that they could bear children;
18 for God‡ had tightly closed every womb in Abimelech's household on account of Abraham's wife Sarah.

It becomes immediately evident that this story is a doublet of the J tradition preserved in 12:10–20. Since this is the first use made of the elusive E source in the composition of Genesis, it is impossible to tell in what sequence the story originally stood in relation to the rest of the Abraham narrative. We may probably assume, however, that it was approximately where the Yahwist placed it in his version, toward the beginning of Abraham's career in Canaan. Abraham and Sarah are represented as coming for the first time into a land whose ways are unknown to them (vs. 11), and Sarah rather obviously is presumed to be a young and sexually appealing woman. By inserting the story where he has, the Redactor has

---

† The MT has "what did you see?" The two verbs are very similar in Hebrew spelling.
‡ So the Samaritan Pentateuch and some LXX evidence. The MT has "Yahweh," probably under the influence of 21:1 following.

unavoidably created the anomaly of a ninety-year-old Sarah attracting Abimelech's attention (that is, by following the P chronology of 12:4b, 17:17, and 21:5 which has been made the structure of Genesis). On the other hand, a special poignancy is now added to the basic theme of the story, which is to bring out the total protection which the Lord draws over his elect in order to fulfill his promises. In its present redactional position the story is concerned with a Sarah who is already carrying Abraham's son (so 18:10, 21:1, J), that Isaac who, rather than Ishmael, will be the bearer of God's covenant (17:19, P). The peril to the working out of the divine purposes unwittingly raised by Abimelech, therefore, is more acute than in the Elohist's original construction. As a consequence, the birth of Isaac (JEP) in chapter 21 will be greeted as a greater than ever overcoming of the obstacles which human weakness and obliviousness interpose in vain to the sure working out of a committed providence.

The geography of vs. 1 is somewhat confusing. We seem to have an E correspondent to the J of 12:9 which also had Abraham making his way south after entering Canaan; here he *journeyed on to the region of the Negeb* as before, and finally *settled between Kadesh and Shur* (associated with Hagar and Ishmael in 16:7.14, J). This would put us considerably south indeed, much farther south than any of the haunts which the other sources customarily associate with Abraham. And, in fact, in the next breath he is said to have *stayed in Gerar,* in all probability the present-day Tell Abu Hureira, a good eighty kilometers to the north, which 21:32.34 quite properly locates near Beer-sheba "in the land of the Philistines." Does this indicate, as some believe, that vss. 1a and 1b derive from separate sources? More likely, in our view, is Gunkel's guess, that something has been left out of this E story at the very beginning, in keeping with the fragmentary and supplementary way in which this stratum of tradition has been worked into the dominant J and P narrative. Gunkel supposed that once this story, like that of 12:10–20, might have told of Abraham's moving out of the Negeb to escape a famine, here to Gerar, however, rather than to Egypt.

Already when discussing the earlier J story we reviewed the major differences which distinguish this version with its higher sensitivities from its more rough-hewn prototype. The Elohist is almost embarrassingly diffuse in his efforts to exculpate Abimelech of all blame—even though in the same breath he likewise palliates the less than straightforward conduct of Abraham, there is no doubt that Abimelech emerges as the more generous and attractive of the two men. This, despite the fact that a divine visitation *on account of Abraham's wife Sarah* had afflicted Abimelech's household (vss. 17–18): it was the biblical belief that wrong and evil were objective facts calling for retribution, even when they were the result of inadvertence. Abimelech's simplicity in respect to honesty and cleanhandedness is matched by his generosity in ridding himself of the undeserved blame that had attached to his house. Pharaoh had enriched Abraham for Sarah's sake before the fact, but afterward he had wanted only to see Abraham's back on his way out (cf. 12:19–20). Abimelech, on the contrary, invites the patriarch to *settle wherever you please* in the land of Gerar and showers upon him gifts to the tune of *a thousand shekels* weight *of silver,* let us say the then value of eleven and a half kilos of silver, or some twenty-five pounds of it. All of this, he says to Sarah with extreme delicacy, he has given *your brother* that it may *serve you as a vindication before all who are with you:* literally, that they may "turn a blind eye" (so the New English Bible) to all that appeared to have taken place and recognize instead that *your honor has been preserved with everyone.*

The story of the birth of Isaac now follows, recounted by all three of our sources. The unwinding of the strands can be subject to some discussion, but the general lines of division are clear. First the J version:

> **21** The LORD took note of Sarah as he had said he
> would; he did for her as he had promised . . .
> 6b [Sarah said:] "All who hear of it will laugh with me.
> 7 Who would have told Abraham," she added, "that
> Sarah would nurse children! Yet I have borne him a
> son in his old age."

We see the fulfillment of the promise of 18:10. Yahweh *took note of Sarah* (literally, "he visited her") as he had said he would, a year hence, when he sat before Abraham's tent by the terebinth of Mamre. Sarah duly bears Abraham a son *in his old age.* The *laugh with me* of vs. 6b (again "laughter" is associated with the name of Isaac) is probably better taken as "laugh at me": what is meant is the good-natured ribaldry of neighborhood wives chaffing and bantering over the birth of a child to one of their number who had long been judged to be over the age for such novelties.

The P version causes little difficulty:

> 2 Sarah became pregnant and bore Abraham a son in
> 3 his old age, at the set time that God had stated. Abra-
> ham gave the name Isaac to this son of his whom
> 4 Sarah bore him. When his son Isaac was eight days
> old, Abraham circumcised him, as God had com-
> 5 manded. Abraham was a hundred years old when his
> son Isaac was born to him.

This birth is in fulfillment of the promise of 17:21, *at the set time that God had stated* there. Abraham names his son, as stipulated by 17:19, and he circumcises him according to the covenant law of 17:12. The *hun-*

dred years of Abraham (vs. 5) corresponds with the chronology of 17:21.24.

The rest of the birth notice comes from E. It is not so much important as such as it is the introduction to a fairly important doublet of a previous passage from J.

> 6a Sarah then said, "God has given me cause to laugh
> 8 . . ." Isaac grew and on the day of the child's weaning Abraham held a great feast.
> 9 Sarah noticed the son whom Hagar the Egyptian had borne to Abraham playing with her son Isaac*;
> 10 so she demanded of Abraham: "Drive out that slave and her son! No son of that slave is going to
> 11 share the inheritance with my son Isaac!" Abraham was greatly distressed, especially on account of his
> 12 son Ishmael. But God said to Abraham: "Do not be distressed about the boy or about your slave woman. Heed the demands of Sarah, no matter what she is asking of you; for it is through Isaac that
> 13 descendants shall bear your name. As for the son of the slave woman, I will make a great* nation of him also, since he too is your offspring."
> 14 Early the next morning Abraham got some bread and a skin of water and gave them to Hagar. Then, placing the child on her back,* he sent her away. As she roamed aimlessly in the wilderness of
> 15 Beer-sheba, the water in the skin was used up.
> 16 So she put the child down under a shrub, and then went and sat down opposite him, about a bowshot away; for she said to herself, "Let me not watch to see the child die." As she sat opposite him, he*
> 17 began to cry. God heard the boy's cry, and God's messenger called to Hagar from heaven: "What is the matter, Hagar? Don't be afraid; God has heard
> 18 the boy's cry in this plight of his. Arise, lift up the boy and hold him by the hand; for I will make of
> 19 him a great nation." Then God opened her eyes, and she saw a well of water. She went and filled the skin with water, and then let the boy drink.
> 20 God was with the boy as he grew up. He lived in
> 21 the wilderness and became an expert bowman, with his home in the wilderness of Paran. His mother got a wife for him from the land of Egypt.

---

* See the commentary.

In this case the "laughter" motif connected with the appearance of Isaac seems to be nothing except the expression of sheer joy (vs. 6a). In the Elohist narrative there is nothing about a child born to parents of old age, only the birth of a man-child that calls for celebration. *The day of the child's weaning* (an event rather late for a Semitic child, up to three years after birth: cf. 1 Samuel 1:23–24, 2 Maccabees 7:27) is one of the fairly universal family sacraments of simpler societies which by such events clock the stages of growth into full and independent human existence. The rite of circumcision, all-important to P, is mentioned neither by J or E. Though ancient in practice, circumcision may have had no special religious significance for the Israelites at the time the J and E traditions were being formed.

There can hardly be any doubt that vss. 9–21 constitute an E parallel to the J story of Hagar in chapter 16. The divergences between the two versions are immediately apparent, and it is they that made it possible for the story to be told twice with some verisimilitude of sequence rather than as a simple repetition. In the J passage Hagar was big with child, but here in E she has already given birth. The cause of her expulsion is not, accordingly, her uppity ways as in J, but rather the innocent circumstance of her being the mother of a child whom Sarah viewed as a threat to the inheritance of her own son. It is not clear whether the legal background which defined Hagar's status in Abraham's household has been remembered in E as it was in J. Abraham displays considerably more emotional ties with Hagar and her child than he did in chapter 16, understandably, perhaps, because in the latter he can see his own flesh and blood living before his eyes. Only at God's express command does he accede to Sarah's demand that he *drive out that slave and her son,* and only after having received the assurance that this child, too, will be favored along with his son Isaac.

The redactional placement of the story has led to the inevitable kind of inconsistencies that we have remarked before when the same sort of thing has been done. In the story before us, Hagar's son is obviously still an infant, not the hulking lad of sixteen or seventeen that he would have to be did the chronology of the Priestly author apply (cf. 16:16, 21:5). The Redactor has ignored the inconsistencies with admirable aplomb, but they did disturb later scribes who have tampered with the text in those places which we have marked above with asterisks. (We say later scribes and not the Redactor because in each instance the evidence of the Septuagint and other ancient versions indicates the correct, pre-Masoretic reading of an original that has been translated by the NAB in preference to the MT.) Thus in vs. 9 *with her son Isaac,* present in the LXX, is lacking in the MT. The suggestion is that it has been deliberately omitted in order to obscure the picture which the storyteller wanted to draw, of two boys of roughly the same age romping together as boys will, a picture ordinarily provoking no reaction more severe than adult indulgence, but in this case provocative to a jealous mother who broods on the possible implications of the undiscriminating social equality of childhood. A bonus for the scribe who struck the words from the text was that a now ambiguous *playing* (from the same verbal root that accounts for the "laughter" endemic in the Isaac stories) was left indeterminately applied to Hagar's son, a term which later rabbinic exegesis could interpret to mean that he had been overseen doing something reprehensible (cf. Paul's use of the text in Galatians 4:29). The same inclination to denigrate Abraham's descent through Hagar in favor of Israel's inheritance through Isaac *may* be responsible for the MT's omission of *great* in vs. 13 (though it has been allowed to stand in vs. 18). Certainly a tendentious change has been made in the MT of vs. 14 where, with the sacrifice of good Hebrew syntax, not Hagar's child (the reviser, of course, thinking of the teen-age Ishmael) but rather the *skin of water* has been placed *on her back* by Abraham. And finally, in vs. 16 the wailing of a thirsty infant in the wilderness ("he") has been changed into Hagar's weeping of adult despair ("she"). (It is true that in vs. 17 *the boy's cry* still appears in the Hebrew, but this cry, literally "voice," could easily be understood as the unuttered and unvocalized plight of an unfortunate being which has come to the Lord's attention.)

An interesting feature of this story is that the name of Ishmael never appears in it. (The "Ishmael" of vs. 11 above is not attested by the Hebrew or by any other witness to the original text but has been simply supplied by the NAB.) Though the Elohist has preserved the tradition that had Abraham's son by Hagar destined to become *a great nation,* and though in vs. 21 he and his descendants are localized in the same general area to which the Yahwist had assigned the Ishmaelites (16:14, 25:18; contrast P in 25:12–16), it would appear that this biblical author had either forgotten or did not care about Israel's Arabian cousins whom the other sources knew as the sons of Ishmael. Hagar's son disappears from the story almost as anonymously as he entered it.

The delicacy of touch that characterizes the work of the Elohist is very apparent in this little episode. Abraham not only is said to be *distressed* over the imminent departure of Hagar and her and his son, his distress is dramatized in the pathetic scene of vs. 14 which summons the reader's imagination to supply for the storyteller's deliberate silences. Hagar has been informed of her fate, of course, and after a tearful and sleepless night she stands numbed and submissive before Abraham's tent which is now no longer home for herself and her child. Abraham can hardly meet her eyes as he embraces his son for the last time and then makes what to both father and mother must seem a most pitiful and inadequate gesture toward humanity: a mouthful of food, a few swallows of water for two living beings on foot in the wilderness that leads to Egypt. Abraham, it is true, has God's assurance that it will go well with his son, but like all assurances that are rested on faith, it has to contend with grim and present realities that seem to contradict it. As for Hagar, who has no assurance of any kind, she can only despair as she proceeds to make her way *aimlessly in the wilderness of Beer-sheba,* wandering without hopeful purpose till *the water in the skin was used up.* Her pathos depicted with a few masterful strokes in vs. 16 is a further indication of the concern which the Elohist shows for those who people his stories, who are turned by him from traditional names and faceless figures into living, everyday, suffering and rejoicing human beings.

Various elements in common link this story with the J narrative of chapter 16. *God's messenger* calls to Hagar here as Yahweh's messenger encountered her there. Here the messenger calls to her *from heaven:* a further example of the tendency to "spiritualize" the communication between God and man by making it less anthropomorphically direct (like the revelation to Abimelech in a dream of 20:3–7), even though in vs. 12 God simply "says" something to Abraham. In vs. 19 there is a *well of water* as in chapter 16, though nothing is made of it as a sacred site. *The wilderness of Paran* where the Elohist leaves Hagar's son corresponds sufficiently well, as we have already said, with the geographical termination of chapter 16, as does the way of life ascribed to him: the *expert bowman* was the mainstay of Bedawin society (cf. Isaiah 21:17). That *his mother got a wife for him from the land of Egypt* signals in E as in J (and contrary to P) his passing from further consideration in the history of the Hebrew patriarchs.

22 About that time Abimelech, accompanied by Phicol, the commander of his army, said to Abraham: "God
23 is with you in everything you do. Therefore, swear to me by God at this place that you will not deal falsely with me or with my progeny and posterity, but will act as loyally toward me and the land in
24 which you stay as I have acted toward you." To
25 this Abraham replied, "I so swear." *Abraham, however, reproached Abimelech about a well that*
26 *Abimelech's men had seized by force.* "I have no idea who did that," Abimelech replied. "In fact, you never told me about it, nor did I ever hear of it until
27 now." Then Abraham took sheep and cattle and gave them to Abimelech and the two made a pact.
28 *Abraham also set apart seven ewe lambs of the flock,*
29 *and Abimelech asked him, "What is the purpose of these seven ewe lambs that you have set apart?"*

30 *Abraham answered, "The seven ewe lambs you shall*
   accept from me that thus I may have your acknowl-
31 *edgment that the well was dug by me."* This is why
   the place is called Beer-sheba; the two of them took
32 an oath there. *When they had thus made the pact in*
   Beer-Sheba, Abimelech, along with Phicol, the
   commander of his army, left and returned to the
   land of the Philistines.
33 *Abraham planted a tamarisk at Beer-sheba, and*
   there he invoked by name the LORD, *God the Eter-*
34 *nal.* Abraham resided in the land of the Philistines
   for many years.

There can be no question at all about the composite character of this
passage; it is, in fact, fairly much the parade example of how parallel traditions have sometimes been combined to make up a single story. The two
components were sufficiently alike that they could be welded together
without difficulty, yet separately each is an independent narrative. (The
NAB, translating a now unified story into English idiom, here and elsewhere by creating subordinate clauses, introducing connectives, etc., has
inevitably obscured the lines of demarcation of the separate pieces that
make it up. Thus the "however" of vs. 25 and the "also" of vs. 28 are har-
monizations not in the original text. "When they had thus made the pact in
Beer-sheba" is in the Hebrew: "And they cut a covenant in Beer-sheba.")
The one story, which picks up the narrative thread left hanging at 20:18,
tells of a simple pact of friendship entered into by Abimelech and
Abraham. In it Beer-sheba, where the event is represented as taking place,
is etymologized as "the well (*beer*) of the oath (*shaba*)": *the two of them*
took an oath there (sham nishbe'u sheneyhem in the alliteration of the
original). The second story, which we have italicized above, describes a
covenant that settles a dispute that had arisen over a well. Beer-sheba in
this case derives its name from the *seven (sheba) ewe lambs of the flock*
which Abraham *set apart* in token of his rightful claim to the well, demanding in return Abimelech's quitclaim which is the substance of *the*
pact in Beer-sheba into which the two of them entered. By the older critics
this italicized portion of our text was assigned to the Yahwist, despite the
fact that there is a J doublet of the story in 26:23–33 which features Isaac
instead of Abraham. More recent critics tend to regard it simply as an isolated piece of tradition which the Elohist came across when gathering his
material and which he found it congenial to interweave with the rest of his
narrative. As we shall see, it still makes a great deal of sense to consider
these verses J material, whatever may have been their original relationship
to the Yahwistic history and whosoever may be the hand that is responsible
for their inclusion in the actual book of Genesis.

Contrary to the indication of vs. 34 which picks up from 20:15 and has Abraham residing *in the land of the Philistines,* that is, in the neighborhood of Gerar (20:1), the action of this piece occurs to the southeast, at *Beer-sheba,* another sacred *place* where oaths are taken and covenants solemnly entered into. Today a mound known as es-Seba, Beer-sheba was not a center of sedentary population until the time of Iron Age Palestine (after 1200 B.C.), but it had long been a place of resort both in the Bronze Age and in the earlier Chalcolithic. It is for E Abraham's customary home (cf. 22:19) in place of the Mamre-Hebron favored by J and P; the J tradition tends to associate Isaac more than Abraham with Beersheba.

The covenant of friendship which Abimelech seeks with Abraham is the rather natural outcome of his experience in chapter 20. Abraham, the friend of God, is patently one whom any man would be well advised to have on his side. At the same time, the presence of *Phicol, the commander of his army,* underscores the technicalities of the case, that Abimelech is the superior of the two parties to the pact, and that he is binding Abraham to himself with an oath of fealty. What is being depicted is a suzerainty treaty, a device by which overlords of the ancient Near East exacted pledges of loyalty and mutual support from their vassals in exchange for the benefits they had bestowed on them. Here Abimelech reminds Abraham of his past beneficence and especially of the liberal grant recorded in 20:15: *the land in which you stay* is, after all, Abimelech's. At least for the purposes of this story Beer-sheba is counted within Abimelech's sphere of influence, even though vs. 32 distinguishes it from "the land of the Philistines."

"The land of the Philistines" is an anachronism here, like calling the city of Peter Stuyvesant New York or naming the legendary Arthur of Camelot king of Britain. The Philistines, we have observed more than once, are no more ancient in the land of Canaan than the Israelites themselves, for all that it was from them that Palestine came to be called.

The companion story of a covenant by which a dispute over a well was resolved undoubtedly corresponds with everyday facts of patriarchal life even more closely than those which could envisage a suzerainty treaty. We have already seen the importance of wells in this society and in this land. By his gift and petition to Abimelech Abraham again assumes the posture of the inferior covenant partner. However, what was of chief interest to the biblical author was to make it clear that the well or wells of Beer-sheba (the name to him meant "seven wells": cf. the parallel in 26:12–33) went back to none other than the great forefather of Israel.

Beer-sheba was for Israel a sacred place of oracle and pilgrimage (cf. Amos 8:14). In vs. 33, in the wont of J, Abraham "claims" Beer-sheba for Israel: he *planted a tamarisk,* the sacred tree, and *he invoked* Yahweh *by name.* Yahweh's name is coupled with that of *God the Eternal,* El

Olam, doubtless a local title like that of Elyon, Roi, Shaddai, etc., which were extracted from Canaanite life and assimilated into Yahwism by a route we have already surveyed.

22 Some time after these events, God put Abraham to the test. He called to him, "Abraham!" "Ready!"
2 he replied. Then God said: "Take your son Isaac, your only one, whom you love, and go to the land of Moriah. There you shall offer him up as a holocaust
3 on a height that I will point out to you." Early the next morning Abraham saddled his donkey, took with him his son Isaac, and two of his servants as well, and with the wood that he had cut for the holocaust, set out for the place of which God had told him.
4 On the third day Abraham got sight of the place
5 from afar. Then he said to his servants: "Both of you stay here with the donkey, while the boy and I go on over yonder. We will worship and then come
6 back to you." Thereupon Abraham took the wood for the holocaust and laid it on his son Isaac's shoulders, while he himself carried the fire and the
7 knife. As the two walked on together, Isaac spoke to his father Abraham: "Father!" he said. "Yes, son," he replied. Isaac continued, "Here are the fire and the wood, but where is the sheep for the
8 holocaust?" "Son," Abraham answered, "God himself will provide the sheep for the holocaust." Then
9 the two continued going forward. When they came to the place of which God had told him, Abraham built an altar there and arranged the wood on it. Next he tied up his son Isaac, and put him on top of
10 the wood on the altar. Then he reached out and took
11 the knife to slaughter his son. But the LORD's messenger called to him from heaven, "Abraham, Abra-
12 ham!" "Yes, Lord," he answered. "Do not lay your hand on the boy," said the messenger. "Do not do the least thing to him. I know now how devoted you are to God, since you did not withhold from me
13 your own beloved son." As Abraham looked about, he spied a ram caught by its horns in the thicket. So he went and took the ram and offered it up as a
14 holocaust in place of his son. Abraham named the site Yahweh-yireh; hence people now say, "On the mountain the LORD will see."

This is without any doubt whatsoever the most important contribution that the Elohist has made to the story of Abraham. In Romans 4:19–22 Paul rhapsodizes on Abraham's faith which never questioned or doubted God's promise; and although he does not allude to this passage it cannot fail to have been in his mind, for it exactly epitomizes a faith of this kind which the Bible so confidently ascribed to Abraham. This is true of the passage precisely as it stands in the Elohist's narrative even without advertence to its redactional position in the completed work of Genesis which is of course the way Paul knew it. Already in 21:9–21 the author has movingly depicted the final removal of Hagar's son from Abraham's house over all his protestations and only at the express command of God, who had unaccountably sided with the jealous Sarah. God had then assured him that all would go well, since it was through Isaac that his name would endure in his descendants. But now what? He is directed to slay this child of promise, still a tender boy, and thus leave himself as he was before, alone in the world without prospect for the future. The word of God is quite inexorable in its demands and makes no effort at all to minimize what will be their consequence: *take your son Isaac, your only one, whom you love.* But Abraham's *Ready!* has been no idle response to the divine summons, even though he could hardly have been prepared for the enormity of what he is now required to do. As before, the Elohist leaves it to the reader to imagine all that goes on in the patriarch's mind and soul as he matter-of-factly sets about making the mundane preparations necessary for the fateful journey to which he has been called.

So terrible is the thing Abraham feels he must do, even though it has been commanded of him by God, he cannot bring himself to reveal it to his companions. Thus he dissembles *to his servants,* taking refuge in circumlocutions: *We will worship and then come back to you.* The same dissimulation he makes to Isaac, when the latter innocently inquires about *the sheep for the holocaust.* Hardly a commentator has been able to resist the invitation which the Elohist has extended to fill in with imagination and empathy all that is presupposed between the *as the two walked on together* of vs. 7 and *the two continued going forward* of vs. 8—the turmoil in Abraham's being, who nevertheless speaks calmly and with the conventional affection to the questioning of his son, and Isaac's growing awareness that something badly out of the ordinary is about to happen. The understatement with which the author has so briefly sketched the circumstances of this tragic walk of father and son up the hillside is maintained to the end, as the climax of the scene is reached and passed. Only the grim essentials are related. Silently, we may suppose, Abraham heaps up a few stones to form a rough altar, spreads out on it the sticks of wood which his son has carried for his own sacrificial pyre, and readies the knife and fire with which the holocaust is to be accomplished. It could not be in silence, however, that he at last reveals to Isaac who is to be the victim of the sacrifice, as he binds his arms and legs and lays him on the cruel couch that has been prepared for him. Are we to think of Isaac as pleading against this unsuspected fate or as numbly acquiescing to the actions of his suddenly unnatural father? And what of his future feelings, even though Abraham's hand was stayed at the end? There are events, and this is surely one of that kind, which can never be forgotten, which rather determine the attitudes of a lifetime. To none of these questions does the biblical author offer an answer. His attention is riveted on the sole issue of Abraham's faith in God's promise, which stood the ultimate test of willing compliance with an awful command of obedience (cf. Hebrews 11:17–19).

Commentators have often sought in this passage clues to an earlier message that it may have possessed, as concerns the rejection by Israel of human sacrifice, to be specific, for which instead animal sacrifice was substituted. It has been the tendency of recent writers to scout this idea as being foreign to the story's obvious purpose, yet there is still probably much to be said for it. It will be noted that at the outset Abraham finds nothing monstrous or extraordinary about the suggestion that God's will demands a human sacrifice; what is monstrous is that *he* personally, in the face of a promise that now seems about to be broken, should have to sacrifice his *only* son. The alacrity with which he responds to the test of his faith also is proof of the compatibility which he thought to exist between the substance of the command and the One who had issued it. And, to be sure, human sacrifice, and particularly child sacrifice, was widely practiced by Israel's Semitic neighbors, including those who could boast of superior cultural attainments. It assumed a variety of forms, sometimes as the ultimate sacrifice to speak to the deity in great need (2 Kings 3:27), sometimes the routine offering to satisfy the blood lust of a particular god (2 Kings 23:10), sometimes the "first fruits" which, whether of field or flock or family, by universal custom belonged to God (Exodus 22:28), sometimes as part of a consecratory rite in founding a new place (1 Kings 16:34). One of the sadder aspects of Canaanite archeology is the constant recurrence of infant skeletons buried beneath the thresholds of city gates and houses, evidence of the tiny lives that had been sacrificed to ward away evil and ensure divine protection. Both in Israel's laws and in the words of its prophets and historians human sacrifice is excoriated as a heathen abomination, but the same sources leave us in no doubt that it was often practiced by Israelites all the same, and that it was sometimes regarded by these as compatible with the worship of Yahweh. Even Micah 6:7, which mentions infant sacrifice only to score its futility, lays it alongside libations and animal sacrifices which under the circumstances were also unacceptable, as though all of these were equally thinkable forms of worship and the means of expiating sin.

It cannot be determined whether in the strictly Israelite period of their history the people who claimed the ancestry of Abraham ever knew a time when human sacrifice had been sanctioned by law and custom. Certainly they knew of its prevalence among their relatives and neighbors, however, and they must have surmised that their own ancestors, of the same flesh and blood of these relatives and neighbors, had done similar dreadful things, in the time when Israel was not yet and their fathers worshiped other gods. It would be surprising were there no record at all, no awareness shown, of the development that once took place in religious history, of the new insight that was afforded into the nature of God and his requirements, which accounts for such diametrically opposed outlooks on human sacrifice as that of Israel on the one hand and that of the rest of its cultural world on the other. We can only suggest that Genesis 22:1–14 may be read as the record of such a development, or at least a part of it. Much depends on what is understood by the word or will or revelation of God, on what, in other terms, is the image of God as it imprints itself upon the mind and conscience of man. By now we have become accustomed to the casual way in which God and man converse in these patriarchal stories, so accustomed that our ears may be deadened to all that this naïve language is trying to say to them. That *God said* to Abraham that he should take his son and *offer him up as a holocaust* means that to a man of proved religious sensitivity it once came as an inner conviction that his highest duty required of him to destroy his only heir in service of some greater good. That later *the* LORD's *messenger called to him from heaven* and told him that no such thing was desired of him means that this same man arrived at a new conception of what is pleasing to God, or even, if you will, a new conception of God himself. Surely, something more than trivial change of fancy and whim is being insinuated here. If we must resist the temptation to read into these stories more than they intended to say or other than they intended to say, we must also not succumb to the opposite temptation to hold their meaning to the paltry and parsimonious when they would have it generous. Israel did, after all, almost alone of its compeers raise its eyes to a vision of God and religion that relegated the otherwise respectable institution of human sacrifice to the dank backwaters of superstition and barbarism. It ought not seem strange that its great forefather Abraham should have been thought to anticipate this enlargement of the human spirit even as he has anticipated so much else that is Israelite in the pages of Genesis.

The *ram caught by its horns in the thicket* that appears providentially as the substitute sacrifice for Isaac echoes a theme common in ancient folklore, which often dwells on the last-minute aborting of a human sacrifice.

It is also possible that in this instance there was once a religious or other significance attached to this particular figure that now escapes us. The early excavations of ancient Ur turned up an attractive image of this very thing, a ram entangled by its horns in a bush, its forelegs threshing in the air; but whether the effigy satisfied any need or purpose beyond the artistic, we do not know.

Related to the matter of religious backgrounds still detectable in this story is certainly the determination of the sacred place of which it was once a cult legend. The rule according to which the earlier *Ortsgebundenheit* of the narrative has had to yield to later concerns, whether of a more particularist popular interest or of a more universalist vision of the divine or simply of the exigencies of good storytelling, finds no exception here. Abraham and his God are the focus of the Elohist's attention and that of Genesis. Nevertheless, it is evident that place was an important factor in the formation of the story at its beginning, and had this factor been lacking it is likely enough that the story would never have been.

The place which must bear this responsibility was not *the land of Moriah* of vs. 2. Moriah turns up only once again in the Hebrew Bible, in 2 Chronicles 3:1, where it is the name given to a scene of divine apparition which became the site of the Jerusalem temple. Undoubtedly there is a tendentious connection between these two references. Has an editor of the Genesis text introduced Moriah into vs. 2, changing it from something else, because of its Jerusalemite connotations? Or has the Chronicler, rather, named the temple mound Moriah because of the Abraham and Isaac story which he knew from Genesis? It would be difficult to decide between the two alternatives. What is virtually certain, in any case, is that Moriah did not stand in the Genesis text as the Elohist originally composed it. Its later insertion, however, from whatever source, in all likelihood accounts for some of the rest of the text in its present form. By a benign popular etymology Moriah can be taken to mean something like "the vision of Yahweh." Once this name had been connected with the height of Abraham's sacrifice and had been so interpreted, it doubtless became the route whereby the same or another editor substituted in vs. 14 and then in vs. 11 for the "God" (Elohim) which the Elohist had put there the repeated "Yahweh" which we do not find elsewhere in his work. The *will see* with the Deity as subject of vs. 14 obviously has the *God himself will provide* of vs. 8 for its antecedent (literally, "God will see to [it] himself," *elohim yireh-lo*). By all accounts, then, the *Yahweh-yireh* of vs. 14 is secondary, dependent on the "etymology" of Moriah.

It is impossible to determine what original word lies concealed in the Moriah of the MT. The other witnesses to the text strongly suggest that it was something of similar spelling, but unfortunately they cannot tell us what the spelling precisely was and even less what the word meant. For "the land of Moriah" the Samaritan Pentateuch, Symmachus (one of the Jewish translators of the Hebrew Bible into Greek in early Christian times when an effort was being made to supplant the LXX), and the Latin Vulgate offer "the land of (the?) vision." This rendering would presuppose the Hebrew *mareh*. On the other hand, the LXX has "the high land," indicating that it read here the *moreh* of 12:6 which it also translated there "high." The ancient Syriac version, for its part, has "the land of the Amorites." It seems to be clear enough from this confusion of sounds that we are not likely to discover the scene of Abraham's sacrifice from any examination of vs. 2. We can only conjecture by ranging elsewhere in the text.

The ingenious proposal offered decades ago by Hermann Gunkel has, to our knowledge, never been bettered and still commends itself as eminently plausible. Gunkel observed, as others have before and after him, the incidence not only of the *elohim yireh* of vs. 8, but also the *yere elohim* of vs. 12 (*devoted you are to God*) and the *yar . . . ayil* of vs. 13 (*he spied a ram*), all of whose assonances seemed to converge toward the etiology not of a site named Yahweh-yireh, as now in vs. 14, but rather of something like Jeruel or Jeriel (variants of the same name, like the Penuel and Peniel of Genesis 32:31–32). Both these names can be verified in Israelite tradition: Jeriel a clan in the territory of Issachar (1 Chronicles 7:2), and Jeruel (in the LXX, Jeriel) a wasteland in the region of Judah, between En-gedi and Jerusalem in the neighborhood of Tekoa (2 Chronicles 20:16.20), a three-day march from Beer-sheba (cf. Genesis 22:4.19). The latter Jeruel/Jeriel especially could very easily have been the sacred place which the story of 22:1–14 intended to celebrate by popular etymology, before the intrusion of the Moriah that dictated Yahweh-yireh. (The real etymology would have been "El has founded [the place]," cf. [Jeru]-Salem of 14:18.) To the objection that Jeruel plays no major role in biblical history and is otherwise unknown as a sanctuary, Gunkel appropriately pointed out that it is only from the stories of Genesis that we are apprised of other significant places like Beer-lahai-roi (16:14), Mahanaim (32:3), Mamre (13:18, etc.), and Machpelah (23:17–20, etc.).

It is at least a thinkable thought, therefore, that at an obscure shrine in the desert of Judah at a time that we cannot even imagine, it was brought in to the heart of man not only that God preferred obedience to sacrifice but also that there were sacrifices that he did not want at all.

> 15 Again the LORD's messenger called to Abraham
> 16 from heaven and said: "I swear by myself, declares the LORD, that because you acted as you did
> 17 in not withholding from me your beloved son, I will bless you abundantly and make your descend-

ants as countless as the stars of the sky and the
sands of the seashore; your descendants shall take
18 possession of the gates of their enemies, and in your
descendants all the nations of the earth shall find
blessing—all this because you obeyed my command."
19 Abraham then returned to his servants, and they
set out together for Beer-sheba, where Abraham
made his home.

Aside from vs. 19, which completes and concludes the story of vss.
1–14, this little section is a supplement to what has gone before in the
words and in the spirit of J (cf. 12:2–3, 15:5), whatever may be its relation to the regular source material of Genesis. Something extra is being
added: not only is Abraham's obedience rewarded with the continued life
of his son, the previous promises of great progeny and archetypical blessing are reiterated. And they are reiterated with an oath: this time not the
oath of covenant ritual (15:18) but the oath of one who must swear by
himself since there is none other by whom he may swear (cf. Amos 4:2).

20 Some time afterward, the news came to Abraham:
"Milcah too has borne sons, to your brother Nahor:
21 Uz, his first-born, his brother Buz, Kemuel (the
22 father of Aram), Chesed, Hazo, Pildash, Jidlaph and
23 Bethuel." Bethuel became the father of Rebekah.
These eight Milcah bore to Abraham's brother
24 Nahor. His concubine, whose name was Reumah,
also bore children: Tebah, Gaham, Tahash and
Maacah.

This genealogy is J's: P has some of the relationships otherwise (Aram
the son of Shem in 10:22 and Uz the son of Aram in 10:23), and E has
no genealogies. In 11:29 (J) neither of Abraham nor *Nahor* was issue
named; now of the latter by *Milcah* his wife and *Reumah his concubine*
twelve sons are listed (like Ishmael's in 17:20, 25:13–16, P), all of
whom turn out to be Semitic relatives of the Israelites, mainly though not
exclusively resident in the homeland of Aram Naharaim. The Redactor's
purpose in inserting the genealogy here appears in vs. 23: *Bethuel became
the father of Rebekah,* and the Yahwist is about to tell the story of Rebekah in chapter 24.
As far as *Uz* and *Aram* are concerned, see the commentary on 10:22–
23 above. *Buz,* like Uz, is probably Edomite, the Assyrian Bazu, between
Teman and Dedan (Jeremiah 25:23). *Kemuel* is unknown; possibly it is
the name of a remembered ancestor rather than of a people. *Chesed,* as

we have seen (above on 11:31), is the eponymous ancestor of the Chaldeans, the Amorite conquerors of Babylonia who were also Edomite by extraction (cf. Job 1:17). *Hazo,* in Assyrian inscriptions mentioned with the Bazu above, was probably in the same region. *Pildash* and *Jidlaph* are unknown quantities. *Bethuel,* as appears from chapter 24, along with *Rebekah,* are intended to be historical persons. *Tebah* was a city near Damascus, an Aramean conquest of David (2 Samuel 8:8). *Gaham* is unknown. But *Tahash* may be identified with the Tahshi of the Amarna letters, a site somewhere in the Lebanon, therefore fittingly associated with *Maacah,* a region south of Mount Hermon (Joshua 13:11, 2 Samuel 10:6.8).

23 The span of Sarah's life was one hundred and twenty-
2 seven years. She died in Kiriath-arba (that is, Hebron) in the land of Canaan, and Abraham per-
3 formed the customary mourning rites for her. Then
he left the side of his dead one and addressed the
4 Hittites: "Although I am a resident alien among
you, sell me from your holdings a piece of property for a burial ground, that I may bury my dead
5 wife." The Hittites answered Abraham: "Please,†
6 sir, listen to us! You are an elect of God among
us. Bury your dead in the choicest of our burial sites.
None of us would deny you his burial ground for
7 the burial of your dead." Abraham, however, began
to bow low before the local citizens, the Hittites,
8 while he appealed to them: "If you will allow me
room for burial of my dead, listen to me! Intercede
9 for me with Ephron, son of Zohar, asking him to
sell me the cave of Machpelah that he owns; it is
at the edge of his field. Let him sell it to me in
your presence, at its full price, for a burial place."

Genesis 23 is the work of the Priestly author. Just as E reached its culmination of the Abraham story in the patriarch's great act of obedience, and as J will reach it in the provision of a wife for Isaac (chapter 24), P finds the realization of Abraham's full life accomplished in the acquisition of the family tomb of *Machpelah,* where Abraham himself will eventually repose (25:7–10). The fact that Abraham purchases this burial ground in his hundred and thirty-seventh year (vs. 1, cf. 17:17) while nothing else is recorded of him for the rest of his thirty-eight allotted years (cf. 25:7)

† Here and in vss. 11 and 14 "please" is a reasonable conjecture used to translate an obscure Hebrew expression.

testifies to the importance that the Priestly author attached to this event. It explained how it was that Abraham, though only a *resident alien* in the land of Canaan, nevertheless gained for himself and his descendants a holding that came to be revered as the last resting place of Israel's ancestors. (We have already explained that the resident alien, the *ger wetoshab,* was an outsider with a "permanent residence visa" who enjoyed the protection of the local laws and acknowledged duties toward them. By his landlessness he was distinguished from the full citizen, and by his protected status he differed from the *nokri,* the true foreigner, who had no rights at all.) We do not know how ancient in Israel was the tradition that linked Hebron with "the tombs of the patriarchs": the great mosque of Hebron, el-Haram el-Ibrahimi el-Khalil, which claims to be built over the cave of Machpelah, obviously can date only from the time of the Arab conquest of Palestine in the seventh Christian century, but before that there was a Byzantine church there, and even earlier the site had been enclosed by Herod the Great (37–4 B.C.), whose massive Roman masonry still survives at the site. This present Genesis story leads us to suspect that at least several centuries before Herod there was at or near Hebron a place venerated as the tomb of Abraham and his family, just as one has later been venerated by Jews, Christians, and Muslims, whether or not the place was in every instance the same. Aside from the precise determination of the place, which is presently impossible and probably always was, it is the acquisition itself of *a* place that was of chief importance to the biblical author. Machpelah signified to him an earnest, the first fruits, of Israel's eventual possession of the land: Abraham, so to speak, had already staked a claim for himself and those who would spring from him.

The scene is *Kiriath-arba,* which is vaguely identified with Hebron, just as Mamre has been and will be again in vs. 19, and as Machpelah is, though these places are also distinguished. Hebron itself was not founded until about 1700 B.C. (cf. Numbers 13:22). Kiriath-arba, which in Joshua 14:15 is fancifully named after a certain Arba, one of the aboriginal Anakim ("giants"), actually means "the city of four" (four quarters, hills, intersecting roads—all these have been conjectured). It may be identifiable with a hill overlooking Hebron called er-Rumeideh, on which are ruins carrying the name el-Arba'in. Wherever, it was hither that Abraham repaired after having *performed the customary mourning rites for* the dead Sarah, and here he *addressed the Hittites.*

As we already know, the Hittites of the Bible are rarely or never the Hittites known to the historian of ancient Anatolia (central Turkey on a modern map), an Indo-European people with a language and cultural traditions related to ours of "the west," who between the sixteenth and fifteenth centuries B.C. and again from the fourteenth to the beginning of the twelfth century maintained redoubtable kingdoms in Asia Minor. Hittites there surely were in Abraham's time—they make their first appearance around the beginning of the second millennium B.C.—but they were not in Canaan: Hittite records, which are copious, show that they never penetrated farther south than Damascus. We should ordinarily have no difficulty in concluding that by "Hittites" in this story P means nothing more than the people insinuated by 9:27 (see the commentary) or 10:15 or 15:20 (all J), like the "Perizzites" of 13:7 (also J) simply another of the indigenes of Canaan (cf. 26:34, 27:46, 36:2, all P), possibly distinguished as non-Semites in the process. Alternative theories, however, have been proposed to account for the Hittites of Genesis 23. One of these is that the people in question were proto-Hittites, earlier inhabitants of Asia Minor who were displaced by the Hittites and who might, some of them, have migrated into Palestine. Another and more elaborate theory was that of Sir Leonard Woolley, based on some distinctive pottery evidence which he had discovered both in Anatolia and southern Palestine, which persuaded him that the Hittites of this chapter could have been part of a migration from the original Hittite homeland in the Caucasus: this part could have split off and gone south after passing the upper reaches of the Tigris and Euphrates while the main group continued on westward eventually to establish the early Hittite kingdom in Asia Minor.

One reason for trying to get some kind of authentic Hittites into the Canaan of Abraham's time was the attractive persuasion that chapter 23 of Genesis had preserved the memory of some peculiarities of Hittite law which it could hardly have done save through an early contact with Hittites. After about 1200 B.C. with the destruction of the "new" Hittite empire, knowledge of Hittite law was lost and would only be regained in our own times through archeological discovery and deciphering. Thus, for example, in vss. 11–15 below the negotiations between Abraham and Ephron could be interpreted as involving a nicety of legalism known from §§ 46–47 of the Hittite Code. In Hittite legal practice obligations were attached to things as well as persons. If a man acquired a whole field, certain feudal services (precisely what, we do not know) which were attached to it now devolved upon him, whereas if he purchased only a part of it these services continued to be the responsibility of the primary owner. It might seem that in expressing interest only in *the cave of Machpelah at the edge of his field* Abraham was attempting to avoid acquiring the feudal obligations now held by Ephron, and that by insisting on an all-or-nothing purchase of both field and cave Ephron was showing himself no less eager to be rid of these obligations. The story can be read with such a background in mind, of course, but it need not be. It has also been noted as significant that in vs. 17 the trees of the field are mentioned, since one characteristic of Hittite contracts was the exact enumeration of the trees in a parcel of land that passed from one owner to another. The point doubtless is significant, since the biblical text in this respect as in others faithfully records Near Eastern contractual detail; but the counting of trees was not confined to Hittite contracts.

It would appear that it is somewhat precarious to build large hypotheses on rather slender foundations. The story of Genesis 23 makes incontestable sense without recourse to an exotic milieu that can only be conjectured, and while it does presuppose a knowledge of certain legalities, they were everyday legalities for which the Priestly author or his source required no special information. The Hittites of Kiriath-arba were, as far as we know for sure, like the rest of the Hittites of the Bible—that is, anything but Hittites!

One antiquarian note that is properly sounded in this story is Abraham's concern over a proper burial for his dead wife. The Amorite nomads with whom Abraham is associated more often than not by the biblical traditions are known archeologically to have been the most careful tomb-builders of ancient Palestine. The Bible, of course, is not really interested in antiquarian authenticity so much as it is in validating the patriarchs' stake in the Land of Promise. And in telling a good story while doing so. Though the Hittites receive Abraham with courtly deference and invite him to make free use of their gravesites, the patriarch will not be beholden to them or dependent on their sufferance. He does, nevertheless, match and even exceed them in gestures of politeness, for he is, after all, asking of them a favor and a privilege. Because he is a resident alien and therefore not legally entitled to own land, if an exception is to be made for him it can only be with the concurrence of all the city fathers. This exception the Hittites are at first reluctant to grant, aware, no doubt, of the dangers inherent in setting such a precedent. Nevertheless, as Abraham presses his request and becomes specific about the holding he desires, indicating its owner sitting in their midst, the assembly evidently registers its assent to the proposal. They remain in session now to serve as the witnesses to the bargain that will be struck between Abraham and Ephron.

> 10 Now Ephron was present with the Hittites. So Ephron the Hittite replied to Abraham in the hearing of the Hittites who sat on his town council:
> 11 "Please, sir, listen to me! I give you both the field and the cave in it; in the presence of my kinsmen I
> 12 make this gift. Bury your dead!" But Abraham, after bowing low before the local citizens, addressed
> 13 Ephron in the hearing of these men: "Ah, if only you would please listen to me! I will pay you the price of the field. Accept it from me, that I may
> 14 bury my dead there." Ephron replied to Abraham,

15 "Please, sir, listen to me! A piece of land worth
four hundred shekels of silver—what is that between you and me, as long as you can bury your
16 dead?" Abraham accepted Ephron's terms; he
weighed out to him the silver that Ephron had stipulated in the hearing of the Hittites, four hundred
shekels of silver at the current market value.
17 Thus Ephron's field in Machpelah, facing Mamre,
together with its cave and all the trees anywhere
18 within its limits, was conveyed to Abraham by purchase in the presence of all the Hittites who sat on
19 Ephron's town council. After this transaction, Abraham buried his wife Sarah in the cave of the field
of Machpelah, facing Mamre (that is, Hebron) in
20 the land of Canaan. Thus the field with its cave was
transferred from the Hittites to Abraham as a burial
place.

The *give* of vs. 11 is exactly the same word which NAB has translated
sell once in vs. 4 above and twice in vs. 9. To give something in exchange
for money or some other consideration is, of course, to sell it. We are im-
mersed here in the language conventions of ancient oriental trading,
which, for that matter, are neither inscrutably oriental nor exclusively ancient. Having been discreetly brought into the proceedings as a negotiator
and no longer a mere councilor, Ephron plays his role to the hilt. First, he
expresses his willingness to sell, and not only to sell the bit of property
that Abraham had begged for, but to make available a much ampler and
worthier plot of land for a family cemetery: *both the field and the cave in
it.* Far from objecting to this offer, Abraham probably expected it: it was
part of the ritual that purchases be modest in proposal and generous in
disposal. (It is instructive to compare with this episode the story of
David's purchase of the threshing floor of Araunah the Jebusite told in 2
Samuel 24:18–25.) It would have been unthinkable for Ephron prematurely to put a price on this "gift" which his magnanimity had directed
him to proffer this favored outlander; to elicit such information some additional ceremony is required on Abraham's part. Finally it is produced, as
with the casual wave of a hand Ephron dismisses the distasteful subject
once for all, mentioning by the by that *four hundred shekels of silver*
would be considered by any fair judgment an equitable exchange for the
piece of land that is under discussion. We have no way of being sure, but
we may doubtless surmise with the greatest probability that it was a noble
sum indeed that Ephron exacted. Four hundred shekels would be about
forty-six kilos or over one hundred pounds of silver. David bought the

temple site and the materials for sacrifice for fifty silver shekels (2 Samuel 24:24). In any case, Abraham paid the stipulated price without protest. It undoubtedly pleased the biblical author to record that the patriarchal tombs at Machpelah had passed from Hittite ownership into that of the Hebrews by no deed of condescension from the inhabitants of Canaan but only through a munificent gesture of Israel's great ancestor. (In like manner, the Chronicler's rewriting of 2 Samuel 24:24 in 1 Chronicles 21:25 has David pay out to Araunah [Ornan] six hundred shekels of *gold!*)

So Machpelah *was conveyed to Abraham by purchase,* and there the patriarch *buried his wife Sarah,* in the same tomb that would eventually receive his own body. The Priestly author has now told us all that he knew about Abraham. So also has the Yahwist, as it now appears, since the long story that follows in chapter 24 introduces him only for a final time, as a man who commissions a trusted servant to execute his last will and testament by finding a suitable wife for his son Isaac. There can be no doubt that this J story represents a deathbed request, and that in the interim between commission and fulfillment Abraham has ceased to be. Under these circumstances, it is all the more interesting that the Yahwist has chosen to protract the narrative the way he has, seemingly out of the sheer joy of garrulous storytelling. That it is, indeed, a story well told, there can be no question. No effort at all has been made to economize on detail in order to speed the flow of the Redactor's grand design.

> **24** Abraham had now reached a ripe old age, and the
> 2 LORD had blessed him in every way. Abraham said
> to the senior servant of his household, who had
> charge of all his possessions: "Put your hand un-
> 3 der my thigh, and I will make you swear by the
> LORD, the God of heaven and the God of earth, that
> you will not procure a wife for my son from the
> 4 daughters of the Canaanites among whom I live, but
> that you will go to my own land and to my kindred
> 5 to get a wife for my son Isaac." The servant asked
> him: "What if the woman is unwilling to follow me
> to this land? Should I then take your son back to
> 6 the land from which you migrated?" "Never take my
> son back there for any reason," Abraham told him.
> 7 "The LORD, the God of heaven, who took me from
> my father's house and the land of my kin, and who
> confirmed by oath the promise he then made to me,
> 'I will give this land to your descendants,' he will
> send his messenger before you, and you will ob-
> 8 tain a wife for my son there. If the woman is un-
> willing to follow you, you will be released from this

9 oath. But never take my son back there!" So the
servant put his hand under the thigh of his master
Abraham and swore to him in this undertaking.

This longest of the early patriarchal stories of Genesis has often been
called a novelette. In inverse proportion to its size, it might be thought, is
its protagonist, who is a mere servant. However, it becomes quickly evident that much more is involved here than a tale about, and by, Abraham's chief servitor: it was a story prized for a number of values
without which the patriarchal history would have been considered incomplete, and in consequence it was told and retold in loving detail and doubtless with embellishments as a perennial reminder to Israel of all that
Abraham's call had meant and what was signified by the coming of
Rebekah, Israel's second mother. The story is certainly the Yahwist's, but
there is evidence here and there both of compilation and of more recent
adaptation. Modern critics have given up the attempt to discern in its
make-up the residue of an elaborate composition from sources or a series
of recensions such as were once proposed by Gunkel and Otto Procksch.
Most of what was then deemed to be the evidence of such things now
tends to be put down to an original narrative prolixity—admittedly, not
the Yahwist's usual wont—made wordier still by subsequent transmission.
We may be sure that the repetitiveness which we occasionally find a bit
overwhelming was not so sensed by the authors and editors of the Bible.
To them it was a beautiful story, expertly constructed, of which they
would not sacrifice a single word. By whatever process it has come about,
Genesis 24 emerges as a unique literary form in its environment, and there
is very little else in Genesis against which it may be properly measured.

Abraham had now reached a ripe old age: Gunkel believed that 25:5
originally followed this verse; in any case, the perspective seems to be that
of a deathbed commission. Now that *the* LORD *had blessed him in every
way,* Abraham plans to crown a full life by seeing to the preservation of
his descent as he knows the Lord would have it, with the marriage of his
son to one of his own kind and not to a woman of the Canaanite peoples.
This concern corresponds with the endogamous pattern we have observed
before in the Terahites, a pattern which will be repeated in the marriages
of Isaac's son Jacob. The *senior servant* to whom Abraham entrusts his
commission undoubtedly holds the same position as the Eliezer of 15:2
who was destined to be his heir in default of natural issue, but in this story
he is entirely anonymous. The extreme seriousness of the commission is
underlined by the imposition of a solemn oath. To swear by placing the
hand under one's *thigh* seems to be a euphemism for touching the
genitalia: in Genesis 46:26 and Exodus 1:5 the NAB's "direct descendants" is, literally, "who issued from his thigh." In Genesis 47:29 (J)

Jacob, or Israel, in another deathbed performance, requires the same kind of oath of his son Joseph. No doubt we are witnessing a ceremony far more ancient than Israel or the Hebrews which reverenced the organ of generation as the seat of life and the symbol of its sacredness: the same mentality that found expression in phallic worship and fertility ritual. Reverence for life is not, at bottom, a bad thing, nor an unworthy value to swear by. Nevertheless, Israel had something better, which is reflected in this story. Abraham's servant swears his oath not by life but by Yahweh the Author of life. *The God of heaven and the God of earth,* which is to say, the God of the universe, may be the formulation of a theology later than the Yahwist's, but it is not one that would have been alien to his thought (cf. 18:25).

The substance of Abraham's commission is precisely defined. From it, it is seen at once why an emissary and not Isaac himself is sent to Abraham's *own land and kindred* (contrary to the later story of both J and P which has Jacob repair to Aram Naharaim at the behest of his parents). So mindful is Abraham of the Providence that has guided his steps to the land of Canaan and of the oath by which the Lord confirmed this land to be the possession of his descendants (15:18) that there must be no slightest turning back. *Never take my son back there for any reason.* The same Lord will surely see to it that a willing woman will be found from among his own to embark on the path which he took so long ago to join her lot with his family's and become a part of the new world. The old world has its uses, but it is not there that the future lies. It is a page of history that has been turned once and for all. Of all this Abraham is quietly confident. He humors his servant's practical and sensible reservation about the success of his mission, but he knows, all the same, that no real difficulty will arise. The story is the more impressive, perhaps, for the lack of theophany, vision, divine messenger, or other vehicle by which revelation is customarily delivered to man. Here is only the mind of one who has walked a road so far that he now knows its every bend.

> 10 The servant then took ten of his master's camels,‡
> and bearing all kinds of gifts from his master, he
> made his way to the city of Nahor in Aram Na-
> 11 haraim. Near evening, at the time when women go
> out to draw water, he made the camels kneel by
> 12 the well outside the city. Then he prayed: "LORD,
> God of my master Abraham, let it turn out favorably
> for me today and thus deal graciously with my
> 13 master Abraham. While I stand here at the spring
> and the daughters of the townsmen are coming out

‡ With the LXX, the NAB omits a superfluous "and he made his way."

14 to draw water, if I say to a girl, 'Please lower your jug, that I may drink,' and she answers, 'Take a drink, and let me give water to your camels, too,' let her be the one whom you have decided upon for your servant Isaac. In this way I shall know that you have dealt graciously with my master."

15 He had scarcely finished these words when Rebekah (who was born to Bethuel, son of Milcah, the wife of Abraham's brother Nahor) came out with a jug

16 on her shoulder. The girl was very beautiful, a virgin, untouched by man. She went down to the spring

17 and filled her jug. As she came up, the servant ran toward her and said, "Please give me a sip of water

18 from your jug." "Take a drink, sir," she replied, and quickly lowering the jug onto her hand, she

19 gave him a drink. When she had let him drink his fill, she said, "I will draw water for your camels, too,

20 until they have drunk their fill." With that, she quickly emptied her jug into the drinking trough and ran back to the well to draw more water, until

21 she had drawn enough for all the camels. The man watched her the whole time, silently waiting to learn whether or not the LORD had made his errand

22 successful. When the camels had finished drinking, the man took out a gold ring weighing half a shekel, which he fastened on her nose,* and two gold bracelets weighing ten shekels, which he put on her wrists.

23 Then he asked her: "Whose daughter are you? Tell me, please. And is there room in your father's house

24 for us to spend the night?" She answered: "I am the daughter of Bethuel the son of Milcah, whom

25 she bore to Nahor. There is plenty of straw and fodder at our place," she added, "and room to

26 spend the night." The man then bowed down in

27 worship to the LORD, saying: "Blessed be the LORD, the God of my master Abraham, who has not let his constant kindness toward my master fail. As for myself also, the LORD has led me straight to the house of my master's brother."†

---

* "Which he fastened on her nose" is supplied from the SP; not in the MT. Cf. vs. 47.
† So the ancient versions; the MT has "kinsmen."

Abraham's servant sets forth with a noble entourage, befitting the man whom Yahweh had so abundantly blessed with wealth as men then accounted wealth (vs. 35). Not for the first or the last time does one who has prospered in a world of new horizons return, in person or by surrogate, to dazzle the stay-at-homes with visions of what has been made both possible and actual in the land of opportunity. He takes *ten of his master's camels* not only to bear *all kinds of gifts from his master* but also to transport an honor guard of other retainers (cf. vss. 23.32). *He made his way to the city of Nahor:* as we have seen above, Nahor (Nahur) is the attested name of a city in Aram Naharaim as well as that of a brother of Abraham (cf. 11:22–27, P; 11:28–30, 22:20–24, J). It is not certain which meaning is intended here, but in any event neither Nahor, Abraham's brother, nor Bethuel his son (11:29, 22:20–23, J) appear in the story except as names; the male head of Rebekah's household is her brother Laban (vs. 29 and following). We can only assume that in the storyteller's mind both Nahor and Bethuel were now dead. If by "the city of Nahor in Aram Naharaim" the Yahwist intended only to designate the place where Nahor had once resided and where his descendants now were, undoubtedly he meant the city of Haran (cf. 27:43, 29:4–5, J).

Later on Jacob, Rebekah's son, will find his own wife by a well (cf. 29:1–14, J). Here his mother is destined to be discovered *by the well outside the city,* where Abraham's servant makes temporary camp *at the time when women go out to draw water* (cf. 1 Samuel 9:11). Certainly this is the best opportunity for a man at his leisure to survey the nubile maidens of a given town. But this man is also in a hurry. With all the confidence of his master in the working of divine providence, he does not hesitate to organize a strategy and stipulate a sign for the Lord to give him, in all of which he expects 100 per cent co-operation from above. The proposed sign, however, is nothing merely arbitrary, but rather contains its own simple logic and promise of self-fulfillment. The camels of this and the other patriarchal stories are, as we have seen above, anachronisms; but there was nothing anachronistic about an Israelite author's acquaintance with the ways of camels and their proverbial thirst. For a girl to provide a wayfarer with drink on his request was only to be expected as an elementary mark of civility and minimal virtue. For her to offer spontaneously to run back and forth between well and trough till the wants of ten tired and demanding camels had been completely assuaged, that was something else entirely. Here indeed must be a jewel of a woman, and a pearl beyond price!

Shrewdly the servant *watched her the whole time,* until the deed had been done. It was easy enough to make a generous gesture, but harder to carry through with it. Only *when the camels had finished drinking* was he satisfied that his call for a sign had been answered, and therefore that

Yahweh *had made his errand successful.* Not only is he satisfied, however, he concludes that his mission is now a *fait accompli* and proceeds to bring it to a speedy end. The ten and a half shekels of gold that he showers upon the bewildered Rebekah could hardly have been thought by her or her family to be just a recompense for hospitality: they are, rather, at least a portion of the *mohar,* the bride price, which Deuteronomy 22:29 calcu- lated at the value of fifty silver shekels. Only when he has bestowed this gift, so sure is he that what he is about is absolutely right, does he inquire of the identity of the maiden who stands before him and of the possibility of being received into her home. He now learns for the first time what we have known since vs. 15, that the girl to whom the Lord had directed him is Isaac's first cousin once removed, that Yahweh has indeed led him *straight to the house of* his *master's brother,* to fulfill to the letter Abraham's desire that his son have a wife from not only his own land but also from his own kindred (vs. 4 above).

28 Then the girl ran off and told her mother's
29 household about it. Now Rebekah had a brother
30 named Laban. As soon as he saw the ring and
the bracelets on his sister Rebekah and heard
her words about what the man had said to her,‡
Laban rushed outside to the man at the spring.
When he reached him, he was still standing by
31 the camels at the spring. So he said to him:
"Come, blessed of the LORD! Why are you staying outside when I have made the house ready
32 for you, as well as a place for the camels?" The
man then went inside; and while the camels were
being unloaded and provided with straw and fodder, water was brought to bathe his feet and the
33 feet of the men who were with him. But when
the table was set for him, he said, "I will not eat
until I have told my tale." "Do so," they replied.
34/35 "I am Abraham's servant," he began. "The
LORD has blessed my master so abundantly that
he has become a wealthy man; he has given him
flocks and herds, silver and gold, male and fe-
36 male slaves, and camels and asses. My master's
wife Sarah bore a son to my master in her old
age, and he has given him everything he owns.
37 My master put me under oath, saying: 'You shall
not procure a wife for my son among the daugh-

‡ NAB has rearranged vss. 29–30.

38 ters of the Canaanites in whose land I live; instead, you shall go to my father's house, to my
39 own relatives, to get a wife for my son.' When I asked my master, 'What if the woman will not
40 follow me?' he replied: 'The LORD, in whose presence I have always walked, will send his messenger with you and make your errand successful, and so you will get a wife for my son
41 from my own kindred of my father's house. Then you shall be released from my ban. If you visit my kindred and they refuse you, then, too, you shall be released from my ban.'
42 "When I came to the spring today, I prayed: 'LORD, God of my master Abraham, may it be your will to make successful the errand I am en-
43 gaged on! While I stand here at the spring, if I say to a young woman who comes out to draw water, Please give me a little water from your
44 jug, and she answers, Not only may you have a drink, but I will give water to your camels, too—let her be the woman whom the LORD has decided upon for my master's son.'
45 "I had scarcely finished saying this prayer to myself when Rebekah came out with a jug on her shoulder. After she went down to the spring and drew water, I said to her, 'Please let me
46 have a drink.' She quickly lowered the jug she was carrying and said, 'Take a drink, and let me bring water for your camels, too.' So I drank,
47 and she watered the camels also. When I asked her, 'Whose daughter are you?' she answered, 'The daughter of Bethuel, son of Nahor, born to Nahor by Milcah.' So I put the ring on her nose
48 and the bracelets on her wrists. Then I bowed down in worship to the LORD, blessing the LORD, the God of my master Abraham, who had led me on the right road to obtain the daughter of
49 my master's kinsman for his son. If, therefore, you have in mind to show true loyalty to my master, let me know; but if not, let me know that, too. I can then proceed accordingly."

Abraham's servant, as yet not knowing Rebekah's circumstances, had asked about reception in her father's house (vs. 23), using the conventional term for the family hearth. Now *the girl ran off and told her mother's household about* all that had happened: obviously, a conscious effort is being made to indicate that Rebekah's father was no more. Her mother, on the other hand, while she is mentioned again (vss. 53.55), plays no part at all in the story, and evidently she had not left behind even her name in the tradition (unlike Rebekah's grandmother Milcah, cf. vss. 15.24). Her brother Laban now becomes the standard second party in the action that follows, after the excited Rebekah has hastened homeward (presumably not forgetting her water jug) to report on the marvelous event that has befallen her by the city well. Laban's instant reaction *as soon as he saw the ring and the bracelets,* his rush to secure this prize of a traveler so prodigal with gold, and the fulsomeness of the invitation he presses upon him, all are described with sardonic humor, in anticipation of the figure that Laban will cut later on in his dealings with Jacob (chapter 29, 30:25–43, etc.). It is typical of the Yahwist's narrative technique that in vss. 31 and 50–51 he has Laban address Abraham's servant in the name of Yahweh, even though he knows him to be the worshiper of other gods (see below on 30:53, J). This, however, may also be thought of as a piece of conventional politeness, since the servant has already revealed to Rebekah who is his master and the name of his master's God (cf. vs. 27 above), and such intelligence would easily have been included in Rebekah's breathless account to her family of what had so recently occurred in her meeting with the stranger.

Protocol demands that the needs of the guest be satisfied before the transaction of any business. Hence the weary beasts of burden were *unloaded and provided with straw and fodder, water was brought to bathe* the servant's *feet and the feet of the men who were with him* (we tend to forget about these from time to time), and *the table was set for him.* But the servant will not have it so. First he must tell his tale, which is one that we as well as he now know by heart. What would be inadmissible repetition on the part of a stenographic recorder of minutes, however, permits the teller of a story to exercise his art expansively. The servant's tale thus adds some subtleties to the narrative that it would not otherwise possess.

There are some slight variations in this part of the story that differentiate it from the rest, some of which have significance and some of which do not. Throughout vss. 28–49 it is a "spring" rather than a "well" at which the encounter with Rebekah occurs. In the preceding vss. 10–27, however, the two words have been used indifferently to refer to the same thing, so that for the purpose of the story they appear to be synonymous. Synonyms, too, are the "ban" of vs. 41 quoting vs. 8 and "oath" that was spoken of there, in view of vs. 37 which also has "oath." But in vss. 39–41 it is clearly not by accident that the servant omits any mention of Abraham's vehement and reiterated insistence that on no account may

Isaac ever be taken to Aram Naharaim (vss. 6.8). Tact forbids any such reference, along with any advertence to the election of Abraham and the promise of the land on which the ban was premised, since in neither of these will Laban share nor would he be expected to understand them. In recompense, in vs. 41 Abraham's charge is paraphrased to envisage the possibility not only of the prospective bride's reluctance to follow the servant back to Canaan but also of the refusal of his kindred to permit the marriage; in either case, the servant's commission will have been fulfilled. He is thus in a position, giving his audience time for deliberation as he squeezes the last narrative drop out before them, at last in vs. 49 to put to them the question direct. What is it to be: yes or no?

50 Laban and his household* said in reply: "This thing comes from the LORD; we can say nothing to
51 you either for or against it. Here is Rebekah, ready for you; take her with you, that she may become the wife of your master's son, as the LORD has said."
52 When Abraham's servant heard their answer, he
53 bowed to the ground before the LORD. Then he brought out objects of silver and gold and articles of clothing and presented them to Rebekah; he also gave costly presents to her brother and mother.
54 After he and the men with him had eaten and drunk, they spent the night there. When they were up the next morning, he said, "Give me leave to re-
55 turn to my master." Her brother and mother replied, "Let the girl stay with us a short while, say ten days;
56 after that she may go." But he said to them, "Do not detain me, now that the LORD has made my errand
57 successful; let me go back to my master." They answered, "Let us call the girl and see what she her-
58 self has to say about it." So they called Rebekah and asked her, "Do you wish to go with this man?"
59 She answered, "I do." At this they allowed their sister Rebekah and her nurse to take leave, along with
60 Abraham's servant and his men. Invoking a blessing on Rebekah, they said:
"Sister, may you grow
     into thousands of myriads;
And may your descendants gain possession
     of the gates of their enemies!"

* Conjecture: reading *betho* in place of MT *bethuel*, "his house" rather than "Bethuel."

61 Then Rebekah and her maids started out; they
mounted their camels and followed the man. So the
servant took Rebekah and went on his way.

In vs. 49 above Abraham's servant had asked his hosts to declare their
willingness to exchange with his master *hesed we-emeth,* covenant or
familial fidelity, *true loyalty,* or not: otherwise, he would know whether to
proceed, literally, "either to the right or the left." In vs. 50 Laban proves
himself to be an adept master at an even more refined oriental circumlocution. *"This thing comes from the* LORD," he says piously. *"We can say
nothing to you either for or against it."* And yet it is clear that he has, indeed, declared in favor of the proposal, as appears from his further words
in vs. 51 and the servant's reaction in vs. 52. What Laban is torn between
is the present possession of an obviously precious sister who could command an untold amount in the bridal market and a concrete offer of about
120.75 grams or roughly four troy ounces of gold against the expectations
of a man who—it is said—has received of his father everything he owns in
flocks and herds, silver and gold, male and female slaves, and camels and
asses (vs. 35). Laban is willing to commit himself to the opportunity at
hand, but he would also like to improve upon it if possible (cf. vs. 55).

The commitment is sufficient for Abraham's servant. He proceeds to bestow the remainder of the *mohar* on Rebekah, *objects of silver and gold
and articles of clothing,* and then what Laban had been looking forward
to: *to her brother and mother* also he *gave costly presents.* Only after this,
the transaction completed to his satisfaction, do *he and the men with him*
presume to partake of the hospitality offered them, to eat and to drink and
to spend the night.

Up to this point the conduct of all has been impeccable. On the morrow,
however, the servant commits an almost unheard-of breach of the social
canons by asking immediate *leave to return to my master.* He knows that
this proposal will be countered; we can only suppose that he has anticipated matching wits with the wily Laban and has therefore resolved to join
the battle on his own terms. The rejoinder of his hosts quite probably
takes him aback, however, suggesting a delay that far exceeds what polite
convention would demand. The *a short while, say ten days* of the NAB
translation above renders a curious Hebrew which has it, literally, "days,
or ten." This could mean, as Benno Jacob argued, "a year, or ten
months." At any rate, a prolonged stay was being requested, partly understandable under the circumstances without the need of further explanation,
but also partly explained by Laban's desire to see more of Abraham's
bounty which continued hospitality would elicit. But the servant has a
trump card which he displays immediately to bring the game to a conclusion ere it has hardly begun. Laban yesterday would venture neither a yea

nor a nay lest he intrude in the affairs of the Lord? So be it. *Do not detain me, then, now that the* LORD *has made my errand successful; let me go back to my master.* Laban cannot argue against his own piety; he can only be expected to acquiesce gracefully.

Which is what he does. *Let us call the girl and see what she herself has to say about it.* Thus far scant attention has been given to Rebekah's feelings in this matter that concerned her more than anyone else. Marriage, in the majority view of most of the Old Testament, was far too serious a subject to be left to the discretion of the young, including the young people who were to be the marriage partners. In arranging this particular marriage neither Rebekah nor Isaac has been consulted. Instead, complete reliance has been placed on the prudence of Abraham's servant both to choose wisely a suitable woman and to represent to her family the worthiness of her suitor. Indeed, Rebekah now knows more about Isaac than he of her, and she undoubtedly knew more about him than most other maidens of her peer group would have known of their prospective husbands. And now at the end her consent is, after all, solicited: *Do you wish to go with this man?* It may be that legal technicalities were involved. Nuzi marriage contracts sometimes required the bride's consent when it was a brother rather than her father who arranged the marriage. Assyrian law protected a girl's right to stay in her own homeland: she could not be wed to a foreigner in a strange land against her will.

The epithalamion or wedding blessing of vs. 60 is a rare form in the Old Testament (late examples in Ruth 4:11–12, Tobit 7:12). It is, almost inevitably, also a fertility blessing (ancient examples in Genesis 49:25–26, Deuteronomy 33:13–17). Its martial, conquistador-like tone should not occasion surprise. Like so many other formulas that the Bible has made applicable to the ordinary state of man and woman in the particulars of their human life (see above on 1:26–28), this one, too, is doubtless the "democratization" of language that had its original setting in the circumstances of a royal consort (cf. Psalm 45:17–18). The reiterated address of *sister* Rebekah in vss. 59–60, along with the "household" references of vss. 28 and 50 (corrected text), of course point to a larger family of Rebekah than simply a mother and brother, though nothing has been said of the other members before or will be said after.

This larger family is also implied in what follows, as Rebekah, having assented to what fortune has brought her, dutifully accompanies Abraham's servant on the route back from Aram Naharaim to Canaan. With her go *her nurse,* undoubtedly the family retainer who had cared for her from babyhood, and *her maids,* the other body servants whom she had at her disposal. *They mounted their camels and followed the man:* the caravan that had once set out from Abraham's tent now returns to it doubled in strength. Abraham's munificence has been felt in Aram Naharaim, and so will Laban's be in Canaan.

62 Meanwhile Isaac had gone from† Beer-lahai-roi and
63 was living in the region of the Negeb. One day toward evening he went out . . . in the field, and as
he looked around, he noticed that camels were ap-
64 proaching. Rebekah, too, was looking about, and
65 when she saw him, she alighted from her camel and
asked the servant, "Who is the man out there, walking through the fields toward us?" "That is my master," replied the servant. Then she covered herself
with her veil.
66 The servant recounted to Isaac all the things he had
67 done. Then Isaac took Rebekah into his tent;† he
married her, and thus she became his wife. In his
love for her Isaac found solace after the death of
his mother Sarah.

The conclusion of the story is in many respects quite opaque. At its beginning Abraham seemed to be on his deathbed, as we observed at the
time, and in vs. 36 above Abraham's servant had almost spoken of his
master in the past tense, reporting to Rebekah's family that the inheritance
had already passed to Isaac (whose name, curiously, never came up at all
in the marriage negotiations). Apparently he did not expect to find Abraham still alive on his return, even though he was making his return
with a certain dispatch, ahead of schedule. Somewhere along the line, ex-
pectation has become certainty: the servant reports not to Abraham but to
Isaac, and it is Isaac whom he identifies to Rebekah as his master.
Abraham, therefore, is dead. The Redactor of Genesis, of course, cannot
allow this to be, since he plans to tell of the patriarch's death only in the P
version of 25:7–11. Therefore various things have been done to the
Yahwist's narrative. The NAB in vs. 67 has undoubtedly correctly
translated *into his tent,* omitting the "Sarah his mother" which in the MT
is added ungrammatically at this point. This latter phrase NAB has transferred to the end of the verse, yielding the translation *after the death of his
mother Sarah* (the MT has simply, "after his mother"). What is most
likely is that the Yahwist originally wrote here "after the death of his father," having included at some previous stage in his chronicle a notice of
Abraham's death which was subsequently suppressed. The Redactor presumably changed the ending of the story to make it look back instead
to the P account of Sarah's death and burial in chapter 23, thus leaving
himself free to bring in the later P fragment of 25:7–11 below.

† See the commentary.

There is some confusion, too, as regards Isaac's movements in the story and where exactly we are when we come to the end of it. The NAB, in concert with probably most other modern versions of Genesis, has translated an obscure and ambiguous Hebrew text so as to read that *Isaac had gone from Beer-lahai-roi and was living in the region of the Negeb.* Beer-lahai-roi has been mentioned only once before (16:14, J), not as the place of residence of any of Abraham's people, to be sure, yet as a site sanctified by one of his own in the same fashion that the Yahwist often pictures him sanctifying other sites. If we are to preserve the "from" of vs. 62 (other translations, however, are possible), we may imagine the author now bringing Isaac back to the Negeb (presumably to Beer-sheba, cf. 26:23, J) from the wasteland farther to the south where he had resided for some undisclosed reason, and that it was here, therefore, that he received Rebekah. If this is so, it is a good guess that 25:11b (J), the only other text which names Beer-lahai-roi, and precisely in connection with Isaac, originally had a place earlier on in the Yahwist's narrative (see below on 25:1–6). This hypothesis strikes the present writer as preferable to most of its alternatives. Whatever be the truth of the matter, we have an additional indication that the J story has been tampered with and rearranged by the Redactor.

One day toward evening Isaac *went out* to do something we know not what *in the field.* The NAB has wisely refrained from assigning any meaning here to a Hebrew verb which has been so variously translated by both ancient and modern versions that it is apparent all attempts to render it on present information can be only educated guesswork. Whatever it might tell us about Isaac, therefore, remains hidden. We simply find Abraham's son presiding over his encampment when, presumably by prior arrangement, *he noticed that camels were approaching.* Rebekah, too, no doubt has been alerted to the proximate meeting with her destined husband, *the man out there.* When he is dutifully pointed out for her, *she covered herself with her veil.* The veiling of a bride, sometimes as a wedding ritual, sometimes as a garb for all of wedded life, has been a custom of many peoples and many times. It accounts for purdah, for the dress of the Muslim wife and of the medieval nun, and for some of the bridal *couture* of the modern Western world.

It has often been remarked that Isaac first married Rebekah, and that he then came to love her: not at all the sequence with which we are ordinarily familiar. Neither is it the inevitable sequence of the Old Testament, for that matter, as chapter 29 (J) will also show. Nevertheless, it was undoubtedly the sequence that governed the marriage of most of our fathers and mothers through countless generations, and which made possible the romanticism which freer and more leisurely societies can indulge in virtue of the practicalities of the past.

The following verses of chapter 25 are also J, but their location within the Yahwist's narrative is subject to discussion. Already 25:5 has been anticipated by 24:36, as we saw above. Furthermore, as we have also observed, 25:11b looks like the presupposition of 24:62. It seems to be a fair assumption that what we are now reading here for the first time the Redactor of Genesis read at some earlier point in this copy of the J chronicle, and that for purposes of his own he saw fit to move to this place.

> 25 Abraham married another wife, whose name was
> 2 Keturah. She bore him Zimran, Jokshan, Medan,
> 3 Midian, Ishbak and Shuah. Jokshan became the
>   father of Sheba and Dedan. The descendants of
>   Dedan were the Asshurim, the Letushim, and the
> 4 Leummim. The descendants of Midian were
>   Ephah, Epher, Hanoch, Abida and Eldaah. All of
>   these were descendants of Keturah.
> 5 Abraham deeded everything that he owned to his
> 6 son Isaac. To his sons by concubinage, however,
>   he made grants while he was still living, as he sent
>   them away eastward, to the land of Kedem, away
> 11b from his son Isaac . . . who made his home near
>   Beer-lahai-roi.

As in other genealogies of the kind, the rationale of the generations is far from clear. Two descendants are attributed to the second "son" in the primary list of six, and five to the fourth in line; none to any of the others. For good measure, however, three "descendants" make up a third generation ascribed to the second in the line of the second in the line. These latter, who are obviously the plural names of peoples, are suspect as being expansions intruded into a tree which originally listed only eponymous ancestors. They were, nevertheless, intruded into a right place. *The Asshurim* (not the Asshur of 10:22, but of vs. 18 below, cf. Numbers 22:24), *the Letushim, and the Leummim,* we may confidently assume, were Arabic tribes, peoples with whom the Israelites acknowledged kinship through Abraham, "Semites" therefore (though in the P genealogy of 10:7 *Sheba and Dedan* appear as "descendants of Ham").

Keturah, poor thing, who shows up nowhere else in the Bible (except in the paraphrase of 1 Chronicles 1:32), has always been an embarrassment to the biblical expositor. She is obviously the mother of Israel's Arab cousins, yet this post previously seemed to have been pre-empted by Abraham's Egyptian concubine Hagar (16:12, J; 17:20, P; cf. 25:12–18, P; 21:18.21, E). As it turns out, however, the J author has to this point not attempted to trace the descent of any of these names except as they related to Israel's Semitic ancestry and family relationships. The attempt of medieval rabbis to identify Keturah with Hagar was both misguided and unnecessary. These verses, contrary to vss. 12–16 below (P), are the J accounting for the Arabs of the steppe, who spring from Keturah.

Zimran (the LXX has either Zemran, Zebran, or Zembran) may be Zabram, the home of a tribe in Saudi Arabia west of Mecca. *Jokshan* is very likely the Joktan of 10:26–28, who there as here is the "father" of Sheba. *Midian* is the Midianites, cf. 4:2b–16 above. *Medan* (see 37:36) and *Ishbak* are otherwise unknown, but *Shuah* appears to be a place in Arabia or Idumea (cf. Job 2:11).

The secondary generations, as far as we know, are also Arabian. *Ephah* (cf. Isaiah 60:6) is certainly such. *Abida* is most probably such, a place which in Assyrian texts is put in the same region as Ephah. *Epher, Hanoch,* and *Eldaah* are all good Semitic names, but their relation to our present context is unknown.

In vss. 5–6 Abraham's *sons by concubinage* (literally, "sons of concubines") are treated quite differently from the way Hagar's would have been under the presuppositions of the arrangement described in the J story of chapter 16. Keturah (and possibly other concubines as well?) was simply a secondary wife, the commonplace of a polygamous society, not a substitute wife taken for the purpose of bearing an heir. Law and custom protected the rights of children born of such unions, but there would be no question of their sharing in an estate alongside the legal heirs. That the question could never even rise, Abraham distances these of his descent from his son Isaac and pensions them off *while he was still living.* The biblical author doubtless expects us to recognize in this action both the patriarch's generosity and his prudent foresight. *Eastward, to the land of Kedem* ("the east") is a pleonasm. Kedem and the Kedemites appear variously in several Old Testament references; here the Syrian-Arabian desert seems to be the rather vague designation indicated.

This datum from J about Abraham's alien wives really interferes with the standard salvation history that leads through Isaac to Jacob without interruption. The Redactor, to his credit, has included it, though as a kind of footnote. We may be sure that he was much more comfortable with the following P verses that told of Abraham's demise, a satisfying end to the preceding saga. As we have already seen, the second part of vs. 11 belongs to J, and we show it here with italics.

7 The whole span of Abraham's life was one hundred
8 and seventy-five years. Then he breathed his last,
  dying at a ripe old age, grown old after a full life;
9 and he was taken to his kinsmen. His sons Isaac and
  Ishmael buried him in the cave of Machpelah, in
  the field of Ephron, son of Zohar the Hittite, which

10 faces Mamre, the field that Abraham had bought
from the Hittites; there he was buried next to his
11 wife Sarah. After the death of Abraham, God
blessed his son Isaac, *who made his home near
Beer-lahai-roi.*

The death of Abraham, as far as the redaction of Genesis is concerned, has been recorded only by the P tradition, which apparently had nothing in it about Ishmael's having been dismissed from Abraham's household (contrast 16:12, J; 21:20–21, E). Hence he appears here as just another son of Abraham, burying his father in the family tomb at Machpelah (chapter 23, P), one brother the equal of another in a common family affair. The eventual difference, however, is signaled in vs. 11a: *after the death of Abraham, God blessed his son Isaac.* Neither in P nor in any of the other sources of Genesis is any reason given for divine election. It is simply said that one line was chosen and another was not. Ishmael might have been the choice rather than Isaac, but it was not so: such is the ecumenical message of P, which grinds no finely honed ideological ax. Arabs, Arameans, Philistines, Kushites—all these could as easily have been Yahweh's choice as Israel proved to be (cf. Amos 9:7). The Priestly author, whose loyalty to Jewish priorities is certainly untarnished and without the admixture of any revisionist qualifications, nevertheless is a theologian before he is ethnic or nationalist or otherwise sectarian. God chose Isaac, that was the fact, and with this fact he had to grapple.

In keeping with this openness to what might have been the theoretical possibilities, P concludes his story of Abraham with a genealogy of Ishmael, the twelve tribes who sprang from him according to the promise of 17:20 (P). The final vs. 18, which we italicize, has nothing to do with the genealogy but introduces a geographical note that corresponds most closely with the J narrative that ended off at 16:14.

12 These are the descendants of Abraham's son
Ishmael, whom Hagar the Egyptian, Sarah's
13 slave, bore to Abraham. These are the names of
Ishmael's sons, listed in the order of their birth:
Nebaioth (Ishmael's firstborn), Kedar, Adbeel,
14/15 Mibsam, Mishma, Dumah, Massa, Hadad,
16 Tema, Jetur, Naphish and Kedemah. These are
the sons of Ishmael, their names by their vil-
lages and encampments; twelve chieftains of as
many tribal groups.
17 The span of Ishmael's life was one hundred and
thirty-seven years. After he had breathed his last
18 and died, he was taken to his kinsmen. *The Ish-*

*maelites ranged from Havilah-by-Shur, which is
on the border of Egypt, all the way to Asshur;
and each of them pitched camp in opposition to
his various kinsmen.*

These are the descendants: we hardly realize it, yet this is the beginning of another of the Priestly author's *toledoth.* The genealogy of Ishmael now plays a completely diminished role in the over-all history of Genesis which the Redactor has put together; it will disappear with the *toledoth* of Isaac in vs. 19 below which begins the Saga of Jacob.

The twelve tribes of Ishmael are, like Keturah's children in the J genealogy above, Arabs of the Syro-Arabian desert. Some of the names are identifiable while others are not. *Nebaioth* appears again in 28:9 and 36:3 (both P) where, *à choix,* an association or dissociation is set up in relation to the "Canaanites" of the land. In Isaiah 60:7 both Nebaioth and *Kedar* are mentioned in the company of other recognized Arab sites like Midian, Ephah, and Sheba. Isaiah 21:16 and 42:11 also clearly make Kedar out an Arabian name, while "the dark tents of Kedar" (cf. Song of Songs 1:5) is a byword for the dwellings of the Bedawin Arab, then as now woven by preference from the black hair of goats. *Adbeel* is likely the Idibiel of Assyrian records, an Arabian place-name. So also *Dumah* (the "Dumah" of Isaiah 21:11 has been corrected in the NAB to "Edom," but there is an oasis Dumat el-Ghandal in the Syrian desert), *Tema* (cf. Isaiah 21:14 and the oasis Teima in northwest Arabia), and *Jetur,* a name that lies behind the Itureans of classical times, inhabitants of the Anti-Lebanon around Mount Hermon. We may feel fairly confident that the other names which have escaped further reference in the Bible or in other Near Eastern sources belonged to the same category. The "Yahwistic" vs. 18 which describes the life-style of the Ishmaelites in terms of Genesis 16:12 (J) agrees with P in determining their habitat: on *Havilah* see Genesis 2:11 (J), 10:7 (P), and 10:29 (J); on *Shur* see 16:7 (J) and 20:1 (E); and for *Asshur* cf. vs. 3 above.

The span of Ishmael's life . . . For reasons we can only imagine, the Priestly author has Ishmael live for forty-eight years after the death of Abraham (cf. 17:24, 25:7). That *he was taken to his kinsmen* even as Abraham was (vs. 8) is a further indication that for this author Ishmael no less than Isaac was remembered as a revered and venerable father of the past, despite his not being in the direct line that led from Abraham to Israel.

III. The Saga of Jacob

1. Esau's Birthright

19 *This is the family history of Isaac, son of Abraham;*
20 *Abraham had begotten Isaac. Isaac was forty years*
old when he married Rebekah, the daughter of
Bethuel the Aramean of Paddan-aram and the sis-
21 *ter of Laban the Aramean.* Isaac entreated the LORD
on behalf of his wife, since she was sterile. The LORD
heard his entreaty, and Rebekah became pregnant.
22 But the children in her womb jostled each other so
much that she exclaimed, "If this is to be so, what
good will it do me!" She went to consult the LORD,
23 and he answered her:

"Two nations are in your womb,
two peoples are quarreling while still within
you;
But one shall surpass the other,
and the older shall serve the younger."

24 When the time of her delivery came, there were
25 twins in her womb. The first to emerge was reddish,
and his whole body was like a hairy mantle; so they
26 named him Esau. His brother came out next, gripping Esau's heel; so they named him Jacob. *Isaac*
was sixty years old when they were born.
27 As the boys grew up, Esau became a skillful hunter,
a man who lived in the open; whereas Jacob was a
28 simple man, who kept to his tents. Isaac preferred
Esau, because he was fond of game; but Rebekah
29 preferred Jacob. Once, when Jacob was cooking a
30 stew, Esau came in from the open, famished. He
said to Jacob, "Let me gulp down some of that red
stuff; I'm starving." (That is why he was called

31 Edom.) But Jacob replied, "First give me your
32 birthright in exchange for it." "Look," said Esau,
"I'm on the point of dying. What good will any
33 birthright do me?" But Jacob insisted, "Swear to me
first!" So he sold Jacob his birthright under oath.
34 Jacob then gave him some bread and the lentil stew;
and Esau ate, drank, got up, and went his way. Esau
cared little for his birthright.

Bench marks with which we are now quite familiar easily identify the italicized vss. 19–20 and 26b as P. The character of the main strand of the narrative, however, has not always been so readily defined. It is plain that much of it is J, but whether all of it is has been disputed. Older critics, mainly on the basis of supposed discrepancies and doublets in the rest of the tradition, detected an Elohist influence at work in the story (e.g., vss. 21–26a=J, vss. 27–28=JE, and vss. 29–34=E). A more relaxed approach to literary analysis has persuaded most present-day commentators that it is unnecessary to look beyond the Yahwist, however, to account for most of what we read here, and this opinion has been adopted by this commentary.

The family history of Isaac is the Priestly author's *toledoth* introducing yet this further segment of Genesis which, as we already know, is rather the history of Jacob than of Isaac. According to its fragmentary notice *Isaac was forty years old when he married Rebekah:* the J Isaac of chapter 24 for whom a wife was sought and found with Abraham's kindred was surely thought of as younger than this, but of course the Priestly chronology is always artificial. *Paddan-aram* is the P term for Aram Naharaim: it means something like "the land of Aram" (cf. Hosea 12:13). *Bethuel* and, particularly, *Laban* are here called *the Aramean,* i.e., a descendant of Aram (10:23, P), a Semite, but not, perhaps, as in the genealogy of 22:20–24 (J), a Terahite along with Abraham and a Nahorite (cf. 11:24–26 P)? It would probably be hypercritical to raise an objection on this score. Also in chapter 31 (JE) Laban is "the Aramean": see the commentary there.

As though to underscore the preoccupation that the story will have with Jacob rather than with Isaac, by a series of quick jumps we are immediately plunged *in medias res:* an oracle of birth, the birth itself of the twins, and then, suddenly, a scene from the youth or early manhood of Jacob and Esau. The abruptness of these transitions contrasts strangely with the leisurely pace set for so much of the Jacob narrative later on. We learn that Isaac, too, was frustrated at first in his desire for issue owing to the sterility of his wife, only to be informed with the same breath that the frustration was removed at the source. Nothing of a patient waiting and hoping, nothing of a surrogate wife, no suspense: the J doublet in 26:6–11 of the E narrative of chapter 20 is, in consequence, a rather jejune reiteration of a now threadbare patriarchal theme. Perhaps a plus of this hasty *mise en scène* is that Isaac, in distinction to his father and his sons, is presented throughout the few episodes that treat of his adult life as a strict monogamist, content with the one wife brought to him from Aram Naharaim and whom he loved.

The compression of the narrative obscures more than usually the cultic background that so often peeps through these old stories. The language of Isaac's *entreated* and of Yahweh's *heard his entreaty* (the verb *'athar*) is that of cultic prayer and response, as is Rebekah's *consult* (the verb *darash*) and the answering oracle of vs. 23. We are at some sacred place where prophet or priest mediates divine revelation to the clients of the local deity. For the biblical author, of course, the deity is Yahweh, but absolutely nothing is made of the professional means or methods by which his intervention was sought; even for J, a determination of this kind would have been an anachronism. And therefore nothing is made of the place either where all this occurred, whether it was Beer-lahai-roi (25:11b, J) or Beer-sheba (28:10, J).

The theme of hostile twins whose mutual opposition manifests itself already while they are still in their mother's womb is a frequent enough detail of myth and folklore. Biblical tradition has adapted it to the careers of Edom and Israel, two peoples closely bound to each other by ties of blood and history who were destined to live in constant enmity and border warfare. The response of vs. 23, in answer to Rebekah's rather incoherent cry of perplexity, is modeled on the gnomic, often cryptic type of pronouncements which emanated from the oracular shrines of antiquity. (*The older* and *the younger* of the NAB are less ambiguous than the Hebrew, which has simply "the great," "the small." "Older" and "younger," in any case, are distinctions that apply only improperly to twins.) The rivalry between Jacob and Esau developed in the stories that follow (of J and E, not of P) will figure the later power struggle waged between Israel and Edom. In the Jacob and Esau stories Esau is not only the "older" but also the "greater" of the two brothers from the consideration of material wealth and power and political dominion. The oracle, however, looks to the future, to Israelite times, when Edom had been subjugated during David's conquests and reduced to a vassaldom of his little empire (2 Samuel 8:14). After the division of the united kingdom of David and Solomon Edom remained subject to Judah but eventually regained its sovereignty as a by-product of one of the periodic shuffles of power in the Near East (cf. 2 Kings 16:6). Even later, when Judah had fallen on evil days, Edom did not hesitate to assist in its fall, and therefore was remembered by Israel as the jackal to the lion of Babylon which had devoured Jerusalem and the

Land of Promise (cf. Psalm 137:7–8). In the postexilic restoration of Jerusalem, Geshem the Arab, who was probably governor of Edom for the Persian empire, was one of those who opposed the rebuilding of a Jewish state in Palestine (cf. Nehemiah 2:19, 6:1–6). Idumea, as Edom came to be called in classical times, was forcibly converted to Judaism during the Maccabean wars; and by an irony not lost on the Jews who had to endure his reign, Herod the Great was the son of an Idumean.

There is more than a bit of heavy-handed whimsey to the wordplays that are indulged in vss. 25–26. *The first to emerge was reddish,* i.e., he was *admoni, and his whole body was like a hairy mantle* (that is, *se'ar*), *so they named him Esau.* "Esau" itself had no popular etymology in Israelite Hebrew, it appears, but associated ideas certainly did. Edom is *admoni,* the red land, the land of the red clay, just as man, *adam,* essentially a pinkish creature in the biblical author's view, had been formed out of *adamah,* the red earth (Genesis 2:7, J). The "hairy" bit about Esau relates him, obviously, to Seir, the name of the region of Edom where Esau made his home (Genesis 32:4, J). In both instances Esau's identity is accorded by geography, but physical characteristics draw attention to it. Hairiness or shagginess seems to have been *eo ipso* a mark of incivility: "shaggy with hair is his whole body," is said of the semi-human Enkidu in the Gilgamesh epic. Similarly, there was a prejudice against the ruddy or redheaded person, for reasons that are unclear, which existed not only in the ancient Near Eastern world but well into the time of Western Christianity as well. Judas Iscariot was depicted in medieval art as a redhead! Rosalind will have it of Orlando that "his very hair is the dissembling colour"—that is, red—while Celia insists that it is rather "something browner than Judas'." In respect to Esau, therefore, the author's wordplays go beyond mere cleverness and insinuate a bias against him from the beginning.

All the same, the wordplay brought to bear on *Jacob* in vs. 26 is not entirely friendly either. In 27:36 (J) below Jacob's name will be explained by Esau as proper to one who is a supplanter, an overreacher. Here an intimation is given of the same thing by a neutral observer, the biblical narrator himself, who remarks on a child born from the womb already *gripping* his brother's *heel* (*'aqeb*): *so they named him Jacob.* Unlike Esau's, we do have a fair idea of what the real etymology of Jacob's name was. The name Jacobel or its equivalent, of which Jacob is undoubtedly a shortening, is known from Egyptian, Mesopotamian, and Palestinian sources indifferently: the meaning would be something like "may (the) god give strength."

That Esau should have become *a skillful hunter* and thus pleased his father who *was fond of game,* whereas Jacob, the homebody, *was a simple man, who kept to his tents* and was favored by Rebekah, sets up a not unusual family scenario that plays equally well in today's suburbia as in the steppes of the Bronze Age Negeb. Preparation is being made for the story of chapter 27 in which the fierce protectiveness of the mother comes to grips with Isaac's doting senility, a confrontation out of which no real good can come to anyone and in which everyone, both parents and both sons, lose something. Straight away, however, the distinction of the brothers' separate ways of life is preface to the well-known episode of Esau's sale of his birthright. It, too, is a tale that does little to the credit of either of the participants in it. From it has come the proverbial English "mess of pottage" to characterize the trifling exchange for which a thing of great value is thoughtlessly bartered away, an expression popularly thought to derive from the Authorized (King James) Version of A.D. 1611 but is not there, and actually is much older.

The biblical author intends by this story an indictment of Esau: *Esau cared little for his birthright* is the Aesopian moral by which the reader is invited to judge the conduct of a man who has shown himself to be brutish and wholly bereft of any sense of values. Coming back to the family encampment *from the open,* his hunt this time evidently having been fruitless, and *famished,* Esau finds Jacob at the evening fire quietly *cooking a stew*—of what, Esau evidently does not know. No matter, he must *gulp down some of that red stuff* and that immediately; the language is deliberately chosen to heighten the exaggerated urgency of Esau's appetite, to which everything else must be subordinated: "Give me a gulp of the red, that red there!" (The "red" [*adom*] is a further etiology for Edom, as the parenthetical gloss somewhat superfluously points out.) The cry *I'm starving* is heard often enough on social occasions and need be nothing more than conventional hyperbole or even polite appreciation of a well-laden table. But Esau is dead serious. *I'm on the point of dying. What good will any birthright do me?* Thus he dismisses as of no account what Jacob holds most precious and greedily receives in its stead *some bread and the lentil stew.* It is probably an additional irony of the author that the exchange was such a humble, commonplace dish, whatever may have been the red delicacy that Esau had anticipated. So *Esau ate, drank,* wiped his mouth with the back of his hand, we may suppose, *got up, and went his way,* ready for sleep after a full belly, leaving his brother enriched with all that it was in his power to give him.

The modern reader is doubtless more disposed to censure Jacob for taking advantage of his brother's weakness than an Israelite author would have been, who could not forget the Edom and Israel for which Esau and Jacob stood. We should not imagine, nevertheless, that his attitude toward Jacob was one of unqualified approval. The character of Jacob is by far the most carefully and subtly delineated of all the patriarchal figures, and from these legends he emerges as the most clearly defined human being with a personality that develops and matures. We shall see more of this development as we go along; for the moment, it is probably fair to say that the author thought of him as a young man rather too clever for his own good, with whom one would be well advised to read the fine print of any contract with a cautious eye. Given the premises, however, he would have applauded Jacob's insistence in pressing Esau to an oath. A hasty promise may be taken back, an oath never. An oath, like a blessing or a curse (see chapter 27), may be repented of, but never withdrawn. Not even one so lacking in the amenities as Esau could afford to repudiate his solemn word to which both God and the indispensable order of man's world served as guarantors. Primogeniture, the first birthright, both in ancient and in later times has carried with it the perquisites of a privileged status, with both social and economic implications. From a Nuzi contract we know that it was possible for an elder son to sell his first birthright to a younger brother (three sheep were the price of the transaction). What Jacob did, then, while ethically questionable, was perfectly legal—a distinction that earlier and later entrepreneurs have found it convenient to make. Thus far and in chapter 27 Jacob will be shown with his eye to the main chance plotting his own way in a competitive world, and so he will appear again in subsequent chapters. God's designs upon him, which do not necessarily coincide with his own shrewd planning, are revealed in the same chapters playing a kind of counterpoint.

2. Stories About Isaac

The following section, which takes up most of chapter 26, testifies to the paucity of information which the biblical traditions had preserved about Isaac in his own right. The Yahwist—for it is obviously the Yahwist to whom we are indebted for these verses—has done his best to supply for the lacuna by assembling a series of vignettes that might equally well apply, at least for the most part, to any other patriarchal figure. They are, in fact, mainly a reiteration of what has been said about Abraham, either in conscious duplication of words which the Yahwist earlier pronounced in Abraham's favor or in Yahwistic doublets of stories which the Elohist told featuring Abraham. The whole is timeless in relation to what precedes and follows it: Isaac and his wife are a young couple, as in 24:67, unencumbered by the young adult sons of 25:27–34, and certainly decades removed from the advanced age they have attained by chapter 27. Perhaps in recompense for the prevailing anonymity of the second of the patriarchs in this passage, twice within its short compass Isaac is made the recipient of Yahweh's revelation (vss. 2–5 and vs. 24).

> 26 There was a famine in the land (distinct from the earlier one that had occurred in the days of Abraham), and Isaac went down to Abimelech, king of
> 2 the Philistines in Gerar. The LORD appeared to him and said: "Do not go down to Egypt, but continue
> 3 to camp wherever in this land I tell you. Stay in this land, and I will be with you and bless you; for to you and your descendants I will give all these lands, in fulfillment of the oath that I swore to your father
> 4 Abraham. I will make your descendants as numerous as the stars in the sky and give them all these lands, and in your descendants all the nations of the
> 5 earth shall find blessing—this because Abraham obeyed me, keeping my mandate (my commandments, my ordinances and my instructions)."

The *famine in the land* of course recalls the J story of Abraham beginning in 12:10; the Redactor has taken note of the similarity by the distinction he has introduced in the parenthesis—unless it is the Yahwist's own parenthesis, which he has attached in order to be able to repeat his earlier story in a new context. The NAB has continued the allusion to 12:10 by having it that *Isaac went down to Abimelech,* whereas the Hebrew says only that he "went to" him. Wherever Isaac is supposed to have been at this time, at Beer-lahai-roi (25:11b) or Beer-sheba (26:33), he would hardly have gone "down" to Gerar, which is to the north in either case. As in 21:34 (E), in this sequence of chapter 26 Abimelech and his subjects are anachronistically termed *the Philistines.*

The promise to Isaac also evokes 12:10 by its prohibition that he *not go down to Egypt* but rather *camp wherever in this land I tell you.* It is not that "this land" refers specifically to Gerar (whether Gerar ever became part of the Israelite federation is in doubt): *all these lands* which Yahweh guarantees to Isaac *in fulfillment of the oath* he swore to Abraham are those of 15:18–21 (J), that is, the land of Canaan as distinct from the land of Egypt. The words of the promise to Isaac are a pastiche of those formerly made to Abraham, according to J (12:3, 15:5.18–21). In vs. 5 the reference to Abraham's obedience up to *keeping my mandate* are doubtless the Yahwist's, but the parenthetical *my commandments, my ordinances and my instructions* would appear to be one of those rare Deuteronomic expansions which have touched Genesis at some state of its development (cf. Deuteronomy 5:31, 6:1, 7:11, etc.).

6/7 So Isaac settled in Gerar. When the men of the
place asked questions about his wife, he answered,
"She is my sister." He was afraid, if he called her
his wife, the men of the place would kill him on
account of Rebekah, since she was very beautiful.
8 But when he had been there for a long time, Abimelech, king of the Philistines, happened to look
out of a window and was surprised to see Isaac
9 fondling his wife Rebekah. He called for Isaac and
said: "She must certainly be your wife! How could
you have said, 'She is my sister'?" Isaac replied, "I
thought I might lose my life on her account."
10 "How could you do this to us!" exclaimed Abimelech. "It would have taken very little for one of
the men to lie with your wife, and you would have
11 thus brought guilt upon us." Abimelech therefore
gave this warning to all his men: "Anyone who
molests this man or his wife shall forthwith be put
to death."

That this story is a triplet version of the one found in 12:10–20 (J) and
chapter 20 (E), has already been stated more than once. Both by reason
of its arbitrary location in the Isaac narrative and the laconic sparseness of
its detail, it is the most colorless and the least intriguing of the three passages. Commentators and critics have been at odds as to whether its peculiarities would indicate for it an earlier or rather a later date in the adaptation of the common tradition that underlies all three accounts. Some have
argued that its very brevity is indication of its relative antiquity, of the
primitive telling of events that was subsequently elaborated with particulars and significant pauses; others, more persuasively, have maintained
that it is precisely the elimination of these "scandalous" elements that
marks the verses before us as the final stage in the transmission of a now
fairly harmless and pointless anecdote. Nothing much remains except the
motif of Isaac's deception, which is perhaps palliated by the spectacle of
the Philistines' bellicose attitude depicted in vss. 12–22. Abimelech, it is
true, retains a vestige of the "noble pagan" role in which the Elohist cast
him in chapter 20; but it is a reminiscence only, the performance of a man
speaking for the record rather than from any deep conviction. Not even
Rebekah, let alone Isaac, seems to have been put in any real jeopardy at
any time. And for the Yahwist as well as for the Redactor of Genesis, in
view of the sequence with 25:21–34, no question of a threat to the patriarchal succession ever rises. One can hardly avoid the impression that here
the story has been found to be more useful at space-filling than at adding
any genuine dimension to the patriarchal history.

In vs. 2 above Isaac was enjoined to *continue to camp* in the land, and he will be seen again in vss. 17–22 camping in the environs of *the Wadi Gerar* (somewhere in the neighborhood of the intersecting arroyos known today as the Wadi Gazzeh and the Wadi esh-Sheriah). But from vs. 8 it appears that his "settling" in Gerar (vs. 6) entailed a bit of city dwelling (which would not have precluded the farming activity attributed to him in vs. 12). At least, it is the most logical assumption that when *Abimelech, king of the Philistines, happened to look out of a window and was surprised to see Isaac fondling his wife Rebekah,* he was watching goings-on in an adjoining house (just as David espied Bathsheba in 1 Samuel 11:2). "Fondling" is undoubtedly a biblical metaphrase like the current English metaphrase "making love." It is also, in the Hebrew, of the same root that accounts for the "laughing" and "playing" otherwise exploited in the Isaac stories—this is the last time the pun will be indulged.

12 Isaac sowed a crop in that region and reaped a hundredfold the same year. Since the LORD blessed him,
13 he became richer and richer all the time, until he
14 was very wealthy indeed. He acquired such flocks and herds, and so many work animals, that the Phil-
15 istines became envious of him. (The Philistines had stopped up and filled with dirt all the wells that his father's servants had dug back in the days of his fa-
16 ther Abraham.) So Abimelech said to Isaac, "Go away from us; you have become far too numerous
17 for us." Isaac left there and made the Wadi Gerar
18 his regular campsite. (Isaac reopened the wells which his father's servants* had dug back in the days of his father Abraham and which the Philistines had stopped up after Abraham's death; he gave them the same names that his father had given
19 them.) But when Isaac's servants dug in the wadi
20 and reached spring water in their well, the shepherds of Gerar quarreled with Isaac's servants, saying, "The water belongs to us!" So the well was called Esek, because they had challenged him there.
21 Then they dug another well, and they quarreled
22 over that one too; so it was called Sitnah. When he had moved on from there, he dug still another well; but over this one they did not quarrel. It was

* The ancient versions have "his father's servants"; the MT only "his father Abraham."

called Rehoboth, because he said, "The LORD has
now given us ample room, and we shall flourish in
the land."

In 12:16 because of Sarah Abraham had been enriched by the Egyptians, and again in 20:14–16, this time in spite of Sarah, Abimelech had
laden him with wealth; now, still in conjunction with the story of the "im-
periled ancestress," Isaac becomes rich, but entirely through his own
efforts. This is the first mention of agriculture as a pursuit of any of the
patriarchs. Farmers in the Near East, as in various other countries today,
worked their fields by day and returned to their town or village by night
(cf. Mark 15:21); they did not habitually live on the land. That Isaac
reaped a hundredfold the same year describes an extraordinary yield, but
not an impossible one. Yahweh's blessing, to which the patriarch's increasing affluence is ascribed, is the benison of providence and not of miracles.
It does presuppose, however, an arrangement that Genesis 23 (P) had envisaged only as a once-for-all exception in patriarchal life: namely, that
any of the ancestors of Israel had actually owned a stake in the land of
Canaan.

Contrary to the general purport of chapter 20 which had Abraham and
Abimelech part on the friendliest of terms, here considerable attention is
given to a protracted dispute between the two parties, or at least between
their separate agents and retainers, and in vs. 27 below Isaac interprets
Abimelech's decree of separation in vs. 16 as an act of hostility. It would
appear from the J part of 21:22–34 (that is, vss. 25–26), however, which
corresponds with vss. 26–31 below, that something like the altercation described above lay behind the pact between Abraham and Abimelech as
conceived by that version. In vss. 15 and 18 above parenthetical and
redactional allusion is made to multiple wells which had been dug at Beer-
sheba by Abraham, though these go unmentioned in the Abraham story itself (note, however, 21:30.32a, J, where the number "seven" is being accounted for). A fair assumption is that there was once told about
Abraham something like what is told about Isaac in these verses, and that
for some reason the former story was omitted in the composition of Genesis. A good guess would be that this Yahwistic story was passed over there
and rather included here, by the Redactor or by the Yahwist himself, because there was already ample material at his disposal which related to
Abraham and far too little which related to Isaac.

The names of the wells under discussion in vss. 20–22 probably referred
to actual sites in the region between Gerar and Beer-sheba, though of
course they have been given popular etymologies to correspond with the
details of the story. Of these the most probably identifiable is *Rehoboth*
(literally, "wide spaces"), so called because Yahweh had at last provided

ample room, breathing space, respite: southwest of Beer-sheba a few miles is the Wadi Shutnet er-Ruheibeh. The same modern name might preserve the *Sitnah* ("opposition") of our story. For *Esek* ("challenge"), on the other hand, *because they had challenged him there,* there is no known point of reference.

> 23/24 From there Isaac went up to Beer-sheba. The same night the LORD appeared to him and said: "I am the God of your father Abraham. You have no need to fear, since I am with you. I will bless you and multiply your descendants for the
> 25 sake of my servant Abraham." So he built an altar there and invoked the LORD by name. After he had pitched his tent there, his servants began to dig a well nearby.
> 26 Abimelech had meanwhile come to him from Gerar, accompanied by Ahuzzath, his councilor,
> 27 and Phicol, the general of his army. Isaac asked them, "Why have you come to me, seeing that you hate me and have driven me away from
> 28 you?" They answered: "We are convinced that the LORD is with you, so we propose that there be a sworn agreement between our two sides— between you and us. Let us make a pact with
> 29 you: you shall not act unkindly toward us, just as we have not molested you, but have always acted kindly toward you and have let you depart in peace. Henceforth, 'The LORD's blessing be
> 30 upon you!'" Isaac then made a feast for them,
> 31 and they ate and drank. Early the next morning they exchanged oaths. Then Isaac bade them farewell, and they departed from him in peace.
> 32 That same day Isaac's servants came and brought him news about the well they had been digging; they told him, "We have reached wa-
> 33 ter!" He called it Shibah; hence the name of the city, Beer-sheba, to this day.

After an appearance of Yahweh which paraphrases the one to Abraham in chapter 15, Isaac who had gone *up to Beer-sheba built an altar there and invoked the LORD by name.* The formula, we recognize, is one in which the Yahwist delights, with which he has previously associated Abraham with the sacred places of Shechem (12:7), Bethel (12:8, 13:4), and Hebron (13:18). That Isaac is so associated with Beer-sheba may say something about the *Ortsgebundenheit* of the Isaac legends. However, we must also acknowledge the secondary character of these Isaac stories in the Yahwist's narrative, remembering as well that in 21:33, which we have confidently assigned to J, it is Abraham who "claims" Beer-sheba for Israel. In vs. 25 not only the *altar* but also the *well* (cf. vss. 32–33) has an undoubted religious significance (cf. 16:14). Along with the sacred tree or trees (cf. 12:6, 13:18, 14:13, 18:1, 21:33), the well (*beer*) or spring (*ain* or *en* in our translations) is an habitual concomitant of the sacred resorts of cult and oracle. This is only natural, since they were also the oases of a parched land, the places where there could be a gathering of people: *qahal,* which translates into Greek both as *ekklesia*=church, and *synagoge*=synagogue.

The pact solemnized in vss. 26–31 certainly is a J version of the E part of 21:22–32, exception made for the detail that Isaac rather than Abraham is the second party to Abimelech, and also that here the covenant heals a wound as well as solidifies a friendship. In this instance Abimelech comes to Abraham not only with *Phicol, the general of his army,* as before, but also with *Ahuzzath, his councilor,* that is, his official adviser: this is a state visit. The terms of covenant are much as they were before; this time, however, there is a covenant meal (vs. 30), as was the frequent use in such transactions (cf. 31:54). Then as now, sharing a common meal, particularly a festive meal, was a concrete sign of friendship and reconciliation. The name of the well which Isaac's servants bring in is intended to supply yet another etymology of Beer-sheba. (In strict point of fact, Sheba may have been a divine name in Canaan, as it certainly was in Assyria.) *Shibah* was doubtless understood by the MT to mean "seven" (cf. 21:30), but it is also conceivable that the Yahwist originally wrote *shebuah,* "oath" (cf. vs. 31: *they exchanged oaths*). In either case, the association is appropriate. Beer-sheba, as we have seen, was for Israelites the place of "the seven wells," and it was in Israelite times as in times before a shrine of pilgrimage and oath-taking (cf. Amos 8:14).

3. Jacob Goes Abroad

This segment of Genesis, which in the Redactor's scheme of things has to do with the separate destinies of Jacob and Esau determined in part by their choice of wives, properly begins with the following P verses that conclude chapter 26.

34 When Esau was forty years old, he married Judith,
    daughter of Beeri the Hittite, and Basemath, daugh-
35 ter of Elon the Hivite. But they became a source of
    embitterment to Isaac and Rebekah.

These verses are continued at 27:46 in the P narrative which had its
own accounting for Jacob's departure from Canaan; they originally had no
connection with the J story immediately following. In P there was nothing
about a rivalry between Esau and Jacob or about Jacob's supplanting Esau
by purchase or by ruse. In the Priestly author's perspective Esau simply
debased himself by his marriage with the women of the land, thus provoking his father's displeasure and his consequent blessing of Jacob (28:1),
who is sent back to Paddan-aram to get a proper wife. In the Redactor's
context the verses have probably been placed here to soften the bad impression created by the ruthless and unscrupulous conduct portrayed of
Rebekah and Jacob in chapter 27. Esau, in other words, is being
presented (as in the J story of 25:27–34) as one of those types with
which one need not be overnice in dealing.

Beeri the Hittite is without doubt a "Hittite" in the sense we have now
noted several times over in Genesis, namely one of the natives of the land
of Canaan. So also is *Elon the Hivite.* ("Hivite" here the NAB has derived
from the ancient versions; the MT has "Hittite" again, doubtless under the
influence of 36:2.) The Hivites we saw at 10:17 (J), simply as one of the
many names used for Canaanites. Though they appear with relative frequency in the Bible, it is conceivable that "Hivites" is a deformation of the
better-known "Horites" (in Hebrew the words are very similar: חוי and
חרי). The Horites were mentioned in 14:6. Just as there were real Hittites
so were there real Horites: the Hurrians, a non-Semitic people originally
from the Armenian region who during the fifteenth and fourteenth centuries B.C. maintained (under an Aryan ruling class) the powerful kingdom of Mitanni north of Haran, and who before and after this were scattered throughout Mesopotamia (Nuzi was a Hurrian city), Syria, and
Palestine. The Israelites became acquainted with the Hurrians at the time
of their "conquest" of Canaan, but it is fairly certain that there were none
there in what we think to be patriarchal times. The Horites (and Hivites)
of Genesis are, therefore, in all likelihood, like the Philistines of chapter
26, popular anachronisms in respect to the indigenous population.

Judith (curiously, the name will later mean "Jewess") is not listed
among Esau's wives in the intriguing catalogues of chapter 36. *Basemath*
is, but there she is neither Hittite, Hivite, nor Horite, but rather an Ishmaelite.

What now follows is the J story of Rebekah's and Jacob's deception of
Isaac, a veritable drawing of the wool over another's eyes, whatever may

have been the inspiration of that figure of speech. All of a sudden Isaac is decrepit, blind, on his deathbed like Abraham in chapter 24, and disposed to give his dying blessing to his favored son. All this is not so in the Priestly version of Isaac's blessing of Jacob (28:1–5), but even there we shall be seeing Isaac for the last time, and Jacob will return to him only to bury him (35:27–29).

27 When Isaac was so old that his eyesight had failed him, he called his older son Esau and said to him, 2 "Son!" "Yes, father!" he replied. Isaac then said, "As you can see, I am so old that I may now die at 3 any time. Take your gear, therefore—your quiver and bow—and go out into the country to hunt some 4 game for me. With your catch prepare an appetizing dish for me, such as I like, and bring it to me to eat, so that I may give you my special blessing before I die."

5 Rebekah had been listening while Isaac was speaking to his son Esau. So when Esau went out into the 6 country to hunt some game for his father,* Rebekah said to her son Jacob, "Listen! I overheard your fa- 7 ther tell your brother Esau, 'Bring me some game and with it prepare an appetizing dish for me to eat, that I may give you my blessing with the LORD's ap- 8 proval before I die.' Now, son, listen carefully to 9 what I tell you. Go to the flock and get me two choice kids. With these I will prepare an appetizing 10 dish for your father, such as he likes. Then bring it to your father to eat, that he may bless you before 11 he dies." "But my brother Esau is a hairy man," said Jacob to his mother Rebekah, "and I am 12 smooth-skinned! Suppose my father feels me? He will think I am making sport of him, and I shall 13 bring on myself a curse instead of a blessing." His mother, however, replied: "Let any curse against you, son, fall on me! Just do as I say. Go and get me the kids."

14 So Jacob went and got them and brought them to his mother; and with them she prepared an appetiz- 15 ing dish, such as his father liked. Rebekah then took the best clothes of her older son Esau that she had

---

* "For his father" is the LXX; the MT has "and bring it."

> in the house, and gave them to her younger son Ja-
> 16 cob to wear; and with the skins of the kids she cov-
> ered up his hands and the hairless parts of his neck.
> 17 Then she handed her son Jacob the appetizing dish
> and the bread she had prepared.

We see immediately why the Redactor found it advisable to preface to this story the little section of P which already insinuated that Esau was a man destined to be rejected. For, despite our recent memory of the hearty gobbler of lentils whose senses were dulled except to the growling of his stomach, it is hard not to feel sympathy for this uncouth but as yet harmless fellow when we are made privy to the scheme being contrived against him by his more agile-witted mother and brother whose ethical sense is also less than acute. Rebekah plays the Lady Macbeth role, or the role of Beatrice Cenci, but opposite a highly receptive cognate and an extremely docile Giacomo: Jacob is worried only by the prospect that the plan may run foul and leave him with a frightful heritage in place of none at all. The Yahwist merely tells the story and does not moralize. Hosea 12:3–4 and Jeremiah 9:3, however, are witness to other Israelite recollections of the same Jacob tradition, which was not recalled in total pride. For that matter, even in Genesis the connivers connive only to their own frustration. Rebekah, who has already discarded one son, has to send the other into exile, never to see him again. Jacob is forced to desert his homeland. The conspirators gain nothing for their pains and leave casually in their wake an embittered and disillusioned old man and a callow innocent to whom a cause for hatred has been revealed for the first time.

We have been prepared by 25:28 for the little scene of vss. 1–4 above and thus find it altogether familiar even though we see it for the first and only time. Isaac—we wish that we had a better picture of him than the one- or two-dimensional line sketches of the preceding stories have been able to afford us—now mindful of the uncertainty of life and the certainty of death that may visit him at any time, summons to his bedside the son with whom he has always felt at ease to give him a final blessing. Countless must have been the occasions before when the two of them sat down together to enjoy the fruits of the chase and to relive, the older man vicariously, the events of the day's hunt and their common interests, while the other male of the household took his solitary meal apart, wrapped in his own thoughts and self-sufficient in his exclusion. As all idyls must, this one is coming to an end. There will be one last simple symposium, and then Isaac will bestow his *special blessing* on the son in whom he has found fulfillment and fellowship. This, literally, "blessing of the soul," which Rebekah in vs. 7 characterizes as *with the LORD's approval* ("before the face of Yahweh"), probably retained for the biblical authors some of the aura that more primitive religious conceptions had attached to it, that is, of the transmission of *mana,* the vital fluid, of one personality to another. We shall see this contention borne out in the conversation between Isaac and Esau below.

Rebekah, we must imagine, had been listening in on the deliberations of her menfolk as Sarah was in 18:10. (It is interesting to note, by the way, that the classical figure of the mother-in-law, either as a force for solidarity or for discord in the family, never enters into the patriarchal stories. The mothers of the patriarchal wives are either non-existent or mere shadows, while the wives themselves, contrary to the odds of actuarial statistics, habitually predecease their husbands and know not the fulfillment of daughters-in-law. Esau's wives in 26:34–35, 27:46, 28:6–9 make up only an apparent exception to this rule. If the wives and mothers of the patriarchs tend to act in similar ways, it is not from any agreement among them but simply out of the manner of woman as male authors thought this manner to be.) Immediately she devises a stratagem that appears to her absurdly simple and which must succeed by its very simplicity: Jacob shall substitute for the absent Esau and take in his stead the blessing of a blind and doddering Isaac! *Two choice kids* will provide the *appetizing dish* Isaac has asked of his son Esau. Will Isaac be unable to tell the difference between goat flesh and the venison he has so often delighted in? Probably not, but no matter: nothing ventured, nothing gained. Jacob, willing but fainthearted, raises the obvious objection: to pass himself off as Esau will require not only play-acting but physical traits he has no power to conjure, which separate him from his brother far more decisively than wild meat can be distinguished from tame. Impatiently, Rebekah dismisses these scruples. She is fully aware of the hazards, but her will is iron and her nerves are steel. *Let any curse against you, son, fall on me!* So much for Jacob's superstitious fears. Men must be indulged their ratiocinations that produce parliaments and debating societies, but meanwhile someone else has to get at the business that has to be done. *Just do as I say!*

Improvising as she goes, Rebekah attires Jacob in *the best clothes of her older son Esau.* These would have been the garments Esau wore on rare and festive occasions, but which, the narrative presupposes, breathed with the distinctive odor that he carried with him from his efforts afield with the bow. That they were ready to Rebekah's hand is, of course, understandable from the fact that in this J story, contrary to the P perspective of 26:34–35, Esau was still a young unmarried man living in the common family tent. Even taking into account the societies which relish body odors (at least in certain situations) rather than obliterate them routinely by frequent bathing, and conceding the relative inefficiency of ancient laundering processes, there is something more than a bit fantastic about this entire motif of clothing that reeks of Esau. Similarly with what follows: that even a blind and befuddled old man was to be fooled into taking goatskins for human body hair, be the body ever so hirsute as the hairy Ainu's. To try to rationalize in these areas is a little like searching a doctoral dissertation for its excursions into whimsey and high humor or to pursue the crisp logic of a television commercial. By their very outrageous character these devices pass the pragmatic test of good storytelling; and, as the sequel shows, they work!

18 Bringing them† to his father, Jacob said, "Father!" "Yes?" replied Isaac. "Which one of my sons are
19 you?" Jacob answered his father: "I am Esau, your first-born. I did as you told me. Please sit up and eat some of my game, so that you may give me your
20 special blessing." But Isaac asked, "How did you succeed so quickly, son?" He answered, "The LORD,
21 your God, let things turn out well with me." Isaac then said to Jacob, "Come closer, son, that I may feel you, to learn whether you really are my son
22 Esau or not." So Jacob moved up closer to his father. When Isaac felt him, he said, "Although the
23 voice is Jacob's, the hands are Esau's." (He failed to identify him because his hands were hairy, like those of his brother Esau; so in the end he gave him
24 his blessing.) Again he asked him, "Are you really
25 my son Esau?" "Certainly," he replied. Then Isaac said, "Serve me your game, son‡ that I may eat of it and then give you my blessing." Jacob served it to him, and Isaac ate; he brought him wine, and he
26 drank. Finally his father Isaac said to him, "Come
27 closer, son, and kiss me." As Jacob went up and kissed him, Isaac smelled the fragrance of his clothes. With that, he blessed him, saying,
   "Ah, the fragrance of my son
      is like the fragrance of a field
      that the LORD has blessed!
28   "May God give to you
      of the dew of the heavens,
   And of the fertility of the earth
      abundance of grain and wine.

---

† "Bringing them" is indicated by the ancient versions; the MT has "and he came."
‡ So the LXX; in the MT: "the game of my son."

29   "Let peoples serve you,
         and nations pay you homage;
     Be master of your brothers,
         and may your mother's sons bow down to you.
     Cursed be those who curse you,
         and blessed be those who bless you."

30 Jacob had scarcely left his father, just after Isaac
   had finished blessing him, when his brother Esau
31 came back from his hunt. Then he too prepared an
   appetizing dish with his game, and bringing it to his
   father, he said, "Please, father, eat some of your
   son's game, that you may then give me your special
32 blessing." "Who are you?" his father Isaac asked
   him. "I am Esau," he replied, "your first-born son."
33 With that, Isaac was seized with a fit of uncontrollable trembling. "Who was it, then," he asked, "that
   hunted game and brought it to me? I finished eating it* just before you came, and I blessed him.
34 Now he must remain blessed!" On hearing his father's words, Esau burst into loud, bitter sobbing.
35 "Father, bless me too!" he begged. When Isaac explained, "Your brother came here by a ruse and car-
36 ried off your blessing," Esau exclaimed, "He has
   been well named Jacob! He has now supplanted me
   twice! First he took away my birthright, and now he
   has taken away my blessing." Then he pleaded,
37 "Haven't you saved a blessing for me?" Isaac replied: "I have already appointed him your master,
   and I have assigned to him all his kinsmen as his
   slaves; besides, I have enriched him with grain and
38 wine. What then can I do for you, son?" But Esau
   urged his father, "Have you only that one blessing,
   father? Bless me too." Isaac, however, made no re-
39 ply,† and Esau wept aloud. Finally Isaac spoke
   again and said to him:
     "Ah, far from the fertile earth
         shall be your dwelling;
         far from the dew of the heavens above!
40   "By your sword you shall live,
         and your brother you shall serve;

---

* The conjectured meaning of the MT's "I ate of all."
† This sentence is from the LXX, not in the MT.

But when you become restive,
you shall throw off his yoke from your neck."

Jacob enters his father's presence, accoutered and provisioned for the great deception. The reader of these verses and of vss. 41–45 which continue and conclude the story can hardly be unaware of the reasons that prompted earlier critics to discover variant sources at work here, for the multiple repetitions are undeniable and provide incontrovertible evidence that Jacob's theft of Esau's blessing had been celebrated in Israelite saga and romance by more than one storyteller whose craft had been challenged to supply the imaginative details of his fancy. Twice Isaac calls on Jacob to draw near him, once that he may feel the hairiness of his skin (vs. 22), once that he may smell his clothing (vs. 26), and in each case a blessing is the result of the inquiry (vs. 23 and vss. 27–29). After the deception, once Isaac tells Esau that his blessing has been given beyond recall to another and Esau cries disconsolately (vss. 33–34), and again, with greater detail, he tells him that his brother has stolen his blessing, and Esau weeps aloud (vss. 35–38). The common connective is Jacob's substitution of himself for Esau with a bogus offering of freshly killed game. These phenomena do indeed point to a conflation of materials, but rather of the Yahwist who has combined them skillfully in vss. 1–17 and less so in the remaining verses of the chapter than of a Redactor who had joined together entirely disparate and independent traditions.

Which one of my sons are you? is a perfectly natural question of the recumbent Isaac, whose reveries are suddenly interrupted by a sharp *Father!* Esau has been with him only a short while before and has been sent on a mission. Jacob is not in the habit of seeking out his father, but long-established reticences have a way of disappearing in the nearness of death. So, then, it is Esau after all, Isaac learns, as Jacob tells his first lie. *How did you succeed so quickly, son?* is another natural question. Isaac's understandable puzzlement easily turns to skepticism which is not dissipated quickly by Jacob's second and more horrendous lie, the mawkish, sanctimonious, incredibly hypocritical attribution of his here and now presence to the beneficent designs of Yahweh, Isaac's God. Commentators are fond of vs. 27—the kiss of perfidy—as marking the high-water mark of Jacob's iniquity, but a sensitive Israelite reader would without doubt feel that anything Isaac's son did after vs. 20 could only be anticlimax. Isaac imposes the tactile test, against which, we have already agreed, Jacob is armed with a fairly childish device, and professes himself content with the result: it is, indeed, Esau who stands before him. Hardly in mitigation of Jacob's and Rebekah's cynical exploitation of an old man's folly, but in some measure to explain how it must have seemed to them almost quixotic to let the opportunity slip by, the storyteller invites us to remark on the ease with which Isaac allowed himself to be gulled.

Isaac consumes the counterfeit game, again without demur, then applies a further test, which once more the pseudo-Esau passes handily. But now a paradox! The smell of Esau, which was supposed to evoke the chase and the open wild which were dear to Isaac's memories, evokes no such thing at all. Rather, it is *like the fragrance of a field that the* LORD *has blessed!* The blessing to which Isaac is finally prompted in vs. 28 is the invocation of a God of fertility of the sky and land, a blessing like that of the Joseph tribes in Genesis 49:25–26, Deuteronomy 33:13–17. It is the blessing of an agricultural people expressed in the kind of formula that we would expect to have been emitted on the occasion of one of Israel's great feasts, the Unleavened Bread (the Passover), Leviticus 23:10–14, or the Feast of Weeks, Leviticus 23:15–21, or the Feast of Tents, Leviticus 33:33–43. Obviously, what has happened in the Yahwistic story of Genesis is a coming to the fore of what Jacob and Esau symbolize—that is, Israel and Edom—rather than the drama of Isaac's two sons. The blessing has nothing to do with the real Esau or the pseudo-Esau or even the real Jacob, but only with the eponymous ancestor of the twelve tribes of Israel/Jacob. This impression is borne out by vs. 29, which, while also "democratizing" a benison of the style once pronounced over an ambitious king (*Let peoples serve you, and nations pay you homage*), applies it specifically to this one people that will *be master of your brothers,* who will *bow down to you:* not only Edomites, but also Ishmaelites (or the children of Keturah), Moabites, and Ammonites. *Cursed* or *blessed be those who curse* or *bless you:* the touchstone is resistance to or acceptance of the Israelite hegemony, which is willed by Yahweh.

As we know, the patriarchal narratives hardly ever ascribe an agricultural life to Israel's forefathers in Canaan. This is understandable, since these traditions generally attempt to reconstruct an earlier age in which it was thought that the pursuits of the before-Israel had been nomadic and pastoral, not the bucolic and peasant society with which the biblical authors were familiar, a land of small industries in wine and oil, with a little metal and other mineral worths, some trading here and there at the crossroads of commerce, tolls taken along the way from buyers and sellers, and so forth. The nomadic, at least the semi-nomadic, backdrop of Israelite history represented in the patriarchal history undoubtedly has its basis in fact, though it also became a source of romance and fable: the Rechabites of Jeremiah 35 (cf. 2 Kings 10:15–16) were doubtless to their contemporaries as various fundamentalist sects are to us today, building on a biblical past that never really was and looking to a biblical future that cannot be. Be that as it may, in vss. 27–29 antiquarian interests are entirely abandoned and Israel is blessed as it would have wanted to be blessed in its hardly won homeland.

Now enters the plodding Esau, fresh with his kill, which, all unsuspecting, he prepares into a tasty dish to set before his father. *"Who are you?"* asks Isaac. Esau must have been thunderstruck. Who am I? Instants ago he had been sent to fetch fresh food; and this he has done, and with dispatch. Haply, however, Isaac is equally as confused as his elder son: he is *seized with a fit of uncontrollable trembling* (the horror of Isaiah 21:4, Ezekiel 26:16), as he recognizes, now without the need of puerile testing, that his authentic first-born waits on his next word. *"Who was it, then?"* he stammers in this extremity; who had the access and the knowledge to perpetrate on a dying father the enormity that has now been revealed? The question needs only to be asked to be answered, by father and son alike. *"He has been well named Jacob,"* cries Esau, since *"he has now supplanted me twice"*—the word association we have noted above at 25:26.

In Isaac's response to Esau in vs. 33 and the subsequent dialogue between father and son the irrevocable and independent nature of the "special blessing" is well brought out (see above on vs. 4). It is quite obvious that in the mind of the author and his readers a blessing was more than a matter of words and pious wishes; once uttered, even in error, it was effective of the good it pronounced and could neither be recalled nor transferred to another. In part, such ideas are tributary to the almost superstitious awe in which the spoken word was held: "word" and "deed" being virtually interchangeable concepts, for good or for ill the blessing or the curse respectively worked its effect by its very pronouncement. In addition, this blessing is, indeed, "special": Isaac has, so to speak, expended in it all his capability of vital communication, so that there is nothing left for the real Esau (vs. 37). In the face of the piteous despair of his twice betrayed son, now bereft of his heritage for once and all, Isaac must remain mute and helpless.

The "blessing" of Esau, when it finally comes, looks to be an afterthought in the narrative and quite evidently has been worded to describe Edom and the Edomites in relation to Israel's history, just as the earlier blessing described the historical Israel itself. We are reminded in vss. 39–40 both of the lines spoken of Ishmael in 16:12 (J) and of the oracle of 25:23 (J) in this evocation of a warlike, brawling people inhabiting a harsh and inhospitable land, whose further destiny is one of subjection to others. *But when you become restive, you shall throw off his yoke from your neck* seems, on the face of it, to envision the time when the Edomites had regained their independence from Israel and Judah, and therefore, a time well beyond that of the Davidic and Solomonic purview which is normally attributed to the Yahwist. There were, however, even in Solomonic times, Edomite insurrections like that narrated in 1 Kings 11:14–22.25

and probably others as well, which could easily have been portrayed as "throwing off the Israelite yoke." And it is also possible, though less likely, that E. A. Speiser's conjecture could be correct, that the allusion is to earlier relationships between the pre-Israel on one hand and the predecessors of Edom on the other.

41 Esau bore Jacob a grudge because of the blessing his father had given him. He said to himself, "When the time of mourning for my father comes, I will kill
42 my brother Jacob." When Rebekah got news of what her older son Esau had in mind, she called her younger son Jacob and said to him: "Listen! Your brother Esau intends to settle accounts with you by
43 killing you. Therefore, son, do what I tell you: flee
44 at once to my brother Laban in Haran, and stay with him a while until your brother's fury subsides
45 [until your brother's anger against you subsides] and he forgets what you did to him. Then I will send for you and bring you back. Must I lose both of you in a single day?"

The sympathy which Esau's plight engendered begins to fade away as we learn of his murderous designs, even though the feelings that prompt them are understandable. Rebekah, adept at discovering Esau's plans as she had those of his father, again counsels her beloved younger son. Isaac, whose imminent demise is contemplated in vs. 41, is obviously in no position to be consulted. Before, Abraham had insisted that on no account should any son of his return to the ancestral home in Mesopotamia (24:6, J), but now conditions have changed. Rebekah wagers, not without cause, on the mercurial and impulsive character of Esau: his moods will pass into others, as they have before. But her final words are fraught with exquisite irony for the biblical writer: *Must I lose both of you in a single day?* She means, of course, to forestall the slaying of Jacob at Esau's hands and then the almost inevitable death of Esau himself in the ensuing blood vengeance exacted by kin and clan (cf. 2 Samuel 14:7). In reality, she has indeed lost both of her sons in this single day. Esau, in fact, she had lost long ago, and Jacob she now loses by thinking to save him. She does not know it, but her craft has played itself out. Never will she make good on her promise to *send for you and bring you back.*

According to J, therefore, Jacob's reason for going to Haran was to escape the wrath of Esau. According to the P story that follows, however, which takes up from 26:34–35 above, he was sent there by Isaac and Rebekah together to get a wife, and the reason for his being blessed rather than Esau (28:1.3–4), about which Esau learns in 28:6, is that, unlike his elder brother, he had not married Canaanite women. Isaac is, of course, no longer on his deathbed. In the P chronology he was sixty years old at the time of the birth of Jacob and Esau (25:26b), one hundred when Esau took his wives (26:34), and all of one hundred and eighty when he died (35:28).

46 Rebekah said to Isaac: "I am disgusted with life because of the Hittite women. If Jacob should also marry a Hittite woman, a native of the land like these women, what good would life be to me?"
28 Isaac therefore called Jacob, greeted him with a blessing, and charged him: "You shall not marry a
2 Canaanite woman! Go now to Paddan-aram, to the home of your mother's father Bethuel, and there choose a wife for yourself from among the daugh-
3 ters of your uncle Laban. May God Almighty bless you and make you fertile, multiply you that you may
4 become an assembly of peoples. May he extend to you and your descendants the blessing he gave to Abraham, so that you may gain possession of the land where you are staying, which he assigned to
5 Abraham." Then Isaac sent Jacob on his way; he went to Paddan-aram, to Laban, son of Bethuel, the Aramean, and brother of Rebekah, the mother of Jacob and Esau.
6 Esau noted that Isaac had blessed Jacob when he sent him to Paddan-aram to get himself a wife there, charging him, as he gave him his blessing, not to
7 marry a Canaanite woman, and that Jacob had obeyed his father and mother and gone to Paddan-
8 aram. Esau realized how displeasing the Canaanite
9 women were to his father Isaac, so he went to Ishmael, and in addition to the wives he had, married Mahalath, the daughter of Abraham's son Ishmael and sister of Nebaioth.

Though quite sketchy, the entire substance of the P "family history of Isaac" (25:19), that is, the story of Jacob and Esau, seems to have been preserved by Genesis. It has, however, been distributed piecemeal and by way of supplement among the far more interesting and lively stories of J and E, from which it differs in many respects besides length. In P there is no enmity between Jacob and Esau, and nothing really reprehensible is ever ascribed to either of the two brothers (it is not even certain that P regards Esau as the ancestor of the Edomites). Discrepancies of such mag-

nitude can hardly be construed as other than a deliberate effort on the part
of this later theologian of Israel's history to reshape the contours of the
older traditions which for various reasons were now felt to be inappropriate. That the earlier and the more recent nevertheless coexist in the present text of Genesis is additional proof, if we needed one, that the Redactor and the Priestly author of this work are quite distinct persons with
separate objectives and values. And it is fortunate for us that it is so, since
we would be ever so much the poorer had only the Priestly narrative been
permitted to survive as the total substitute for J and E.

Still, it must not be our thought that the Priestly author's contribution is
minimal here or is in any way to be denigrated. We have had sufficient experience of the theology of P by now to know that it can be rarely
dismissed as of little consequence. The figure of Jacob in this theology by
no means forms any exception to that rule.

Walter Gross called attention not too long ago to the common traits
possessed by the P sections dealing with Jacob in Genesis (28:3–4,
35:6.9–15, 48:3–4), which are six: they all invoke *God Almighty* (El
Shaddai, P's name for the patriarchal God, cf. 17:1); they all feature *the
blessing* of this God; Jacob is the recipient of the blessing; he is promised
numerous progeny, as Abraham was; precisely, he will become *an assembly of peoples* (so also in 48:4, though the NAB has translated "an assembly of tribes"; in 35:11 appears "an assembly of nations"); and, as
was to Abraham, there is promise of eventual *possession of the land*. The
P treatment of Jacob is at once an evocation and an extension of the treatment of Abraham, with this shift of emphasis, that whereas Abraham is
presented pre-eminently as the man of God's covenant, Jacob is the man
of blessing *par excellence*.

So far P builds on the suggestions of the older traditions. The covenant
with Abraham of chapter 17 is the P version of the J story of chapter 15.
We have just seen in the J chapter 27 the centrality of blessing in the career of Jacob, and we shall have other instances of the same thing below.
But there is more to the question than this. What is this "assembly"
(*qahal*) of peoples/nations which Jacob will become according to the
terms of his reiterated blessing in P? It can hardly be dissociated from the
"host of nations" predicted of Abraham in 17:4. As we saw then, the
dominant concept of covenant in chapter 17 was of one that embraced a
larger Israel, not a narrow one (see especially on 17:23–27), as was already insinuated by calling it the "everlasting" pact (17:7), thus linking it
with the covenant of Noah in 9:16. Let us have no mistakes about it, the
Priestly author was a thoroughgoing Israelite who believed in the chosenness of his people and the heritage of the Land of Promise which was
its concrete expression. But he was not a nationalist. His notion of
religion, of the right relation of man to God, had been conceived in the

womb of a broader experience of the human condition than had been vouchsafed to the poets and chroniclers of Israel's wars and triumphs over its neighbors in the days of conquest and empire. He had known defeat, the loss of his land, the need to find new sureties for old, and thereby he had learnt compassion for those who shared his weaknesses and wished to share with them his strengths. If his ecumenism was not quite what we would desiderate as a present ideal, it was nonetheless admirable for being a necessary stage on the way toward the ideal.

> Let not the foreigner say,
>   when he would join himself to the LORD,
>   "The LORD will surely exclude me from his people . . ."
>   . . . The foreigners who join themselves to the LORD,
>   ministering to him,
> Loving the name of the LORD,
>   and becoming his servants—
> All who keep the sabbath free from profanation
>   and hold to my covenant,
> Them I will bring to my holy mountain
>   and make joyful in my house of prayer;
> Their holocausts and sacrifices
>   will be acceptable on my altar,
> For my house shall be called
>   a house of prayer for all peoples (Isaiah 56:3.6–7).

This is proselytism, admittedly. It explains, nonetheless, why the prerogatives of man—all man—in creation and the terms of the covenant with Noah—that is to say, with existing man—were no less dear to the Priestly author than the stipulations of the Sinaitic covenant. And it explains why, other than from a desire simply to compress an ancient narrative, P did not choose to isolate Ishmael from Isaac nor to put enmity between Jacob and Esau nor to rehearse such additional ancient themes as had once nourished religious fervor but which he now considered passé and embarrassingly particularistic.

It remains to be seen that Esau, who in P is not Jacob's enemy, in vss. 6–9 tries to learn from his brother's example and please his parents in compensation for the grief he has caused them unwittingly. Jacob had been sent to seek a wife from his mother's kindred? Well, then, Esau will seek one from his father's kindred: this should make up for the wives he had first chosen, *the Hittite women* of vs. 46, *native of the land* of Canaan. *So he married Mahalath, the daughter of Abraham's son Ishmael and sister of Nebaioth.* Mahalath appears only here. In 36:3 Esau's wife who is the daughter of Ishmael and sister of Nebaioth is named Basemath. (Nebaioth was Ishmael's first-born according to 25:13, P.) Furthermore, according to 36:2, the daughter of Ishmael no less than the Hittite and Hivite women is listed among "the Canaanites." Ishmael, it should be noted, as far as P is concerned was still living in Isaac's neighborhood at the age of about one hundred and fourteen years (16:16, 17:24–25, 25:17.26b, 26:34).

The final verses of this section can be divided equally between J and E: they begin a long narration of Jacob's voyage to and from Mesopotamia, and of his experiences there, in which P evinces hardly any interest at all. Purely arbitrarily, we shall indicate the E segments with italics.

10 Jacob departed from Beer-sheba and proceeded to-
11 ward Haran. *When he came upon a certain shrine, as the sun had already set, he stopped there for the night. Taking one of the stones at the shrine, he put it under his head and lay down to sleep at that spot.*
12 *Then he had a dream: a stairway rested on the ground, with its top reaching to the heavens; and God's messengers were going up and down on it.*
13 And there was the LORD standing beside him and saying: "I, the LORD, am the God of your forefather Abraham and the God of Isaac; the land on which you are lying I will give to you and your de-
14 scendants. These shall be as plentiful as the dust of the earth, and through them you shall spread out east and west, north and south. In you and your descendants all the nations of the earth shall find
15 blessing. Know that I am with you; I will protect you wherever you go, and bring you back to this land. I will never leave you until I have done what I promised you."
16 When Jacob awoke from his sleep, he exclaimed, "Truly, the LORD is in this spot, although I did not
17 know it!" *In solemn wonder he cried out: "How awesome is this shrine! This is nothing else but an abode of God, and that is the gateway to heaven!"*
18 *Early the next morning Jacob took the stone that he had put under his head, set it up as a memorial*
19 *stone, and poured oil on top of it.* He called that site Bethel, whereas the former name of the town had been Luz.
20 *Jacob then made this vow: "If God remains with me, to protect me on this journey I am making and to give me enough bread to eat and clothing to wear,*

21 *and I come back safe to my father's house, the* LORD
22 *shall be my God. This stone that I have set up as a
memorial stone shall be God's abode. Of everything
you give me, I will faithfully return a tenth part to
you.*"

There is a rather abrupt transition from 27:45 to vs. 10 of this passage; however, it is possible that the Redactor has suppressed a verse or two of the J narrative in view of this insertion of the P 28:1–5, especially vs. 5. At any rate, Jacob quits his father's home which since 26:33 has been localized at Beer-sheba and begins his journey toward the ancestral homeland in Haran. Both versions of the tradition have him now undergo a significant experience at Bethel, a sacred place which the Yahwist has previously associated with Abraham, who "claimed" it for Israel (12:8, 13:3–4), but which most certainly did originally have its primary connection in history with the northern patriarchal figure of Jacob/Israel. (Possibly the secondary nature of the Abraham tradition is indicated by its having him build his altar and invoke Yahweh by name not precisely at Bethel itself but "between Bethel and Ai.") In the narrative as it had finally developed, with Jacob/Israel made the grandson of Abraham and given a youth in Canaan before his career in Aram Naharaim, the initial experience at Bethel takes the form of a temporary farewell to the Land of Promise in which he is assured of the protection of his fathers' God while on his way. Undoubtedly chapter 35 below better situates Bethel in the historical chronology of the "wandering Aramean who went down to Egypt with a small household and lived there as an alien" (Deuteronomy 26:5b).

It would be difficult to overestimate the importance of Bethel in Israelite history. In the time of Amos and Hosea it was a chief sanctuary (cf. Amos 5:5, 7:10–13; Hosea 10:5), and so it remained until the Deuteronomic reform of King Josiah (640–609 B.C.), which obliterated the "country" shrines and their priesthoods in favor of an exclusively Jerusalemite cult (cf. 2 Kings 23:15). In prophetic eyes it had become a source of seduction to Israel both as a scene of syncretistic worship—the provocation of the Deuteronomic reform—and of a chauvinistic priesthood and prophetic corps who nourished false hopes and nationalist complacency (it is so remembered by Jeremiah 48:13); but it had known better days. Bethel had been one of the chief sanctuaries and places of assembly for Israel before the coming of the monarchy (cf. Judges 20:18.26, 21:2; 1 Samuel 7:16), and it had been present at the birth of Israelite prophecy (cf. 2 Kings 2:2–3.23). It had, of course, been "Canaanite" before it became Israelite: Judges 1:22–25 ascribes its conquest to "the house of Joseph," by which undoubtedly the tribe of Ephraim is meant (cf. 1 Chronicles

7:28). When such a conquest occurred, the paraphernalia and appurtenances of the focal holy place were transferred from one deity to another with practiced ease—not unlike the Bargello Apollo, who became a David when his quiver was translated into a slingshot under Michelangelo's steady chisel. It is very plain that for both J and E it was important for Bethel to have an Israelite prehistory, which they found in the Jacob/Israel father figure who was remembered there.

The memory, the cultic legend, has been more vividly preserved in the E story than in the J, as is appropriate, since the Elohist presumably possessed the closer control of the northern traditions to which Jacob properly belongs. E knows the conformation of the Bethel countryside: "the desolate stony hollow among the barren hills," in Sir James Frazer's words. He evidently did not know, though we know from archeology, that Bethel was already an inhabited site in the Middle and Late Bronze periods, safely within any patriarchal age. He speaks of *a certain shrine* and of Jacob making a pillow of *one of the stones at the shrine* (the Hebrew for this is simply "the place") because of Bethel's eventual character as a holy place, but he also ascribes this sacred character to the revelation made to Jacob in his dream and to his anointing there of a memorial stone. It seems to be presupposed that Jacob does, indeed, chance upon this isolated spot midway in his journey and that he picks at random the hard bed whereon to lay himself. No one is more surprised than he when he discovers (in vss. 17 and 22) that this place is the *abode of God* (in Hebrew, *beth Elohim*, i.e., Bethel). What makes this intelligence known to him is the vision of the *stairway* which *rested on the ground, with its top reaching to the heavens* (the latter clause is not exactly the same as the J "with its top in the sky" of 11:4, but it may have similar Near Eastern resonances). What is this "stairway" (*sullam*)? Though the word occurs only here in the Hebrew Bible, its basic meaning hardly seems to be in doubt. Somehow, Bethel is envisioned as a quintessential meeting place of God and man—exactly what a shrine or sanctuary is supposed to be—a place where *God's messengers* are constantly *going up and down* bearing petitions and responses, therefore a *gateway to heaven*. The stairway itself? Some think of the very terrain surrounding Bethel, the stepped hillsides which could suggest to a receptive imagination a facility for comings and goings between heaven and earth. And some think of Esagila and the other ziggurats of Babylonia (see above on 11:4) where the temple below was considered to be the appearance place (through oracles) of the god who dwelt at the top, inaccessible except through his priestly intermediaries who walked the ramp (*sullam* can mean a ramp) connecting the upper and lower levels of the "holy mountain." The ziggurat was not a feature of Israelite religious tradition, but the symbolized mountain of revelation certainly was, and not only for Israel but for countless other religions, the Christian included.

According to vs. 18 Jacob, following the recognition brought home to him of this holy place, woke the next morning and *set up the stone that he had put under his head as a memorial stone, and poured oil on top of it.* In other words, he consecrated a *massebah.* The *massebah* was without question a routine fixture of Canaanite shrines and, like the stone knives of circumcision (Exodus 4:25, Joshua 5:2) and the unhewn stones which were the fabric of Israelite altars (Exodus 20:25), it was a link with the distant past when all our fathers literally worshiped stocks and stones for the only reason that they were the sole matériel of cult. Like the sacred tree the *massebah* was unquestionably connected with fertility worship; in some religions this association is very apparent in the phallus or vulva form given to the stone, though most of the *masseboth* recovered by Palestinian archeology seem to have been simple slabs. In Israelite religion the sacred stones of the inherited holy places became "memorial stones" tied in with the deeds of ancestors rather than with any sympathetic magic once related to fertility cult. When Israelite women came to Bethel and rubbed their fingers over its sacred stone as their Canaanite sisters had done before them, they remembered the deeds of their ancestor Jacob, or they were supposed to, just as they were supposed to forget the connotations the stone may have held for other pieties. The hermeneutical effort may not always have been successful, just as it was not always successful in the translation, say, of Aztec idols into *santos.*

(Though it has nothing to do with the interpretation of Genesis, it is of passing interest to take note of the legend which has identified with Jacob's pillow the Stone of Scone also called the Stone of Destiny or King Edward's stone, which rests beneath the coronation throne of Britain's sovereigns. Of good Scottish rock, this stone on which the Celtish kings of the north had been crowned was brought from the Abbey of Scone to Westminster Abbey by Edward I in 1296 and has remained there since, except when it was borrowed for a while by Scottish nationalists in the 1950s.)

The story of the sacred stone at Bethel invites several other comments. First of all, and rather exceptionally, this stone itself and not only the place where it has been erected is *God's abode;* the stone itself is Bethel (vs. 22). Further, the Bethel with which the stone is identified was the name of a Canaanite deity (like Roi, Elyon, Olam, Shammai) as well as of a cult center of this deity. (Jeremiah 48:13, which we cited above, has already indicated this by pairing off with Bethel of the Israelites the god Chemosh in whom the Moabites had foolishly trusted.) Below in 31:13 (E) the NAB has translated "I am the God who appeared to you in Bethel" (and so most other modern versions), but the Hebrew actually says, word for word: "I am the God Bethel (*or*, El Bethel) who appeared to you." Moreover, Bethel must have been a deity of more than usual prestige and tenacity in the Canaanite pantheon and its adaptation by Israelite Yahwism. Aramaic papyri of the Persian period (fifth century B.C.), records of a Jewish colony on the island of Elephantine near the first cataract of the Nile in Egypt, show that Bethel was then and there a revered divine figure, the exact relationship of which to Yahweh, the principal object of the colony's worship, is not altogether clear. Assyrian and Babylonian documents of a century or so earlier likewise testify to a god Bethel worshiped in the Semitic west, presumably in Phoenicia and Syria. And it is to this same region, which had once included Canaan, that Philo of Byblos, attempting to explain Semitic mythology to a Greek audience at the end of the first or beginning of the second Christian century, attributed regard for a god whom he called Baitylos (the LXX transliteration for Bethel-the-place was Baithel). Baitylos, said Philo, descended from Ouranos, that is, from heaven. This is an interesting note, since *baitylos* or *baitylion* is the word used by Philo and later writers in Greek for the sacred stones (anglicized as bætyls or betyls), usually meteorite in origin, which were thought to be spirit-possessed and potent in divers ways. These disparate yet associated patterns seem to be refractions of a common Semitic lore surrounding the name of Bethel, of which Genesis 28:10–22 has retained some of the elements.

One has the impression that the Pentateuchal traditions were not quite as at ease with the divine name Bethel as they were with some others which they did not hesitate to appropriate to the God of Israel. Nevertheless, they had no scruples about accepting the sanctuary of Bethel as a shrine of their God. The nationalist Israel and the Israel of popular cult were of the same mind, as we have seen; their enthusiasm for Bethel even exceeded that of the Pentateuch. But it was not so with the prophets, as we have also seen, nor with the later historical writings which were inspired by the prophets. Here (cf. Amos 3:14, 4:4, 5:5; Hosea 4:15, 10:5; Jeremiah 48:13; 2 Kings 23:15, etc.) Bethel uniformly is portrayed as a site of otiose and obscene ritual, whose reigning deity cannot be squared with the Yahweh of Israel's historical encounter.

It is perhaps in keeping with E's more than halfhearted acceptance of Bethel and its tradition that in vss. 20–22 Jacob is seen initiating a covenant with God rather than the other way round. (In vs. 21 *the* LORD *shall be my God* is a redactional insertion: originally, Bethel itself: *this stone that I have set up as a memorial stone shall be God's abode* is the *quid* of the *pro quo* that Jacob proposes: *If God remains with me . . .*) This kind of covenant is dangerously close to what the prophets proclaimed as totally wrong about Israel's supposed relationship with its God: the notion that, in contradiction with Hosea 6:6 or Amos 5:21–24 or Isaiah 1:11–14, justification may be achieved through works, self-chosen works, which somehow must win the divine favor, rather than through trust in God's mercy which chooses whom it wills and asks only humble obedience (cf. Isaiah 7:9b; Micah 6:8). It is part of the genius of the Jacob story of Genesis, however, that its hero matures spiritually and otherwise during the course of the narrative. The *tenth part* which Jacob promises to return of his goods and produce is in accord with the tithing that was customary at Bethel (cf. Amos 4:4).

The J version of the Bethel story takes the form of a theophany, also in a dream (vs. 16). It is not unlike other J passages in Genesis. Yahweh *standing beside him* repeats the Hebrew of 18:2. There is a repetition of the promise of the land to the patriarch and his descendants (cf. 13:15), and of plentiful progeny like *the dust of the earth* (cf. 15:5), which will *spread out east and west, north and south* (cf. 13:14–15) and be a sign of blessing for *all the nations of the earth* (cf. 12:3). There is no question here of any initiative except on the part of the "God of the fathers," *the God of your forefather Abraham and the God of Isaac.* In vs. 19b probably a redactional gloss has identified *Bethel* with *Luz*. The two places were originally nearby each other (cf. Joshua 16:2), but later tradition, for reasons that are not entirely clear, made them one and the same.

The combined JE narrative of Bethel, even though each strand of tradition may tell an incomplete story and the union of the two is artificial, undoubtedly has something to tell us about the evolution of patriarchal religion and about patriarchal religion in evolution toward the Yahwism of Israel. As we have tried to intimate in the treatment above, neither J nor E has a primitive legend of Bethel and Jacob on which the other has built and elaborated. Rather, the stories are distinct, and each is separately primitive and developed. Primitive with J is the concept of the ancestral God, the God of the fathers of clan or tribe, bound to no specified land or sacred place, who accompanied wandering Amorites and Arameans like Abraham and Jacob in their migrations from east to west and back again. Developed in J, of course, is the naming of this God Yahweh, a step which could be taken only after much growth in history and in the spirit. Developed, too, is the association with the God of the fathers of the promise of the land, which really grew out of his identification with the Elim of Canaan's sanctuaries. Primitive in E is the cult legend of Bethel, the covenant of Bethel, and El Bethel himself. Developed is the idea of this God as one who will be with Jacob wherever he goes, whose power will be as much at work in Aram Naharaim as it is in this holy place. It is rather evident that from neither J nor E can we reconstruct what was the "pure" form of the patriarchal religion: both sources presuppose the ultimate syncretism which it achieved in the Yahwistic religion of Israel and can recall only imperfectly this or that quality of it that had once been thrown into the syncretic melting pot. We can, however, and we must, try to take due cognizance of these qualities en route to discovering the relation of Genesis to the rest of the Pentateuch.

Patriarchal religion, as far we can determine it, resulted from a fusion of the ancestral El with the El of Canaan's shrines. Above (see on 14:18–20) we suggested that whether these Elim (Elyon, Olam, Roi, et al.) were popularly thought of as one or several, a common basis in any case existed to account for the identification that seems to have taken place. The best evidence that we have for this common basis is Canaanite mythology of about 1500 B.C., and according to this mythology, as Frank M. Cross has written: "El can be described neither as a sky-god (like Anu), nor as a storm-god (like Enlil or Zeus), nor as a chthonic god (like Nergal), nor as a grain-god (like Dagan). The only image of El that can combine all of his mythological traits is that of the patriarch. He is the forefather of gods and men, sometimes severe, often indulgent, but always wise in his ways." It is not hard to see why a god of this character—always supposing that the Canaanite mythology we know from northern Syria was in some part the common property of all Canaan and that it was already such property in the patriarchal times—could not have been readily identified with the nomadic god(s) who had entered Canaan from the east.

Nor is it hard to see why Yahwism, when it was introduced into Canaan in the thirteenth century B.C., should not have found a receptive soil in which to be sown that it might grow almost overnight into the dominant faith of Palestine. Yahweh was speedily identified with El: with all the Elim that we have seen up to now, mainly in the Yahwist's narrative, and with others, such as the El Berith of Judges 7–9 (Shechem, cf. chapter 34 below). He was not, except in unauthorized popular cult, identified with Baal, the "active" god who had replaced the "retired" El in headship of the Canaanite pantheon. Baal and everything in Canaanite rite and ritual that could be associated with him were declared totally and inescapably incompatible with Yahwism (cf. 1 Kings 18), while El and everything in Canaanite rite and ritual that could be reasonably associated with him, titles, attributes, traditions, usages, and even a few strange notions, were cheerfully assimilated. The assumption is, which the patriarchal legends reinforce, that the Israel which emerged in Palestine from a coalition of foreign and indigenous components was able to count on, among the latter, a fifth column already prepared for a new religious adventure, a people or peoples whose god or gods were yearning to have their horizons broadened and their ambients augmented. If Yahwism was a practical that later became a theoretical monotheism, we may consider the patriarchal religion to have been a practical monotheism that grew out of a henotheism.

Where all of this leaves us with regard to what we have remarked on

11:27–32 above is not entirely clear. We can only repeat that the patriarchal tradition is not of one piece, and that those who are on one page represented as comfortable polytheists might equally well appear on the next as monotheists, just as the pastoral Abraham of one chapter may become the army general of the one following. We have to take the material as we find it, and as we find it, what we have written above seems to make the best sense.

4. Jacob and Laban

The first part of the following section seems to form no problem. It is J throughout.

29 After Jacob resumed his journey, he came to the
2 land of the Easterners. Looking about, he saw a well in the open country, with three droves of sheep huddled near it, for droves were watered from that well. A large stone covered the mouth of
3 the well. Only when all the shepherds were assembled there could they roll the stone away from the mouth of the well and water the flocks. Then they would put the stone back again over the mouth of the well.
4 Jacob said to them, "Friends, where are you
5 from?" "We are from Haran," they replied. Then he asked them, "Do you know Laban, son of
6 Nahor?" "We do," they answered. He inquired further, "Is he well?" "He is," they answered; "and here comes his daughter Rachel with his flock."
7 Then he said: "There is still much daylight left; it is hardly the time to bring the animals home. Why don't you water the flocks now, and then continue
8 pasturing them?" "We cannot," they replied, "until all the shepherds are here* to roll the stone away from the mouth of the well; only then can we water the flocks."

* The versions change the voice of the verb, but the meaning stays the same.

9 While he was still talking with them, Rachel arrived with her father's sheep; she was the one who
10 tended them. As soon as Jacob saw Rachel, the
daughter of his uncle Laban, with the sheep of his
uncle Laban, he went up, rolled the stone away
from the mouth of the well, and watered his un-
11 cle's sheep. Then Jacob kissed Rachel and burst
into tears.
12 He told her that he was her father's relative, Re-
13 bekah's son, and she ran to tell her father. When
Laban heard the news about his sister's son Jacob,
he hurried out to meet him. After embracing and
kissing him, he brought him to his house. Jacob
14a then recounted to Laban all that had happened, and
Laban said to him, "You are indeed my flesh and
blood."

Jacob continues his journey to Haran, coming now *to the land of the
Easterners*. This expression (literally, "the land of the sons of Kedem")
may be the result of a later glossing of the text; at least, there would appear to be no connection with the Kedem of 25:6 (J). In vs. 4 the
author may be trying to suggest that *the well* of vss. 2–3 is the now well-
known one of 24:10–27 where Abraham's servant long ago encountered
Rebekah, Jacob's mother. If so, some changes have been made since last
we saw it, though we get the impression from vs. 8 that the arrangement
there described was of long-standing agreement. This well is *in the open
country* and subject to effective communal control, since it must water
many flocks and therefore respond to a share-and-share-alike policy that is
guaranteed by the *large stone* covering it. That Jacob in vs. 10 is able all
by himself to roll aside this stone which is the usual burden of several
husky men may be traceable to a half-remembered tradition that ascribed
to him superhuman strength (perhaps the same thing is intimated in the E
story of the raising of the monolith of Bethel in 28:18). There is a touch
of quiet humor here as there is to some of the other details of the story.
The brash self-assuredness which prompts Jacob to offer the shepherds of
Haran unsolicited advice on the running of their well is one of these details; it is in ironic contrast with the earlier picture of Jacob the recluse,
whose will and initiative were at the passive disposal of a domineering
mother now no longer with him. Ironic, too, is the spectacle of this Jacob
who cannot but *burst into tears* in the presence of his cousin, this Jacob
whose family feeling thus far has tolerated with little qualm the exploitation of his more pedestrian brother and the beguiling of a senile father.
We must be on the alert, it is true, against the temptation to reduce to one

single mold the various narrative themes which the Yahwist combined to create the composite Jacob, but neither should we ignore the artistry of the creation.

It would hardly be Jacob's way to emulate Abraham's servant and propose a sign for the Lord's providential disposition of his affairs: he prefers to steer his own course, at least as he thinks. Yet we are invited to see the hand of Yahweh at work all the same, when without even knowing his exact whereabouts the resolute young man is so suddenly brought to his goal, the home of his kinsman. For the moment the scene is all one of family affection as uncle and nephew warmly embrace and no doubt exchange news about mutual friends and relatives. Jacob's purpose in quitting Canaan, to find refuge and sanctuary among his mother's people, has been achieved. The acquisition of a wife, the purpose of Jacob's journey according to P, is not as yet a concern in the present context. By another tiny flick of irony, however, the author has already permitted us to see Jacob embracing his bride-to-be (vs. 11), even though his emotions on the occasion may have been altogether proper and cousinly. It is this final fillip that adds to the resemblance of this story of Jacob and Laban's daughter to that of Moses and Reuel's daughters in Exodus 2:15b–21 (J).

The Redactor's continuation of the story in the following verses necessitates a transition that is not as smooth as it initially appears to be. Rachel, whom we have already met, is introduced to us again in vss. 16–18, along with her sister Leah. Jacob is, as before, Laban's kinsman, but he lives in the household not as a passing guest but as one of the master's servants. It is even arguable that this portion of the narrative knew nothing of an independent Jacob who had come to Haran from Canaan: he could just as easily have been an orphan or some other poor relation who took up service with a more prosperous and neighboring member of the family. Aside from vs. 14b, which may very well belong with the preceding J episode, it seems we have to do here with a different narrative element, which we hesitantly assign to the Elohist.

> 14b After Jacob had stayed with him a full month,
> 15 Laban said to him: "Should you serve me for nothing just because you are a relative of mine?
> 16 Tell me what your wages should be." Now Laban had two daughters; the older was called Leah, the
> 17 younger Rachel. Leah had lovely eyes, but Rachel
> 18 was well formed and beautiful. Since Jacob had fallen in love with Rachel, he answered Laban, "I will serve you seven years for your younger daugh-
> 19 ter Rachel." Laban replied, "I prefer to give her to you rather than to an outsider. Stay with me."

20 So Jacob served seven years for Rachel, yet they
   seemed to him but a few days because of his love
   for her.
21 Then Jacob said to Laban, "Give me my wife, that
   I may consummate my marriage with her, for my
22 term is now completed." So Laban invited all the
23 local inhabitants and gave a feast. At the night-
   fall he took his daughter Leah and brought her to
   Jacob, and Jacob consummated the marriage with
24 her. (Laban assigned his slave girl Zilpah to his
25 daughter Leah as her maidservant.) In the morning Jacob was amazed: it was Leah! So he cried
   out to Laban: "How could you do this to me! Was
   it not for Rachel that I served you? Why did you
26 dupe me?" "It is not the custom in our country,"
   Laban replied, "to marry off a younger daughter
27 before an older one. Finish the bridal week for this
   one, and then I will give you the other too, in return for another seven years of service with me."
28 Jacob agreed. He finished the bridal week for
   Leah, and then Laban gave him his daughter
29 Rachel in marriage. (Laban assigned his slave girl
   Bilhah to his daughter Rachel as her maidservant.)
30 Jacob then consummated his marriage with Rachel
   also, and he loved her more than Leah. Thus he
   remained in Laban's service another seven years.

In this episode Laban immediately begins to display the character with
which the common tradition had credited him (see above on 24:28–61),
namely of a sharp, closefisted trickster and trader who will not permit sen-
timent or bloodlines to interfere with the business of life. There is a temptation to listen in the narrative for a counterpoint to previous themes asserted by the Yahwist: Jacob the deceiver (27:1–45) is now heroically
deceived by a crude ruse that must have certified him the legitimate butt
for the coarse japery of every nearby hearth and campfire, and he who had
before flaunted and circumvented the rule of the first-born (25:19–34) is
now caught by the same rule without any effective appeal from it (vs. 26).
However, while the biblical author is not above having his fun with Jacob,
neither has he intended to represent him ultimately as anything less than a
worthy father of Israel. The story that we now read does, indeed, feature
the wiliness of Laban, but it is a wiliness that will eventually get him nowhere, and which Jacob will exploit to his own benefit.

"Should you serve me for nothing just because you are a relative of

mine?" Laban asks. We do not know the circumstances under which Jacob came to serve Laban. In a later society a wage earner had to be paid by the day, as he felt the need (Deuteronomy 24:14–15; Leviticus 19:13), but there were probably no laws to regulate the return that should be made to a family member who pitched in his talents and industry to the common endeavor. Laban's proffer of a wage contract was probably less dictated by anything to which he was strictly required than it was to his esteem in the countryside and his public *noblesse oblige.*

Laban was undoubtedly agreeably surprised by Jacob's offer—and we must not forget that it was Jacob's offer. Knowing his man, Jacob has set terms which he is confident Laban cannot turn down. (Later, according to Deuteronomy 22:29, fifty silver shekels will be set as fair compensation for a nubile girl.) Besides, he is in love and not disposed to haggle. Both of Laban's daughters are now introduced to the reader, since both will become Jacob's wives, though his offer extends to only one. *Leah,* says the NAB, *had lovely eyes, but Rachel was well formed and beautiful.* Older translations made out Leah's eyes to be "weak" (the adjective is the "tender" of 18:7, the "frail" of 33:13, etc.), but this one follows a recent tendency to think of them as limpid and melting, a mark of beauty even if not as striking as Rachel's shapely figure and more opulent good looks. No matter, for *Jacob had fallen in love with Rachel,* and it is for her alone that he will serve seven years. Laban quickly seals the bargain, not without a further reference to their kinship, however, which insinuates that this rather than self-interest dictates his acquiescence: *I prefer to give her to you rather than to an outsider. Stay with me* is not, of course, an invitation to hospitality; it is simply a brief assertion of the terms of Jacob's indenture.

The deceit which Laban practices upon Jacob—and his own daughter Rachel—in the situation described in vss. 21–27 would have been made possible by the prevailing social customs. The bride would have been veiled from her husband (cf. 24:65 above) until she was brought to him in the darkness of the nuptial chamber; probably there was not much more to the marriage "ceremony" than this. Also, we may surmise that the wedding feast, an expansive celebration of seven days' duration (vs. 27), would already have made its contribution to the dulling of wits and instincts that in normal circumstances were more alert and on guard. Jacob's righteous indignation on the morrow is met by Laban with the same aplomb he displays on a later occasion (cf. 31:43), and now as then he brushes aside all charges of misconduct by a pious appeal to law and custom. Now as then, too, he feigns a magnanimous gesture. After the decent interval that is Leah's due—his concern for the feelings of this other daughter whom he has drawn into his machinations is touching—there will be not one bride but two! (Hidden somewhere in this happy prospect is the consideration that a lavish and expensive wedding feast can as easily satisfy the proprieties owed to the wedding of two daughters as it can of one.) The Rachel for whom Jacob has longed will also become his wife forthwith. Only, Jacob must, on his honor now, undertake another seven years of service. Probably from having no other choice, Jacob agrees. It is also possible, though less likely (cf. 30:28 below), that different terms were to govern the second seven-year tour of duty. In any case, in no other way did this love story, for it is a love story in its fashion, seem destined to have a happy ending. Marriage with two sisters, forbidden by later law (Leviticus 18:18), was obviously no problem for these earlier traditions.

Discussing 16:1–6 above, which, as we shall soon see, has a definite relevance to 29:31–30:24 below, we had occasion to refer to Nuzi evidence which has helped to clarify the social background that underlay what otherwise had seemed a rather peculiar arrangement contrived by husband, wife, and concubine. Nuzi confirmed that it was the right, or even the obligation, of a childless wife to provide her husband with a surrogate through whom he might generate an heir, who through the fiction of law would be counted her own child. The Nuzi marriage contract that offered this confirmation also specified, marginally, the name of the slave girl who had been "assigned as her maid" to the bride at the time of the wedding. It is a reasonable assumption that this maid was the one destined to be the surrogate wife in case of need. It is likewise reasonable to assume that the Nuzi clause has a biblical echo in vss. 24 and 29 above which the NAB has parenthesized, according to which *Laban assigned his slave girl Zilpah/ Bilhah to his daughter Leah/Rachel as her maidservant*. Older critics wanted to assign these verses to P because of 16:3 and 46:18.25, which certainly do originate with the Priestly author, and because of 30:4.9, which certainly do not. Already 16:2 (J) has presumed a situation explicable in Nuzi terms quite on its own, and there is no reason that vss. 24 and 29 of this present passage should not do the same, whether we assign them to E, as we have, or to J, as other commentators prefer.

Introduction of Nuzi parallels offers another intriguing possibility of further defining Jacob's station in Laban's ménage other than the obvious one of husband of his daughters. The Nuzi marriage contract to which we referred in the paragraph above, which named the maid assigned to the bride by her father, was also a contract of adoption by which the father of the bride constituted the bridegroom his heir. At Nuzi adoption and marriage seem to have been habitually associated. Since its publication in 1926 by C. J. Gadd, one of the Nuzi contracts in particular which envisions this dual relationship has been very often brought into conjunction with the Jacob and Laban story and has entered into many commentaries on Genesis because of its supposed close approximation of the family arrangements that story presupposes. We cite it here, and in order to give full weight to the comparison we have substituted for the original Hurrian names in the document those which are the presumed biblical counterparts:

> Tablet of adoption whereby Laban, the son of Bethuel, has adopted Jacob, the son of Isaac. As long as Laban lives, Jacob will assure him food and clothing. When Laban dies, Jacob will be his heir. If Laban has a son of his own, he will divide the inheritance equally with Jacob, but it is the son of Laban who will take Laban's gods. If Laban has no son of his own, then Jacob shall take Laban's gods. Further, Laban has given his daughters Leah and Rachel to be the wives of Jacob. If Jacob takes another wife, he loses all rights to Laban's goods, land, and buildings.

The suggestion is that the contract thus adapted to the biblical situation both suits it admirably well and explains some of its ensuing developments, these considerations being given full credit: (1) Laban's sons, who appear only in 30:35 and 31:1, did not exist at the time of Jacob's marriage and adoption. (2) After these sons had been born, Laban's household gods belonged to them. Hence Laban's concern over them and the wrongfulness of Rachel's appropriating them, according to the story of 31:19.30–35. (3) Jacob's secret flight from Laban was necessitated by his still being legally bound to him during his lifetime. Jacob and his wives and all that he had taken with him were still Laban's legitimate possessions, even as he claims in 31:43. (4) In 31:50 Jacob is reminded of his oath not to marry other wives outside the family, which is in accord with the final clause of the Nuzi contract. This clause would not have been broken by his union with his wives' maids, of course, since they had been given by Laban to his daughters precisely for that purpose, that there be no need for Jacob ever to follow a roving eye to obtain elsewhere the fulfillment of children of his own.

It must certainly be confessed that the suggested parallel is most attractive and that it does afford a plausible explanation for some of the details of the story. For others, however, it is less successful in this function, while still others must be ignored or submitted to a bit of Procrusteanism if they are to fit the hypothesis. We will discuss these details as they come up in the narrative. It must also be acknowledged that little if anything in the story itself that we have just read, not even the cryptic references in vss. 24 and 29 to the maids given the two sisters, would have led anyone who did not know of the Nuzi practice to imagine anything like it in the lives of Jacob and Laban, Leah and Rachel. (Laban, after all, had given not one maid but several to Rebekah on the occasion of her marriage, cf.

24:61.) Nor does it appear that the biblical authors who transmitted these traditions possessed any awareness of such a possible state of affairs as they went about composing their narratives; very often they presuppose other types of arrangement which are either incompatible with it or reconciled with it only with difficulty. These are not peremptory arguments against the suggested interpretation, for we know that the writers of Genesis have often through the accurate retention of tradition maintained contact with a past that they did not fully understand. We shall be in a better position to judge the validity of the Nuzian connection once we have seen the story as a whole.

The verses that follow, concerning the birth and the naming of Jacob's children, and the incident complexities of a polygamous and rather highly uxorious household, are the result of a conflation of parallel stories from J and E. Though it might seem that little is to be gained from it in this particular instance, we have attempted to indicate by italics what we consider to be the E elements, thus distinguishing the two sources. The distinction is admittedly quite chancy when it comes to deciding which verses belong to whom; all that we really know is that a distinction has to be made somehow. As E. A. Speiser chose to understate the matter, "the borderline between *J* and *E* is sometimes uncertain in this section."

31 When the LORD saw that Leah was unloved, he made her fruitful, while Rachel remained barren.
32 Leah conceived and bore a son, and she named him Reuben; for she said, "It means, 'The LORD saw my
33 misery; *now my husband will love me.*'" She conceived again and bore a son, and said, "It means, 'The LORD heard that I was unloved,' and therefore he has given me this one also"; so she named him
34 Simeon. Again she conceived and bore a son, and she said, "Now at last my husband will become attached to me, since I have now borne him three
35 sons"; that is why she† named him Levi. Once more she conceived and bore a son, and she said, "This time I will give grateful praise to the LORD"; therefore she named him Judah. Then she stopped bearing children.
30 When Rachel saw that she failed to bear children to Jacob, *she became envious of her sister. She said to*
2 *Jacob, "Give me children or I shall die!" In anger Jacob retorted, "Can I take the place of God, who*

† So the versions; the MT has "he."

3 *has denied you the fruit of the womb?" She replied,*
"Here is my maidservant Bilhah. Have intercourse
with her, and let her give birth on my knees, so that
4 *I too may have offspring, at least through her." So*
she gave him her maidservant Bilhah as a consort,
5 and Jacob had intercourse with her. *When Bilhah*
6 *conceived and bore a son,* Rachel said, *"God has*
vindicated me; indeed he has heeded my plea and
given me a son." Therefore she named him Dan.
7 *Rachel's maidservant Bilhah conceived again and*
8 *bore a second son, and Rachel said, "I engaged in a*
fateful struggle‡ with my sister, and I prevailed."
So she named him Naphtali.
9 When Leah saw that she had ceased to bear children, she gave her maidservant Zilpah to Jacob as
10 a consort. So Jacob had intercourse with* Zilpah,
11 and she conceived and bore a son. Leah then said,
12 "What good luck!" So she named him Gad. Then
Leah's maidservant Zilpah bore a second son to Ja-
13 cob; and Leah said, "What good fortune!"—meaning, "Women call me fortunate." So she named him
Asher.
14 One day, during the wheat harvest, when Reuben
was out in the field, he came upon some mandrakes
which he brought home to his mother Leah. Rachel
asked Leah, "Please let me have some of your son's
15 mandrakes." Leah† replied, "Was it not enough for
you to take away my husband, that you must now
take my son's mandrakes too?" "Very well, then!"
Rachel answered. "In exchange for your son's mandrakes, Jacob may lie with you tonight."
16 That evening, when Jacob came home from the
fields, Leah went out to meet him. "You are now to
come in with me," she told him, "because I have
paid for you with my son's mandrakes." So that
17 night he slept with her, *and God heard her prayer;*
18 *she conceived and bore a fifth son to Jacob. Leah*
then said, "God has given me my reward for having
let my husband have my maidservant"; so she

‡ Literally, "in wrestlings of Elohim."
* These words have been supplied from the LXX.
† So the LXX; the MT="to her" (*lah* in place of *leah*).

19 *named him Issachar. Leah conceived again and*
20 *bore a sixth son to Jacob; and she said, "God has*
   brought me a precious gift. This time my husband
   will offer me presents, now that I have borne him
21 six sons"; so she named him Zebulun. Finally, she
   gave birth to a daughter, and she named her Dinah.
22 *Then God remembered Rachel; he heard her prayer*
23 and made her fruitful. *She conceived and bore a*
   son, and she said, "God has removed my disgrace."
24 So she named him Joseph, meaning, "May the LORD
   add another son to this one for me!"

In the form of a story about the successive births of Jacob's sons by his wives and their two maids, this segment of our tradition lists the eponymous ancestors of the Israelite "tribes," that is, of the different peoples who federated together to make up what later came to be known as the nation Israel. The list here, with the addition of Benjamin, whose birth is not told until 35:16–20, is the same as that of 35:22b–26 and chapter 49. Usually, however, the "tribes" of Israel are listed as they are in Ezekiel 48:1–7.23–27, omitting Levi and substituting Manasseh and Ephraim for Joseph. The reasons for the discrepancy are entirely historical, rooted in the fact that the tribal names were originally geographical before they became personal eponyms. There never was a territory called "Joseph," but regions which bore the titles of Ephraim and Manasseh were incorporated into the tribal tradition under the guise of "Joseph-tribes" (cf. 48:8–20). The "tribe" of Levi probably forms the lone exception to the geographical rule that otherwise obtained: from the beginning the Levites seem to have been a social class within the federation rather than residents of any given territory. Jacob's daughter Dinah appears in vs. 21 to prepare for the story of chapter 34; she otherwise plays no part in any of the tribal lists.

By whatever listing system, the Israelite tribes are habitually numbered as twelve. This number, which is as significant for the New Testament as it was for the Old, we have already seen turn up in the patriarchal lists (cf. 25:12–16). The rationale of the number twelve has been variously riddled in this particular connection. It is, for one thing, part of the ancient Mesopotamian six-base system which still affects some of our mathematics, and it has had mystical connotations through the ages: twelve, for example, is the number of the signs of the zodiac and of the members of the human body (the notion that lies behind Judges 29:29). In Greek history there is a pattern of twelve city-states making up an amphictyony which surrounded a single central sanctuary: maintenance of the sanctuary was rotated among the components of the league month to month throughout the year. The same amphictyonic structure was proposed by the late

Martin Noth as accounting for the twelve-tribe system of Israel, and for a long time this theory enjoyed pride of place in the critical study of Old Testament history. Indeed, there are some strong parallels which still argue in its favor. More recent reflection and study, however, have caused scholars to question whether any one of the premonarchical Israelite sanctuaries (Shechem, Gilgal, Bethel, Shiloh, etc.) was at any one time or successively central to an entire federation. The federation itself, while it undoubtedly existed, may have assumed different structures and strengths at various points in time, and also, it may be more realistic to think of several federations rather than of a single one. It is conceivable that the eventual twelve-tribe pattern in Israel, even though it has some genuine historical roots, is as such a legendary reconstruction of the premonarchical past which was the product rather than the cause of the nation that took shape under David and Solomon. We shall have occasion to return to this subject when we examine chapter 49 of Genesis.

The tribal names as they appear in this story all have been given popular etymologies. These have no correspondence with "real" history, it is true, but they are nonetheless important for tying Israel's ancestors firmly to the only history that it would ever have of them, which is this counting of the fruit of Jacob's marriages. The associations are purely verbal and made-to-order:

Reuben	*J:* "saw my misery" (*ra'ah be'oni*)
	E: "will love me" (*ye'ehabani*) ‡
Simeon	"heard" (*shama*)
Levi	"will become attached" (*yillaweh*)
Judah	"I will give grateful praise" (*odeh*)
Dan	"has vindicated me" (*dananni*)
Naphtali	"I engaged in struggle" (*naftule niftalti*)
Gad	"good luck" (*gad*)
Asher	"good fortune" (*asheri*)
Issachar	"my reward" (*sekari*)
Zebulun	*E:* "brought me a gift" (*zebadani zebed*)
	J: "will offer me presents" (*yizbeleni*)
Joseph	*E:* "has removed" (*asaf*)
	J: "may he add" (*yosef*)

Leah was unloved (literally, "was hated": the Hebrew is not given to fine distinctions) in comparison with Rachel both because she had not been sought by Jacob in the first place and also because of the part she had to take in the deception played on him. The ground is laid for a new variation on the theme of the barren patriarchal wife: not man but God

‡ The original verb here, as Gunkel thought, may have been closer to the spelling of Reuben, before J and E were joined together.

decides the course of providential history, and through Leah rather than through the bride of Jacob's own choice will the greater number of Israelite tribes count their origin. At the same time, when the Lord does at last "remember" Rachel it will be for the birth of Joseph, who as a personality dominates the final portion of Genesis and as a people undeniably presided over the birth of the nation Israel as none other of the tribes did.

Rachel's use of Bilhah in 30:3–8 certainly resembles Sarah's of Hagar in chapter 16 and argues for the kind of legal arrangement we discussed above on 29:14b–30. *Let her give birth on my knees* signifies acknowledgment of a child as one's own (cf. 50:23; Job 3:12); *so that I too may have offspring, at least through her* certainly implies childbearing through surrogate. It is to be noted, too, that in every case it is always Rachel and Leah who name the children, whether they are of their own bodies or of their maids'. The same kind of recourse is much more difficult to predicate of Leah and Zilpah in vss. 9–13, however. Leah, after all, has more than proved her fruitfulness, and there arises no question of providing an heir or otherwise fulfilling her wifely duties. Rather, female rivalry would seem to be at issue and not male legalities.

The J story of the mandrakes in vss. 14–16 is an unfinished fragment. It is altogether likely that it began an account of how Rachel finally obtained fruitfulness and became the mother of Joseph through the application of an old home remedy; and it is equally likely that the Redactor has cut the story short because he and those of his generation no longer deemed it entirely proper. The mandrake or mandragora was not an ordinary food plant but one to which various narcotic and medicinal powers were ascribed, including those of the love draught and the fertility potion. The human form of its divided root (which has contributed by popular etymology to the English "man-drake") called forth these associations for ancient and modern peoples alike in Asia, Europe, and Africa; the Hebrew word for it (*dudai*) relates to "lover" (*dod*), and the fact that its fruit resembles that of the tomato plant doubtless explains why European settlers once gave the name "love apple" to this American perennial. Whatever may have been the original sequel to Rachel's purchase of the mandrakes, however, whatever may have *made her fruitful* (literally, "opened her womb") as J had first told the story, it is made clear in the E of vs. 22 that because *God remembered Rachel* and *heard her prayer* she gave birth to Joseph. The J etymology of Joseph's name in vs. 24 might suggest that once in this version, contrary to the E story of 35:16–20, the conception and birth of Benjamin followed soon on, rounding out the full muster of Jacob's twelve sons. But as we shall see, the location of Benjamin in the chronology of Jacob's family is at best unclear in all the sources.

We turn now to the amusing and somewhat perplexing story of how

Jacob came to collect his "wages" from the wily Laban. The story is amusing, at least to the rough tastes of the campfire gathering among which it
first circulated to the tune of many approving guffaws, as it accurately documents a duel of wits between a favored ancestor and his adversary in-law.
The humor is broad, yet not cruel, since no one is ever really hurt but only
outreached a bit. It is perplexing because it is obviously a composite of
onetime parallel accounts of the same thing, which invites us to inquire
about the presence of sources that have gone into its production. Older
critics without hesitation distributed the verses between J and E, and always in the same computation, but recent commentators have tended to
assign the whole to J. With some reluctance, we find ourselves in
agreement with the later school. There is no doubt that the story is a composition from variants on a common theme, but the technique of composition is authorial rather than redactional: it is a technique that we have already accepted as not atypical of the Yahwist. Accordingly, we put this
section in sequence with the J of vs. 24, recognizing at the same time the
contrary indications that would argue against our doing any such thing.

25 After Rachel gave birth to Joseph, Jacob said to
26 Laban, "Give me leave to go to my homeland. Let
   me have my wives, for whom I served you, and my
   children, too, that I may depart. You know very
27 well the service that I have rendered you." Laban
   answered him: "If you will please . . .
   "I have learned through divination that it is because
28 of you that God* has blessed me. So," he continued,
   "state what wages you want from me, and I will pay
29 them." Jacob replied: "You know what work I did
   for you and how well your livestock fared under
30 my care; the little you had before I came has grown
   into very much, since the LORD's blessings came
   upon you in my company. Therefore I should now
31 do something for my own household as well." "What
   should I pay you?" Laban asked. Jacob answered:
   "You do not have to pay me anything outright. I
   will again pasture and tend your flock, if you do this
32 one thing for me: go through your whole flock today and remove from it every dark animal among
   the sheep and every spotted or speckled one among
33 the goats.† Only such animals shall be my wages. In

* "God" is the reading of the ancient versions; the MT has "Yahweh."
† A partially conjectural reading is being followed here that differs somewhat from
the MT.

the future, whenever you check on these wages of
mine, let my honesty testify against me: any animal
in my possession that is not a speckled or spotted
34 goat, or a dark sheep, got there by theft!" "Very
well," agreed Laban. "Let it be as you say."
35 That same day Laban removed the streaked and
spotted he-goats and all the speckled and spotted
she-goats, all those with some white on them, as
well as the fully dark-colored sheep; these he left
36 . . . in charge of his sons. Then he put a three days'
journey between himself and Jacob, while Jacob
continued to pasture the rest of Laban's flock.
37 Jacob, however, got some fresh shoots of poplar,
almond and plane trees, and he made white stripes
in them by peeling off the bark down to the white
38 core of the shoots. The rods that he had thus peeled
he then set upright in the watering troughs, so that
they would be in front of the animals that drank
from the troughs. When the animals were in heat as
39 they came to drink, the goats mated by the rods,
and so they brought forth streaked, speckled and
40 spotted kids. The sheep, on the other hand, Jacob
kept apart, and he set these animals to face the
streaked or fully-colored animals of Laban. Thus he
produced special flocks of his own, which he did
41 not put with Laban's flock. Moreover, whenever the
hardier animals were in heat, Jacob would set the
rods in the troughs in full view of these animals, so
42 that they mated by the rods; but with the weaker
animals he would not put the rods there. So the fee-
ble animals would go to Laban, but the sturdy ones
43 to Jacob. Thus the man grew increasingly prosperous, and he came to own not only large flocks but
also male and female servants and camels and asses.

The attentive reader will already have seen why this story is judged to
be a composite. Not once but a couple of times Jacob calls to Laban's attention the service he has rendered him and announces his intention to see
to his own household, and not once but twice does Laban respond by an
offer of wages. Jacob does not and then does demand compensation, and
what he asks for eventually in vss. 32–34 is not precisely what he obtains
through his own devices in vss. 37–42. (The discrepancy is more evident
in other translations than in the NAB, which follows the lead of the ancient
versions in approximating the sense of vs. 32 to that of vs. 35.) There is a

bewildering display of adjectives applying to the animals of Laban's flocks, more than is necessary, one feels, unless they are the residue of multiple descriptions. And, as the NAB indicates by its ellipses in vss. 27 and 35, there are unfilled gaps in the text which suggest that the author had either too little or too much material to work with when he composed his narrative.

All this is bound to be of relatively small interest, however, since it hardly affects the interpretation that the biblical author has intended us to attach to the story. *After Rachel gave birth to Joseph* presupposes, of course, at least the J contribution to the combined narrative of 29:31–30:24 preceding, and the *for whom I served you* of vs. 26 implies as original in the J tradition (unless, indeed, this verse is really E, as older critics maintained) some kind of family arrangement like that told about in the Elohist's story of 29:14b–30. Jacob's proposal of a new work contract, nevertheless, is here premised less on his faithful completion of the terms of an old one than it is on an appeal to equity in view of the prosperity that has come to Laban through his service. Far from rebuffing the argument, Laban eagerly acquiesces in it and even volunteers corroboration of his own: he has inquired of Yahweh (cf. 25:22) and has ascertained that because of Jacob he has been blessed. (We judge "Yahweh" to be original in vs. 27 rather than the NAB's "God." Later transmitters of the text, but hardly the Yahwist himself, experienced scruples over putting the name of Yahweh on Laban's lips or having the God of Israel respond to an act of divination.) We need not suspect any insincerity on Laban's part in acknowledging the justice of Jacob's claim, for all that he was also reluctant to lose an extraordinarily valuable worker to whom it had not occurred to him previously to offer any wages.

Jacob's terms, at least in the resultant form they assume in the story as we have it above, must have seemed ingenuously agreeable to Laban and have occasioned him an audible sigh of relief. In Near Eastern flocks sheep and goats are pastured together (cf. Ezekiel 34:17; Matthew 25:32), and the rule is white sheep, black goats; *a speckled or spotted goat, or a dark sheep* are the rare exceptions to this rule. It is, then, a meager enough reward that Jacob was requesting. Already the canny old man was turning over in his mind the scheme he immediately put to work in vss. 35–36, whereby he planned to reduce Jacob's chances from minimum to nil. Had he not been so occupied in his own cleverness, he might have turned a more suspicious ear to what he was hearing, and even, perhaps, a cynical ear when the words *let my honesty testify against me* surfaced in the discussion—for Jacob, of course, also had plans of his own. The two men, uncle and nephew, father-in-law and son-in-law, had had numerous years of living together in which to take each other's measure, but quite plainly it was Jacob and not Laban who had proved to be the apter pupil in this common school of learning.

In vs. 35 we discover for the first time that Laban has sons; they reappear in 31:1, which is also J. Above, discussing the possibility of a Nuzi background for the story of 29:14b–30, we allowed for the later birth of these sons to add a codicil to the adoption-marriage arrangement which the story might presume. We must also admit an alternative, however. The alternative is, simply, that in J Laban has sons, and in E he does not. In the E part of chapter 31 the story of 29:14b–30 will be picked up again (cf. especially vs. 41), but we do not know, even despite 30:26 above (if it is J and not E after all), what the Yahwist has as the equivalent of this earlier, Nuzi account. At all events, the biblical author intends only to say in these verses that Laban adopted a shrewd ruse to frustrate Jacob's interests in his flocks by the elementary device of separating by *a three days' journey in charge of his sons* that only part of them which could be of use to his son-in-law. Laban reckoned, of course, without the counterruse of Jacob. He also overreached himself by making possible (cf. 31:19.22 below) entirely on his own hook Jacob's later departure by stealth.

A modern husbandman would hardly try to breed his flocks by adhering to the Jacob schedule of vss. 37–42. It was by the lights of its time, however, quite scientific. First, by producing alternate stripes of dark and light in the *rods of poplar, almond and plane trees* which Jacob *set upright in the watering troughs* frequented by Laban's goats when they *were in heat,* he managed to produce from them a breed of *streaked, speckled and spotted kids.* (The white stripes had counteracted the dominant black otherwise typical of the goat.) Then he had the sheep—white, we recall—couple in full view of the streaked goats that he had so far produced, and so they gave birth to uncharacteristically darker animals which would fall to his lot. Thus he gained by his wits a large flock of pied goats and mottled sheep, a very unusual thing, and soon the source of abundant wealth, *not only large flocks but also male and female servants and camels and asses.* As an added tweak of his father-in-law's nose, Jacob selected for his genetic improvements only the better animals and left the culls for Laban. There is no point in trying to justify these machinations ethically any more than there is to reconcile them with a contemporary notion of how prenatal influences can be transmitted to fetal life. The *poplar* (*libneh*) and the *white stripes* (*lebanoth*) which Jacob peeled down *to the white core* (*laban*) *of the shoots* obviously play on the name of Laban.

In the final chapter of this Laban and Jacob epic we again return to a composite of J and E. This time E is in the dominance and will be indicated as such by roman type, while we shall point out the J contributions by the use of italics.

31 *Jacob learned that Laban's sons were saying, "Jacob has taken everything that belonged to our father, and he has accumulated all this wealth of his by* **2** *using our father's property."* Jacob perceived, too, that Laban's attitude toward him was not what it **3** had previously been. *Then the* LORD *said to Jacob, "Return to the land of your fathers, where you were born, and I will be with you."*

4 So Jacob sent for Rachel and Leah to meet him **5** where he was in the field with his flock. There he said to them: "I have noticed that your father's attitude toward me is not as it was in the past; but the **6** God of my father has been with me. You well know **7** what effort I put into serving your father; yet your father cheated me and changed my wages time after time. God, however, did not let him do me any **8** harm. Whenever your father said, 'The speckled animals shall be your wages,' the entire flock would bear speckled young; whenever he said, 'The streaked animals shall be your wages,' the entire **9** flock would bear streaked young. Thus God reclaimed your father's livestock and gave it to me. **10** Once, in the breeding season, I had a dream in which I saw mating he-goats that were streaked, **11** speckled and mottled. In the dream God's messenger **12** called to me, 'Jacob!' 'Here!' I replied. Then he said, 'Note well. All the he-goats in the flocks, as they mate, are streaked, speckled and mottled, for I have seen all the things that Laban has been doing **13** to you. I am the God who appeared to you in Bethel,‡ where you anointed a memorial stone and made a vow to me. Up, then! Leave this land and return to the land of your birth.' "

14 Rachel and Leah answered him: "Have we still an **15** heir's portion in our father's house? Are we not regarded by him as outsiders? He not only sold us; he has even used up the money that he got for us! **16** All the wealth that God reclaimed from our father really belongs to us and our children. Therefore, do, **17** just as God has told you." *Jacob proceeded to put* **18** *his children and wives on camels,* **and he drove off**

‡ Literally, "I am El Bethel who appeared to you . . ."

**with all his livestock and all the property he had
acquired in Paddan-aram, to go to his father Isaac
in the land of Canaan.**

The boldfaced type indicates the rare occurrence of P in these verses, a fragment which remains from the narrative that once continued and complemented 27:46–28:9.

Like Abraham (see above on 12:1–9), Jacob is summoned by his God—in J Yahweh, in E the God with whom he had covenanted at Bethel —to make his way from Haran to the land of Canaan. The divine will is manifested, as is so frequently the case, to the accompaniment of events that cause it to emerge as the dictate of a sense of what must be done. In J the envy and hostility of Laban's sons convince Jacob that his welcome in their midst has long been worn out and that any hopes he has for a tranquil future will have to be realized somewhere else. In E it is the conduct of the old man himself which prepares Jacob for the idea that a severance of their relations is desirable. We note that while some of the details in the "salary" arrangements between Jacob and Laban are the same in the E of vss. 6–13 and the J of chapter 30 above, the two traditions have quite gone their separate ways in developing their stories. In E the color factor which was to be the determinant of those animals which would fall to Jacob's share has been Laban's initiative, and he has changed it at will to suit, as he hoped, his own advantage. The thought expressed by these verses is sometimes a bit opaque, but the general idea is clear: E will have it that Jacob's prosperity had been achieved not through his successful finessing of an opponent in a game of sharp and questionable play on both sides but rather through the providence of a God who had evened the unfair odds that had been declared against him. With regard to "the God of Bethel" see above on 28:10–22.

Some of the other particulars of the E story are not too clear. Jacob summons his wives *to meet him where he was in the field with his flock.* Nothing more or less may be meant than that he was assuring privacy for a family council, though we may also be asked to admire Jacob's conscientiousness in refusing to leave the work he had contracted to do. What is intriguing is the council itself. On the one hand, it permits Jacob an elaborate justification of himself in the presence of his womenfolk, a gesture of male vanity not unfamiliar to the Bible. It also implies, however, that Jacob is not a totally free agent. Not only must he have Leah's and Rachel's consent that they and their children go with him to Canaan—the legalities presupposed by 24:57–59 may be involved—he must also implicate them in a covert flight which Laban apparently has both the power and the right to prevent if he chooses. It is not, as Gerhard von Rad would have it, that Jacob was proposing the "unusual" dissolution of a *father's house* (*beth ab*, vs. 14), the extended family which was "the real owner of the land worked by individual families." The extended family, normally made up of four generations (Leviticus 18:6–17), certainly existed, but nowhere does it appear to have impinged on the autonomy of the basic family structure of Israel, the union of husband and wife and children. Furthermore, nowhere else in these chapters does it appear that Jacob was in any way bound to the land; like his ancestors before him and his descendants after him he was a sojourner, a wayfarer. His contract with Laban, in J or in E, was purely personal.

Are we, then, brought back to the putative situation of 29:14b–30 (E), to the possibility that a legal arrangement only half remembered by the biblical writer has been preserved here, according to which Jacob was bound to Laban in an adoption-marriage relationship? It is difficult to give an unqualified yes to this question. Jacob does not talk like an heir seeking to avoid family squabbles over testamentary details. He does not talk at all like one who has any stake whatever in remaining where he is in Laban's environment, who would have to defend his certain rights against other certain rights. He talks merely like one who is fed up with an unsatisfactory work agreement in which he can see no clear future for himself or his family, and he wants to escape it by whatever means he can.

Leah's and Rachel's response to Jacob only adds to the confusion. First of all, they set his mind at ease: they are even more willing than he to sever their ties with Laban and to join their husband whither his God is beckoning him. Why? Not, obviously, because of bothersome technicalities by which men set store, but because of solid and practical realities. They are, for one thing, *regarded by* their father *as outsiders*, as *nokriyoth*, foreigners, servant maids in the household rather than those who have *an heir's portion* therein. Laban no longer treats them as his daughters but has abandoned them to the fate of the man they have married: he himself has cast their lot with Jacob rather than with himself. *He not only sold us; he has even used up the money that he got for us!* The "sold" and the "used up" (literally, "eaten") of this verse have their parallels in Nuzi sources, referring to the *mohar* or bridal price paid in a marriage (cf. Genesis 34:12), and might, at first glance, reinforce the suspicion that a Hurrian background lurks behind this story. But where, in any of the preceding episodes in the Jacob-Laban story, has it appeared that Jacob paid a *mohar* for either Rachel or Leah? We seem to be dealing with this issue here for the first time, not as something with which we have already been familiarized. In short, it is impossible to extract a truly coherent account from the data we have before us that will correspond exactly with any suggested paradigm. *"All the wealth that God reclaimed from our father,"* Jacob's wives loyally profess, echoing his faith and his interpretation of past events, *"really belongs to us and our children"—lebanenu,* "to our children," and not to Laban.

19 *Now Laban had gone away to shear his sheep,* and Rachel had meanwhile appropriated her father's
20 household idols. Jacob had hoodwinked Laban the Aramean by not telling him of his intended flight.
21 *Thus he made his escape with all that he had. Once he was across the Euphrates, he headed for the highlands of Gilead.*
22 *On the third day, word came to Laban that Jacob*
23 *had fled.* Taking his kinsmen with him, *he pursued him for seven days until he caught up with him in*
24 *the hill country of Gilead.* But that night God appeared to Laban the Aramean in a dream and warned him. "Take care not to threaten Jacob with any harm."
25 When Laban overtook Jacob, Jacob's tents were pitched in the highlands; *Laban also pitched his*
26 *tents there, on Mount Gilead.* "What do you mean," Laban demanded of Jacob, "by hoodwinking me and carrying off my daughters like war captives?
27 *Why did you dupe me by stealing away secretly? You should have told me, and I would have sent you off with merry singing to the sound of tam-*
28 *bourines and harps.* You did not even allow me a parting kiss to my daughters and grandchildren!
29 What you have now done is a senseless thing. I have it in my power to harm all of you; but last night the God of your* father said to me, 'Take care not to
30 threaten Jacob with any harm!' *Granted that you had to leave because you were desperately home-sick for your father's house,* why did you steal my
31 gods?" *"I was frightened,"* Jacob replied to Laban, *"at the thought that you might take your daughters*
32 *away from me by force.* But as for your gods, the one you find them with shall not remain alive! If, with my kinsmen looking on, you identify anything here as belonging to you, take it." Jacob, of course, had no idea that Rachel had stolen the idols.
33 Laban then went in and searched Jacob's tent and

* This is a plural in the Hebrew: not Jacob's only, but his and his entourage's.

Leah's tent, as well as the tents of the two maidservants; but he did not find the idols. Leaving
34 Leah's tent, he went into Rachel's. Now Rachel
had taken the idols, put them inside a camel cushion,
and seated herself upon them. When Laban had
rummaged through the rest of her tent without find-
35 ing them, Rachel said to her father, "Let not my lord
feel offended that I cannot rise in your presence; a
woman's period is upon me." So, despite his search,
36 he did not find his idols. *Jacob, now enraged, up-
braided Laban.* "What crime or offense have I committed," he demanded, "that you should hound me
37 so fiercely? Now that you have ransacked all my
things, have you found a single object taken from
your belongings? If so, produce it here before your
kinsmen and mine, and let them decide between us
two.

38 *"In the twenty years that I was under you, no ewe
or she-goat of yours ever miscarried, and I have
39 never feasted on a ram of your flock. I never
brought you an animal torn by wild beasts; I made
good the loss myself. You held me responsible for
40 anything stolen by day or night. How often the
scorching heat ravaged me by day, and the frost by
41 night, while sleep fled from my eyes!* Of the twenty
years that I have now spent in your household, I
slaved fourteen years for your two daughters and
six years for your flock, while you changed my
42 wages time after time. If my ancestral God, the God
of Abraham and the Awesome One of Isaac, had not
been on my side, you would now have sent me away
empty-handed. But God saw my plight and the fruits
of my toil, and last night he gave judgment."

Already in vs. 18 the Priestly author had Jacob make his departure from
Paddan-aram, and in 33:18 he will be seen safely back in Canaan, with
nothing intervening described. It will be remembered that only in P (as far
as we know) had Jacob come to Laban's house expressly to obtain a wife,
and it is not likely that in this tradition there was ever anything resembling
the J and E theme of enmity between uncle and nephew. No more than to
illustrate the historical rivalry between Edom and Israel (see above on
27:46–28:9) does P show any interest in using the patriarchal legends to

emblemize the relationship of Israel to Aram with pejorative implications for the latter.

In both J and E, for reasons which, we have seen, are never made entirely clear, Jacob's leave-taking of Laban's presence must take the form of a *flight*, an *escape*. According to J, *Laban had gone away to shear his sheep*, removing himself by a three days' journey (cf. vs. 22 and 30:36 above); a sheepshearing was a major social occasion, accompanied by entertainment and feasting over a period of some days (cf. 2 Samuel 13:23–28). It is perhaps significant in our context that neither Jacob nor any of his people have any part in Laban's festivities. Anyway, Laban's absence and his exclusion of Jacob from his company facilitate the hasty assembling and provisioning of a caravan and its setting forth south and west toward Canaan, *across the Euphrates* and *headed for the highlands of Gilead*. E includes a delightful play on words in vss. 19b–20, repeated by Laban in vss. 26.30b, which it is impossible to reproduce in translation: *Rachel had meanwhile appropriated* (literally, "she stole") *her father's household idols,* and *Jacob had hoodwinked Laban* (literally, "he stole his heart"). This latter idiom, which has its almost exact equivalent in other languages, "means to deprive someone of insight, to deceive him" (Hans Walter Wolff): "heart" in Hebrew is the same as our "mind," the seat of knowledge, understanding, forethought (cf. Psalm 44:22; Proverbs 15:11, etc.).

The theft of Laban's heart is more readily explicable than the theft of his "household idols" (*teraphim*) by Rachel: in vs. 30b Laban identifies these simply as *my gods*. We remember the lines in Gadd 51, the Nuzi document which we cited above in connection with 29:14b–30 (E), in which the gods of the testator figured importantly in the contractual obligations assumed by the parties. They were, it would appear, the prima-facie credentials of the chief heir or paterfamilias in the family succession. Thus, it has been thought, Rachel's "appropriation" of Laban's *teraphim* on the eve of her departure from her father's house was to ensure the legitimacy of Jacob's claim to the inheritance for which he had bargained in good faith and for which he had long labored. The hypothesis has its likelihood, especially in view of the fact that Laban's natural sons, who by Nuzi terms would have had the right to his gods before Jacob, make their appearance only in J and have no place at all in this E story. But there are difficulties to give us pause. For one thing, Jacob seems to be totally unaware of what is going on, though we might suppose he would have had more than a passing interest in securing the rights he had acquired by the toil he describes so eloquently below. He is not only ignorant of Rachel's action, he thinks the idea that anyone should have done such a thing preposterous and ludicrous: he is brought to the limit of making a foolish oath (vs. 32) taken without heed of the possible consequences (like Saul's in 1

Samuel 14:23b–46 or Jephthah's in Judges 11:30–40). And furthermore, in Nuzi law the household gods descend and have their efficacy after the testator's death, not while he is yet alive. In no way does it seem that a living Laban could have been much affected by Jacob's having his lares and penates, except that he understandably wanted his property restored. And Jacob, as we have said, besides not even knowing that he has these things, is interested only in putting distance between himself and his father-in-law, not in inheriting his goods.

The *teraphim* turn up elsewhere in the Hebrew Bible. Whatever they were originally, they made no uniform imprint on the tradition, a good sign that they were half-forgotten things like Urim and Thummim and the Ephod and a number of other cultic devices of the distant past. In Hosea 3:4 *massebah* (cf. 28:18), *ephod* (cf. Exodus 28:15–30), and *teraphim* are mentioned together in the same breath, apparently as three externals along with a fourth, "sacrifice," of an Israelite worship that was deemed to be rubrically proper. In 1 Samuel 19:13.16 the *teraphim* (here by exception taken as a singular rather than a plural) assume a man-sized form, but otherwise (as in vss. 34–35 above, quite evidently) they are small objects, entirely compatible with the hearth deities familiar to us from ancient Rome, from popular Catholicism, and from the Canaan of even Israelite times which cast clay *astartes* by the thousands. There is no reason to conclude that the *teraphim* which Rachel brought with her from Aram Naharaim were anything other than family talismans which were dear to her and which she was later forced by her husband to abandon at Bethel (cf. 35:4). Laban wanted these heirlooms even more than his daughter did, and of course he had the right to them that she did not.

Laban successfully overtakes Jacob *in the hill country of Gilead,* which will lend a geographical index to the pact enacted in vss. 43–54. Meanwhile, according to the E of vs. 24 (cf. vs. 42) God has intervened, as he already had in vss. 10–13, to persuade Laban to deal magniloquently if not magnificently with Jacob, forgoing his "rights" (which probably means his *force majeure*) in favor of beneficence. Therefore neither in J nor in E does Laban assert any claim that he has on Jacob aside from those of family piety and natural decency. Had Jacob only done what he did through regular channels, Laban says, there would be no problem. A parting kiss *to daughters and grandchildren:* how little disposition he had shown for such affection before, we know, but now no matter. Family piety may also be considered the title under which Laban presses his complaint in the one area where both God and man must surely agree his grievance is real: who has stolen away his house gods? Alas, in this quest, too, the old intriguer is doomed to disappointment. Jacob, blissfully ignorant of his wife's theft, is not only not put to any disadvantage by Laban's accusation, he is rather reinforced by it and by the subsequent fruitless search of his belongings in the righteous disdain he feels for Laban and his methods: what now happens is simply the latest in a long line of consistently gratuitous indignities he has had to endure at the hands of his bullying father-in-law. As for Rachel, she proves herself to be her father's daughter, though hardly in such a way as to give joy to her sire, even had he penetrated her stratagem.

Now Jacob experiences that orgastic pleasure which is sometimes the undeserved reward of one not overscrupulous in his own dealings who discovers himself unassailably in the moral advantage over another who has misused him. And he is not slow to savor the pleasure. In E his protestations against Laban take over a familiar form as he rehearses the circumstances of his fourteen years' service for Laban's daughters (29:14b–30) and an ensuing *six years* (only here given as six) of labor *for your flock* during which the proprietor had tried to bilk him by changing the terms of their contract at his whim (vss. 6–7 above). He gives credit, as he did before when speaking to his wives (in vss. 10–13), to the God whom Laban himself has acknowledged (vs. 29), for having protected his interests then and lately: *last night he gave judgment.* This *ancestral God,* however, he now names not El Bethel but *the God of Abraham and the Awesome One of Isaac.* The same "Awesome One of Isaac" appears as the name of the Deity by whom Jacob swears in the covenant of vs. 53b below. The title, probably, has not been borrowed from any of the pre-Israelite shrines of Canaan (though one is tempted to think of the Mizpah of vs. 49 or the Mahanaim of 32:3 in this connection), but was more likely simply a surrogate for "the God of Isaac" popularized in Israelite cult and poetry.

If we were to take vs. 41 to be in literal conjunction with 30:25, as the Redactor, undeniably, has invited the literalist to read the text, then we would have to assume that all of Jacob's twelve children from Reuben to Joseph (29:31–30:24) were conceived and born within a seven-year period (cf. 29:23–30). Not impossible given four wives, certainly, but certainly impossible when one of the wives, Leah, has borne seven of the children and experienced the while a period of unproductivity (29:35). The conflation of sources has something to do with this rather curious narrative product, of course, but over and beyond is the character of saga that penetrates both sources and declares them outside the literalist's bounds. Computations of this kind are exactly the sort of thing that poses pseudo-problems for biblical interpretation.

In J Jacob speaks not so much like a servant who has been abused and cheated as he does like one whose dedicated and honest labor has never been properly appreciated but instead was ignored and not even niggardly rewarded. *No ewe or she-goat of yours ever miscarried:* this testifies both to Jacob's care and to his integrity, for Laban can lay no claim to any lamb or kid unaccounted for. *I have never feasted on a ram of your flock* again certifies both that Jacob has purloined nothing of Laban's and also that Laban has offered him nothing out of generosity. *I never brought you an animal torn by wild beasts:* Jacob has never taken the legal recourse to excuse himself of unavoidable depredation on the flocks consigned to his care (Exodus 22:12); rather, he simply absorbed the loss. All this (conveniently overlooking his own manipulation of providence in 30:25–43?) under a conscienceless and ruthless taskmaster day by harsh day and night by frigid night. And all this—here J agrees with E—for twenty years, a small generation of man.

> 43 Laban replied to Jacob: "The women are mine, their children are mine, and the flocks are mine; everything you see belongs to me. But since these women are my daughters, I will now do something for them
> 44 and for the children they have borne. Come, then, we will make a pact, you and I; the LORD† shall be a witness between us."
> 45 Then Jacob took a stone and set it up as a memorial
> 46 stone. *Jacob said to his kinsmen, "Gather some stones." So they got some stones and made a mound,*
> 47 *and they had a meal there at the mound.* Laban called it Jegar-sahadutha, but Jacob called it Galeed.
> 48 *"This mound," said Laban, "shall be a witness from now on between you and me." That is why it was*
> 49 *named Galeed*—and also Mizpah, for he said: "May the LORD‡ keep watch between you and me
> 50 when we are out of each other's sight. If you mistreat my daughters, remember that even though no one else is about, God will be witness between you and me."
> 51 *Laban said further to Jacob: "Here is this mound,* and here is the memorial stone *that I have set up*
> 52 *between you and me. This mound shall be witness,* and this memorial stone shall be witness, *that, with hostile intent, neither may I pass beyond this mound into* your territory nor may you pass beyond it into
> 53 mine. *May the God of Abraham and the God of Nahor [their ancestral deities]* maintain justice between us!"*

† Not in the Hebrew. The LXX has: "that there may be a witness . . ."
‡ The LXX has "God," probably rightly.
* Undoubtedly a redactional gloss.

Jacob took the oath by the Awesome One of Isaac.
54 He then offered a sacrifice on the mountain and invited his kinsmen to share in the meal. When they
had eaten, they passed the night on the mountain.
32 Early the next morning, Laban kissed his grandchildren and his daughters goodbye; then he set out on
2 his journey back home, while Jacob continued on his
own way. Then God's messengers encountered Ja-
3 cob. When he saw them he said, "This is God's encampment." So he named that place Mahanaim.

Laban affects to be singularly unimpressed by Jacob's oratory: four
times he reasserts his ownership over all that is in the possession of his
son-in-law, stopping short only of declaring Jacob himself still bound to
him. But however we are to construe his claim, either as having a legal
basis never made unambiguously clear or simply as a piece of bluff dependent on the naked power that allows him to do what he chooses to do,
it adds up to nothing much more than bluster. He has been inhibited by
God from harming Jacob in any way, legally or illegally, and therefore he
must make the best of a very bad bargain. What shall he do, then, after all
this mustering of his forces for a punitive expedition that, after all, has
come to nought? He gropes for a face-saving device. *Since these women
are my daughters,* he triumphantly concludes, *I will now do something for
them and for the children they have borne.* It was little enough he had
done before, and it is even less now. He will make a pact with Jacob,
which will do little more than signify his agreement to the *fait accompli*
with which Jacob has already presented him.

The covenant between Laban and Jacob is recorded by both J and E. In
E it is marked by a *memorial stone* which obviously implies a play on
words with *Mizpah* (i.e., *massebah* and *misepah*) as well as with the *keep
watch* (*yisep*) of vs. 49. That there was a memorial stone there strongly
suggests the presence of a cult legend, and there is no doubt that Mizpah
of Gilead was a cult center in early Israelite times (cf. Judges 10:17,
11:11.29). Whether in our text there is enough evidence to make us look
for the residue of a local cult tradition is another matter. As we have already insinuated above, we consider the LORD of vss. 44 and 49 in the
NAB to be incorrect readings of the text. Rather, we would suspect that in
view of the designation of Laban as "the Aramean" in vss. 20.24 above,
the E version of the Laban-Jacob covenant is a variant on the J story,
which is a reminiscence of an ancient boundary agreement between
Arameans and Israelites (cf. the *his kinsmen* of vs. 54). This, despite the
evident effort of the biblical author to personalize the pact as one of
Laban's belated concern for his daughters and their children, not only in

vss. 43–44 but also in vss. 49–50, and in the touching farewell of 32:1. In vs. 50 something is said about the Semitic notion of a solemn oath and its consequences: *remember that even though no one else is about, God will be witness between you and me.* The covenant is ratified in vs. 54 not only with *a sacrifice* (as in the E version of the ratification of the covenant of Sinai in Exodus 24:3–8) but also with a *meal* (as in the J version of the same event, Exodus 24:1–2.9–11). *The mountain* of this verse is, of course, "the highlands" of vs. 25 above.

The J story of the covenant between Laban and Jacob more overtly recalls a non-aggression pact between Aram and Israel that lurks somewhere in the remembered past of a source that is very much attuned to national memories. Here the sign of the covenant is *a mound* of stones, a cairn, which even to this day is in the Near East a conventional memorial of an agreement. The mound is called by Laban *Jegar-sahadutha,* which is a passable Aramaic equivalent of Jacob's *Galeed* (i.e., *gal 'ed,* "the mound of witness"), which evokes, of course, Mount Gilead (vs. 25 above) where all this occurs. To the separate names of the mound obviously correspond *the God of Abraham and the God of Nahor* of vs. 53, which (as the gloss in the text correctly indicates) means the Gods separately revered by Jacob and Laban, even though the Yahwist doubtless thought of them as one and the same God. Again (vs. 46) a covenant *meal* seals the bargain. Gilead, generally considered to be that part of the Transjordan bounded on the north by the Yarmuk and on the south by the Jabbok, throughout most of Israelite history was reckoned to be integral to that Land of Promise which lay mostly to the west of the Jordan, that is, the land of Canaan, or, in later terms, Palestine. Always, however, it was a land in dispute. The main disputant with Israel of Gilead's autonomy was, in the biblical authors' time, Aram (cf. Amos 1:3–5, for example). It would be impossible to determine at what time and under what circumstances the pact of vss. 46–48.51–53 was established between Israelites and Arameans that banished the latter irrevocably from the land of Gilead. All that we can be very sure of is that it was a pact soon broken which had left behind it a heap of stones no more negotiable than later scraps of paper have come to be in the currency of modern statecraft.

The Elohist concludes the story of Jacob and Laban in 32:1–2a, returning Laban to his home and sending Jacob on his way; but in vss. 2b–3, with hardly a break in his stride, he adds that *God's messengers encountered Jacob.* What are we to make of this unusual transition? For one thing, we are being given a popular/historical etymology for the *place Mahanaim,* a site that can be located with fair certainty east of the Jordan on the Jabbok and which certainly figured prominently in Israelite history (cf. 2 Samuel 2:12.29, 17:24.27; 1 Kings 4:14, etc.). Jacob says, *"This is God's encampment"—mahaneh elohim=mahanaim.* But such can hardly be the whole purpose of these verses. God's "messengers," we know by now, are avatars for God himself. We seem to have in this fragmentary note a parallel to the even more perplexing narrative of vss. 23–33 below, in which Jacob is confronted on his entrance to the land to which he has been bidden and which is yet forbidden to the casual interloper by a divine protector whose conditions must be satisfied as the price of entry. Here the theme is not pursued, but we are forewarned that he who has contended with man—Laban—will now have to contend with God (see vs. 29 below). Thus the passage provides a fitting end to the rather lengthy Jacob and Laban episode.

5. Jacob the Patriarch

There seems to be no problem whatever about assigning the following small section to J. It is the Yahwist's conception of how a fearful Jacob returning from Aram Naharaim planned to meet up with a potentially hostile Esau (cf. 25:21–34, 27:1–45) and of the prudent measures he accordingly took.

4 Jacob sent messengers ahead to his brother Esau in 5 the land of Seir, the country of Edom, with this message: "Thus shall you say to my lord Esau: 'Your servant Jacob speaks as follows: I have been staying with Laban and have been detained there 6 until now. I own cattle, asses and sheep, as well as male and female servants. I am sending my lord this information in the hope of gaining your 7 favor.'" When the messengers returned to Jacob, they said, "We reached your brother Esau. He is now coming to meet you, accompanied by four 8 hundred men." Jacob was very much frightened. In his anxiety, he divided the people who were with him, as well as his flocks, herds, and camels, into 9 two camps. "If Esau should attack and overwhelm one camp," he reasoned, "the remaining camp may 10 still survive." Then he prayed, "O God of my father Abraham and God of my father Isaac! You told me, O LORD, 'Go back to the land of your birth,

11 and I will be good to you.' I am unworthy of all the
acts of kindness that you have loyally performed
for your servant: although I crossed the Jordan
here with nothing but my staff, I have now grown
12 into two companies. Save me, I pray from the hand
of my brother Esau! Otherwise I fear that when he
comes he will strike me down and slay the mothers
13 and children. You yourself said, 'I will be very
good to you, and I will make your descendants
like the sands of the sea, which are too numerous
to count.' "

14a After passing the night there . . .

We are probably not supposed to inquire too closely into the inner logic
of the story or its total harmony with the rest of the Jacob saga. After
twenty years, a period which Jacob manages to insinuate was an unwanted
hindrance to normal family relations—*staying with Laban and detained
there until now*—he seems to assume that nothing has changed since he
and Esau were boys together, that his twin brother must still bear against
him the grudge for past injuries that precipitated his earlier flight. Further,
though how we know not, Jacob appears to be well aware of Esau's capability of doing him real harm, now that—again through some unexplained
transformation—he has become a powerful chieftain who commands a
formidable private army. Jacob's mention of his own affluence in vs. 6 is
doubtless intended to suggest a willingness to share and to let Esau know
that he may have freely by benevolence what it is not necessary for him to
wrest away by force. The message is, perhaps, a bit naïve, but it also has
about it a dignity that is muted in the obsequiousness of the following
chapter—though it is also true that Jacob's fulsomeness there can partly
be excused by the relief that he undoubtedly felt.

Jacob's messengers return with a report that he finds ominous. Anticipating the worst, he divides his caravan *into two camps* (this expression,
translated *two companies* in vs. 11, allows the Yahwist to call to mind the
Mahanaim of vs. 3); the entirely pragmatic purpose of this measure,
which seems to be forgotten in the verses that follow, is simply to provide
for survivors of an attack that is deemed almost certain. The Yahwist will
not have us believe, however, that Jacob has entirely given himself over to
despair: in vss. 10–13 he is discovered in the hithertofore unusual posture
of humble, reliant prayer, anxiously waiting on providence instead of trying to anticipate it. In vs. 13 reference is made to the earlier J 28:13–15,
and in vs. 10 the J of 31:1.3 is recalled. There is no reason to regard
Jacob's prayer as a pious intrusion into the text, nor is there any incom-
patibility between it and the precautions he had taken. It may be thought,

however, that the Yahwist has introduced it from another, parallel context, perhaps compressing his narrative in the process. That might explain *the Jordan here* of vs. 11, since the surrounding context still supposes the action to be taking place well within the Transjordan. (An alternative hypothesis is to presume that "Jordan" has been for some reason substituted for an earlier "Jabbok.") In any case, the geography of chapters 31–33 is not necessarily always consistent.

The temporal clause into which the NAB has cast vs. 14a obscures its original character as the conclusion of a preceding episode rather than the introduction to a new one. "And he passed the night there" is the letter of the Hebrew, essentially the same formula that concludes the following verses, which constitute the E parallel to the J story we have just seen.

14b Jacob selected from what he had with him the fol-
15 lowing presents for his brother Esau: two hundred
   she-goats and twenty he-goats; two hundred ewes
16 and twenty rams; thirty milch camels and their
   young; forty cows and ten bulls; twenty she-asses
17 and ten he-asses. He put these animals in charge of
   his servants, in separate droves, and he told the servants, "Go on ahead of me, but keep a space be-
18 tween one drove and the next." To the servant in
   the lead he gave this instruction: "When my brother
   Esau meets you, he may ask you, 'Whose man are
   you? Where are you going? To whom do these ani-
19 mals ahead of you belong?' Then you shall answer,
   'They belong to your brother Jacob, but they
   have been sent as a gift to my lord Esau; and Ja-
20 cob himself is right behind us.'" He gave similar
   instructions to the second servant and the third and
   to all the others who followed behind the droves,
   namely: "Thus and thus shall you say to Esau,
21 when you reach him; and be sure to add, 'Your
   servant Jacob is right behind us.'" For Jacob
   reasoned, "If I first appease him with gifts that pre-
   cede me, then later, when I face him, perhaps he
22 will forgive me." So the gifts went on ahead of
   him, while he stayed that night in the camp.

We do not know what, in the E story of the boyhood of Jacob and Esau that has not been preserved by Genesis, were the correspondents of the J of 25:27–34 and 27:1–45, the grievances that had set brother against brother and were now a source of anxiety to Jacob coming into the ambit of his powerful and presumably long-memoried twin. Perhaps they were nothing so serious as those represented by the Yahwist. The *appease him* of vs. 21 is a fair enough translation, but the verb need not refer to anything objectively expiable; in like manner, *perhaps he will forgive me* in this same verse is possibly too explicit: "perhaps he will be favorable to me" would do equally well. Benno Jacob is one who has pointed out the relevance of this passage to Proverbs 16:14–15 (where "appease" is translated "pacify" by the NAB): Jacob may merely have been taking account of "the evil things that are in the childish hearts of kings" as he prepared to meet with a local suzerain who had it in his power and at his whim to spoil or favor him, with or without regard to family ties.

The camp is divided again, now not in two but in multiple divisions, and not as a survival measure but for the purpose of simultaneously stimulating and slaking a desert lord's thirst for placating gifts, as is adequately explicated by Jacob's reasoning in vs. 21. About five hundred and eighty animals are involved in the "gift," a truly noble and exuberant gesture that must challenge a kindred spirit to equal flamboyance. The challenge is not issued in vain, as we see below.

In vss. 21–22 the word "face" (*panim*) occurs five times, usually in idioms untranslatable literally. The reference to the Peniel episode that follows—no matter who is responsible for this—is unmistakable. Similarly, the "gifts" (*minhah*) and the "camp" (*mahaneh*) of vs. 22 can hardly have no connection with the Mahanaim of vs. 3 above (E).

And now we come to a really perplexing passage, which could as easily flow from vs. 14a as from vs. 22b, or—and this may be the most obvious conclusion—from neither one nor the other. Older critics took the easier course of distributing it between J and E, and indeed it does contain elements that suggest both sources. The more recent commentators who strive for an economy of source material tend to assign it to a single strand of tradition, which generally turns out to be J. Undoubtedly it has more in common with J than it does with any other thing in Genesis, but not so much as to make the attribution easy and certain. We prefer to recognize here a crucial redactional section which has been brought in from a combination of earlier source materials. The importance of these verses is undeniable, whencever the Redactor chose to draw them.

> 23 In the course of that night, however, Jacob arose,
> took his two wives, with the two maidservants and
> his eleven children, and crossed the ford of the
> 24 Jabbok. After he had taken them across the stream
> 25 and had brought over all his possessions, Jacob was
> left there alone. Then some man wrestled with him
> 26 until the break of dawn. When the man saw that he
> could not prevail over him, he struck Jacob's hip at
> its socket, so that the hip socket was wrenched as

27 they wrestled. The man then said, "Let me go, for
   it is daybreak." But Jacob said, "I will not let you
28 go until you bless me." "What is your name?" the
29 man asked. He answered, "Jacob." Then the man
   said, "You shall no longer be spoken of as Jacob,
   but as Israel, because you have contended with di-
30 vine and human beings and have prevailed." Jacob
   then asked him, "Do tell me your name, please."
   He answered, "Why should you want to know my
31 name?" With that, he bade him farewell. Jacob
   named the place Peniel, "Because I have seen God
   face to face," he said, "yet my life has been spared."
32 At sunrise, as he left Penuel, Jacob limped along be-
33 cause of his hip. That is why, to this day, the Israelites do not eat the sciatic muscle that is on the
   hip socket, inasmuch as Jacob's hip socket was
   struck at the sciatic muscle.

The story begins on a confusing note. Penuel, where the action takes
place, is usually identified with the modern Tulul edh-Dhahab, a neighbor
of Succoth (cf. 33:16) north of the Jabbok (cf. Judges 8:8–9.16–17; an
inscription of Pharaoh Shishak preserved at Karnak celebrating his invasion of Palestine around 924 B.C. [briefly mentioned in 1 Kings
14:25–27] also lists Penuel in close conjunction with Succoth). Yet here
Jacob is said to have *crossed the ford of the Jabbok.* After having sent on
ahead *his two wives, with the two maidservants and his eleven children*
(either this story knows nothing of Dinah or she is omitted on the principle that women do not count) along with *all his possessions* (a thing
which vss. 14b–22 seem to presume has already occurred, at least in part),
are we to suppose that he retraced his path back to the northern heights
and *was left there alone* for his strange encounter? Besides being unexplained, such a casual crossing of "the profound ravine of the Jabbok," as
Sir James Frazer called it, is not lightly to be imagined:

The gorge is, in the highest degree, wild and pictur-
esque. On either hand the cliffs rise almost perpen-
dicularly to a great height; you look up the precipices
or steep declivities to the skyline far above. At the bottom of this mighty chasm the Jabbok flows with a
powerful current, its blue-grey water fringed and hidden, even at a short distance, by a dense jungle of tall
oleanders, whose crimson blossoms add a glow of
colour to the glen in early summer. The Blue River,
for such is its modern name, runs fast and strong. Even

in ordinary times the water reaches to the horses' girths, and sometimes the stream is quite unfordable, the flood washing grass and bushes high up the banks on either hand.

What, we might ask, is Jacob about, cutting short his sleep to undertake this formidable fording of the Jabbok in the middle of the night, transporting men, women, children, and untold numbers of cattle and goods? Furthermore, why cross the Jabbok at all, either north to south or south to north? Jacob's meeting with Esau (33:1–16) is not geographically located for us, it is true, but when next we are told of his whereabouts it is either Succoth (33:17, J) or Shechem (33:18.19, P and E), both of which are to the north of the Jabbok. All of this adds up to at least one conclusion, which is that the story of vss. 23–33 is not of a piece with the rest of the Jacob narrative.

What, then, is it a piece of? The relevance of the Jabbok (Hebrew *yabboq*) peeps through, no doubt, in vs. 25, when we get to the heart of the story and are told that Jacob *wrestled* (*ye'abeq*) with *some man until the break of dawn.* Several venerable mythological motifs are at work here. One is the theme of the river-god or spirit who must be placated or whose conditions must otherwise be met as the price of crossing the boundaries which he protects. Though in vs. 25 (cf. 18:2) Jacob's wrestling partner is *some man* (*ish:* "someone" might be a better rendering in the context; "the man" of the NAB's vss. 26, 27, 28, and 29 is not in the original but has been supplied by the translator), in vss. 29 (*elohim,* "god," "divine being") and 31 it becomes quite plain that a superhuman, God-like character is the one with whom he has *contended* at the Jabbok. Another theme is that of the supernatural being whose power is restricted to the night and disappears with daybreak (vs. 27).

Within the story are other confusions. In vs. 26 "the man" cannot prevail over Jacob (we recall the extraordinary strength attributed to him in 29:10) and therefore magically lames him, yet in vs. 27 he is still in Jacob's hold and has to plead for release. Jacob demands a blessing in return, instead of which he is given a new name; but when he in turn asks the name of his opponent, his request is airily dismissed as naïve and childish and is not answered. Who, then, won in the struggle? In vs. 29 "the man" tells Jacob that he has *contended with divine and human beings and have prevailed,* but in vs. 31 Jacob is content, having *seen God face to face,* with the less triumphal result that *my life has been spared.* It is instructive to compare with this Genesis account of Jacob the lines of the prophet Hosea (of the latter part of the eighth century B.C.) which obviously depend on the same traditions, without necessarily sharing the conclusions that Genesis has drawn from them:

The LORD has a grievance against Israel:
    he shall punish Jacob for his conduct,
    for his deeds he shall repay him.
In the womb he supplanted his brother [Genesis 25:26, J],
    and as a man he contended with God [this story];
He contended with the angel and triumphed,
    [the "angel" and the "triumph" are Hosea's]
    entreating him with tears.
    [another detail which does not appear in Genesis]
At Bethel he met God [Genesis 28:13–15, 31:3, J]
    and there he spoke with him:
The LORD, the God of hosts,
    the LORD is his name!
You shall return by the help of your God,
    if you remain loyal and do right
    and always hope in your God (Hosea 12:3–7).

What did Genesis, finally, intend to say by utilizing this extraordinary story which was part of the lore which surrounded the ancestral figure of Jacob? For one thing (cf. the P of 35:6.9–13.15 below, associated with Bethel as in Hosea 12:5), it celebrates the change of Jacob's name to Israel, that is, to the eponymous ancestor of the Israelites, who claimed their common descent from Jacob. The real meaning of "Israel" is unknown— is it related to the Jeshurun ("darling" in the NAB) of Deuteronomy 32:15, 33:5.26; Isaiah 44:2? In Genesis it is etymologized from *saritha*, "you have contended," and *elohim*, God (hence vs. 29). Secondly, a popular etymology is given by the story to the place Penuel or Peniel (so in vs. 31; the two forms seem to have coexisted indifferently), which, we have seen, was a significant site in early Israelite history. *Jacob named the place Peniel* because there he had seen God face to face: *elohim panim el-panim*. And finally, a dietary law is explained (vs. 33) which, despite *the Israelites do not eat . . . ,* never became a part of the Torah or Talmud of Israel or Judaism. Whatever may have been the ancient taboo against eating *the sciatic muscle that is on the hip socket*—Theodor Gaster has reminded us of the thigh as symbolic of the seat of life, cf. 24:2 above—it was not a rule that survived in later Israel; it is one, however, that may very well testify to the antiquity of the materials on which the Redactor of Genesis could depend for this complement to the story of Jacob.

So far we have not really answered the question of what the passage means in the context of Genesis. If Penuel, Israel, and Jabbok all have their names hidden in the narrative at the beckon of the careful reader and reciter, they are nevertheless secondary to the purpose of the biblical author, who had more important issues to consider than ancient geography or ethnology. Did the story originally envisage Jacob's journey *into* and not *out of* Aram Naharaim? The crossing of the Jabbok might raise the question. But again, this is another question than the one of what has been made of the story by Genesis.

At the risk of oversimplification, we would suggest that the biblical message of the story lies in vs. 29. A Jacob previously adept at dealing with men (Esau, Isaac, Laban, and soon Esau again) has now *contended with* God and has similarly *prevailed* in a way that this tale can hardly adequately explain but can only symbolize. Jacob has had an experience of the divine that has changed him (his limp is an at least temporary reminder of the change). In the chapters that follow he will assume both as an individual and as the embodiment of the Israel to come a worthier posture of a man more sensitive to the higher values both human and divine (we will see, for example, his rebuke of Simeon and Levi in 34:30, the purification of his camp in 35:2). At the same time, he has learnt that a genuine relationship with God does not reside in mere passivity, rejoicing in election and waiting on providence (the prayer in vss. 10–13); it entails as well personal effort, a striving, wrestling with the divine will and purposes. "Victory" is less the objective of such a contending than are understanding and involvement. The poetry of the book of Job was to explore this truth of religion in beautiful detail. It may be thought that the strange story of vss. 23:33 was by comparison an ill-suited vehicle for the conveyance of the same truth in the book of Genesis, but we have ample precedent in these pages for the parabolic use of quite primitive myth and legend to expound ideas of equal sublimity.

The refusal of the divine being to reveal his name (vs. 30) exhibits on the one hand the half-superstitious reluctance of many peoples, ancient and modern, to submit themselves to the control of others, which in some fashion is bestowed by making known their name. It also reminds us, on the other hand, of Yahweh's response to Moses in Exodus 3:14. (The original sense of "I am who am" is not that this is the divine "name" for which Moses has asked but rather that the God who speaks to him is ineffable.) Jacob is brought to the realization that the God whom he has *seen face to face* is not to be named, and so he names Peniel instead.

We now return to Jacob's meeting with Esau for which preparation had been made in 32:4–22 and which has been delayed by the preceding story. The section that follows is by some authors ascribed whole and entire to the Yahwist, but most find in it traces of the Elohist's work. For reasons that we think will be made clear in the commentary, we consider a number of the verses to be E, and these we have put in italics.

> 33 Jacob looked up and saw Esau coming, accompanied
> by four hundred men. So he divided his children

2 among Leah, Rachel and the two maidservants, putting the maids and their children first, Leah and her
3 children next, and Rachel and Joseph last. He himself went on ahead of them, bowing to the ground
4 seven times, until he reached his brother. *Esau ran
to meet him, embraced him, and flinging himself
on his neck, kissed him as he wept.*

5 *When Esau looked about, he saw the women and
children. "Who are these with you?" he asked.* Jacob
answered, "They are the children whom God has
6 graciously bestowed on your servant." Then the
maidservants and their children came forward and
7 bowed low; next, Leah and her children came forward and bowed low; lastly, Rachel and her chil-
8 dren* came forward and bowed low. *Then Esau
asked, "What did you intend with all those droves
that I encountered?" Jacob answered, "It was to
9 gain my lord's favor." "I have plenty," replied Esau;
10 "you should keep what is yours, brother." "No, I
beg you!" said Jacob. "If you will do me the favor,
please accept this gift from me, since to come into
your presence is for me like coming into the presence
of God, now that you have received me so kindly.
11 Do accept the present I have brought you; God
has been generous toward me, and I have an abundance." Since he so urged him, Esau accepted.*

12 Then Esau said, "Let us break camp and be on our
13 way; I will travel alongside you." But Jacob replied: "As my lord can see, the children are frail.
Besides, I am encumbered with the flocks and herds,
which now have sucklings; if overdriven for a single
14 day, the whole flock will die. Let my lord, then,
go on ahead of me, while I proceed more slowly at
the pace of the livestock before me and at the pace
15 of my children, until I join my lord in Seir." Esau
replied, "Let me at least put at your disposal some
of the men who are with me." But Jacob said, "For
what reason? Please indulge me in this, my lord."
16 So on the same day that Esau began his journey back
17 to Seir, Jacob journeyed to Succoth. There he built
a home for himself and made booths for his livestock. That is why the place was called Succoth.

---

* This seems to be a mistake of the NAB. The MT has "Joseph and Rachel"; the
LXX and the Syriac "Rachel and Joseph."

In view of the elaborate preparations that Jacob had made to protect himself against a supposedly vengeful Esau, the actual encounter between the two brothers comes as a seeming anticlimax: Esau willingly accepts the role of the beneficent lord in which Jacob has eagerly cast him. The J story is not complete, and we are not told in it the cause of Esau's benevolence, but presumably the ceremonial servility of Jacob and his caravan is enough to capture his good will, at least temporarily. As before in J (32:7) Esau has his *four hundred men* with him, and also as before (32:8) Jacob divides his people into groups, though now not two but three, and no longer to salvage a remnant in case of attack but rather to enhance the ritual of greeting. There may be vestige of the defensive idea in the distribution of the groups, since *the two maidservants and their children* will be the first to meet up with the unpredictable Esau, then *Leah and her children,* and last of all the beloved *Rachel and Joseph.* But if so, it seems to be quite forgotten when Jacob runs on ahead of the whole troupe to perform the first obeisance. *Bowing to the ground seven times* is not an invention of Genesis to heighten the impression of Jacob's subservience but was a conventional mark of fealty attested to by the Amarna letters.

In E the gifts which Jacob had sent on ahead of him by stages (32:14b–22) have had their intended effect and assured Esau's coming in friendship; he wants only to be introduced to his brother's family and to encircle them all in his embrace. We may confidently assume that his inquiry about the intent of *all those droves* in vs. 8 is a rhetorical question and that his demurrer about accepting them which is overcome by Jacob's insistence is conventional politeness.

Neither does E have a complete story. When J takes up again in vs. 12 we quickly discover that Esau's good feeling toward Jacob has been premised on the assumption that his brother will join him in his domain *in Seir* (see 25:25, 32:4, both J), there undoubtedly to pursue the same vassal type of relationship that he has taken on himself at their meeting. Jacob, of course, has no intention of doing any such thing, and more than a trace of the "old" Jacob surfaces in the dickering that ensues, in which he manages to persuade Esau to "go on ahead" and not even leave behind a force of his own men to oversee Jacob's subsequent movements. For all his panoply of success and power, Esau is as easily gulled as he was so long ago. Once again Jacob has contended with men and prevailed. The threat which Esau promised has been circumvented and he is now free to make his way in peace to the land of Canaan for which he had set out.

According to this J story, however, Jacob first takes up residence east of the Jordan (and north of the Jabbok) at *Succoth* ("booths" or "tents," hence the associative etymology of vs. 17). Succoth, as we have already noted, which is usually identified with the modern Tell Deirallah, had a close association in Israelite history with Penuel. In the E of vs. 10 above the presence of God (pene elohim) is considered to be a further allusion to Penuel, whether or not it is related to the story of 32:23–33. The obvious sense of vs. 17 is that Jacob and his retinue made their home for some considerable time at Succoth.

In the other Genesis sources there is no mention of a stay at Succoth. These three concluding verses of this chapter consist of a brief summary account in the manner of P, which we have italicized, and a lengthier though still short narrative which appears to be E, both of which make Shechem the first patriarchal center in the Land of Promise (see above on 12:1–9).

18 *Having thus come from Paddan-aram, Jacob arrived*
   safely at the city of Shechem, which is in the land of
19 *Canaan,* and he encamped in sight of the city. The
   plot of ground on which he had pitched his tent
   he bought for a hundred pieces of bullion from the
20 descendants of Hamor, the founder of Shechem. He
   set up a memorial stone there and invoked "El, the
   God of Israel."

Shechem, the site of which (Tell Balatah) has been thoroughly explored by archeology, lay well within the limits of Cisjordan Palestine, roughly on a line westward from Penuel and Succoth. It was a thriving city in the Bronze Age, the time in which we locate the patriarchs, and, with brief interruptions, it remained so throughout Israelite and later Jewish history; it was finally destroyed, as so many other cities were, by the Romans. Its importance for early Israel was considerable. In Joshua 24 it is represented as the place where the tribes of Israel assembled to consolidate their conquest of the land, and where they took solemn oaths and made covenant with Yahweh at his sanctuary. Even after David and Solomon had made Jerusalem the political and religious capital of the Israelite nation, it was to Shechem—some forty miles north of Jerusalem—that Solomon's son and successor Rehoboam went to be proclaimed king by "all Israel" (1 Kings 12:1). It is no wonder, then, that just as the Yahwist had Abraham build an altar at Shechem (12:7), the Elohist should be interested in representing Jacob as erecting there a *massebah,* his favored cult object.

In vs. 20 Jacob invokes at Shechem *El, the God of Israel.* In early Israelite times, according to Judges 9:46, the city-god of Shechem was El-berith, "El (or god) of the covenant"; in Judges 8:33, 9:4 it is Baal-berith, "Baal (or lord) of the covenant," doubtless the same deity. In vs. 19 the Shechemites are called *descendants* (literally, "sons") *of Hamor, the founder* (literally, "father") *of Shechem.* These phrases can be read in the sense of the following chapter, in which Shechem and Hamor have become the proper names of persons actually living, but they can also be read in another way. *Hamor* means "ass." If we recall the covenant ritual of 15:7–12 above, together with the circumstance that at Mari an ass substituted for the calf of Jeremiah 34:18, it is conceivable that "sons of Hamor" (cf. Judges 9:28) meant something like "covenant fellows," consonant with the Shechemites' worship of an El-berith. Another interesting fact is that nowhere in the Heptateuch is it ever mentioned that Shechem, for all its importance in Canaan before and after the coming of Israel, was part of the Israelite "conquest." Rather, it is simply assumed without further explanation that it was a fitting assembly place for Israel and its cult as soon as ever Yahwism obtained hegemony in the Land of Promise. The story of Judges 9 even gives the impression that in Israel's early days Israelites (who worshiped Yahweh) and Canaanites (who worshiped Baal) lived together in Shechem side by side. The archeology of Shechem also confirms that during the period (thirteenth century B.C.) which we associate with the "conquest" there was no violent interruption of its civic life (as there certainly was at various other sites which the Bible represents as falling to Israelite arms). May we assume, therefore, that vs. 20 remembers a political and religious change in Shechem, when, for many of its citizens at least, the God of its covenant became identified with the God of Israel's covenant (under the name of El, understandably, and not of Baal, which remained distinctive of Canaan)? This is at least a possibility.

Perhaps something of this kind is insinuated in vs. 19 when, by exception, Jacob is said to have *bought* and therefore owned the land on which he—Israel—camped at Shechem. *A hundred pieces of bullion* translates "one hundred *kesitahs*." We do not know what was this monetary weight or value.

The casual reader may be able to pass from these verses into the following chapter as though the one flows from the other with the inevitability of day and night; but it is not so, as we shall see. The Redactor, to be sure, has done his best to make it so, and we must respect his intentions. But we begin with another source that constitutes the basic narrative: J, by the feel of it, indicated by the presence of Dinah, the castigation of Simeon and Levi, among other things. But the story has also been amplified, and in significant ways. The amplification contributes to some of the suggestions that have been provoked by the E verses above, but it is impossible to say whether it was, indeed, from the Elohist that the Redactor took it. We show it below in italics.

34 Dinah, the daughter whom Leah had borne to Jacob,
   went out to visit some of the women of the land.
2 When Shechem, son of Hamor the Hivite,† who was
   chief of the region, saw her, he seized her and lay

---

† The LXX has "Horite": see above on 26:34.

3 with her by force. Since he was strongly attracted to Dinah, daughter of Jacob, indeed was really in love with the girl, he endeavored to win her affection. 4 *Shechem also asked his father Hamor, "Get me this girl for a wife."* 5 Meanwhile, Jacob heard that Shechem had defiled his daughter Dinah; but since his sons were out in the fields with his livestock, he held his peace until 6 they came home. *Now Hamor, the father of She-* 7 *chem, went out to discuss the matter with Jacob,* just as Jacob's sons were coming in from the fields. When they heard the news, the men were shocked and seethed with indignation. What Shechem had done was an outrage in Israel; such a thing could not be 8 tolerated. *Hamor appealed to them, saying, "My son Shechem has his heart set on your daughter. Please* 9 *give her to him in marriage. Intermarry with us; give your daughters to us, and take our daughters for* 10 *yourselves. Thus you can live among us. The land is open before you; you can settle and move about* 11 *freely in it, and acquire landed property here."* Then Shechem, too, appealed to Dinah's father and brothers: "Do me this favor, and I will pay whatever you 12 demand of me. No matter how high you set the bridal price, I will pay you whatever you ask; only give me the maiden in marriage."

We have, it appears, a story and a story made out of a story. First is the J narrative of Dinah, who *went out to visit some of the women of the land.* Where? The last we heard of Jacob in J he was in Succoth beyond the Jordan (33:17). The next we know of his whereabouts (35:21) puts him in the vicinity of Jerusalem, if the Migdal-eder of Genesis is the same as that of Micah 4:8. The story of 37:12–20 (J) locates him near Hebron, obviously in Cisjordan Canaan, far to the south of Shechem, whither, rather unbelievably, he dispatches his tender son Joseph. The episode that lies before us could have happened anywhere: *Shechem, son of Hamor the Hivite,* and afterward simply *Shechem,* we may be sure are redactional names devised to denote the originally anonymous *chief of the region* whose private little tragedy the Yahwist first recorded. The supplement to the story, which dealt expressly with the city Shechem, has contributed to it the eponyms of Shechem and Hamor. Obviously, the passage of some time is presupposed: Jacob's children are grown.

The Yahwist's tale is a simple one, which has been tiresomely repeated

throughout most of human history. The local squire, used to taking what
he wants when and where he finds it, oppresses a comely peasant maiden.
Then he discovers that he is in love, and he resolves to do the noble thing.
He takes the girl to his house (cf. vs. 26 below), where by this time she
was probably not unwilling to go (vs. 3), and formally seeks her hand in
marriage. He could not have been unaware, however insulated he was
from the lower life that throve about him, of the feelings that a powerless
father could only choke back in anguish (vs. 5); but he is sure that the
honor he will bestow and the *mohar* he will pour into the family coffers
will heal all wounds. He reckons, however, without knowledge of the sense
of propriety that dictated the morals of countless generations of Israelites:
an outrage in Israel; such a thing could not be tolerated (cf. Judges 19:30;
2 Samuel 13:12).

The supplement has built on this story by turning it into an overture by
the Shechemites, sparked by the young man Shechem and fueled by his
father Hamor, to propose a general miscegenation between the two peoples. Shechem wants one of Jacob's women for a wife, and Hamor proposes that not only this request be granted but that there be reciprocal
intermarriages and that, in fact, Jacob and his family be absorbed into the
indigenous community. The proposal is put in terms of a *quid pro quo* but
it amounts to a surrender: that Jacob could *acquire landed property here*
is a gift which the God of Israel has reserved to himself. Jacob does not
have it in his power to accept this gift from any man, but only from God.
The land is open before you (vs. 10) is reminiscent of 13:14–17 (J):
here, however, a tempter proffers what only God can guarantee (cf.
Matthew 4:1–11; Luke 4:1–13).

> 13 Jacob's sons replied to Shechem *and his father
>   Hamor* with guile, speaking as they did because their
> 14 sister Dinah had been defiled. *"We could not do
>   such a thing,"* they said, *"as to give our sister to an
>   uncircumcised man; that would be a disgrace for us.*
> 15 *We will agree with you only on this condition, that
>   you become like us by having every male among you
> 16 circumcised. Then we will give you our daughters
>   and take yours in marriage; we will settle among you
> 17 and become one kindred people with you. But if you
>   do not comply with our terms regarding circumci-
>   sion, we will take our daughter and go away."*
> 18 Their proposal seemed fair to *Hamor and his son
> 19 Shechem.* The young man lost no time in acting in
>   the matter, since he was deeply in love with Jacob's
>   daughter. Moreover, he was more highly respected

20 than anyone else in his clan. *So Hamor and his son Shechem went to their town council and thus pre-*
21 *sented the matter to their fellow townsmen:* "*These men are friendly toward us. Let them settle in the land and move about in it freely; there is ample room in the country for them. We can marry their daughters and give our daughters to them in mar-*
22 *riage. But the men will agree to live with us and form one kindred people with us only on this con-dition, that every male among us be circumcised as*
23 *they themselves are. Would not the livestock they have acquired—all their animals—then be ours? Let us, therefore, give in to them, so that they may settle among us.*"
24 All the able-bodied men of the town agreed with *Hamor and his son* Shechem, *and all the males, in-cluding every able-bodied man in the community,*
25 *were circumcised. On the third day, while they were still in pain,* Dinah's full brothers Simeon and Levi, two of Jacob's sons, took their swords, advanced against the city *without any trouble, and massacred*
26 *all the males.* After they had put *Hamor and his son* Shechem to the sword, they took Dinah from
27 Shechem's house and left. *Then the other sons of Ja-cob followed up the slaughter and sacked the city*
28 *in reprisal for their sister Dinah's‡ defilement. They seized their flocks, herds and asses, whatever was*
29 *in the city and in the country around. They carried off all their wealth, their women, and their children, and took for loot whatever was in the houses.*
30 Jacob said to Simeon and Levi: "You have brought trouble upon me by making me loathsome to the inhabitants of the land, the Canaanites and the Perizzites. I have so few men that, if these people unite against me and attack me, I and my family
31 will be wiped out." But they retorted, "Should our sister have been treated like a harlot?"

Again a simple and rather sad story has been built into an ethnic saga about the perennial theme of Juliet and her Romeo, Maria and Tony. In J Shechem makes his bid to Dinah's father and brothers, offering the *amende honorable* after his less than chivalrous conduct in the past and

‡ The name "Dinah" does not appear in the Hebrew of this passage.

the proposal of full marriage at any price. (The bride, we may assume—for we never see her again—was expecting her family to sustain her honor by naming a respectable price.) Whatever the *mohar* was that the Israelites feigned to conclude the affair (vss. 13.18), Shechem accepted the demand as he said he would (vs. 12), and at the same time he secured the consent of his city fathers to his wedding with the alien in their midst (vss. 19.24). But only to their common betrayal. Simeon and Levi take the occasion of Shechem's unawareness to sneak into his city, seek out his house, slay him, and restore to her family circle, whether or not she was inclined by now to remain a part of it, their sister Dinah. It is not a very pleasant story, but one in which *omertà* looms more important than does a decent respect for the opinion of mankind.

The supplement tells an even grimmer tale. According to it, for no really proportionate cause the sons of Israel—all of them, not merely Simeon and Levi—seize the opportunity afforded by the Shechemites' offer of alliance to trick them, then to slaughter them and sack and loot their city. These verses assume that the Shechemites, Hivites or Horites (vs. 2 above, probably R), were uncircumcised, non-Semites, an assumption which may preserve an authentic historical recollection. They also presuppose, in patriarchal times, a violent Israelization of Shechem, a thing which, we have seen, is not claimed for the actual period of Israelite conquest by biblical documents or supported by archeological evidence, but which might be suggested by 48:22 (JE) below. This, too, may be history. Circumcision as the *sine qua non* condition of covenant between Israelites and Shechemites may well be an anachronism, but it is not at all hard to believe that a tradition had been faithfully handed down which recorded a pre-Israelite assimilation of Shechem, by treaty and/or the tactics of terror, into one or another of the tribal elements that later joined to make up the federation of Israel. In 48:22 Shechem is assigned to Joseph by Jacob: variously in the Bible the city is ascribed to the territories of Ephraim or Manasseh, both of which are "Joseph" tribes.

Circumcision, whatever is to be said of it historically, is of course integral to the supplementary narrative of chapter 34. It explains, not altogether plausibly, but plausibly enough for the purpose of the story, how the sons of Israel were able to take over a town suddenly bereft of its male defenders and therefore have their will prevail. We do not expect to find in stories of this kind a clinical realism but rather should look for the sort of themes that would appeal to rough humor and rouse the chuckles of the fairly low audience for whom they were designed, who doubled with merriment at the thought of "the uncircumcised" (cf. Judges 15:18, etc.). Later, more cultivated peoples have likewise felt themselves superior to others whose speech sounded to their untuned ears like *bar bar* rather than proper Greek, or, as history rolled on, like Greek rather than proper English or French or German, or whose quirky customs tended to deviate

from those of Athens or Isfahan or Peoria. The true measure of a paro-
chial society is that it has constituted itself a measure, knowing none other.

We would like to see, in the J conclusion to the original story in vss.
30–31, a loftier repudiation of the violence of Simeon and Levi than simply Jacob's complaint that his life has been made more difficult among *the
Canaanites and the Perizzites* (see above on 15:20–21, J), who are capable of taking revenge for the murder of Shechem and easily overwhelming
his relatively minor forces. At least, however, he recognizes that the opposition may have a legitimate grievance. His obdurate sons will not concede
even this much in their single-minded and stupidly stolid dedication to the
honor of a sister for whom they have hithertofore probably lifted never a
finger. They have acted without thinking to assuage their feelings of family
disgrace, whereas Jacob, equally sensible of the affront (vs. 5), had *held
his peace* and reflected on what should be done. Perhaps nothing would
have come of Jacob's lucubrations, but certainly nothing good could come
from what his sons have done. Jacob does know that right and wrong have
neither their beginning nor their end in the exclusive interests of his family
circle.

What comes next, the conclusion to the Jacob story, seems to be basically Elohistic, except for some routine insertions that bear all the ear-
marks of P. We indicate the latter, conventionally, with italics.

> **35** God said to Jacob: "Go up now to Bethel. Settle
> there and build an altar there to the God who
> appeared to you while you were fleeing from
> 2 your brother Esau." So Jacob told his family
> and all the others who were with him: "Get rid of
> the foreign gods that you have among you; then
> 3 purify yourselves and put on fresh clothes. We
> are now to go up to Bethel, and I will build an
> altar there to the God who answered me in my
> hour of distress and who has been with me
> 4 wherever I have gone." They therefore handed
> over to Jacob all the foreign gods in their pos-
> session and also the rings they had in their ears,
> and Jacob buried them beneath the terebinth
> 5 near Shechem. Then, as they set out, a terror
> from God fell upon the towns round about, so
> that no one pursued the sons of Jacob.
> 6 *Thus Jacob and all the people who were with
> him arrived in Luz* [*that is, Bethel*] *in the land of
> 7 Canaan.* There he built an altar and named the
> place Bethel,* for it was there that God had re-

---

* The Hebrew has El Bethel; see above on 28:10–22.

vealed himself to him when he was fleeing from his brother.

8 Death came to Rebekah's nurse Deborah; she was buried under the oak below Bethel, and so it was called Allon-bacuth.

9 *On Jacob's arrival from Paddan-aram, God ap-*
10 *peared to him again and blessed him. God said to him:*

"*You whose name is Jacob*
shall no longer be called Jacob,
but Israel shall be your name."

11 *Thus he was named Israel. God also said to him:*
"*I am God Almighty;*
be fruitful and multiply.
A nation, indeed an assembly of nations,
shall stem from you,
and kings shall issue from your loins.
12 *The land I once gave*
to Abraham and Isaac
I now give to you;
And to your descendants after you
will I give this land."

13/14 *Then God departed from him.* On the site where God had spoken with him, Jacob set up a memorial stone, and upon it he made a libation
15 and poured out oil. *Jacob named the site Bethel, because God had spoken with him there.*

16 Then they departed from Bethel: but while they still had some distance to go on the way to Ephrath, Rachel began to be in labor and to suf-
17 fer great distress. When her pangs were most severe, her midwife said to her, "Have no fear!
18 This time, too, you have a son." With her last breath—for she was at the point of death—she called him Ben-oni; his father, however, named
19 him Benjamin. Thus Rachel died; and she was buried on the road to Ephrath [that is, Bethle-
20 hem]. Jacob set up a memorial stone on her grave, and the same monument marks Rachel's grave to this day.

It has often been remarked that vss. 1–5 read like the proclamation and inauguration of a solemn cultic event. Jacob is instructed, how we are not told, by God (*Elohim*) to *go up* (the language of pilgrimage) *to Bethel* and there to *build an altar to the God* (*El*) who had appeared to him while he was fleeing the wrath of Esau. The reference, there can hardly be any doubt, is to 28:11–12.17–18.20–22 (E): El Bethel is being designated the God of Israel's worship, even as the El of Shechem had previously been so declared (33:20, E). In keeping with this new consecration of his family, Jacob requires of them that they abandon their *foreign gods*—the biblical author probably intends us to think, first of all, of Rachel's *teraphim* (31:19b.30b.32–35, E), but also probably not only of these—which they do, along with *the rings they had in their ears* (probably the author had in mind the well-known crescent earrings of the ancient Near East which proclaimed their wearer to be a devotee of the Semitic moon-god). Jacob buries all these paraphernalia beneath the sacred tree at Shechem (cf. 12:6, J), signifying that a clean break is being made with the past and that an entirely new chapter will begin in Bethel. Consonant with this gesture, he exhorts his people to *purify yourselves* (another cultic term, indicating the satisfaction of ritual proprieties) *and put on fresh clothes,* which from the dawn of man's religious experience has been made a sacrament to symbolize new life and new identity.

It is also possible to agree with recent scholars who think the biblical narrative is a reinterpretation of an ancient pilgrimage rite which originally was not concerned with the abandonment of one god for another but simply with the desire to avoid ritual "contamination" (cf. Ezekiel 44:19). Various Near Eastern archeological sites have revealed deposits of god figurines, other images, and ornaments which had been deliberately buried at holy places (like *the terebinth near Shechem*). These deposits, some of which date from most ancient times, the Middle Bronze Age and before, testify to a widespread practice whose purpose or purposes have been variously interpreted by scholars, one of which, however, could easily have been that of Muslim pilgrims to Mecca who still preserve a pre-Islam use of leaving behind their clothing and other personal effects at some point of departure lest these offend the sanctity of the place of their destination. (It has been suggested by one author that such a deposit was known to exist at Shechem and is here being given an etiology.) Only later, in the opinion of these scholars, was this conventional and temporary abandonment of everyday possessions on the part of pilgrims turned by the author of Genesis into a renunciation of "foreign" gods, following the formulations of Joshua 24:14.23, Judges 10:16, 1 Samuel 7:3 (which are generally accounted Deuteronomic).

As far as we can see, there is no conflict between this hypothesis and the other which commentators since Albrecht Alt have entertained, that in this story can be discovered an Israelite or proto-Israelite memory of a time when the center of tribal cult shifted or was transferred from Shechem to Bethel, an event that may very well have been periodically re-enacted in liturgy by those elements of the later Israel who first treasured up the Jacob-Israel legend and contributed it to the common fund of the patriarchal history. As we pointed out above in the commentary on 12:1–9, it is also a plausible conjecture that this supposed pilgrimage from Shechem to Bethel of early Israel may have been responsible not only for the route that is assigned to Jacob in these present chapters but also for the one that was earlier ascribed to Abraham and presumably modeled upon it.

It is proper in vs. 7 that Jacob should build an altar at Bethel, where before (28:18, E) he had only anointed a memorial stone. It is somewhat more difficult to understand in this E narrative, however, why in vs. 14 he should be represented as erecting the *massebah* all over again, complete with the ritual of libation and oil. Some have suggested here the presence of another source, but the conjecture seems both arbitrary and hardly likely under the circumstances. Like J and P, the Elohist has occasionally combined narrative strands that are not internally consistent. Ordinarily the Redactor has smoothed away these rough transitions, but not so here. Why, we may venture to think, is that he interpreted the *massebah* of vs. 14 in the same sense as that of vs. 20, namely as a grave marker for an important ancestor or ancestress (cf. vs. 8).

This fairly obvious solution to one problem, at the same time, merely opens up another one that calls for a comparable resolution. Why should *Rebekah's nurse Deborah*—the one woman has not been heard of since 27:46 and the other has never been mentioned at all except anonymously in 24:59—become, or her grave become, a place of resort for generations of Israelites who gave it the plaintive name "the oak of weeping" (vs. 8)? The best guess is that there was a "Deborah's tree" near Bethel which had had some deep significance for early Israel (cf. Judges 4:5) and to which various etiologies were assigned. With the passing of time—not much time is needed—people and places and things tend to mix together and one become the other. Thus we have inherited a Veronica in Christian hagiography who was probably once the *vera eikon,* "true image" of the face of the Lord imprinted on a venerated portrait that succeeded in finding a legend and a person to give it identity. We cannot even guess the details of the local legend that surrounded the site of Allon-bacuth and why the Deborah ("bee") with whom it came to be associated should have been identified as Rebekah's nurse.

Only in vs. 5 (redactional?) is there an advertence to the context of chapter 34. The *terror from God* (this expression only here, but equivalents in Exodus 23:27; 1 Samuel 14:15, etc.) perhaps asserts an at least apparent exception to the rule we predicated of the patriarchal narratives when commenting on chapter 15 above: it comes close to the idea of the God of Israel entering the lists with his people and fighting with them in their "holy" war against the Gentiles (cf. Judges 5:4–23), contributing manifestations of his almighty power to their force of arms. Jacob and his family retire from Shechem unhampered and unhindered because the might of their God intimidates any who might want to harm them.

In vss. 6.9–13.15 we have the P parallel to the story of Jacob's religious experience at Bethel, the change of his name to Israel, the identification of the God of Bethel with the God of his fathers, the naming of Bethel in commemoration of these events, and the promise of progeny and of the land. All these details have been spelt out more imaginatively in the J and E traditions which we have already examined.

The last several verses record the birth of Benjamin and the death of Rachel. The site of these events is designated by E as *Ephrath* in the Cisjordan of Palestine near Bethel; in vss. 24–26 below (P), Benjamin is said to have been born in Mesopotamia. Ephrath, first of all, was a place near Ramah of Benjamin (1 Samuel 10:2; Jeremiah 31:15), not the Bethlehem with which later tradition (so the gloss of vs. 19) associated it (cf. Micah 5:1; Matthew 2:5–8). The "tomb of Rachel," therefore, which is dutifully pointed out to the tourist of the Holy Land in the environs of Bethlehem (and which is a quite routine Muslim mausoleum) is more of a monument to piety than to the mother of Joseph and Benjamin. Wherever the tomb of Rachel, actual or imagined, may have actually lain in Israelite times (vs. 20), we cannot locate it today. The area of Benjamin (the word means "southerners") encompassed an area of less than a hundred square miles north of Jerusalem (Bethlehem lies to the south). There, wherever, *Rachel began to be in labor and to suffer great distress.* And there she gave birth to a son whom she was willing to name in her sorrow *Ben-oni,* "the son of my affliction." Naturally a father could allow no name of this kind to rest on a child of his generation, and therefore *Benjamin* is called "son of the right hand," a title of honor in Israel (cf. Psalm 68:28) which, however, we have already indicated, historically meant nothing more or less than "of the south" ("left" was "north" and "right" was "south," since the one pointing directions was assumed to be facing east).

The verse and a half that immediately follow, there seems to be no doubt, belong to J. Their theme is picked up later on, as we shall see.

> 21 Israel moved on and pitched his tent beyond Mig-
> 22a dal-eder. While Israel was encamped in that region,
>   Reuben went and lay with Bilhah, his father's con-
>   cubine. When Israel heard of it, he was greatly of-
>   fended.†

Firstly, Jacob is now called Israel by preference, a trait that is more typical of the Yahwist than of the other sources in the chapters that follow.

† The final clause is a perhaps unnecessary addition taken from the LXX.

Migdal-eder, we have pointed out above, was a site in the vicinity of Jerusalem (cf. Micah 4:8), which never came into the sphere of Israelite domination until the days of David. The incident of Reuben's intercourse with Bilhah, which figures in later biblical history (cf. 49:3–4; 1 Chronicles 5:1), we shall consider below.

Finally, the Priestly author catalogues the sons of Israel, mainly as they have been previously listed by J and E, and ends the story of Isaac, entirely in his own fashion:

> 22b/23 The sons of Jacob were now twelve. The sons
> of Leah: Reuben, Jacob's first-born, Simeon,
> 24 Levi, Judah, Isaachar, and Zebulun; the sons
> 25 of Rachel: Joseph and Benjamin; the sons of
> 26 Rachel's maid Bilhah: Dan and Naphtali; the
> sons of Leah's maid Zilpah: Gad and Asher.
> These are the sons of Jacob who were born to
> him in Paddan-aram.
> 27 Jacob went home to his father Isaac at Mamre,
> in Kiriath-arba [that is, Hebron], where Abra-
> 28 ham and Isaac had stayed. The lifetime of Isaac
> was one hundred and eighty years; then he
> 29 breathed his last. After a full life, he died as
> an old man and was taken to his kinsmen. His
> sons Esau and Jacob buried him.

The children of Jacob are listed here as they appear in the JE of 29:31–30:24, except that Dinah (who is mentioned only by J) finds no notice at all and Benjamin is ascribed to Jacob's Mesopotamian period, apparently in total ignorance of the poignant story of vss. 16–20 above. As we will see in the Joseph story that follows, both Benjamin and Rachel —the latter, save for the very tardy reference in 49:31–32, at one with the indifference that the biblical traditions usually display with regard to the further circumstances of patriarchal women—are often represented in ways that are not entirely consistent even within the same source.

Jacob returns *to his father Isaac at Mamre,* which is where he was when last located by P (25:9–11a). In the J story of 27:1–45 Isaac was already on his deathbed at the time Jacob left him for Aram Naharaim, and by the implied chronology of both J and E some thirty years or so must have passed since then. In respect to the actual number of years elapsed the explicit chronology of P is even more extraordinary, since in it (cf. 25:26b, 26:34) a good eighty years will have gone by before Isaac breathes his last at *one hundred and eighty years.* But of course we do not look for correspondence in this matter between JE and P, and the Priestly calculations do not relate to historical realities. In P, which knows nothing of a

prior alienation between Esau and Jacob or of the former's early settlement in Edom, the two sons are on hand to bury their father together just
as Isaac and Ishmael had done for their father before (cf. 25:9). Though
it is not explicitly stated here, Isaac was also buried in the same place as
Abraham, in the cave of Machpelah, facing Mamre (cf. 49:31).

6. Edomites

At the end of what we have designated the Saga of Jacob, before he em-
barks on the final part of Genesis, the Story of Joseph, the Redactor has
appended the chapter that follows, which is a compilation of early chronicles concerning the Edomites. Some of it is obviously P, and all of it may
indeed be attributable to the Priestly author's zeal in assembling ancient
material, bits of which can be reasonably construed as Edomite traditions
rather than Israelite. The editing of the compilation, however, whether by
P or R, has been neither thorough nor serious. Not only are there conflicts
and inconsistencies from section to section within the chapter, the P of
these verses occasionally disagrees with what was previously written in P.
It is fitting, nevertheless, that the entire chapter should bear, in one form
or another, the signature of that author who is the least particularistic of
all those who have contributed to Genesis, whose concern extends to all of
Abraham's descendants and, for that matter, to all of Noah's and of
Adam's.

36 These are the descendants of Esau [that is, Edom].
2 Esau took his wives from among the Canaanite
women: Adah, daughter of Elon the Hittite; Oholibamah, granddaughter through Anah of* Zibeon
3 the Hivite; and Basemath, daughter of Ishmael and
4 sister of Nebaioth. Adah bore Eliphaz to Esau;
5 Basemath bore Reuel; and Oholibamah bore Jeush,
Jalam and Korah. These are the sons of Esau who
were born to him in the land of Canaan.
6 Esau took his wives, his sons, his daughters, and all
the members of his household, as well as his live-

* So the LXX, the SP, and the Syriac. The MT makes Anah (cf. vss. 24–25 below)
into a daughter of Zibeon.

stock comprising various animals and all the property he had acquired in the land of Canaan, and
went to the land of Seir,† out of the way of his
7 brother Jacob. Their possessions had become too
great for them to dwell together, and the land in
which they were staying could not support them be-
8 cause of their livestock. So Esau settled in the high-
9 lands of Seir. [Esau is Edom.] These are the descendants of Esau, ancestor of the Edomites, in the
highlands of Seir.

10 These are the names of Esau's sons: Eliphaz, son
of Esau's wife Adah; and Reuel, son of Esau's wife
11 Basemath. The sons of Eliphaz were Teman,
12 Omar, Zepho, Gatam and Kenaz. (Esau's son Eliphaz had a concubine Timna, and she bore Amalek
to Eliphaz.) These are the descendants of Esau's
13 wife Adah. The sons of Reuel were Nahath, Zerah,
Shammah and Mizzah. These are the descendants of
14 Esau's wife Basemath. The descendants of Esau's
wife Oholibamah—granddaughter through‡ Anah
of Zibeon—whom she bore to Esau were Jeush,
Jalam and Korah.

The reader sees immediately that the text is conflated: Vss. 1–5 and
9–14 agree where they are parallel, but they tend to repeat each other mechanically; both in vss. 1 and 9 the Priestly author solemnly announces the
toledoth of Edom, and the parallel between the two passages has been
heightened by the insertion of a couple of glosses.

To the contrary, these verses give a somewhat different accounting for
Esau's wives and their backgrounds and ancestry. In 26:34 Esau was married to Judith, daughter of Beeri the Hittite, and Basemath, daughter of
Elon the Hivite (Hittite in the MT). In 27:46 both of these were called by
Rebekah Hittites, and in 28:8 they are considered to be Canaanites, distinct from Mahalath, the daughter of Ishmael, whom Esau later married
(28:9) to make amends for the displeasure he had caused his parents by
taking in marriage women of the land of Canaan. Here Judith has disappeared. There is a *daughter of Elon the Hittite,* all right, but her name is
Adah rather than Basemath. There is, in turn, a *Basemath,* but now she is
the *daughter of Ishmael and sister of Nebaioth,* taking the place of the
Mahalath who has gone the way of Judith. In addition, or in recompense,
there is a newcomer, *Oholibamah, granddaughter through Anah of Zibeon*

† "Seir" comes from the Syriac (cf. vs. 8). In the MT there is a blank.
‡ The same note applies for Anah here as above in vs. 2.

the Hivite. And all of these women are simply "Canaanites," following the fairly usual pattern of Genesis, which is to make free with the indigenous ethnic names it has inherited from its legends more for the sake of literary variety than from any serious intent to distinguish one Canaanite from another.

The names of Esau's descendants, it seems, are mainly authentically Edomite, or at least those of other Arab peoples hardly distinguishable from those who eventually made up the realm of Edom. *Eliphaz* was the name of one of the "friends" of Job (Job 2:11, etc.), certainly in that book an Edomite chieftain: the Eliphaz of Job comes from *Teman* (cf. vs. 11 here). *Reuel* is, in the J tradition, the name of Moses' father-in-law (Exodus 2:18), a Midianite (on the Midianites, see 4:2b–16 above). The sons of Oholibamah (the name doubtless has some connection with *ohel,* "tent") can only be guessed at: *Jeush* may be related to an Arabian divine name; *Jalam* appears to be derived from the word for "wild goat"; and *Korah,* later counted in Israel as a Judahite (1 Chronicles 2:43) or Levitical clan (1 Chronicles 9:19), is suspect of being an aboriginal Canaanite or Edomite family (remembered in the titles to numerous Psalms) which, like the Calebites, the Kenites, and various others, was eventually adopted into the Israelite nation and given a history to match. *Omar* is not otherwise attested in the Bible, but the name (related to *emir,* "prince") is Arabic. With *Zepho* and *Gatam* we cannot do much, but *Kenaz* was definitely an Edomite family related to the Calebites which later became part of Israel (cf. Joshua 14:14). *Amalek,* the eponymous ancestor of the Amalekites (cf. 14:7), represents a nomadic tribe of the Negeb of Palestine (Numbers 13:29), contiguous to Edom. *Nahath* may be the Mahanath of vs. 23 below, but if so we are not much the wiser about his identity in this context. Similarly *Shammah* and *Mizzah.* Nahath, however (in 2 Chronicles 31:13), and Shammah (in 1 Samuel 16:9) later turn up as Israelite names, as does *Zerah* (Genesis 38:30), the last being a Judahite clan which (cf. the titles to Psalms 88–89 and 1 Kings 5:11) probably entered into Israel from Edom by the route of the Korahites.

In vss. 6–8 we have the Priestly version of Esau's settlement in Seir (glossed as Edom), here an entirely peaceful separation from Israel at the end rather than at the beginning of their life together, in a brief narrative that recalls the E of 13:6.12 on which it has probably been modeled.

> 15 The following are the clans of Esau's descendants.
>   The descendants of Eliphaz, Esau's first-born: the
> 16 clans of Teman, Omar, Zepho, Kenaz, Korah,*
>   Gatam and Amalek. These are the clans of Eliphaz
>   in the land of Edom; they are descended from

---

* Korah's clan is omitted by the SP.

17 Adah. The descendants of Esau's son Reuel: the
clans of Nahath, Zerah, Shammah and Mizzah.
These are the clans of Reuel in the land of Edom;
18 they are descended from Esau's wife Basemath. The
descendants of Esau's wife Oholibamah: the clans
of Jeush, Jalam and Korah. These are the clans of
19 Esau's wife Oholibamah, daughter of Anah. Such
are the descendants of Esau [that is, Edom] according to their clans.

Nothing much but some tedious repetition for copyist and reader is
added by this evident doublet of the genealogies above. It has suppressed a
few details in the interests of economy, given Korah a dual descent from
Esau (if, indeed, Korah's name really belongs in vs. 16), and more overtly
acknowledged that we are talking about clans and not individual persons
(though we are no stranger by now to the convention which associates
peoples by the device of a family tree). The wives and the descendants are
otherwise as they were before.

20 The following are the descendants of Seir the Horite,
the original settlers in the land: Lotan, Shobal, Zib-
21 eon, Anah, Dishon, Ezer and Dishan; they are the
Horite clans descended from Seir, in the land of
22 Edom. Lotan's descendants were Hori and Hemam,
23 and Lotan's sister was Timna. Shobal's descendants
were Alvan, Mahanath, Ebal, Shepho and Onam.
24 Zibeon's descendants were Aiah and Anah. (He is
the Anah who found water† in the desert while he
25 was pasturing the asses of his father Zibeon.) The
descendants of Anah were Dishon and Oholibamah,
26 daughter of Anah. The descendants of Dishon‡ were
27 Hemdan, Eshban, Ithran and Cheran. The descend-
28 ants of Ezer were Bilhan, Zaavan and Akan. The
29 descendants of Dishan were Uz and Aran. These
are the Horite clans: the clans of Lotan, Shobal,
30 Zibeon, Anah, Dishon, Ezer and Dishan; they were
the clans of the Horites, clan by clan, in the land of
Seir.

In the perspective of Pentateuchal history (cf. Deuteronomy 2:12), the
aboriginal inhabitants of Edom were the Horites, who were displaced by
Esau and his descendants just as Israel and his descendants displaced the

---

† "Water" is the conjectural but probable meaning here of a Hebrew that is obscure.
‡ The MT has here "Dishan" for "Dishon," an understandable scribal mistake.

Canaanites in their Promised Land. Accordingly, an eponymous ancestor *Seir* is here assigned to these Horites who had left only the memory of their names in the land of Edom. Seir, which we have seen is habitually interchangeable with Edom to designate this region, probably originally referred to the mountain range (cf. "the highlands of Seir" in vs. 8 above and elsewhere) which rises several thousand feet above sea level west of the Arabah and south of the Dead Sea; ultimately the name was transferred to the whole countryside in which the mountains lay and which they dominated.

The Horites, we know (see above on 26:34), who may at the same time be the same as the Hivites (note that Zibeon is a Horite in vs. 20 and a Hivite in vs. 2), are the biblical equivalent of the people whom students of the history of the ancient Near and Middle East know as the Hurrians. Unfortunately, nothing can be made of this biblical tradition of a Hurrian prehistory in Edom except the most likely judgment that it is in error, of a piece, very probably, with P's discovery of Hittites at Hebron in chapter 23. All of the names of vss. 20–30, as far as we can determine them at all, are Semitic and not Hurrian; and there is no evidence in either Hurrian or Edomite records to support a Hurrian presence in patriarchal or prepatriarchal Edom. We have to do, therefore, with another of those popular anachronisms that characterize the handling of ancient ethnic names by the sources of Genesis.

Nevertheless, these verses are not bereft of all historical interest or of relevance to the understanding of Genesis. For one thing, we note in this name list a preponderance of those ending in -an or -on, which long ago were shown by W. F. Albright to be typical of the nomenclature of pre-Israelite Canaan. (Cf. Hem*an* the Ezrahite of Psalm 88:1 who is one of the sons of Korah [vs. 14 above, etc.] and Eth*an* the Ezrahite of Psalm 89:1 [cf. also 1 Kings 5:11, etc.]. In Albright's view "Ezrahite" [related to the Zerah of vss. 13.17, etc.] means "aboriginal," i.e., one of the former natives of the land.) For another thing, we cannot ignore the fact that "Hurrian" is a Semitic name, applied to the people in question not by themselves but by others (even as a modern people who call themselves *die Deutschen* are known by English speakers as "Germans," and what Europeans and Americans identify as "Egypt" is a land that its own inhabitants recognize as *al-Misr*). A persistent etymology of "Hurrian" in Semitic (the *Hori* of vs. 22) is "cave" (Hebrew *hor,* Akkadian *hurru*), which may not be simply an afterthought of folk humor: it could have meant from the beginning troglodyte, cave dweller, primitive, aboriginal, native. It is not unusual, as we have remarked before, for a people of limited experience and social horizons to apply to another that is badly known a pejorative or at least a patronizing name. The example we previously instanced was that of the Philistines, whose name by association with

Israelite prejudice became roughly the equivalent of "clowns," certainly synonymous with the uncultured and the uncultivated (a usage which Thomas Carlyle absorbed from the casual German scholarship of his time and so introduced into English literature), even though by most criteria men use to measure culture the Israelites were the inferiors of the Philistines. Even today people not innately mean or stupid will nevertheless concoct crude jokes and canards about other peoples whose language and folkways seem funny to them only because they are unshared and unfamiliar. What we are leading up to here is the suggestion that biblical tradition under the rubric "Horites" may be able to tell us nothing, indeed, about the historical Hurrians, yet perhaps something about the early inhabitants of southern Palestine. In particular, the *Lotan* of vs. 20 who gave his name to a clan (vs. 29) strongly reminds us of the Lot of the Arabah after whom the Arabs have named the Dead Sea, whom other tradition, it is true, has connected with the story of Abraham, though not very securely, and whom that same tradition (19:30–38) made a cave dweller.

Several of the names in this list (Zibeon, Anah, Oholibamah, there Hivites of the land of Canaan; Timna, not further identified) have already appeared in vss. 1–14. Some of them are recognizably Arabic, and some, as before, have other incarnations elsewhere in Israel's records, testimony to their once having been borne by inhabitants of a greater Canaan who were at length assimilated into the Israelite tribal system. Thus *Shobal* in 1 Chronicles 2:50–52 is a Calebite, as is *Mahanath; Shepho* does not, but his brother *Onam* does show up in 1 Chronicles 2:26 as a Jerahmeelite and Judahite. To this day the Bedawin of the steppes of the Negeb and the Arabah show a partiality for animal names. Here we have a goodly number of them: *Zibeon* probably means "hyena"; *Anah* is the Arabic for "ass" (the little saga of vs. 24 memorializes this association); *Dishon* in Deuteronomy 14:15 is some kind of antelope; and *Aiah* in Deuteronomy 14:13 is a species of predatory bird. *Eshban* is an Arabic word for "red," recalling the many similar terms we have already seen brought into connection with Edom, the red land; and *Uz,* as we saw above (10:23, a Semite by way of Aram; 22:21, this time, like Lot, a nephew of Abraham), is an undeniably Edomite name, of a district and, probably, a clan with which Israel acknowledged bonds of kinship and common tradition. Various other names in these verses could call for attention, but the reader will probably have concluded by now that quite enough time has been spent on the matter. At least, we have seen enough to know that Genesis has not simply invented random and rootless names to people these genealogies.

31 The following are the kings who reigned in the land
of Edom before any king reigned over the Israelites.

32 Bela, son of Beor, became king in Edom; the name
33 of his city was Dinhabah. When Bela died, Jobab,
   son of Zerah, from Bozrah, succeeded him as king.
34 When Jobab died, Husham, from the land of the
   Temanites, succeeded him as king. He defeated the
   Midianites in the country of Moab; the name of his
35 city was Avith. When Husham died, Hadad, son of
36 Bedad, succeeded him as king. When Hadad died,
   Samlah, from Masrekah, succeeded him as king.
37 When Samlah died, Shaul, from Rehoboth-on-the-
38 River, succeeded him as king. When Shaul died,
   Baal-hanan, son of Achbor, succeeded him as king.
39 When Baal-hanan died, Hadar* succeeded him as
   king; the name of his city was Pau. (His wife's
   name was Mehetabel; she was the daughter of Ma-
   tred, son of Mezahab.)

Edomites, Moabites, Ammonites, and others, together with the Israelites
were Western Semitic peoples who carved out little realms for themselves
at about the same time in history, in the thirteenth century B.C., along the
eastern coast of the Mediterranean Sea south of the Aramean territories
westward of the Euphrates and as far inland to the east as the desert
would allow. The Israelites, as we know, admitted to kinship with most of
these other peoples, as well as with the Arameans to the north and others
even more remote to the east. Indeed, they were all essentially the same
people, distinguished only by historical experience, just as Low and High
Germans parted company long ago over historic issues far more important
than the substitution of a z for a t, or, conversely, as Englishmen accepted
the Danish egg but could not long abide Danegeld and Danelaw. The historical experience which distinguished Israelites from their neighbors and
cousins was the Yahwistic covenant. Some of these neighbors and cousins
might dissolve the distinction by crossing over into the covenant, as we
have good reason to suspect that countless Edomites did. Some might, for
whatever reasons, never make the transitions: that Moabites and Ammonites were forever excluded from union with Israel (Deuteronomy
23:4) undoubtedly points to some historical facts about which we can
only guess. As for the other inhabitants of the land, principally those
whom the Bible reckons as Canaanites or Amorites, no relationship was
acknowledged. These peoples, or this people, also of the same Western

---

* The name ought to be Hadad. So it is in the SP, the Syriac, and many manuscripts
of the MT (cf. 1 Chronicles 1:50). The NAB has acknowledged this evidence in its
critical notes and opted for the correction, but strangely has balked at changing the
printed text. (We remember that Hebrew d is easily confused with r.)

Semitic stock which in point of fact had contributed to Israel their sons and daughters at Shechem and elsewhere to build the covenant, and from whom many if not most of the Israelites consequently counted their descent and ancestry, remained now only a residue of unbelievers, to be reckoned with Hittites, Horites, and other discarded peoples who had been cleared away to make room for the Lord's own. And of course, there was no commerce with the Philistines, the non-Semitic people who had invaded Palestine from the sea in the same thirteenth century B.C., and who had secured the enclave on the coast from which they were never successfully dislodged throughout all of Israel's history.

In view of this history it is not difficult to credit an authentic record of *the kings who reigned in the land of Edom before any king reigned over the Israelites* as being in the possession of an Israelite author. Neither would an Israelite author have any reluctance about attributing an earlier coming of monarchy to Edom than to Israel: monarchy was the law of the nations (1 Samuel 8:5), but Israel had had peculiar scruples in adjusting to this law (1 Samuel 8:7–8), and these scruples were respected in later theology. If we find it strange that an Israelite author, nevertheless, should make such a point of chronicling long-dead Edomite kings in a history of Israel, several considerations must be borne in mind. First, in the free and easy chronology of the Pentateuch, Edom (Esau, as we are frequently reminded) already existed in patriarchal times, long before the coming of Israel into the land. Therefore a list of Edomite kings, whatever its actual historical provenance, could be included in a partiarchal narrative without conscious anachronism. This leads to the second consideration. A sequence of Israelite kings, in a narrative devoted to a remote pre-Israel, *would* be a glaring anachronism, by anybody's standards. Secondly, therefore, the tradition has taken occasion from the Edomite source to indicate the only fulfillment it could of the divine promise that kings would spring from the loins of Abraham and Isaac (17:6.16, P; the same promise is made to Jacob in 35:11, P). And finally, in the perspective of P, who is the collector of these bits and pieces, or of R, who shares his views, Edom has been a concern of the Lord no less than Israel. Edom for the sake of Israel, no doubt, but still a concern.

What immediately strikes one in the Edomite king list is its lack of any evidence of a dynastic succession. Most of the kings are identified by city and by family, all of which differ. However these eight men came to be king—by election, by charismatic or prophetic designation, or by conquest —they ruled in their own right and not by inheritance. This situation may have commended itself and evoked nostalgic memories for an Israelite author, however he might have been committed to the tradition of a Davidic dynasty as a matter of policy, when he recalled that not only Saul (1 Samuel 9–10) but also David himself (1 Samuel 16:1–13, 2 Samuel 2:1–6) had thus been constituted king of Israel, not to mention the fact that in the subsequent divided kingdom the Israel of the north had continued to be so governed by occasional kings (cf. 2 Kings 9:1–13, etc.). Genesis was put together in a time when charismatic leadership signified an act of faith in the past if not a fact of present reality (the Deuteronomic book of Judges, for example). We can hardly imagine the Yahwist author looking for a similar precedent in the historical records of an Edom which had been humbled and subjugated by David.

Bela, son of Beor reminds one immediately of the soothsayer Balaam, son of Beor, of Numbers 22:5. Balaam was from Pethor on the Euphrates in the land of Amaw. Both of these geographical names seem to have turned up in cuneiform sources (though there is a persistent view that "pethor" really means "sorcerer"), pointing to a place near Carchemish in northern Syria (cf. Numbers 23:7), so that it is not likely the two persons were the same. Bela, for that matter, is a common enough Western Semitic name (Benjaminite, for example, in Genesis 46:21), as probably was Beor. Unlike *Bozrah* and *the land of the Temanites* (Amos 1:12, etc.), *Dinhabah, Masrekah,* and *Pau* are otherwise unknown as Edomite sites. *Rehoboth-on-the-River* would normally indicate a place on the Euphrates, which could hardly have been in Edom; but such names have a way of traveling, just as before and after rivers have crossed continents and oceans, and cities and lakes have circumnavigated the globe.

Jobab is a Semitic, Arabian name in Genesis 10:29. *Zerah* we have seen. *Husham* and *Hadad,* under various forms, appear often in the Bible, and the latter (1 Kings 11:14, etc.) is definitely Edomite. Most of the rest of these names it would be of little profit to pursue further. It is at least an interesting curiosity, however, that in vs. 38 a *Shaul* (the same as Saul, the first king of Israel) is succeeded by a *Baal-hanan* (probably meaning "Baal has been merciful"). By some, David, who succeeded Saul in Israel, is thought to be the Elhanan of 2 Samuel 21:19, the son of Jair from Bethlehem, who killed Goliath the Philistine. But there are other explanations of this seeming coincidence.

> 40 The following are the names of the clans of
> Esau individually according to their subdivisions
> and localities: the clans of Timna, Alvah, Je-
> 41/42 theth, Oholibamah, Elah, Pinon, Kenaz, Teman,
> 43 Mibzar, Magdiel and Iram. These are the clans
> of the Edomites, according to their settlements
> in their territorial holdings. [Esau was the father
> of the Edomites.]

We end, for good measure, with a final listing of *the clans of Esau* which partly agrees and also radically differs with everything that has gone before. The historical value of this strange roster is, to say the least, questionable; the eleven clans do not even have the advantage of adding up to a significant number. Only *Kenaz* and *Teman* appear as they were in vs. 15 above. *Timna,* on the contrary, who in vs. 12 was a concubine of Eliphaz and in vs. 22 a Horite, the sister of Lotan, now becomes the name of a clan, unthinkable for a woman. Similarly *Oholibamah,* in vss. 2.5.14.18.25 the daughter of Anah, in vs. 2 a Hivite, and in vs. 25 a Horite. The other names are new. Is *Alvah* the Alvan of vs. 23? Or *Jetheth* the Ithran of vs. 26? (The LXX has *Iether* for Jetheth.) *Elah* is thought to be the Elath of the Gulf of Aqabah, the port city of Edom. *Pinon,* we can be sure, is the Punon of Numbers 33:42–43, today Khirbet Fenan on the east side of the Arabah north of Petra by some thirty-eight kilometers. *Mibzar* may be Petra itself, or rather one of its dependencies: the word means "fortress." The two other names are not identifiable.

IV. The Story of Joseph

1. Joseph and His Brothers

37 Jacob settled in the land where his father had
2 stayed, the land of Canaan. This is his family history. When Joseph was seventeen years old, he was tending the flocks with his brothers; he was an assistant to the sons of his father's wives Bilhah and Zilpah, and he brought his father bad reports about them.

The first of these verses is in reality the conclusion of the Priestly author's story of Jacob's career as the founder of Israel; it is in logical sequence with 35:29. The second verse, however, does properly begin the Joseph story, which, as far as P is concerned, has not only been unimaginatively digested in the way that is usual with this source, but has also been so grudgingly used by the Redactor of Genesis, who has discarded the rest, that it is now impossible to reconstruct what contribution it may once have made to this final portion of our book. The *toledoth* (*family history*) of Jacob is, of course, the chronicle that is to follow, the account of his descendants, which as we presently have the story—almost exclusively from J and E—is mainly confined to the doings of Joseph, Jacob's youngest son so far (apart from what is related in the E of 35:16–20, which has no bearing on the chapters that lie ahead). We can guess from vs. 2 that P as well as J and E, for whatever reasons, restricted his attention to Joseph among the sons of Israel; but we cannot prove this. The chronological note of *seventeen years* corroborates the guess, and it will be further confirmed below; as before, the Priestly author devises periods and life-spans only for those persons who are significant to him.

Joseph is here a shepherd and subservient to his elder brothers, as he is in the major JE story that follows. Only here, his duty is restricted *to the sons of his father's wives Bilhah and Zilpah,* that is, to Dan and Naphtali, Gad and Asher, sons/tribes who figure not at all in the following narrative and hardly at all in the subsequent Israelite history that we know. (We are presuming, of course, that the distribution of Jacob's "sons" was in P as it is also in the JE of 29:31–30:24.) Thus it is that the hatred of Joseph by his brothers, a theme common to all the sources, is in P confined to only four of them, motivated by his talebearing concerning some unspecified deeds of theirs. We would like to be able to follow this story to the end and learn its implications, but the Redactor has prevented us. He directs us now to the JE amalgam which is the substance of the Genesis story of Joseph.

This story, as we pointed out earlier in our introduction, is rather different from the stories that have gone before. "The same sources are there, yet in ways less than subtle they are different." These chapters "separate themselves from the rest of the patriarchal history through an orientation and inspiration that are peculiarly theirs, which betray an influence at work that has not touched the sources elsewhere." First of all (and these "firsts" were already noted, for the most part, by Hermann Gunkel over three quarters of a century ago), the Joseph story is not a saga made up of unmatched pearls laid side by side—a perfect description of so much of the Yahwist's work in the earlier chapters of Genesis—but a *Novelle,* a short story, a *roman.* Nor is it simply a matter of having tightened up in this case a narrative that is or can be looser in others: along with the shift in genre there is also a change in attitude and priorities. The cult sagas or myths that lurk in the background of J and to a less extent of E in the Abraham and Jacob stories are not to be discerned here at all. There are no theophanies (46:1–5, E, is the probative exception to the rule). Taking the place of the divine intervention in its conventional modes are dreams and the interpretation of dreams (a skill) and the art of divination (likewise a skill). And there is even a more striking distinction yet, from the standpoint of folk and religion: that whereas before in J or E Gentiles like Abimelech or Laban could be portrayed as crypto-Yahwists sharing basically the same theology and moral code with their patriarchal guests, in the Joseph story the separate identity of Egypt and its ways becomes paramount, and the relation of Joseph to these ways and to those of his father and brethren remains an unresolved issue, if issue it was, which never dissolves simplistically into an accommodation with Israelite orthodoxy.

All this being so, it is not hard to see why Gerhard von Rad should have conceived of a "wisdom" leitmotiv directing the Joseph narrative, whether in J or E, as it developed on the soil of Palestine. "Wisdom" was in Israel both a literary tradition and a way of thought. As a way of thought it tended to be international and ecumenical, secular rather than doctrinaire, depending more on reason and common sense than on appeal to revealed religion to shape an outlook on life and to find therein solutions for life's many problems. It took an interest, purely for their own sake, in the many facets of nature and of the human phenomenon—even as the Joseph story is interested in such varied items as the protocol of the Egyptian court, Egyptian words and customs, the process of mummification, and the like, all of which it found curious and worth thinking about. Joseph himself appears in the story in one of the classic guises of the wisdom professor: the royal counselor and adviser in the practical business of statecraft. Egypt was proverbial in Israel for its wise men (cf. 1 Kings 5:10), and there are numerous traces of its wisdom tradition in the "wisdom" literature of the Old Testament.

Von Rad thought of the Joseph story as a product of an "older" wisdom school—one which, without being irreligious, nevertheless had for its ideal the "wise and discerning man" (Genesis 41:33) who was guided by prudence and experience rather than by the revealed Law of God which in later wisdom writings is identified with wisdom itself (as in Sirach 24, for example). As William McKane has pointed out, however, the figure cut by Joseph in our story is not all that "secular": Joseph attributes his powers to the working of God, and he is recognized by Pharaoh as one possessed of the Spirit of God (41:16.38). Further, in his other dealings Joseph is directed by Hebrew piety (cf. 39:9) as well as by shrewdness and sagacity. But there would seem to be little problem about accepting the major thesis, that in theme and in technique the Joseph story of Genesis is wisdom-inspired, whether the wisdom be of an earlier or a later appropriation in Israelite letters.

We therefore must be forewarned that the "J" and the "E" of the sections that follow are of a different discipline from that of their counterparts in chapters 1–36 of Genesis. We still see the correspondences between them, but we also see many changes. Gone, for the most part, are the theological and cultural interests that combined to shape the other patriarchal sagas. Rather, it is the genius of the Joseph tradition to have shaped the sources and imprinted on them its distinctive character, which is one rather free of theology and ideology. Under the powerful influence of this tradition the two sources produced separate versions of a common story which are remarkably parallel in thought and detail, and the Redactor selected what he evidently considered to be the better parts of each to make up the narrative we now possess in Genesis. The closest analogue to what has happened here is what happened earlier on in the composition of the Genesis flood story, where the Redactor also had to work with parallel versions of an equally powerful and formative tradition and assembled from them a narrative which made the best use of both. Nevertheless, we must confess without dissimulation that the Joseph story presents more unresolved problems for the documentary hypothesis and asks more serious questions about it than does any other part of Genesis.

The story, as it begins, seems to be J:

3 Israel loved Joseph best of all his sons, for he was the
child of his old age; and he had made him a long
4 tunic. When his brothers saw that their father loved
him best of all his sons,* they hated him so much
that they would not even greet him.

Israel is the title which the Yahwist habitually attributes to Jacob in the
Joseph story. That Jacob preferred Joseph to the rest of his sons because
he was the child of his old age is not entirely consonant with the earlier JE
account of 29:31–30:24 which merely made Joseph the most recent in a
line of children born to a Jacob in the full vigor of his manhood. Neither is
it entirely consonant with what will come later in this same story, when it
will appear that Benjamin and not Joseph is the child of Jacob's old age.
Benjamin is not mentioned at all for the present, and it is likely that in this
tradition he was thought of as having been born only after Joseph was
taken into Egypt. The most natural acceptation of the situation sketched in
the verses above is that of an aging father showing a marked favoritism for
a youngest child in whom he sees a reflection of his own vanished youth,
with whom he can also play the role of a doting parent as he can no longer
with the strapping young men who are his other sons. Not an unusual pass
in human annals, and one that has more than once contributed to deep
and irreversible tragedy.

At all events, whereas P attributed the bad blood between Joseph and
his brothers, or some of them at least, to Joseph's having informed on
them in some matter or other, in J it is Jacob's partiality to Joseph that
causes the alienation. The *long tunic* which Jacob made for Joseph is the
"coat of many colors" of older translations. The meaning of the Hebrew
expression is not certain, but present-day opinion inclines to the idea that
the sumptuousness of the garment rather than its colors distinguished it.
Probably it was ankle-length, or perhaps sleeved; the outer garb of the
common man, on the contrary, was short and sleeveless. Gunkel undoubtedly caught the significance of the tunic rightly when he judged it to be the
mark of a pampered youth who had never been initiated into the
workaday world.

Finally, the Elohist—for it is to E that we must probably assign the following verses—has yet another explanation for the hostility of Jacob's
other sons toward their younger brother: his dreams of grandeur. Dreams
will play a major role in the subsequent development of the Joseph story.

5 Once Joseph had a dream, which he told to his
6/7 brothers:† "Listen to this dream I had. There we

---

* So the LXX, the SP, and manuscript evidence. The standard MT has "his brethren."
† The MT adds from vs. 8 "and they hated him all the more."

were, binding sheaves in the field, when suddenly
my sheaf rose to an upright position, and your
sheaves formed a ring around my sheaf and bowed
8 down to it." "Are you really going to make yourself king over us?" his brothers asked him. "Or
impose your rule on us?" So they hated him all the
9 more because of his talk about his dreams. Then
he had another dream, and this one, too, he told
to his brothers. "I had another dream," he said;
"this time, the sun and the moon and eleven stars
10 were bowing down to me." When he also told it to
his father,‡ his father reproved him. "What is the
meaning of this dream of yours?" he asked, "Can
it be that I and your mother and your brothers are
11 to come and bow to the ground before you?" So his
brothers were wrought up against him but his father pondered the matter.

The two dreams of Joseph do not indicate a conflation of parallels here
but are rather a peculiarity of the Elohist's story: in 40:5–19 Joseph interprets two separate dreams of Pharaoh's courtiers, and in 41:1–7 Pharaoh
himself experiences two dreams in sequence, both of which, as here, convey the same message. It is hardly difficult to understand why Joseph's
brothers should have an animosity against him or why his father was disturbed and concerned. It is not that Joseph has committed any offense precisely, for dreams, it is assumed by all, are a means of divine revelation
not subject to the control of the dreamer. Nevertheless, the habit of
beheading the messenger of unpleasant tidings is ingrained in human nature and history, as contemporary experience can still testify. (Recall the
plaintive appeal of Obadiah to Elijah in 1 Kings 18:7–15.) The meaning
of the dreams is apparent to his brothers, to Jacob, and certainly to a sus-
piciously ingenuous Joseph. He is destined to dominate over his brothers
and even to surpass his father and mother in the eyes of men and in the
dignity and acclaim that it is within the power of men to bestow. In 42:6
(E) Joseph's brothers do literally *come and bow to the ground before*
him, and it is possible that in some other portion of the Elohist's narrative
that has not been retained by the Redactor a similar gesture was attributed
to his father and mother. But the biblical author is also thinking of the
later history of Israel, when the "Joseph" tribe of Ephraim dominated the
tribal confederation and assumed unchallenged leadership over it, so that
Joseph became indeed "the prince among his brothers" (49:26). Even
after the coming of the monarchy and then the separation in two of a once

‡ The MT adds "and to his brothers."

united kingdom, Ephraim remained to the end identified with the larger, wealthier, and politically more significant north that retained the name of Israel. For the northern prophet Hosea "Ephraim" and "Israel" are interchangeable titles. The Elohist source, which displays northern influences, would most logically take note of the later superiority of Joseph-Ephraim forecast in the earliest of the dreams which were to determine the course of Joseph's life in different ways.

The first of Joseph's dreams seems to presuppose (like 26:12, 27:27–28 above, both J) an agricultural life for Joseph and his brothers rather than the usual pastoral one that shows up again when the J story is resumed in vs. 12. Here, too, Joseph is a field laborer along with the rest and not the spoilt idler of vss. 3–4. The *sheaves* which *bowed down* to the sheaf of Joseph anticipates the later episode of 42:6, of the brothers kneeling before the dispenser of Egypt's grain (cf. also 50:18). The explicitness of *to make yourself king over us,* however, may, as we suggested above, look beyond the immediate confines of the Joseph story to the later history that it foreshadowed, when there was a literal Ephraimite kingship in Israel. The dream of *the sun and the moon and eleven stars* evidently has the same general meaning as that of the sheaves, but it is more mysterious in its conception. Are we to think of Joseph as a twelfth star in this vision—the text does not really say so—and thus imagine behind it some kind of zodiacal signification? Apparently not; the heavenly luminaries are simply random symbols tossed up by the surrealism of dream stuff: with Benno Jacob we agree that sun, moon, and a cluster of stars all in confluence is totally unreal. From vs. 10 it is plain that in the purview of this story Rachel is yet alive, therefore that the E account of her death in 35:16–20 was unknown to this portion of the tradition. By the same token, as we suggested earlier, the birth of Benjamin probably did not occur until later on in the Joseph story as it is developed in these present chapters, or as it has been drawn upon selectively to make up these chapters. Here as elsewhere in the traditions, however, Joseph nonetheless has eleven brothers. We have already warned that exact consistency of detail has been no hobgoblin to frighten the Redactor of Genesis.

The remainder of this chapter has been produced by a skillful binding together of the sources we designate J and E. The latter we indicate by italics in the paragraphs below.

> 12 One day, when his brothers had gone to pasture
> 13 their father's flocks at Shechem, Israel said to Jo-
> seph, "Your brothers, you know, are tending our
> flocks at Shechem. Get ready; I will send you to
> 14 them." "I am ready," Joseph answered. "Go then,"

he replied; "see if all is well with your brothers and
the flocks, and bring back word." So he sent him off
from the valley of Hebron. When Joseph reached She-
15 chem, a man met him as he was wandering about
in the fields. "What are you looking for?" the man
16 asked him. "I am looking for my brothers," he answered. "Could you please tell me where they are
17 tending the flocks?" The man told him, "They have
moved on from here; in fact, I heard them say, 'Let
us go on to Dothan.'" So Joseph went after his
18 brothers and caught up with them in Dothan. *They
noticed him from a distance,* and before he came up
19 to them, they plotted to kill him. *They said to one
20 another: "Here comes that master dreamer! Come
on, let us kill him and throw him into one of the
cisterns here; we could say that a wild beast devoured him. We shall then see what comes of his
dreams."*
21 *When Reuben heard this, he tried to save him from
22 their hands, saying, "We must not take his life. Instead of shedding blood,"* he continued, *"just throw
him into that cistern there in the desert; but don't
kill him outright." His purpose was to rescue him
23 from their hands and restore him to his father.* So
when Joseph came up to them, they stripped him of
24 the long tunic* he had on; *then they took him and
threw him into the cistern, which was empty and
dry.*
25 They then sat down to their meal. Looking up, they
saw a caravan of Ishmaelites coming from Gilead,
their camels laden with gum, balm and resin to be
26 taken down to Egypt. Judah said to his brothers:
"What is to be gained by killing our brother and
27 concealing his blood? Rather, let us sell him to these
Ishmaelites, instead of doing away with him ourselves. After all, he is our brother, our own flesh."
28 His brothers agreed. They sold Joseph to the Ishmaelites for twenty pieces of silver.
*Some Midianite traders passed by, and they pulled
Joseph up out of the cistern and took him to Egypt.*
29 *When Reuben went back to the cistern and saw that*

* See the commentary.

30 *Joseph was not in it, he tore his clothes, and returning to his brothers, he exclaimed: "The boy is gone!*
31 *And I—where can I turn?"* They took Joseph's
tunic, and after slaughtering a goat, dipped the tunic
32 in its blood. They then sent someone to bring the
long tunic to their father, with the message: "We
found this. See whether it is your son's tunic or
33 not." He recognized it and exclaimed: "My son's
tunic! *A wild beast has devoured him!* Joseph has
34 been torn to pieces!" *Then Jacob rent his clothes, put
sackcloth on his loins,* and mourned his son many
35 days. Though his sons and daughters tried to console him, he refused all consolation, saying, "No, I
will go down mourning to my son in the nether
world." *Thus did his father lament him.*
36 *The Midianites,*† *meanwhile, sold Joseph in Egypt
to Potiphar, a courtier of Pharaoh and his chief
steward.*

One story has been made from two, a better story, perhaps, from the
best components of the others, but it is still possible to discern the contours of the originals despite their having been separately truncated when
they were stitched together. As J would have it, the brothers have *plotted
to kill* Joseph before he catches up with them at Dothan. When he arrives,
they first strip him of the hated *long tunic* that had so long epitomized for
them all that was detestable about their younger brother; *then they sat
down to their meal* to deliberate what they were to do with him. Over the
horizon appears *a caravan of Ishmaelites coming from Gilead,* and *Judah*
persuades the rest of his brethren—Judah, of course, being a special hero
for the Yahwist tradition—not to kill Joseph after all but rather to sell him
into slavery by means of these international entrepreneurs. Which they do.
Thereafter they dip the famous tunic in goat's blood and pass it off to
Jacob as evidence they had found of Joseph's having *been torn to pieces*
by wild animals somewhere along the way. In the E story the brothers
similarly resolve to destroy Joseph as they see him approaching them in
the distance. This time their plans are firmed up quickly and without
delay: they will *kill him and throw him into one of the cisterns* nearby;
then they will report *that a wild beast devoured him.* The brother of compassion is now *Reuben,* who talks his fellows into merely casting Joseph
into the cistern without killing him first. Reuben intends to rescue him
covertly *and restore him to his father.* But meanwhile, after the brothers

† Here, literally, "Medanites," a variant of "Midianites." In vs. 17 the first "Dothan"
is actually spelt "Dothain." Cf. the Penuel and Peniel of 32:23–33.

have left their encampment, *Midianite traders passed by, pulled Joseph up out of the cistern and took him to Egypt,* where they sold him *to Potiphar, a courtier of Pharaoh and his chief steward.* On his secret return to the cistern Reuben is disconsolate to find that Joseph has vanished; now he can only go along with the story on which the brothers has agreed and tell Jacob that *a wild beast has devoured* Joseph. Why Reuben, a "Leah" son of Jacob like Judah, should be the flawed "hero" of this Elohistic story is not altogether clear. Probably it is because in the traditions he held pride of place as first-born: E does not take into account 35:22 and 49:4, Reuben's disinheritance.

In vs. 23, which above we have assigned to J, there is with some likelihood a conflation of the two sources, a redactional signal that here the stories merged. This fact has been obscured in the NAB, which understandably attempts to elicit from the received text as smooth a rendering as possible in preference to making obvious its unevennesses. Quite literally we read in this verse: "They stripped him of his *kuttoneth* (his outer garments), of the *kethoneth passim* he had on." Probably *kuttoneth* is E language: the brothers, having accepted Reuben's counsel not to kill Joseph outright, first strip him before casting him into the cistern where he will presumably die of hunger and exposure. The *kethoneth passim* (the "long tunic" of the NAB) is, as always, the property of J: this is Joseph's distinctive robe which, later spattered with blood, Jacob will accept as proof evident of his son's death by predatory beasts somewhere on his journey.

The Yahwist's prelude in vss. 12–17 is curious in several respects. In 35:21 (J) Jacob was last seen at Migdal-eder in the neighborhood of Jerusalem, and in 35:27 (P) he was at Mamre, in Kiriath-arba, identified with Hebron. Here also, if we are to take vs. 14b at face value, the family residence is in the south, in *the valley of Hebron.* It is difficult to reconcile this indication with the logic of the story as it unfolds, however. Shechem was several days' journey to the north of Hebron. What would Jacob's sons be doing pasturing his flocks so far afield? And of what could he be thinking, to send on such an arduous and dangerous passage the tender son of his old age? For such a trivial mission, it can be added: *see if all is well with your brothers and the flocks, and bring back word.* It makes much better sense to imagine as the original locale of the story the vicinity of Shechem, where the traditions earlier placed Jacob; the Yahwist, with his partiality for southern sites, in particular for Hebron with its Abrahamic associations, would have made the change in disregard of the other possibilities. If this hypothesis is correct, Jacob's sending Joseph out on a casual errand becomes quite credible: perhaps little more lay behind it than a father's thought that a day's outing would do his stay-at-home son no harm.

In this construction the brothers' movement to Dothan, some fifteen kilometers to the north of Shechem, is as understandable as their removal to Shechem from Hebron was not. Other details of the story also fall in line. Joseph *wandering about in the fields* near Shechem and encountered by *a man*—another shepherd, no doubt—who directed him toward Dothan was not nearing the end of a long and wearisome journey to which only a few more miles must now be added, he was rather faced with the choice of abandoning the small commission with which his father had entrusted him, dispensable time wasted over no great thing, or of embarking on a genuine voyage that will commit him to perils Jacob had never anticipated when he sent him forth. Foolishly, perhaps, paradoxically foolishly for one whose name is later to be equated with wisdom and common sense, Joseph takes the road to Dothan, thus setting in motion the chain of events that add up to the Joseph story. For their part, the brothers of Joseph react with a certain logic. They have long entertained a hatred for their younger brother (vs. 4 above), but they could hardly do anything about it as long as the object of their hate was safe beneath the shelter of the family roof. Now, for the first time, he has forfeited his protection. Even the short distance between Shechem and Dothan allows for innumerable pitfalls where a favorite son can be lost and buried forever. Joseph's thoughtless enthusiasm comes up against his brothers' grim determination and loses in the contest.

Dothan (the Tell Dotha of modern Palestinian archeology) also has other meanings for the Joseph story. It was an Early and Middle Bronze settlement well within the limits that can be assigned to the patriarchal age by anyone's computation, just as it was a thriving city in the days of Elisha's Iron Age (cf. 2 Kings 6:13) and continued for several centuries afterward. Far more important, it was part of a caravan route which proceeded from Mesopotamia through *Gilead* to Egypt (cf. vs. 25), frequented by *Ishmaelites* and other wandering merchants who brought from the east *gum, balm and resin* to satisfy Egyptian demand for such commodities useful in liturgy, medicine, and embalming. The *Midianites* (25:1–6 above, cf. 4:2b–16) of the E story also appear as Arab *traders*. We have no way of estimating the value of the *twenty pieces of silver* which the brothers received from the Ishmaelites; they were interested, in any case, less in realizing a profit from Joseph than in effectively removing him from the scene, a service which the Midianites also perform at no expense to anyone. Both the Ishmaelite merchants and the Midianite traders of these verses are seen doubling as slave-runners, which has usually been deemed a detestable occupation even by those who took the peculiar institution of slavery for granted, as the societies of Old Testament times certainly did. The slave was in principle a foreigner, a reminder that in the Near East slavery began as an act of clemency toward war prisoners, who were sentenced to labor rather than to death. Israelite law made it a capital offense for anyone forcibly to enslave a fellow Israelite, a feat that could be accomplished only by kidnaping him and shipping him abroad (cf. Exodus 21:16; Deuteronomy 24:7), precisely as happens to Joseph in this story.

In the Elohist's narrative both Reuben and Jacob give vent to their frustration and grief with the oriental extravagance that includes the rending of clothing, doubtless a relief to the feelings however ineffectual a remedy of their cause. The Yahwist has Jacob mourn in a quieter sort of way, but perhaps more eloquently for all that. We can only imagine the spirit in which *his sons and daughters tried to console him:* the same sons, it must be, whose unnatural cruelty, lies, and deception had transported him beyond all consolation. (The plural "daughters" may, at the same time, be another hint at the different reckoning—indeed, a reckoning that seems to follow no fixed rules—that here and there obtains in the Joseph story.) In vs. 35 occurs the first of the Yahwist's references (the others are 42:38 and 44:29.31) to Sheol, *the nether world,* the place whither the shades of the dead were thought to "descend." None of these references, unlike some others elsewhere in the Old Testament, betrays the slightest desire to speculate about the nature or the conditions of Sheol; they simply speak, dramatically but stereotypically, of a sorrow that ends only with the grave, or of one that leads to an early grave.

Potiphar, the *courtier of Pharaoh and his chief steward* to whom Joseph was sold in Egypt according to E, in keeping with the tenor of these chapters bears an authentically Egyptian name (the same as the Potiphera of 41:45). It means—or it meant, before Hebrew spelling and pronunciation deformed it—something like "the gift of Re," that is, of the sun-god. We shall see more of Potiphar below.

2. Judah and Tamar

Scarcely has the distinctive Joseph story been begun when it is interrupted by a chapter that apparently has nothing to do with it, which reverts to the "old" character of the patriarchal sagas with their interest in Palestinian sites, clans, and other etiologies. There can hardly be any doubt that this chapter did, as a matter of fact, originally have no connection with the Story of Joseph and that it is, therefore, in some sense an intrusion here. It does not seem to be an arbitrary intrusion introduced by the Redactor of Genesis, however, as though he had a scrap of odd material lying about which he had some compulsion to use and which he could fit in nowhere else. Rather, it was the Yahwist, who was unregenerately more at home and at ease with the content and method of the saga sources than with the "wisdom" genre of the Joseph traditions on which he had now embarked. Though hardly for this reason alone, and, in fact, not consciously for this reason at all, by the forcible entry of chapter 38 into the surrounding J version of the story of Joseph, the Yahwist has constituted the latter more recognizably his own than it otherwise would be, simply because it now contains so much more that is compatible with his usual interests and tastes.

Text and commentary will indicate how unmistakable is the attribution of chapter 38 to the Yahwist, by every criterion of language, style, and focus of concern. Why, we may ask nevertheless, do we now read it here, just as the Joseph story is scarcely under way?—why especially this when, as we have conceded, the two stories were originally quite unconnected? The answer must be that the Yahwist inherited the story of chapter 38 just about as he handed it on, and he was prevented by its content from placing it anywhere else in his narrative, always provided that he wanted to preserve the Joseph story intact, as he obviously did. The story concerns an adult Judah who is separated from the rest of his brothers and leads a life apart in the south of Palestine. This combination of circumstances hardly allows for a positioning of the story anywhere earlier in the saga, when Judah was too young, or is presumed still part of the common family, or in any case is in the wrong part of the country. Neither could it be put immediately before the Joseph story, for in the Yahwist's version of that story Judah must be on hand with the rest of his brothers to get the thing launched, as we have just seen. Once the story of Joseph in Egypt is well begun with chapter 39 there is no longer any opportunity to interrupt it without inflicting literary violence to revolt a less sensitive artist than the Yahwist; and besides, the ensemble of Judah and his brothers is soon required again to carry the story on to its desired conclusion. Finally, the story of Judah and Tamar could not be postponed to the end of the book, for by then Judah's entire family has migrated to Egypt, there to remain. Therefore there is a certain inevitable logic to the Yahwist's solution of his problem, the way he found to unite the discrete or at least to effect, despite themselves, a symbiosis of elements that had never thought to meet, much less to embrace. In chapter 38 the passing of a long time is presumed; originally, of course, the time was indefinitely long and ever after. The Yahwist turned redactor now expects us to imagine that during these same years Joseph was rising from slave to vizier in Egypt and building a power structure there.

We shall now see what it was about chapter 38 that captured the Yahwist's interest and caused him to take with it the trouble that he did.

38 About that time Judah parted from his brothers and
pitched his tent near a certain Adullamite named
2 Hirah. There he met the daughter of a Canaanite
named Shua, married her, and had relations with
3 her. She conceived and bore a son, whom she*
4 named Er. Again she conceived and bore a son,
5 whom she named Onan. Then she bore still another
son, whom she named Shelah. They were in Chezib
when he was born.

6 Judah got a wife named Tamar for his first-born,
7 Er. But Er, Judah's first-born, greatly offended the
8 LORD; so the LORD took his life. Then Judah said
to Onan, "Unite with your brother's widow, in fulfillment of your duty as brother-in-law, and thus
9 preserve your brother's line." Onan, however, knew
that the descendants would not be counted as his;
so whenever he had relations with his brother's
widow, he wasted his seed on the ground, to avoid
10 contributing offspring for his brother. What he did
greatly offended the LORD, and the LORD took his
11 life too. Thereupon Judah said to his daughter-in-
law Tamar, "Stay as a widow in your father's house
until my son Shelah grows up"—for he feared that
Shelah also might die like his brothers. So Tamar
went to live in her father's house.

About that time the Yahwist doubtless understands to be the period
when Joseph was being taken down into Egypt by the Ishmaelites (39:1,
J, corresponds with 37:36, E), after the false evidence of his death had
been presented to his father Jacob, who thereafter remained disconsolate
and, probably, aloof from his other children. The original context of the
story, if any there was, we of course do not know. *Judah parted from his
brothers:* the Shephelah, the Judean downs, will be the geographical locale of the following story. In this fact may lie a further explanation of
why (in the hypothesis espoused above) the Yahwist in 37:14 changed
the residence of Jacob and his sons from the neighborhood of Shechem to
that of Hebron. From the highlands Judah easily "parted" (literally, "went
down") to *Adullam* (later associated with David, 1 Samuel 22:1, and frequent in Israelite history) and *Chezib* (probably the Achzib of Joshua
15:44; Micah 1:14), towns in the low country a few kilometers apart and
about fifteen kilometers to the north and west of Hebron. Later there is

---

* So the SP and some manuscripts of the MT; the standard MT has "he." In J, it will
be remembered, the mother usually names the child (as in vss. 4–5).

mention of a *Timnah* to which Judah "went up": Joshua 15:57 lists a Timnah in the highlands which may be the modern Khirbet Tibneh, north and east of Adullam on the edge of the Shephelah. Between Adullam and Timnah, according to vs. 14 below, was *Enaim,* otherwise unknown unless it is—as it very likely is—the Enam of Joshua 15:34, put there in the company of Adullam. This Judahite geography, whose sounds sang in the Yahwist's ear and filled his mind with historical memories, is the necessary stage setting for the saga of Judah and his descendants which intrigued him even more.

That Judah "parted from his brothers," that he *pitched his tent* among the Adullamites, that he married *the daughter of a Canaanite* and had sons by her, some of whom survived and others did not, that he had (vs. 12 and after) other liaisons with the people of the land resulting in other offspring—all this is stuff from the loom of fable, on which the tapestried figures of men are woven of fibers and threads spun from the legends and sagas of clans and lesser tribes. It is a good guess that the tribe of Judah, destined under David and Solomon to assume hegemony in Israel and thereafter to determine most of what we know as Old Testament history and theology, was in point of historical fact a latecomer into the Israelite federation and nation. It is an equally good guess that a chronicle such as we have in this chapter was one of the tardy credentials provided by the later tradition to certify presence at the creation for this tribe after all, whatever had been its real antecedents.

The Song of Deborah (Judges 5), an ancient poem and perhaps the most ancient of all Israelite poems, which celebrates a decisive victory in Canaan sometime in the twelfth century B.C., provides a somewhat uncertain roster of the tribes who constituted the amphictyony, or whatever we are to call it, which preceded Israel's nationhood. Ephraim is there, Joseph therefore, along with Benjamin: the two Rachel tribes. Two other names occur that probably can be counted along with Joseph: Machir (part of Manasseh, cf. Genesis 50:23) and Gilead (another part of Manasseh, cf. Numbers 26:29). So far, then, four tribes, not always the ones that appear in Genesis. The two Bilhah tribes, Dan and Naphtali, are also listed in the Song, bringing the tally to six. And there is one Zilpah tribe, Asher (Gad, on the contrary, is not mentioned). Finally, of the Leah tribes only three are named: Zebulun, Issachar, and Reuben. The Song of Deborah, the oldest Israelite tradition, testifies to a ten-tribe league. Since it calls the roll of these tribes both to lavish praise on faithful companions in arms and to heap scorn on the slackers and delinquents, we may safely assume that the *Appell* is complete, that there were no other tribes to name.

The remaining "Leah" tribes, therefore, Levi, Simeon, and Judah, enter into Israel only at a later stage in the tradition. Simeon and Levi we have seen together in the J of Chapter 34 above, and we shall see them joined again in 49:5–7 below. Levi is a case apart in Israelite tribal history, and it need not occupy our attention for the present. Historically, Simeon was never anything but a subdivision of Judah. That is to say, Simeon was absorbed by Judah at some early period, and its clans which had once been Edomite became Judahite before they were eventually certified as Israelite. What we see in this present chapter 38 is how Judah itself was born from the people of Canaan and Edom, from clans like Onan and Shelah, Perez and Zerah. (The saga, of course, puts the history backward, tracing the genealogy of offspring of an eponymous Judah.) That Reuben, Simeon, Levi, and Judah were remembered in the tradition as the earliest of Jacob's children, the oldest of the tribes of Israel, undoubtedly speaks to an historical fact that they were indeed ancient on the soil of Palestine, where Israel actually begins. They were not, however, part of that earliest Israel supposed by the Song of Deborah, the coalition of peoples that had first formed in response to the gospel of Yahwism. That Israel which had once known no Judah, however, by the time of the J history not only had digested Judah within its system, it had in a way also been digested by it: Judah had become the quintessential Israel (cf. 49:8–12). So was the Boston of the Brahmins inherited by an alien race.

The proper names of this chapter are mainly tribal, but some are merely personal, to contribute verisimilitude to the story. *Hirah*, near whom Judah *pitched his tent*, may be a variant on the common Canaanite name Hiram. In vss. 12 and 20 below Hirah is Judah's *friend*, which we may assume is a technical term for one allied with him by covenant. Here and in what follows no effort is made to conceal the fact that the Judahite clans were also Canaanite (this tradition does not share the revulsion of 24:3, J, or 28:1, P, against intermarriage with the people of the land). No name is given to Judah's Canaanite wife, however, unless *the daughter of . . . Shua* is a roundabout way of saying Bathshua, the name which appears in 1 Chronicles 3:5 as the equivalent of Bathsheba (and in the NAB of this verse has simply been changed to Bathsheba). Possibly there is some significance intended by the dissemblance of this woman's identity whereas that of *Tamar*, likewise a Canaanite, no doubt, is accentuated in the story: the former woman mothered Judahite clans that did not survive or that survived hardly, while the latter was remembered as the ancestress of those for whose sake this story was first told. Tamar (which means "palm tree") was another common Canaanite and Palestinian name; it was borne by one of David's daughters and by a granddaughter (cf. 2 Samuel 13, 14:27).

Er (in 1 Chronicles 4:21 a descendant of Shelah), *Onan* (the Onam of 36:23?), *Shelah* (in Numbers 26:20 mentioned along with Perez and Zerah), *Perez,* and *Zerah* (Edomite in 36:13.17.33, Simeonite in Numbers 26:13) are all clan names. The Cozeba of 1 Chronicles 4:21–22 may explain why in vs. 5 above Chezib has been brought into conjunction with Shelah: possibly the same place is meant in both spellings, and an ancient association is being recalled. As will be made clear at the end of the chapter (vs. 29), the eventual pre-eminence of the Perez clan in Judah is the main point being driven at in this story; but the other names and events contained in it also had their importance for the biblical author, and we would be wrong were we to judge them mere narrative embellishments. Indeed, the average reader today will inevitably find the Perez etiology rather less compelling of his interest other than other features of the story for what they reveal about the values and priorities of those among whom it developed and took shape. Precisely because it is a very good story that has been elaborated with great care, it reveals these quite plainly.

When the author says that Er, Judah's first-born and Tamar's first husband, *greatly offended* Yahweh without specifying exactly how, it is not, as some have supposed, that Er's offense was something too frightful to be named, nor is it, as others have supposed, that it was the same as the offense of Onan (the nature of which they misunderstood). Er's offense is not the point at issue; it is simply presupposed. The premature death of a young husband was a tragedy which the mind of biblical man refused to ascribe to fate or chance. God had caused this thing, and since God acts neither aimlessly nor arbitrarily, he must have been provoked by some capital crime. This logical sequence from effect to cause is of course reversed in narration: Er sins, Yahweh ends his life. It is the well-nigh universal persuasion of the Old Testament that natural disasters, bodily afflictions, shortened life, spiritual anguish all had their explanation in the unhealthy habits and misconduct of those on whom these sufferings were visited. John 9:2 is good indication that the persuasion was still very much alive in the New Testament era. There was and is something to be said in favor of the belief, though the book of Job is a monument to another wisdom which is its measure; essentially, it merely affirmed the principle of inherent retribution, which has a certain amount of empirical evidence on its side—and some opposed to it, or at the most inconclusive, as the Old Testament also knew. In these days of psychosomatics and ecologistics the same principle, or one very like it that has been suitably secularized, has collected respectable corroborative evidence of its own.

There is no question about what was Onan's offense, because of which Yahweh *took his life too*. After Er had died without issue, Judah enjoined upon his second son his *duty as brother-in-law*, that is, that he marry Tamar *and thus preserve your brother's line*. This duty was in fulfillment of the so-called levirate law (from the Latin *levir*, "brother-in-law"), which we find formulated only once in the Law of Moses, in Deuteronomy 25:5–10, but there in terms that make it sound very much like what is presupposed by Genesis. In the fourth chapter of the book of Ruth some similar kind of marriage arrangement involving a near relative is brought into being, though this time the family property seems to have been more at stake than the family name. It would appear that the levirate was just one exemplification of what the Hebrews understood by the concept of *ge'ullah,* "redemption" or "vindication." It was the next of kin who was the usual *go'el,* redeemer, avenger, savior, acting in various capacities depending on the nature of the *ge'ullah* that was to be performed. In the times of blood vengeance the *go'el* tracked down the murderer and exacted life for life. Boaz was the *go'el* of his kinsman Elimelech in Ruth 4, purchasing his land from his widow and marrying his widowed daughter-in-law so as to "raise up a family for the departed on his estate." In chapter 32 of the book of Jeremiah, the prophet is summoned to an act of *ge'ullah,* to exercise his "first claim" to the field of his cousin Hanamel at Anathoth, to preserve intact the family estate lest it be acquired by a profit-seeking stranger. The *go'el* who would normally ensure descent for one who had died without children so as to continue his line and name was the man's own brother, but Boaz is evidence that other next of kin could also serve, and in vs. 26 below Judah acknowledges that he himself had the obligation once he had withheld his son Shelah from Tamar. The institution of "redemption" and the levirate belongs to a society in which the family is all, to be preserved in its various identities by its own resources, and a society which either lacks or spurns the recourses that have been developed in other legal systems to attain the same ends. The institution seems to have been peculiarly Israelite. (Quite appropriately, therefore, Yahweh is sometimes called Israel's *go'el,* e.g., in Isaiah 44:24, 47:3: "redeemer" in the NAB). The sometimes alleged parallel to the levirate in Hittite law most probably was instead an application of the legal principle that a man could inherit his dead brother's wife along with the rest of his chattels; quite a different thing.

It was Onan's refusal of the sacred duty of the *go'el,* his selfishness and his lack of love and loyalty to his brother and family that *greatly offended* Yahweh and brought about his speedy demise. His offense was doubtless compounded by his hypocrisy, since he pretended to undertake the obligation and to all appearances did his duty, while at the same time he made sure that the whole purpose of the relationship would be thwarted. The means he took to ensure this result, or rather, to ensure that there would be no result, has contributed to our language since the beginning of the 1700s the term "onanism"—which, curiously, was first a "learned" circumlocution for male masturbation before it came to apply to the *coitus interruptus* or withdrawal that Genesis obviously has in mind. As far as this practice is concerned, there can hardly be any doubt that the biblical author would have judged Onan's conduct to be odd, bizarre, perhaps even disgusting; but for him this was not the sin of Onan, only the means he took to commit his sin.

Besides, though Onan and Er appear in this story as brothers, we must not lose sight of their representative character in Judah's tribal history. W. F. Albright believed that the biblical names hid those of the Awnanu and Ya'urru, Habiru peoples of the First (Amorite) Dynasty of Babylon. Whether or not we can be so precise, the biblical story is about clans rather than individuals, and it has no real interest in trying to specify the sins of any single historical person.

We have mentioned Ruth a couple of times: Ruth and Tamar are joined not only by the levirate custom, or by a form of it, but also by their common determination to fulfill themselves in offspring by recourse to extraordinary measures. Tamar has another association in Israelite tradition and legend: with Sarah, for example, the "unlucky wife" of Tobit 3:7–9, the woman who devours her husbands and to whom one gives a son in marriage at his own peril. Judah succumbs to this superstition. *Stay . . . until my son Shelah grows up* must have offered as fictitious a timetable to Tamar as it was intended to be by Judah, a hollow show of respect for the commitments he had contracted in Canaan. The subsequent story makes it rather plain that Tamar knew and Judah knew and Shelah knew that vs. 11 describes a charade, a subterfuge. Judah had failed his duty, with or without the compliance of Shelah, whose "youth" is another imponderable for us. The stage was cleared, then, for the next act, which becomes entirely Tamar's.

12 Years passed, and Judah's wife, the daughter of Shua, died. After Judah completed the period of mourning, he went up to Timnah for the shearing of his sheep,† in company with his friend Hirah the 13 Adullamite. When Tamar was told that her father-in-law was on his way up to Timnah to shear his 14 sheep, she took off her widow's garb, veiled her face by covering herself with a shawl, and sat down at the entrance to Enaim, which is on the way to Timnah; for she was aware that, although Shelah was now grown up, she had not been given to him in 15 marriage. When Judah saw her, he mistook her for a 16 harlot, since she had covered her face. So he went over to her at the roadside, and not realizing that she was his daughter-in-law, he said, "Come, let me have intercourse with you." She replied, "What will you pay me for letting you have intercourse with

† So with vs. 13. The MT has "to his sheepshearers."

17 me?" He answered, "I will send you a kid from the flock." "Very well," she said, "provided you leave a
18 pledge until you send it." Judah asked, "What pledge am I to give you?" She answered, "Your seal and cord, and the staff you carry." So he gave them to her and had intercourse with her, and she con-
19 ceived by him. When she went away, she took off
20 her shawl and put on her widow's garb again. Judah sent the kid by his friend the Adullamite to recover the pledge from the woman; but he could not find
21 her. So he asked the men of the place, "Where is the temple prostitute, the one by the roadside in Enaim?" But they answered, "There has never been
22 a temple prostitute here." He went back to Judah and told him, "I could not find her; and besides, the men of the place said there was no temple prostitute
23 there." "Let her keep the things," Judah replied; "otherwise we shall become a laughingstock. After all, I did send her the kid, even though you were unable to find her."

His wife dead, Judah is left alone: we are being prepared for the readiness with which he approaches Tamar in her harlot guise. (Interestingly, this entire chapter seems to presuppose a monogamous society, which can further account for Onan's reluctance to have children by Tamar if she was to be his only wife and the children were not to be his.) *Shelah was now grown up:* whether he was also married or not is not stated, but at all events Tamar now knows of a certainty what she had suspected all along, that this man was not to become her husband despite all law and custom to the contrary. Therefore—and at high time, one might think—she decides to take action of her own. She seizes on the occasion of a sheep-shearing, that time of festivity when wine flowed freely and the normal rules of conduct might be counted on to be relaxed (cf. 1 Samuel 25:8; 2 Samuel 13:27–28). As we see, she did not count in vain. As he makes his way *up to Timnah* after his *period of mourning,* Judah is, together *with his friend Hirah,* the proverbial out-of-towner, the conventioner, a visiting sheikh with his little entourage, ready for diversion.

Widow's weeds probably tended to be worn permanently (cf. 2 Samuel 14:2), as they are still in some parts of the world today. Tamar's "disguise" as a harlot, on the contrary, consisted not in what she wore but in her displaying herself publicly by the wayside as a woman available for commerce (cf. Jeremiah 3:2; Ezekiel 16:25). There was nothing out of the way in the *shawl* with which *she veiled her face,* but it was necessary in order that Judah not recognize her, just as it was necessary that she doff *her widow's garb* in which he was used to seeing her. We are left to imagine how she managed to sustain the deception during their brief relationship somewhere near *the entrance to Enaim.*

Judah's proposition, or his acceptance of Tamar's tacit proposition, is straightforward and traditional, and the biblical author has no moral judgment to pass on it. Tamar, of course, though she plays the harlot is not one, and therefore she does not really care about the price which convention requires her to demand for the mutual transaction. The price, however, to be delivered in kind, permits her to get what she is truly interested in, the *pledge* which she shrewdly stipulates shall be Judah's very identity, his *seal and cord* and *the staff* he carried. The seal and cord, that is, a cylinder incised with a distinctive design, bored through lengthwise and strung with a cord by which it was worn about the neck, when rolled across the wet clay of a cuneiform tablet imprinted the signature and attestation of the single person who bore them. It was originally a Babylonian device, but along with the identifying staff which was also Babylonian, it emigrated westward and became quite common in Palestine. In effect, what Judah does is surrender his ID card, which he expects to be quickly redeemed, but which Tamar retains for her own purposes.

In vs. 15 it is said that Judah perceived Tamar to be a *zonah,* which is the common or garden Hebrew word for "harlot." In vss. 21–22, however, when Judah sends Hirah to recover his pledge, the conversation is all about a *qedeshah* (literally, "a consecrated woman"), a *temple prostitute.* The temple prostitute, a routine fixture of the Near Eastern fertility cults, would have been a familiar and expected figure in the southern Canaan where Judah dwelt. Is this later talk between Judah and Hirah and between Hirah and the men of Enaim an attempt to raise the level of the business that had taken place from the squalid use made of a common whore to the socially quite acceptable visitation of a hierodule? Judah, we note, is much concerned about his dignity in this episode: he sends a deputy to redeem his pledge rather than go himself, and when the pledge is not immediately recoverable he forgoes further inquiry, lest he *become a laughingstock.* Or did Tamar, herself a Canaanite, pass herself off as indeed a temple prostitute? In either case, we may be sure that it was all one to Judah and that the Yahwist likewise understood that it was all one to him. He was not accusing his hero of a *communicatio in sacris.*

> 24 About three months later, Judah was told that his
> daughter-in-law Tamar had played the harlot and
> was then with child from her harlotry. "Bring her
> 25 out," cried Judah; "she shall be burned." But as
> they were bringing her out, she sent word to her

father-in-law, "It is by the man to whom these things belong that I am with child. Please verify," she added, "whose seal and cord and whose staff
26 these are." Judah recognized them and said, "She is more in the right than I am, since I did not give her to my son Shelah." But he had no further relations with her.
27 When the time of her delivery came, she was found
28 to have twins in her womb. While she was giving birth, one infant put out his hand; and the midwife, taking a crimson thread, tied it on his hand, to note
29 that this one came out first. But as he withdrew his hand, his brother came out; and she said, "What a breach you have made for yourself!" So he was
30 called Perez. Afterward his brother came out; he was called Zerah.

Tamar has conceived by Judah (vs. 18 above), and after the first trimester of her pregnancy the fact becomes plain for all to see. That a double standard of morality was applied to men and to women is likewise plain. However, it is assumed that Tamar was guilty of having committed adultery, and all ancient societies dealt very harshly with the adulterous wife. The fact that Judah takes action against her rather than her own father in whose house she lives (vs. 11) indicates that her "harlotry" was interpreted not simply as the dalliance of a mature widow for whom no subsequent marriage had been arranged (widows usually had a hard time of it to acquire another husband), but rather as the crime of an affianced woman against a man and his family to whom she was legally bound. This can hardly mean anything other than a unilateral obligation by which Tamar was held to be Shelah's wife in all respects despite his never having been given to her as husband. If this arrangement sounds grossly unfair, of course it was, as Judah more or less admits in vs. 26. All the same, we probably do him no injustice if we surmise that he discovered in Tamar's apparent disgrace an easy way out of the continuing embarrassment she caused him by her very existence, and that he pronounced sentence on her the more willingly for this reason.

Judah's command is to *bring her out* that *she shall be burned*. The later Law of Moses decreed burning for a priest's daughter who would disgrace her father by fornication (Leviticus 21:9), but for adultery the penalty was death by stoning (Deuteronomy 22:23–24). It is while *they were bringing her out,* that is, preparing to take her to the place of execution, that *she sent word* to Judah and also his "pledge" which she had carefully kept against such an opportune moment as this. In vss. 25–26 there is a very close literary parallel with 37:32–33 which can hardly be entirely co-incidental but is rather an additional confirmation of the common J authorship of these two chapters. The closeness of the parallel is dissembled somewhat in the free translation of the NAB, but it can be readily perceived in a more literal rendering:

37:32–33 They then sent . . . and they said . . . Please examine . . . and he recognized it and said . . .

38:25–26 She sent . . . and she said . . . Please examine . . . and he recognized and said . . .

Judah confesses his offense and the rightness of what Tamar had done; *but he had no further relations with her* is the acknowledgment that her life has now been fulfilled in the offspring that he will accept as his own. Later tradition would make explicit what the Yahwist doubtless implies, namely that Tamar's stratagem was praiseworthy and that hers was a character to be remembered with reverence (cf. Ruth 4:12). Nothing more is said, however, of her relation to either Er or Shelah.

In vss. 27–30 recurs the familiar theme of the twins who are destined to vie with each other even from the womb. *Perez* means "breach"; as a proper name it is here made to refer to the one twin's shouldering aside the other in order to be born first. *Zerah,* a word which can denote the glow of the rising sun in Hebrew and which in cognate Semitic languages resembles a term for the color red, evidently is given a popular etymology to connect with the *crimson thread* which the midwife tied about the wrist of the child who had first put forth his hand. In the tradition represented by Ruth 4:18–22, 1 Chronicles 2:5–15, Perez was the ancestor of David. If this tradition was already known to the Yahwist, it offered him a powerful incentive to include at all costs this Judahite story wherever he could in his chronicle; and we are shown another connection between Tamar and Ruth, the Canaanite and the Moabite who were ancestresses of the great king and of the Great King (cf. Matthew 1:3.5).

3. Joseph in Egypt

As we resume the Joseph story we are still in the company of J, as we shall be through this entire chapter that now follows.

> **39** When Joseph was taken down to Egypt, a certain
> Egyptian (Potiphar, a courtier of Pharaoh and his

chief steward) bought him from the Ishmaelites who
2 had brought him there. But since the LORD was with
him, Joseph got on very well and was assigned to
3 the household of his Egyptian master. When his
master saw that the LORD was with him and brought
4 him success in whatever he did, he took a liking to
Joseph and made him his personal attendant; he put
him in charge of his household and entrusted to him
5 all his possessions. From the moment that he put
him in charge of his household and all his possessions, the LORD blessed the Egyptian's house for Joseph's sake; in fact, the LORD's blessing was on everything he owned, both inside the house and out.
6a Having left everything he owned in Joseph's charge,
he gave no thought, with Joseph there, to anything
but the food he ate.

The NAB has rightly put parentheses about the reference to Potiphar in vs. 1b: it is redactional, borrowed from 37:36, the E story which takes up again in chapter 40. Here we have the sequel to 37:28: having been taken to Egypt by *the Ishmaelites,* Joseph is sold to *a certain Egyptian* (who remains anonymous throughout the rest of the chapter). Instead of select-ing parts from the two traditions J and E which separately described Joseph's first experiences in Egypt, the Redactor has put them in se-quence, harmonizing them into a single account; this, of course, has been frequently done in Genesis. It is well that the choice was so made, for we should be the poorer had either version been entirely or substantially omit-ted.

The Yahwist tells of a Joseph who was so obviously protected and blessed by the Lord that he speedily rose from newly imported slave to trusted overseer and master of a household in all but the name. Even when a contretemps casts him down from this lofty perch and reduces him to a state even lowlier than the one in which he began, within this tempo-rarily more confined ambit he repeats the process all over again, quickly obtaining the highest position to which he can aspire. In this introduction is presaged Joseph's later assumption of the post of second-in-command of all Egypt, a story which we do not have from the Yahwist but which was probably a course of events similar to that detailed by the Elohist below.

That Joseph's Egyptian master put everything in his hands and *gave no thought to anything but the food he ate* expresses a reservation motivated by no lack of trust but rather by religious or dietary taboos (see below on 43:32, J).

6b Now Joseph was strikingly handsome in countenance
7 and body. After a time, his master's wife began to
8 look fondly at him and said, "Lie with me." But he
refused. "As long as I am here," he told her, "my
master does not concern himself with anything in
9 the house, but has entrusted to me all he owns. He
wields no more authority in this house than I do,
and he has withheld from me nothing but yourself,
since you are his wife. How, then, could I commit
so great a wrong and thus stand condemned before
10 God?" Although she tried to entice him day after
day, he would not agree to lie beside her, or even
stay near her.
11 One such day, when Joseph came into the house to
do his work, and none of the household servants
12 were then in the house, she laid hold of him by his
cloak, saying, "Lie with me!" But leaving the cloak
in her hand, he got away from her and ran outside.
13 When she saw that he had left his cloak in her hand
14 as he fled outside, she screamed for her household
servants and told them, "Look! my husband has
brought in a Hebrew slave* to make sport of us!
He came in here to lie with me, but I cried out as
15 loud as I could. When he heard me scream for help,
he left his cloak beside me and ran away outside."
16 She kept the cloak with her until his master came
17 home. Then she told him the same story: "The Hebrew slave whom you brought here broke in on me,
18 to make sport of me. But when I screamed for help,
19 he left his cloak beside me and fled outside." As
soon as the master heard his wife's story about how
20 his slave had treated her, he became enraged. He
seized Joseph and threw him into the jail where the
royal prisoners were confined.
21 But even while he was in prison, the LORD remained
with Joseph; he showed him kindness by making the
22 chief jailer well-disposed toward him. The chief jailer
put Joseph in charge of all the prisoners in the jail,
and everything that had to be done there was done

* "Slave" is inserted here by the NAB (cf. vs. 17), which supposes that the word
('bd) dropped out of the text because of its similarity to the contiguous "Hebrew"
('bry). Another confusion of the Hebrew d and r.

23 under his management. The chief jailer did not concern himself with anything at all that was in Joseph's
charge, since the LORD was with him and brought
success to all he did.

The story of Joseph and the lusty wife of his Egyptian master is the
jewel of the Yahwist's anthology. (The lady is popularly known as "Potiphar's wife" because of the redactional vs. 1b. The same redaction has
created the anomaly of Potiphar's having a wife in the first place, since he
was the *saris* of Pharaoh: an E term found in 37:36, 39:1b, and 40:2.7,
translated "courtier" by the NAB. *Saris* is a common Semitic word for
"eunuch.") The story has many parallels in world literature. Gaster instances the myths of Phaedra and Hippolytus, Anteia and Bellerophon,
Astydameia and Peleus, Biadice and Phrixus. It is interesting, however,
that the closest parallel is Egyptian, in the Tale of the Two Brothers, a
story known from a papyrus of the thirteenth century B.C. In the Egyptian
tale the prologue is much the same as in Genesis, only the epilogue differs
radically. Joseph the high-minded subaltern, his uxorious and credulous
superior, and the frustrated and wanton wife all have their exact counterparts in the Egyptian story, and, as in Genesis, the proffered seduction is
refused for the noblest of reasons. Joseph will not repay the confidence
placed in him by committing *so great a wrong* for which he would *stand
condemned before God.* (We are not to be surprised that "God" rather
than "Yahweh" occurs here in this J narrative, for Joseph is speaking to
an Egyptian in terms he wants her to understand.) We have observed
above the horror in which adultery was held by Israelite tradition.
Similarly in Egypt, adultery or attempted adultery was a high crime. It is
this fact as well as spite, then, and the fury like which hell hath none, that
explains the woman's denunciation of Joseph. Having gone so far she must
go further yet, for there is no retreat possible. If the truth of what has
taken place gets out, as easily it might, she could be in grave danger.
Therefore she strikes the first blow, gaining the tactical advantage of giving evidence rather than having to deny it.

Joseph has left behind evidence hard to explain away by relinquishing
his cloak, which was doubtless the only apparel he had on: he had come
into the house to do his work. We may imagine him fleeing naked from the
unwelcome embrace of his temptress across the courtyard which separated
his master's quarters from his own. And of course, Joseph was both a
slave and a foreigner, as the woman is careful to emphasize in vss. 14 and
17, therefore one whose word could hardly be preferred even by a liberal
master to the word of his own wife who was also his honor. For the meaning of "Hebrew" here, see above on 14:13.

In the Tale of the Two Brothers the faithless wife is killed by her husband when the falsely accused, his younger brother, proves his innocence by rather gruesome means. Joseph has no such immediate vindication; the initial reaction of his master is to have him thrown into prison. If imprisonment was to be the extent of the punishment of a slave held guilty of the attempted rape of his master's wife, the mildness of the Egyptian's retaliation is truly astounding. Perhaps we are supposed to think of Joseph as held in custody pending a direr judgment, even as Pharaoh's "chief baker" in the E story that follows was removed from house arrest only to be executed. But then again, we cannot press the logic of events too closely in these narratives. Obviously Joseph cannot be allowed to die or suffer irreversible harm, for it now must be told how he rose to power in Egypt. Hence the author, having done with this episode, moves on to the next without bothering overmuch to tidy up. There is nothing about accusations, defense, trials, or other processes. Joseph must be found in *the jail where the royal prisoners were confined,* and that is where the author places him.

Thus begins the second stage of Joseph's career in Egypt, a stage which the Yahwist is not destined to pursue beyond a few more verses, since the Redactor chose to reproduce the Elohist's parallel instead. We can but surmise how the Yahwist handled the story, which breaks off with the first verse of the following chapter, also J and doubtless originally in sequence with vs. 23 as it is now:

> **40** Some time afterward, the royal cupbearer and baker
> gave offense to their lord, the king of Egypt.

In 39:20–23, after noting that Joseph's prison was also where the king's prisoners were kept, the author tells how once again through the providence of Yahweh Joseph rose to a position of trust and pre-eminence in the domain which fate had thrust upon him. So the scene is set for the introduction of *the royal cupbearer and baker,* who, having given *offense to their lord, the king of Egypt,* are (though it is not said so explicitly in this shortened account) put into this prison and thus come in contact with Joseph, the trusty in charge. How did Joseph exploit this contact, according to J? We shall never know, for at this point the Elohist takes over, for the rest of chapter 40 and for much of chapter 41. The transition was eased for the Redactor by the sameness of the royal officials in both stories, who in E, however, are the "chief" cupbearer and the "chief" baker, and of "Pharaoh" rather than "the king of Egypt." With redactional refinements which we shall observe in due course, the narrative on which we now embark is Elohistic, the original continuation of 37:36.

> 2 Pharaoh was angry with his two courtiers, the chief
> 3 cupbearer and the chief baker, and he put them in
> custody in the house of the chief steward (the same

4a jail where Joseph was confined). The chief steward
assigned Joseph to them, and he became their attendant.

Let us orient ourselves and see where we are in this story of Joseph,
both as the Redactor of Genesis intends us to be and as the sources allow
us to be. In the E of 37:36 the Midianites who had extracted Joseph from
the cistern in Canaan and transported him to Egypt eventually sold him to
Potiphar, a courtier of Pharaoh and his chief steward. It would appear
that in these verses above we have what was once the immediate sequel to
37:36. The *chief steward* here is Potiphar, as he was before. Now that the
Redactor has identified Potiphar with the "certain Egyptian" of the preceding J story (39:1b), however, his name cannot be permitted to occur
again, and therefore it has probably been suppressed once or twice in the
course of this narrative. Along with such presumed deletions there have
also been obvious suppletions introduced into the text. The NAB notes
one in vs. 3b above, the parenthetical reference which seeks to equate *the
house of the chief steward* with the *jail where Joseph was confined;* but
again in vs. 5 below (which largely uses the language of J), and in vs. 15
and 41:14 which use *dungeon* in place of *jail,* insertions have been made
to harmonize chapters 39–40. In the original perspective of E, *the chief
cupbearer and the chief baker,* important functionaries in Pharaoh's court,
had not been cast into a common prison but were remanded to the custody
of the highest functionary of all, Pharaoh's major-domo, and were in his
home, where his house slave Joseph was assigned to tend to their wants.

All these courtiers are in the Hebrew *sarisim,* eunuchs. The employment
of castrated males at court and in the civil and even military service was
known to the Israelites from Mesopotamian practice, but the practice did
not obtain in Egypt. Neither did *saris* originally mean eunuch in the now
technical sense: the word is a loan from the Akkadian, where it literally
said "head man," that is, "counselor" (similarly the Greek *eunouchos,*
which by etymology is "keeper of the bed," that is, "chamberlain"). It is
conceivable, therefore, that the biblical author intended by the term nothing more than the "courtiers" of the NAB, reaching back to its earliest
significance. It is more likely, however, that he did think of these men as
eunuchs in the sense the word had acquired from the usage of the East, a
usage which he mistakenly ascribed to the Egyptians.

4b After they had been in custody for some time,
5 the cupbearer and the baker of the king of Egypt
who were confined in the jail both had dreams on
the same night, each dream with its own meaning.
6 When Joseph came to them in the morning, he no-

7 ticed that they looked disturbed. So he asked Pharaoh's courtiers who were with him in custody in his
master's house, "Why do you look so sad today?"
8 They answered him, "We have had dreams, but
there is no one to interpret them for us." Joseph
said to them, "Surely, interpretations come from
9 God. Please tell the dreams to me." Then the chief
cupbearer told Joseph his dream. "In my dream," he
10 said, "I saw a vine in front of me, and on the vine
were three branches. It had barely budded when
its blossoms came out, and its clusters ripened into
11 grapes. Pharaoh's cup was in my hand; so I took
the grapes, pressed them out into his cup, and put
12 it in Pharaoh's hand." Joseph said to him: "This
is what it means. The three branches are three days;
13 within three days Pharaoh will lift up your head and
restore you to your post. You will be handing Pharaoh his cup as you formerly used to when you
14 were his cupbearer. So if you will still remember,
when all is well with you, that I was here with you,
please do me the favor of mentioning me to Phar-
15 aoh, to get me out of this place. The truth is that I
was kidnaped from the land of the Hebrews, and
here I have not done anything for which I should
have been put into a dungeon."

Making his morning rounds in service to the involuntary house guests of
his master the chief steward, Joseph finds them glum and brooding over
the troubled night that each has spent separately. Both have dreamed puzzling dreams, and both share the common frustration that in their temporary isolation from their normal resources *there is no one to interpret* their
dreams for them. Egypt set great store by dreams—this is part of the authentic Egyptian flavor of the Elohistic story of Joseph—and professional
oneirocritics were a customary feature of the Egyptian scene (cf. 41:8).
Joseph, with his superior Hebraic wisdom, casually brushes aside their
problem as of no consequence. With serene confidence in divine guidance
he undertakes to divine for them the meaning of what they have dreamed.
Not, one might conclude, that his task was all that difficult: for the purposes of the story the "dreams" have been made more or less to order, and
their sense is fairly transparent.

A somewhat grim play on idiom is involved in the expression "lift up
the head" which occurs several times in this chapter. In vs. 13 Joseph uses
it to signify the coming restoration to favor of the cupbearer: figuratively

bowed in humble petition before his absolute master, the courtier will be permitted to raise his eyes once more and walk as a free man to resume his former duties. In vs. 19 below the phrase takes on a quite different and unpleasantly literal signification, while again in vs. 20 both meanings are implied together along with a neutral third which is their presupposition: to lift up someone's head is to call him to mind, to bring up his case for consideration.

Joseph hopes to have won a friend at court by having been the channel of such a favorable prognosis. In vs. 15 he summarizes the sadness of his plight: kidnaped from his homeland and sold into a life of menial slavery, here and now the servant of men who are themselves under restraint and out of favor. In E there has been nothing up to this point of Joseph's having mildly prospered in Egypt under Yahweh's protection. The *dungeon* of vs. 15 and 41:14 is redactional, as we know. It is the same word (literally, "pit," "hole") that was the "cistern" where the Midianites first found Joseph in 37:28b.

> 16 When the chief baker saw that Joseph had given this
> favorable interpretation, he said to him: "I too had
> a dream. In it I had three wicker baskets on my
> 17 head; in the top were all kinds of bakery products
> for Pharaoh, but the birds were pecking at them out
> 18 of the basket on my head." Joseph said to him in
> reply: "This is what it means. The three baskets
> 19 are three days; within three days Pharaoh will lift up
> your head† and have you impaled on a stake, and
> the birds will be pecking the flesh from your body."
> 20 And in fact, on the third day, which was Pharaoh's
> birthday, when he gave a banquet to all his staff,
> with his courtiers around him, he lifted up the heads
> 21 of the chief cupbearer and chief baker. He restored
> the chief cupbearer to his office, so that he again
> 22 handed the cup to Pharaoh; but the chief baker he
> impaled—just as Joseph had told them in his inter-
> 23 pretation. Yet the chief cupbearer gave no thought
> to Joseph; he had forgotten him.

We may impute more than a little naïveté to the chief baker, who apparently thought he was to receive a favorable interpretation of his dream just because the chief cupbearer had. If not the baker, certainly the reader has already scanned the dream for its share of bad omens. We do not for-

† The MT adds, "from you."

get, however, that in the mind of the ancients the bearer of a revelation was frequently regarded as the one responsible for it, or put another way, it was within Joseph's power, if he worked at it hard enough, to divine good as well as evil from the courtier's dream. If such was the mentality, the cupbearer's failure to remember Joseph once his fortunes were restored becomes all the more inexcusable. The baker's silence, on the other hand, is quite as understandable as it was brief: he had no cause to thank Joseph.

It is not entirely clear by what manner of death the baker met his end at Pharaoh's command. Where the NAB has *impaled on a stake,* older translations are likely to read "hanged on a tree," but perhaps pretty much the same thing is intended by both expressions. The verb in question does mean "hang" or "suspend," but it probably described a disposition of the body following execution rather than a means of execution itself. The condemned was not hanged by the neck until dead in the time-honored Anglo-Saxon fashion; rather, his dead body was hung up or impaled for all to see and remember as a cautionary example (cf. Deuteronomy 21:22). The Assyrians, who were as fond of documenting their own atrocities as modern military machines have been, decorated the walls of their palaces and other public buildings with bas-reliefs by the acre depicting impaled enemy soldiers. These men had been pierced through the upper body and suspended face downward from the tops of poles. This was not, then, the utterly barbarous kind of impalement execution described by Henryk Sienkiewicz in his novels about the Tartar wars. If we take vs. 19 at its face value, we might conclude that the chief baker was beheaded, even though the "from you" omitted by the NAB may indeed be the later gloss of a scribe loath to permit the text to be anything less than clinically explicit.

Also the first part of the following chapter is Elohistic, in immediate sequence with the preceding. Not until Joseph actually comes to power in Egypt does the Yahwistic chronicle rejoin this one.

> **41** After a lapse of two years, Pharaoh had a dream.
> 2 He saw himself standing by the Nile, when up out
> of the Nile came seven cows, handsome and fat;
> 3 they grazed in the reed grass. Behind them seven
> other cows, ugly and gaunt,‡ came up out of the
> Nile; and standing on the bank of the Nile beside
> 4 the others, the ugly, gaunt cows ate up the seven
> 5 handsome, fat cows. Then Pharaoh woke up. He
> fell asleep again and had another dream. He saw

‡ In vss. 3, 19, 20, 27 the MT has vacillated between *raqqoth,* "gaunt," and *daqqoth,* "thin." The meaning of the text is hardly affected.

seven ears of grain, fat and healthy, growing on a
6 single stalk. Behind them sprouted seven ears of
7 grain, thin and blasted by the east wind; and the
seven thin ears swallowed up the seven fat, healthy
ears. Then Pharaoh woke up, to find it was only a
dream.

8 Next morning his spirit was agitated. So he summoned all the magicians and sages of Egypt and
recounted his dreams to them; but no one could in-
9 terpret his dreams for him. Then the chief cupbearer spoke up and said to Pharaoh: "On this oc-
10 casion I am reminded of my negligence. Once, when
Pharaoh was angry, he put me and the chief baker
11 in custody in the house of the chief steward. Later,
we both had dreams on the same night, and each of
12 our dreams had its own meaning. There with us was
a Hebrew youth, a slave of the chief steward; and
when we told him our dreams, he interpreted them
for us and explained for each of us the meaning of
13 his dream. And it turned out just as he had told us:
I was restored to my post, but the other man was
impaled."

14 Pharaoh therefore had Joseph summoned, and they
hurriedly brought him from the dungeon. After he
shaved and changed his clothes, he came into Phar-
15 aoh's presence. Pharaoh then said to him: "I had
certain dreams that no one can interpret. But I
heard it said of you that the moment you are told
16 a dream you can interpret it." "It is not I," Joseph
replied to Pharaoh, "but God who will give Pharaoh
the right answer."

Dreams in the E narrative have thus far influenced Joseph's life, though
not spectacularly to its enrichment; dreams will now deliver him from slavery and make him vizier of Egypt. The dreams of Pharaoh are a trifle
more complicated than those of the chief cupbearer and chief baker, but in
principle there is little to choose between them, since these too have been
designed by the storyteller for a predetermined end and exploit a symbolism that does not lie far below the surface. Naturally, there is the phantasmagory proper to dreams: emaciated cattle, doomed by their physiology in
Egypt and elsewhere to be perpetual herbivores, nevertheless eat up their
sleek and compliant cousins on the bank of the Nile, and spears of wheat
blighted by the southeast sirocco (Deuteronomy 28:22) swallow up their
sibling spears on the same stalk of grain. Still, the imagery is fairly plain.

Prosperity is to be overtaken by destitution. Prosperity is the *handsome and fat cows* who emerge from their cooling and protective bath in the Nile, prosperity is the *fat and healthy ears of grain,* spelt or common wheat, no doubt—these are the ordinary signs of a healthy economy within the limited horizons of the pre-industrial world; and if these signify good times, it really takes very little thought to know what is meant by the scrawny cattle and shriveled kernels that succeed and overwhelm them. We can only experience some amaze that *all the magicians and sages of Egypt*—the sweep of experts at Pharaoh's command is, of course, limitless —cannot come up with even the slightest hint about what these dreams have portended. They cannot be allowed, of course, just as the Egyptian magicians of Exodus 7–8 cannot be allowed to accomplish what Moses and Aaron will do, and as the magicians, enchanters, sorcerers, and Chaldeans of Nebuchadnezzar's court in Daniel 2 cannot be allowed to interpret a dream whose substance and meaning have been revealed only to the Israelite Daniel. Correspondingly, in vs. 16 Joseph is afforded the opportunity to correct the misapprehension of Pharaoh: the interpretation of dreams does not depend on a learnt or professional skill, but is alone made possible by the enlightenment of God.

The impotence of Pharaoh's professional dream scanners serves to jog the memory and the conscience of his cupbearer. *After a lapse of two years* he finally remembers Joseph and brings him to the attention of the court. We now see an additional reason for Joseph's having been lodged by E in the house of the chief steward—the redactional "dungeon" here merely gets in the way—since this would mean that he was somewhere within easy access of *Pharaoh's presence.* That Joseph *shaved and changed his clothes* first was doubtless due to a prompting of protocol as well as of the practical. The Egyptians were a clean-shaven people, abhorring the ways of barbarians whom, along with serfs, they pictured in their art as bearded.

17 Then Pharaoh said to Joseph: "In my dream, I was
18 standing on the bank of the Nile, when up from the
Nile came seven cows, fat and well-formed; they
19 grazed in the reed grass. Behind them came seven
other cows, scrawny, most ill-formed and gaunt.
Never have I seen such ugly specimens as these in
20 all the land of Egypt! The gaunt, ugly cows ate up
21 the first seven fat cows. But when they had consumed them, no one could tell that they had done
so, because they looked as ugly as before. Then I
22 woke up. In another dream, I saw seven ears of

23 grain, fat and healthy, growing on a single stalk. Behind them sprouted seven ears of grain, shriveled
24 and thin and blasted by the east wind; and the seven
thin ears swallowed up the seven healthy ears. I have
spoken to the magicians, but none of them can give
25 me an explanation." Joseph said to Pharaoh: "Both
of Pharaoh's dreams have the same meaning. God
has thus foretold to Pharaoh what he is about to
26 do. The seven healthy cows are seven years, and the
seven healthy ears are seven years—the same in
27 each dream. So also, the seven thin, ugly cows that
came up after them are seven years, as are the seven
thin, wind-blasted ears; they are seven years of fam-
28 ine. It is just as I told Pharaoh: God has revealed to
29 Pharaoh what he is about to do. Seven years of great
abundance are now coming throughout the land of
30 Egypt; but these will be followed by seven years of
famine, when all the abundance in the land of Egypt
will be forgotten. When the famine has ravaged the
31 land, no trace of the abundance will be found in the
land because of the famine that follows it—so ut-
32 terly severe will that famine be. That Pharaoh had
the same dream twice means that the matter has
been reaffirmed by God and that God will soon
bring it about."

Pharaoh proves himself to be a good storyteller, recalling his dreams
with a vividness of detail and observation that marks an improvement over
the more matter-of-fact account in vss. 1–7 above. Dramatic effect
required their retelling rather than being simply referred to in indirect discourse, and we are also permitted to gain the impression that by now
Pharaoh has told his tale often enough to have made a good thing out of
it. Joseph proceeds to unlock the meaning of the dreams that had baffled
Egypt's "magicians."

Numbers figure in these dreams as they do in the preceding ones with
which Joseph has been involved. Here they stand for years. Famine in
Egypt resulted from the failure of the Nile to inundate and thus silt the
otherwise unproductive land along its banks with rich alluvial soil borne
along by the river from sources far to the south. The annual flooding of
the Nile consequently spelled the difference between life and death for
most of the inhabitants of Egypt. And this flooding, and the degree of it,
were quite unpredictable. A seven years' absence of inundation was without doubt unusual, but there is reason to believe that it happened. On the

island of Siheil near the first cataract of the Nile, not far from where a high dam now seeks to control the waters of modern Egypt and free it from the river's cruel whims, a stone inscription records a period of seven years during which there was no overflow. The inscription is relatively late (about 200 B.C.), but it purports to describe a very ancient happening indeed, from about the twenty-eighth century B.C. The document is tendentious and may have been an exercise in pious fiction: like the Donation of Constantine it provides "historical" validation for priestly privilege that was exempt from secular law and taxation (cf. Genesis 47:22.26). It does, in any case, show that a seven-year famine was "thinkable" in Egyptian tradition and not a farfetched idea at all.

In the remainder of this chapter J is heard from once again. We know this with utmost certainty because of the two parallel versions of essentially the same story which from time to time we can see being developed side by side. This certainty does not extend to every particular of the combined narrative, however, and other authors may legitimately differ in their assignment of the E and J verses. Neither can we reconstruct adequately what must have taken place in the suppressed part of the J history, that part which told how Joseph came to be introduced to Pharaoh, which the Redactor rejected because he preferred the E story of Pharaoh's dreams. We can only surmise that, through the offices of the royal cupbearer and baker into whose company Joseph had been thrown—not as their servant but as the one who had them in his charge (cf. 39:22–40:1, J)—he was somehow brought to the position of ultimate preferment which had several times already been presaged for him by J and which only in E has appeared as a total reversal of his previous fortunes. The basic text remains E and we indicate it in normal type. The parts that look like J we have put in italics. And there is a lone half verse that can only be P, a mere scrap of tradition unheralded and unpursued, which we have printed in boldface.

33 "Therefore, let Pharaoh seek out a wise and discerning man and put him in charge of the land of Egypt.
34 *Pharaoh should also take action to appoint overseers,* so as to regiment the land during the seven
35 years of abundance. *They should husband all the food of the coming good years, collecting the grain under Pharaoh's authority, to be stored in the towns*
36 *for food.* This food will serve as a reserve for the country against the seven years of famine that are to follow in the land of Egypt, so that the land may not perish in the famine."
37 This advice pleased Pharaoh and all his officials.
38 "Could we find another like him," Pharaoh asked his officials, "a man so endowed with the spirit of

39 God?" So Pharaoh said to Joseph: "Since God has
   made all this known to you, no one can be as wise
40 and discerning as you are. You shall be in charge
   of my palace, and all my people shall dart at your
   command.* Only in respect to the throne shall I
41 outrank you. *Herewith," Pharaoh told Joseph, "I*
   place you in charge of the whole land of Egypt."
42 *With that, Pharaoh took off his signet ring and put*
   it on Joseph's finger. He had him dressed in robes
   of fine linen and put a gold chain about his neck.
43 *He then had him ride in the chariot of his vizier,*
   and they shouted "Abrek!" before him. Thus was
44 *Joseph installed over the whole land of Egypt. "I,*
   Pharaoh, proclaim," he told Joseph, "that without
   your approval no one shall move hand or foot in
45 *all the land of Egypt." Pharaoh also bestowed the*
   name of Zaphenath-paneah on Joseph, and he gave
   him in marriage Asenath, the daughter of Potiphera,
46 *priest of Heliopolis.*† **Joseph was thirty years old**
   when he entered the service of Pharaoh, king of
   Egypt.

   After Joseph left Pharaoh's presence, he traveled
47 throughout the land of Egypt. During the seven
   years of plenty, when the land produced abundant
48 crops, *he husbanded all the food of these years of*
   plenty‡ that the land of Egypt was enjoying and
   stored it in the towns, placing in each town the crops
49 *of the fields around it. Joseph garnered grain in*
   quantities like the sands of the sea, so vast that at
   last he stopped measuring it, for it was beyond meas-
   ure.

50 Before the famine years set in, Joseph became the
   father of two sons, born to him by Asenath, daugh-
51 ter of Potiphera, priest of Heliopolis. He named his
   first-born Manasseh, meaning, "God has made me
   forget entirely the sufferings I endured at the hands
52 of my family"; and the second he named Ephraim,
   meaning, "God has made me fruitful in the land of
   my affliction."

* A conjectural reading: the meaning of the verb is uncertain.
† The LXX ends here. The MT adds "and Joseph went forth over the land of Egypt,"
doubtless an intrusion from the surrounding context.
‡ "Of plenty" comes from the LXX and the SP. It may not have been in J at all.

53 When the seven years of abundance enjoyed by the
54 land of Egypt came to an end, the seven years of
famine set in, just as Joseph had predicted. Although there was famine in all the other countries,
food was available throughout the land of Egypt.
55 *When hunger came to be felt throughout the land of*
Egypt and the people cried to Pharaoh for bread,
Pharaoh directed all the Egyptians to go to Joseph
56 *and do whatever he told them. When the famine had*
spread throughout the land, Joseph opened all the
cities that had grain* and rationed it to the Egyp-
tians, since the famine had gripped the land of
57 *Egypt. In fact, all the world came to Joseph to ob-*
tain rations of grain, for famine had gripped the
whole world.

The reader who has kept with us thus far and who has taken note of the peculiarities of the last few chapters should not experience too much trouble divining the reasons that have persuaded us to divide the text as we have. In E, having just given his own example of what it is to be *a wise and discerning man,* Joseph pointedly suggests to Pharaoh that such a person be *put in charge of the land of Egypt.* In J, under what advantages of access and persuasion we do not know, Joseph advises Pharaoh *to appoint overseers* who will *husband all the food* of the land in granary towns that it may be rationed in time of need. Implied in this proposal, too, is that Pharaoh should designate someone to oversee the overseers; yet the proposals are not exactly the same. The "wise and discerning man" of E who will *regiment the land* (the verb is in the singular) will be exacting a tax out of which the reserve will be built (the NAB's "regiment" actually means "to take a fifth," cf. 47:23–26), whereas the overseers, apparently, simply will supervise the entire grain production of the land and turn it into a state-run enterprise. Appropriately, the response of Pharaoh, even though it produces much the same effect in either case, namely the elevation of Joseph to second-in-command throughout Egypt, envisions a different office in the two sources. In E Joseph is constituted "master of the palace" (cf. 45:8), an exceedingly important official charged with the finances of the kingdom, but in J he becomes *vizier* (in vs. 43 *mishneh,* literally "second man"), an even more important official who was Pharaoh's lieutenant for all the administrative details of the land. Both these offices are known from Egyptian inscriptions. There was nothing to prevent their being held by one person, as indeed did sometimes occur, and as the

---

* A conjectural reading in debt to vss. 35 and 48, suggested by the LXX, the SP, and the Syriac.

Redactor evidently thought occurred with Joseph. We shall consider the historical possibilities involved later on.

The Joseph who in J speedily became plenipotentiary in his master's house, then in the prison where treachery had cast him, now—and we repeat, we know not precisely by what route—is made so over all of Egypt. The vizier was "keeper of the royal seal," hence the *signet ring* which is *put on Joseph's finger* by Pharaoh. The *robes of fine linen* (for "fine linen" the Hebrew text has *shesh,* an Egyptian loan-word) and *gold neck chain* (the Hebrew can mean "*the* gold chain," perhaps referring to a ceremonial emblem of office and not merely to a random token of honor bestowed by Pharaoh) were both the characteristic garb of Egyptian dignitaries, as we know from Egyptian art. The vizier, like many lesser nobles before and after him, had criers to run before his chariot to clear the way in crowded places. The *Abrek* of vs. 43 is of uncertain meaning. In the Vulgate Jerome conjectured that the word had something to do with the Hebrew root *brk,* "knee," therefore that it was a command to bow down, to genuflect. Modern scholars tend to look for an underlying Egyptian expression, which they find in one which says, literally, "take to heart," that is, "take care," or, simply, "attention!" Certainly the name given to Joseph by Pharaoh and the name of the wife also given to him are authentically Egyptian. *Zaphenath-paneah* seems to be a deformation of the Egyptian for "God speaks: he is the living." *Asenath* was a common enough Egyptian name, indicating a person who had been put under the patronage of the goddess Neith. *Potiphera,* we have already observed, is the same as the Potiphar of 37:36: both J and E knew that a person of this name had a relation to Joseph in Egypt, but they had gone their separate ways in identifying the relationship. *Heliopolis* ("city of the sun") is the classical equivalent of the "On" of the Hebrew text (standing for the Egyptian "Anu"), the name of the holy city of the Egyptian sun-god and seat of his all-powerful priesthood. (The site of On lies a few miles northeast of the modern Cairo.) It was only natural that the Hebrew Joseph on assuming the office of Pharaoh's vizier should take an Egyptian name and an Egyptian wife. It is at the same time typical of the traditions of Genesis 37–50 that no point is made one way or the other (just as none was made of Judah in chapter 38) of Joseph's taking a non-Hebrew wife—the daughter of an Egyptian priest, no less!—or about the implied accommodation of patriarchal religion and customs to those of Egypt. The question will rise again below.

Both in J and E Joseph quickly takes over the office he has assumed and consolidates his power in Egypt. In both traditions food is available in Egypt despite the fact that famine has now gripped the land, for the foresight of Joseph has made appropriate provision. And in both traditions a general cataclysm is supposed, not one of Egypt alone: *there was famine in all the other countries* (E), and "all the world came to Egypt to obtain rations of grain from Joseph, for famine had gripped the whole world" (which is the J of vs. 57, better than the NAB translation above). Preparation is being made for the journey of Joseph's brothers from Canaan which is about to take place.

In E Joseph has sons born to him during the lush years, before the beginning of the seven famine years. (The "born to him by Asenath, daughter of Potiphera, priest of Heliopolis" of vs. 50b is probably redactional, borrowed from vs. 45b.) Both sons are given significant names in the conventional mold. *Manasseh* (Hebrew *menashsheh*) is related to *God has made me forget,* etc. (*nashshani,* or perhaps *nishshani*), and *Ephraim* to *God has made me fruitful,* etc. (*hiphrani*). The doleful tone of these popular etymologies owes something to the E narrative in which they have been embedded, since in E Joseph's career in Egypt up to the moment of his deliverance by Pharaoh had been consistently a sad one.

4. Joseph and His Brothers Revisited

The story that follows continues for the most part in chapter 42 with the Elohist's narrative, though a few verses have been inserted from J, which we italicize. There were these two traditions of the reunion of Joseph and his brothers which were remarkably parallel, and which the Redactor of Genesis combined by taking the first part from E (chapter 42) and the second from J (chapters 43–44), inserting editorial adaptations as they were necessary for harmony. The E story highlights Reuben (42:22.37) as it did before (37:21–22.29–30), and the J story highlights Judah (43:3–5.8–10) as it did before (37:26–27). E has Simeon kept as a hostage for Benjamin (42:18–24), a detail that is lacking in the J story (except for the obviously redactional 43:23b). In E the brothers find their money that they took to Egypt in their "sacks" after they return to Canaan (42:35), while in J they discover it in their "bags" along the way home (42:27–28, 43:20–21). In both versions of the tradition it seems to be taken for granted that Benjamin is a young boy whom Joseph has never seen, separated by many years from the rest of his brothers, while at the same time the age gap between Joseph and the brothers who sent him into exile has vanished.

42 When Jacob learned that grain rations were available in Egypt, *he said to his sons: "Why do you keep gap-*

2 *ing at one another?* I hear," he went on, "that rations of grain are available in Egypt. Go down there and buy some for us, that we may stay alive rather 3 than die of hunger." So ten of Joseph's brothers went down to buy an emergency supply of grain 4 from Egypt. It was only Joseph's full brother Benjamin that Jacob did not send with the rest, for he 5 thought some disaster might befall him. *Thus, since there was famine in the land of Canaan also, the sons of Israel were among those who came to procure rations.*

6 It was Joseph, as governor of the country, who dispensed the rations to all the people. When Joseph's brothers came and knelt down before him with 7 their faces to the ground, *he recognized them as soon as he saw them. But he concealed his own identity from them and spoke sternly to them. "Where do you come from?" he asked them. They answered, "From the land of Canaan, to procure food."*

8 When Joseph recognized his brothers, although they 9 did not recognize him, he was reminded of the dreams he had had about them. He said to them: "You are spies. *You have come to see the naked-* 10 *ness of the land." "No, my lord," they replied. "On the contrary, your servants have come to procure* 11 *food. All of us are sons of the same man.* We are honest men; your servants have never been 12 spies." *But he answered them: "Not so! You have* 13 *come to see the nakedness of the land."* "We your servants," they said, "were twelve brothers, sons of a certain man in Canaan; but the youngest one is at present with our father, and the other one is 14 gone." "It is just* as I said," Joseph persisted; "you 15 are spies. This is how you shall be tested: unless your youngest brother comes here, I swear by the 16 life of Pharaoh that you shall not leave here. So send one of your number to get your brother, while the rest of you stay here under arrest. Thus shall your words be tested for their truth; if they are untrue, as 17 Pharaoh lives, you are spies!" With that, he locked them up in the guardhouse for three days.

* The language of 41:28 (E) is supplied here in what is apparently a defective MT.

Though J and E differ in style and vocabulary, and each has its own reminiscences of earlier narration, there is no substantial difference in the present story they have to tell. There is famine in the land of Canaan as there was in Abraham's day (12:10, J) and in Isaac's day (26:1, J), and while Abraham had gone down into Egypt and Isaac had not, a middle course is found by Jacob, who sends his sons to buy food there, holding back Benjamin his youngest who has replaced Joseph at the center of his affections.

That Joseph, *governor of the country,* should personally have *dispensed the rations to all the people* hardly seems realistic, but it is necessary for the development of the story. Joseph immediately recognizes his brothers: one can easily forget the face of an individual person, but hardly the identity of a group of ten habitually associated with one another; and as they *knelt down before him with their faces to the ground he was reminded of the dreams he had about them* (37:5–11, E). That they should have failed to recognize him is entirely understandable. The Joseph they had known as a boy they presumed to be dead (vs. 22), and here they were in the presence of a man. A man, further, who in name, dress, language (cf. vs. 23), and all other externals was a thoroughgoing Egyptian, and not merely that but an Egyptian official of the highest order. Who could have even wildly imagined that he was Joseph? For his part, Joseph plays his assumed role to the limit. He seasons his speech with Egyptian oaths, and he feigns to share in the paranoid Egyptian fixation on spying by foreigners. His brothers, he asserts, *have come to see the nakedness of the land,* to spy out its vulnerabilities to attack, just as Asiatics of the north and Africans of the south are perpetually trying to do. We might even add that Joseph further establishes his Egyptian credentials by adopting what has thus far been shown a sovereign measure in Egypt to respond to an offense or to postpone decision on one: he has his brothers *locked up in the guardhouse* for a few days.

What is the rationale of the game which Joseph plays with his brothers? As will eventually appear, he has thought out a devious and "wise" method of ensuring the reunion of his entire family in Egypt, where they will not only be saved from the uncertainties of life in Canaan but will also participate in all the good things that his wealth and position can make possible. For this reunion to be successfully accomplished his brothers and father must be gradually conditioned for it, earn it, in fact, so that at the end their taking up residence in Egypt will be not only a willing acquiescence in a proposal but eager acceptance as well, the relief that men find in the unexpected happy termination of proceedings that boded only pain and trouble. Undeniably, however, Joseph also intends his brothers to suffer for their past misdeeds, as it is only right that they should. At first he allows them to contemplate the possibility of imprisonment for all save one of their number indefinitely till Benjamin be brought to Egypt. Next he will "mitigate" this sentence by imposing another that is scarcely less agreeable to them, and he has other schemes in mind to harass them and keep them off balance. Credibility has been unwittingly given by the brothers themselves to Joseph's otherwise arbitrary demand that they fetch Benjamin from Canaan. In their anxiety to rebut his pretended charge of espionage they have dwelt on the circumstances of their family, thinking to persuade him of their way of life totally alien to careers of spying. Now they must make good on their claims and prove they are what they said they are.

> 18 On the third day Joseph said to them: "Do this, and
> 19 you shall live; for I am a God-fearing man. If you
> have been honest, only one of your brothers need
> be confined in this prison, while the rest of you may
> go and take home provisions for your starving fam-
> 20 ilies. But you must come back to me with your
> youngest brother. Your words will thus be verified,
> 21 and you will not die." To this they agreed. To one
> another, however, they said: "Alas, we are being
> punished because of our brother. We saw the an-
> guish of his heart when he pleaded with us, yet we
> paid no heed; that is why this anguish has now come
> 22 upon us." "Didn't I tell you," broke in Reuben, "not
> to do wrong to the boy? But you wouldn't listen!
> 23 Now comes the reckoning for his blood." They did
> not know, of course, that Joseph understood what
> they said, since he spoke with them through an in-
> 24 terpreter. But turning away from them, he wept.
> When he was able to speak to them again, he had
> Simeon taken from them and bound before their
> 25 eyes. Then Joseph gave orders to have their con-
> tainers filled with grain, their money replaced in
> each one's sack, and provisions given them for their
> 26 journey. After this had been done for them, they
> loaded their donkeys with the rations and departed.
> 27 *At the night encampment, when one of them opened*
> *his bag† to give his donkey some fodder, he was*
> *surprised to see his money in the mouth of his bag.*
> 28 *"My money has been returned!" he cried out to his*
> *brothers. "Here it is in my bag!" At that their hearts*

------

† With the LXX, cf. vs. 28 and 43:12 (J). The MT has the "sack" of vs. 25 (E).

sank. Trembling, they asked one another, "What is this that God has done to us?"

29 When they got back to their father Jacob in the land of Canaan, they told him all that had happened
30 to them. "The man who is lord of the country," they said, "spoke to us sternly and put us in custody‡ as
31 if we were spying on the land. But we said to him: 'We are honest men; we have never been spies.
32 There were twelve of us brothers, sons of the same father; but one is gone, and the youngest one is at
33 present with our father in the land of Canaan.' Then the man who is lord of the country said to us: 'This is how I shall know if you are honest men: leave one of your brothers with me, while the rest of you* go home with rations for your starving families.
34 When you come back to me with your youngest brother, and I know that you are honest men and not spies, I will restore your brother to you, and you
35 may move about freely in the land.'" When they were emptying their sacks, there in each one's sack was his moneybag! At the sight of their moneybags,
36 they and their father were dismayed. Their father Jacob said to them: "Must you make me childless? Joseph is gone, and Simeon is gone, and now you would take away Benjamin! Why must such things
37 always happen to me!" Then Reuben told his father: "Put him in my care, and I will bring him back to you. You may kill my own two sons if I do not re-
38 turn him to you." *But Jacob† replied: "My son shall not go down with you. Now that his full brother is dead, he is the only one left. If some disaster should befall him on the journey you must make, you would send my white head down to the nether world in grief."*

On the third day is, we know, the frequent biblical index to the passing of a crisis, transition to a new state, fulfillment of past promise. In given instances the index points to an event of great moment: the salvation of a people (Hosea 6:2; Esther 5:1) or, in the New Testament, the resur-

---

‡ "In custody" has been omitted by error in the MT, appears in the LXX; cf. 40:3.
* "The rest of you" is supplied from the LXX; cf. vs. 19.
† "Jacob" has been supplied by the NAB; the Hebrew has only "he" implicit in the verb.

rection of a Savior. Usually the moment is not that great. In Genesis so far we have seen Abraham and Isaac reach the mountain of sacrifice on the third day (22:4, E), Laban learn of Jacob's flight on the third day (31:22, J), the Shechemites fall prey to Israel on the third day (34:25, probably E), and, in the E story of 40:20 above, the realization of Joseph's predictions to the chief cupbearer and chief baker. Here a relatively minor development occurs. Joseph comes to his hapless brothers with the good news that the most of them will not have to languish in prison: they may take advantage, all but one of them, of the compassion of *a God-fearing man* who is willing to believe, provisionally, in their talk of *starving families* back home who need the grain of Egypt. But there must be no mistaking kindness for softheadedness. One of their number will remain as hostage to the rest and to their return with their *youngest brother,* the only proof that will be accepted that they are the innocent Hebrew family they profess to be and not, after all, a band of spies.

The brothers agree of course, since they have no alternative. Privately, as they think, they vent their frustration on one another, dredging up the memory of the long-ago betrayal of their lost brother—and, even as Pharaoh remembered his dreams, recalling the memory in more poignant detail than was contained in the earlier narration of chapter 37—which they correctly interpret as the author of the nemesis that has now overtaken them. That Joseph weeps (as he often does again both in J and E, in 43:30, 45:1–2.15) overhearing their heated and remorseful recriminations is the biblical writer's way of suggesting the total lack of vengeful feeling with which he has undertaken the chastisement of his brothers. More than once during the painful experiences that he will inflict upon them his natural instinct for disclosure and reconciliation will threaten to surface, and he must steel himself to persevere in his plan. The plan now calls for the shackling of Simeon, to remove any doubt about the seriousness of the present enterprise: either they return with Benjamin or their brother is lost to them forever. We are probably to assume that Simeon was Joseph's choice for hostage, the eldest of the brothers after Reuben, who in E is Joseph's champion.

The covert replacing of the money which had been used to buy Egypt's grain is an ambiguous element in the story. For one thing, it permits Joseph to make a grand gesture worthy of the princely figure he has become. But it is also a twisting of the screw of doubt and uneasiness which Joseph has deliberately clamped upon all his dealings with the brothers. Certainly nothing he had done or said to them up to this point would have prepared them to expect gifts from him. Either a ghastly mistake has been made, or they have been entrapped. If mistake it was, though a mistake of such dimensions can hardly be imagined, it is sure to be held against them: the careless clerks responsible will by now have detected their error and found ways to shift the blame for it. More likely it is a trap set by that strange autocrat who has already caused them so much grief: he will now, under the pretext of theft, have further cause to proceed against them. They know at last—the effect that was intended—how uncomfortable it can be to stand or fall at the mercy and whim of another, and that compassion that they once did not extend they now want very badly. If they do not return to Egypt they have lost Simeon, and if they do return it may be to slavery or worse (cf. 43:18). They are nicely boxed in, hardly believing it all could have happened. Therefore the discovery of the moneybags is cause for dismay and consternation, for father and sons in vs. 35 when it occurs at the end of their journey home, for the brothers alone in vss. 27–28 when it takes place along the way according to the J parallel inserted by the Redactor.

The Redactor was not at his editorial best when he incorporated these J verses into the E narrative. Perhaps he was not satisfied with E's simple assertion that *they and their father were dismayed* when Joseph's brothers found the money during their unpacking, and therefore he got in the direct discourse and the more vivid reaction described by J even at the expense of the logic of the story. Perhaps, too, he thought the logic could be saved somewhat by letting it be said that only *one of them opened his bag at the night encampment*—leaving us to imagine no one else similarly occupied or all so devoid of curiosity that they would not check to see whether they had been similarly favored? From 43:21 it is quite clear that in the J account all of the men found their money at the encampment en route. In J the money had been put in the bags in which they carried their provisions, but in E (cf. vs. 25) the provisions were loaded separately, and the money would not have been discovered until they reached home and turned out the sacks in which they had transported the hard-won foodstuffs of Egypt. It would be somewhat anomalous elsewhere in the J narrative for "Israelites" among themselves to refer to their guiding Deity as "God" rather than "Yahweh," as the brothers do in vs. 28; but in this wisdom-oriented J section of the Joseph story the sacred name does not necessarily have the import that it possesses for the other patriarchal sagas. Besides, "God" in the sense of "fate" or "destiny" or "providence" is as readily usable by J as by any other source (cf. 27:28, J), and that seems to be the sense in which it is used here.

Likewise J, though some commentators would disagree, is the final vs. 38. In the E narrative Jacob is most disturbed by the prospect that he must now send Benjamin to follow Simeon and Joseph down into the insatiable maw of Egypt. This thought of giving up yet another son is more repugnant to him than any other, crowding out of his consideration the circumstance of vs. 35 and focusing it entirely on the story that his sons had told him in vss. 30–34. Even Reuben's eloquent appeal in vs. 37 (in which we learn that Jacob's eldest son was himself a man of some family, with concerns and responsibilities of his own) may not have moved him greatly. Still, we can hardly believe that Jacob—the Israel of the J narrative (cf. the note on vs. 38 above)—could have proclaimed such an adamantine refusal to traffic further with Egypt as he is represented doing at the end of this chapter unless he was reckoning with different counters than the story has supplied him with thus far. In the J narrative that now begins and extends through the following two chapters there is no Simeon in durance vile back in Egypt, there is only a Jacob who is given the option of bargaining Benjamin against future need. For the moment he can decline the bargain and refuse a further journey without losing anything at all. On the *nether world* of vs. 38, cf. the J of 37:35.

43 Now the famine in the land grew more severe.
2 So when they had used up all the rations they had brought from Egypt, their father said to them, "Go
3 back and procure us a little more food." But Judah replied: "The man strictly warned us, 'You shall not appear in my presence unless your brother is
4 with you.' If you are willing to let our brother go with us, we will go down to procure food for you.
5 But if you are not willing, we will not go down, because the man told us, 'You shall not appear in my
6 presence unless your brother is with you.' " Israel demanded, "Why did you bring this trouble on me by telling the man that you had another brother?"
7 They answered: "The man kept asking about ourselves and our family: 'Is your father still living? Do you have another brother?' We had to answer his questions. How could we know that he would say, 'Bring your brother down here'?"
8 Then Judah urged his father Israel: "Let the boy go with me, that we may be off and on our way if you and we and our children are to keep from starv-
9 ing to death. I myself will stand surety for him. You can hold me responsible for him. If I fail to bring him back, to set him in your presence, you can hold
10 it against me forever. Had we not dillydallied, we could have been there and back twice by now!"

In J the brothers are under no compulsion to return to Egypt, and in fact they have reason to be wary of such a thing in view of the ambiguous conditions under which they quitted the country before. No concern for an imprisoned brother but only the continuing agony of *the famine in the land* provokes a second journey. Jacob himself proposes it, and it now falls the duty of the J hero Judah to remind his father (or perhaps to tell him for the first time: 42:38 might originally have had another location in the narrative) that there can be no discussing this thing unless Benjamin is to accompany them. From vs. 7 it would appear that in the earlier part of the J story which we do not have it was the persistent questionings of Joseph, under what pretense we have no way of saying, that elicited the fatal information about Benjamin, rather than the brothers' having eagerly volunteered it in their desire to prove that they were not spies.

Judah's offer to go surety for Benjamin lacks the eloquence of Reuben's in the E of 42:37. If we can assume that the story of chapter 38 had already been assimilated by the Yahwist when these lines were being composed, it might be that it was thought inappropriate to bring up the question of Judah's children. He speaks trenchantly, however, and to the point: the NAB of vs. 10 is an excellent translation which beautifully captures the urgency of the Hebrew—much better than the "hesitated" of 19:16 (also J) with which the same verb was rendered there.

> 11 Their father Israel then told them: "If it must be so, then do this: Put some of the land's best products in your baggage and take them down to the man as gifts: some balm and honey, gum and resin, and pis-
> 12 tachios and almonds. Also take extra money along, for you must return the amount that was put back in the mouths of your bags; it may have been a mis-
> 13 take. Take your brother, too, and be off on your
> 14 way back to the man. May God Almighty dispose the man to be merciful toward you, so that he may let your other brother go, as well as Benjamin. As for me, if I am to suffer bereavement, I shall suffer it."
> 15 So the men got the gifts, took double the amount of money with them, and, accompanied by Benjamin, were off on their way down to Egypt to present
> 16 themselves to Joseph. When Joseph saw Benjamin with them, he told his head steward, "Take these men into the house, and have an animal slaughtered and prepared, for they are to dine with me at noon."
> 17 Doing as Joseph had ordered, the steward conducted
> 18 the men to Joseph's house. But on being led to his house, they became apprehensive. "It must be," they thought, "on account of the money put back in

our bags the first time, that we are taken inside; they
want to use it as a pretext to attack us and take our
19 donkeys and seize us as slaves." So they went up to
Joseph's head steward and talked to him at the en-
20 trance of the house. "If you please, sir," they said,
"we came down here once before to procure food.
21 But when we arrived at a night's encampment and
opened our bags, there was each man's money in
the mouth of his bag—our money in the full amount!
22 We have now brought it back. We have brought
other money to procure food with. We do not know
23 who put the first money in our bags." "Be at ease,"
he replied; "you have no need to fear. Your God
and the God of your father must have put treasures
in your bags for you. As for your money, I received
it." With that, he led Simeon out to them.
24 The steward then brought the men inside Joseph's
house. He gave them water to bathe their feet, and
25 got fodder for their donkeys. Then they set out
their gifts to await Joseph's arrival at noon, for they
26 had heard that they were to dine there. When Joseph
came home, they presented him with the gifts they
had brought inside, while they bowed down before
27 him to the ground. After inquiring how they were,
he asked them, "And how is your aged father, of
28 whom you spoke? Is he still in good health?" "Your
servant our father is thriving and still in good
29 health," they said, as they bowed respectfully. When
Joseph's eye fell on his full brother Benjamin, he
asked, "Is this your youngest brother, of whom you
told me?" Then he said to him, "May God be gra-
30 cious to you, my boy!" With that, Joseph had to
hurry out, for he was so overcome with affection for
his brother that he was on the verge of tears. He
went into a private room and wept there.
31 After washing his face, he reappeared and, now in
control of himself, gave the order, "Serve the meal."
32 It was served separately to him, to the brothers, and
to the Egyptians who partook of his board. (Egyptians may not eat with Hebrews; that is abhorrent to
33 them.) When they were seated by his directions according to their age, from the oldest to the youngest,
34 they looked at one another in amazement; and as

portions were brought to them from Joseph's table,
Benjamin's portion was five times as large as anyone
else's. So they drank freely and made merry with
him.

As usual, the Yahwist is at his best when he challenges the reader's
imagination, inviting him to paint in from his own cheerful or rueful memory colors of empathy over the bold lines of his drawing. Jacob allows
himself to be persuaded that Benjamin must, after all, go down to Egypt.
Therefore he resolves to put the best possible face on the matter, requiring
his sons to take with them *as gifts the land's best products,* things much in
demand in Egypt (cf. 37:25, J) and therefore the ironic wealth of a
famine-stricken people which could not use them for the sustenance of life.
The *balm and honey, gum and resin* named here were probably all the
saps and exudations of various trees and fruits. The sons of Israel must
also take extra money to show good faith, just in the hope that the mysterious return made to them previously had been a mistake and was not a
trap set for them. Having taken these precautions, Jacob has acted as
wisely as he knows to make the best of a situation that all of them feel is
none too good. His prognosis remains less than optimistic: *if I am to
suffer bereavement, I shall suffer it.*

As would follow from our analysis of the source distribution of these
chapters, the reference in vs. 14 to *your other brother* (viz. the Simeon of
E) is redactional. Quite probably the entire verse has been supplied by the
Redactor. Elsewhere *God Almighty* (El Shaddai) is a name favored by P
(17:1, 28:3, 35:11, and 48:3); it appears also in 49:25, a passage that
we discuss below.

Hardly are the brothers, *accompanied by Benjamin, off on their way
down to Egypt* when they are already there, seen first by Joseph from a
distance. The Yahwist wastes no time getting to the heart of his story,
which as always is the interaction between Joseph and his brothers and its
effects on them all. Here no narrative detail is spared as Joseph is allowed
to pursue his way of "wisdom" with the sons of Israel, deliberately
prolonging their anxiety and aggravating it by his mercurial conduct. Here
they come, these rustics from Canaan, uneasy about the reception they are
likely to get, and at once their worst fears seem to be realized. Invited into
the palace of the highest and mightiest they have ever met in or out of
Egypt, they can no way believe they have happened upon a social occasion. The only business that such a lord can have with men of their station
is the sadly familiar one of the way of the powerful with the powerless, the
way of victimization and exploitation. And so, they conclude that the pre-
monition of doom they once experienced on the road back to Canaan
(42:28) had been a true omen of a now present disaster. These are little

people, of course, and they think little thoughts: because a few donkeys represent to them the world's wealth, they can conceive of this lord of the land scheming to divest them of their liberty and property by baroque ruses, never considering how insignificant they and theirs must be in the calculations of such a person and what little recourse he would need for specious legalities if he chose to crush them at his will. We can picture the tolerant amusement of *Joseph's head steward* as they touch his sleeve *at the entrance of the house* and recite to him the story they have long rehearsed—a true story, indeed, but rehearsed nonetheless—of how they had before quitted Egypt with grain unpaid for. There is perhaps irony intended by the evasive and noncommittal response put on the steward's lips: the God whom they had once suspected of demonic designs on their future (42:28) instead *must have put treasures in your bags for you.*

From the steward's further statement that he had received their money the first time round, we might surmise that it was with him rather than with Joseph directly that the brothers had dealt in the J narration of their earlier journey to Egypt. For this reason it is not inappropriate that at the end of vs. 23 it is the steward who *led Simeon out to them,* releasing the bound hostage before the appearance of Joseph, who according to E had put him in bondage. These obviously redactional words, however, which seek to harmonize further the E and J accounts, could hardly have been inserted with any degree of verisimilitude at a later point in the J story, which has two further scenes to display.

The first scene is the meeting of Joseph with his brothers in their full strength, Benjamin now included. Finally persuaded that they have been brought to Joseph's house for no more sinister purpose than a midday meal, the brothers wash themselves and lay out the modest gifts they have brought to ingratiate themselves with the great man, who now returns home at the appointed time. Unfortunately, the Yahwistic narrative does not at this moment shed any additional light on the motives that had impelled Joseph's brothers to bring Benjamin with them on their second journey without fail or on the title by which Joseph had imposed on them this requirement. We are simply treated to a low-key spectacle of family reunion, recognized as such to the full by only one of the participants, in which by small talk the continued well-being of a common father is verified and by observation, probably for the first time, the identity of a younger brother is recognized. Joseph's emotional outburst on the occasion clearly results from looking into the face of his only full brother, in whom he can see the image of both his father and his mother: we do not presuppose here the moving story of Rachel's death at Benjamin's birth in 35:16–20 (E). We may readily assume the wonderment of Joseph's brothers over his erratic ways, but by now they must have concluded that what would be accounted bizarre and manic in their familiar workaday world could hardly even occasion remark in the mad hatter's land of Egypt's potentates.

The other scene is the banquet. The biblical author expects us to be amused at this interlude, as indeed we should be. With their enormous burden of worry lifted from their shoulders, as they think, and all unaware of the cruelest jest of all that Joseph is about to play on them, the brothers abandon themselves to the spirit of the present moment, heedless of any other that is to come and oblivious to all the others that have passed. Though for one instant they may have *looked at one another in amazement* because of Joseph's seating arrangements which betrayed a privy knowledge of their family precedences, they quickly dissipate their mystification, banishing it from their minds lest it get in the way of their determined euphoria, or at least file it for delayed consideration along with so many other queer memorabilia they have collected in their Egyptian ventures. *They drank freely and made merry with him* means, of course, that they became mildly and pleasantly drunk. There seem to have been three tables at the banquet, one apart for Joseph, as befitted his rank, one for *the Egyptians who partook of his board*—Joseph's home is the manor of a feudal lord—and a third for "the Hebrews." The principle of separation observed here is authentically Egyptian: "the antipathy of the Egyptians for everything foreign was proverbial in antiquity" (Benno Jacob). Specifically, Egyptians honored dietary laws and taboos which precluded their dining with those who did not share them or who carried about with them eating tools that had been used on forbidden foods. (Tables were not set with knife and fork: everyone carried on his person instruments to dress his food.) Benno Jacob points out appositely that the *may not* of vs. 32b ascribes to the Egyptians the same kind of ritual purity and propriety that forbade to Jews under the Torah certain foods and certain kinds of conduct (cf. Deuteronomy 12:17, 14:3; and also Genesis 31:35; Numbers 9:6; Deuteronomy 16:5; where the same formulas tend to recur). The parallel was undoubtedly sensed by the Redactor, and it may have shaped the language in which he chose to transmit the Yahwist's narrative. Finally, we might comment on the *five times as large* of vs. 34. Sending a choice bit from host to diner is a conventional sign of courtesy and hospitality observed to this day in the Near East. (Jesus does this for Judas according to John 13:26.) We may imagine that the rite was enacted repeatedly during this festive meal. "Five times" no doubt is an indeterminate number, half the "round number" of ten, therefore equal to "several"; but the repeated incidence of "five" in the Joseph story (besides here, also in 45:22, 47:2.24, all J) might indicate as well some esoteric symbolism that it once had either for Egypt or for Israel.

44 Then Joseph gave his head steward these instructions: "Fill the men's bags with as much food as

they can carry, and put each man's money in the
2 mouth of his bag. In the mouth of the youngest one's
bag put also my silver goblet, together with the
money for his rations." The steward carried out Jo-
3 seph's instructions. At daybreak the men and their
4 donkeys were sent off. They had not gone far out of
the city when Joseph said to his head steward: "Go
at once after the men! When you overtake them,
say to them, 'Why did you repay good for evil? Why
5 did you steal the silver goblet from me?‡ It is the
very one from which my master drinks and which
he uses for divination. What you have done is
wrong.' "
6 When the steward overtook them and repeated these
7 words to them, they remonstrated with him: "How
can my lord say such things? Far be it from your
8 servants to do such a thing! We even brought back
to you from the land of Canaan the money that we
found in the mouths of our bags. Why, then, would
we steal silver or gold from your master's house?
9 If any of your servants is found to have the goblet,
he shall die, and as for the rest of us, we shall be-
10 come my lord's slaves." But he replied, "Even
though it ought to be as you propose, only the one
who is found to have it shall become my slave, and
11 the rest of you shall be exonerated." Then each of
them eagerly lowered his bag to the ground and
12 opened it; and when a search was made, starting
with the oldest and ending with the youngest, the
13 goblet turned up in Benjamin's bag. At this, they
tore their clothes. Then, when each man had re-
loaded his donkey, they returned to the city.

This time the Israelites are not permitted to go a day's journey on their
way home but are stopped *not far out of the city.* We must supply the details: they have recovered from the prior day's feasting, someone has
provisioned their beasts of burden, and *at daybreak the men and their
donkeys were sent off.* They may be yet a touch befuddled as they seek out
their mounts—asses, we note, and not the anachronistic camels that nose
their way into other Genesis accounts—but they are hardly prepared for
the refinements of harassment Joseph has thought up to torment them one
last time. The instruction to *put each man's money in the mouth of his bag*

‡ "Why . . . me" has been supplied from the LXX; it is omitted by the MT.

sounds like a mechanical repetition of what was done the time before when the brothers left Egypt; the money is never mentioned again, even though according to vs. 12 each one's bag was thoroughly searched when they were overtaken by Joseph's steward. This time it is the *silver goblet* nestled among Benjamin's possessions that will cause them grief.

From vss. 5 and 15 below we learn that Joseph was practiced in divination. The silver goblet was employed for this purpose in addition to its being, apparently, his favorite table cup. Perhaps divination was thought to go with the office which Joseph held, or perhaps a talent of this kind was simply part of the common tradition by which he was remembered: in E Joseph is an interpreter of dreams (albeit with divine help), and dream-reading is another form of divination (some of the would-be interpreters of Pharaoh's dreams in 41:8.24 were styled "magicians"). The goblet would indicate that what is in question here is water divination. Water divination was widespread in the ancient Near East, where it assumed various forms. Water in the cup might be mixed with a few drops of oil, and the resulting configuration on its surface would be "read" for its significance. Or the shimmering surface itself might be "read" as one "reads" a crystal ball. Or it might be the pattern of drops that fell from the goblet when it was upended or tilted in pouring that provided the means of augury. The biblical author records, he does not judge, Joseph's capacity as a diviner, despite the fact that Israelite law repudiated divination as a heathen superstition and a crime punishable by death (cf. Leviticus 19:31, 20:6; Deuteronomy 18:10–11). At best, Joseph's personal theology in his career as Egypt's vizier and husband of a daughter of a priest of Heliopolis (41:45) has been left vague and cloudy in the Bible. The "God" on whom Joseph calls in both J and E seems to be the God both of Pharaoh and of the Hebrews of Canaan. "Wisdom" ideology doubtless contributed to this syncretism. But we will have to return to the subject of Joseph's origins and religion a few pages below.

Arrested by Joseph's steward who, as his alter ego, readily identifies his own "I" and "mine" with the "he" and "his" of his master, the brothers, conscious of no wrongdoing and instead well aware of the proofs of their rectitude which they had so shortly before demonstrated, are provoked into a rash oath. Their father Jacob (in the E story of 31:32–35) had once uttered such an oath and had been vindicated, but only through the ingenuity of his wife. These men stand naked before the wiles of one who has already bested them at every turn, and against whom they have no defender. With exquisite irony their blustering invitation to death and general enslavement is rebuffed by the steward, who manages to emerge as a force of moderation and sweet justice, mitigating to kindly limits a retribution which, we know, is merited by none of them at all. Sure of their innocence, they eagerly dump their goods on the ground. And just as surely, the fatal *goblet turned up in Benjamin's bag*. Grinding their teeth at this last evil deal that fate has handed them, they are afforded no other option but to reload their donkeys with their scattered belongings and return to the city.

14 As Judah and his brothers reentered Joseph's house, he was still there; so they flung themselves on the
15 ground before him. "How could you do such a thing?" Joseph asked them. "You should have known that such a man as I could discover by divi-
16 nation what happened." Judah replied: "What can we say to my lord? How can we plead or how try to prove our innocence? God has uncovered your servants' guilt. Here we are, then, the slaves of my lord —the rest of us no less than the one in whose pos-
17 session the goblet was found." "Far be it from me to act thus!" said Joseph. "Only the one in whose possession the goblet was found shall become my slave; the rest of you may go back safe and sound to your father."
18 Judah then stepped up to him and said: "I beg you, my lord, let your servant speak earnestly to my lord, and do not become angry with your servant, for you
19 are the equal of Pharaoh. My lord asked your servants, 'Have you a father, or another brother?'
20 So we said to my lord, 'We have an aged father, and a young brother, the child of his old age. This one's full brother is dead, and since his is the only one by that mother who is left, his father dotes on him.'
21 Then you told your servants, 'Bring him down to me
22 that my eyes may look on him.' We replied to my lord, 'The boy cannot leave his father; his father
23 would die if he were to leave him.' But you told your servants, 'Unless your youngest brother comes back with you, you shall not come into my presence
24 again.' When we returned to your servant our father,
25 we reported to him the words of my lord. "Later, our father told us to come back and buy some food
26 for the family. So we reminded him, 'We cannot go down there; only if our youngest brother is with us can we go, for we may not see the man if our young-
27 est brother is not with us.' Then your servant our father said to us, 'As you know, my wife bore me two
28 sons. One of them, however, disappeared, and I had to conclude that he must have been torn to pieces by

29 wild beasts; I have not seen him since. If you now take this one away from me, too, and some disaster befalls him, you will send my white head down to the nether world in grief.'

30 "If then the boy is not with us when I go back to your servant my father, whose very life is bound up

31 with his, he will die as soon as he sees that the boy is missing; and your servants will thus send the white head of our father down to the nether world in grief.

32 Besides, I, your servant, got the boy from his father by going surety for him, saying, 'If I fail to bring him back to you, father, you can hold it against me for-

33 ever.' Let me, your servant, therefore, remain in place of the boy as the slave of my lord, and let the

34 boy go back with his brothers. How could I go back to my father if the boy were not with me? I could not bear to see the anguish that would overcome my father."

The entire point of this section is the beautifully eloquent plea of Judah, which both fulfills and justifies the questionable logic with which Joseph has pursued the "instruction" of his brothers and at the same time prompts us to ask whether Joseph was, after all, really such a wise and considerate man as he had thought himself to be when he embarked on his devious course of action. Judah's plea is a deep and penetrating rebuke, no doubt about it, as is acknowledged in the J of 45:1 that follows. It is also a vindication of what Joseph has done: here is one who stands ready to substitute himself as a sacrificial offering in place of his brother, to lay down his life for a friend. A great enlargement has taken place, then, in the soul of the Judah who earlier (37:25–28) could think of no other alternative to the murder of his brother than to sell him into slavery. And we may suppose that Judah's spiritual growth in some measure was that of his brothers: thus Joseph had achieved his purpose and converted his brethren to a view on man that transcended the horizons surrounding their particular hearthstones.

But at the same time Joseph has overreached himself. Judah rebukes him first when he brushes aside Joseph's pretense of supernal intelligence and acknowledges that one and all he and his brothers are guilty as charged. Earlier commentators, bred to the accepted wisdom that an innocent man must automatically protest his innocence, wondered about this act of Judah's. Events of our own recent past in war and politics, however, may help us to understand better the psychology at work here. Caught in the meshes of processes he neither understands nor can control, and obsessed by feelings of guilt for a crime of which he believes his inquisitor to be ignorant, Judah seizes the opportunity to bring his ordeal to an end and to atone for his misdeeds by confessing to the offense with which he is charged. The charge is false, but the guilt is real; and at last the cat-and-mouse game which Joseph has been playing will be finished. If Joseph can rejoice in this cheap victory he has won by adopting the tactics of a bully and a tyrant, then let him. It is Judah who has really won in a way, since he has turned Joseph into the dispenser of justice that he is now only pretending to be, leaving him unaware of the fact and knowing only that he is the persecutor of innocent and helpless men. And in truth, Joseph's response to Judah's surrender in vs. 17 seems somewhat lame and embarrassed, even though it is also a forcible reiteration of his steward's words in vs. 10 above.

The sharpest rebuke to Joseph, however, is in the moving plea of vss. 18–34 wherein Judah seeks to substitute himself for Benjamin so as to spare his father unbearable anguish. It must suddenly occur to Joseph, to his chagrin, that he has been surpassed in his love and concern for the father who had preferred him to all his other sons. Whatever plan he had had in chastening his errant brothers, the plan had also entailed the suffering of an innocent old man, and he had scarcely been aware of it. The storyteller builds Judah's lengthy speech into a magnificent climax, after which there can be only the inevitable denouement. If Joseph had intended to fret his brothers further, he intends it no more. Judah's humble eloquence has triumphed.

In the final scenes of this story played out in chapter 45 the two narrative sources again join forces. The part that we judge to be J appears in roman, while E is in italic type. The reader should as before experience no trouble in recognizing the reasons for most of our decisions, though certainly not every commentator will agree with all of them.

> **45** Joseph could no longer control himself in the presence of all his attendants, so he cried out, "Have everyone withdraw from me!" Thus no one else was about when he made himself known to his brothers. *2 But his sobs were so loud that the Egyptians heard 3 him, and so the news reached Pharaoh's palace. "I am Joseph," he said to his brothers. "Is my father still in good health?" But his brothers could give him no answer, so dumbfounded were they at him.* 4 "Come closer to me," he told his brothers. When they had done so, he said: "I am your brother Jo-5 seph, whom you once sold into Egypt. But now do not be distressed, and do not reproach yourselves for

having sold me here. *It was really for the sake of
saving lives that God sent me here ahead of you.*
6 *For two years now the famine has been in the land,
and for five more years tillage will yield no harvest.*
7 *God, therefore, sent me on ahead of you to ensure
for you a remnant on earth and to save your lives*
8 *in an extraordinary deliverance.* So it was not really
you but God who had me come here; and he has
made of me a father to Pharaoh, lord of all his
household, and ruler over the whole land of Egypt.*
9 "Hurry back, then, to my father and tell him: 'Thus
says your son Joseph: God has made me lord of all
10 Egypt; come to me without delay. You will settle in
the region of Goshen, where you will be near me—
you and your children and grandchildren, your
11 flocks and herds, and everything that you own. *Since
five years of famine still lie ahead, I will provide for
you there, so that you and your family and all that*
12 *are yours may not suffer want.' Surely, you can see
for yourselves, and Benjamin can see for himself,*
13 *that it is I, Joseph, who am speaking to you.* Tell my
father all about my high position in Egypt and what
you have seen. But hurry and bring my father down
14 here." Thereupon he flung himself on the neck of his
brother Benjamin and wept, and Benjamin wept in
15 his arms. *Joseph then kissed all his brothers, crying
over each of them; and only then were his brothers
able to talk with him.*

In both versions of the story an emotional outburst on Joseph's part
precedes the disclosure of his identity to his brothers. What in the E version provoked the outburst we cannot now know: it hardly could have
been anything comparable to the Judah speech of 44:18–34 dwelling on
the sorrows of Jacob, since in such a context the question of Joseph in vs.
3 would be an inanity. That question, incidentally, is not the polite inquiry
about health and welfare that the slightly harmonizing translation of the
NAB has made of it but rather, as the Hebrew literally has it, a search for
vital information: "Is my father still alive?" In E Joseph does not obtain
this vital information until vs. 15 when at last his brothers, struck dumb at
his sudden revelation, find their tongues and begin *to talk with him*. Meanwhile in J he has already issued detailed instructions about the message

* The NAB follows the LXX and the SP; the MT is slightly different.

that is to be brought to Jacob, summoning him to a life of prosperity and ease in Egypt for himself and his whole family.

In J Joseph *made himself known to his brothers* in complete privacy, even secretively (cf. vs. 4, *come closer to me*), while in E *the news reached Pharaoh's palace*, with the results that we will see in vss. 16–20 below. In both versions Joseph excuses his brothers of blame in the circumstances that brought him to Egypt; he prefers to ascribe the whole affair to God, who thus in his providence ensured the salvation of Israel. Both the *remnant* and the *deliverance* (literally, "survival" or "survivors") of vs. 7 are consecrated terms of Old Testament theological language to designate the effect of divine intervention in Israel's history, preserving it from ultimate disaster. And in both versions, with the use of insignificantly varying titles as before, Joseph is named Pharaoh's vicegerent and *ruler over the whole land of Egypt*. In vs. 8 *father to Pharaoh* is the Hebrew equivalent of an expression that was actually used in Egypt to refer to the vizier.

The region of Goshen we shall consider below.

16 *When the news reached Pharaoh's palace that Joseph's brothers had come, Pharaoh and his courtiers*
17 *were pleased. So Pharaoh told Joseph: "Say to your brothers: 'This is what you shall do: Load up your animals and go without delay to the land of Canaan.*
18 *There get your father and your families, and then come back here to me; I will assign you the best land in Egypt, where you will live off the fat of the*
19 *land.' Instruct them further:† 'Do this. Take wagons from the land of Egypt for your children and your wives and to transport your father on your way back*
20 *here. Do not be concerned about your belongings, for the best in the whole land of Egypt shall be yours.' "*
21 The sons of Israel acted accordingly. *Joseph gave them the wagons, as Pharaoh had ordered,* and he
22 supplied them with provisions for the journey. He also gave to each of them fresh clothing, but to Benjamin he gave three hundred shekels of silver and
23 five sets of garments. Moreover, what he sent to his father was ten jackasses loaded with the finest products of Egypt and ten jennies loaded with grain and
24 bread and other provisions for his journey. As he

† So the LXX; the MT has "You are instructed."

sent his brothers on their way, he told them, "Let
there be no recriminations on the way."

25 *So they left Egypt and made their way to their fa-*
26 *ther Jacob in the land of Canaan. When they told*
him, "Joseph is still alive—in fact, it is he who is
ruler of all the land of Egypt," he was dumbfounded;
27 *he could not believe them. But when they recounted*
to him all that Joseph had told them, and when he
saw the wagons that Joseph had sent for his trans-
28 *port the spirit of their father Jacob revived.* "It is
enough," said Israel. "My son Joseph is still alive! I
must go and see him before I die."

In E's story Joseph's father and brothers and their families are called
down to Egypt not only with Pharaoh's foreknowledge but actually at his
own insistence. The Egyptian court spontaneously adopts Joseph's cause
and interests as its own, and orders go forth to facilitate the journey and to
assure the Hebrews of a warm and generous welcome. So lavish is
Pharaoh in his promises—*do not be concerned about your belongings*—he
almost overshadows the here-and-now practicality of Joseph, who in J
showers gifts on the departing brothers for themselves and their father. We
note again in vs. 22 the occurrence of "five" as a significant number. If E
wants to underscore Pharaoh's unflagging gratitude to the "man endowed
with the spirit of God" (41:38) whom he elevated to second-in-command
in Egypt and his devotion to all his concerns, it is the intent of the
Yahwist, in whose work Pharaoh never assumes any distinct personality of
his own, to stress the completeness of Joseph's reconciliation with his family and his desire to compensate for the grief he has caused. *Let there be
no recriminations on the way* is probably an injunction to the same end:
the past is past, and there is nothing to be gained by trying to assign to it
guilt and innocence, to determine who was the injurer and who the in-
jured. Everyone will be better off for concentrating on what is to be.

Jacob was dumbfounded (not the same Hebrew expression so translated
in vs. 3 above) implies an interesting bit of primitive physiology. Literally,
"his heart was cold, sluggish": the Hebrew "heart" is the Greek "mind";
Jacob could not bring his senses to bear immediately on the strange intelligence his sons had brought him, and therefore *he could not believe them.*
But eventually, when he had heard their tale and seen the evidence of
Pharaoh's wagons, *the spirit of their father Jacob revived,* that is, "he
again drew breath," his vital powers were renewed and he was able to
think clearly again. The *It is enough* of J that concludes this section
presupposes a similar argumentation and display of exhibits have established credibility for the astounding thing which Jacob is expected to

believe. Believe it he does at last, and we are prepared for the next, final, and fatal act of the patriarchal drama, when Israel—at the beckon of the wise Joseph—descends freely and willingly into that place which forever after will be known in song and story as "the land of Egypt, that place of slavery" (Deuteronomy 5:6, etc.).

5. Israel in Egypt

As we enter upon this ultimate episode of Genesis, the one in which the beginning of Israel's experience of Egypt purports to be told, it will be useful to have in mind a few facts about the Egypt with which we are concerned, or at least with which the biblical authors expect us to be concerned.

Egypt and Mesopotamia, geographically, politically, and culturally, were the twin hammers of history that pounded the anvil of Canaan and Israel. There are many similarities between the two. Just as Mesopotamia has a right to the title of cradle of civilization, inventor of writing, originator of the arts and crafts, so does Egypt have a like right. And just as Mesopotamia lived in virtue of its two great rivers, Egypt was the creation of its one: the Greek historian Herodotus of the fifth century B.C. coined the phrase that has been made the cliché of every commentator when he called Egypt "the gift of the Nile."

We have already seen the importance of the Nile for the prosperity of Egypt. Egypt must be the most oblong country in the world in terms of arable land, since for all practical purposes it consists of about six hundred miles, say nine hundred and fifty kilometers, of Nile riverbank from south to north, until it widens into the Nile delta and the river reaches its mouth at the Mediterranean Sea. The Nile originates about twenty-five hundred miles or four thousand kilometers south of its mouth in Lake Victoria in Uganda, though its meandering course down to the sea adds to its total length another three eighths of the crow-flight distance. This river, from source to mouth, is the so-called White Nile. At Khartoum in the Sudan the White Nile is joined by the Blue Nile, another river which flows in from the mountains of Ethiopia. Between Khartoum and Aswan there are six cataracts, and at the last of these (or the first, of course, counting from north to south) the classical Egypt begins. Rain hardly falls in Egypt, and then only in the delta region; the level of the Nile, and the annual inundation that brings with it the precious fertile soil, depends on the rainy season in Ethiopia and the consequent cresting of the Blue Nile as it descends into Egypt. When the Nile overflows in Egypt the color of the silt which has been brought down from the heights and is spread throughout the land, sparingly until the delta is reached and then lavishly, gives rise to the name of the Red Nile.

From Egypt's southern extremity at the first cataract of Aswan north to Memphis, on the edge of the delta and near the modern Cairo, there are about four hundred miles of land. This is southern or Upper Egypt. From Memphis on to the sea there are another hundred miles: Lower Egypt. In the earliest times these were separate countries, and in recorded Egyptian history they remained separate, distinguished by characteristic flora, fauna, and other features. The Egyptian Pharaoh was known as "the lord of the two lands," and the Hebrew for Egypt, Mizraim, is a dual.

Since Manetho, a Greco-Egyptian historian of the fourth–third century B.C., whose works have been preserved fragmentarily by other ancient authors and principally, in what concerns us here, by the Jewish historian Josephus (about A.D. 37–100), it has been customary to distribute the history of old Egypt over thirty "dynasties." Modern Egyptologists still employ the distribution, though they combine it more recent criteria for dividing up the many centuries of Egypt's past as the abundance of its archeology and inscriptions has revealed them

We know that there was an archaic or predynastic period before Egypt was ever united, and that after it was united two "dynasties" reigned over it maybe a half millennium at Memphis in Lower Egypt—an obscure age which, it is sobering to reflect, exceeds by twice and a half again the years of the American Republic. Then came the Old Kingdom, the third to the fifth of Manetho's dynasties, eight hundred years (2850–2052 B.C.) which witnessed the building of the great pyramids and a vast amount of history that does not concern us. Between the Old and the Middle Kingdom, the period of the sixth to the eleventh dynasty, there was a time of decadence when the government moved back and forth between Memphis and Thebes in Upper Egypt. Now and later, though in theory the land may have been governed by a single Pharaoh, in practice the administration was often in the hands of local aristocracies and gentries, and it is possible that sometimes the "Pharaoh" or "king of Egypt" of Old Testament traditions might have been no more than the nearest Egyptian princeling with whom outlanders would come into contact. Such a possibility might be present, were we pressed to treat the story as a piece of history, in respect to Abraham's visit to Egypt according to the J of 12:10–20. Above we considered this story within the context of the Middle Kingdom (2052–1778 B.C.), the Twelfth Dynasty, a period of two and three quarters centuries which witnessed one of the apogees of Egyptian culture and influence. It is tempting to dwell on this Middle Kingdom history as well as that of the New Kingdom (1610–1085 B.C.) which succeeded it, the latter especially for its intimate connection with what is incontestably historical about the origins of Israel (e.g., the Amarna letters of 1413–1358 B.C., the first mention of "Israel" on a stele of Pharaoh Merneptah, about 1220 B.C., etc.). However, our present interest is confined to a much more obscure and poorly documented era of little more than a century and a half of Egyptian history that could just possibly shed some light on the biblical story of Joseph.

Anarchy, incursions, and disintegration accompanied the decline of the Twelfth Dynasty and introduced a midtime (1778–1610 B.C.) of confusion and uncertainty, an age which the *condottieri* would have found challenging and homelike. This period is that of Manetho's dynasties thirteen to seventeen, of which the first two and the last ruled from Thebes in Upper Egypt while the other two, the fifteenth and the sixteenth, had their capital in the Nile delta, at a place that has been called variously Tanis, Avaris, or Zoan. These dynasties north and south were not sequential but probably concurrent. We have to do with those of Lower Egypt, which Manetho ascribed to the Hyksos.

Hyksos is the Greek spelling of an Egyptian expression which Manetho thought meant "shepherd kings" but which more likely should be rendered "foreign rulers." According to Manetho the Hyksos seized power in Egypt by invasion, but it is more probable that their regime was secured by a series of coups d'état in Lower Egypt. The Hyksos seem not to have been a distinct race or people but rather the ruling class among a mixed population movement that poured into Egypt just as Amorites and other peoples had moved into Canaan. (A parallel situation in the ancient Near East was the kingdom of Mitanni of 1500–1370 B.C. on the upper Euphrates, a Hurrian population ruled by an Aryan aristocracy.) Both Hurrian and Semitic names turn up among the Hyksos, the latter predominating, and it is not difficult to imagine that their strength derived both from the mercenaries who had been called in from time to time to fight in Egypt's internecine wars and from the normal seepage of peoples that freely penetrated its supposedly secure boundaries. However they came to power, come to power they did. They fought throughout their whole history with the Theban regimes of Upper Egypt, and they generally prevailed; usually they were content to hold Lower Egypt and accept a token tribute from the south. Their religion was a syncretism of the Western Semitic combined with the native Egyptian, and their culture was basically that of Phoenicia/Canaan. Withal, they were the lords of Egypt and capable of a chauvinism for their adopted country more than the equal of any of its natives, following a not uncommon pattern for a populace of recent immigration.

The Hyksos, who exercised a vigorously innovative influence on a highly traditional country, are credited with introducing the war chariot into Egypt (cf. 41:43) and thereby bringing in the horse (cf. 47:17; however, excavations at the fortress of Buhen or Wadi Halfa in the Sudan have disclosed the skeleton of a horse that has been dated in the Twelfth Dynasty). Archeologists also recognize a distinctive type of fortification which they style "the Hyksos wall." There seems to be no doubt that in the normal course of events an extensive record of this age would have been preserved for us in the sandstone hieroglyphs, the obelisks, and the other well-nigh imperishable devices by which the kings of Egypt kept their names alive, often undeservedly, for centuries and millennia to come. The Egyptians, however, had a way of erasing the memory of their antecedents when it suited them to do so. Queen Hatshepsut of the New Kingdom whose massive temple-tomb is one of the enduring wonders of the Valley of the Kings in Upper Egypt devoted much of her royal time to chiseling away the name of her predecessor incised in the stones of Karnak, and later on Ramses III would thwart any like diminution of his heroic figure by having his inscriptions cut several times the normal depth into the walls of his palaces. It is altogether understandable why a proud people like the Egyptians of the New Kingdom would not care to be reminded of what they must have regarded as an ignominious chapter in their history, once the Hyksos had been finally expelled by a new and vigorous Theban dynasty. For whatever reason, documentation of the Hyksos age is very sparse.

We do know enough about it, however, to consider it a plausible historical background for the Joseph story. For a Semite to rise to high station in Hyksos Egypt would not have been at all unthinkable. (Interestingly, there is evidence that one of the Hyksos bore the name "Jacob.") This is not to rule out the possibility, or probability, that in the biblical legend Joseph's stature has been exaggerated, just as the lineage by which he is linked to the tribes of Israel may be in part or in whole artificial. In its traditions Israel remembered at the beginning and the end of an Egyptian experience men of Egyptian names, Zaphenath-paneah and Moses, the first of whom had provided it with security and survival in Egypt while the other, when times had radically changed, had led it to freedom out of Egyptian serfdom. An "historical Joseph" is by no means as integral to this tradition as is an "historical Moses": Moses, or the memory of Moses, is one of the constitutive elements of Israel's coming-to-be, while Joseph's connection with the pre-Israelite tribal system is at best shaky and undefined. Nevertheless, for the historical reality of both these men there are good probabilities. In the rise and fall of the Hyksos in Egypt, however unsatisfactory may be our access to this episode in history, we may justly presume to have some kind of instrument by which the Joseph and Israel stories of these chapters of Genesis may be removed from the realm of pure romance into that of formative fact, vague and shadowy though its outlines may be.

Chapter 46 begins with a few verses that appear to be mainly E. There are also some traces of J, however, and it seems as though there are vestiges of two separate accounts of the departure for Egypt that have been mingled into one. We shall not attempt to sort out typographically the separate elements which the Redactor has mixed together here.

> **46** Israel set out with all that was his. When he arrived
> at Beer-sheba, he offered sacrifices to the God of his
> 2 father Isaac. There God, speaking to Israel in a vi-
> sion by night, called, "Jacob, Jacob!" "Here I am,"
> 3 he answered. Then he said: "I am God, the God of
> your father. Do not be afraid to go down to Egypt,
> 4 for there I will make you a great nation. Not only
> will I go down to Egypt with you; I will also bring
> you back here, after Joseph has closed your eyes."
> 5 So Jacob departed from Beer-sheba, and the sons of
> Israel put their father and their wives and children
> on the wagons that Pharaoh had sent for his trans-
> port.

It is our guess that in these verses the Redactor has rather composed a free account of his own using the material of J and E than he has tried to interweave the sources by preserving the separate strands. Jacob is now Jacob, now Israel. He sets out for Egypt on his own resolve (cf. 45:28, J), and he is instructed to go there *in a vision by night* by *the God of his father Isaac,* the El of Beer-sheba. In 21:22–34 there is a combined E and J story which recalls Abraham's experience of this God at Beer-sheba, and in 26:23–25 (J) the same God, conventionally identified with Yahweh, indeed appeared to Isaac. So it is that the theophany—the only one in the whole of the Joseph story—is colored by the language of both J and E and looks back to narrative antecedents in both; in the *great nation* of vs. 3 there is even a reminiscence of the P of 35:11. All of this looks more like free composition than the combining of sources.

I will also bring you back here in vs. 4 refers to the story of the return of Jacob's body to Canaan told by both P and J in 49:29–50:14 below. Undoubtedly the biblical author has in mind at the same time, however, the "return" of all Israel to the Land of Promise after the exodus from Egypt, the final fulfillment of the covenants made with the patriarchs in these divine appearances.

Jacob's journey to Egypt is continued with vs. 28 below. At this point, though, the Redactor chooses to interrupt the narrative inserting a section from P which has its own account of the descent prefaced to a genealogy. It is for the sake of the genealogy that P has been introduced here, although as we shall see it fits in somewhat curiously with the surrounding JE context.

6 They took with them their livestock and the possessions they had acquired in the land of Canaan. Thus Jacob and all his descendants mi-
7 grated to Egypt. His sons and his grandsons, his
daughters and his granddaughters—all his descendants—he took with him to Egypt.

8 These are the names of the Israelites, Jacob and
his descendants, who migrated to Egypt.

9 Reuben, Jacob's first-born, and the sons of Reu-
10 ben: Hanoch, Pallu, Hezron and Carmi. The
sons of Simeon: Nemuel,* Jamin, Ohad, Jachin,
Zohar, and Shaul, son of a Canaanite woman.

11 The sons of Levi: Gershon, Kohath and Merari.

12 The sons of Judah: Er, Onan, Shelah, Perez and
Zerah—but Er and Onan had died in the land of
Canaan; and the sons of Perez were Hezron and
13 Hamul. The sons of Issachar: Tola, Puah, Ja-
14 shub† and Shimron. The sons of Zebulun: Sered,
15 Elon and Jahleel. These were the sons whom
Leah bore to Jacob in Paddan-aram, along with
his daughter Dinah—thirty-three persons in all,
male and female.

16 The sons of Gad: Zephon,‡ Haggi, Shuni, Ez-
17 bon, Eri, Arod‡ and Areli. The sons of Asher:
Imnah, Ishvah, Ishvi and Beriah, with their sister Serah; and the sons of Beriah: Heber and
18 Malchiel. These were the descendants of Zilpah,
whom Laban had given to his daughter Leah;
these she bore to Jacob—sixteen persons in all.

19 The sons of Jacob's wife Rachel: Joseph and
Benjamin.

20 In the land of Egypt Joseph became the father of
Manasseh and Ephraim, whom Asenath, daughter of Potiphera, priest of Heliopolis, bore to

---

* Here and in Exodus 6:15 the MT has Jemuel; Nemuel agrees with Numbers 26:12 and 1 Chronicles 4:24.

† Puah and Jashub are read with 1 Chronicles 7:1 and ancient versions; the MT differs.

‡ These two names are so read with the SP and the LXX; cf. Numbers 26:15.17.

21 him. The sons of Benjamin: Bela, Becher, Ash-
bel, Gera, Naaman, Ahiram,* Shupham,* Hu-
22 pham* and Ard. These were the sons whom
Rachel bore† to Jacob—fourteen persons in
all.
23/24 The sons of Dan: Hushim. The sons of Naph-
25 tali: Jahzeel, Guni, Jezer and Shillem. These
were the sons of Bilhah, whom Laban had given
to his daughter Rachel; these she bore to Jacob
—seven persons in all.
26 Jacob's people who migrated to Egypt—his direct descendants, not counting the wives of Jacob's sons—numbered sixty-six persons in all.
27 Together with Joseph's sons who were born to
him in Egypt—two persons—all the people comprising Jacob's family who had come to Egypt
amounted to seventy persons in all.

Immediately we notice some strange things. The NAB has aptly selected
the verb *migrated* to characterize this descent of *Jacob and all his descendants* down into Egypt, for indeed it has the solemnity and finality of a
movement from one land and its way of life into another, not unlike the
migration of the Terahites from Mesopotamia to Canaan (11:31–32,
12:4b–5, P). That earlier migration had also been signaled by genealogies
of the principals (25:7–11a.12–17, P). Interrupted by the Isaac episode
concerning which the P source had very little to say, the migration theme
was resumed in the story of Jacob's coming to Canaan from Paddan-aram
(31:18, P, is almost a carbon copy of vs. 6 above), again accompanied by
a genealogy in the fashion of the one here (cf. 35:22b–26, P). Thus we
have in these verses the record of a further family relocation which follows
patterns set in the past, not the response to Joseph's urgent summons as J
would have it, and certainly not an acceptance of Pharaoh's invitation to
abandon personal possessions and flock to the good life of Egypt as E has
told the story. We have no way of knowing what conformations the story
of Joseph in Egypt would have taken on in the P tradition, since the
Redactor has shown us so very little of it; we can only be sure that it
differed more than a bit from the JE chronicle.

It is also strange that in vs. 7 "all" of Jacob's descendants should be
defined as *his sons and his grandsons, his daughters and his grand-*

* These three names have been reconstituted from a corrupted MT by the use of
Numbers 26:38–39 and 1 Chronicles 8:4–5; see the commentary.
† So the SP, the Syriac, etc.; the MT has "the sons of Rachel who was [*sic*] born to
Jacob."

daughters, who are presumably to be named in the genealogy that follows, while as it turns out there are numerous sons and grandsons mentioned in it, but only one daughter and one granddaughter, and then, to make up for the deficiency, two unheralded great-grandsons. The genealogy poses many other problems than this one, however. Benjamin, the tender lad whom Jacob could not allow from his sight in the preceding chapters, is here the father of nine living sons (ten, in the uncorrected MT). It seems to be an inescapable conclusion that the genealogy has been introduced not only to the disregard of the JE story of Joseph but also as an afterthought in the P narrative itself. It was originally an independent and traditional list of some of Jacob's descendants in the first and occasionally the second generations, fairly identical with those which appear in different order in 1 Chronicles 2:3–5, 4:24, 5:3.27, 7:1.6.12.13.30–31, 8:1–10 and in Numbers 26, spread over the chapter, which has only secondarily been made a component of the present story. There seems to be little point in pursuing a further commentary on these names, some of which we have seen before and some of which we have not, all of which in any case appear in one form or another as clans in the later Israelite federation.

The *seventy persons* of vs. 27 was simply a traditional, "round" number for the descendants of Jacob (cf. Exodus 1:5, P, and Deuteronomy 10:22), but some editor of the text before us had resolved to come up with an exact seventy, which he achieved by adding the thirty-three of vs. 15 to the sixteen of vs. 18 to the fourteen of vs. 22 and the seven of vs. 25. (The LXX totted up a number seventy-five, in which it was followed by Acts 7:14.) The computation is artificial, as a quick look at the whole genealogy will show. It is hard to tell whether in vs. 21 "fourteen" has been arrived at by generating for Benjamin another son or the other son had already appeared through a bad distribution of Hebrew consonants: the NAB presupposes *w'ḥyrm wšwpm wḥwpm* whereas the MT has *'ḥy wr'š mpym wḥpym*—four names have emerged from three, contrary to the evidence of Numbers and Chronicles. Neither is the *sixty-six persons* of vs. 26 a realistic figure. What seems to have happened is that someone simply subtracted from the seventy given in vs. 27 four counters that would represent the two sons of Joseph born in Egypt, Joseph who had preceded Israel into Egypt, and Jacob himself who was not to be computed in the number of his "descendants."

It is comforting to return to the "standard" Joseph story which without question in the following section has drawn exclusively on the J source.

> 28 Israel had sent Judah ahead to Joseph, so that he
>   might meet him in Goshen.‡ On his* arrival in the

‡ MT: "that he might appear before him in Goshen."
* MT: "their." In both readings the NAB follows the SP and the Syriac.

29 region of Goshen, Joseph hitched the horses to his
chariot and rode to meet his father in Goshen. As
soon as he saw him, he flung himself on his neck and
30 wept a long time in his arms. And Israel said to Joseph, "At last I can die, now that I have seen for
myself that Joseph is still alive."
31 Joseph then said to his brothers and his father's
household: "I will go and inform Pharaoh, telling
him: 'My brothers and my father's household, whose
home is in the land of Canaan, have come to me.
32 The men are shepherds, having long been keepers of
livestock; and they have brought with them their
flocks and herds, as well as everything else they
33 own.' So when Pharaoh summons you and asks what
34 your occupation is, you must answer, 'We your servants, like our ancestors, have been keepers of livestock from the beginning until now,' in order that
you may stay in the region of Goshen, since all shepherds are abhorrent to the Egyptians."
47 Joseph went and told Pharaoh, "My father and my
brothers have come from the land of Canaan, with
their flocks and herds and everything else they own;
2 and they are now in the region of Goshen." He then
presented to Pharaoh five of his brothers whom he
3 had selected from their full number. When Pharaoh
asked them what their occupation was, they answered, "We, your servants, like our ancestors, are
4 shepherds. We have come," they continued, "in order to stay in this country, for there is no pasture for
your servants' flocks in the land of Canaan, so severe has the famine been there. Please, therefore, let
5a your servants settle in the region of Goshen."† Pharaoh said to Joseph, "They may settle in the region
of Goshen; and if you know any of them to be qualified, you may put them in charge of my own livestock."

Judah, who is the only one of Joseph's brothers to have a role assigned
him in the Yahwist's narrative, here serves as an advance messenger for
Jacob to announce his coming. *The region of Goshen* is the Yahwist's
name for the area of Egypt in which the Israelites settled, generally assumed to be the Wadi Tumilat region of the northeastern Nile delta. This

† The NAB has rearranged vs. 5 to agree with the LXX.

is the Egypt known to "Asiatics," who frequently settled there, and it was also near the capital of the Hyksos. Here was ample grazing land well suited to shepherds, and to secure residence there Joseph's brothers are carefully instructed to identify themselves as such. That *all shepherds are abhorrent to the Egyptians* is a datum not elsewhere attested, but it is not unusual for settled and nomadic peoples to hold each other in mutual distrust and animosity. The sense of Joseph's allusion to this Egyptian prejudice seems to be that by obtaining leave to dwell in Goshen the Israelites would not only be in a land ideal for their life-style but also in one where they could live in peace and privacy, shunned by the surrounding Egyptians.

The Yahwist's story of Israel's entry into Egypt takes the form of a tearful reunion of a son long thought dead with an aged father who now looks forward only to a tranquil death. Joseph, who has arranged the removal of his family with all their possessions from Canaan to Egypt to share in the life he can offer them, now presents them to Pharaoh and obtains the royal permission to settle them in the place he had chosen—the *five of his brothers* who constitute a select delegation continues the persistent "five" that crops up in the J version of the Joseph story. A different accounting of the first encounter between Egypt and Israel occurs in the following verses.

5b Thus, when Jacob and his sons came to Joseph in Egypt, and Pharaoh, king of Egypt, heard about it, Pharaoh said to Joseph, "Now that your father
6 and brothers have come to you, the land of Egypt is at your disposal; settle your father and brothers in
7 the pick of the land." Then Joseph brought his father Jacob and presented him to Pharaoh. After Ja-
8 cob had paid his respects to Pharaoh, Pharaoh asked
9 him, "How many years have you lived?" Jacob replied: "The years I have lived as a wayfarer amount to a hundred and thirty. Few and hard have been these years of my life, and they do not compare with the years that my ancestors lived as wayfarers."
10 Then Jacob bade Pharaoh farewell and withdrew from his presence.
11 As Pharaoh had ordered, Joseph settled his father and brothers and gave them holdings in Egypt on the
12 pick of the land, in the region of Rameses. And Joseph sustained his father and brothers and his father's whole household, down to the youngest, with food.

Here Pharaoh takes the initiative, informing Joseph that his father and brothers have arrived in fulfillment of the order he had issued on learning of the relationship (45:16–20, E). Unprompted, Pharaoh decrees that they shall reside *in the pick of the land* (cf. 45:18.20, E). In vs. 11 this area is designated as *the region of Rameses*. Rameses (the Raamses of the book of Exodus) is here an anachronism, since the city acquired this name only in the time of Ramses II of the nineteenth Egyptian dynasty (about 1301–1234 B.C.), who named it after himself; by this name it would have been especially remembered by the Israelites, for at the time of the exodus it was again the capital of Egypt and a place of Israelite oppression (cf. Exodus 1:11). The Bible identifies Rameses with Avaris, the Hyksos capital, which it likewise calls Zoan and Tanis.

These verses are ascribed by some commentators to E and by others to P. We would like to agree with the first of these opinions, but it must be admitted that vss. 7–10—which for that matter could be lifted from the text without disturbing the sequence of vss. 6.11—do have all the characteristics of P. Here Jacob is introduced to Pharaoh and replies to a polite interrogation about his health and welfare with a computation of his age that fits the P chronology. *A hundred and thirty* years may be calculated as *few and hard* only in comparison with the ages of Abraham and Isaac, which according to P were one hundred and eighty and one hundred and seventy-five respectively. Jacob describes his life and that of his fathers as *wayfarers:* the same term (sometimes paraphrased in the NAB) occurs elsewhere in 17:8, 28:4, 36:7, and 37:1 (all P). The term, which likens the patriarchal life to a homeless wandering (not precisely the "pilgrimage" in a spiritual sense which some earlier commentators wanted to find in the text), contrasts with the *holdings in Egypt* which Joseph obtained for his brethren according to vs. 11. "Holding" is also a P term, later designating Israel's title to the land of Palestine as a permanent possession in distinction to the Deuteronomic theology which considered it to be "on loan" at the Lord's sufferance. Here the word serves to continue and complete the "migration" interpretation of Israel's descent into Egypt expressed by 46:26 above (P).

Having brought Israel to Egypt (the P story will be ended with another little fragment in vss. 27–28 below), the Redactor—or his sources, indeed —loses interest in pursuing the subject further. Instead, there has been appended an apparently totally unrelated section from J which has obviously nothing to do directly with the history of Israel but which nonetheless was judged to be germane to the history that Israel wanted to remember about Egypt.

13 Since there was no food in any country because of
the extreme severity of the famine, and the lands of
Egypt and Canaan were languishing from hunger,

14 Joseph gathered in, as payment for the rations that
   were being dispensed, all the money that was to be
   found in Egypt and Canaan, and he put in it Phar-
15 aoh's palace. When all the money in Egypt and Canaan was spent, all the Egyptians came to Joseph,
   pleading, "Give us food or we shall perish under
16 your eyes; for our money is gone." "Since your
   money is gone," replied Joseph, "give me your livestock, and I will sell you bread in return for your
17 livestock." So they brought their livestock to Joseph,
   and he sold them food in return for their horses,
   their flocks of sheep and herds of cattle and their
   donkeys. Thus he got them through that year with
18 bread in exchange for all their livestock. When that
   year ended, they came to him in the following one
   and said: "We cannot hide from my lord that, with
   our money spent and our livestock made over to my
   lord, there is nothing left to put at my lord's disposal
19 except our bodies and our farm land. Why should
   we and our land perish before your very eyes? Take
   us and our land in exchange for food, and we will
   become Pharaoh's slaves and our land his property;
   only give us seed, that we may survive and not perish, and that our land may not turn into a waste."
20 Thus Joseph acquired all the farm land of Egypt for
   Pharaoh, since with the famine too much for them to
   bear, every Egyptian sold his field; so the land
21 passed over to Pharaoh, and the people were reduced to slavery,‡ from one end of Egypt's territory
22 to the other. Only the priests' land Joseph did not
   take over. Since the priests had a fixed allowance
   from Pharaoh and lived off the allowance Pharaoh
   had granted them, they did not have to sell their
23 land. Joseph told the people: "Now that I have acquired you and your land for Pharaoh, here is your
24 seed for sowing the land. But when the harvest is in,
   you must give a fifth of it to Pharaoh, while you
   keep four-fifths as seed for your fields, and as food
   for yourselves and your families [and as food for

‡ So the LXX and the SP; the MT has tried (by substituting the root 'br for 'bd) to
make Joseph's action innocuous: "and he removed the people to cities."

25 your children]." "You have saved our lives," they
answered. "We are grateful to my lord that we can
26 be Pharaoh's slaves." Thus Joseph made it a law
for the land in Egypt, which is still in force, that
a fifth of its produce should go to Pharaoh. Only
the land of the priests did not pass over to Pharaoh.

The Israelites, who as we have seen in these stories were intrigued by
things Egyptian, were especially intrigued by the fact that "that land of
slavery" from which they had been freed was inhabited by a people who
took serfdom for granted as an everyday way of life. It is a fact that the
Egypt of the Middle Kingdom, a feudal state of private property which at
the same time had a lively sense of social justice and "the rights of man,"
in the New Kingdom changed into a despotism under which everything in
the land belonged to Pharaoh and some powerful nobles. With a bland
disregard—accompanied, of course, by a probable ignorance—of the real
historical circumstances under which this situation had come to pass,
Israelite tradition liked to ascribe this development in Egypt to the instru-
mentality of the patriarchal figure Joseph. We may find this a questionable
accolade to be stored up for the memory of a popular hero, and whoever
tampered with the text to produce the MT of vs. 21 also evidently thought
the attribution to be less than admirable; but there is no mistaking the
original meaning. Israel's dedication to personal freedom and private initiative was whole and entire, and the Israelites could only be puzzled by
a society that could tolerate any other state of affairs. Knowing that such a
contrary state of affairs was, nevertheless, tolerated by those Egyptians
from whose atrocious system they had once been freed by the mercy of
God, they indulged a dark and sardonic humor in the reflection that it had
been brought into being by one of their own.

This story is in logical sequence with 41:55–57 above (J). First the
Egyptians pay for their rations of grain, then they turn over their livestock,
and eventually they surrender their lands and their persons. This is the
story of the subjugation of Egypt: the "and Canaan" of vss. 13, 14, and
15 has been mechanically added in echo of 41:57. As observed above,
Hyksos horses turn up for the first time in the Bible in vs. 17 (the
"horses" of 46:29 above have been supplied *ad sensum* by the NAB). The
20 per cent income tax—another of those "fives" beloved of the Yahwist
—is featured in vss. 24–26; this, too, was a curious concept to the
Israelites, and cheerfully ascribed by them to the doing of Joseph. Exemp-
tion from the tax and immunity to state control of the land enjoyed by *the
priests* according to vss. 22 and 26 together with their *fixed allowance
from Pharaoh* are certainly genuine Egyptian phenomena: the priesthood
of Heliopolis was a law to itself which no Pharaoh dared to challenge.

Throughout this story "famine" has been understood as dearth of grain for food, without consideration given to the abundant flocks of sheep and herds of cattle that were presumably available for man's sustenance both in Canaan and Egypt and which obviously had whereon to feed and grow fat. It would be frivolous to press the logic of the story in any detail. The sons of Israel did not eat of their flocks in Canaan but drove them to Egypt because it was necessary for them to escape the famine in Canaan by removing to Egypt. The Egyptians sold their livestock and then themselves not because of any taboos about the eating of meat but because it was necessary that the famine of Egypt be made by Joseph the means of changing the Egyptian social system.

The following two verses conclude the P story of Jacob's coming to Egypt, in sequence with either vs. 7 or vs. 27 of chapter 46. It could be argued that the first of the verses is J rather than P (in sequence with vs. 5a above), but it does not seem worthwhile to make an issue of it.

> 27 Thus Israel settled in the land of Egypt, in the region of Goshen. There they acquired property, were
> 28 fertile, and increased greatly. Jacob lived in the land of Egypt for seventeen years; the span of his life came to a hundred and forty-seven years.

6. The Passing of Jacob

Having brought Israel to Egypt, the biblical narrative quickly loses most of its interest in things Egyptian and proceeds to tell the end of the Jacob saga. There are several traditions of Jacob's "last will and testament." The first begins in an easily identifiable form, which can only be J.

> 29 When the time approached for Israel to die, he called his son Joseph and said to him: "If you really wish to please me, put your hand under my thigh as a sign of your constant loyalty to me; do not let me
> 30 be buried in Egypt. When I lie down with my ancestors, have me taken out of Egypt and buried in
> 31 their burial place." "I will do as you say," he replied. But his father demanded, "Swear it to me!" So Joseph swore to him. Then Israel bowed at the head of the bed.

According to J, Jacob had made the journey to Egypt with no higher ambition than to see for a last time the son whom he had given up for lost so long ago and then to die (cf. 46:30). Whereas in the P narrative he lived for a further seventeen years after his arrival in Egypt (vs. 28 above), we have the impression here that death was a soon consequence of this fateful removal to what was to become the place of Israel's thralldom. For the oath ritual to which Jacob submitted Joseph, see above on 24:2 (J). Burial with one's ancestors in the family gravesite was the much desired sequel to death in the Israelite mind, a sign that the life now sadly but inevitably terminated had been lived worthily and in true faith with the ideals inherited from the past. For a man to obtain no proper burial place was accounted a great evil (cf. 1 Samuel 31:10–13; 2 Samuel 21:1–14; Jeremiah 22:18–19). Satisfied that his dying wish will be honored, *Israel bowed at the head of the bed*. The sense of this expression, which has puzzled translators and commentators since at least the time of the Septuagint, seems to be that Jacob, lacking the strength to perform the conventional gesture of gratitude and homage (a profound bow to the ground, cf. vs. 12 below), did what he could by solemnly nodding his head on his pillow.

All three of the sources used by the Redactor of Genesis appear to have included among Jacob's last acts his requirement of appropriate burial and his adoption of Joseph's sons as his own, "naturalizing" them as Israelites. We have just seen the burial request according to J (which, as we shall see from 50:10 below, doubtless envisaged a different site from that of either P or E), and the blessing of Ephraim and Manasseh in the J version will appear in vss. 8–20 later on. In the immediately following section we have E's introduction to both themes, one of which will never be completed in the ensuing narrative, and also P's account of how Ephraim and Manasseh came to be Israelite. Here we indicate E in roman type and P in italic.

48 Some time afterward, Joseph was informed, "Your father is failing." So he took along with him his two
2 sons, Manasseh and Ephraim. When Jacob was told, "Your son Joseph has come to you," he rallied his strength and sat up in bed.
3 *Jacob then said to Joseph: "God Almighty appeared to me at Luz in the land of Canaan, and blessing*
4 *me, he said, 'I will make you fertile and numerous and raise you into an assembly of tribes, and I will give this land to your descendants after you as a*
5 *permanent possession.' Your two sons, therefore, who were born to you in the land of Egypt before I joined you here, shall be mine; Ephraim and Manas-*

seh shall be mine as much as Reuben and Simeon
6 *are mine. Progeny born to you after them shall re-*
main yours; but their heritage shall be recorded in
7 *the names of their two brothers.* I do this because,
when I was returning from Paddan, your mother*
Rachel died, to my sorrow, during the journey in Canaan, while we were still a short distance from Ephrath; and I buried her there on the way to Ephrath
[that is, Bethlehem]."

In the E version of events, in keeping with the fact that it was Pharaoh
who had summoned Jacob to Egypt and had informed Joseph of his coming (cf. 45:16–20, 47:5b–6), father and son do not seem to have been
living in the close proximity and intimacy in Egypt that are presumed in
the J story; Joseph is told of the imminent demise of Jacob by concerned
outsiders and thereupon hastens to his father's bedside, bringing with him
his own two sons. The presence of *Manasseh and Ephraim*—in that order,
pending the reversal to be effected in vss. 8–20—prepares for the theme of
the blessing/adoption of Joseph's sons by Jacob. Nothing really prepares
for vs. 7, however, a seemingly pointless reference to Rachel's death and
burial *on the way to Ephrath* according to the E story of 35:16–20. (The
NAB's *I do this because* in this verse is not in the Hebrew and, in fact,
makes little sense, since there is no logical connection between Rachel's
gravesite and the preceding vss. 3–6 from P concerning the adoption of
Ephraim and Manasseh.) The only explanation of vs. 7 that commends itself as reasonable is that the verse is an uncompleted fragment of a direction which Jacob gave for his burial in a family tomb, in this case not the
Machpelah of P (49:29–32) but rather in Ephrath with Rachel.

The intervening vss. 3–6 are incontestably P. They refer to and paraphrase the divine promise given to Jacob at Bethel (cf. 35:6.9–12, P),
and they perpetuate terminology like "assembly" of tribes, nations, peoples (cf. above 28:3 and 35:11, P) and "permanent possession" (or
"holding," see above on 47:11 and cf. 17:8, 23:4.9.20, all P). Perhaps in
keeping with their Priestly character, these verses have a legalistic flavor.
Jacob, recalling the terms of the divine dispensation given at Bethel,
orders the succession by which Joseph's sons may be counted among the
tribes of Israel. Joseph himself is passed over, reflecting the historical reality that there was no tribe named Joseph in the Israelite federation or nation. Instead, *Ephraim and Manasseh shall be mine as much as Reuben*
and Simeon are mine: though in the legend these were grandsons rather
than sons of Jacob, they are to be equated with the others of his immedi-

---

* "Your mother" comes from the LXX and the SP; it is lacking in the MT.

ate descent who become the eponymous ancestors of Israelite tribes. The supposition is, apparently, that while yet living Jacob can adopt Joseph's sons as his own, but he cannot make the same provision for other sons who may be born at some future time. *Progeny born to you after them shall remain yours* obviously entertains the possibility of there being later children of Joseph who will remain his both naturally and legally, and who may find a place in Israelite history only indirectly, reckoned as descendants rather than as equals of their siblings: *their heritage shall be recorded in the names of their two brothers.* It is a bit on the curious side that P should take the time to spell out these legalities, since in point of fact no other sons than Ephraim and Manasseh are ascribed to Joseph in Israel's traditions and no other Joseph clans or tribes figure in its genealogies save these and their natural descendants.

The second part of the P story of Jacob's farewell, the determination of his place of burial, will appear below in 49:29–33. The rest of chapter 48 contains the JE version of Jacob's acceptance of Joseph's sons, which in these sources takes the form of a blessing rather than an adoption. That Jacob blesses the sons twice, in vss. 15–16 and again in vs. 20, that the first blessing disturbs the sequence of vss. 14.17, are conventional indications that parallel accounts have been fused into one. From then on, however, it is difficult to separate the source convincingly by recognizing the constants of language and theme which ordinarily identify them. It seems preferable to conclude that here once more the Redactor has permitted himself more than the usual latitude in assembling his material, mingling the trademarks of J and E to produce a homogeneous effect that otherwise would be less apparent. We shall not attempt, therefore, to isolate the one from the other element in this passage and will rather deal with it as the redactional unity that it is.

> 8 When Israel saw Joseph's sons, he asked, "Who are
> 9 these?" "They are my sons," Joseph answered his
> father, "whom God has given me here." "Bring them
> to me," said his father, "that I may bless them."
> 10 (Now Israel's eyes were dim from age, and he could
> not see well.) When Joseph brought his sons close
> 11 to him, he kissed and embraced them. Then Israel
> said to Joseph, "I never expected to see your face
> again, and now God has allowed me to see your
> descendants as well!"
> 12 Joseph removed them from his father's knees and
> bowed down before him† with his face to the

† "Before him" comes from the LXX and the Syriac.

13 ground. Then Joseph took the two, Ephraim with
his right hand, to Israel's left, and Manasseh with his
14 left hand, to Israel's right, and led them to him. But
Israel, crossing his hands, put out his right hand
and laid it on the head of Ephraim, although he was
the younger, and his left hand on the head of Ma-
15 nasseh, although he was the first-born. Then he
blessed them‡ with these words:

"May the God in whose ways
    my fathers Abraham and Isaac walked,
The God who has been my shepherd
    from my birth to this day,
16   The Angel who has delivered me from all harm,
    bless these boys
That in them my name be recalled,
    and the names of my fathers, Abraham and
      Isaac,
And they may become teeming multitudes
    upon the earth!"

17 When Joseph saw that his father had laid his right
hand on Ephraim's head, this seemed wrong to him;
so he took hold of his father's hand, to remove it
18 from Ephraim's head to Manasseh's, saying, "That
is not right, father; the other one is the first-born;
19 lay your right hand on his head!" But his father resisted. "I know it, son," he said, "I know. That one
too shall become a tribe, and he too shall be great.
Nevertheless, his younger brother shall surpass him,
and his descendants shall become a multitude of na-
20 tions." So when he blessed them that day and said,
"By you shall the people of Israel pronounce blessings; may they say, 'God make you like Ephraim
and Manasseh,'" he placed Ephraim before Manasseh.
21 Then Israel said to Joseph: "I am about to die. But
God will be with you and will restore you to the
22 land of your fathers. As for me, I give to you, as to
the one above his brothers, Shechem, which I captured from the Amorites with my sword and bow."

‡ This is the LXX; the MT has "And he blessed Joseph," so as not to anticipate the
blessing of vs. 20.

The original context of this composite account of Jacob's meeting with Joseph's sons is obviously the earliest moments of his arrival in Egypt which, contrary to the P chronology of 47:28, doubtless closely corresponded with the time of his death and leave-taking, though probably not quite as closely as vs. 1 above would now make it. The emotion-packed encounter of the faltering and nearly blind Jacob (like his father before him in chapter 27, J) with the sons of his own long-lost son in vss. 8–11 looks like a sequel or accompaniment to the reunion at Goshen according to 46:28–30 (J). The blessing of vss. 12–14.17–20 presupposes no less the situation of vs. 2 above (E), when Jacob *rallied his strength and sat up in bed*. It appears from vs. 12 that Joseph first set his sons upon *his father's knees* that he might adopt them as his own (cf. 30:3, 50:23, both E), somewhat in the fashion of the P pronouncement in vss. 3–6 above. In gratitude for this acceptance, Joseph *bowed down before him with his face to the ground*. But there is to be more to the blessing than only a validation of the rightful place of Ephraim and Manasseh within the roll of Israelite tribes. In addition there is reasserted the theme of election, specifically of the election of one brother rather than the other and of the later rather than the prior, a theme which is particularly beloved of the Yahwist: Abel (then Seth) is chosen over Cain (chapter 4), Japheth supersedes Ham in the order of precedence after Shem (9:18–27), Isaac is preferred to Ishmael, Jacob to Esau, Perez to Zerah (38:27–30), Judah over his elder brothers (cf. 49:8). In this story Joseph brings his sons before his father in the proper order, so that his first-born will be in the place of honor, at Jacob's right hand. When Jacob crosses his arms in bestowing his blessing, thus reversing Joseph's protocol, the latter naturally thinks that blindness or senility has befuddled the mind of the aged patriarch and seeks to rectify the mistake. But Jacob has in his final breaths been gifted with prophetic insight, which counts for more than the wisdom of Joseph. Once again, we must recognize the presupposition of the biblical author, according to which the blessing of Jacob was not a prediction but rather the cause of the effect to follow. (Even as Isaac's blessings in chapter 27 decided the fate of Jacob and Esau.) It is now determined that Manasseh, though destined to become a great tribe, will be surpassed by Ephraim in Israel's history, as indeed it was.

The language of the blessings ascribed to Jacob echoes traditional formulas. The "ways of God" (vs. 15) are the revelation of God, his manifestation in history through his own deeds of what is right and just and therefore of what is right and just for those who would follow him (cf. Deuteronomy 32:3–4; Hosea 14:10). This God *in whose ways* Jacob's fathers have walked is first characterized as *shepherd* (cf. 47:24). "Shepherd" was a not unusual title in the ancient Near East for a ruler, civil or religious (cf. Jeremiah 23, for example), though not generally in the beneficent sense with which Psalm 23 and later John 12 have made us familiar: the image of "the good shepherd." The shepherd of a people earliest became a derived concept from the everyday scene of the herdsman bullying and driving a giddy and irresponsible flock of antic animals into pastures they could never find for themselves, which were ultimately for their own good but only because they were first of all for his good. The shepherd's crook was originally a symbol of power and control, not of "pastoral" guidance. The context of Genesis, however, shows that the concept of the "gentle" shepherd of Psalm 23 has prevailed in this text. Similarly, this God appears as an *Angel* (which we may doubtless understand as "divine presence," see on 16:7 above and thereafter) and as *go'el* (this is the *who has delivered me* of the NAB, see on 38:6–11 above). Under these titles an expansive blessing for a glorious future is called forth from God not unlike that pronounced over Jacob himself in 27:28–29.

The second blessing of vs. 20, preceded by the separation of Ephraim and Manasseh, is likewise traditional. That Ephraim and Manasseh should become so signally blest that their names become proverbial for all the good that God can bestow on his servants is a thought begun in 12:3 and repeated thereafter.

And there is, finally, a blessing for Joseph himself, or a bequest, or something similar for which we have no specific term, which the biblical author has made the complement of the blessing of Ephraim and Manasseh. In vs. 21 there is in Jacob's words to Joseph an almost verbatim anticipation of Joseph's to his brothers in 50:24. Whereas there, however, Joseph is preparing to put his brothers under oath with regard to the disposition of his dead body (as, indeed, Jacob will soon lay a similar charge on all his sons according to the P of 49:1a.29–33), here a quite different perspective is in view. The restoration *to the land of your fathers* which Jacob promises to Joseph no doubt is of the same kind as that of the divine assurance given to Jacob at Beer-sheba (see above on 46:4, JE), that is, that his bones will find their final repose in an ancestral earth (cf. Exodus 13:19). But here as there an additional meaning lies below the surface, which in this instance becomes immediately apparent. *I give to you* must envisage a donation not to the "personal" but to the "tribal" Joseph: *as to the one above his brothers* invites comparison with 49:26b below. The NAB is one of the few modern translations which put *Shechem* in the text as a proper name, though probably all agree that it is indeed being referred to by a less than obscure play on words. The *shechem* which Jacob gives to Joseph means "shoulder" (as in 24:15.45, 49:15, etc.); that it can also mean "mountain slope" (RSV) or "ridge of land" (NEB) or something like is possible, but it is also guesswork. That in the context of vs. 22 it means, or is the equivalent of, "portion" (so in the older English translations) is a persuasion as old at least as the Latin Vulgate: in this acceptation Jacob is figured as distributing the Promised Land like a householder dividing a slaughtered animal, adding a choice portion (the shoulder? cf. 1 Samuel 9:23–24) to the lot of a favored one (cf. 1 Samuel 1:4–5). Whatever the allusion, the city of Shechem, which in later Israelite history was associated both with Ephraim and Manasseh, was because of its great prestige one of the jewels of the Joseph tribes, and certainly with this city our passage is concerned. In the commentary on chapter 34 above we laid out the hypothesis of a Shechem that was Israelite before the "conquest," hence capable of being inherited in patriarchal times long before the regular portions of the land were assigned to the tribes according to the legend of Joshua 13–21. Problems remain: here Jacob seems to vaunt his acquisition, boasting of a Shechem *which I captured from the Amorites* (not, be it noted, the Hamorites or Hivites of 34:2) *with my sword and bow,* while in chapter 34 he rather deprecated the violence that had taken place at Shechem and wanted no share or profit from it. But it would not be unusual for there to be variant and even contradictory stories surrounding the same event, with different sensitivities to its moral implications.

Benno Jacob offered a deceptively simple solution to the problem posed by vss. 21–22. As he read the text, Joseph's father did indeed speak of Shechem, but only to designate it the site of his son's eventual grave in Palestine (cf. Joshua 24:32). The site was on ground which Jacob had bought from the Shechemites (Genesis 33:19), with such wealth, therefore, as he had obtained "with his sword and bow."

With the penultimate chapter of Genesis that follows we enter upon a final section of this book that has seen and still does see more than its fair share of controversy. It is poetry, most of it, and very old poetry at that, comparable to other passages like Deuteronomy 33, Judges 5, or the Balaam oracles of Numbers 23–24, all of which have their roots in a premonarchical Israel of the tribal federation(s) which we associate with the period "of the judges." Because it is quite ancient poetry, the original text has been vulnerable to the ravages of time and is therefore in a state more than usually open to the corrective suggestions of critical commentators. Because it was inspired by tribal interests only remotely connected with the historical religion of the Old Testament, the nowadays reader may find it hard to share its concerns over regional geography and assorted clan lore that can appear rather peripheral to *Heilsgeschichte.* This reader must simply be reminded that it was nevertheless of such stuff that the earliest fabric of Genesis was woven, and it is obvious that one of the authors of Genesis at least thought it very important to hoard up some of the antique skeins.

What has happened in this chapter is very easy to see. A Priestly "last words of Jacob" which had to do with his final resting place (49:1a.29–33) and which parallels the J of 47:29–31 and the E of 48:7 above has been interpolated by the poetry of 49:1b–27 and joined to this new-found context by the addition of vs. 28. Below we indicate the P verses and the redaction indifferently by the use of italics. The poetry needs further explanation, however.

It is, first of all, a collection which predated the Redactor of Genesis and was gathered to correspond with a literary form that already existed and would continue to exist for centuries to come in the ancient world without regard to specific place or culture. The posture of the aged patriarch, father, or master, who on his deathbed decrees the fate of his descendants, sons, or disciples is classical not only in the Old Testament (Genesis 27, Deuteronomy 33, Joshua 23–24, etc.) but also in nonbiblical antiquity (Socrates' farewell discourse, the Testaments of the Twelve Patriarchs, etc.) and in the New Testament (John 14–17). The form was set and was fairly universal: the additional note, that the word of prediction was also a word of determination—undoubtedly important here for the biblical author—was likewise not unprecedented, since it was generally assumed that a dying man had some vision into the future that was denied to others. The form explains the collection, therefore, though it does not explain the bits and pieces of poetry that someone collected to make it up. Some of the poetry, and therefore the collection of it, can hardly predate the J tradition itself: 49:4 is explained by 35:22 (J), 49:5 by the J of chapter 34, and 49:22–26 is certainly dependent on the story of Joseph's rise to supremacy over his brothers in Egypt, a story told by J as well as by E.

Was J, therefore, the collector of this poetry or the author of some of it? Much of it is older than J and all of it could very well have been used by J, but it is next to impossible to determine where it could have been reasonably fitted into the J schema as we have been able to reconstruct it. Neither, of course, does it adjust comfortably to the environment of P—a source to which some other critics have wanted to assign it—where it is, we repeat, an interpolation. It seems to be, in the last analysis, a collection of poetic fragments relating to the several tribes of Israel according to the categories of 29:31–30:22 and 35:16–20 that had been gathered together and cast into a conventional testamentary mold independently of the usual source material of Genesis, which the Redactor found ready to hand and of which he made grateful use to solemnize Jacob's last farewell to his sons. The existence of material of this kind, we know by now, was not at all extraordinary in the time of the formation of Genesis.

49 *Jacob called his sons and said:* "Gather around, that
I may tell you what is to happen to you in days to
come.

2 "Assemble and listen, sons of Jacob,
    listen to Israel, your father.
3 "You, Reuben, my first-born,
    my strength and the first fruit of my manhood,
    excelling in rank and excelling in power!
4 Unruly as water, you shall no longer excel,
    for you climbed into your father's bed
    and defiled my couch to my sorrow."

Reuben was a Transjordanian tribe which roamed north of the Arnon parallel with Judah to the west and which in covenantal times (cf. Judges 5:15b–16) was hardly to be depended upon in any state of federational emergency; as a matter of fact, it seems to have evaporated as a political force early in Israelite history (cf. Deuteronomy 33:6). Here the decline of the tribe is attributed to the gaucherie of its eponymous ancestor as related in 35:22 above. Some tradition that we do not know and have no means to evaluate had dictated that the obscure Reuben should once have been counted the first of Jacob's sons: we can only guess about the pre-Israelite history of this once proud people. The *to my sorrow* of vs. 4 is a conjectural translation resolving an uncertain Hebrew text.

5 "Simeon and Levi, brothers indeed,
    weapons of violence are their knives.
6 Let not my soul enter their council,
    or my spirit be joined with their company;
For in their fury they slew men,
    in their willfulness they maimed oxen.
7 Cursed be their fury so fierce,
    and their rage so cruel!
I will scatter them in Jacob,
    disperse them throughout Israel."

In Deuteronomy 33:8–11 Levi is lavishly praised for its true-believer response to Moses' call to action according to the story of Exodus 32:25–29. Simeon is not mentioned there at all. Neither tribe shows up in the roll called in Judges 5. Here is brought to mind the landlessness of both these tribes, their "scattering," therefore, among the other tribes of Israel by whose sufferance alone they retained a name and an identity. The scattering of these peoples was historical, but it was also consequent on different circumstances, though here it is made a common retribution for the action of the eponymous Simeon and Levi at Shechem according to the J story of chapter 34. The reference is not 100 per cent sure: *their knives* in vs. 5 is a guess, even though an educated guess, about the meaning of the Hebrew; and vs. 6b reproaches the brothers for a maiming of cattle about which Genesis 34 says nothing. But there would seem to be small doubt that these verses do refer to the earlier story.

Simeon was originally a people which inhabited the southern reaches of Judah and was eventually absorbed into it (cf. Joshua 19:1–9). The Simeonites did not thus automatically become Judahites as did various clans of Edomites, Calebites, Kenites, and others (cf. Joshua 14:6–16), for their tribal distinctiveness was remembered. However, they were probably never of great consequence in the Israelite league, since they were an appendage to Judah from the beginning; in Deuteronomy 33 Simeon is not mentioned at all.

Levi was likewise probably a latecomer into Israel, a fact which may explain its landlessness. It is debated whether there was ever a tribe of Levi in the sense of the other tribes, with a district and territory of its own; the "Levitical cities" of Numbers 35:2–8 and Joshua 21:3–42 are rightly judged by modern scholars to have been the ideal rather than a real possession of the Levites. It is far likelier that Levi was originally a social class rather than a geographically determined people, a nomadic caste like the itinerant smiths or the Rechabites (who were also Kenites, cf. 1 Chronicles 2:55 and see above the introduction to 4:2b–16) which did not at first adapt to the settled ways of the rest of Israel to which it was joined but instead continued a restless and wandering way of life that literally dispersed it through Israel. In times when land became all in determining political and individual identity, the landless person and the landless people were inevitably thrown on the mercy of others as the condition of their survival. Hence the Levites frequently appear along with widows, orphans, resident aliens, and other deprived persons as the objects of charity to which Israel was exhorted in its laws (cf. Deuteronomy 12:12.18.19, 14:27.29, etc.). Later—later than the composition of Genesis 49:5–7, rather evidently—Levi obtained a fresh and unique standing in the society of Israel by being assigned the functions of a professional priesthood (so in Deuteronomy 33:8–11). The process by which this transformation took place is quite unknown to us, and need not concern us here.

The animosity shown toward Simeon and Levi in these verses makes them stand out in contrast to the treatment meted out to the other tribes, even to the Reuben who is also deprecated. Who is the *I* of vs. 7b who decrees the scattering and dispersal of these peoples? In the literary fiction of the patriarchal testament it is of course Jacob who speaks, but in the original setting, in which both *Jacob* and *Israel* appear as a people and a land, such could hardly have been the case. Rather, these verses sound like a prophetic oracle, in which the "I" of prophecy is the Deity whose message the prophet proclaims. Why should there have been a prophetic censure in the name of Israelite religion? We have already proposed Genesis 34 as the referent of these verses just as 35:22 seems to be the referent for the demotion of Reuben in vss. 3–4: offenses of various "sons" of Israel (=the legendary figures of saga) which account for the lot in Palestine of corresponding "sons of Israel" (=the Israelites who bear this or that tribal name). Some authors have thought that another kind of historical reminiscence might have been shared between the legend of chapter 34 and this oracle about Simeon and Levi. Could it be that chapter 34 recalls a pre- or proto-Israelite assault on Ephraimite Shechem by a band of Levites and Simeonites, an assault which did not ultimately succeed and which was condemned by Israelite opinion and thus by Israel's God? If so, another interpretation might be given Genesis 48:22, where Israel bequeaths to Joseph (Ephraim) the Shechem he had won by sword and bow. But here we do not really have sufficient grounds for profitable speculation.

> 8 "You, Judah, shall your brothers praise
> —your hand on the neck of your enemies;
> the sons of your father shall bow down to you.
> 9 Judah, like a lion's whelp,
> you have grown up on prey, my son.
> He crouches like a lion recumbent,
> the king of beasts—who would dare rouse him?
> 10 The scepter shall never depart from Judah,
> or the mace from between his legs,
> While tribute is brought to him,
> and he receives the people's homage.
> 11 He tethers his donkey to the vine,
> his purebred ass to the choicest stem.
> In wine he washes his garments,
> his robe in the blood of grapes.
> 12 His eyes are darker than wine,
> and his teeth are whiter than milk."

The tribe of Judah came into pre-eminence with the coming of the monarchy under David, and this fragment of poetry doubtless dates from that time. In the opinion of many scholars, Judah had never been part of Israel until the monarchy or shortly before it: in Judges 5 there is no mention of Judah, and from Deuteronomy 33:7 it may be plausibly conjectured that Judah was then in a tentative state of *rapprochement* with an Israelite league, striving to overcome geographical and political barriers that stood in its way. Here in Genesis, of course, Judahite priority among the "sons" of Israel is ascribed to it by default, after the passing over of Reuben, Simeon, and Levi.

To the disregard of vs. 26 below which accords supremacy among the tribes to "Joseph," in vs. 8 Judah is acclaimed not only victor over all its external enemies but also the acknowledged leader of all the Israelite tribes. This condition, reiterated in vs. 10 and mythicized in vss. 11–12, can hardly be dissociated from the circumstances of the Davidic monarchy, circumstances which overcame Israelite prejudice against kingship through prophetic pronouncement (cf. 2 Samuel 7:8–16; Psalm 89) and which contributed to Israelite religion a dimension of messianism that was to be developed in many stages to come. Judah is represented in vs. 10 in a royal estate, with *the scepter* and *the mace* (the rules of parallelism would indicate that the same insigne is meant) *between his legs*. In both vss. 8 and 10 we hear the language typical of a royal oracle promising peace, prosperity, and uncontested domination. The *while tribute is brought to him* of vs. 10, however, conjecturally resolves a long-standing controversy over the meaning of this verse by slightly emending the Hebrew text. The emendation is quite acceptable and suits the messianic aura otherwise sustained by the passage (cf. Isaiah 18:7). Similarly vss. 11–12, which ascribe paradisaical conditions to the reign of Judah (compare Isaiah 11:1–9). In such times the impossible becomes routine. Animals may be tethered to valuable vinestocks without fear of loss and spoilage, so plentiful they are. Wine (the parallel *blood of grapes* is a Canaanite expression) exists in such abundance that it may be put to the improbable use of washing clothes. Judah is pictured as thoroughly sated with the good things of life: the text of vs. 12 can be, and probably should be, translated "his eyes are dark from wine, his teeth are white from milk." If the paradise envisaged here seems to be rather like that of *The Green Pastures,* it is only just to recognize that it was the image of a people whose aspirations were indeed modest and who were generally deprived of even that little to which they aspired. With David had come a quickening of national pride, freedom from the fear of foreign domination, and hope for a bright future founded on the rock of divine promise. All this and more constituted the Davidic ideal, retrojected here into a poem about Judah. The same ideal would also inspire later poetry, prophecy, and noble deeds, time and again in Israel's history. Later still, a people conscious of having been touched by the liberating power of God would find it natural to call the agent of their salvation by the name of the Son of David.

In vs. 9 Judah is likened to *a lion*. The imagery may be thought self-explaining, since it occurs elsewhere in old Israelite poetry (Numbers 23:24, 24:9); but it is also peculiarly Judahite. There is archeological evidence that the lion was a divine symbol in Judah long before the rise of Israel, and an eighth-century Judahite prophet thought it appropriate that the Yahweh of Jerusalem should roar like a lion when pronouncing his judgment against all Israel (cf. Amos 1:2).

13 "Zebulun shall dwell by the seashore
   [This means a shore for ships],
     and his flank shall be based on Sidon.
14 "Issachar is a rawboned ass,
     crouching between the saddlebags.
15 When he saw how good a settled life was,
     and how pleasant the country,
   He bent his shoulder to the burden
     and became a toiling serf.
16 "Dan shall achieve justice for his kindred
     like any other tribe of Israel.
17 Let Dan be a serpent by the roadside,
     a horned viper by the path,
   That bites the horse's heel,
     so that the rider tumbles backward.
18 "[I long for your deliverance, O LORD!]"

Nothing very remarkable is said of Zebulun, even if we accept various plausible suggestions that have been made to improve on the text. Assonances abound in this poetic anthology: the *you, Judah, shall your brothers praise* of vs. 8 is *yehudah attah yoduka aheyka* in Hebrew, and in vs. 14 it is *yissakar harmo,* in vs. 16 *dan yadin,* and in vs. 19 below *gad gedud yegudennu.* Thus it may be that *zebulun . . . yizbol* (rather than the present . . . *yishkon*) was the original reading of vs. 13, i.e., "Zebulun shall *rule* the seashore" (cf. Deuteronomy 33:19 where Zebulun along with Issachar is accounted a maritime province). We are being told, apparently by a poet whose reach for the facts far exceeded the grasp of which he was capable in central Palestine, that the territory of Zebulun bordered the Mediterranean Sea, was contiguous with Phoenicia, and drew its wealth from nautical commerce. None of these assumptions seems to have been correct, or at least they were never correct for any appreciable amount of time. Zebulun was an inland people sandwiched between Asher and Issachar westward of the Sea of Galilee in northern Palestine. But even had the geography of the poetry run true, nothing much of consequence would be added to the enlargement of our spirit. We do know that Zebulun rallied to the Israelite banner as a sturdy ally in the formative age that determined the destiny of a land and a people (cf. Judges 5:18).

Issachar, which inhabited the northwest bank of the fertile Jordan valley (cf. Joshua 19:17–23), comes in for a separate kind of mention, quite different from that of Deuteronomy 33:18, which simply puts it in affluent league with Zebulun. Here Issachar is caricatured as a docile and over-laden beast of burden submitted to domestication with all its assurance of fodder and security in preference to the uncertainties and risks that inevitably attach to the free life. The poetry denigrates a people that has chosen to become *ish sakar,* a wage earner, rather than remain its own master. A demeaning existence for an Israelite tribe! Issachar is content to live in harmony with Canaanite overlords, to work for them and make with them a common future. Whether this condition of Issachar was before or after the battle of Taanach, we do not know. In the moment of decision, Issachar cast its lot with Israel (cf. Judges 5:15).

Dan shall achieve justice for his kindred: both in legend and in fact, the Danites seem to have been a people of southern Palestine (cf. Joshua 19:40–48) who migrated to the north (Judges 18). The comparison of Dan with *a horned viper by the path* seems to be based on the disproportion of size to the capability for fatal damage. Just as a tiny serpent can bring down both rider and mount by a skillful thrust at the horse's heel, so Dan, a small tribe, will wreak havoc on formidable adversaries by stealthy attacks on their exposed flanks. The new location of Dan, the northernmost extent of what later became the kingdom of Israel, put it in a position of control of the trade routes from the north and the east, and also, therefore, in a position of dispute and contention.

The ejaculation in vs. 18 has always been a puzzler for commentators. By placing it within brackets the NAB indicates what is the probable case, that it is a gloss on the text introduced by some pious scribe motivated by we can only guess what thought had occurred to him in his reading of it. All the attempts that have been made to count it among the utterances of the "Jacob" of this chapter and to relate it as such to the context in which it is found remain unconvincing. As it happens, it is the last verse of Genesis in which the divine name Yahweh appears.

19 "Gad shall be raided by raiders,
    but he shall raid at their heels.
20 "Asher's produce is rich,
    and he shall furnish dainties for kings.
21 "Naphtali is a hind let loose,
    which brings forth lovely fawns."

The NAB has slightly revised the Hebrew text in producing these three verses. The few emendations are quite standard and are presupposed in most modern translations, therefore there seems to be no need to call the reader's attention to them here.

Neither is much of consequence communicated by the verses. As observed above, vs. 19a is a piece of heavy Hebrew alliteration. Gad, a Transjordan tribe, dwelt in the midst of nomadic peoples for whom the *razzia* was a way of life. Deuteronomy 33:20–21 also celebrates the fierceness of Gad, which evidently gave better than it received in these warlike exchanges. In Deuteronomy 33:23–25 as well as here it is the advantageous geography of Asher and Naphtali, and their consequent prosperity, that are called to attention. The two tribes were contiguous, and both doubtless profited from their proximity to the mercantilism of the Phoenicians to the north and along the littoral. Asher was indeed a maritime tribe, but it did not possess the ports of Acco, Sidon, or Achzib which were vaguely in its territory (cf. Judges 1:31); none of the Israelite peoples were seafarers, and, as a matter of fact, the Palestinian seacoast south of Asher was and is not suited to commerce, offering no natural ports such as are to be found in the north. In the Song of Deborah both Dan and Asher (Dan by this time also a northern people bordering Phoenicia and "spending his time in ships" while Asher "rests in his coves") are rebuked for their indifference to the Israelite effort against Sisera whereas Naphtali is praised for its rallying to the cause (cf. Judges 5:17–18); according to Judges 4:6 Barak, Israel's leader in the decisive battle at Taanach, was a chieftain of Naphtali.

> 22 "Joseph is a wild colt,
>   a wild colt by a spring,
>   a wild ass on a hillside.
> 23 Harrying and attacking,
>   the archers opposed him;
> 24 But each one's bow remained stiff,
>   as their arms were unsteady,
> By the power of the Mighty One of Jacob,
>   because of the Shepherd, the Rock of Israel,
> 25 The God of your father, who helps you,
> God Almighty, who blesses you,
> With the blessings of the heavens above,
>   the blessings of the abyss that crouches below,
> The blessings of breasts and womb,
> 26   the blessings of fresh grain and blossoms,
> The blessings of the everlasting mountains,
>   the delights of the eternal hills.
> May they rest of the head of Joseph,
>   on the brow of the prince among his brothers."

One need only glance at an alternative translation, old or recent, of these verses in order to see how much the NAB has had to rely on conjecture in its rendering of this ancient poetry. In view of its exaltation of Joseph (i.e., Ephraim) at the expense of all his other brothers, it is safe to assume that this segment of the poetic collection long antedates the section concerning Judah and may, indeed, be the oldest part of all; certainly it is the part that has been most damaged and worried out of shape in its transmission to us. It is not possible to attain certainty concerning the correct translation to be given various individual words and figures in the passage, though the general sense of the whole emerges clearly enough. Uncertainties of translation apart, interpretation of specifics is further hampered by unevennesses of thought and abrupt transitions which strongly suggest that parts of the poem have been lost along the way or were deliberately dropped for one reason or another. Even with—or perhaps, especially with—the most accurate possible translation, the verses project a confused and kaleidoscopic image of mixed metaphors and oddly connected concepts very much like a stream of consciousness. This is the only one of the tribal pronouncements that contains a blessing, the sole one that could justify the title "blessings of Jacob" which was traditionally bestowed on this collection following the lead of the editorial vs. 28 below.

In vs. 22 Joseph is called *ben porath*—the *p-r-th* is doubtless intended to evoke Ephrath, i.e., Ephraim. Because *porath* appears to be a feminine participle meaning "being fruitful" or "bearing fruitfully," because *a spring* is immediately mentioned, and because in the final line the Hebrew seems to talk about "daughters" who "run" (ungrammatically, however) along or upon a "wall," ancient translators and commentators made what they could of these curious conceits by settling for an agricultural figure: Joseph is likened to a bough, the "son" of a fruitful vine or tree planted by a spring, whose branches or tendrils (the "daughters") spread over a wall, like ivy perhaps. Not too happy a solution, one might think, but still a good try out of a desperate swamp. In the NAB, as is obvious, the image has altered radically. The word *porath* has been taken as hiding a feminine form of *pere,* "wild ass" (this term was applied to Ishmael in 16:12 above); thus, as the son of a female wild ass Joseph is *a wild colt* and *a wild colt by a spring,* where one may be rightly found as surely as any tree or vine. The daughters and their running have disappeared through a rereading of the Hebrew consonants in concert with some cognate Arabic words to yield yet another expression meaning *a wild ass.* And finally, the "wall" of the last line has been benignly interpreted as a natural wall, a grassy mount or *hillside.* This rendition, riddled with conjecture though it be, has the definite advantage of replacing an agricultural figure with an animal one: feral imagery seems to have been a convention in these tribal poems (cf. vss. 9.14.17.21.27 here; Deuteronomy 33:17 where Joseph is a wild ox, also vss. 20 and 22 of that chapter; Numbers 23:22.24, 24:8–9; Genesis 16:12). In any case the probable intention of the poetic author is being served by this translation as well as by the other, which is to represent Joseph as leading the nomadic ideal of an open, free, and unhindered life.

In vs. 23 the figure changes (unless we are to think, rather improbably, of hunters attacking a wild ass with bow and arrow; certainly they are not assaulting a tree or a vine). Now Joseph is a warrior surrounded by adversaries on every side. The *attacking* of the NAB probably better renders the sense of an obscure Hebrew verb that other translations would make read "they shot at him," for the NAB is also probably correct in its understanding of vs. 24a, namely that the attacking archers were unable to get off their shots because of the divine power of Joseph's Protector who robbed their bows of their spring and weakened their drawing arms. This Protector is called *the Mighty One of Jacob:* probably "Jacob" is in this acceptation a people rather than the person who is supposedly speaking these lines, for elsewhere the parallel expression "Mighty one of Israel" occurs in Old Testament poetry. The "mighty one" of this title undoubtedly once meant "bull" (as it still does in biblical Hebrew when given a slightly different pronunciation): the bull, both in image and by name, was in frequent use in the ancient Near East to signify deity, having the connotations of power and fertility; altars were frequently "horned" (cf. Exodus 27:2, etc.) to the same purpose. In these verses divine titles are employed that have a strong Canaanite flavor, which would later be avoided for that reason, and which in the present Hebrew text may have been deliberately obscured by pious editors and scribes by slight alterations which most translations quietly ignore. Thus God is also called *the Shepherd* (see above on 48:15) and *the Rock of Israel:* the latter occurs only here (it is not the same "Rock" repeatedly invoked in Deuteronomy 32 and elsewhere in Old Testament poetry), but its sense is not hard to find and there is evidence that it was a divine title in Canaan. *The God of your father* might preferably be rendered "El your Father," since the context is only artificially "patriarchal" and "El the Father" is a well-attested title in Canaanite literature. *God Almighty,* El Shaddai, is already familiar to us.

With vs. 25 the address has turned from the third to the second person, though somewhere along the line it will unobtrusively slip back into the third person where it will end. With the *who blesses you* of the same verse the narration dissolves into an invocation which more than sustains the exotic tone already set by the roll of divine names. As the strongly parallel Deuteronomy 33:13–17 indicates, and as Canaanite parallels also confirm, we are in the presence of traditional formulas and a traditional genre. This is that rare thing in Israelite poetry, an agricultural blessing, of which we have had above a small scrap in 27:28. The fertility blessings usual in the patriarchal narrative, we know, take an entirely different form, derived from the royal oracle and not from a reliance on the chthonian and empyrean forces thought to reside in *the heavens, the abyss,* the *breasts and womb, the mountains* and *hills.* All these forces, personified and deified in Canaanite mythology, appear here only half shed of their mythology. *The abyss that crouches below* (the same in Deuteronomy 33:13) clearly exemplifies what we mean: this is the *tehom* of Genesis 1:2, but personified here as it is not there. (Only here and in the Deuteronomy passage does the biblical *tehom* figure as a source of blessing.)

The NAB of vs. 26a breaks the pattern, it is true. But this is the rendition of a highly conjectural emendation of a Hebrew text that may very well have been deliberately corrupted at some time in order to get rid of an even more explicit mythological heritage. The present Hebrew text admittedly has little resemblance to what we imagine the original poetry to have been; the present Hebrew text is not even poetry at all. What the NAB has done is take its consonants: *brkt 'byk gbr 'l brkt hry 'd,* reread them as: *brkt 'byb wgb'l brkt hrry 'd,* and emerge with the translation: *the blessings of fresh grain and blossoms,* etc. There is the temptation to propose alternative emendations, but of course they would remain equally problematical.

The prince among his brothers corresponds with "the one above his brothers" of 48:22. In this poem there is no doubt that Joseph represents supremacy in Israel.

> 27 "Benjamin is a ravenous wolf;
>   mornings he devours the prey,
>   and evenings he distributes the spoils."
> 28 *All these are the twelve tribes of Israel, and this is what their father said about them, as he bade them farewell and gave to each of them an appropriate*
> 29 *message. Then he gave them this charge: "Since I am about to be taken to my kindred, bury me with my fathers in the cave that lies in the field of Ephron*
> 30 *the Hittite, the cave in the field of Machpelah, facing on Mamre, in the land of Canaan, the field that Abraham bought from Ephron the Hittite for a bur-*
> 31 *ial ground. There Abraham and his wife Sarah are buried, and so are Isaac and his wife Rebekah, and*
> 32 *there, too, I buried Leah—the field and the cave in*
> 33 *it that had been purchased from the Hittites." When Jacob had finished giving these instructions to his sons, he drew his feet into the bed, breathed his last, and was taken to his kindred.*

Benjamin was a small but important tribe in the Israelite federation. It paid its dues in the great battle at Taanach (cf. Judges 5:14), and from it —rather than from Ephraim, then in decline, or from Judah, still on the rise—came Saul, the first leader of the federation who resembled the king of a nation. The secret of its success, before it was eventually overwhelmed by history in the shape of David's charisma and a rebirth of Ephraimite nationalism following Solomon, was its ruthless and warlike character (cf. Judges 3:15–30; 1 Chronicles 8:40, 12:1–2; 2 Chronicles 14:7, etc.). It is this proverbial character that is celebrated in vs. 27.

It has become quite evident by now that there can be considerable discrepancy between the "sons of Israel" as they are listed in the genealogies of Genesis, twelve sons of a man named Jacob, and as they actually figured in history, even the history presupposed by Genesis 49, disparate peoples separated by time and tradition and geography who came together through a complex of circumstances only vaguely hinted at in Genesis to construct the nation Israel. If it has done nothing else, the poetry of this chapter has served to remind us of the great gulf that divides textbook history from the history that Richard Niebuhr called internal, that is, the history which a people creates for itself and in which it discovers its identity.

The *farewell* and *appropriate message* of the editorial vs. 28 is the NAB's way of dissipating the inappropriate "blessings" of which the text literally speaks. What has gone before in this collection of poetry hardly adds up to a series of blessings, of course, but nevertheless that is what the editor called them, following the convention of chapter 27, 48:8–22, etc.

The final verses of chapter 49, originally in sequence with vs. 1a, is the P account of Jacob's last charge to his sons immediately preparatory to his death, requiring that his body be brought back to the ancestral cave-tomb at Machpelah, a locale that was obviously of great import to the Priestly tradition (cf. chapter 23, 25:9). Only here we are told we might have surmised it earlier, that Isaac and Rebekah were buried there (cf. 35:29) and that Leah also found there a final resting place. The conclusion and fulfillment of this episode are in 50:12–13 below.

7. The Passing of Joseph

There remains one chapter of Genesis, which appears to fall neatly into three unequal parts. First there is a fairly detailed J account of Joseph's acquittal of his vow to return his father's body to a burial place with his ancestors (cf. 47:30–31, J). Partially inserted into this story are the P vss. 12–13 which conclude 49:1a.29–33 above, a parallel narrative which also brings Jacob back to Canaan, though to a different place. And finally, there is an E conclusion which does not obviously presuppose either of the preceding but rather begins to set the scene for a drama that will be played out beyond the boundaries of Genesis, to which Genesis has been only prologue.

50 Joseph threw himself on his father's face and wept
2 over him as he kissed him. Then he ordered the
physicians in his service to embalm his father. When
3 they embalmed Israel, they spent forty days at it,
for that is the full period of embalming; and the
4 Egyptians mourned him for seventy days. When that
period of mourning was over, Joseph spoke to Pharaoh's courtiers, "Please do me this favor," he said,
5 "and convey to Pharaoh this request of mine. Since
my father, at the point of death, made me promise
on oath to bury him in the tomb that he had prepared for himself in the land of Canaan, may I go
up there to bury my father and then come back?"
6 Pharaoh replied, "Go and bury your father, as he
made you promise on oath."
7 So Joseph left to bury his father; and with him went
all of Pharaoh's officials who were senior members
of his court and all the other dignitaries of Egypt,
8 as well as Joseph's whole household, his brothers,
and his father's household; only their children and
their flocks and herds were left in the region of
9 Goshen. Chariots, too, and charioteers went up with
him; it was a very large retinue.
10 When they arrived at Goren-ha-atad, which is beyond the Jordan, they held there a very great and
solemn memorial service; and Joseph observed
11 seven days of mourning for his father. When the
Canaanites who inhabited the land saw the mourning at Goren-ha-atad, they said, "This is a solemn
funeral the Egyptians are having." That is why the
place was named Abel-mizraim. It is beyond the Jordan.

And from the same source:

14 After Joseph had buried his father he returned to
Egypt, together with his brothers and all who had
gone up with him for the burial of his father.

There can be no doubt that all this continues the J story and, for that
matter, ends it as far as Genesis is concerned. Jacob's bowing "at the head
of the bed" in 47:31 (J) was the last gesture of a dying man who must
now be wept over and his will carried out. After his emotional release,
Joseph orders *the physicians in his service to embalm his father*. The em-

balming of the dead was as much a curiosity to non-Egyptians in the ancient world as it has become a curiosity to non-Americans in the modern world. The Egyptian process was, it is true, far more complicated and drawn out than the cosmetic folkway with which we are familiar, since the end was not simply to pretend away the reality of death for a few days before interment removes the body from sight and mind; mummification went the step beyond of trying to deny death entirely, of constituting the body forever proof against decay and corruption and thus affording the soul an enduring place of residence where life might go on indefinitely. It is typical of the Joseph story that it passes no religious judgment on the embalming of Jacob and later of Joseph, though for the Egyptians mummification was a highly religious expression, involving ritual, prayers, and incantations as well as herbs and canopic jars. The story says only that *they spent forty days at it, for that is the full period of embalming:* Egyptian texts of the time would indicate that the biblical author was minimally informed on his point, since the total operation involved in preserving and wrapping the body took considerably more than forty days. The *seventy days* over which *the Egyptians mourned him,* however, seems to reflect authentic Egyptian custom.

As is usual in J, Joseph is not in direct contact with Pharaoh, even though he is his vizier, and therefore he requests leave to go to Canaan through the members of Pharaoh's court. (The *courtiers* of vs. 4 are not the *sarisim,* eunuchs, of the E story; the NAB has paraphrased the Hebrew, which speaks of "the house of Pharaoh.") There is no sign, however, of any diminution of Joseph's power or favor at court, since all to the contrary Pharaoh's response is truly royal and generous. In picturing a gigantic procession of Israelites from Goshen to Canaan accompanied by the most prestigious of Egypt's nobles and court officials, the biblical author by this exaggeration may intend an ironic reflection on the circumstances of a later and far more significant exodus from Egypt, when Israel fled for its life before Pharaoh's army, pursued by those *chariots and charioteers* (cf. Exodus 14:7, J) who are now its honor guard.

Above in commenting on 48:7 we proposed that for E the burial place of Jacob was the tomb of Rachel near Ephrath. In 47:30 (J) Jacob specified the place merely as the one where his ancestors were buried. From the present vss. 10–11 it appears we must conclude that that place was in the Transjordan, unless for some reason the twofold *which is beyond the Jordan* is an addition to the original text. It is conceivable that this is so, that the Redactor inserted this phrase—thereby charting a Goshen-to-Hebron itinerary that should have caused more wonderment to the locals than the strange goings-on at Abel-mizraim—all in order to distance more firmly Goren-ha-atad from the Machpelah where, following P, he had decided that Jacob was to be buried. It seems doubtful, however, that such a geographical translation could have been effected. *Goren-ha-atad,* which means something like Thornbush Threshers (*goren,* "threshing floor," was a generic name which attracted regional determinants, as with our "-burgs" and "-villes" and "Forts"), looks like a place that was known and for which a popular etiology was being sought in the story for the associated name *Abel-mizraim.* The etiology offered is "mourning of the Egyptians"; the name really meant Something- "creek" or "field" or the like. We cannot identify this site, but there is no reason to think that it did not actually exist, on the other side of the Jordan, on some ancestral ground of Jacob/Israel (perhaps in the vicinity of Mahanaim or Penuel, JE, cf. chapter 32). In any case, there can be no doubt that the *seven days of mourning* and the *very great and solemn memorial service* held at Goren-ha-atad is the J version of the burial of Jacob with his fathers, in a construction of the events that differs markedly from the story told by the Priestly author, whose two final verses in Genesis now follow.

> 12 Thus Jacob's sons did for him as he had instructed
> 13 them. They carried him to the land of Canaan and
>   buried him in the cave in the field of Machpelah,
>   facing on Mamre, the field that Abraham had bought
>   for a burial ground from Ephron the Hittite.

Perhaps at this stage we can understand better why the Priestly author has been so intent on putting the patriarchs and their families at rest in Hebron. Machpelah is, we have been continually reminded, *the field that Abraham had bought for a burial ground from Ephron the Hittite.* It was not a tomb which Jacob had made for himself (contrary to the purport of vs. 5 above from J), in some ancestral place of pre-Israelite associations hallowed, no doubt, by pre-Israelite cult and religion. It was, rather, firmly in the land of the patriarchal sojourn, tied to the memory of the first patriarch of all and to none other before him, in a spot which was a constant reminder to the patriarchs that the land was still alien and not yet theirs by right of possession, in which nevertheless through Abraham's purchase there was one corner of a foreign field forever Israel. As in the P of 25:9–10 and 35:29, the burial of Jacob here is the acquittal of a simple family duty performed by sons for their father; there is no room for the intrusion of the Egyptians, their burial customs, or their funereal rites.

> 15 Now that their father was dead, Joseph's brothers
>   became fearful* and thought, "Suppose Joseph has
>   been nursing a grudge against us and now plans to
>   pay us back in full for all the wrong we did him!"

---

* So the Syriac and Vulgate; the MT, using the same Hebrew consonants, has "saw."

16 So they approached† Joseph and said: "Before your
17 father died, he gave us these instructions: 'You shall
say to Joseph, Jacob begs you to forgive the criminal wrongdoing of your brothers, who treated you
so cruelly.' Please, therefore, forgive the crime that
we, the servants of your father's God, committed."
When they spoke these words to him, Joseph broke
18 into tears. Then his brothers proceeded to fling
themselves down before him and said, "Let us be
19 your slaves!" But Joseph replied to them: "Have no
20 fear. Can I take the place of God? Even though you
meant harm to me, God meant it for good, to
achieve his present end, the survival of many peo-
21 ple. Therefore have no fear. I will provide for you
and for your children." By thus speaking kindly to
them, he reassured them.

The final segment of this chapter and of the book of Genesis beginning
with vs. 15 corresponds better with the characteristics of E than with any
other. There is no presupposition of an intervening visit to Canaan and the
passing of considerable time as demanded by the J story: here, quickly on
the demise of their father, the brothers take stock of their perhaps changed
fortunes with the removal of their protector and begin to fear that retribution may, after all, now catch up with them. The *criminal wrongdoing* to
which they confess could fit the circumstances of either the J or the E version of what they had done to Joseph long ago, but Joseph's reassurances
in vss. 19–21 are a reiteration of the E parts of chapter 45 more than of
anything else in that combined story. In vs. 18 the brothers again fulfill to
the letter the dream prophecies of 37:5–10. In vs. 17 they make mention
of the patriarchal God, which only E does in these chapters (cf. 46:1–4,
48:15–16, and vs. 24 below), if we except the conventional use of "Yahweh" in the J of chapter 39. Finally, Joseph appears here in the typical E
posture of the God-directed wise man who is careful to subordinate himself throughout to the divine power that leads him in all his ways.

This final glance at Joseph and his brothers permits the author to indulge a taste for irony which proves that his estimate of their separate
characters differed little from that of the Yahwist (especially in chapter
43), who has dealt with them most in this story. Those who are of small
spirit and petty ways can hardly credit another who is more powerful with
good will in their behalf simply out of brotherly feeling and piety. It is not
the way they have acted, nor is it the way they would act were the posi-

---

† So with some of the ancient versions; the MT has "they instructed."

tions reversed. They must invent—for surely it is an invention—a safe-conduct uttered in their favor by a dying father whose claim on Joseph's affections was proved and could be counted on to stay the avenging hand they fear simply because it can always descend despite all assurances that it will not. Joseph's tears, which are frequent in E, are perhaps here tears of exasperation as well as of familial concern. He does not even remark on the brothers' thin story: it is of no consequence. Probably there was nothing he could ever do that would forever quiet the apprehensions of these mistrusting souls. He can only tell them again what he has told them before and allow them to wait on his continued beneficence as the proof of his words. Their own characters have doomed them to live with an anxiety which neither word nor deed will ever finally remove, the nemesis of their own mean thoughts and selfish schemings.

> 22 Joseph remained in Egypt, together with his father's
> 23 family. He lived a hundred and ten years. He saw
> Ephraim's children to the third generation, and the
> children of Manasseh's son Machir were also born
> on Joseph's knees.
> 24 Joseph said to his brothers: "I am about to die. God
> will surely take care of you and lead you out of this
> land to the land that he promised on oath to Abra-
> 25 ham, Isaac and Jacob." Then, putting the sons of
> Israel under oath, he continued, "When God thus
> takes care of you, you must bring my bones up with
> you‡ from this place." Joseph died at the age of a
> hundred and ten. He was embalmed and laid to rest
> in a coffin in Egypt.

It may be that the Redactor has introduced a few phrases from J into these final verses. It is twice mentioned that Joseph's age was *a hundred and ten years; the sons of Israel* (still here literally meant and not in the sense "Israelites") is typical of J; and it is J who remarked on the Egyptian practice of embalming in vss. 2–3 above, here applied to Joseph in vs. 26, though vs. 25 speaks only of *my bones* and not of an embalmed body.

Joseph concludes his days realizing what most men of antiquity would have accounted a totally fulfilled life. To see one's children and one's children's children *to the third generation* was to obtain the best reward that earthly life can give, to know that one's name is secure in men's annals, that one's life will go on in a remembering progeny, that such immortality as men can have is now assured. The hundred and ten years that Joseph

‡ "With you" is not in the MT but has been added on the testimony of the other ancient witnesses to the text.

lives do not come from the Priestly author's chronology, though they may have later been integrated into it. They are, rather, a last Egyptian touch in this story. Repeatedly in Egyptian sources a hundred and ten years appears as the ideal life-span, the age of utter and complete fulfillment.

Israelite interests predominate at the end. That *the children of Manasseh's son Machir were also born on Joseph's knees* means that Joseph adopted and recognized them as his own, anticipating somewhat the legalistic pronouncement of 48:5 by which Ephraim and Manasseh were certified as Israelite tribes. In the Song of Deborah (Judges 5:14) Machir appears in the tribal list in place of Manasseh, another indication of the fluidity of the tribal relationships in their real history which the Pentateuchal traditions have romanticized. It is incongruous that Joseph, so much younger than most of his other brothers, should die before they and that they should outlast his satisfyingly full life, but of course this is a detail required by the legend, so that he, too, with the foresight of the dying may predict "what is to happen in days to come." The *take care of you* of vss. 24 and 25 is a rather jejune translation of a fairly technical term of biblical theological vocabulary: this is the "visitation" which God makes either in judgment or salvation, his solemn intervention in human history that determines the lot of his people. The exodus is in view, when Israel will go forth to claim the land *promised on oath* by God to the patriarchs. The *you* of the brothers surrounding Joseph's bed thus in vision dissolves into the *you* of the tribes who will bear their names when they settle the Land of Promise. Until that time, much is to be endured, and along with Joseph's bones, Israel must bide *in Egypt*.

> Then a new king, who knew nothing of Joseph, came to power in Egypt . . . Taskmasters were set over the Israelites to oppress them with forced labor . . . But the LORD said, "I have witnessed the affliction of my people in Egypt and have heard their cry of complaint against their slave drivers, so I know well what they are suffering . . . Come, now! I will send you to Pharaoh to lead my people, the Israelites, out of Egypt!" . . . After that, Moses and Aaron went to Pharaoh and said, "Thus says the LORD, the God of Israel: Let my people go" . . . Now, when Pharaoh let the people go . . . Moses also took Joseph's bones along, for Joseph had made the Israelites swear solemnly that, when God should come to them, they would carry his bones away with them . . . After Moses, the servant of the LORD, had died, the LORD said to Moses' aide Joshua, son of Nun: "My servant Moses is dead. So prepare to cross the

Jordan here, with all the people, into the land I will give the Israelites" . . . Thus Joshua captured the whole country, just as the LORD had foretold to Moses. Joshua gave it to Israel as their heritage, apportioning it among the tribes. And the land enjoyed peace . . . The bones of Joseph, which the Israelites had brought up from Egypt, were buried in Shechem in the plot of ground Jacob had bought from the sons of Hamor, father of Shechem, for a hundred pieces of money. This was a heritage of the descendants of Joseph . . . (Exodus 1:8.11a, 3:7.10, 5:1a, 13:17a.19; Joshua 1:1–2, 11:23, 24:32).

Index

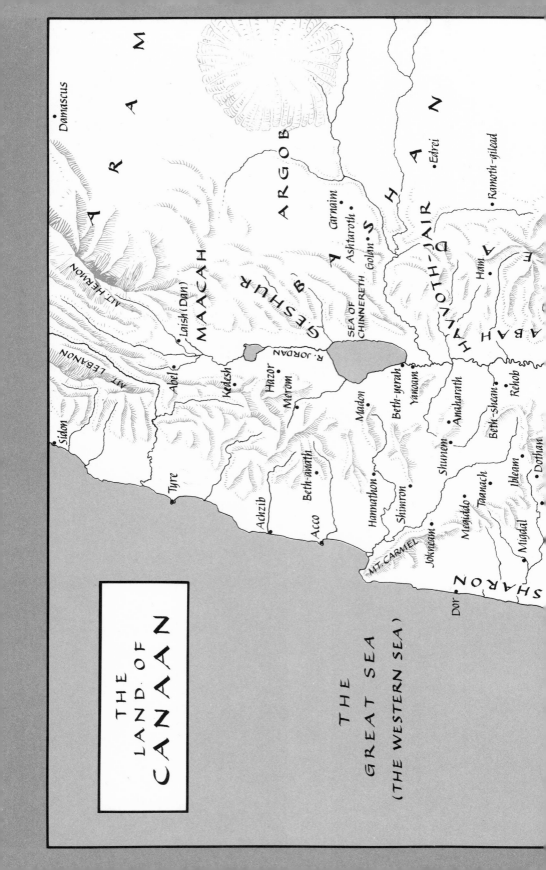

THE
LAND OF
CANAAN

THE
GREAT SEA
(THE WESTERN SEA)

Damascus

A R A M

MT. HERMON

MT. LEBANON

Sidon

Tyre

Achzib

Acco

MT. CARMEL

Dor

SHARON

Jokneam

Megiddo

Taanach

Ibleam

Migdal

Dothan

Shimron

Hannathon

Madon

Merom

Hazor

Kedesh

Abel

Laish (Dan)

MAACAH

GESHUR

R. JORDAN

SEA OF CHINNERETH

Golan

Ashtaroth

Carnaim

ARGOB

S

HAVOTH-JAIR

BASHAN

Edrei

Ramoth-gilead

Ham

ABAH

Rehob

Beth-shan

Anaharath

Shunem

Beth-yerah

Yanoam

Jabbok

Beth-anath